Cases for Leadership and Leadership Standards

Case for Leadership	Vision	Student Learning Professional Development	In-School Environment	Community Collaboration	Ethics	General Context
Rash Decision? (p. 34)		X	X	X	X	X
Cooperative Learning (p. 78)		X	X			X
Problems at West High (p. 120)	X	X	X	X		X
Reverse the Decline (p. 159)		X	X			
Surprise at St. Clair (p. 198)		X	X	X	X	X
Conflict at WHS (p. 234)	X	X	X	X	X	X
A Reading War (p. 266)		X	X	X		X
A Mandate for Higher Accountability (p. 295)	X	X	X			X
Teachers Council (p. 333)	X		X	X		X
Scandal at Placido High (p. 369)		X		X	X	X
Leadership and Reform (p. 406)	X	X	X	X	X	X
Anonymous Letter (p. 426)		X	X	X	X	X
Snubbing Creationists? (p. 428)	X	X	X	X	X	X
Crossing the Line or Only a Crush? (p. 430)		X	X	X	X	X
Leading to Change, Changing to Lead (p. 433)	X	X	X	X	X	X
Motivational Challenge (p. 434)	X	X	X	X	X	X
Parental Demand (p. 436)		X	X	X	X	X
Dilemma at Urban High (p. 438)	X	X	X	X	X	X
Litigation, Religion, & Politics (p. 439)		X	X	X	X	X

Seventh Edition

EDUCATIONAL ADMINISTRATION

Theory, Research, and Practice

Wayne K. Hoy
The Ohio State University

Cecil G. Miskel
The University of Michigan

Boston   Burr Ridge, IL   Dubuque, IA   Madison, WI   New York   San Francisco   St. Louis
Bangkok   Bogotá   Caracas   Kuala Lumpur   Lisbon   London   Madrid   Mexico City
Milan   Montreal   New Delhi   Santiago   Seoul   Singapore   Sydney   Taipei   Toronto

The McGraw·Hill Companies

Mc Graw Hill | **Higher Education**

EDUCATIONAL ADMINISTRATION: THEORY, RESEARCH, AND PRACTICE
Published by McGraw-Hill, a business unit of The McGraw-Hill Companies, Inc., 1221 Avenue of the Americas, New York, NY, 10020. Copyright © 2005, 2001, 1996, 1991, 1987, 1982, 1978 by The McGraw-Hill Companies, Inc. All rights reserved. No part of this publication may be reproduced or distributed in any form or by any means, or stored in a database or retrieval system, without the prior written consent of The McGraw-Hill Companies, Inc., including, but not limited to, in any network or other electronic storage or transmission, or broadcast for distance learning.
Some ancillaries, including electronic and print components, may not be available to customers outside the United States.

This book is printed on acid-free paper.

1 2 3 4 5 6 7 8 9 0 FGR/FGR 0 9 8 7 6 5 4

ISBN 0-07-287568-2

Vice President and Editor in Chief: *Emily Barrosse*
Executive editor: *David S. Patterson*
Senior development editor: *Cara Harvey*
Executive marketing manager: *Pamela S. Cooper*
Media producer: *Shannon Gattens*
Lead project manager: *Susan Trentacosti*
Senior production supervisor: *Carol A. Bielski*
Associate designer: *Srdjan Savanovic*
Cover design: *Amanda Kavanaugh*
Cover image: *© L&M SERVICES B.V. Amsterdam 20040506*
Typeface: *10/12 Palatino*
Compositor: *Carlisle Communications, Ltd.*
Printer: *Quebecor World Fairfield Inc.*

Library of Congress Cataloging-in-Publication Data

Hoy, Wayne K.
  Educational administration : theory, research, and practice / Wayne K. Hoy, Cecil G. Miskel—7th ed.
    p. cm.
  Includes bibliographical references and index.
  ISBN 0–07–287568–2 (softcover)
  1. School management and organization—United States. I. Miskel, Cecil G. II. Title.
LB2805.H715 2005
371.2'00973—dc22

                                                            2004054253

www.mhhe.com

Dedicated to Anita and Sue

ABOUT THE AUTHORS

Wayne K. Hoy   received his B. S. from Lock Haven State College in 1959 and his D. Ed. from The Pennsylvania State University in 1965. After teaching at Oklahoma State University for several years, he moved to Rutgers University in 1968, where he was a distinguished professor, department chair, and Associate Dean for Academic Affairs. In 1994, he was selected as the Novice G. Fawcett Chair in Educational Administration at The Ohio State University. His primary professional interests are theory and research in administration, the sociology of organizations, and the social psychology of administration.

In 1973, he received the Lindback Foundation Award for Distinguished Teaching from Rutgers University; in 1987, he received the Alumni Award for Professional Research from the Rutgers University Graduate School of Education; in 1991, he received the Excellence in Education Award from The Pennsylvania State University; in 1992, he received the Meritorious Research Award from the Eastern Educational Research Association; and in 1996 he became an Alumni Fellow of The Pennsylvania State University. He is past secretary-treasurer of the National Conference of Professors of Educational Administration (NCPEA) and is past president of the University Council for Educational Administration (UCEA). In November 2003 he was awarded the Roald Campbell Lifetime Achievement Award in Educational Administration.

Professor Hoy is coauthor with D. J. Willower and T. L. Eidell of *The School and Pupil Control Ideology* (1967); with Patrick Forsyth, *Effective Supervision: Theory into Practice* (1986); with C. J. Tarter and R. Kottkamp, *Open Schools—Healthy Schools: Measuring Organizational Climate* (1991); with C. J. Tarter, *Administrators Solving the Problems of Practice* (1995, 2004); with C. J. Tarter, *The Road to Open and Health Schools* (1997); with D. Sabo, *Quality Middle Schools* (1998); and with his wife, Anita Woolfolk Hoy, *Instructional Leadership: A Learning-Centered Guide* (2003). He is also on the editorial boards of the *Journal of Educational Administration* and *Leadership and Policy in Schools*.

Cecil G. Miskel is a professor of Educational Administration and Policy at the University of Michigan. From 1988 to 1998, he was the Dean of the School of Education at Michigan. He served the University of Utah as a professor and chairperson of the Department of Educational Administration from 1982 to 1983 and professor and dean of the Graduate School of Education from 1983 to 1988. He also spent 12 years at the University of Kansas, where he held such positions as assistant, associate, and full professor of educational administration as well as associate dean for research administration and associate vice-chancellor for research, graduate studies, and public service. His public school experience includes being a science teacher and principal in the secondary schools of Oklahoma.

Professor Miskel holds an undergraduate degree in science education from the University of Oklahoma, and Master of Science and Doctor of Education degrees from Oklahoma State University. He teaches graduate classes and guides scholarly inquiry in school organization, administration, and policy. His current research program deals with reading policy at the state and national levels. He served as editor of the *Educational Administration Quarterly* for the 1987 and 1988 volumes and has been a member of its editorial board for nine years. Professor Miskel has received the William Davis Award for the most outstanding article published in Volumes 16 and 19 of the *Educational Administration Quarterly*. In addition to being a coauthor of the seven editions of *Educational Administration: Theory, Research, and Practice,* Professor Miskel has published widely in a variety of scholarly journals. Professors Hoy and Miskel are also editors of a book series on *Theory and Research in Educational Administration* (2002, 2003, 2004).

CONTENTS IN BRIEF

CONTENTS

CHAPTER 12   *One Last Time: A Review of
                 the School as a Social
                 System 410*

PREFACE

In *Educational Administration: Theory, Research, and Practice*, we make two assumptions about the study and practice of educational administration:

1. A substantive body of knowledge about educational organizations is available but often neglected by both professors and administrators.
2. Administrative practice can become more systematic, reflective, and effective when guided by sound theory and research.

Thus, we summarize and review relevant knowledge and demonstrate its utility in solving problems of practice. An open social-systems model of schools provides the overarching conceptual framework that organizes and relates this theory and research for educational administrators.

APPROACH

- Our approach is a pragmatic one, selecting the theories and research that are most useful and discarding those that are not. At the heart of our social-systems model are four critical elements of organizational life—structure, individual, culture, and politics, each discussed in a separate chapter. These elements interact and situate a chapter on teaching and learning in schools. The environmental chapter provides a set of opportunities and constraints for the schools; and the outcomes of the school are examined in the chapter on effectiveness. Four key administrative processes are analyzed in chapters on deciding, motivating, communicating, and leading, which remain central to effective administration. New theories and contemporary research are incorporated into our analyses of teaching, learning, and leading. Because the basic aim of educational administrators is to solve real problems, we provide an authentic case for leadership at the conclusion of each chapter. We believe that to make full use of the content of this text that students must first *understand* the materials (a constructivist perspective), then they must *remember* them (a cognitive perspective), and then they must *apply and practice* them (a behavioral perspective)—the three learning views developed in the second chapter.

NEW TO THE SEVENTH EDITION

- **New Knowledge.** More than 200 new citations were added and about the same number eliminated in this edition as we bring administrators and prospective administrators the most current information, but we also make a special effort to keep the classic analyses of such giants in the field as Max Weber, Peter Blau, Alvin Gouldner, Amitai Etzioni, B. F. Skinner, Bernard Weiner, Vygotsky, Piaget, Henry Mintzberg, John Dewey, James March, and Herbert Simon, to mention just a few.

- **Expanded Coverage of Learning and Teaching.** Chapter 2 summarizes the latest theory and research on teaching and learning, one of the few educational administration books that deals with these central functions of schooling.
- **Reformulated Treatment of School Effectiveness.** Chapter 8 offers elaborated perspectives on school performance, accountability, and improvement, especially comprehensive school reform. It also provides an extensive treatment of school accountability, including the movement to standards, testing, rewards, and punishments.
- **Expanded Features.** Each chapter now includes *TIP* application questions, *A Case for Leadership* (an authentic and challenging problem of practice), and a *Key Assumptions and Principles* summary feature. All features were designed to help students confirm and apply what they learn.
- **A Collection of Cases for Educational Leadership.** A collection of eight cases is now available at the conclusion of the text. These additional cases provide students with extra practice in a variety of situations as they apply their knowledge to actual leadership challenges.
- **New Coverage of the Council of Chief State School Officers Standards (ISLLC Standards).** New to this edition is a demonstration of how the new standards are addressed with actual administrative cases. All of the leadership cases in the book are summarized in the *Case Matrix,* which classifies each case in terms of the standards addressed.

FEATURES

Each chapter includes the following features:

- **Preview.** At the beginning of each chapter the student will find a Preview, which is a brief outline of the key points to be covered in that chapter. We suggest that students take time to study the preview, which is deliberately short and terse, because it provides a road map of the chapter.
- **Theory into Practice (TIP).** Exercises to make the book more practical and user-friendly have been added in this edition. Throughout each chapter students will be confronted with a number of TIPs, practical issues and application exercises, which require them to test their understanding of theory and to suggest applications to contemporary problems.
- **A Case for Leadership.** Each chapter includes a real case to challenge students to apply the ideas and concepts developed in the chapter and to demonstrate their leadership initiative.
- **Key Concepts.** Key concepts in each chapter are identified in bold. Students should take the time to check themselves to make sure they understand and can define these concepts.
- **Key Assumptions and Principles.** New to this edition, located at the conclusion of each chapter, this feature provides a brief summary of the crucial generalizations in the chapter.

ACKNOWLEDGMENTS

Thank you to the instructors who provided feedback on the sixth edition to help guide our revision of the text:

John J. Battles, *George Washington University*

Perry Berkowitz, *The College of St. Rose*

Walter Keith Christy, *University of Arkansas at Little Rock*

Denise P. Dunbar, *Tennessee State University*

Ernest Johnson, *University of Texas, Arlington*

Jason P. Nance, *The Ohio State University*

Winston D. Pickett, *Tennessee Technological University*

James Sinden, *North Carolina State University*

Karen L. Stevens, *Tennessee State University*

Our colleagues and students continue to be important sources of ideas and criticism. We would like to thank Terry Astuto, New York University; James Bliss, Rutgers University; Eric Camburn, University of Michigan; Jane Coggshall, University of Michigan; David K. Cohen, University of Michigan; Michael DiPaola, College of William and Mary; Roger Goddard, University of Michigan; Patrick Forsyth, Oklahoma State University; Ronald Heck, University of Hawaii; Sam Hwan Joo, Chungnam National University; Megan Tschannen-Moran, College of William and Mary; Rodney Ogawa, University of California-Santa Cruz; Gail Schneider, University of Wisconsin, Milwaukee; Page Smith, University of Texas at San Antonio; Mengli Song, American Institutes for Research; Scott Sweetland, Ohio State University; C. J. Tarter, St. John's University; Brian Rowan, University of Michigan; Charles Teddlie, Louisiana State University; Cynthia Uline, Ohio State University; Frank Walter, Ohio State University; and Anita Woolfolk Hoy, Ohio State University. Finally, we owe a special thanks to all our students who have helped enrich the explanations and ground the theories with their experiences. A special thanks to Eileen McMahon, Thomas Reed, Nancy-Nestor Baker, Michael DiPaola, Harry Galinsky, and John Tarter, who drew upon their experiences in schools to write Cases for Educational Leadership.

Wayne K. Hoy
Cecil G. Miskel

THE SCHOOL AS A SOCIAL SYSTEM

Although we set out primarily to study reality, it does not follow that we do not wish to improve it; we should judge our researches to have no worth at all if they were to have only a speculative interest. If we separate carefully the theoretical from the practical problems, it is not to the neglect of the latter; but, on the contrary, to be in a better position to solve them.

Emile Durkheim
The Division of Labor in Society

PREVIEW

1. Organizational theory is a set of interrelated concepts, definitions, and generalizations that systematically describes and explains patterns of regularities in organizational life.

2. The functions of theory are to explain, to guide research, to generate new knowledge, and to guide practice.

3. Theory informs practice in three important ways: it forms a frame of reference; it provides a general model for analysis; and it guides reflective decision making.

4. The evolution of organizational thought and theory can be viewed using three competing systems perspectives: rational, natural, and open.

5. A rational-systems perspective views organizations as formal instruments designed to achieve organizational goals; structure is the most important feature.

6. A natural-systems perspective views organizations as typical social groups intent on surviving: people are the most important aspect.

7. An open-systems perspective has the potential to combine rational and natural elements in the same framework and provide a more complete perspective.

8. Schools are open social systems with five important elements or subsystems: the structural, the individual, the cultural, the political, and the pedagogical. Organizational behavior is a function of the interaction of these elements in the context of teaching and learning.

9. The teaching-learning process is the technical core of the school social system; it is a complex process that can be usefully viewed from three perspectives— the behavioral, cognitive, and constructivist.

10. The environment is also a critical aspect of organizational life; it not only provides resources for the system but also provides additional constraints and opportunities.

11. We posit a congruence postulate: Other things being equal, the greater the degree of congruence among the elements of the system, the more effective the system.

12. Our open-systems model of schools provides a conceptual basis for organizational analysis and administrative problem solving.

The systematic study of educational administration is as new as the modern school; the one-room schoolhouse of rural America did not need specialized administrators. Research on administration and development of theories of organization and administration are relatively recent phenomena. Before exploring conceptual perspectives of educational administration, however, we need a basic understanding of the nature and meaning of organizational theory. Consequently, we begin the chapter by defining theory and science and discussing the interrelationships among theory, research, and practice.

THEORY

Much of the skepticism about theory is based on the assumption that educational administration is incapable of becoming a science. This is a skepticism that has plagued all social sciences. Theory in the natural sciences, on the other hand, has attained respectability not only because it necessarily involves precise description, but also because it describes ideal phenomena that "work" in practical applications.

Most people think that scientists deal with facts whereas philosophers delve into theory. Indeed, to many individuals, including educational administrators, facts and theories are antonyms; that is, facts are real and their meanings self-evident, and theories are speculations or dreams. Theory in educational administration, however, has the same role as theory in physics, chemistry, biology, or psychology—that is, it provides general explanations and guides research.

Theory and Science

The purpose of all science is to understand the world in which we live and work. Scientists describe what they see, discover regularities, and formulate theories (Babbie, 1990). Organizational science attempts to describe and explain regularities in the behavior of individuals and groups within organizations. Organizational scientists seek basic principles that provide a general understanding of the structure and dynamics of organizational life (Miner, 2002).

Some researchers view science as a static, interconnected set of principles that explains the universe in which we live. We view **science** as a dynamic process of developing, through experimentation and observation, an interconnected set of propositions that in turn produces further experimentation and observation (Conant, 1951). In this view the basic aim of science is to find general explanations, called *theories*. Thoughtful individuals trying to understand how things work create theories; however, no theory is ever taken as final because a better one may be devised at any time. Indeed, one of the basic strengths of science is that it is self-critical and self-corrective (Willower, 1994, 1996). The norms of science and theory are oriented toward open-mindedness, public communication of results, and impersonal criteria of assessment (Zucker, 1987).

As the ultimate aim of science, theory has acquired a variety of definitions. Donald J. Willower (1975) provides a parsimonious definition: theory is "a body of interrelated, consistent generalizations that serves to explain" (p. 78). We suggest a more comprehensive definition of theory in educational administration based on the work of Fred N. Kerlinger (1986). **Theory** is a set of interrelated concepts, assumptions, and generalizations that systematically describes and explains regularities in behavior in educational organizations.

Concepts are the basic building blocks of theory. They are abstract terms that have been given special definitions. Because they have specific connotations, concepts help us agree on the meaning of terms and their abstractness ensures generality. **Generalizations** are statements that indicate the relation between two or more concepts. Theories provide general explanations of phenomena; they provide a coherent and connected story about why acts, events, and behavior occur (Sutton and Staw, 1995). Most of the concepts, generalizations, and theories in this book are in the middle range—that is, they are somewhat limited in their scope rather than all-embracing. They are attempts to summarize and explain some of the consistencies found in school organizations.

Theories are by nature general and abstract; they are not strictly true or false but rather useful or not. Theories are useful to the extent that they generate accurate predictions about events and help us understand and influence behavior. Albert Einstein, one of the greatest theorists of all times, and Leopold Infeld (Einstein and Infeld, 1938) capture the essence of theorizing in the following quotation:

> In our endeavor to understand reality we are somewhat like a man trying to understand the mechanism of a closed watch. He sees the face and the moving hands, even hears its ticking, but he has no way of opening the case. If he is ingenious he may form some picture of a mechanism, which could be responsible for all the things he observes, but he may never be quite sure his picture is the only one, which could explain his observations. He will never be able to compare his picture with the real mechanism, and he cannot even imagine the possibility of the meaning of such a comparison. (p. 31)

Theory and Reality

Reality exists, but our knowledge of it always remains elusive and uncertain. It should not be surprising that different individuals often draw different conclusions from the same perceptual experiences because they hold different theories that affect their interpretation of events (Carey and Smith, 1993). Our knowledge consists of our theories. The form of the theory, however, is less important than the degree to which it generates useful understanding. Ultimately, research and theory are judged by their utility (Griffiths, 1988).

The use of theory in organizational analysis seems indispensable to reflective practice. The beginning student of educational administration may ask, "Do these theories and models really exist?" Our position is the same as Mintzberg's (1989). The models, theories, and configurations used to describe organizations in this book are mere words and pictures on pages, not reality itself. Actual organizations are much more complex than any of these representations; in fact, our conceptual frameworks are simplifications of organizations that underscore some features and neglect others. Hence, they distort reality. The problem is that in many areas we cannot get by without theoretical guidance (implicit, if not explicit theories), much as a traveler cannot effectively navigate unknown territory without a map.

Our choice is not usually between reality and theory but rather between alternative theories. Mintzberg (1989) captures the dilemma nicely:

> No one carries reality around in his or her head, no head is that big. Instead we carry around impressions of reality, which amount to implicit theories. Sometimes these are supplemented with explicit frameworks for identifying the concepts and interrelating them—in other words, with formal theories, built on systematic investigation known as research, or at least on systematic consideration of experience. In fact, some phenomena cannot be comprehended without such formal aid—how is one to develop an implicit theory of nuclear fission, for example? (p. 259)

We all use theories to guide our actions. Some are implicit and others are explicit; in fact, many of our personal implicit theories are formal ones that have been internalized. To paraphrase John Maynard Keynes, practical administrators who believe themselves to be exempt from any theoretical influences are usually the slaves of some defunct theory. Good theories and models exist, and if we do our job well in this book, they will exist where all useful knowledge must exist—in our minds. Reality is not in our heads, but we begin to understand it in the course of acting, adjusting, and refining our theories and models (Selznick, 1992; Hoy, 1996).

Theory and Research

Research is inextricably related to theory; therefore, many of the misconceptions and ambiguities surrounding theory are reflected in the interpretation of the meaning and purpose of research. Kerlinger (1986: 10) provides a formal definition: "Scientific research is systematic, controlled, empirical, and critical investigation of hypothetical propositions about the presumed relations among natural phenomena." This definition suggests that research is guided by hypotheses that are empirically checked against observations about reality in a systematic and controlled way. Results of such tests are then open to critical analyses by others.

Haphazard observations followed by the conclusion that the facts speak for themselves do not qualify as scientific research; in fact, such unrefined empiricism can distort reality and does not lead to the systematic development of knowledge. Well-conceived surveys and ethnographic studies for the express purpose of developing hypotheses are at times useful starting points in terms of hypothesis and theory development. Ultimately, however, knowledge in any discipline is expanded by research that is guided by hypotheses that are derived from theory. In brief, facts from research are not as important as the general patterns and explanations that they provide.

Hypotheses

A **hypothesis** is a conjectural statement that indicates a relationship between at least two concepts or variables. The following two examples illustrate this point.

- The stronger the collective teacher efficacy of a school, the higher the level of mathematics achievement in the school.
- The greater the external pressure from the community on their schools, the higher the level of academic achievement.

Several observations can be made about these hypotheses. First, each hypothesis specifies the relationship between at least two variables. Second, each clearly and concisely describes that relationship. Third, the concepts of each hypothesis are such that each could be empirically tested. For example, the first hypothesis expresses the relationship between collective teacher efficacy and mathematics achievement, both concepts that can be measured as variables. Schools that have high collective efficacy are predicted to have higher student achievement levels in mathematics. Such hypotheses bridge the gaps between theory and research and provide a means to test theory against observed reality; in fact, they are developed from theory. For example, the first hypothesis can be derived from efficacy theory discussed in Chapter 4. The second hypothesis can be derived from the conceptual perspectives on organizational climate provided in Chapter 5.

The hypothesis is the researcher's bias. If it is deduced from a theory, the investigator expects that it will be supported by data. Hypothesis testing is essential to the development of knowledge in any field of study. Support of the hypothesis in empirical research demonstrates the usefulness of the theory as an explanation. The fact that knowledge depends in part upon unsupported theories and assumptions should not cause discouragement. The goal of organizational researchers is to test our assumptions and theories, refining explanations and reformulating the theories as more data are gathered and analyzed.

The basic form of knowledge in all disciplines is similar; it consists of concepts, generalizations, and theories, each dependent on the one preceding it (Willower, 1963). Figure 1.1 summarizes the basic components of theory that are necessary to the development of knowledge. It shows that concepts are eventually linked together into generalizations that in turn form a logically consistent set of propositions providing a general explanation of a phenomenon (a theory). The theory is empirically checked by the development and testing of hypotheses deduced from the theory. The results of the research provide the data for accepting, rejecting, reformulating, or refining and clarifying the basic generalizations of the theory. Over time, with continued empirical support and evidence, the generalizations develop into principles that explain the phenomenon. In the case of organizational theory, principles are developed to explain the structure and dynamics of organizations and the role of the individual in organizations. Theory is both the beginning and the end of scientific research. On the one hand, it serves as the basis for generating hypotheses that describe and predict observable behavior. On the other hand, the ultimate objective of all scientific endeavors is to develop a body of substantive theory, that is, to provide reliable general explanations. Good theories help us understand and solve all kinds of problems from the ordinary to the complex.

Theory and Practice

Theory is directly related to practice in at least three ways. First, theory forms a frame of reference for the practitioner. Second, the process of theorizing provides a general mode of analysis of practical events. And third, theory guides decision making.

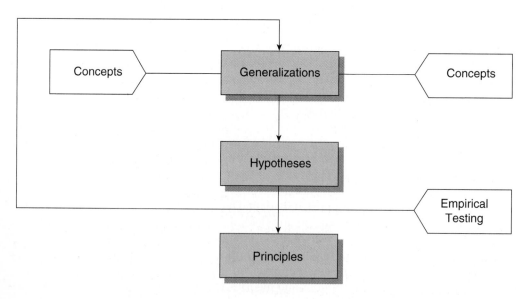

FIGURE 1.1   *Theoretical System*

Theory gives practitioners the analytic tools and a frame of reference needed to sharpen and focus their analyses of the problems they face (Dewey, 1933). Administrators so armed can develop alternative solutions to pragmatic problems. It is wrong, however, to think that any social science theory can supply definitive programs and immediate solutions. Theory does not directly generate immediate applications to practical problems. As William James (1983) noted, what is needed is an intermediary inventive mind to make the application, by using its own originality and creativity. There is no substitute for reflective thinking.

Administrators themselves maintain that the most important qualification for their jobs is the ability to use concepts. It is a mistake, however, to assume that the ability to label aspects of a problem by using theoretical constructs from sociology or psychology automatically provides a solution to a problem. Designating a problem as one of role conflict, goal displacement, or cognitive processing, for instance, does not in itself solve the problem; it may, however, organize the issues so that a reasonable plan of action can emerge.

The theory-practice relationship goes beyond using the concepts of theorists to label the important aspects of a problem. The scientific approach provides a way of thinking about events, a mode of analysis, for both theorists and practitioners alike. Indeed, the scientific approach is the very embodiment of rational inquiry, whether the focus is theoretical analysis and development, a research investigation, organizational decision making, or problem solving at the personal level. A good general description of this approach is found in John Dewey's (1933) analysis, *How We Think*. The process involves identifying a problem, conceptualizing it, proposing generalizations in the form of hypotheses that provide answers to the problems, deducing the consequences and implications of the hypotheses, and testing the hypotheses.

Some differences do exist in the specific ways that theorists, researchers, and practitioners implement and use the scientific approach, but the differences are a matter of degree of rigor and level of abstraction rather than approach. Theorists operate on a higher level of abstraction and generality than researchers, who test hypotheses. Practitioners, in turn, operate on an even lower level of abstraction than researchers because they are primarily concerned with specific problems and events in their organizations.

Similarly, theorists and researchers typically use the scientific approach more rigorously than practitioners, and for good reason. Theorists usually preface their propositions with the phrase "other things being equal," and researchers attempt to control all other variables except those under study. In contrast, practitioners function in a world where other things typically are not equal and all variables are not controllable. Practitioners are constrained by their positions, responsibilities, authority, and the immediacy of their problems. Although they do not abandon a reflective approach, practitioners are forced to be more flexible in applying the scientific method. For example, educational administrators are probably less concerned than theorists or researchers with generalizability—that is, the extent to which their solutions work for other administrators in other districts. Nonetheless, the approach of theorists, researchers, and thoughtful practitioners is basically the same; it is a systematic and reflective one.

One final relationship between theory and practice needs to be mentioned—theory guides administrative decision making. We can define administration as both the art and the science of applying knowledge to administrative and organizational problems. Arthur Blumberg (1984, 1989) calls it a craft. Such definitions imply that administrators have access to knowledge needed for making decisions. Without theory, however, there is virtually no basis for knowledge because the meaningful research that provides information presupposes a theory. Unfortunately, theory and research in educational administration continue to make only modest gains at best. Nonetheless, reflective administrators are more likely to be guided by theories, as imperfect as they are, than by impulse or the biases of dubious beliefs. Erroneous beliefs and bias will never disappear, but they can be held in check by mental habits that promote sound reasoning (Gilovich, 1991). Theories are no substitute for thought, but they are guides for making decisions and solving problems.

Administrative theory does influence practice. The evolution of organizational thought and theory over the last century, can be described in a number of ways. We view the history of organizational thought through a series of systems lenses.

A SYSTEMS PERSPECTIVE

The system concept has a rich history in the physical as well as the social sciences. Both Alfred N. Whitehead (1925) and George C. Homans (1950) have observed that the idea of an organized whole, or system, occurring in an environment is fundamental and essential to science.

A significant development in the analysis of organizational behavior is the distinction between open and closed systems. Early system analyses of the school (Getzels and Guba, 1957) viewed organizations as closed systems—that is, sealed off from the outside world. Explanations were given in terms of the internal workings of the organization with little or no attention to external constraints in the environment. Today, however, few contemporary organizational theorists accept the premise that organizations can be understood in isolation of events occurring externally; in fact, Marshall Meyer (1978: 18) argues, "the issue of open versus closed systems is closed, on the side of openness."

Although contemporary organizational thought is anchored in modern social science, three competing systems perspectives have emerged and continue, each with its share of advocates. W. Richard Scott (1987b, 1992, 1998) calls them the rational-systems, natural-systems, and open-systems perspectives. These three popular views of organizations are relatively distinct, yet they are partly overlapping, partly complementary, as well as partly conflicting; and each has its antecedents in earlier organizational thought. Drawing heavily from Scott's (1992, 1998) work, each will be discussed in some detail.

Rational System: A Machine Model

The **rational-systems perspective** views organizations as formal instruments designed to achieve specific organizational goals. Rationality is the extent to which a set of actions is organized and implemented to achieve predetermined goals with maximum efficiency (Scott, 1992). The rational approach has its early roots in the classical organizational thought of the scientific managers.

Scientific Management: The Beginning

Frederick Taylor, the father of the **scientific management** movement, sought ways to use people effectively in industrial organizations. Taylor's background and experience as laborer, clerk, machinist, supervisor, chief drafter, and finally, chief engineer reinforced his belief that individuals could be programmed to be efficient machines. The key to the scientific management approach is the machine metaphor.

Taylor and his associates thought that workers, motivated by economics and limited by physiology, needed constant direction. In 1911 Taylor (1947) formalized his ideas in *Scientific Management*. A sampling of his ideas reveals the flavor of his managerial theory. Taylor and his followers—the human engineers—focused on physical production, and their **time and motion studies** sought workers' physical limits and described the fastest method for performing a given task (Barnes, 1949: 556–67). They believed that by systematically studying a work task and timing how long it took to perform various tasks they could determine the most efficient way to complete the task. Although Taylor's work had a narrow physiological focus and ignored psychological and sociological variables, he demonstrated that many jobs could be performed more efficiently. He also helped the unskilled worker by improving productivity enough to raise the pay of unskilled nearly to that of skilled labor (Drucker, 1968).

Whereas Taylor's human engineers worked from the individual worker upward, the administrative managers worked from the managing director downward. Henri Fayol, like Taylor, took a scientific approach to administration. Fayol was a French mining engineer and successful executive who later taught administration. According to Fayol (Urwick, 1937: 119), administrative behavior consists of five functions—planning, organizing, commanding, coordinating, and controlling. Luther Gulick (1937) later amplified these functions in answer to the question, "What is the work of the chief executive?" He responded, "POSDCoRB," an acronym for his seven administrative procedures: planning, organizing, staffing, directing, coordinating, reporting, and budgeting.

To the administrative managers, **division of labor** was a basic principle of organization. Accordingly, the more a task could be broken down into its components, the more specialized and, therefore, the more effective the worker would be in performing the task. To complement the division of labor, tasks were grouped into jobs, and these jobs were then integrated into departments. Although the criteria for division could pose conflicting demands, division of labor and the departmentalization it entailed were necessary aspects of management. Moreover, breaking tasks into components allows for routinized performance, that is, **standardization** of work.

Span of control, or the number of workers supervised directly, was a second principle. In subdividing from the top downward, each work unit had to be supervised and coordinated with other units, and the span of control considered to be most effective was 5 to 10 subordinates. This rule of thumb is still widely used in building administrative organizations. A single executive, with power and authority flowing uniformly from the top to the bottom, heads the pyramid-shaped structures stemming from this second principle.

A third operating tenet of the administrative manager was the **principle of homogeneity** of positions. According to Gulick (1937), a single department could be formed of positions grouped in any of four different ways: major purpose, major process, clientele, or location.

- *Major purpose* joined those who shared a common goal.
- *Major process* combined those with a similar skill or technology.
- *Clientele* or material grouped those who dealt with similar clients or materials.
- Organization based on *location* or geographic area brought together those who worked together regardless of function.

Organizing departments in these four ways presents obvious problems. For example, should a school health activity be placed in a department of education or of health? How one answers the question will alter the nature of the service. Homogenizing departments in one of the four ways does not homogenize them in all ways. "The question is not which criterion to use for grouping," James D. Thompson (1967: 57) has observed, "but rather in which priority are the several criteria to be exercised?"

Both the human engineers and the scientific managers emphasized formal or bureaucratic organization. They were concerned with the division of labor, the allocation of power, and the specifications for each position; they conspicuously neglected individual idiosyncrasies and the social dynamics of people at work. This perspective, aptly termed a "machine model," implies that an organization can be constructed according to a blueprint, as one would build a bridge or an engine (Worthy, 1950).

As detailed by Roald Campbell and his colleagues (1987), developments in educational administration parallel those in the broad field of administration. Similar to Taylor's scientific managers, although lacking the rigor of the human engineers, early students of educational administration such as Franklin Bobbit (1913) looked at organizational behavior from the vantage point of job analyses. They observed administrators at work, specifying the component tasks to be performed, determining more effective ways to perform each task, and suggesting an organization to maximize efficiency. Raymond E. Callahan's (1962) analysis of schools and of the "cult of efficiency," concentrating on the period from 1910 through 1930, clearly indicates the influence of the scientific managers in the literature on schools.

It would be incorrect, however, to view Taylor's scientific management as a passing fad; in fact, Kanigel (1997) argues that Taylorism has been absorbed into the living tissue of modern organization as well as into American life itself. Taylor's obsession with time, order, productivity, and efficiency translates today into our fascination with electronic organizers, mobile phones, voice mail, and beepers, all to keep us productive and efficient. Today, Taylorism may be intellectually out of fashion, but few deny its lasting impact on American society. For better and worse, Taylorism lives on.

Contemporary Rational Systems: A Structural View

For those who have a rational-systems perspective, behavior in organizations is seen as purposeful, disciplined, and rational. The concerns and concepts of rational-systems theorists are conveyed by such terms as "efficiency," "optimization," "rationality," and "design." Furthermore, emphasis is placed upon the limitations of individual decision makers in the context of organizations; hence, the notions of opportunities, constraints, formal authority, rules and regulations, compliance, and coordination represent key elements of rationality. Contemporary rational-systems theorists stress goal specificity and formalization because these elements make important contributions to the rationality and efficiency of organizations (Scott, 1998).

Goals are the desired ends that guide organizational behavior. Specific goals direct decision making, influence the formal structure, specify the tasks, guide the allocation of resources, and govern design decisions. Ambiguous goals hinder rationality because without clear goals, ordering alternatives and making rational choices are not possible; hence, even when the general organizational goals are vague (as they often are in education), the actual daily operations are guided by specific objectives. Educators may argue endlessly about the merits of progressive and traditional education, but within each school considerable agreement develops around issues such as graduation requirements, discipline policies, and school regulations.

Formalization, or the level of rules and job codification, is another feature that makes organizations rational; formalization produces standardization and regulation of work performance. Rules are developed that precisely and explicitly govern behavior; jobs are carefully defined in terms of acceptable behaviors; role relations are defined independently of personal attributes of incumbents; and sometimes the work flow itself is clearly specified. Formalization is the organization's means to make behavior predictable by standardizing and regulating it. As Simon (1947: 100) cogently states, "Organizations and institutions permit stable expectations to be formed by each member of the group as to the behavior of the other members under specific conditions. Such stable expectations are an essential precondition to a rational consideration of the consequences of action in a social group."

Formalization also contributes to the rational functioning of the organization in a number of other important ways (Scott, 1992). It makes visible the structure of the organizational relationships; thus, to improve performance managers can modify formal structures. Management by objectives (MBO); planning, programming, and budgeting systems (PPBS); strategic planning; and performance evaluation and review techniques (PERT) are examples of technical tools managers use to facilitate rational decision making. Formal structure also promotes discipline and decision making based on facts rather than emotional ties and feelings; in fact, formalization reduces to some extent both positive and negative feelings that members have toward each other. As Merton (1957: 100) observes, "Formality facilitates the interaction of the occupants of offices despite their (possibly hostile) private attitudes toward one another." Moreover, formalization renders the organization less dependent on particular individuals. The replacement of individuals is routinized so that appropriately trained individuals can be replaced with minimal disturbance. Even leadership and innovation needs are addressed by formalization. As Seldon Wolin (1960: 383) notes, "Organization, by simplifying and routinizing procedures, eliminates the need for surpassing talent. It is predicated on average human beings."

For those committed to attaining organizational goals, rationality and formalization are the hallmarks of the quest. How can structures be created and designed to get the job done efficiently? Rational-systems theorists respond with a set of guiding principles that includes division of labor, specialization, standardization, formalization, hierarchy of authority, narrow span of control, and the exception principle. Division of labor subdivides the task into its basic components and leads to specialization. Specialization in turn yields increased expertise and together with standardization of the task promotes efficient and effective responses to routine tasks. Moreover, formalization promotes standard operating procedures in the form of a system of rules and regulations. The exception principle, however, dictates that superiors must deal with exceptional situations not covered in the rules. Finally, a hierarchy of authority coordinates and controls organizational behavior by providing a unity of command, that is, top-down structure, which promotes disciplined compliance to administrative directives. The formal organization was critical, as was the belief that organizations could be designed to be efficient and effective by adhering to the preceding principles of organization.

Perhaps the greatest shortcoming of the rational-systems perspective is its rigid conception of organization. As James G. March and Herbert Simon (1958) have observed, the structure and functioning of an organization may be greatly affected both by events outside the organization and by events imperfectly coordinated within it, and neither of these occurrences can be fixed in advance. Contemporary critics also note the undue emphasis on parts rather than the whole. Senge and his colleagues (Kofman and Senge, 1993; Senge, 1990), for example, argue that restricting attention to the parts of an organization and believing that optimizing each part amounts to maximizing the whole is shortsighted because it neglects the primacy of the whole, forces artificial distinctions, and denies the systemic functioning of organizations.

TIP: THEORY INTO PRACTICE

Name each person in your school who has formal authority over teachers. What is the role of each? Their titles? How much formal authority do they have and how do they exert it? Give specific examples. Describe the division of labor and specialization in the school. Is there a narrow or broad span of control? How fixed or flexible is the curriculum? How much independence do teachers have to make their own decisions? How would you characterize the formal organization of your school?

Natural System: An Organic Model

The **natural-systems perspective** provides another view of organization that contrasts with the rational-systems perspective. The natural-systems perspective had its early roots in the human relations approach of the 1930s; it developed in large part as a reaction to the scientific managers and perceived inadequacies of the rational-systems model.

Human Relations: The Beginning

Mary Parker Follett was a pioneer in the human relations movement. She wrote a series of brilliant papers dealing with the human side of administration and argued that the fundamental problem in all organizations was developing and maintaining dynamic and harmonious relationships. In addition, Follett (1924: 300) thought that conflict was "not necessarily a wasteful outbreak of incompatibilities, but normal process by which socially valuable differences register themselves for enrichment of all concerned." Despite Follett's work, the development of the human relations approach is usually traced to studies done in the Hawthorne plant of the Western Electric Company in Chicago. These studies are basic to the literature describing informal groups, and the study of informal groups is basic to an analysis of schools.

The **Hawthorne studies** (see Roethlisberger and Dickson, 1939) began with three experiments conducted to study the relation of quality and quantity of illumination to efficiency in industry. The first illumination experiment was made in three departments. The level of illumination intensity in each department was increased at stated intervals. The results were puzzling. Increased production rates did not correspond with increased lighting, nor did production decline with reduced illumination.

In a second experiment, a test group in which illumination intensities were varied was compared to a control group with illumination held constant. Both groups showed increases in production rates that were not only substantial but also nearly identical.

Finally, in a third experiment, when the lighting for the test group was decreased and that for the control group held constant, the efficiency of both groups increased. Furthermore, the production rates increased in the test group until the light became so poor that the workers complained they could no longer see what they were doing.

The results were neither as simple nor as clear-cut as the experimenters had originally anticipated. Two conclusions seemed justified: employee output was not primarily related to lighting conditions; and too many variables had not been controlled in the experiments. The startling nature of the findings stimulated more research.

Two Harvard professors—Elton Mayo, an industrial psychologist, and Fritz Roethlisberger, a social psychologist—were retained to continue studying the relationship between physical conditions of work and productivity. The company suspected that psychological as well as physiological factors were involved. From 1927 through 1932 the two researchers continued the Hawthorne studies in a series of experiments that have since become research classics in the social sciences. One generalization became clear almost immediately. The workers' behavior did not conform to the official job specifications. An informal organization emerged that affected performance. **Informal organization** is an unofficial social structure that emerges within the organization that has informal leaders as well as informal norms, values, sentiments, and communication patterns.

The researchers found that informal patterns of interactions developed as soon as the men were put together to work on tasks. Friendships formed and well-defined groups emerged. These informal cliques were evident in interaction patterns both on and off the job. For example, one clique, rather than another, engaged in certain games during off-hours. Even more important than the different interaction patterns were the informal norms that emerged to govern behavior and unify the group. Too much work, and one was a rate buster. Too little work constituted the equally serious informal offense of chiseling. A no-squealing norm also emerged; no group member should say anything that might injure a fellow member. Other norms included not acting officiously or self-assertively; one was expected to be a "regular guy" and not to be noisy and anxious for attention and leadership.

The work group enforced respect for informal norms through ostracism, sarcasm, and invective to pressure deviant members. One mechanism to enlist compliance was binging—a quick, stiff punch on the upper arm. The bing was not physically damaging, nor was it meant to be; it was a symbolic gesture of group displeasure.

Much activity in the group countered formal role prescriptions. Workers did not stick to their jobs as prescribed but frequently traded jobs, had informal contests, and helped each other. The group also restricted production. Group norms defined a fair day's work below management's expectations, although not so far below so as to be unacceptable. Most work was done in the morning. Faster workers simply slowed their pace earlier or reported less work than they had accomplished to save production for slow days. The informal production levels were consistently maintained, even though higher production was possible. Because the group was on a piece rate, higher output would have meant higher wages. Thus, behavior was a function of group norms, not economic incentives. The experiments at the Hawthorne plant were the first to question many of the basic assumptions of human engineers and scientific managers, but others soon followed and reinforced the importance of the informal organization.

Although these findings date from the 1930s, they remain important. The human relations approach, however, is not without its detractors. Amitai Etzioni (1964) suggests that the human relations approach grossly oversimplifies the complexities of organizational life by glossing over the realities of work. Organizations have conflicting values and interests as well as shared ones; they are a source of alienation as well as human satisfaction. Worker dissatisfaction is just as likely to be symptomatic of real underlying conflicts of interests as to be indicative of a lack of understanding of the situation. Put simply, organizations are often not one big "happy family." Contemporary critics of the human relations movement (Clark et al., 1994; Scott, 1998) also argue that the concern for workers was not authentic; rather, management used it as a tool or strategy to manipulate subordinates. Nevertheless, one conclusion is clear: the human relations approach tempered the scientific managers' concentration on organizational structure with an emphasis on employee motivation and satisfaction and group morale.

The impact of the Hawthorne studies on schools was evident in writing and exhortation on democratic administration. The ill-defined watchword of the period was "democratic"—democratic administration, democratic supervision, democratic decision making, and democratic teaching. As Roald Campbell (1971) noted, this emphasis on human relations and democratic practices often meant a series of prescriptions as to how conditions ought to be and how persons in an organization ought to behave. Supposed "principles of administration" abounded, but they were usually no more than the observations of successful administrators or the democratic ideologies of college professors. In the 1940s and early 1950s, educational administration, as a democratic approach, was long on rhetoric and woefully short on research and practice (Campbell, 1971).

Contemporary Natural Systems: A Human Resources View

While rational-systems proponents conceive of organizations as structural arrangements deliberately devised to achieve specific goals, natural-systems advocates view organizations as primarily social groups trying to adapt and survive in their particular situation. Natural-systems analysts generally agree that goal specificity and formalization are characteristics of organizations, but they argue that other attributes are of much greater significance; in fact, some maintain that formal goals and structures have little to do with what is actually happening in organizations (Scott, 1998; also see Etzioni, 1975; Perrow, 1978).

The natural-systems view focuses on similarities among social groups. Thus, organizations, like all social groups, are driven primarily by the basic goal of survival—not by specifically devised goals of particular institutions. Gouldner (1959: 405) captures the essence of the natural-systems approach when he states, "The organization, according to this model, strives to survive and to maintain its equilibrium, and this striving may persist even after its explicitly held goals have been successfully attained. This strain toward survival may even on occasion lead to the neglect or distortion of the organization's goals." Survival, then, is the overriding goal. Formal organizations are viewed not primarily as means for achieving specific ends but as vehicles for individuals to satisfy their human needs. People are valuable human resources for the organization.

Just as the natural-systems analysts generally disregard goals as important attributes of organizations, they also view as unimportant the formal structures constructed to achieve goals. Although they acknowledge that formal structures do exist, they argue that behavior in organizations is regulated primarily by informal structures that emerge to transform the formal system. Thus, a natural-systems perspective emphasizes the informal organization rather than the formal, people rather than structure, and human needs rather than organizational demands. Individuals in organizations are never simply hired hands but bring along with them their heads and hearts. They enter the organization with their own needs, beliefs, values, and motivations. They interact with others and generate informal norms, status structures, power relations, communication networks, and working arrangements (Scott, 1992).

In sum, goals and structure do not make organizations distinctive; in fact, formal features of organization are overshadowed by more generic attributes such as the desire for the system to survive, characteristics of the individuals, and informal relationships. Whereas the rational-systems perspective stresses the importance of structure over individuals, the natural-systems approach emphasizes individuals over structure. In the stark terms of Warren G. Bennis (1959), the rational-systems focus is on "structure without people," whereas the clear reversal of priorities in the natural-systems model produces an orientation of "people without organization."

Thus far we have traced the development of organizational thought from its early beginnings in scientific management and human relations to its contemporary systems perspectives—rational and natural (see Figure 1.2).

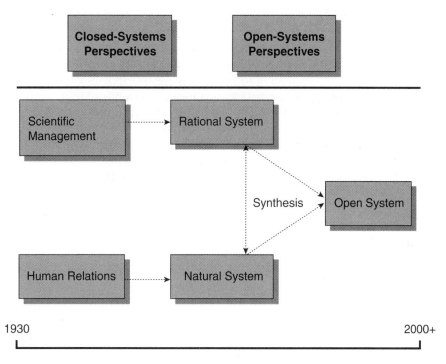

FIGURE 1.2 *Growth and Development of Organizational Thought*

The early systems perspectives were closed, but they have given way to open-systems views. Virtually everyone now agrees that organizations are open systems, and viewing them in this way provides a framework for a synthesis of the formal, rational elements of organizational life with the informal, natural ones. We turn next to a discussion of the open-systems approach to organizations and schools.

TIP: THEORY INTO PRACTICE

Name each person in the organization who has informal power but does not have formal authority. Why does each person have such power? Where do they get their power? Describe the important informal norms that exist in your school. How do the informal and formal leaders get along? Give some examples of their cooperation. What group of teachers is the "in-group"? Does the group have a rival? How do the informal groups get along? How much conflict is there between those with formal authority and those with only informal authority? What is the conflict about? Give some examples.

OPEN SYSTEM: AN INTEGRATION

The **open-systems perspective** was a reaction to the unrealistic assumption that organizational behavior could be isolated from external forces. Competition, resources, and political pressures from the environment affect the internal workings of organizations. The open-systems model views organizations as not only influenced by environments, but also dependent on them. At a general level, organizations are easily pictured as open systems. Organizations take inputs from the environment, transform them, and produce outputs (see Figure 1.3). For example, schools are social systems that take resources such as labor, students, and money from the environment and subject these inputs to an educational transformation process to produce literate and educated students and graduates.

Because the rational-system approach, particularly the scientific managers, ignored the impact of individual needs and social relations and because the natural-systems, especially the human relations proponents, discounted formal structure, both of these systems perspectives are limited and incomplete. Clearly both the formal and informal as well as structure and people are critical to understanding organizations. An open-systems perspective supplies such a vantage point.

Chester I. Barnard (1938) was one of the first to consider both views in his analysis of organizational life in Functions of the Executive. The product of Barnard's years as president of Bell Telephone Company of New Jersey, this book offers a comprehensive theory of cooperative behavior in formal organizations. Barnard provided the original definitions of formal and informal organizations and cogently demonstrated the inevitable interaction between them. Barnard (1940) himself summarized the contributions of his work in

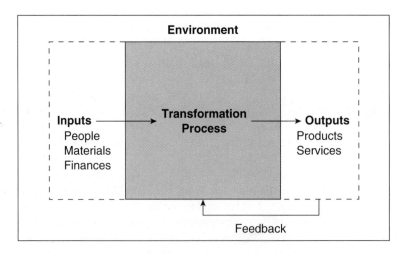

FIGURE 1.3   *Open System with Feedback Loop*

terms of structural and dynamic concepts. The structural concepts he considered important were the individual, the cooperative system, the formal organization, the complex formal organization, and the informal organization. His important dynamic concepts were free will, cooperation, communication, authority, the decision process, and dynamic equilibrium.

Herbert Simon (1947), in *Administrative Behavior,* extended Barnard's work and used the concept of organizational equilibrium as a focal point for a formal theory of work motivation. The organization was seen as an exchange system in which inducements are exchanged for work. Employees remain in the organization as long as they perceive the inducements as larger than their work contributions.

The organization, although providing the framework, information, and values for rational decisions, is limited in its ability to collect and process information, search for alternatives, and predict consequences. Therefore, questions are resolved through satisficing rather than through optimizing. In Simon's view, no best solution exists to any given problem, but some solutions are more satisfactory than others (see Chapter 9).

Another important theoretical formulation of organizations (see Chapter 3) evolved from the writings of Max Weber (1947). Although many of Weber's views are consistent with those espoused by the scientific managers, Weber's discussions of bureaucracy and authority have provided present-day theorists with a starting point in their conceptions of organizations as social systems that interact with and are dependent upon their environments. It remained to Talcott Parsons (1960), however, to stress the importance of the environment on the organization and anticipate a conception of the organization as an open system—a social system dependent on and influenced by its environment.

The open-systems model has the potential to provide a synthesis by combining the rational and natural perspectives. Organizations are complex and dynamic. They have formal structures to achieve specified goals, but are composed of people who have their own idiosyncratic needs, interests, and beliefs that often conflict with organizational expectations. Thus, organizations have planned and unplanned features, rational and irrational characteristics, and formal and informal structures. In some organizations rational concerns dominate the relationships and natural, social relationships predominate in others. In all organizations, however, both rational and natural elements coexist within a system that is open to its environment.

Some scholars argue that contemporary organizations are either open, natural systems or open, rational systems, which are adaptations to different kinds of environments (Lawrence and Lorsch, 1967). Our view is that schools are open systems confronted with both rational and natural constraints that change as the environmental forces change; to neglect either the rational or the natural elements is shortsighted. Open-systems theory is our general framework for exploring the conceptual foundations of educational administration in this text. Although many theories are discussed in our analyses, the open-systems perspective is the overarching framework that underscores four internal subsystems that interact to influence organizational behavior: the structural, cultural, individual, and political systems. The key concepts, assumptions, and principles of each of the three systems perspectives are summarized at the end of this chapter in Table 1.2.

TIP: THEORY INTO PRACTICE

Which is more important in your school, the formal or the informal organization? Why? What area does each control? Where do you fit into the power relations in your school? What improvements would you try to make to the formal and informal relations in your school if you became the principal? Why? Who are the people in your school whose voices have been silenced and why? Finally, analyze the leadership behavior of your principal. To what extent does she or he rely on the formal organization and informal organization to get things done? What is the balance between the two? Which is more important? From your view is the balance good or could it be improved? How?

KEY PROPERTIES OF OPEN SYSTEMS

An open system is concerned with both structure and process; it is a dynamic system with both stability and flexibility, with both tight and loose structural relationships. The organization as an arrangement of roles and relationships is not static. To survive, the organization must adapt and to adapt, it must change. The interdependence of the organization and its environment is critical. Instead of neglecting the environment, as the rational-systems perspective does, or seeing it as hostile, as is the case with the natural-systems perspective, "the open-systems model stresses the reciprocal ties that bind and interrelate the organization with those elements that surround and penetrate it. Indeed, the environment is even seen to be the source of order itself" (Scott, 1987b: 91).

There is some agreement about the key properties and processes that characterize most social systems. We begin by presenting, defining, and discussing nine central concepts. An open system is a set of interacting elements that acquires *inputs* from the outside, transforms them, and produces outputs for the environment. People, raw materials, information, and money are the typical inputs for organizations. In the *transformational process,* these inputs are changed into something of value called *outputs,* which are then exported back into the environment. Outputs are usually products and services, but they may also include employee satisfaction and other by-products of the transformation process. Classrooms, books, computers, instructional materials, teachers, and students are critical inputs for schools. Ideally, students are transformed by the school system into educated graduates, who then contribute to the broader environment, or society. These three elements of an open system are illustrated in Figure 1.3.

The system's capacity for feedback facilitates the repetitive and cyclic pattern of "input-transformation-output." *Feedback* is information about the system that enables it to correct itself. Formal communication structures—PTA and various advisory councils—and informal political contacts are established inside and outside the school building to provide feedback to the school. Unlike mechanical systems, however, social systems do not always use the information to change. The superintendent of a school system who receives information about falling SAT scores and increased difficulties of graduates to get jobs and enter the colleges of their choice can use this information to identify factors within the system that are contributing to the problem and take corrective action. Yet not all superintendents choose to act. Hence, although feedback provides self-correcting opportunities, the potential is not always realized.

Systems have *boundaries*—that is, they are differentiated from their environments. The boundaries are less clear for open than for closed systems, but they do exist. Are parents part of the school system? It depends. In some schools they are considered part of the schools and in others they are not. Regardless of whether parents are considered to be inside the boundaries, schools expend substantial energy in boundary-spanning activities such as parent-teacher meetings, community service projects, and adult education programs.

The *environment* is anything outside the boundaries of the system that either affects the attributes of the internal components or is changed by the social system itself (see Chapter 7 for a detailed consideration of external environment). For a specific school, district policies, central administrators, other school buildings, and the community are important features of the school's environment. Although organizational environment is typically understood to refer to conditions external to the organization, the clear separation of the organization from its environment is virtually impossible when applied to open systems such as schools. In practice, however, some administrators attempt to control the openness of the school. For example, only appropriate clientele are allowed into the school building, people from the street are locked out, and visitors are required to sign in at the principal's office.

The process by which a group of regulators acts to maintain a steady state among the system components is called *homeostasis*. A biological analogy illustrates the concept: when an organism moves from a warm environment to a cold one, homeostatic mechanisms trigger reactions to maintain body temperature. Similarly, in a school building, crucial elements and activities are protected so that overall stability is maintained. Systems that survive tend to move toward a steady state—equilibrium. This steady state, however, is not static. Energy from and to the environment is continuously imported and exported. Although forces that seek to maintain the system counter any force that threatens to disrupt the system, systems do exhibit a growth dynamic. Events that throw the system out of balance are addressed by actions that are calculated to move the system toward a new state of balance, or equilibrium. As administrators are well aware, disruptive stresses upset this equilibrium and create temporary periods of disequilibrium. A community group may demand that a course such as sex education be deleted. This causes disequilibrium, but the system either changes itself or neutralizes the disruptive forces impinging on it; that is, it restores equilibrium.

The tendency for any system to run down—to cease to exist—is called *entropy*. Open systems can overcome entropy by importing energy from their environment. Organizations, for example, seek to maintain a favorable position with respect to their environments by adapting to changing environmental demands. Pressure from a state department of education for new programs typically results in accommodation to those demands, albeit with more taxes and resources for the system.

The principle of *equifinality* suggests that systems can reach the same end from different initial positions and through different paths. Thus, no one best way exists to organize and, likewise, there is no one best way to reach the same end. For instance, schools may select a variety of means (e.g., discovery learning, independent projects, interactive technologies) to achieve improvements in critical thinking skills of students.

SOCIAL-SYSTEMS MODEL: BASIC ASSUMPTIONS

The notion of a social system is a general one. It can be applied to social organizations that are carefully and deliberately planned or to those that emerge spontaneously. The school is a system of social interaction; it is an organized whole comprising interacting personalities bound together in an organic relationship (Waller, 1932). As a social system, the school is characterized by an interdependence of parts, a clearly defined population, differentiation from its environment, a complex network of social relationships, and its own unique culture. As with all formal organizations, analysis of the school as a social system calls attention to both the planned and unplanned—the formal and informal—aspects of organizational life.

Thus far in our discussion of systems we have made several implicit assumptions. Let us now make these and others explicit as we examine the school as a social system. We have gleaned these assumptions from the literature, but the primary sources are Jacob W. Getzels and Egon G. Guba (1957); Jacob W. Getzels, James Lipham, and Ronald F. Campbell (1968); Charles E. Bidwell (1965), and W. Richard Scott (1998, 2003).

- Social systems are open systems. Schools are affected by the values and resources of the community, by politics, and by history.
- Social systems are peopled. People act on the basis of their needs as well as their roles.
- Social systems consist of interdependent parts, characteristics, and activities that contribute to and receive from the whole. When one

part is affected, a ripple goes through the social system. For example, when the principal is confronted by parental demands for new courses, not only is the principal affected directly but also the teachers and students are affected.

- Social systems are goal oriented. Indeed they often have multiple goals. In a school, student learning and control are just two of many goals. The central goal of any school system is the preparation of its students for adult roles.
- Social systems are structural. Different components are needed to perform specific functions and allocate resources. School systems have division of labor (e.g., math and science teachers), specialization (e.g., teachers, guidance counselors, and administrators), and hierarchy (superintendent, principals, assistant principals, and teachers).
- Social systems are normative. Formal rules and regulations as well as informal norms prescribe appropriate behavior.
- Social systems are sanction bearing. The norms for behavior are enforced with reward and punishment. Formal mechanisms include expulsion, suspension, termination, tenure, and promotion. Informal sanctions include the use of sarcasm, ostracism, and ridicule.
- Social systems are political; power relations inevitably enter into social relations.
- Social systems have distinctive cultures, that is, a dominant set of shared values that influence behavior.
- Social systems are conceptual and relative. The social systems construct is a general one that applies to social organizations regardless of size. For one purpose, a classroom can be considered a social system. For other purposes, the school or school district may be taken as a social system.
- All formal organizations are social systems. But all social systems are not formal organizations.

These assumptions suggest that a school consists of a number of important elements or subsystems that affect organizational behavior.

KEY ELEMENTS OF THE SCHOOL SOCIAL SYSTEM

All social systems have some activities and functions that are accomplished in a fairly stable fashion. For example, if we conceive of society itself as a social system, then the routine and imperative functions of educating, protecting, and governing are performed by educational, legal, and governmental institutions. Regardless of the nature of the social system, patterns of behavior become regular and routine.

When the accomplishment of an objective requires collective effort, individuals often set up organizations specifically designed to coordinate the activities and to furnish incentives for others to join them in this purpose. Such an organization—explicitly established to achieve certain goals—is a **formal organization.** Our concern is with the school social system as a formal organization.

Figure 1.4 pictures the major elements, or subsystems, of a social system. Behavior in formal organizations is influenced not only by structural and individual elements but also by cultural and political elements. *Structure* is defined in terms of formal bureaucratic expectations, which are designed and organized to fulfill the goals of the organization. The *individual* is viewed in terms of the needs, goals, beliefs, and cognitive understandings of work roles; the individual provides the energy and capacity to achieve the organization's goals. *Culture* is the shared work orientations of participants; it gives the organization special identity. *Politics* is the system of informal power relations that emerge to resist other systems of control. Further, all the elements and interactions within the system are constrained by important forces from both the *technical core* and the *environment;* the system is open. Finally, formal organizations as social systems must solve the basic problems of adaptation, goal achievement, integration, and latency if they are to survive and prosper.[1]

The model of formal organization that we are proposing takes all of these factors into consideration. We begin by examining internal elements of the system and then discuss the impact of the environment and technical core (teaching-learning process) on the school and its outcomes.

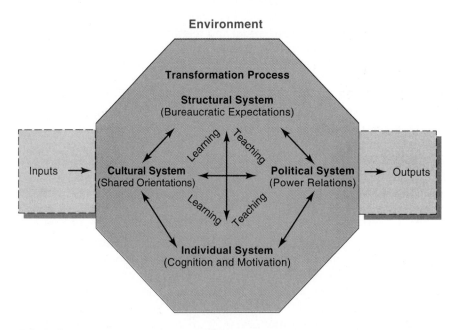

FIGURE 1.4   *Internal Elements of the System*

Structure

Bureaucratic expectations are formal demands and obligations set by the organization; they are the key building blocks of organizational structure. **Bureaucratic roles** are defined by sets of expectations, which are combined into positions and offices in the organization. In schools, the positions of principal, teacher, and student are critical ones and each is defined in terms of a set of expectations. The bureaucratic expectations specify the appropriate behavior for a specific role or position. A teacher, for instance, has the obligation to plan learning experiences for students and has the duty to engage students in a pedagogically effective manner. Bureaucratic roles and expectations are the official blueprints for action, the organizational givens of the office.

Some formal expectations are critical and mandatory; others are more flexible. Many roles are not precisely prescribed; that is, the expectations associated with most positions are wide ranging. This range of freedom makes it feasible for teachers with quite different personalities to perform the same roles without undue tension or conflict (Parsons and Shils, 1951). Roles derive their meaning from other roles in the system and in this sense are complementary. For example, it is difficult, if not impossible, to define either the role of student or that of teacher in a school without specifying the relationship of teacher to student. Likewise, the role of principal is dependent on its relationship to the roles of teacher and student.

From a vast array of vague and contradictory expectations, formal organizations select a few general bureaucratic expectations that are reasonably consistent with the organization's goals. These expectations often are formalized, codified, and adopted as official rules and regulations of the organization; they may delineate such things as arrival times, building assignments, and job descriptions. Specialization—the expectation that employee behavior will be guided by expertise—complements the rules and regulations. Thus, a teacher is expected to behave in appropriate ways based on the school's rules and the expertise demanded by the instructional job.

Put simply, formal organizations such as schools have structures composed of bureaucratic expectations and roles, a hierarchy of offices and positions, rules and regulations, and specialization. Bureaucratic expectations define organizational roles; roles are combined into positions and offices; and positions and offices are arranged into a formal hierarchy of authority according to their relative power and status. Rules and regulations are provided to guide decision making and enhance organizational rationality, and labor is divided as individuals specialize in tasks. Some structures facilitate the operation of the organization and others hinder, and undoubtedly, behavior in an organization is determined in part by the structural arrangement of the school.

Individual

The fact that a social unit has been formally established does not mean that all activities and interactions of its members conform strictly to structural requirements—the official blueprint. Regardless of official positions and elaborate bureaucratic expectations, members have their own individual needs, beliefs, and cognitive understandings of their jobs.

Just as not all expectations are relevant for the analysis of organizational behavior, not all individual needs are relevant to organizational performance. What are those facets of the individual that are most instrumental in determining an individual's organizational behavior? We postulate several important cognitive aspects of the individual: needs, goals, beliefs, and cognition. Work motivation constitutes the single most relevant set of needs for employees in formal organizations. We will elaborate extensively later, but for now work needs are defined as basic forces that motivate work behavior.

Cognition is the individual's use of mental representations to understand the job in terms of perception, knowledge, and expected behavior. Workers seek to create meaningful, coherent representations of their work regardless of its complexity. They learn what their job is about by monitoring and checking their own behavior. Their needs, personal beliefs, goals, and previous experiences become the bases for constructing organizational reality and interpreting their work. Their motivation and cognition are influenced by such factors as beliefs about personal control and competence, individual goals, personal expectations for failure and success, and work motives. In brief, the salient aspects of the individual system are personal needs, beliefs, goals, and cognitive orientations to work.

Although we have examined the influence of structural (S) and individual (I) elements separately, behavior is a function (f) of the interaction of bureaucratic role expectations and the relevant work orientations of the organizational member [$B = f(S \times I)$]. For example, the evaluation of the teaching staff is affected by district policy as well as by the principal's own needs. The rules and regulations state that the principal is expected to evaluate each teacher at given intervals with a specified evaluation instrument. The principal acts as a result of this policy. Each principal's behavior differs in the evaluation meetings, perhaps because of individual cognition and motivational needs. One building administrator who has a great personal desire for social acceptance from the teachers may treat these sessions as an opportunity for friendly socializing rather than for evaluating. But another principal, lacking such a need for social acceptance, may follow the book and remain analytical in the evaluation. The two principals are affected by both elements, but the first is more influenced by individual needs and the second by bureaucratic role expectations.

The ratio of bureaucratic expectations to individual work needs, which at least partly determines behavior, will vary with the specific type of organization, the specific job, and the specific person involved. Figure 1.5 presents pictorially the general nature of this interaction. Vertical line A represents a hypothetical situation in which the proportion of behavior controlled by the bureaucratic structure is relatively large; line B (at the right) represents the situation in which behavior is primarily controlled by individual needs.

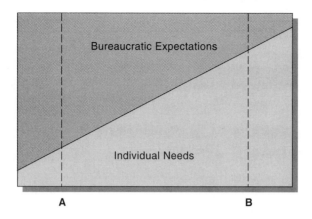

FIGURE 1.5   *Interaction of Bureaucratic and Individual Elements Affecting Behavior*

Military organizations commonly are considered to be represented by line *A*—more bureaucratic control—whereas research and development organizations are better represented by line *B*. Most schools probably fall between these two extremes. Free, open-concept, or Montessori schools would be close to line *B*. Church-related schools are typically thought to be closer to line *A*. Where do administrators and students fall in this regard? Individuals differ; some tend toward line *B*—free spirits—and some toward line *A*—bureaucrats. In our example of the two principals in evaluation sessions, the first with a high need for social acceptance would be near line *B* and the second closer to line *A*.

Culture

There is a dynamic relationship between bureaucratic role demands and individual work needs as people are brought together in the workplace. Organizations develop their own distinctive cultures. As organizational members interact, shared values, norms, beliefs, and ways of thinking emerge. These shared orientations form the culture of the organization. Culture distinguishes one organization from another and provides members with a sense of organizational identity (Hellriegel, Slocum, and Woodman, 1992; Daft, 1994). In a school, shared beliefs and informal norms among teachers have a significant impact on behavior. Culture provides members with a commitment to beliefs and values beyond themselves; individuals belong to a group that is larger than themselves. When the culture is strong, so is their identification with the group and the influence of the group.

Culture represents the unwritten, feeling part of the organization (Daft, 1994). Communication of feelings is easy among peers, especially friends. Shared orientations help maintain cohesiveness and feelings of personal integrity, self-respect, and belonging. Because many interactions in organizations are informal, they are personal and not dominated by authority. They furnish opportunities for the individual to maintain his or her personality against the attempts of the bureaucratic organization to submerge, if not destroy, it (Barnard, 1938). Members receive important rewards from the group and group norms are significant in guiding their behavior. For example, accepted informal procedures, not formal rules, may develop among the teachers for disciplining students; in fact, the custodial informal norms for controlling students become the criteria for judging "effective" teaching in many schools. Good control is equated with good teaching.

Behavior in formal organizations is influenced not only by structural and individual elements but also by emergent values and shared orientations of the work group. Organizational culture, with its important group norms, values, and beliefs, is another powerful force that affects organizational behavior.

Politics

Structure represents the formal dimension of the school social system, whereas the personal aspect of the system is represented in the individual. Culture is the collective dimension of the system that blends the formal with the personal to create a system of shared beliefs. But it is the political dimension that spawns the informal power relations that emerge, often to resist other systems of legitimate control. Members who work within the confines of the structure, culture, and individual systems usually contribute directly to the needs of the organization at large. Structure provides formal authority; culture generates informal authority; and the individual brings the authority of expertise to the organization. Politics, in contrast, is typically informal, often clandestine, and frequently illegitimate. It is illegitimate because it is behavior usually designed to benefit the individual or group at the expense of the organization. Consequently, most politics is divisive and conflictual, pitting individuals and groups against each other and against the organization at large (Mintzberg, 1983a; Pfeffer, 1992).

Politics, however, is an inevitable part of organizational life. There are always those who want to seize power for their own personal ends. In its extreme, one can conceive of an organization "as a mass of competing power groups, each seeking to influence policy in terms of its own interest, or, in terms of its own distorted image of the [organization's] interest" (Strauss, 1964: 164). Power relations get played out in a variety of ways: political tactics and games, bargaining, and conflict resolution. Members are invariably forced to play the power game of politics. Allison (1971: 168) puts it succinctly, "Power . . . is an elusive blend . . . of bargaining advantages, skill, and will in using bargaining advantages. . . ." Although politics is informal, divisive, and typically illegitimate, there is little doubt that it is an important force influencing organizational behavior.

To understand organizational life one must look at both formal and informal as well as legitimate and illegitimate forms of power. Hence, structure, individual, culture, and politics are critical elements of the social systems; these elements can become individual frames or lenses to view organizational behavior, but remember behavior is a function of the *interaction* of these elements.

Technical Core: Teaching and Learning

All organizations have a technical core that is concerned primarily with the major mission of the social system. In schools the teaching-learning process is the core of the organization. All other activities are secondary to the basic mission of teaching and learning, which shapes the administrative decisions in schools. Learning occurs when there is a stable change in an individual's knowledge or behavior; there is no one best explanation of learning because it is a complex cognitive process. Different theories of learning have different implications for teaching depending on what is to be learned. Administration does not happen in a vacuum—behavioral, cognitive, and constructivist perspectives of learning provide the setting for school decision making (see Chapter 2).

Environment

As a general definition, environment is everything that is outside the organization. But unlike physical systems, social systems are open; hence, the boundaries are much more ambiguous and the environment more intrusive. There is no doubt that environment is critical to the organizational functioning of schools. It is the system's source of energy. It provides resources, values, technology, demands, and history—all of which place constraints and opportunities on organizational action.

Which features of the environment are most salient for constraining behavior in schools? There is no quick or simple answer. Both broad and specific environmental factors influence the structure and activities of schools. Larger social, legal, economic, political, demographic, and technological trends have a potentially powerful impact on schools, but the effects of such general environmental forces are by no means clear. In contrast, interested constituencies and stakeholders, such as parents, taxpayers, unions, regulatory agencies, colleges and universities, state legislatures, accrediting agencies, and educational associations, have more immediate and direct effects on schools. But again the results are not certain.

The degree of uncertainty, the degree of structure or organization, and the degree of scarcity in the environment condition the response of the school to environmental factors. School decision makers monitor the environment for information, and their perceptions determine to a large degree the future directions of the organization. Schools, like all organizations, attempt to reduce uncertainty and control their environments; therefore, administrators often resort to strategies to minimize external effects. Moreover, if the groups and organizations of the environment are highly organized, then the school is faced with a potent set of demands and constraints, and the result will likely be compliance. Finally, schools compete in an environment made up of various resource pools. If resources of a particular kind are scarce, then the internal structure and activities will develop in ways that will facilitate their acquisition.

In brief, schools are open systems that are affected by external forces. Although there is basic agreement on the importance of the environment, its complexity makes analysis difficult. Nonetheless, we need to consider what factors individually and in relation to others create the basic external demands, constraints, and opportunities to which schools respond. We will return to a detailed analysis of the environment in Chapter 7.

Outcomes

A school, then, can be thought of as a set of elements—individual, structural, cultural, and political. However, behavior in organizations is not simply a function of its elements and environmental forces; it is a function of the interaction of the elements. Thus, organizational behavior is the result of the dynamic relationship among its elements. More specifically, behavior is a function of the interaction of structure, individual, culture, and politics as constrained by environmental forces. To understand and predict the behavior in schools, it is useful to examine the six pairs of interactions among the elements in terms of their harmony. We posit a **congruence postulate:** other things being equal, the greater the degree of congruence among the elements of the system, the more effective the system.[2] For example, the more consistent the informal norms and the formal expectations, the more likely the organization will be to achieve its formal goals. Likewise, the better the fit between individual motivation and bureaucratic expectations, the more effective the performance. In Table 1.1, examples of critical questions concerning the congruence of each pair of key elements are outlined.

Performance outcomes are indicators of goal accomplishment. Performance outcomes include such indicators as achievement, job satisfaction, absenteeism, and overall performance quality. In any case, the critical aspects of behavior are defined by the outputs of the system. The model assumes that the effective achievement of these behavioral outcomes is a function of the degree of congruence among the system elements. Hence, organizational effectiveness is the degree to which actual outcomes are consistent with expected outcomes. The key elements, their interactions, the demands and constraints of the environment, and the behavioral outcomes are summarized in Figure 1.6.

Internal Feedback Loops

The social-systems model pictured in Figure 1.6 also has both internal and external feedback mechanisms. For example, the formal school structure and the informal groups both attempt to influence individual behavior (Abbott, 1965b).

TABLE 1.1

Congruence between Pairs of Key Elements

Congruence Relationships	Crucial Questions
Individual ↔ Structural	To what extent do individual work needs enhance bureaucratic expectations?
Individual ↔ Culture	To what extent are shared orientations of organizational culture consistent with individual work needs?
Individual ↔ Politics	To what extent do power relations conflict with individual work needs?
Structural ↔ Cultural	To what extent do the bureaucratic expectations reinforce the shared orientations of the cultural system?
Structural ↔ Political	To what extent do the power relations undermine bureaucratic expectations?
Political ↔ Culture	To what extent do the power relations conflict with and undermine the shared orientations of the culture?

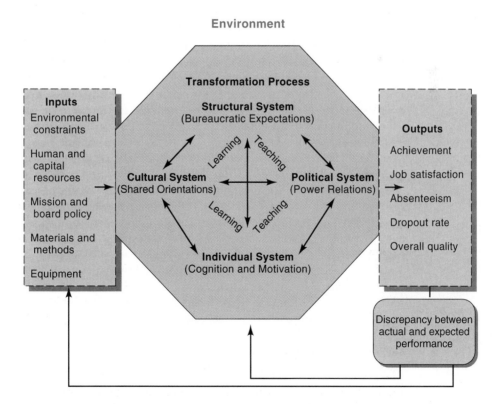

FIGURE 1.6   *Social-Systems Model for Schools*

Feedback informs individuals how the bureaucratic structure and the informal organization view their behavior. Although the bureaucracy has formal mechanisms and the work group informal ones, both have internal feedback loops.

The formal school organization provides an official definition of the position, its rank in the hierarchy, and a set of expected behaviors that go with it. In fact, the bureaucratic structure has an established incentive pattern for ensuring appropriate behavior. If the school bureaucracy approves of an individual's performance, positive rewards reinforce his or her behavior. If that person's behavior is evaluated as inferior, positive incentives are reduced and negative incentives are increased.

Informal groups similarly influence behavior. As our discussion of the Hawthorne studies explained, group norms control behavior. In the school building, norms exist within and among all informal peer groups. For example, teachers expect their peers to act appropriately to control students. If a teacher fails to maintain discipline in the classroom, the other teachers apply sanctions: sarcasm and ostracism in the teachers' lounge can have devastating effects on an individual.

External Feedback Loops

Behavior in schools also is monitored through external feedback loops. The culture of the community provides environmental constraints that directly influence bureaucratic expectations, group norms, and organizational goals that indirectly influence individual needs. In spite of attempts by a school to isolate itself, it remains open to community, state, and national forces. The introduction of AIDS education into the school curriculum, for example, rarely goes unnoticed by the public. In fact, organized community groups provide important inputs about what they consider the goals and outcomes of an acceptable AIDS education program.

Social behavior in a school is thus affected directly by at least four internal elements, or subsystems—structure, individual, culture, and politics—all occurring in the context of teaching and learning. Moreover, as Figure 1.6 illustrates, internal and external feedback reinforce appropriate organizational behavior. When there is a discrepancy between expected and actual outcomes, the feedback loops inform individuals and groups inside and outside the system.

The social-systems model gives a dynamic view of the school, with the feedback mechanisms and elements providing the action components. Good, bad, and neutral events occur constantly, and the dynamic nature of the system becomes even more evident when we consider the ways that students, teachers, and administrators affect one another's behavior. Systems analysis focuses on how the totality—elements and activities—produces a given result. The dynamic result is not predictable with complete accuracy because of the infinite variations that can occur as bureaucracy, subgroups, and individuals modify goals, express values, and exert power through leadership, decision making, and communication.

THE SCHOOL AS A LEARNING ORGANIZATION

It should be abundantly clear by now that organizational life is complex because it is part of an intricate network of social relationships. The full meaning of any event can only be understood in the context of the system; that is, by contemplating the whole rather than isolated parts of the system. Such an approach has been termed "systems thinking" (Senge, 1990), and it fits well into viewing the school as a social system.

Schools are service organizations that are committed to teaching and learning. The ultimate goal of the school is student learning; in fact, its very existence is based on such activity. Schools more than any other kind of organization should be **learning organizations.** They should be places where participants continually expand their capacities to create and achieve, where novel patterns of thinking are encouraged, where collective aspirations are nurtured, where participants learn how to learn together, and where the organization expands its capacity for innovation and problem solving (Senge, 1990; Watkins and Marsick, 1993). A complementary definition of a learning organization is one in which the participants pursue common purposes with a collective commitment to routinely assessing the value of those purposes, modifying them when appropriate, and continually developing more effective and efficient ways to achieve those purposes (Leithwood and Louis, 1998).

Although the concept of learning organization has gained widespread notoriety since Senge's pioneering analysis of the art and practice of the learning organization (1990), the literature has been long on theoretical analysis and short on research evidence, a condition that led Weick and Westley (1996) to comment that "there appear to be more reviews of organizational learning than there is substance to review (p. 40)." Empirical research, however, is just beginning to emerge in schools (Ben-Peretz and Schonmann, 1998; Leithwood, Jantzi, and Steinbach, 1998, and Louis and Kruse, 1998) that supports the compelling theoretical rationale of schools as learning organizations.

If schools are to be effective learning organizations, they must find ways to create structures (Chapter 3) that continuously support teaching and learning (Chapter 2) and enhance organizational adaptation; develop organizational cultures and climates that are open, collaborative, and self-regulating (Chapter 5); attract individuals who are secure, efficacious and open to change (Chapter 4); and prevent vicious and illegitimate politics from displacing the legitimate activities of learning and teaching (Chapter 6). Transformational leadership (Chapter 11), open and continuous communication (Chapter 10), and shared decision making (Chapter 9) are mechanisms that should and can enhance organizational learning in schools. The challenge is to create schools that have the capacity to respond effectively not only to contemporary problems (Chapter 7), but also to new and emerging issues of school effectiveness (Chapter 8).

A CASE FOR LEADERSHIP

Rash Decision?

Imagine that you are the superintendent of the Indianola School District. The town of Indianola is a suburban community 10 miles south of a large midwestern city. The town of 30,000 people has become increasingly more professional and diverse as young professionals have moved into the community to complement the old-time community residents who are mostly blue- and white-collar workers. As you pick up the morning paper, you are startled to find the following account:

An Indianola eighth grader is spending seven days at home on suspension after being accused of assaulting a teacher with a weapon: poison ivy. After classmates reported her, Angela Kim, 14, admitted to her parents and school officials that she had rubbed the plant on the chair of her science teacher, Tom Jones, at Oak Street Middle School. Angela was upset at Jones; she accuses Jones of treating her differently from other students because she is Asian, said her mother, Angie Kim. The family is Korean.

Jones did not develop a rash, but middle school Principal Chris Smith said the district's policy defines a weapon as a gun, knife, dangerous object, or chemical. Principals can suspend students for up to seven days without consulting the central office, and that is precisely what he did last Thursday. "If you do something to hurt someone else and do it on purpose, it's wrong," the principal exclaimed.

Angela's father, Hop Kim, is meeting today with the principal to ask that the suspension be reconsidered. Mr. Kim said his daughter complained to him about Jones earlier in the school year. "She said he called her names and treated her differently than he did other kids," Mr. Kim said. "I told her she might have misunderstood him. I tried to blame it on her. I told her to respect her teachers and pay more attention in class and not pay so much attention to personal conflict." But, "Now I am not sure. Maybe the atmosphere of the school is poor. How could the principal suspend my daughter, who is an honor student and who

has never been in trouble, without talking to her parents before taking such drastic action?"

Mr. Kim emphasized that he did not seek news media attention, noting that Fred Reiss, a friend of his, called the *News*. Reiss, an Indianola resident and attorney, said the school's punishment is excessive and he urged the Kims to fight the decision. He believes that the punishment is a reaction to incidents around the country, including the shooting deaths at Columbine High School in Colorado.

"This is not going to give any serious credibility to the issue of weapons possession in the schools," Reiss said. "Is someone going to be punished because they're carrying peanuts? Leaves? We need to have any punishment fit the offense."

Family members say Angela gathered the leaves, which were near the school, because the teacher and her classmates were harassing her; in fact, "the teacher was doing nothing to prevent other students from making fun of her. She is a very good kid," Mrs. Kim said. "She is a spelling bee champion in schools. She never made any trouble." She simply lashed out because she thought the teacher insulted her. The parents admit that what she did was wrong, but they say they are worried about her safety and emotional health because this issue has been blown out of proportion. "We moved to Indianola because we believed it would be a good place to raise our children and now we find that the school does not support people who are of a different race or color." Principal Smith admitted that Angela Kim was not a troublesome student, but he is adamant that the offense was serious and warrants a seven-day suspension. "We have zero tolerance for violence in this school," he exclaimed.

When pressed on the charges of teacher and student racism, the principal simply rejected the charges as "groundless fabrications." Angela will get her homework assignments and, according to district policy, will be allowed to make up 60 percent of her work for credit. For his part, Mr. Kim

(Continued)

A CASE FOR LEADERSHIP *(Concluded)*

says things are out of control, and he blames the principal and teacher for not setting a good example. "This is America," he says, "everyone should be treated fairly and with respect."

- Should you, as superintendent, get involved?
- Do you need to touch base with the principal before the meeting or "keep your hands off"?
- What implications does this case have for the structure and procedures of the school? For district policy? For the culture of the school? For student-teacher relations?

- Consider the relationship between the news media and the school. Does the press treatment seem fair?
- Could racism be a problem?
- Can the school function as a learning organization, that is, learn from this incident? How?

SUMMARY AND SUGGESTED READINGS

Theory is not simply idealistic speculation, nor is it "common sense." Because facts do not speak for themselves, a framework is needed to give facts meaning. Organizational theory provides that framework and functions in the same way theory does in the natural sciences and in the other social sciences: it provides an explanatory system connecting otherwise unrelated information. In addition, theory gives direction to empirical research; it may generate new knowledge, and it serves as a rational guide to action as well. Theory is refined through research, and when theory, in the light of research findings, is applied to individual action, it is transformed into practice. Such application is neither simple nor mechanical; it involves an inventive and creative mind.

We trace the history of organizational theory and thought by using three systems perspectives: rational, natural, and open. First, a rational-systems perspective views organizations as formal instruments designed to achieve organizational goals; structure is the most important feature. A natural-systems perspective views organizations as typical social groups intent on surviving: people are the most important aspect. Finally, an open-systems perspective is used to combine rational and natural elements in the same framework and provide a more complete perspective.

Our social-systems model calls attention to rational and natural aspects of organizational life. Contemporary theory and research are used to elaborate the components of the model: organizational structure, the individual, climate and culture, politics, teaching and learning, environment, and effectiveness. In addition, key administrative processes are used to influence the interaction among these social system elements. Significant bodies of knowledge inform attempts to decide, communicate, and lead in school organizations. Each of the following chapters considers in substantial detail the major theoretical and research underpinnings of the social-systems model and its administrative processes. Our approach in this text is pragmatic, pluralistic, and empirical: we try to select the best theories (traditional and nontraditional), frameworks, and research that will help administrators understand and explain the complex nature of order and change in organizations.

All students should read two classic analyses of social systems: Getzels and Guba's (1957) treatment of the school as a social system and Katz and Kahn's (1966) pioneering development of open-systems theory. Senge's contemporary work, *The Fifth Discipline* (1990), is a popular and perceptive attempt to use systems thinking to build "learning organizations." Scott's (2003) comprehensive treatment of systems perspectives is difficult, but worth the effort. Finally, Thomas Greenfield and Peter Ribbins (1993) provide a critical analysis of organizational theory in general and social-systems theory in particular.

We recommend several other insightful discussions of the utility of organizational theory for practice and research (DiMaggio, 1995; Sutton and Staw, 1995; Weick, 1995, 1999). Calas and Smircich (1997) present an interesting set of readings on post-modern management theory. The evolution of organizational thought has been treated comprehensively by a number of other scholars (Burrell and Morgan, 1980; Gross and Etzioni, 1985; Miner, 2002; Scott, 2003; Clark et al., 1994). Gareth Morgan (1986, 1997) provides a useful alternative and novel way of viewing organizations. He uses metaphors to develop images of organizations that represent important partial truths about them. Contemporary organizational theory, however, is not without its critics (Greenfield and Ribbins, 1993; English, 1998, 2003; Foster, 1986; Maxey, 1995). Finally, for two attempts to map the domain of knowledge in educational administration see Hoy, Astuto, and Forsyth (1994) and Donmoyer, Scheurich, and Imber (1994). For a recent historical assessment of the impact of scientific management, read *The One Best Way* (Kanigel, 1997).

Many journals contain research relevant to educational administration. Two journals in education that link administrative theory and research are the *Educational Administration Quarterly* and the *Journal of Educational Administration*. *Planning and Changing, The Journal of School Leadership,* and *The Canadian Administrator* are examples of research journals that focus on the application of research and theory to practice in educational administration. Finally, a great many administrative journals publish important papers from all areas of administration; they include such journals as the *Academy of Management Journal, Academy of Management Review, Administrative Science Quarterly, Journal of Management Inquiry, Organizational Behavior and Human Decision Processes, Organizational Science,* and *Personnel Psychology.*

KEY ASSUMPTIONS AND PRINCIPLES

HISTORICAL ROOTS → CONTEMPORARY SYSTEMS PERSPECTIVES

Scientific Management
(Focus: Organizational Goals)
(Time Frame: 1900–1930)

Pioneers
- Taylor
- Fayol
- Gulick
- Urwick
- Weber

→ **Rational Systems Perspective**
(Focus: Formal Organization, Rationality, and Efficiency)
(Time Frame: Contemporary)

Key Concepts
- Goals
- Division of labor
- Specialization
- Standardization
- Formalization
- Hierarchy of authority
- Narrow span of control
- Control
- Rationality
- Formal organization

Key Assumptions and Principles
1. Organizations exist primarily to accomplish their goals.
2. Division of labor leads to specialization.
3. Specialization promotes expertise.
4. Standardization of tasks produces efficiency.
5. Formalization of activities improves efficiency.
6. Hierarchy promotes disciplined compliance.
7. A narrow span of control improves supervision.
8. Administrative control is essential for efficiency.
9. Rationality in decision making promotes efficiency.
10. Formal organization can be designed to maximize efficiency.

Human Relations
(Focus: Individual Needs)
(Time Frame: 1930–1960)

Pioneers
- Follet
- Mayo
- Rothlisberger
- McGregor

→ **Natural Systems Perspective**
(Focus: Informal Organization, Organizational Culture, and Natural Groupings)
(Time Frame: Contemporary)

Key Concepts
- Survival
- Needs
- Individuals
- Social structure
- Informal norms
- Empowerment
- Broad span of control
- Culture
- Teams
- Informal organization

Key Assumptions and Principles
1. Organizations are primarily social groups adapting and surviving.
2. Individual needs are the primary motivators of organizational performance.
3. Individuals are more important than structure in achieving effectiveness.
4. Individuals organize themselves informally on basis of interests.
5. Unofficial norms and procedures are often more important than formal ones.
6. Shared decision making promotes effectiveness.
7. A broad span of control enhances teacher autonomy and effectiveness.
8. Organizational culture mediates the effects of structure.
9. Teamwork is the key to organizational success.
10. Informal structures are more important than formal ones.

Social Science
(Focus: Integration)
(Time Frame: 1960–present)

Pioneers
- Weber
- Barnard
- Simon
- Parsons
- Weick
- Katz & Kahn

→ **Open Systems Perspective**
(Focus: Interdependence, Integration, and Contingencies)
(Time Frame: Contemporary)

Key Concepts
- Interdependence of the organization and its environment
- Integration
  - Of organizational goals and human needs
  - Of rational and natural features
  - Of tight and loose couplings
  - Of planned and unplanned activities
  - Of formal and informal perspectives
- Contingency theory

Key Assumptions and Principles
1. All organizations are open systems that interact with their environment.
2. Organizational behavior is a function of the interaction of organizational structure and individual needs.
3. All organizations have both rational and natural features.
4. Organizations need both loose and tight couplings to succeed.
5. Politics pervades organizational life.
6. Organizations have two interactive faces: a formal and an informal.
7. There is no one best way to organize, to motivate, to decide, to lead, or to communicate; the effectiveness of such processes is contingent upon a variety of circumstances.

NOTES

1. Our model is primarily a synthesis and extension of the work of Getzels and Guba (1957); Abbott (1965b); Leavitt, Dill, and Eyring (1973); Scott (1987, 1987b, 2003); Mintzberg (1983a); Nadler and Tushman (1983, 1989); Lipham (1988).
2. Many theoretical formulations have proposed such an assumption. For example, see Getzels and Guba (1957); Etzioni (1975); and Nadler and Tushman (1989).

CHAPTER 2

THE TECHNICAL CORE

Learning and Teaching[1]

Knowledge is not a copy of reality. To know an object, to know an event, is not simply to look at it and make a mental copy or image of it. To know an object is to act on it. To know is to modify, to transform the object, and to understand the process of this transformation, and as a consequence to understand the way the object is constructed.

Jean Piaget
Development and Learning

PREVIEW

1. The technical core of all schools is teaching and learning.

2. Learning occurs when experience produces a stable change in someone's knowledge or behavior.

3. There are three general learning perspectives—behavioral, cognitive, and constructivist—each of which helps us understand learning and teaching.

4. Many students confuse negative reinforcement and punishment; reinforcement strengthens behavior, but punishment suppresses or weakens behavior.

5. Learning objectives, mastery learning, and direct instruction (often including review, presentation, guided practice, checks for understanding, and independent practice) are applications of behavioral learning approaches.

6. Cognitive explanations of learning highlight the importance of prior knowledge in focusing attention, making sense of new information, and supporting memory.

7. Information processing is a cognitive theory of memory that describes how information is taken in, processed, stored in long-term memory (in the forms of episodes, productions, images, and schemas), and retrieved.

8. Learning strategies and tactics such as underlining, highlighting, and graphing are applications of the cognitive approach.

9. Constructivist views explain learning in terms of the individual and social construction of knowledge. Knowledge is judged not so much by its accuracy as by its usefulness.

10. There are three varieties of constructivism—rational, dialectical, and radical.

11. Situated learning emphasizes the idea that learning is specific to the situation in which it is learned and difficult to transfer.

12. Features of constructivist applications include complex real-life tasks, social interaction, shared responsibility, multiple representations of content, and student-centered teaching.

13. Three promising applications of the constructivist approach are inquiry or problem-based learning, cognitive apprenticeships, and cooperative learning.

Talcott Parsons (1960) was the first to propose three distinct levels of structure in the organization—the technical, managerial, and institutional. The technical level or **technical core** is the system of organizational activity where the actual "product" of the organization is produced; in schools it is exemplified by the teaching and learning in the classroom. The managerial system, the next level up, is responsible for administering the internal affairs of the organizations and for mediating between the organization and the environment. Finally, at the top is the institutional level, whose function is to connect the organization to the environment, specifically to provide legitimacy for the organization in terms of the larger social context. In the case of schools, the board of education is the chief formal mechanism of the institutional level and its function is to legitimate school activities to the community at large. Parsons (1960) makes the point that there are qualitative breaks in the line-authority relations at each point where the levels come together. Although the managerial level is the primary focus of this book on administration, the other levels are also important because they provide critical points of articulation between the school and its student-clients and the school and its citizen-clients.

Just as the institutional level draws attention to the organizational constraints of the environment (see Chapter 7), the technical level underscores the significance of teaching and learning in administrative decision making. In the case of schools the technical function is the process of teaching and learning, the heart and soul of all educational organizations. We are remiss in the analysis of the school as a social system if we do not examine the technical core of the school—the teaching-learning process—because it shapes many of the administrative decisions that must be made (Rowan, 1998; Rowan, Raudenbush, and Cheong, 1993).

LEARNING: A DEFINITION

When we hear the word "learning," many of us think of ourselves in school studying for an exam or learning how to drive a car or learning a new song or mastering a new computer program. We learn subjects, skills, and appropriate behavior for a host of social situations. Learning is clearly not limited to school, yet in the final analysis that is what school is all about. What is learning? In a broad sense, **learning** *happens when experience produces a stable change in someone's knowledge or behavior.* The change may be intentional or not, but to qualify as learning the change must occur because of experience as the individual interacts with his or her environment. Changes simply due to maturation such as growing taller or getting bald are not instances of learning. Similarly, temporary changes due to illness, fatigue, or short-lived physical deprivations are not part of learning, although, of course, people do learn how to cope with such problems (Hill, 2002).

Our definition of learning indicates that it involves a change in the individual's knowledge or behavior. Although most experts on learning would agree with this general proposition, some would tend to emphasize behavior and others knowledge. Our position is that learning is a complex cognitive process and there is no one best explanation of learning. In fact, different theories of learning offer more or less useful explanations depending on what is to be explained. We emphasize three general theories of learning, each with a different focus:

- *Behavioral* theories of learning stress observable changes in behaviors, skills, and habits.
- *Cognitive* theories of learning underscore such internal mental activities as thinking, remembering, creating, and problem solving.
- *Constructivist* theories of learning are interested in how individuals make meaning of events and activities; hence, learning is seen as the construction of knowledge.

The application of each of these theoretical perspectives has different implications for teaching. Thus our discussion of learning will also provide an analysis of teaching.

A BEHAVIORAL PERSPECTIVE ON LEARNING

The modern behavioral approach to learning emerged from the scholarship of Skinner and his followers, who emphasized the importance of antecedents and consequences in changing behavior. The focus of this perspective is clearly on behavior. Learning is defined as a change in behavior brought about by experience with virtually no concern for the mental or internal processes of thinking. Behavior is simply what a person does in a given situation. Think of a behavior as sandwiched between two sets of environmental influences: its antecedents, which precede it, and its consequences, which follow it (Skinner, 1950). This relationship is shown simply as antecedent–behavior–consequence, or A–B–C. As behavior happens, a given consequence transforms into an antecedent for the next ABC sequence. Behavior, then, is altered by changes in antecedents, consequences, or both. Early behavioral work focused on outcomes or consequences.

Consequences

In the behavioral view of learning, consequences of behavior to a great extent determine whether that behavior will be repeated. In particular, the kind and timing of the consequence either will strengthen or weaken the propensity of an individual to repeat behavior. There are two kinds of consequences—those that reinforce (strengthen) behavior and those that punish (weaken) behavior.

Reinforcement

The common meaning of reinforcement is reward, but in learning theory reinforcement has a specific connotation. A reinforcer is a consequence that strengthens the behavior that it follows; thus by definition, reinforcement increases the frequency or duration of a given behavior. The following diagram shows the process:

$$\text{Behavior} \xrightarrow{\quad\quad\quad} \underset{\text{Reinforcer}}{\overset{\text{CONSEQUENCE}}{}} \xrightarrow{\quad\quad\quad} \underset{\text{Strengthened Behavior}}{\overset{\text{EFFECT}}{}}$$

Research demonstrates that food is almost certain to be a strong reinforcer for a hungry animal, but does it work the same way for people? As one would expect, things are more complicated for people. We don't know why an event acts as a reinforcer for an individual; in fact, there are many competing theories that explain why reinforcement works with people. For example, some psychologists believe that reinforcers satisfy needs. Others argue that reinforcers diminish tensions or stimulate a part of the brain (Rachlin, 1991). The extent to which consequences are reinforcing likely depends on the person's perception of the event and the meaning it holds for the individual. For example, students who are routinely sent to the principal's office for misbehaving in class may be getting reinforcement for such behavior. There is probably *something* about this consequence (getting sent to the office) that is reinforcing for them, even if it doesn't seem desirable to their teachers. Perhaps the behavior provides needed attention or produces status among fellow students. Behaviorists would argue that repeated misbehavior is being reinforced in some way for that student.

Let's examine reinforcement more closely. There are two types—positive and negative reinforcement. **Positive reinforcement** occurs when a behavior produces a new stimulus or motivating force. For example, wearing a cool jacket may produce praise and many compliments for the student. Likewise "tripping and falling down" in class may result in laughter. Of course, if this "clumsy role" is played out repeatedly to the laughter and cheers of classmates, teachers are apt to explain the behavior as simply a way "to get attention." This explanation is a behavioral one; teachers are applying the principle of positive reinforcement to explain the behavior by assuming that the attention is a positive reinforcer for the student. Notice that the behavior is reinforced for the student in spite of the fact that it is not positive from the teacher's perspective. Positive reinforcement of inappropriate behavior is a potential problem for all teachers because often teachers unintentionally reinforce misbehavior of students. In brief, when a consequence strengthens a behavior by providing the *addition* of a stimulus, positive reinforcement has occurred.

In contrast, **negative reinforcement** occurs when the consequence that reinforces or strengthens behavior is obtained by eliminating (*subtracting*) a stimulus. When a particular action leads to stopping or avoiding a negative or aversive situation, that behavior is likely to be repeated because the individual has learned how to avoid something negative or uncomfortable. For example, car manufacturers have equipped their cars with seat belts attached to buzzers. Put the key in the ignition and an irritating buzz erupts, which stops as soon as you attach your seat belt. Thus you are likely to repeat the action of "buckling up" (the behavior is reinforced) because it removes the irritation (eliminates a negative stimulus). In other words, a behavior is reinforced or strengthened by removing a negative or aversive stimulus. Consider the parent who is continually complaining about a teacher and insisting the student's teacher be changed. To eliminate the constant complaining you as the principal change the student's teacher. You have eliminated the aversive situation with the parent, and if there are no further negative consequences, you are likely to repeat your behavior to quell other parents' similar complaints. Eliminating a negative stimulus (in this case a nagging parent) has reinforced your behavior. The "negative" in negative reinforcement does not necessarily mean that the behavior being reinforced is bad, but rather negative implies something is being subtracted from the situation that reinforces behavior. Think of positive and negative as associated with numbers—positive reinforcement *adds* something following behavior that reinforces behavior whereas negative reinforcement *subtracts* something following behavior that strengthens that behavior.

By the way, Skinner did not speculate about why reinforcers increase behavior. He believed that it was useless to talk about "imaginary constructs" such as meaning, habits, needs, or tensions. Skinner simply described the tendency for a given operant to increase after certain consequences (Hill, 2002; Skinner, 1953, 1989).

Punishment

Negative reinforcement is commonly confused with punishment. If you know the difference, you know more than most people. Reinforcement, whether positive or negative, always involves strengthening the behavior. **Punishment** involves weakening or suppressing behavior; that is, behavior followed by punishment is less likely to be repeated in similar situations in the future. Remember, however, that it is the effect of decreasing behavior that defines the consequence as punishment. Different people have different perceptions of what is punishing. Suspension from school is a punishment for some students but not for others. The punishment process is noted simply as follows:

CONSEQUENCE   EFFECT
Behavior ──→ Punishment ──────────→ Weakened or Decreased Behavior

Just as there are two types of reinforcement, there are two kinds of punishment defined in behavioral theory—Type I and Type II. Neither label is very informative so we call Type I **direct punishment** because it occurs when the appearance of the stimulus following the behavior suppresses or weakens the behavior; something is added to suppress behavior. When teachers assign detention, extra work, and lower grades to punish students, they are assigning direct punishment. The second kind of punishment (Type II) is **removal punishment** because a stimulus is removed to punish. For example, when parents or teachers remove a student's privileges, they are engaging in removal punishment; they are removing something that is desired. Thus direct punishment *adds* something to slow or stop behavior and removal punishment *subtracts or deletes* something to decrease or weaken behavior. The interaction of the processes of reinforcement and punishment is summarized in Figure 2.1.

Antecedents

Antecedents are the events preceding behavior. They provide information about which behaviors will lead to positive consequences and which to

	Behavior Supported	Behavior Suppressed
Stimulus Presented	**Positive Reinforcement** • High grades • Honor role • Sport letter	**Direct Punishment** • Detention • Lower grade • Extra homework
Stimulus Removed	**Negative Reinforcement** • Exempt from test • Excused from class • Excused from chores	**Removal Punishment** • No driving for a week • No football this week • No dating this week

Reinforcement and punishment are often confused.

Remember:
Reinforcement always encourages or strengthens behavior.
Punishment suppresses or weakens behavior.

FIGURE 2.1   *Kinds of Reinforcement and Punishment*

negative ones (A→B→C). Perceptive people learn to discriminate among situations; that is, they learn to read the antecedent. When should a principal request more resources to purchase new curriculum materials, after a budget defeat or after a positive story in the local newspaper about your school? The antecedent cue of the principal standing in the hall helps students discriminate the probable consequences of "running in the hall" or perhaps even "sneaking a smoke" in the boys lavatory. People react to such antecedent cues without fully thinking about the process and how their behavior is influenced. Nevertheless, antecedents in the form of cues can be deliberately used.

Cueing is providing an antecedent stimulus just prior to a particular behavior. It is especially useful in preparing for a behavior that must occur at a specific time but is easily forgotten. Cueing furnishes information about which behaviors will be reinforced or punished in a particular situation. A police car sitting under an overpass or simply along the highway provides an instantaneous cue about the consequences of speeding.

Teachers and principals often correct students after the fact. For example, they exclaim, "I cannot believe that you. . . ." The problem is, of course, that the misbehavior has already occurred. The student has only a few choices—to promise not to do it again or to try harder or the more aggressive response, "Leave me alone." None of these reactions is particularly useful, but providing a nonjudgmental cue can help avoid a negative confrontation with the student. For example, for teachers and principals, simply attending an athletic function makes it more unlikely that students will demonstrate poor sportsmanship. Moreover, when students perform appropriately after such a cue, teachers can reinforce student behavior without resorting to punishment.

Prompting is providing an additional cue following the first cue. Sometimes people need extra help in responding appropriately to a cue. Becker and his colleagues (1975) propose two principles for using cues and prompts:

- Make sure the environmental stimulus that you want to become a cue occurs right before your prompt, so students will learn to respond to the cue, not rely only on the prompt.
- Fade the prompt as soon as possible; don't make students dependent on it.

An example of prompting is providing students with a checklist or a "to do list" when they work in pairs as part of peer tutoring. As students learn the procedures, the checklist gradually is withdrawn. When the students have learned the procedures, no written or oral prompts are necessary. They have learned how to react appropriately to the cue of working in pairs; they have learned how to work in peer tutoring. Teachers should continue to monitor the process, praise good work, and correct mistakes. The teacher's role is now one of coaching students to improve their tutoring skills.

TEACHING APPLICATIONS OF THE BEHAVIORAL APPROACH

Experienced and expert teachers make good use of behavioral theory. They apply with care and skill the basic principles of reinforcement and punishment in their teaching and classroom management. Before we provide examples of the contributions of behavioral theory to teaching and learning, we summarize some of the guiding principles:

- Give clear and systematic praise, but only if deserved.
- Recognize genuine accomplishments.
- Set standards for praise based on individual abilities and limitations.
- Attribute the student's success to effort and ability to build confidence.
- Recognize positive behavior in ways that students value.
- Give plenty of reinforcement when students tackle new materials or skills.
- Set clear and specific goals so you know what to reinforce.
- Use cues to help establish new behaviors.
- Use a variety of reinforcers and let students choose among them.
- Try to structure the situation to use negative reinforcement rather than punishment.
- Adapt the punishment to fit the misbehavior (Woolfolk, 2004).

Learning objectives, mastery learning, and direct instruction are specific examples of the application of behavioral theory to classroom teaching. Such approaches are especially useful when the goal is to learn new behaviors or explicit information and when the learning is sequential or factual.

Learning Objectives

There are many different approaches to writing objectives; however, all assume that the first step is to decide what changes should take place in the student—what is the goal of teaching. An **instructional objective** is a clear and unambiguous description of the teacher's educational aims for students.

Robert Mager has developed perhaps the most influential system for writing behavioral objectives. His idea is that objectives should describe what students will be doing to demonstrate their achievement and how a teacher will know when students are successful (Mager, 1975). According to Mager, a good objective has three parts:

1. The objective describes the intended student behavior—what must the student do?
2. The objective lists the conditions under which the behavior will occur—how will this behavior be recognized or tested?
3. The objective gives the criteria for acceptable performance on the behavior—how well has the student done?

Mager argues that students often teach themselves if they are given such well-stated objectives.

Are objectives useful? They can be, but only under certain conditions. First, objectives are more successful in promoting learning with such loosely structured activities as lectures, films, and research projects. With structured materials such as programmed instruction, objectives seem less useful. Second, if the significance of information is unclear from the learning materials and activities themselves, instructional objectives focus students' attention and thus increase achievement (Duchastel, 1979).

The most recent research on instructional objectives tends to favor approaches that combine specific and broad objectives. James Popham (2002), a former proponent of very specific objectives, makes this recommendation:

> Strive to come up with a half dozen or so truly salient, broad, yet measurable instructional objectives for your own classroom. Too many small-scope, hyperspecific objectives will be of scant value to you because, if you're at all normal, you'll soon disregard [them]. On the other hand, a small number of intellectually manageable, broad, yet measurable objectives will not only prove helpful to you instructionally but will also help you answer the what-to-assess question. (pp. 98–99)

Today most school districts still require teachers to complete lesson plans that include learning objectives. Good learning objectives, where the objectives and steps are clearly mapped, can be beneficial and enhance learning. Objectives are not only used in classrooms with students; administrators have used them with varying degrees of success. Management by objectives and goal setting (Locke and Latham, 1990) are organizational attempts to use behavioral theory to improve performance. We discuss both in Chapter 4.

When both the objectives and means to achieve them are clear, how might students also go about learning? The mastery learning approach is consistent with behavioral principles.

Mastery Learning

Mastery learning is based on the assumption that given enough time and the proper instruction, most students can master any learning objective (Bloom, 1968; Guskey and Gates, 1986). To use the mastery approach, a teacher must break down what is to be learned into small units of study. Each unit involves mastering several specific objectives. "Mastery" usually means a score of 80 to 90 percent on some kind of assessment. The teacher informs students of the objectives and the criteria of success for each. Students who do not reach the minimum level of mastery or who reach this minimum but want to improve their performance (thus raising their grades) can repeat the unit. When they think they are ready, they take another form of the unit test. The challenge in mastery learning is to provide appropriate help for students who don't achieve success the first time.

Mastery learning is most useful when the focus of instruction is on key concepts or skills that serve as a foundation for subsequent learning. In mathematics, for example, some students will fall farther and farther behind if they move on to more complex procedures before they master elementary ones. If they don't understand fractions, by the time they reach division of fractions, they will be lost. Mastery learning has been successful when students get the extra time and support—especially through corrective instruction outside class or inside class from peer tutors or cooperative learning group members (Kulik, Kulik, and Bangert-Drowns, 1990; Shuell, 1996).

In practice, mastery learning has not erased achievement differences among students, as some proponents have hoped. Left to work at their own pace, some students will learn much more and leave a unit with much better understanding than others. Some will work much harder to take advantage of the learning opportunities, but others will be frustrated instead of encouraged by the chance to recycle (Grabe and Latta, 1981). Other behavioral approaches are more teacher-centered than mastery learning. Direct instruction is one such approach; it works best when the objectives and the paths to success are clear.

Direct Instruction

The direct instruction procedures described in this section fit a specific set of circumstances because they have evolved from a common strand of inquiry. Researchers have elaborated on direct instruction models by comparing teachers whose students learned more than expected with teachers whose students performed at an expected or average level. The researchers focused on existing teaching practices in American classrooms. Effectiveness was usually defined as average improvement in standardized test scores for a whole class or school. Thus the results hold for large groups, but not necessarily for every student in the group. For example, even when the average achievement of a group improves, the achievement of some individuals may decline (Brophy and Good, 1986; Good, 1996; Shuell, 1996).

The direct instruction models described below apply best to the teaching of **basic skills**—clearly structured knowledge and essential skills, such as science facts, mathematics computations, reading vocabulary, and grammar rules (Rosenshine and Stevens, 1986). These skills involve tasks that can be taught step-by-step and tested by standardized tests. One caveat: the teaching approaches described below are not necessarily appropriate for helping students to write creatively, solve complex problems, or mature emotionally.

Psychologists have identified a direct teaching approach consistent with behavioral theory that helps improve student learning. Barak Rosenshine calls this approach **direct instruction** (1979) or explicit teaching (1988), whereas Tom Good (1983) uses the term "active teaching" for a similar approach. Weinert and Helmke (1995) describe direct instruction as follows:

> (a) The teachers' classroom management is especially effective and the rate of student interruptive behaviors is very low; (b) the teacher maintains a strong academic focus and uses available instructional time intensively to

initiate and facilitate students' learning activities; (c) the teacher insures that as many students as possible achieve good learning progress by carefully choosing appropriate tasks, clearly presenting subject-matter information and solution strategies, continuously diagnosing each student's learning progress and learning difficulties, and providing effective help through remedial instruction. (p. 138)

How do teachers transform these admonitions into actions?

Rosenshine's Six Teaching Functions

Rosenshine and his colleagues (Rosenshine, 1988; Rosenshine and Stevens, 1986) have underscored six teaching functions based on the research on effective instruction. They provide a framework for teaching basic skills:

1. *Review and check the previous day's work.* Reteach if necessary.
2. *Present new material.* Teach in small steps, with many examples and nonexamples.
3. *Provide guided practice.* Question students, give practice problems, and listen for misconceptions. Reteach if necessary. Continue guided practice until students answer about 80 percent of the questions correctly.
4. *Give feedback and correctives based on student answers.* Reteach if necessary.
5. *Provide independent practice.* Let students apply the new learning on their own, either in seatwork, cooperative groups, or homework. The success rate during independent practice should be about 95 percent. This means that students must be well prepared for the work by the presentation and guided practice and that assignments must not be too difficult. The point is for the students to practice until the skills become overlearned and automatic—until the students are confident.
6. *Review weekly and monthly.* Consolidate learning and include some review items as homework. Test often and reteach material missed on the tests.

These six functions are not steps to be blindly followed, but they are all elements of effective instruction. For example, feedback, review, or reteaching should occur whenever necessary and should match the abilities of the students. There are a number of models of direct instruction, but most share the elements presented above. Hunter's Mastery Teaching approach (1982) and Good, Grouws, and Ebmeier's Missouri Math (1983) are other examples of direct instruction.

Criticisms of Direct Instruction

Critics argue that direct instruction is limited to lower-level objectives, is based on traditional teaching methods, ignores innovative models, and discourages students' independent thought and action. Some critics go so far as to claim that direct instruction is based on the *wrong* theory of learning. Teachers break material into small segments, present each segment clearly, and reinforce or correct mistakes, thus *transmitting* accurate understandings from teacher to student. According to these critics, the student is seen as an "empty vessel" waiting to be filled with knowledge rather than an active constructor of knowledge (Anderson, 1989a; Berg and Clough, 1991).

But there is ample evidence that direct instruction can help students learn actively, not passively. Particularly for younger and less experienced learners, student learning without teacher direction and instruction can lead to systematic deficits in the students' knowledge. Without guidance the understandings that students construct are sometimes incomplete and misleading (Weinert and Helmke, 1995). Deep understanding and fluid performance—whether in dance or mathematical problem solving or reading—require models of expert performance and extensive practice with feedback (Anderson, Reder, and Simon, 1995). Guided and independent practices with constructive feedback are keys to the direct instruction model. When specific skills and behaviors need to be learned, a teaching approach consistent with behavioral learning theory makes a lot of sense.

TIP: THEORY INTO PRACTICE

Identify a situation in your school that you would like to change. Think about the participants (students, parents, or teachers) whose behaviors could change for the better to improve the situation. Now identify the possible reinforcers for their current behavior—what desirable outcomes do they achieve for acting in the way that they do or what unpleasant outcomes do they escape? In other words, can you spot positive or negative reinforcement in action?

A COGNITIVE PERSPECTIVE ON LEARNING

The cognitive perspective traces its early roots to the ancient Greek philosophers who discussed the nature of knowledge, the value of reason, and the contents of the mind (Hernshaw, 1987); however, cognitive science was dormant as behaviorism flourished in the early and middle 1900s. By the end of the Second World War, however, cognitive research emerged as the computer revolution and breakthroughs in understanding language developed. Evidence accumulated that people do more than simply respond to reinforcement and punishment. For example, individuals plan their responses, use systems to help them remember, and organize their materials in meaningful and unique ways (Miller, Galanter, and Pribram, 1960; Shuell, 1986). With the growing realization that learning is an active mental process, cognitive psychologists became intrigued with how people think, learn concepts, and solve problems (e.g., Ausubel, 1963; Bruner, Goodnow, and Austin, 1956).

Interest in concept learning and problem solving soon gave way to the puzzle of how knowledge was represented and recalled. Remembering and forgetting were major topics of study in cognitive psychology in the 1970s and 80s. The information-processing model of memory dominated research in cognitive science. Today, there are other models of memory in addition to information processing, and many cognitive theorists have a renewed interest in learning, thinking, and problem solving.

Knowledge and Learning

Current cognitive approaches suggest that one of the most important elements in the learning process is what the individual brings to the learning situation. What we already know determines in large part what we will pay attention to, perceive, learn, remember, and forget (Ashcraft 2002; Greeno, Collins, and Resnick, 1996; Resnick, 1981; Shuell, 1986). Knowledge is both a means and an end; more than the product of previous learning; it also guides new learning.

Recht and Leslie (1988) show the significance of knowledge in understanding and remembering new information. In their study, they identified junior high school students who were either very good or very poor readers, and tested them on their knowledge of baseball. Knowledge of baseball was not related to reading ability. Next, they identified four groups of students: good readers/high baseball knowledge, good readers/low baseball knowledge, poor readers/high baseball knowledge, and poor readers/low baseball knowledge. All the students read a passage describing a baseball game and were tested in a number of ways to see if they understood and remembered what they had read.

The results demonstrated the power of knowledge as a scaffold for new learning. Poor readers who knew baseball remembered more than good readers with little baseball knowledge and almost as much as good readers who knew baseball. Poor readers who knew little about baseball remembered the least of what they had read. A good basis of knowledge can be more important than good learning strategies in understanding and remembering—but extensive knowledge plus good strategy is even better.

The cognitive perspective recognizes different kinds of knowledge—general and domain-specific:

- **General knowledge** applies to a variety of situations. For example, general knowledge about how to read or use a word processor is useful in many situations.
- **Domain-specific knowledge** relates to a particular task or subject. For example, knowing there are nine innings in a game is specific to the domain of baseball.

Another way of categorizing knowledge is as declarative, procedural, or conditional (Paris and Cunningham, 1996; Paris, Lipson, and Wixson, 1983):

- **Declarative knowledge** is "knowledge that can be declared, usually in words, through lectures, books, writing, verbal exchange, Braille, sign language, mathematical notation, and so on" (Farnaham-Diggory, 1994: 468).
- **Procedural knowledge** is "knowing how" to do something such as divide fractions or overhaul an air conditioner—procedural knowledge is demonstrated.
- **Conditional knowledge** is "knowing when and why" to apply declarative and procedural knowledge.

Declarative knowledge is "knowing that" something is the case. The range of declarative knowledge is broad. You can know very specific facts (the average brain has over one hundred billion neurons), or generalities (some trees lose their leaves in autumn), or personal preferences (I hate peas), or personal events (what happened on my first date), or rules (to add fractions, convert each fraction so they have the same denominator and then add the numerators and maintain the common denominator). Small units of declarative knowledge are often organized into larger units; for example, principles of reinforcement and punishment can be organized into a theory of behavioral learning (Gagné, Yekovich, and Yekovich, 1993).

Repeating the rule to add fractions shows declarative knowledge—the student can state the rule—but to show procedural knowledge, the student must demonstrate the knowledge. When faced with fractions to add, the student must perform the procedures correctly. Students or teachers demonstrate procedural knowledge when they solve an equation or correctly translate a French passage.

Conditional knowledge is "knowing when and why" to apply your declarative and procedural knowledge. In many kinds of math problems, it takes conditional knowledge to know *when* to apply one formula rather than another, for example, when to compute area and when to get the volume. It takes conditional knowledge to know when to read a text carefully and when to skim. Conditional knowledge is a stumbling block because it requires correct use of both facts and procedures. Often students know the facts and can do the procedures, but don't apply them at the appropriate time. Table 2.1 summarizes and combines our two systems for describing knowledge. To use knowledge, you must remember it. But how do people remember? What do we know about memory?

Information-Processing Model

The information-processing model is one cognitive perspective of the structure and processes of memory. The model is based on the analogy between

TABLE 2.1

Six Kinds of Knowledge and Examples

	General Knowledge	Domain-Specific Knowledge
Declarative	Hours the bank is open. Highway safety rules.	Lines from Shakespeare's *Hamlet.* Definition of educational leadership.
Procedural	How to use a computer. How to drive a car.	How to solve a quadratic equation. How to progam in C++.
Conditional	When to abandon one approach and try another. When to skim and when to read carefully.	When to use the formula for volume. When to run to the net in tennis.

the mind and the computer; it includes three storage systems: the sensory memory, working (also called short-term) memory, and long-term memory.

- **Sensory memory** is a holding system that maintains stimuli briefly so that perceptual analysis can occur (Bruning, Schraw, and Ronning, 1995).
- **Working memory,** or short-term memory, holds from five to nine bits of information at a time for up to about 20 seconds, which is long enough for processing to occur. Information is encoded and perceptions determine what will be held in working memory.
- **Long-term memory** stores huge amounts of information for long periods of time. Information may be coded verbally or visually or both.

In long-term memory, some information is stored and interrelated in terms of images and schemas—data structures that allow us to represent large amounts of complex information, make inferences, and understand new information.

Information is retrieved from long-term memory by activation; that is, one memory activates other related information. Think about how one memory triggers another as you think about something. Remembering is reconstructing, which leads to accurate, partly accurate, or inaccurate recall. Accurate retrieval depends in part on how the information was learned to begin with. Figure 2.2 is a pictorial summary of an information-processing system. Let's look at this system in more depth.

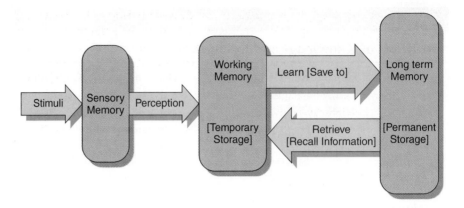

FIGURE 2.2   *Information Processing System*

Sensory Memory

Sensory memory is the initial system that briefly holds stimuli so that perceptional analysis can occur. The meaning we give to the basic information we receive through our senses is called **perception.** Meaning is constructed from both objective reality and our existing knowledge. For example, consider the symbol *I*. If asked what the letter is, you would say "I." If asked what the number is, you would say one. The actual mark remains the same; the perception of it—its meaning—changes with the context and your expectation to recognize either a number or a letter. To a child without the knowledge to perceive a number or a letter, the mark is probably meaningless (Smith, 1975). To recognize patterns rapidly as well as to note specific features, we use existing knowledge about the situation to make meaning.

If all variations in color, movement, sound, smell, temperature, and so on had to be perceived simultaneously, life would be impossible. Thus, we pay attention to some stimuli and ignore others; we select from all the possibilities what we will process. But attention is a limited resource because we can pay attention to only one demanding task at time (Ashcraft, 2002). For example, when you first learned to drive a car, especially if it were a stick shift, there probably was a time when you couldn't both listen to the radio and drive. After practice, however, you could listen to and enjoy the radio and drive without difficulty, but you might turn off the radio when traffic is heavy. Many processes that initially require attention and concentration become automatic with practice. Automaticity, however, is a matter of degree—we are not completely automatic but rather more or less automatic in our performances depending on how much practice we have had (Anderson, 1995). When full attention is critical, we must block out other stimuli.

Attention is the first step in learning. Students cannot process what they don't recognize or perceive. Many factors in the classroom influence student attention. Dramatic displays or actions can draw attention at the beginning of a lesson. A teacher might begin a science lesson on air pressure by pumping the air out of a gallon can until it collapses. Bright colors, underlining, highlighting of written or spoken words, calling on students at random, surprising students, asking puzzling questions, posing challenging dilemmas, changing tasks and teaching methods, as well as changes in voice level, lighting, or pacing can all help get the attention of students. But gaining student attention is only half the battle—keeping them focused and on task is also critical.

Working Memory

Once a stimulus has been registered and transformed into patterns of images or sounds, the information in sensory memory is available for further processing. Working memory is where this new information is held briefly and combined with knowledge from long-term memory. Working memory is sometimes called short-term memory, but as information models have shifted from emphasizing storage to processing, the term "working memory" has replaced "short-term memory." Working memory in some ways resembles the screen of a computer—its content is activated information—what you are thinking about at the moment, your consciousness.

Capacity and Contents

Working memory capacity is limited. In experimental situations, the capacity of working memory is only about five to nine separate new items (chunks of meaningful information) at once (Miller, 1956). For example, when you get a phone number from information, you can usually remember it long enough to dial the number. Get two new phone numbers (14 digits) and most of us are in trouble. We simply cannot recall this much *new* information because we cannot hold it in working memory. In everyday activity we hold more than nine bits of information at once. While you are dialing that seven-digit phone number you just looked up, you have other things "on your mind"—in your memory—such as who you are calling and why. You don't have to pay attention to these things because they are not new knowledge; in fact, some of the processes, like dialing, have become automatic. But imagine that you are in a foreign country and are trying to use an unfamiliar telephone system—you may have trouble remembering the phone number because you are trying to figure out the phone system at the same time.

Some theorists argue that working memory is limited not by the number of bits of information it can store, but rather by the amount of information we can rehearse (repeat to ourselves) in about 1.5 seconds (Baddeley, 1986). The seven-digit telephone number fits this limitation. Recent theories, however, suggest that there are actually two working memory systems—one for language-based information and another for nonverbal, spatial, visual information (Baddeley, 1986; Jurden, 1995). One thing is clear: the duration of information is short in working memory, about 5 to 20 seconds. You may think that a memory system with a 20-second time limit is not useful. Think again. Without this short-term memory, you would have already forgotten what you read in the first part of this sentence before you came to these last few words. Understanding sentences would be difficult to say the least.

Retaining Information in Working Memory

Working memory is fragile. It must be kept activated or the information will be lost. To keep information activated in working memory for longer than 20 seconds, most people need to engage in specific remembering strategies. Rehearsal is one option.

There are two types of **rehearsal** (Craik and Lockhart, 1972) strategies—maintenance and elaborative rehearsal. Maintenance rehearsal is repeating the information in your mind. As long as you repeat the information, it can be maintained in working memory. Such rehearsal is useful for retaining something, like a phone number that you plan to use and then forget. Elaborative rehearsal is associating the information you are trying to remember with something you already know—information from long-term memory. For example, if you meet a parent whose name is the same as your assistant principal's, you don't have to repeat the name to keep it in memory, you just have to make the correct association. Elaborative rehearsal not only improves working memory, but it helps move information from short-term to long-term memory.

A strategy of **chunking** can be used to overcome the limited capacity of working memory. The number of bits of information, not the size of each bit, is the limitation for working memory. You can retain more information if you can group or chunk individual bits of information into meaningful units. For example, if you have to remember the six digits 1, 5, 1, 8, 2, and 0, it is easier to put them together into three chunks of two digits each (15, 18, 20) or two chunks (151, 820). If you can make these changes, then there are only two or three chunks of information to hold at one time rather than six.

Long-Term Memory

Working memory holds the information that is temporarily activated, such as a telephone number you have been given to dial. Long-term memory holds the information that you have learned, for example, telephone numbers you already know.

Capacity and Duration of Long-Term Memory

Information enters working memory very quickly, but to store it in long-term memory (remember it) requires some effort. Whereas the capacity of working memory is limited, the capacity of long-term memory is virtually unlimited. Most of us never approach our capacity of long-term memory, and once information is securely stored in long-term memory, it can remain there indefinitely. Theoretically, although we should be able to remember as much as we want for as long as we want, the challenge is recall, that is, finding the right information when we want it. Access to information requires time and effort because we have to search the vast amount of information in long-term memory, and the less information is used, the harder it is to find.

Contents of Long-Term Memory

Most cognitive theorists distinguish among three kinds of long-term memory: episodic, procedural, and semantic. Memory about information associated with a particular place and time, especially personal memories about the events of your own life, is called *episodic memory.* Episodic memory keeps things ordered; it is where details of a conversation as well as jokes, gossip, or plots from films are stored. Memory for how to do things is called *procedural memory.* It may take a while to learn a procedure—such as how to do a school budget, hit a golf ball, or conduct a school board meeting—but once learned, this knowledge is remembered for a long time. Procedural memories are represented as conditional statements such as, if A occurs, then do B. For example, "If I want to lower resistance to an innovation, involve participants in making decisions," or "To improve student achievement, focus on the academic task." People can't necessarily state all their conditional rules, but they act on them nonetheless. The more practiced the procedure, the more automatic the action (Ashcraft, 2002). *Semantic memory* is memory for meaning; it is the memory of general concepts, principles, and their associations. Two important ways that semantic memories are stored are images and schemas. Let's examine each.

Images are representations based on visual perceptions—on the structure or appearance of the information (Ashcraft, 2002). As we form images, we try to remember or recreate the physical characteristics and spatial structure of information. For example, when asked how many windows are in a given school, most people call up an image of the school "in their mind's eye" and count the number of windows (Mendell, 1971). Images are useful in making many practical decisions such as how a desk might look in your office or how to drive to the next school. Images may also be helpful in abstract reasoning. Physicists, such as Feynman and Einstein, report creating images to reason about complex new problems (Gagné, Yekovich, and Yekovich, 1993; Feynman, 1985).

Schemas (sometimes called schemata) are abstract knowledge structures that organize large amounts of information. A schema is a pattern or guide for understanding an event, a concept, or a skill. My simplified schema for reinforcement is summarized in Figure 2.3—it is a partial representation of knowledge about reinforcement; it tells you what features are typical of a category, what to expect. A schema is a pattern, specifying the "standard" relationships in an object or situation. The pattern has "slots" that are filled with

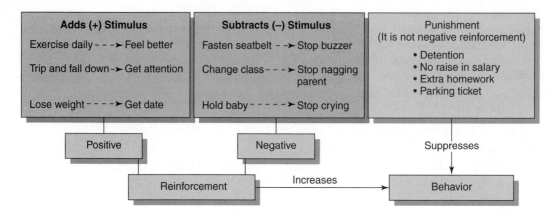

FIGURE 2.3   *Simple Schema for Reinforcement*

specific information as we apply the schema in a particular situation. Schemas are individual. For example, a teacher and a principal may have very different schemas about shared decision making—who makes what school decisions and when, where, and how. In Chapter 9, we have produced an idealized schema for participation in decision making (Figure 9.5); it specifies, when to involve teachers, how to involve them for each situation, the structure of the process, and the various roles of the principal depending on the situation.

Storing and Retrieving Information in Long-Term Memory

How do people "save" information permanently, that is, create semantic, episodic, or procedural memories? How can we make the most effective use of our virtually unlimited capacity to learn and remember? Your initial learning—the way you process the information at the outset—seems to affect its recall. If you integrate new material with information already stored in long-term memory as you construct an understanding, you are more likely to remember. Elaboration, organization, and context aid such integration.

Elaboration is adding meaning to new information by connecting it with already existing knowledge. In other words, we apply our schemas and draw on existing knowledge to construct new meaning as we refine our existing knowledge. Often elaboration occurs automatically. For example, new information about a prior experience of a teacher activates our existing knowledge about that teacher and provides a better and more complete understanding of the teacher.

Information that is elaborated when first learned is easier to recall because elaboration is a form of rehearsal that keeps the material activated in working memory long enough to improve the likelihood of permanent storage in long-term memory. Moreover, elaboration builds extra links to existing knowledge. The more one chunk of information is associated with others, the more routes there are to follow to get to the original chunk. Put simply, you have several "handles" or retrieval cues to recognize or "pick up" the information you might be seeking (Schunk, 2000). The more individuals elaborate new ideas, the more they "make them their own," and the better their understanding memory for the knowledge. We try to help students elaborate by asking them to put information into their own words and by creating examples. Of course, if students elaborate new information by making incorrect connections and developing misguided explanations, unfortunately these misconceptions will be stored and remembered too.

Organization also improves learning. Well-organized material is easier to learn and remember than unorganized bits and pieces, especially when the information is complex. Putting concepts in a structure helps you learn and remember both general definitions and specific examples. Structure serves as a guide back to the information when you need it. For example, knowing the basic dimensions of power (Chapter 7) helps us remember the key aspects of power relationships as well as specific examples of each.

Context is another element of processing that influences learning. The physical and emotional aspects of context—places, how we feel on a particular day, who is with us—are learned along with other information. When you try to remember the information, it helps if the current context is similar to the original one. So studying for a test under "testlike" conditions may result in improved performance. Of course, you can't always go back to the same place you learned something but if you can picture the setting, the time of day, and your companions, you can often prod your memory.

Craik and Lockhart (1972) suggest that the length of time we remember information is determined by how the information is analyzed and integrated with other information; the more completely information is processed, the better our chances of remembering it. For example, if you are asked to sort pictures of dogs based on the color of their coats, you might not remember many of the pictures later, but if asked to determine how likely each dog is to chase you as you jog, you are likely to remember more of the pictures because you will pay attention to details in the pictures, relate features of the dogs to characteristics associated with danger, and so on.

Retrieving Information from Long-Term Memory

When we need information from long-term memory, we search for it. Sometimes the search is conscious, as when you see a familiar face and search for the name, and other times it is automatic, as when you dial a telephone. Think of long-term memory as a huge shed full of tools and supplies ready to be used when needed. Because the shed (long-term memory) is so large and full, it is often difficult to find what you need. The workbench (working memory) is small, but everything is ready for immediate use. But the workbench can get cluttered and supplies (chunks of information) can be lost, fall off, or get covered as one bit of information interferes with another (Gagné, 1985).

Even though the long-term memory network is huge, only a small area can be activated at a given time—the information you are currently using in working memory. Information is retrieved in this network by the spread of activation. When we are thinking about a particular concept, other related knowledge often is activated as well, and the activation spreads through the network (Anderson, 1993; Gagné, Yekovich, and Yekovich, 1993). For example, if you think, "I need to give Susan a makeup exam today," related ideas such as, "I need to change some questions on the test," "I'm behind schedule," and "I need to warm up the car before I leave for school," come to mind. As activation spreads from the "makeup" to "warming the car," the original thought disappears from working memory because of the limited space.

In long-term memory the information is still available, even though you are not thinking about it. If spreading activation does not "find" the needed information, then we might still be able to reconstruct it by using logic, cues, and other knowledge to fill in the missing parts. Unfortunately, sometimes-reconstructed recollections are incorrect. For example, in 1932, F. C. Bartlett conducted a series of famous studies on remembering stories. He read a complex, unfamiliar Native American tale to students at England's Cambridge University. After various lengths of time, he asked students to recall the story. The recalled stories were generally shorter and were reconstructed into the concepts and language of their culture. For example, many students remembered the story of a seal hunt as a "fishing trip," which was more consistent with their experience and schemas.

Forgetting and Long-Term Memory

Information lost from working memory truly disappears; you cannot bring it back. But lost information in long-term memory sometimes can be found with the right cues. Until recently many psychologists believed that nothing was ever lost from long-term memory. But research casts doubts on this belief (Schwartz and Reisberg, 1991). Apparently, information can be lost from long-term memory through two processes: time decay and interference. For example, consider this interesting research finding. Memory for Spanish-English vocabulary decreases for about three years after a person's last course in Spanish, then stays level for about 25 years, then drops again for the next 25 years. Neural connections, like muscles, may grow weak without use (Anderson, 1995). In addition, newer memories may interfere, replace, or obscure older memories, and older memories may interfere with memory for new material.

Nevertheless, long-term memory is remarkable. After a comprehensive analysis of the research, Semb and Ellis (1994) concluded that, "contrary to popular belief, students retain much of the knowledge taught in the classroom" (p. 279). Teaching strategies that encourage student engagement and lead to higher levels of initial learning (such as frequent reviews and tests, elaborated feedback, high standards, mastery learning, and active involvement in learning projects) are associated with longer retention.

Why do some people learn and remember more than others? For those who hold an information-processing view, part of the answer lies in how the information is processed. We have already discussed maintenance rehearsal, elaborative rehearsal, organization, and elaboration. These processes are sometimes called **metacognitive skills,** because the processes can be intentionally used to regulate cognition.

Metacognition and Regulation

Metacognition is an individual's awareness of his or her own cognitive processing and how it works (Meichenbaum, Burland, Gruson, and Cameron, 1985). Individuals use their own knowledge to monitor and regulate their cognitive processes, that is, their reasoning, comprehension, problem solving, learning, and so on. Because people differ in their metacognitive knowledge and skills, they also differ in how efficiently they learn (Brown, Branford, Ferrara, and Campione, 1983; Morris, 1990).

Planning, monitoring, and evaluation are three crucial cognitive skills (Brown, 1987; Nelson, 1996). Planning is deciding how much time to give to a task, what strategies to use, how to begin, what to gather, what order to follow, what to skim, what to focus on, and so on. Monitoring is the awareness of how I'm doing. Is this making sense? Am I trying to go too fast? Do I have it yet? Evaluation is making judgments about the outcomes of thinking and learning. Should I change strategies? Get help? Give up for now? Is this report (proposal, budget, formula, model, action plan, supervisory report, etc.) finished or does it need more work? Many planning, monitoring, and evaluation processes are not conscious, especially among adults and experts. They become automatic; in fact, experts often have difficulty explaining their own processing (Schraw and Moshman, 1995). Fortunately, metacognitive skills can be taught; thus they are an important basis of teaching.

TEACHING APPLICATIONS OF THE COGNITIVE APPROACH

Just as experienced and expert teachers make good use of behavioral theory, they also incorporate sound cognitive approaches in their teaching. Before we provide examples of the contributions of cognitive theory to teaching and learning, we summarize some of the guiding principles:

- Remember that perception and attention are flexible, but limited.
- Make sure that you have the student's attention.
- Guide perception and attention by previous knowledge.
- Help students focus on the most important information.
- Help students make connections between new information and what they already know.
- Recognize that resources and data limitations restrain learning.
- Help students organize information in meaningful chunks.

- Provide students with opportunities to use both verbal stories and visual images.
- Provide review and repetition of information.
- Present information in an organized and clear fashion.
- Focus on meaning, not memorization.
- Make sure that students have the needed declarative knowledge to understand new information.
- Help students learn to manage their resources, know their own cognitive skills, use them deliberately, and monitor comprehension—that is, become self-regulated. (Bruning, Schraw, and Ronning, 1995; Woolfolk, 2004).

Some of the most important applications of cognitive theories are teaching students how to learn and remember by using learning tactics and strategies. Learning strategies are general plans for accomplishing learning goals, an overall plan of attack, whereas tactics are more specific techniques that make up the plan (Derry, 1989). For example, if you are reading this chapter, your overall strategy for learning the material might include the tactics of using mnemonics to remember key terms, skimming the chapter to identify the organization, and then writing sample answers to possible essay questions. Let's examine some useful strategies—underlining, highlighting, note taking, visual mappings, and mnemonics—in more detail.

Most teachers will tell you that they want their students to "learn how to learn." Years of research indicate that using good learning strategies helps students learn and that these strategies can be taught (Hamman et al., 2000). But were you taught "how to learn"? Powerful and sophisticated learning strategies and study skills are seldom taught directly until high school or even college, so students have little practice with these strategies. In contrast, early on students usually discover repetition and rote learning on their own, so they have extensive practice with these strategies. And, unfortunately, some teachers think that memorizing is learning (Hofer and Pintrich, 1997; Woolfolk Hoy and Murphy, 2001). This may explain why many students cling to flash cards and memorizing—they don't know what else to do to learn (Gardner, 1990; Willoughby et al., 1999).

Underlining or Highlighting

If you are like most people, you underline or highlight key phrases in textbooks. Are the words turning yellow or pink at this very moment? Do you outline or take notes? Underlining and highlighting are probably two of the most commonly used strategies among graduate students. Few students, however, know the best ways to underline or highlight, so it is not surprising that many use ineffective strategies. How many times have you looked down to see virtually the entire page highlighted?

Most students underline or highlight much too much. Less is often better and selectivity is crucial. In studies that limit how much students can underline (e.g., to only one sentence per paragraph) learning has improved (Snowman, 1984). In addition to being selective, it helps if you actively transform the information into your own words as you underline or take notes. Don't rely on the words of the book. Think of connections between what you are reading and other things you know. Draw diagrams and pictures to illustrate relationships. Diagrams help you find the missing gaps as well as synthesize what you are trying to learn. Finally, look for organization in the material and use the patterns to guide your underlining (Irwin, 1991; Kiewra, 1988).

Taking Notes

As you sit in class, taking notes, frenetically trying to keep up with your professor, you may wonder if any of it matters. The answer is yes because taking notes has at least two important functions. First, note taking focuses attention and helps encode information so it has a better chance of making it into long-term memory. When you record the key ideas in your own words—translate, connect, elaborate and organize—it helps you process deeply. Even if students don't review their notes before a test, just taking notes appears to aid learning. Like many things, note taking is a skill that requires practice. Students, for example, must be careful that taking notes does not detract from listening and making sense of the presentation. (Van Meter, Yokoi, and Pressley, 1994). Second, notes provide a "permanent" record that permits students to return and review. Students who use their notes to study tend to perform better on tests, especially if they take notes that capture key ideas, concepts, and relationships (Kiewra, 1985, 1989).

Research (Van Meter, Yokoi, and Pressley, 1994) demonstrates that understanding is best when students use note taking to underscore important ideas. As a course progresses, skillful students match notes to their anticipated use. In addition, they make modifications in strategies after tests or assignments, use personal codes to flag difficult material, fill in gaps by consulting other sources (including classmates), and record information verbatim only when required. In general, successful students are strategic about taking and using notes.

Visual Tools

Effective use of underlining and note taking requires an understanding of the structure and organization of the material to be learned. Visual mapping strategies are useful in this regard (Van Meter, 2001). Creating graphic organizers such as concept maps, diagrams, or charts is more effective than simply outlining the text (Robinson and Kiewra, 1995). For example, Armbruster and Anderson (1981) taught students specific techniques for diagramming relationships among ideas presented in a text and found that they improved learning. Mapping relationships by noting causal connections, making comparisons and contrasts, and providing examples improves recall. For instance, it is helpful when students compare one another's "maps" and discuss the differences. Other useful techniques are Venn diagrams, which show how ideas or concepts overlap, and tree diagrams, which demonstrate how ideas branch from each other. Tree diagrams are especially useful, for example, in developing decision-making strategies (see Chapter 9).

Mnemonics

Mnemonics are systematic procedures for improving memory. Many mnemonic strategies use imagery (Levin, 1985; McCormick and Levin, 1987). For example, to remember a grocery list, you might visualize each item in an especially memorable place in your house—perhaps a bunch of bananas hanging from a kitchen plant, a quart of milk on top of the refrigerator, a turkey on top of the stove, and so forth. These places are the pegs that help you remember. So every time you have a list to remember, use the same peg (places) but substitute the objects of the new list.

Acronyms help individuals remember information for long periods of time. An acronym is a form of abbreviation—a word formed from the first letter of each word or a phrase, such as AASA, the American Association of School Administrators. POSDCoRB (Planning, Organizing, Staffing, Directing, Coordinating, Reporting, and Budgeting) is an acronym to recall the seven functions of administration. Another method forms phrases or sentences out of the first letter of each word or item in a list. For example, the question, "How do I cause regularity?" is a good prompt to remember the fundamental features of bureaucracy—*H*ierarchy, *D*ivision of labor, *I*mpersonality, *C*areer orientation, and *R*ules and regulations. Another approach is to incorporate all the items to be memorized into a jingle with rhymes, like "i before e except after c" to help spell certain words.

The mnemonic system that has been most extensively researched in teaching is the keyword method. Joel Levin and his colleagues (Jones, Levin, Levin, and Beitzel, 2000) use a mnemonic (the Three Rs) to teach the keyword mnemonic method:

- Recode the vocabulary item to be learned as a more familiar, concrete keyword—this is the keyword.
- Relate the keyword clue to the vocabulary item's definition through a sentence.
- Retrieve the desired definition.

For example, to remember that the English word *carlin* means old woman, you might recode carlin as the more familiar keyword *car.* Then make up a sentence such as "The old woman was driving a car." When you are asked for the meaning of the word *carlin,* you think of the keyword *car,* which triggers the sentence about the car and the old woman, the meaning. (Jones, Levin, Levin, and Beitzel, 2000).

Teaching strategies based on cognitive views of learning, particularly information processing, highlight the importance attention, rehearsal (practice), and elaboration in learning and provide ways to give students more control over their own learning by developing and improving their own metacognitive processes.

In summary, information processing approaches to learning regard the human mind as a symbol processing system. This system converts sensory input into symbol structures (propositions, images, or schemas), and then processes (rehearses or elaborates) those symbol structures so knowledge can be held in memory and retrieved. The outside world is seen as a source of input, but once the sensations are perceived and enter working memory, the important work is assumed to be happening "inside the head" of the individual (Schunk, 2000; Vera and Simon, 1993). Constructivist perspectives challenge such views.

TIP: THEORY INTO PRACTICE

How is the curriculum in your school helping students develop learning strategies as well as curriculum content? For example, what planning, memory, or monitoring strategies should your students develop to improve their performance on their proficiency tests? How can these strategies be taught as part of the curriculum?

A CONSTRUCTIVIST APPROACH TO LEARNING

Most people who use the term "constructivism" emphasize "the learner's contribution to meaning and learning through both individual and social activity" (Bruning, Schraw, and Ronning, 1999, p. 215). Constructivist perspectives are grounded in the research of Piaget, Vygotsky, the Gestalt psychologists, Bartlett, and Bruner as well as the educational philosophy of John Dewey, to mention just a few intellectual roots. There is no one constructivist theory of learning, but there are constructivist approaches in science and mathematics education, in educational psychology and anthropology, and in computer-based education. Some constructivist theorists such as Vygotsky emphasize the shared and social construction of knowledge; others like Piaget see social forces as less important.

Types of Constructivism

Virtually all the theories in cognitive science include some kind of constructivism because these theories assume that individuals construct their own cognitive structures as they interpret their experiences in particular situations (Palincsar, 1998). But even though many psychologists and educators use the term "constructivism," they often mean very different things

(Marshall, 1996; McCaslin and Hickey, 2001; Phillips, 1997). One way to organize constructivist views is to talk about two forms of constructivism: psychological and social (Palincsar, 1998; Phillips, 1997).

Psychological/Individual Constructivism

Psychological constructivists are interested in individual knowledge, beliefs, self-concept, or identity, so they are sometimes called individual constructivists. They all focus on the inner psychological life of people and how individuals build up their cognitive or emotional structures and strategies (Phillips, 1997). For example, Piaget proposed a sequence of cognitive stages that all humans pass through. Thinking at each stage builds on and incorporates previous stages as it becomes more organized and adaptive and less tied to concrete events. Piaget described how individuals develop *schemes*—the basic building blocks of thinking. Schemes are organized systems of actions or thought that allow us to mentally represent or "think about" the objects and events in our world. Schemes may be very small and specific, for example, the sucking-through-a-straw scheme or the recognizing-a-rose scheme. Or they may be larger and more general—the drinking scheme or the categorizing-plants scheme.

Two processes are applied to schemes. *Assimilation* involves trying to understand something new by applying existing schemes—fitting the new into what we already know. At times, we may have to distort the new information to make it fit. For example, the first time many children see a skunk, they call it a "kitty." They try to match the new experience with an existing scheme for identifying animals. *Accommodation* occurs when a person must change existing ways of thinking to respond to a new situation. We adjust our thinking to fit the new information, instead of adjusting the information to fit our thinking. Children demonstrate accommodation when they add the scheme for recognizing skunks to their other systems for identifying animals. People adapt to their increasingly complex environments by using existing schemes whenever these schemes work (assimilation) and by modifying and adding to their schemes when something new is needed (accommodation).

Piaget's psychological constructivist perspective was less concerned with "correct" representations and more interested in meaning as constructed by the individual. Piaget's special concern was with logic and the construction of universal knowledge that cannot be learned directly from the environment—knowledge such as conservation or reversibility (Miller, 2002). Such knowledge comes from reflecting on and coordinating our own cognitions or thoughts, not from mapping external reality. Piaget saw the social environment as an important factor in development, but did not believe that social interaction was the main mechanism for changing thinking (Moshman, 1997).

Piaget did not make specific educational recommendations. He was more interested in understanding children's thinking. He did express some general ideas about educational philosophy, however. He believed that the main goal of education should be to help children learn how to learn, and that education should "form not furnish" the minds of students (Piaget, 1969, p. 70). Even though Piaget did not design programs of education based on his ideas, many other people have. For example, the National Association for the Education of Young Children has guidelines for developmentally appropriate education that incorporate Piaget's findings (Bredekamp and Copple, 1997).

Some educational and developmental psychologists have referred to Piaget's kind of constructivism as "**first wave constructivism**" or "solo" constructivism, with its emphasis on individual meaning-making (DeCorte, Greer, and Verschaffel, 1996; Paris, Byrnes, and Paris, 2001). "**Second wave**" **constructivism** puts thinking and learning in the context of social situations and cultural practices. Vygotsky's theory is an example of a second wave constructivism.

Vygotsky's Social Constructivism

Lev Semenovich Vygotsky, a Russian psychologist, was only 38 when he died of tuberculosis more than 50 years ago, but he had produced over 100 books and articles. Vygotsky believed that knowledge is socially constructed; that is, knowledge is built upon what participants contribute and construct together. Thus development may proceed differently in different cultural contexts. Social interaction, cultural tools, and activity shape individual development and learning.

Vygotsky believed that *cultural tools,* including real tools (such as printing presses, rulers, and the abacus, along with tools we would add today such as PDAs, computers, and the Internet) and symbolic tools (such as numbers and mathematical systems, Braille and sign language, maps, works of art, signs and codes, and language) play very important roles in cognitive development. For example, as long as the culture provides only Roman numerals for representing quantity, certain ways of thinking mathematically—from long division to calculus—are difficult or impossible. But if a number system has a zero, fractions, positive and negative values, and an infinite number of numbers, then much more is possible. The number system is a cultural tool that supports thinking, learning, and cognitive development. This symbol system is passed from adult to child through formal and informal interactions and teachings.

Vygotsky emphasized that all higher-order mental processes, such as reasoning and problem solving, are mediated by (accomplished through and with the help of) psychological tools, such as language, signs, and symbols. Adults teach these tools to children during day-to-day activities and the children internalize them. Then the psychological tools can help students advance their own development (Karpov and Haywood, 1998). The process is something like this: As children engage in activities with adults or more capable peers, they exchange ideas and ways of thinking about or representing concepts—drawing maps, for example, as a way to represent spaces and places. Children internalize these co-created ideas. Thus, children's knowledge, ideas, attitudes, and values develop through appropriating or "taking for themselves" the ways of acting and thinking provided by their culture and by the more capable members of their group (Kozulin and Presseisen, 1995).

Radical Constructivism

Radical constructivism has become popular in recent years with the rise of post-modern thought and critique in American education; in fact, it has been called a species of post-modernism (Moshman, 1997). Radical constructivists maintain that knowledge is not a mirror of the external world in spite of the fact that experience affects thinking and thinking influences knowledge. All of knowledge is socially constructed, and, more important, some people have more power than others do in defining what constitutes such knowledge. This approach encourages collaboration to understand diverse viewpoints and often challenges traditional bodies of knowledge (Gergen, 1997). It finds no basis for evaluating or interpreting any belief as any better or any worse than any other (Derry, 1992; Garrison, 1995).

A difficulty with this position is that, when pushed to the extreme of relativism, all knowledge and beliefs are equal because all are constructed. This way of thinking offers problems for educators. First, teachers have a professional responsibility to emphasize some values, such as honesty or justice, over others such as bigotry. All beliefs are not equal. As teachers we ask students to work hard to learn. If learning cannot advance understanding because all understandings are equally good, then, as David Moshman (1997) notes, "we might just as well let students continue to believe whatever they believe" (p. 230). Also, it appears that some knowledge, such as counting and one-to-one correspondence, is not constructed but universal. Knowing one-to-one correspondence is part of being human (Geary, 1995; Schunk, 2000). We agree with those scholars and researchers who are critical of the radical constructivist perspective (Chandler, 1997; Moshman, 1997; Phillips, 1997).

These different perspectives on constructivism raise some general questions and disagree on the answers. These questions can never be fully resolved, but different theories tend to favor different positions.

How Is Knowledge Constructed?

One tension among different approaches to constructivism is based on *how* knowledge is constructed. Moshman (1982) describes three explanations.

1. *The realities and truths of the external world direct knowledge construction.* Individuals *reconstruct* outside reality by building accurate mental representations that reflect "the way things really are." Information processing holds this view of knowledge (Cobb and Bowers, 1999).
2. *Internal processes such as Piaget's organization, assimilation, and accommodation direct knowledge construction.* New knowledge is abstracted from old knowledge. Knowledge is not a mirror of reality, but rather an abstraction that grows and develops with cognitive activity. Knowledge is not true or false; it just grows more internally consistent and organized with development.

3. *Both external and internal factors direct knowledge construction.*
    Knowledge grows through the *interactions* of internal (cognitive) and
    external (environmental and social) factors. Vygotsky's description of
    cognitive development through the appropriation and use of cultural
    tools such as language is consistent with this view (Bruning, Schraw,
    and Ronning, 1999). Table 2.2 summarizes the three general
    explanations about how knowledge is constructed.

Knowledge: Situated or General?

A second question that cuts across many constructivist perspectives is
whether knowledge is internal, general, and transferable or bound to the time
and place in which it is constructed. Psychologists who emphasize the social
construction of knowledge and situated learning affirm Vygotsky's notion
that learning is inherently social and embedded in a particular cultural setting (Cobb and Bowers, 1999). What is true in one time and place—such as
the "fact" before Columbus's time that the earth was flat—becomes false in
another time and place. Particular ideas may be useful within a specific community of practice, such as 15th-century navigation, but useless outside that
community. What counts as new knowledge is determined in part by how
well the new idea fits with current accepted practice. Over time, the current
practice may be questioned and even overthrown, but until such major shifts
occur, current practice will shape what is considered valuable.

   Situated learning emphasizes that the real world is not like studying in
school. It is more like an apprenticeship where novices, with the support of
an expert guide and model, take on more and more responsibility until they
are able to function independently. For those who take a situated learning
view, this explains learning in factories, around the dinner table, in high
school halls, in street gangs, in the business office, and on the playground.

   Situated learning is often described as "enculturation," or adopting the
norms, behaviors, skills, beliefs, language, and attitudes of a particular community. The community might be mathematicians or gang members or writers
or students in your eighth-grade class or soccer players—any group that has
particular ways of thinking and doing. Knowledge is seen *not* as individual
cognitive structures but as a creation of the community over time. The practices
of the community—the ways of interacting and getting things done, as well as
the tools the community has created—constitute the knowledge of that community. Learning means becoming more able to participate in those practices,
use the tools, and take on the identity of a member of the community (Derry,
1992; Garrison, 1995; Greeno, Collins, and Resnick, 1996; Rogoff, 1998).

   At the most basic level, situated learning asserts that much of what we
learn is tied to the context in which we learned it (Anderson, Reder, and Simon, 1996, p. 5). Thus, some would argue, learning to do calculations in
school may help students do more school calculations, but may not help them
balance a checkbook because the skills can be applied only in the context in
which they were learned, namely school (Lave, 1997; Lave and Wenger, 1991).
But it also appears that knowledge and skills can be applied across contexts

TABLE 2.2

How Knowledge Is Constructed

What Directs Knowledge Formation?	Assumptions about Learning and Knowledge	Example Theories
External World	Knowledge is acquired by constructing a representation of the outside world. Direct teaching, feedback, and explanation affect learning. Knowledge is accurate to the extent that it reflects the "way things really are" in the outside world.	Information processing
Internal Processes	Knowledge is constructed by transforming, organizing, and reorganizing previous knowledge. Knowledge is not a mirror of the external world. Exploration and discovery are more important than teaching.	Piaget
Both External and Internal Factors	Knowledge is constructed based on social interactions and experience. Knowledge reflects the outside world as filered through and influenced by culture, language, beliefs, interactions with others, direct teaching, and modeling. Guided discovery, teaching models, and coaching as well as the individual's prior knowledge, beliefs, and thinking affect learning.	Vygotsky

that were not part of the initial learning situation, as when you use your ability to read and calculate to do your income taxes, even though income tax
forms were not part of your high school curriculum (Anderson, Reder, and
Simon, 1996). So learning that is situated in school does not have to be
doomed or irrelevant (Berieter, 1997).

Much of the work within constructivist perspectives has focused on
teaching. Many of the new standards for teaching, such as the National Council of Teachers of Mathematics' Curriculum and Evaluation Standards for
School Mathematics and the American Association for the Advancement of
Science's Benchmarks for Science Literacy are based on constructivist assumptions and methods. Many of the efforts to reform and restructure
schools are attempts to apply constructivist perspectives on teaching and
learning to the curriculum and organization of entire schools.

TEACHING APPLICATIONS OF CONSTRUCTIVIST APPROACHES

Expert teachers use good constructivist theories as well as sound behavioral
and cognitive theories. Before we provide examples of the contributions of
constructivist approaches to teaching and learning, we summarize some of
the guiding principles:

- Develop multiple strategies for acquiring and assessing information.
- Frame tasks using processes such as classifying, analyzing, predicting, and creating.
- Organize instruction to facilitate knowledge construction.
- Use raw data and primary sources as well as manipulative, interactive, and physical materials.
- Create a thinking and problem-solving environment.
- Encourage student dialogue both with the teacher and with each other.
- Use coaching and scaffolding to build student understanding.
- Encourage and support student initiative and autonomy.
- Make openness and tolerance basic rules for classroom interaction.
- Alter teaching strategies to keep students' ideas and responses driving forces in the class.
- Make student discovery a primary mission of teaching. (Bruning, Schraw, and Ronning, 1995; Brooks and Brooks, 1993)

"Although there are several versions of the constructivist theories, most
scholars agree that constructivist approaches dramatically change the focus
of teaching by putting the students' own efforts to understand at the center
of educational enterprise" (Prawat, 1992: 357). Let's examine more closely
some of the fundamental dimensions of most constructivist teaching.

Constructivists believe that students should not be given basic skills drills
and simple or artificial problems, but instead should be challenged with complex
situations and "fuzzy" problems, the kind they will find in the world outside the

classroom. Such problems should be embedded in **authentic tasks** and activities, the kinds of situations that students will face as they apply what they are learning to real-world problems (Brown, 1990; Needles and Knapp, 1994).

Many constructivists share Vygotsky's belief that higher mental processes elaborate through social interaction; hence, collaboration in learning is crucial. The Language Development and Hypermedia Group suggests that a major goal of teaching is to develop students' abilities to establish and defend their own positions while respecting the positions of others, a goal that requires exchange—students must talk with each other.

When students encounter only one representation of content—one model, one analogy, or one way to understand complex content—they often oversimplify and try to apply that one approach to every situation. Richard Spiro and his colleagues (1991) recommend that revisiting the same material at different times, in different contexts, for different purposes, and from different conceptual perspectives is a key to mastering advanced knowledge. The idea is not entirely new. Years ago Jerome Bruner (1966) described the advantages of a spiral curriculum, which introduces the fundamental structure of all subjects—the "big ideas"—early in the school years and then revisits the subjects in more and more complex forms over time.

The assumptions we make, our beliefs, and experiences shape what we come to "know." Different assumptions and experiences lead to different conclusions. Constructivists stress the importance of understanding how knowledge is constructed so that students will be aware of the influences that shape their thinking. Then they are able to select, elaborate, and defend positions in a self-critical way while respecting the views of others.

Three examples of constructivist approaches to teaching, which are consistent with these guiding principles, are inquiry and problem-based learning, cognitive apprenticeships, and cooperative learning.

Inquiry and Problem-Based Learning

John Dewey first described his basic **inquiry learning** process in 1910. Although there have been many adaptations of his strategy, the form usually includes the teacher presenting a puzzling event, question, or problem and the students providing these elements (Pasch et al., 1991):

- Formulating hypotheses to explain the problem.
- Collecting data to test the hypotheses.
- Drawing conclusions.
- Reflecting on the original problem and thinking processes needed to solve it.

Sometimes, teachers pose a problem and students ask simple questions to gather data and test hypotheses while the teacher monitors students' thinking and guides the process. Consider the following example that Pasch and her colleagues offer (Pasch et al., 1991):

1. After clarifying ground rules of questioning, the teacher blows softly across the top of an 8½- by 11-inch sheet of paper, and the paper rises. She challenges students to figure out why it rises.
2. Students ask questions to gather more information and to isolate relevant variables. The teacher answers only "yes" or "no." Students ask if temperature is important (no). They ask if the paper is special (no). Does air pressure have anything to do it? (yes). Further questions.
3. Students develop and test causal relationships. In this case, they ask if the movement of air across on top causes the paper to rise (yes). They ask if the fast movement of the air produces less pressure on the top (yes). Then they test their ideas with other materials—for example, thin plastic.
4. Students form a generalization (hypothesis): "If the air on the top moves faster than the air on the bottom of a surface, then the air pressure on top is lessened, and the object rises." Later lessons expand students' understanding of principles and physical laws through further experiments.
5. The teacher leads students in a discussion of their analyses and thinking processes. What were the key variables? How did they determine the cause-and-effect relations?

The inquiry approach has much in common with guided discovery learning. Both require extensive preparation, organization, and monitoring to ensure that students are engaged and challenged (Pasch et al., 1991).

Computer and video technologies can support inquiry and problem-based learning. For example, the Cognition and Technology Group at Vanderbilt University (CTGV 1990, 1993) developed a videodisc-based learning environment for the fifth and sixth graders. The series, *The Adventures of Jasper Woodbury*, challenges students with complex situations that require problem finding, goal setting (including subgoals), and the application of concepts from mathematics, science, history, and literature to solve problems. The situations are complex and lifelike and can be solved using data embedded in the stories. In one adventure, Jasper sets out in a small motorboat and heads to Cedar Creek to inspect an old cruiser he is considering buying. Along the way he has to check maps, use his marine radio, monitor fuel, deal with repair problems, and eventually buy the cruiser. After the purchase, he must determine whether enough fuel and time remain to sail his purchase home before sundown.

The Vanderbilt group calls its problem-based approach, anchored instruction. Their anchor is the rich, authentic, and challenging situation, which provides a reason for setting goals, planning, and using mathematical tools. The aim is to develop useful and flexible knowledge. Initial research suggests that students as young as fourth grade and as old as high school can work with the adventures (CTGV, 1990). Students work in groups to solve the problems, and even group members with limited skills can contribute because they can notice key information in the videotape or sometimes suggest creative ways to approach the situation.

Research on Inquiry and Problem-Based Learning

Inquiry methods are similar to discovery and share some of the same problems, so inquiry must be carefully planned and organized, especially for less prepared students who may lack the background knowledge and problem-solving skills needed to benefit. Some research has shown that discovery methods are ineffective and even detrimental for lower-ability students (Corno and Snow, 1986; Slavin, Karweit, and Madden, 1989). When Ted Bredderman (1983) analyzed the results of 57 comparisons of activity-based learning and more traditional approaches for teaching science, he concluded that activity-based methods were superior to content-based traditional approaches in terms of students' understanding of the scientific method and creativity, but about the same for learning science content.

In 1993, a similar comparison was made of problem-based instruction in medical school. Students learning through problem-based instruction were better at clinical skills such as problem formation and reasoning, but they were worse in their basic knowledge of science and felt less prepared in science (Albanese and Mitchell, 1993). Some students, those who are better at self-regulation, benefit more than others from problem-based methods (Evensen, Salisbury-Glennon, and Glenn, 2001). The best approach may be a balance of content-focused and inquiry or problem-based methods (Arends, 2000).

For example, Eva Toth, David Klahr, and Zhe Chen (2000) tested a balanced approach for teaching fourth graders how to use the controlled variable strategy in science to design good experiments. The method had three phases: (1) in small groups, students conducted exploratory experiments to identify variables that made a ball roll farther down a ramp, (2) the teacher led a discussion, explained the controlled variable strategy, and modeled good thinking about experiment design, and (3) the students designed and conducted application experiments to isolate which variables caused the ball to roll farther. The combination of inquiry, discussion, explanation, and modeling was successful in helping the students understand the concepts.

Cognitive Apprenticeships

Apprenticeships are an effective form of education. By working with a master and sometimes other apprentices, neophytes have learned many skills, trades, and crafts. Why are they effective? Apprenticeships are rich in information because the experts with extensive knowledge guide, model, demonstrate, and correct, as well as provide a personal bond that is motivating. The performances required of the learner are real, important, and grow more complex as the learner becomes more competent (Collins, Brown, and Holum, 1991).

Collins and his colleagues (1989) argue that knowledge and skills learned in school often are irrelevant to the world beyond school. To address this problem, schools sometimes adopt many of the features of apprenticeship, but rather than learning to sculpt or lay bricks, apprenticeships in schools focus on cognitive objectives such as reading comprehension or mathematical problem solving or application of professional skills in internships. Most cognitive apprenticeship models share six features:

- Students observe an expert (usually the teacher) model the task.
- Students get support through coaching or tutoring—including hints, feedback, models, and reminders.
- Conceptual scaffolding—outlines, explanations, notes, definitions, formulas, procedures, and the like—is provided and then gradually reduced as the student becomes more competent and proficient.
- Students continually articulate knowledge—putting their understanding into their own words.
- Students reflect on their progress and compare their problem solving both to an expert's performance and to their own earlier performances.
- Students explore new ways to apply what they are learning—ways they have not practiced at the master's side.

Cooperative Learning

Collaboration and cooperative learning have a long history in American education. In the early 1900s, John Dewey criticized the use of competition in education and urged educators to structure schools as democratic learning communities, and his ideas gained acceptance in the early 1900s; however, cooperation fell from favor in the 1940s and 1950s, as the popularity of competition increased. In the 1960s, there was another swing—back to individualized and cooperative learning structures, stimulated in part by concern for civil rights and interracial relations (Webb and Palincsar, 1996).

Today, evolving constructivist views of learning fuel interest in collaboration and cooperative learning. Two key characteristics of constructivist teaching are complex, real-life learning environments and social interaction. As educators turn to learning in real contexts, "there is a heightened interest in situations where elaboration, interpretation, explanation, and argumentation are integral to the activity of the group and where learning is supported by other individuals" (Webb and Palincsar, 1996: 844). David and Roger Johnson (1999) list five elements that define true cooperative learning groups:

- Face-to-face interaction
- Positive interdependence
- Individual accountability
- Collaborative skills
- Group processing

Students *interact face-to-face* and close together, not across the room. Group members experience *positive interdependence*—they need each other for support, explanations, and guidance. Even though they work together and help each other, members of the group must ultimately demonstrate learning on their own—they are held *individually accountable* for learning, often through individual tests or other assessments. *Collaborative skills* are necessary for effective group functioning. Often these skills, such as giving constructive feedback, reaching consensus, and involving every member, must be taught and practiced before the groups tackle a learning task. Finally, members monitor *group processes* and relationships to make sure the group is working effectively and to learn about the dynamics of groups. They take time to ask, "How are we doing as a group? Is everyone working together?" Let's examine a few of the popular cooperative learning techniques.

Jigsaw

One format for cooperative learning, Jigsaw, emphasizes high interdependence. Each group member is given part of the material to be learned by the whole group and becomes an "expert" on that piece. Students teach each other, so they depend on each other and everyone's contribution is important. A more recent version, Jigsaw II, adds expert meetings in which students who have the same material consult to make sure they understand their assigned part and then plan how to teach the information to their group. After the expert meeting, students return to their groups and bring their expertise to the learning sessions. Finally, students take an individual test on all the material and earn points for their learning team score. Teams work either for rewards or simply for recognition (Slavin, 1995).

Scripted Cooperation

Donald Dansereau and his colleagues have developed a method for learning in pairs called scripted cooperation. Students work cooperatively on some task—reading a selection of text, solving math problems, or editing writing drafts. For example, in reading, both partners read a passage. Then one student gives an oral summary and other comments on the summary, noting omissions or errors. Next the partners collaborate to refine and improve the information—create associations, images, mnemonics, ties to previous work, examples, analogies, and so on. The partners switch the reading and commentary roles for the next passage and continue to take turns until they finish the assignment (Dansereau, 1985; O'Donnell and O'Kelly, 1994).

There are many other forms of cooperative learning. Kagan (1994) and Slavin (1995) have written extensively on cooperative learning and developed and refined a variety of formats. Regardless of the format, the key to learning in groups is the quality of the discourse among the students. Talk that is interpretive—that analyzes and discusses explanations, evidence, reasons, and alternatives—is more useful than talk that is only descriptive. Teachers play an important role in cooperative learning; they are important guides. Effective teachers seed the discussion with ideas and alternatives that push and prod student thinking (Palincsar, 1998). See Table 2.3 for a summary of learning perspectives discussed in this chapter.

Four Learning Perspectives

	Behavioral Skinner	Cognitive Anderson	Individual Constructivist Piaget	Social Constructivist Vygotsky
Knowledge	A fixed body of knowledge to acquire	Fixed body of knowledge to acquire	Changing body of knowledge, individually constructed in the social world—but some understandings clearly superior to others	Socially constructed knowledge; knowledge reflects the outside world as filtered through and influenced by culture, language, beliefs, and interactions with others
Learning	Acquisition of facts, skill, concepts	Acquisition of facts, skill, concepts, and strategies	Active construction and reconstruction of prior knowledge	Collaborative construction of socially defined knowledge and values
	Occurs through explanation, demonstration, and guided practice	Occurs through the effective application of strategies	Occurs through multiple opportunities to connect with what is already known	Occurs through socially constructed opportunities
Teaching	Transmission—telling	Transmission—guiding toward more accurate and complete information	Challenging and guiding students toward a more complete understanding	Teacher and student coconstructing knowledge
Role of Teacher	Supervisor—correct wrong answers	Guide—model effective strategies and correct misconceptions	Guide and facilitator—listen to student's ideas and thinking and guide	Guide, facilitator, and partner—listen to socially constructed knowledge and help coconstruct knowledge
Role of Classmates	Not essential	Not essential, but can facilitate information processing	Not essential, but can stimulate questions and raise questions	Part of the process of knowledge construction
Role of Student	Receiver of information; active in practice	Processor of information; strategy user	Active constructor of knowledge; active thinker and interpreter	Active coconstructor of knowledge; active social participant
Example of Teaching Approaches	Learning objectives; direct instruction	Visual tools—graphs and charts; mnemonic strategies	Conceptual change teaching; pure discovery learning	Cognitive apprenticeship; reciprocal teaching

TIP: THEORY INTO PRACTICE

Think of an important concept in a subject you have taught (ecological niche, point of view, story tone, reciprocal determinism, former/latter, distributive property, democracy . . .). Now plan a lesson on the concept that reflects Piaget's individual constructivism and another lesson exemplifying Vygotsky's social constructivism. What are the main differences between the two perspectives as revealed in your lesson plans?

A CASE FOR LEADERSHIP

Cooperative Learning: Sound Practice or Social Experiment?

This is your second year as principal of Jackson Middle School. The first year was a major adjustment for you because you went directly from being teacher to principal, and most of your energy was focused on keeping the school running smoothly, but this year is different. This year you have a plan to begin to improve the achievement of weak students in Jackson. You have started in a modest way by getting three sixth grade teachers to volunteer to use cooperative learning in their classes. The teachers took a two-course sequence in cooperative learning at the university last summer and now they are well into the second month of the innovation—enjoying the challenge and believing they are making a difference.

You are more than a little upset because you just got a call from Dr. Anita Rodriquez, your superintendent. Dr. Rodriquez has always been very supportive; in fact, it was she who talked you into moving into the principalship. But the phone conversation was troubling. The superintendent reported that she and several of the board members were getting calls from parents about the "cooperative learning experiment," as the parents put it. The superintendent remained supportive, but she concluded her phone conversation with you by saying that she just wanted you to know that there

was opposition to your new cooperative learning experiment and that you should be prepared for some trouble.

Indeed you had personally experienced a number of parental complaints about the cooperative learning program that you had dismissed as the growing pains of the new program. For example, one parent complained that the cooperative learning was "just another passing educational fad" and that she wanted her children to learn the basics. She had attended parochial school as a child and was proud of her no-nonsense education. She concluded that, "learning is not fun and play—it is serious business and hard work." You tried to assure her that her son would learn and perhaps come to enjoy the process of learning, but she left still seemingly unconvinced of the merits of cooperative learning. It was also true that another parent expressed some alarm that the school was "experimenting" with her daughter. In that case, after reviewing some of the facts and purposes of the cooperative leaning program, you thought you were successful in defusing the issue because the parent left feeling much better about school and her daughter. As you reflect further on your interactions, you realize that perhaps there is more resistance than you originally thought—obviously the superintendent and the board are getting complaints. You are committed to the program and

(Continued)

A CASE FOR LEADERSHIP *(Continued)*

want to support the three teachers who volunteered and are moving forward with the innovation.

You decide to talk directly with the teachers about reactions from the parents. An after-school meeting with the three teachers for the purpose of gauging community resistance and assessing the progress of the program yields some surprises. Your teachers have been handling many more negative complaints than you are aware of, yet they are enthusiastic and committed to the program. They believe that they have turned the corner because most of the students are truly enjoying the teamwork, and student performance, especially of the slower students, is definitely improving. What are the parental criticisms of the program?

- The program slows down my child; she is smart and doesn't need help.
- I don't like you experimenting with my kids.
- Competition, not cooperation, is what makes this country great. In the business world, it is dog eat dog.
- My child is going to get lower grades because she is being dragged down by others in her group.
- The kids don't work hard; they play and it is a waste of time.
- My son does all the work for his group and it is not fair.

- I spend all my spare time driving my daughter around to work on group projects with classmates.
- My son does fine on his own; he doesn't like group work.
- Kids in the group are mean to my son; they don't include him; he hates school.

You all agree that too many parents are misinformed about cooperative learning and need to be educated not only about the basic principles undergirding the new program but also about other learning strategies that are occurring in the classroom. To that end you agree, with the help of your cooperative learning teachers, to prepare a short speech for the next PTA meeting. The talk will review the new cooperative learning program, address each of the listed criticisms of the program, and use learning and teaching principles from the behavioral, cognitive, and constructivist perspectives to bolster the teaching and learning program of the school. The aim is to educate and allay parent anxiety.

You are that middle school principal so it is up to you to prepare the speech. Do it.

SUMMARY

The teaching-learning function is the technical core of the school. Although theorists disagree about definitions of learning, most concede that learning occurs when experience causes a change in a person's knowledge or behavior. There is no one best way to teach and no one best explanation of learning. Different theories of learning offer better or worse explanations depending on what is to be explained. Three perspectives on learning—behavioral, cognitive, and constructivist—are especially useful for teachers and educational administrators.

Behavioral views of learning emphasize the role of external events— antecedents and consequences—in changing observable behaviors.

Consequences that increase behaviors are called reinforcers, whereas punishment suppresses or decreases behaviors. The use of learning objectives is an application of behavioral approach in teaching. Learning objectives specify the outcomes of learning so that the final goals or student behaviors are clear. When objectives are clear, students and teachers are more likely to reach them. Mastery learning is another behavioral approach. The teacher breaks down what is to be learned into small units of study such that each unit involves mastering specific objectives. Direct instruction is consistent with behavioral principles and is appropriate for teaching explicit information to groups or the whole class. One framework for direct instruction includes reviewing yesterday's work, presenting new material, giving guided practice, giving feedback and corrections, providing independent practice (or homework), and reviewing weekly and monthly.

Cognitive views of learning focus on the human mind's active attempts to make sense of the world. Knowledge is a central force in cognitive perspectives. The individual's prior knowledge affects what he or she will pay attention to, recognize, understand, remember, and forget. Knowledge can be general or domain-specific and declarative, procedural, or conditional, but to be useful, knowledge must be remembered. One influential cognitive theory is information processing. The model describes how information moves from sensory memory (which holds a wealth of sensations and images very briefly) to working memory (where the information is elaborated and connected to existing knowledge) to long-term memory (where the information can be held for a long time, depending on how well it was learned in the first place and how interconnected it is to other information). People vary in how well they learn and remember based in part on their metacognitive knowledge—their abilities to plan, monitor, and regulate their own thinking. There are many teaching applications of cognitive views including highlighting, mnemonics, imagery, and other learning strategies to help organize and elaborate material.

Constructivist perspectives on learning and teaching, which are increasingly influential today, are grounded in the research of Piaget, Brunner, Dewey, and Vygotsky. The essence of the constructivist approach is that it places the students' own efforts at the center of the educational process. In general, constructivism assumes that people create and construct knowledge rather than internalize it from the external environment, but there are a variety of approaches—three of which are individual, radical, and social. Individual constructivism emphasizes the way individuals construct external reality by using mental representations such as schemas. Radical constructivism rejects the notion that knowledge mirrors the external world and maintains that knowledge is constructed largely by interpersonal interactions and the constraints of culture and ideology. Social constructivism is the middle ground, suggesting that knowledge grows through the interactions of internal (cognitive) and external (environmental, cultural, and social) factors. Constructivists believe that students should not be given stripped-down, simplified problems, and basic skills drills, but instead should deal with complex situations and "fuzzy," ill-structured problems. The use of inquiry learning is one important application of constructivism. Here teachers pose a problem and students ask questions to gather data, formulate hypotheses and test them as the teacher monitors students' thinking and guides the process. The cognitive apprenticeship is another constructivist application. Experts with extensive knowledge guide, model, demonstrate, and correct, as well as provide personal motivation in the performance of real-life tasks. Finally, cooperative learning provides yet another constructivist application in which students work cooperatively in groups to solve complex real-life problems.

KEY ASSUMPTIONS AND PRINCIPLES

1. If the frequency or intensity of a behavior is maintaining or increasing, then something is reinforcing the behavior.
2. If an action allows you to escape or avoid a bad situation, you are likely to repeat the action when faced with the situation again.
3. Current thinking suggests that it is better to have a few important, broad, but measurable instructional objectives for teaching than to have very specific or very general objectives.
4. Direct instruction is effective when the material to be learned is explicit, factual, and hierarchical.
5. Declarative knowledge (knowing what) and procedural knowledge (knowing how) can be used most effectively if you also have conditional knowledge (knowing when and why to apply your knowledge). Many children and adults lack conditional knowledge.
6. When working memory is overloaded, information is lost.
7. Information is easier to remember if is well organized, elaborated (connected to other things you know), and learned in meaningful contexts.
8. Learning strategies need to be explicitly taught and practiced extensively in a variety of situations.
9. There are many different meanings of the term "constructivism" depending on whether the theorists emphasize social and cultural or individual factors in knowledge constructions.
10. Inquiry learning is based on Piaget's theory of cognitive development, which highlights the individual's discovery and invention of knowledge. These methods may not be helpful for less prepared students.
11. Problem-based learning emphasizes Vygotsky's concern with authentic activity in cultural contexts. These methods may be better for understanding process than for learning basic content.

NOTE

1. Wayne K. Hoy and Anita Woolfolk Hoy wrote this chapter jointly.

CHAPTER 3

STRUCTURE IN SCHOOLS

Every organized human activity—from the making of pots to the placing of a man on the moon—gives rise to two fundamental and opposing requirements: the division of labor into various tasks to be performed, and the coordination of these tasks to accomplish the activity. The structure of the organization can be defined simply as the sum total of the ways in which it divides its labor into distinct tasks and then achieves coordination among them.

Henry Mintzberg
The Structuring of Organizations

PREVIEW

1. Five key organizational features define the classic Weberian bureaucracy: division of labor, impersonal orientation, hierarchy of authority, rules and regulations, and career orientation.

2. The Weberian model is criticized because of its dysfunctional consequences, neglect of the informal organization, internal inconsistencies, and gender bias.

3. Rules have both positive and negative consequences for organizational participants; administrators must consider both.

4. Enabling and coercive bureaucracies are two contrasting types of structure, one productive and the other not.

5. Bureaucratic and professional dimensions of organization combine to define four structural arrangements for schools:

Weberian, authoritarian, professional, and chaotic.

6. There is no one best way to organize. Building effective structures demands matching the structure with its goals, environment, technology, people, and strategy.

7. Designing an effective organizational structure also involves balancing a host of countervailing forces created by the basic organizational dilemma of needing both order and freedom.

8. Organizations monitor and control work by mutual adjustment, direct supervision, standardization of work, standardization of outputs, and standardization of skills.

9. The key elements of structure are the strategic apex, middle line, operating core, support staff, and technostructure.

10. School structures vary widely. Some are simple structures; others are machine bureaucracies; a few are professional bureaucracies; some are hybrids; but for some, structure is irrelevant—they are politicized.

11. Structural elements can be tightly and loosely coupled; both arrangements have positive and negative consequences and both exist in schools.

12. A fundamental source of conflict for professionals working in organizations comes from the systems of social control used by bureaucracies and the professions.

13. Organizations accommodate to this conflict by establishing loose structures, developing dual authority structures, or engaging in socialization.

The structural element of the school as social system is found in its formal organization. Max Weber's (1947) classic analysis of bureaucracy is a good beginning point for our discussion of the organizational structure in schools because it is the theoretical basis of most contemporary treatments (e.g., Hall, 1991, 2002; Perrow, 1986; Bolman and Deal, 1997, 2003; Scott, 1998, 2003; Hoy and Sweetland 2000, 2001).

WEBERIAN MODEL OF BUREAUCRACY

Almost all modern organizations, including schools, have the characteristics enumerated by Weber: a division of labor and specialization, an impersonal orientation, a hierarchy of authority, rules and regulations, and a career orientation.

Division of Labor and Specialization

According to Weber, **division of labor** and **specialization** mean "the regular activities required for the purposes of the bureaucratically governed structure are distributed in a fixed way as official duties" (Gerth and Mills, 1946: 196). Because the tasks in most organizations are too complex to be performed by a single individual, division of labor among positions improves efficiency. In schools, for example, division of labor is primarily for instructional purposes. Within that division, subspecialties are based on level—elementary and secondary—and subject—math, science, and other specialties such as reading, bilingual, and special education.

Efficiency increases because division of labor produces specialization, which in turn leads to employees who become knowledgeable and expert at performing their prescribed duties. Such division enables the organization to employ personnel on the basis of technical qualifications. Hence, division of labor and specialization produce more expertise in school personnel.

Impersonal Orientation

Weber (1947: 331) argued that the working atmosphere of a bureaucracy should provide an **impersonal orientation,** "the dominance of a spirit of formalistic impersonality, 'sine ira et studio,' without hatred or passion, and hence without affection or enthusiasm." The bureaucratic employee is expected to make decisions based on facts, not feelings. Impersonality on the part of administrators and teachers assures equality of treatment and facilitates rationality.

Hierarchy of Authority

Offices are arranged vertically in bureaucracies; that is, "each lower office is under the control and supervision of a higher one" (Weber, 1947: 330), which produces a **hierarchy of authority.** This bureaucratic trait is made manifest in the organizational chart, with the superintendent at the top and assistants, directors, principals, teachers, and students at successively lower levels.

Hierarchy is perhaps the most pervasive characteristic in modern organizations. Almost without exception, large organizations develop a well-established system of superordination and subordination, which attempts to guarantee the disciplined compliance to directives from superiors that is necessary for implementing the various tasks and functions of an organization.

Rules and Regulations

Weber (1947: 330) asserts that every bureaucracy has a system of **rules and regulations,** a "consistent system of abstract rules which have normally been intentionally established. Furthermore, administration of law is held to consist in the application of these rules to particular cases." The system of rules covers the rights and duties inherent in each position and helps coordinate activities in the hierarchy. It also provides continuity of operations when there are changes in personnel. Rules and regulations thus ensure uniformity and stability of employee action.

Career Orientation

Because employment in a bureaucratic organization is based on technical qualifications, employees think of their work as a career. Whenever there is such a **career orientation,** Weber (1947: 334) maintains, "there is a system of promotion according to seniority, achievement, or both. Promotion is dependent on the judgment of superiors." To foster loyalty to the organization, individuals with special skills must be protected from arbitrary dismissal or denial of promotion. Employees are protected in the sense that superiors are supposed to make dispassionate decisions. Bureaucracies also institutionalize protection through such deeds.

Efficiency

To Weber (1947: 337), bureaucracy maximizes rational decision making and administrative efficiency: "Experience tends to universally show that the purely bureaucratic type of administrative organization . . . is, from a purely technical point of view, capable of attaining the highest degree of efficiency." Division of labor and specialization produce experts, and experts with an impersonal orientation make technically correct, rational decisions based on the facts. Once rational decisions have been made, the hierarchy of authority ensures disciplined compliance to directives and, along with rules and regulations, a well-coordinated system of implementation and uniformity and stability in the operation of the organization. Finally, a career orientation provides the incentive for employees to be loyal to the organization and to produce extra effort. These characteristics function to maximize administrative efficiency because committed experts make rational decisions that are executed and coordinated in a disciplined way.

Ideal Type

Although Weber's conception of bureaucracy is an **ideal type** that may or may not be found in the real world, it does highlight or emphasize basic tendencies of actual organizations:

- Division of labor (specialization)
- Impersonality
- Hierarchy of authority (centralization)
- Rules and regulations (formalization)
- Career orientation

The ideal type is useful for analytic purposes. As Alvin Gouldner (1950) explains, the ideal type may serve as a guide to help us determine how a formal organization is bureaucratized. Some organizations will be more bureaucratically structured than others. A given organization can be more bureaucratized on one characteristic and less on another. The model, as a conceptual scheme, raises important questions about organizing different kinds of formal bureaucracies. For example, under what conditions are the dimensions of bureaucracy related in order to maximize efficiency? Under what conditions does such an arrangement hinder efficiency?

CRITICISMS OF THE WEBERIAN BUREAUCRATIC MODEL

The Weberian model of bureaucracy has been attacked on a number of fronts. First, Weber is criticized for not being attentive to the dysfunctional features of his formulation. Second, the model has been criticized for its neglect of the informal organization. Third, Weber does not deal with the potential internal contradictions among the elements in the model. Finally, feminists denounce the model as gender biased. We turn to an analysis of each of these criticisms.

Functions and Dysfunctions of the Model

Weber's model of bureaucracy is functional in that application of the principles can promote efficiency and goal attainment. There is, however, the possibility of dysfunctional, or negative consequences—a possibility to which Weber pays limited attention. Let us consider each of the above bureaucratic characteristics or principles in terms of both possible functions and dysfunctions.

Although division of labor and specialization can produce expertise, they also can produce boredom. The literature is replete with instances where such boredom leads to lower levels of productivity or to a search on the part of employees for ways to make their work life more interesting, for example, the Hawthorne Studies discussed in Chapter 1. Indeed, many highly bureaucratized organizations that have experienced the negative consequences of extreme division of labor are enlarging employee responsibility to alleviate boredom.

Impersonality may improve rationality in decision making, but it also may produce a rather sterile atmosphere in which people interact as "nonpersons," resulting in low morale. Low morale, in turn, frequently impairs organizational efficiency.

Hierarchy of authority does enhance coordination, but frequently at the expense of communication. Two of the major dysfunctions of hierarchy are distortion and blockage in communication. Every level in the hierarchy produces a potential communication block because subordinates are reluctant to communicate anything that might make them look bad in the eyes of their superiors; in fact, there is probably a tendency to communicate only those things that make them look good or those things that they think their superiors want to hear (Blau and Scott, 2003).

Rules and regulations, on the one hand, do provide for continuity, coordination, stability, and uniformity. On the other hand, they often produce organizational rigidity and goal displacement. Employees may become so rule oriented that they forget that the rules and regulations are means to achieve goals, not *ends* in themselves. Disciplined compliance with the hierarchy, and particularly with the regulations, frequently produces rigidity and an inability to adjust. Such formalism may be exaggerated until conformity interferes with goal achievement. In such a case, the infamous characteristic of bureaucratic red tape is vividly apparent (Merton, 1957).

Career orientation is healthy insofar as it produces a sense of employee loyalty and motivates employees to maximize effort. Promotion, however, is based on seniority and achievement, which are not necessarily compatible. For example, rapid promotion of high achievers often produces discontent among the loyal, hard-working, senior employees who are not as productive or creative.

The potential dysfunctional consequences of each bureaucratic characteristic are not adequately addressed in Weber's ideal type. Merton, for example, was one of the first to argue that structural arrangements established to maintain reliability and efficiency—rules, disciplined compliance, a graded career, impersonal decision making—can "also lead to an overconcern with strict adherence to regulations which induces timidity, conservatism, and technicism" (1957: 199). Table 3.1 summarizes some of the dysfunctions as well as the functions of the Weberian model. The question now becomes: Under what conditions does each characteristic lead to functional but not dysfunctional consequences? Whatever the answer to this question, the model remains quite useful as both an analytical tool and a guide to scientific research.

Functions and Dysfunctions of Rules

To illustrate the analytic and research usefulness of the model, we focus on Gouldner's (1954) discussion of organizational rules. Almost without exception, large, formal organizations have systems of rules and regulations that guide organizational behavior. For example, most school districts have elaborate policy manuals. Rules are so universally present because they serve important functions.

Organizational rules have an explication function—that is, they explain in rather concise and explicit terms the specific obligations of subordinates. Rules make it unnecessary to repeat a routine order; moreover, they are less ambiguous and more carefully thought out than the hasty verbal command. Rules act as a system of communication to direct role performance.

TABLE 3.1

Functions and Dysfunctions of the Weberian Model

Bureaucratic Characteristic	Dysfunction	Function
Division of labor	Boredom	Expertise
Impersonal orientation	Lack of morale	Rationality
Hierarchy of authority	Communication blocks	Disciplined compliance and coordination
Rules and regulations	Rigidity and goal displacement	Continuity and uniformity
Career orientation	Conflict between achievement and seniority	Incentive

A second function of rules is to screen—that is, to act as a buffer between the administrator and his or her subordinates. Rules carry a sense of egalitarianism because they can be applied equally to everyone. An administrator's denial of a request from a subordinate can be on the grounds that the rules apply to everyone, superior and subordinate alike, and cannot be broken. Subordinate anger is therefore redirected to the impersonal rules and regulations. As Gouldner (1954) explains, rules impersonally support a claim to authority without forcing the leader to legitimize personal superiority; conversely, they permit a subordinate to accept directives without betraying his or her sense of being any person's equal.

Organizational rules may also legitimize punishment. When subordinates are given explicit prior warning about what behavior will provoke sanctions and about the nature of those sanctions, punishment is legitimate. As Gouldner (1954) indicates, there is a deep-rooted feeling in our culture that punishment is permissible only when the offender knows in advance that certain behaviors are forbidden; ex post facto judgments are not permissible. In effect, rules not only legitimize but also impersonalize the administration of punishment.

Rules also serve a bargaining, or "leeway," function. Using formal rules as a bargaining tool, superiors can secure informal cooperation from subordinates. By *not* enforcing certain rules and regulations, one's sphere of authority can be expanded through the development of goodwill among subordinates. Rules are serviceable because they create something that can be given up as well as given use.

For each functional consequence of rules discussed thus far, a corresponding dysfunctional outcome results. Rules reinforce and preserve apathy by explicating the minimum level of acceptable behavior. Some employees remain apathetic because they know how little is required for them to remain secure. When apathy is fused with hostility, the scene is set for "organizational sabotage," which occurs when conforming to the letter of the rule violates the express purpose of the rule (Gouldner, 1954).

Although rules screen the superior from subordinates, that protection may become dysfunctional. **Goal displacement** develops; the means, in this case rules, become ends in themselves. By using rules to make important decisions, administrators may focus attention on the importance of a rule orientation, often at the expense of more important goals.

Another dysfunctional consequence that emerges from the screening and punishment functions of rules is legalism. When rules and punishments are pervasive, subordinates can adopt an extremely legalistic stance. In effect, they become "Philadelphia lawyers," willing and potentially able to win their case on a technicality. In its extreme form, employees may use legalism as an excuse for inactivity in any area not covered by a rule. When an individual is asked why he or she is not performing a reasonable task, the pat answer is "no rule says I have to." To say the least, such extreme legalism creates an unhealthy climate in schools.

The leeway function of rules—not enforcing them in exchange for informal cooperation—involves the ever-present danger of being too lenient. The classic example of this kind of permissiveness is seen in the indulgency pattern described in Gouldner's study of a factory in which few, if any, rules were enforced; although superior-subordinate relations were friendly, productivity suffered. The functions and dysfunctions of rules are summarized in Table 3.2.

School administrators who are aware can avoid the dysfunctional consequences of rules, but the path is not easy. For example, by taking advantage of the screening function of bureaucratic rules, administrators can gain and maintain some control over organizational activities. They anticipate that general and impersonal rules will be "good" because they provide direction without creating status distinctions. Using bureaucratic rules thus maintains control, but it may produce unanticipated consequences. Because bureaucratic rules provide knowledge about minimum acceptable standards (explication function), an unanticipated consequence may be that minimums become maximums (apathy-preserving and goal-displacement dysfunctions), and the difference between actual behavior and expected behavior for goal achievement becomes visible and unacceptable, thereby prompting close supervision. In brief, because the equilibrium originally sought by instituting the bureaucratic rules is upset, the demand for more control is created.

Thus, although rules are used to mitigate some tensions, they may create others. As a matter of fact, rules may actually perpetuate the tensions they were meant to dispel. For example, close supervision can produce high visibility of power relations and a high degree of interpersonal tension; yet the use of rules to reduce tension may unintentionally perpetuate the need for additional close supervision; hence, the cycle begins again. The major problems of low motivation and minimal role performance simply are not solved by more rules.[1]

Educational administrators must learn how to anticipate and avoid the negative consequences of bureaucratic rules. They must ask: How can the functional consequences of rules be maximized and the dysfunctional consequences minimized? Gouldner's (1954) research provides some guidelines.

TABLE 3.2

The Double-Edged Nature of Bureaucratic Rules

Functions	Dysfunctions
Explication ⟷	Apathy reinforcement
Screening ⟷	Goal displacement
Punishment-legitimizing ⟷	Legalism
Leeway ⟷	Indulgency

He maintains that rules having a punishment-centered pattern are most likely to evoke negative consequences. *Either workers or administrators initiate punishment-centered rules,* but not jointly, to coerce the other group to comply; and they result in punishment of one group by the other when the rules are violated, producing tension and conflict.

On the other hand, **representative rules** are initiated and supported by *both* workers and administrators. Although such rules are enforced by the administration and obeyed by subordinates, they result in efforts to educate because rule violations are interpreted as a lack of information. Representative rules are least likely to evoke dysfunctional consequences because they have been jointly initiated, they are generally supported by the parties concerned, and they empower subordinates. Therefore, representative rules, as contrasted with **punishment-centered rules,** are more likely to have the desired functional consequences without many of the unintended dysfunctional consequences.

TIP: THEORY INTO PRACTICE

Give three examples of rules in your school that are useful. Why are they helpful? Now identify three rules in your schools that cause more problems than they solve. Why do they hinder? What guidelines would you use to establish school rules when you are a principal?

Neglect of the Informal Organization

The Weberian model of organization also has been criticized for its omission of the informal structure. **Informal organization** is a system of interpersonal relations that forms spontaneously within all formal organizations. It is a system that is not included in the organizational chart or official blueprint. It is the natural ordering and structuring that evolves from the needs of participants as they interact in their workplace. It contains structural, normative, and behavioral dimensions; that is, it includes informal structure, informal norms, and informal patterns of leadership (Scott, 1992). Teachers, administrators, and students within schools inevitably generate their own informal systems of status and power networks, communication, and working arrangements and structures.

The Development of Informal Organization

As people interact in organizations, networks of informal relations emerge that have important effects on behavior. Official as well as unofficial roles, norms, values, and leaders all shape individual behavior. Informal relations comprise patterns of such social interactions as communicating, cooperating, and competing. When individuals find themselves together in formal organizations, informal interaction inevitably occurs. People talk to each other about personal and social issues. As a consequence, some individuals are liked, others disliked. Typically, people seek continued interactions with those they like and avoid interactions with those they dislike. These informal social exchanges produce differences in social relations among group members and, importantly, define the informal status structure of the group.

A member's status in the group, therefore, depends upon the frequency, duration, and character of interaction patterns with others, and the extent to which others respect the individual in the group. Consequently, some group members are actively sought out, whereas others are avoided; some are admired, others are not; some are leaders, others are followers; and most are integrated as members of a group, although a few are isolated.

The informal interactions produce subgroups; cliques develop within the group structure, some of which have more status, power, and significance than others. Clique membership provides status in the larger group through the prestige of the subgroup. In brief, the differential patterns of interactions among individuals and groups, and the status structure characterized by them, define the social structure of the informal organization.

In addition to the social structure, a normative orientation emerges that serves as a guide for behavior. As individuals engage in social interaction, common conceptions of desirable and acceptable behavior occur. Common values arise to define ideal states of affairs, and social norms develop that prescribe what individuals should do under different situations and the consequences of deviations from those expectations. Norms contain two important features: a general agreement about appropriate behavior and mechanisms to enforce expectations. The distinction between norms and values is sometimes a fuzzy one, but generally values define the ends of human behavior, and social norms provide the legitimate and explicit means for pursuing those ends (Blau and Scott, 2003). Finally, and in addition to the general values and norms that are shared and expected to integrate the group, sets of expectations are differentiated according to the role or status position of the individual in the group. The role of "task master" is quite different from the role of "group comedian"; the role of leader is quite different from the role of follower. In brief, the main components of informal organization are the social structure and normative orientation of the group.

A Hypothetical Illustration in Schools

Imagine the situation of a new school, where the superintendent hires a new principal who in turn hires an entire new staff of teachers, none of whom know each other. At the beginning of the year, we simply have a collection of individuals bound together by the formal requirements of the school and their jobs. The professional staff, however, will quickly become more than the sum of the individuals composing it. Behavior will not only be determined by the formal expectations of the school but also by the informal organization that spontaneously emerges as the participants interact.

As school begins, faculty and staff begin to work together, attend meetings, eat together, socialize in the faculty lounge, and plan school activities. Teacher relations will, in part, be determined by the physical features of the school, such as a faculty lounge, a faculty lunch room, the library, and the arrangement of the classrooms; the technical aspects of the job—for example, department structure, team teaching, and extracurricular responsibilities; and social factors such as the leadership styles of the superintendent and principals. The initial relations of teachers in a school can be examined in terms of formal activities and interactions. Teachers have a need to keep their jobs, and a formal system has been established to achieve school objectives. This formal organization comprises a hierarchy of authority, division of labor, formal rules and regulations, impersonality, and a formal communication structure, developed and implemented to achieve school goals.

A number of consequences follow from the establishment of the initial, formal relations. New sentiments develop that are different from the work-motivated ones that brought teachers together in the first place. The new sentiments are ones of liking and disliking other teachers and groups within the school. Some of the teachers will become well liked and respected; their colleagues will frequently ask them for advice and seek them out. Such sentiments and behavior serve as the basis for an informal ranking of individuals and groups. Moreover, new informal activities will develop, some of which are a direct reaction to the formal organization. For example, the inability of faculty to influence policy through the formal structure may result in informal activities, conversations, and initiatives. New patterns of interaction will elaborate themselves in the school—for example, association in cliques, informal webs of communication, discipline networks centering on informal leadership, and a status structure among groups of teachers. Some informal groups will become more prestigious and powerful than others.

In addition to the informal social structure that develops, a system of informal shared values and beliefs will emerge—the normative orientation. The faculty will define ideal and appropriate behavior. Their ideal, for example, may be a school characterized by hard work, mastery of the basics, an academic orientation, and positive student-teacher relations. To this end, norms emerge to guide teacher behavior: few hall passes will be issued; substantial and meaningful homework assignments will be made; orderly and industrious classrooms will be maintained; and extra help for students will be readily available. If teachers violate these norms, they lose the respect of their colleagues, and social sanctions will be applied. They may find themselves disparaged and isolated by their colleagues. Teachers will also assume specific informal roles; an unofficial teacher spokesperson may serve as a powerful liaison with the principal; another teacher may provide a strong critical voice of school policy in faculty meetings; still another teacher may organize social activities for the faculty; and there may be the teacher who always offers comic relief, especially when events are tense.

The informal organization, then, arises from the formal organization and then reacts to it. The development of group norms, the division into cliques, and the ranking of individuals and subgroups are conditioned directly by the formal structure and indirectly by the school environment. Hence, we can begin with the formal system of the school and argue that the informal is continually emerging from the formal and continually influencing the formal. The formal and informal systems go together; after all, there is only one organization. Yet the distinction is useful because it calls attention to the dynamic nature of organizational life in schools and to the continuous processes of elaboration, differentiation, and feedback in schools. The dynamic character of the informal organization as well as its interplay with the formal organization is summarized in Figure 3.1.

The impact of the informal on the formal organization can be constructive or destructive. For example, the Hawthorne Studies (see Chapter 1) showed that the informal organization restricted production. Evidence also exists, however, that the informal organization can be a constructive force in efficient operation of bureaucratic organizations as well as a mechanism for change. In Chester Barnard's (1938) classic theoretic analysis of organizations, he argued that informal organizations have at least three crucial functions: as effective vehicles of communication, as a means of developing cohesion, and as devices for protecting the integrity of the individual.

FIGURE 3.1   *Elements of the Formal and Informal Organization*

Formal communications systems in organizations such as schools are typically insufficient and are inevitably supplemented by informal ones; in fact, informal communication systems, so-called grapevines, exist in all organizations regardless of how elaborate the formal communications system (Iannaconne, 1962; Hoy and Forsyth, 1986; Robbins, 1991) and are used constructively in effective organizations (Peters and Waterman, 1982). The informal structure provides a channel for circumventing formally prescribed rules and procedures. Many pressing problems emerge for which efficient solutions or communications are not possible within the formal framework; hence, the informal structure assumes added importance. Official communications must be routed through the "chain of command," which often is a long-drawn-out process. Frequently, circumventing the official communication channel through the grapevine appears to be precisely what is necessary for solving crucial problems (Page, 1946; Peters and Waterman, 1982). The knowledgeable and flexible administrator uses the grapevine, thus avoiding the bureaucratic frustration of those who only play it by the book. As a communication vehicle, the grapevine often provides efficient machinery. Indeed, generally speaking, the informal organization is an important device for implementing many important organizational objectives.

Informal organization also can promote cohesion. Patterns of social relationships usually emphasize friendliness, cooperation, and preservation of the group. Informal groups emerge spontaneously and are built on shared interests and friendships. They arise from such simple events as common classroom areas, liking certain colleagues, shared lunch hours, car pools, same planning periods, and other fortuitous activities. Such situations and the accompanying social relationships can provide the social cement that binds faculty by promoting an atmosphere of cordiality and friendliness that is potent enough to cause members to feel that they belong to the group; cohesion and solidarity are the by-products of informal groups (Boyan, 1951; Robbins, 1991).

The informal organization functions to maintain a sense of personal integrity, self-respect, and independence for individuals (Barnard, 1938). Unlike the formal hierarchy, impersonality and formal authority do not dominate the informal. Rather, the informal is an outgrowth of the individual and personal needs of members. It is a means by which teachers can maintain their individual personalities in spite of organizational demands that invariably attempt to depersonalize individuals (Hoy and Forsyth, 1986).

The informal organization exists. It is not an enemy to be eliminated or suppressed; on the contrary, it can be a useful vehicle for improving efficiency. It is irrational to administer a formal organization, such as a school, according to the purely technical criteria of rationality and formality because that ignores the nonrational aspects of informal organization (Blau, 1956). From a theoretical perspective, our position is that administrative practice is enhanced by using both the formal (rational) and the informal (nonrational) components of schools.

Dual Structure of the Bureaucratic Model

Another frequent criticism of the Weberian model is its internal contradictions among certain bureaucratic principles of organization. According to Weber, all characteristics of his ideal type are logically consistent and interact for maximum organizational efficiency; however, both theoretical and empirical analyses indicate that things are not so smooth and integrated in the real world of organizational functioning.

Talcott Parsons (1947) and Gouldner (1954) question whether the guiding principle of bureaucracy is authority based on technical competence and knowledge or authority based on legal powers and discipline. Weber (1947: 339) maintains that "bureaucratic administration means fundamentally the exercise of control on the basis of knowledge." On the other hand, he writes, "The content of discipline is the consistently rationalized, methodically trained and exact execution of the received order, in which all personal criticism is unconditionally suspended and the actor is unswervingly and exclusively set for carrying out the command" (Gerth and Mills, 1946: 196). Hence, Weber is proposing the central importance of discipline as well as expertise. Is bureaucratic administration based primarily on expertise, or is it based on disciplined compliance with directives? Unless one assumes that there will be no conflict between authority based on "technical competence and expertise" and that based on "incumbency in a hierarchical position," the seed of contradiction and conflict rests within these two authority bases that are integral to the Weberian model. In fact, Gouldner (1954) and Constas (1958) suggest that Weber may have been implicitly describing not one but two types of bureaucracy, a conclusion supported by a number of empirical studies (Stinchcombe, 1959; Udy, 1959).

Similarly, Blau and Scott's (2003) analysis of the dual nature of the Weberian model also led them to conclude that Weber failed to distinguish bureaucratic from professional principles. They similarly maintain that bureaucratic discipline and professional expertise are alternative methods for coping with uncertainty. Discipline reduces the scope of uncertainty, whereas expertise provides the knowledge to handle uncertainty. The crux of the problem seems to be that professionals are often employees of bureaucratic organizations; hence, these alternative modes of rationality are frequently mixed, producing strain and conflict. A typical example is the school principal. Does his or her authority reside in the bureaucratic office or in professional expertise? Obviously, a mixture is present and seems to result in some degree of strife.

A Feminist Critique of Bureaucracy

Feminists are often critical of bureaucratic organizations in fundamental ways that go far beyond the common accusation that qualified women in modern organizations do not receive equal treatment or compensation (Scott, 1992, 1998). Joanne Martin (1990b; Martin and Knopoff, 1999), for example, argues that in spite of Weber's analysis of the central features of bureaucracy being gender neutral and universal in his description of administration based on expertise, women are disadvantaged. The emphasis on full-time commitment and extensive training as qualifications for job holding hinders women who routinely confront the conflicting demands of job and family responsibilities. Women often lack equal access to training programs, and discussions of bureaucracy frequently overlook the interdependence of job and family responsibilities, treating work as public and masculine and family as private and feminine (Bose, Feldberg, and Sokoloff, 1987; Martin, 1990a). Hence, bureaucracies are gender biased not only in their *application* of appointment and promotion criteria but also in their *selection* of the criteria (Scott, 1992).

Feminists also argue that bureaucratic structures perpetuate systems of male domination. Ferguson (1984), for one, argues that bureaucracy's patent emphasis on authority, rules, regulations, and rationality recreates paternalistic domination. Bureaucratic structures give priority to masculine virtues and values. Scott (1992: 325) explains, "The principles by which organizations are structured—inequality, hierarchy, impersonality—devalue alternative modes of organizing that are alleged to be more characteristic of women's values: equalitarian and personalized associations." In the same vein, Ferguson (1984) argues that bureaucratic control invades social life by "feminizing" participants—that is, by making them nonassertive and dependent; in fact, women are bound to supportive roles by structures that see feminine characteristics as subordinate and masculine ones as dominant. Male characteristics of independence, rationality, and competitiveness are dominant instrumental features of bureaucracy, whereas the more feminine features of dependence, emotionality, and cooperation are subordinate properties of organizations. The hallmarks of achievement—competition and independence—are quite different from the nurturant expressive behaviors of the feminine style (Gilligan, 1982; Ferguson, 1984). In fact, the feminine side is often repressed and devalued by bureaucracies, creating an oppression of women. Bureaucracies are not caring institutions, but reproducers of patriarchy and reinforcers of patterns of domination (Clark et al., 1994).

Feminist critics also challenge the bureaucratic notion that superior domination though hierarchical patterns of authority is essential to achievement of important goals; in fact, they argue that hierarchy typically restricts the growth of the group and individual members (Denhardt and Perkins, 1976). Moreover, the usual defense of the hierarchical division of labor as a structural device to develop expertise and improve efficiency is seen largely as a guise to conceal the control function of hierarchy. Invariably all workers, but especially women, are isolated, alienated, and depersonalized as communications are mystified and the dominance of bureaucratic control is disguised. Radical feminists make it clear that they are committed to an **antibureaucratic structure** in which

- Groups are decentralized.
- Personal, face-to-face relations are substituted for impersonal rules and regulations.
- Relationships are egalitarian not hierarchical.
- Skills and information are to be shared, not hoarded. (Ferguson, 1984)

FORMAL STRUCTURE IN SCHOOLS

Schools are formal organizations with many of the same characteristics as bureaucratic organizations. Max Abbott (1965a: 45), for example, using the characteristics of the Weberian model developed earlier in this chapter, has concluded: "The school organization as we know it today . . . can accurately be described as a highly developed bureaucracy. As such, it exhibits many of the characteristics and employs many of the strategies of the military, industrial, and governmental agencies with which it might be compared." The bureaucratic model is the one that many school administrators adopt, and this may explain why the model can be used to analyze behavior in schools (Abbott, 1965a; Miles, 1965; Firestone and Herriott, 1981; Abbott and Caracheo, 1988; Corwin and Borman, 1988).

A basic assumption of bureaucracies is that every subordinate has less technical expertise than his or her superior. This assumption certainly does not apply in schools, nor does it apply in other professional organizations. On the contrary, professionals often have more competence and technical expertise than the administrators who occupy a higher level in the organization. Consequently, to find strain and tension in schools between teachers and administrators should not be surprising.

Rather than thinking of schools as bureaucratic or nonbureaucratic, a more useful approach is to examine the degree of bureaucratization with respect to the important components of the Weberian model. Such an approach differentiates types of organizational structures. Richard H. Hall (1962, 1987, 1991), Wayne K. Hoy and Scott R. Sweetland (2000, 2001), and Henry Mintzberg (1979, 1989) are among the contemporary theorists and researchers who have systematically examined structure.

Hall on Bureaucratic Structure

One of the earliest systematic attempts to measure bureaucratization is Hall's (1962) development of an organizational inventory to measure six central characteristics of bureaucratic structure: (1) hierarchy of authority, (2) specialization, (3) rules for incumbents (i.e., those assuming an organizational role), (4) procedure specifications, (5) impersonality, and (6) technical competence. D. A. MacKay (1964) subsequently adapted and modified the organizational inventory in his study of the bureaucratization of schools. He measured bureaucratic patterns in schools using the school organizational inventory (SOI), a questionnaire that operationalizes the same six dimensions of structure.

The interrelationships of these bureaucratic characteristics of schools also have been explored empirically (Kolesar, 1967; Isherwood and Hoy, 1973; Abbott and Caracheo, 1988). Studies indicate that there are two relatively distinct patterns of rational organization rather than one completely integrated bureaucratic pattern. Hierarchy of authority, rules for incumbents, procedural specifications, and impersonality tend to vary together, and specialization and technical competence similarly vary together; however, the two groups are found to be independent of or inversely related to each other.

Organizational Types

In the school, as in other kinds of organizations, the components of Weber's ideal type do not necessarily form an inherently connected set of variables; instead, there are likely to be distinct types of rational organization. These results are summarized in Table 3.3.

In Table 3.3 we have labeled the first set of characteristics "bureaucratic" and the second set "professional." The distinction once again calls attention both to the potential conflict between authority based on technical competence and expertise and that based on holding an office in a hierarchy and to the potential incompatibility between professionalization and bureaucratization. To lump together the bureaucratic and professional patterns in a single

TABLE 3.3

Two Types of Rational Organization in the School Setting

Organizational Characteristics	Organizational Patterns
Hierarchy of authority	Bureaucratic
Rules for incumbents	
Procedural specifications	
Impersonality	
Technical competence	Professional
Specialization	

model of bureaucracy seems to obscure important differences among schools. Indeed, separating two patterns of rational organization and administration makes it possible to explore combinations of the two patterns. For example, if each pattern is dichotomized, as shown in Figure 3.2, then four types of organizations are possible.

A Weberian school structure is one in which professionalization and bureaucratization are complementary; both are high. This pattern is similar to the ideal type described by Weber; hence we call it a **Weberian structure.**

An **authoritarian structure** emphasizes bureaucratic authority at the expense of professional consideration. Authority is based on position and hierarchy. Disciplined compliance to the rules, regulations, and directives is the basic principle of operation. Power is concentrated and flows from top to bottom. Rules and procedures are impersonally applied. The superior always has the last say. Furthermore, promotions to administrative positions typically go to those who have been loyal to the organization and to their superiors. In many respects, this authoritarian structure is similar to the one Gouldner (1954) described as a punishment-centered bureaucracy.

A **professional structure** is one in which substantial decision making is delegated to the professional staff. Members of the staff are viewed as professionals who have the expertise and competence to make important organizational decisions. Rules and procedures serve as guides rather than as strict formats to be applied uniformly. Special cases are likely to be the rule rather than the exception. Teachers have much power in the organizational decision-making process. In brief, decisions are made by those who have the knowledge and expertise to make them. We refer to this type of school structure as professional.

Finally, a **chaotic structure** has a low degree of bureaucratization and professionalization; therefore confusion and conflict typify day-to-day operations. Inconsistency, contradiction, and ineffectiveness are likely to pervade the chaotic structure. Invariably, strong pressures will arise to move toward one of the other structural types.

		Professional Pattern	
		High	Low
Bureaucratic Pattern	High	Weberian	Authoritarian
	Low	Professional	Chaotic

FIGURE 3.2   *Typology of School Organizational Structure*

This typology presents four potential school structures that are quite different and probably have different consequences for teachers and students alike. Henry Kolesar (1967), for example, found that a sense of student powerlessness was significantly higher in authoritarian than in professional school structures. Geoffrey Isherwood and Wayne K. Hoy (1973) uncovered the same finding for teachers in the two types of schools. Overall, the sense of powerlessness among teachers was much greater in authoritarian than in professional structures. But organizationally and socially oriented teachers (those who identify themselves with the values and goals of the organization and of family and friends, respectively) had less of a sense of powerlessness in the authoritarian structure than professionally oriented teachers. Apparently, individual work orientation mediates the relationship between organizational structure and alienation. Teachers with an organizational orientation may not be alienated by authoritarian structures and procedures and indeed may be quite content. Gerald H. Moeller and W. W. Charters' (1966) finding that teachers in highly bureaucratic systems had more sense of power than those in less bureaucratic systems lends support to this speculation.

It is also true that the type of school organizational structure may influence student achievement. Research (MacKay, 1964; B. Anderson, 1971; MacKinnon and Brown, 1994) suggests the possibility that highly bureaucratic structures may have negative effects on student achievement and innovation. Finally, the evidence continues to mount that specialization (professional pattern) and centralization (bureaucratic pattern) are mildly, but negatively related (Hage, 1980; Corwin and Herriott, 1988; Hall, 1991).[2]

Changing School Structures

The classification of school structures into these four structural types seems useful; in fact, the typology can serve as a basis for a theory of school development. Chaotic structures are ineffective and candidates for swift action. Boards of education will be under great pressure from both within and without to bring order to the existing chaos. The typical response is to get "new leadership." The new leadership invariably turns to starkly bureaucratic and authoritarian procedures to gain order. That is, it seems likely that chaotic structures will move to authoritarian ones.

Authoritarian structures are mechanistic. Power and authority rest almost exclusively in a tightly coupled organizational structure; administrators engage in unilateral decision making and teachers are expected to comply with their directives without question. Relations are typically formal, impersonal, and vertical. A single set of clear, formal goals buttressed by bureaucratic authority guide organizational behavior. Instruction is coordinated by administrative enforcement of schedules, rules, and procedures. Expected conflict is moderate—lower than that found in chaotic structures, but higher than that found in Weberian and professional structures. School effectiveness is predicted to be moderate, provided the environment is supportive, stable, and simple.

The next logical step in an evolutionary development of school structure is toward a Weberian configuration. Here the forces of centralization and specialization are balanced. The bureaucratic attributes of hierarchy, rules, procedures, and impersonality complement the technical competence and specialization of teachers. Administrators and teachers share in decision making, with both groups focused on common interests and with both committed to a single set of shared goals. Conflict between teachers and administrators is limited, yet the couplings between organizational parts are moderately tight. In brief, there is an integration of formal and informal properties. School effectiveness is predicted to be high, and such a structure should function most effectively in a simple and stable environment.

Most individuals prefer order to chaos; hence, movement from a chaotic structure to an authoritarian one is relatively straightforward. The challenge, however, of moving an authoritarian school structure to a Weberian or professional one is much more difficult. Our own experience and research (Isherwood and Hoy, 1973; Firestone and Herriott, 1982; Hoy, Blazovsky, and Newland, 1983; Abbott and Carecheo, 1988; Hoy and Sweetland, 2000, 2001) suggest that many schools remain basically authoritarian; they are top-down structures that do not readily evolve into Weberian and professional structures. Moreover, external environmental forces influence school structure. During the last decade there were pressures for movement toward more professional structures as reform in education pressed for teacher empowerment (Goldring and Chen, 1992), school-based management (Malen, Ogawa, and Kranz, 1990; Malen and Ogawa, 1992), decentralization (Brown, 1990; Hill and Bonan, 1991; Bimber, 1993), and a general restructuring of schools (David, Purkey, and White, 1989; Clune and White, 1990), but strong countervailing forces for increased centralization have already muted those forces since the passage of No Child Left Behind legislation. Thus, the pull is now for centralization, standards, and accountability rather than decentralization, professional judgment, and autonomy.

As the occupation of teaching becomes more fully professionalized, a few school structures may evolve from Weberian to professional structures. The professional structure is loose, fluid, and informal. Teacher professionals control decision making; indeed, teacher groups are the dominant source of power. Administrators are subordinate to teachers in the sense that their primary role is to serve teachers and facilitate the teaching-learning process. The burden for integrating the activities of the school rests with the teacher professionals. Professional structures are complex organizations with a highly professional staff, multiple sets of goals, high teacher autonomy, and horizontal rather than vertical relations. Ultimately, the effectiveness of such organizations depends almost exclusively on the expertise, commitment, and service of the teachers. Professional organizations have the potential for high effectiveness in a stable and complex environment, which has confidence in its professionals.

We have proposed a model of school development in which schools move progressively from chaotic to authoritarian to Weberian to professional structures (see Figure 3.3). There is nothing inevitable about the evolution; in fact, we suspect it will be difficult for schools to become professional structures

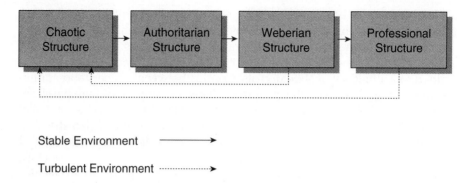

Stable Environment   ⟶

Turbulent Environment   ·················►

FIGURE 3.3   *Predicted Evolutionary Changes in School Structure*

or even Weberian structures in the near future. Moreover, it is likely that many school structures will slip back to chaos as the environment becomes turbulent. Remember also that the four types of structures are ideal types; most schools are variations on these four themes. Nonetheless, the framework should be useful to administrators and students of school organizations as they analyze and attempt to change their own school structures and empower teachers. We now turn to how formalization and centralization can be combined to produce enabling school structures.

Hoy and Sweetland on Structure

Bureaucracies can alienate individual participants, but that is only half the story because research also suggests they can improve worker satisfaction (Michaels et al., 1988), increase innovation (Damanpour, 1991; Craig, 1995), reduce role conflict (Senatra, 1980), and reduce feelings of alienation (Jackson and Schuler, 1985). Indeed, organizational research depicts two conflicting views of the human outcomes of bureaucracy. The negative side suggests that bureaucracy alienates, fosters dissatisfaction, stifles creativity, and demotivates employees, whereas the positive view maintains that it provides needed guidance, clarifies responsibility, reduces role stress, and helps individuals feel and be more effective (Adler and Borys, 1996). How can we reconcile these two views?

Paul Adler and Bryan Borys (1996) offer a possible solution as they interpret formalization as an organizational technology and identify two types of formalization—enabling and coercive. In the Weberian sense, formalization is the extent of written rules, regulations, procedures, and instructions. The notion of enabling and coercive formalization is not unlike Gouldner's (1954) representative and punishment-centered rules. Hoy and Sweetland (2000, 2001) build upon Adler and Borys's (1966) formulation of enabling and hindering formalization to examine the structure of schools.

Let's begin with definitions of the two types of formalization. *Enabling formalization* is a set of procedures that help employees deal more effectively with inevitable problems. Rules and procedures do not have to be designed to make the work foolproof; in fact, they cannot be. Rather what is needed is a flexible set of guidelines or best practices that enable one to deal more effectively with the surprises that occur. For example, a rule not to act until data can be accumulated provides the stimulus for problem solving and is enabling rather than restraining. On the other hand, an automatic detention for talking back to a teacher is punishing and does enable the student to make improvements. *Coercive formalization* is a set of procedures that punishes and attempts to force reluctant subordinates to comply. Rules and procedures become substitutes for commitment rather than complements to it. Instead of giving committed employees access to accumulated organizational learning and best-practice guidelines, coercive procedures are designed to force compliance and extract recalcitrant effort.

Next we consider centralization or the hierarchy of authority of organizations. Similar to formalization, there are two kinds of authority structures. *Enabling centralization* helps employees solve problems rather than getting in the way of their work; it is flexible, cooperative, and collaborative rather than rigid, autocratic, and controlling. Administrators use their power to help teachers and design structures that facilitate teaching and learning. Enabling hierarchy is an amalgam of authority where teachers feel confident and are able to exercise power in their professional roles. *Hindering centralization* refers to a hierarchy and administration that gets in the way rather than helps its participants solve problems and do their work. In such structures, the hierarchy obstructs innovation and administrators use their power and authority to control and discipline teachers.

It should not be surprising that there is a close relationship between formalization (a system of rules, regulations, and procedures) and centralization (hierarchy of authority) in schools; that is, when the rules and procedures are enabling so is the hierarchy and vice versa. Thus school structures can be described along a continuum from enabling to hindering.

An **enabling school structure** is a hierarchy that helps rather than hinders and a system of rules and regulations that guides problem solving rather than punishes failure. In enabling school structures, principals and teachers work cooperatively across recognized authority boundaries while retaining their distinctive roles. Similarly, rules and regulations are flexible guides for problem solving rather than constraints that create problems. In such structures, both hierarchy and rules are mechanisms to support teachers rather than vehicles to enhance principal power.

In contrast, a **hindering school structure** is a hierarchy that impedes and a system of rules and regulations that is coercive. The basic objective of hierarchy is disciplined compliance of teachers; thus, teacher behavior is closely managed and strictly controlled. Both the hierarchy and rules are used to gain control and conformity. The structure is used to ensure that reluctant, incompetent, and irresponsible teachers do what administrators prescribe. The power of the principal is enhanced, but the work of the teachers is diminished.

The contrasting features of these two kinds of school structure are stark. Enabling structures call for two-way communication; viewing problems as learning opportunities; supporting differences; and encouraging trust, cooperation, openness, joint problem solving, and innovation. Hindering structures are typically characterized by top-down, one-way communication, viewing problems as constraints, forced consensus, mistrust, control, and punishment. The processes of developing enabling strategies are ones of participation and problem solving; that is, teachers and principals working together to find ways to solve problems in mutually satisfying ways. Trust is the heart of the enterprise and improvement is the goal. Hindering structures have different strategies, ones of control and enforcement of administrative decisions; principals are intent on watching, controlling, and punishing teachers who do not comply. Principals simply do not trust teachers; and consequently, suspicion, control, and punishment imbue the process.

The administration in an enabling school finds ways to help teachers succeed rather than monitoring teacher behavior to ensure compliance. Let's take one concrete example of enabling structure in terms of the principal's behavior:

> In one school where there was tremendous pressure on everyone to get student proficiency tests above the state average, we found a principal with an open door policy with teachers. She cared for teachers and respected their professional judgments. She was unwilling to tell teachers how to get the scores up, and instead was a colleague working with them on this difficult problem. She demonstrated her commitment to them and problem solving by working long and hard with teachers. One hallmark of her supportive behavior was that teachers knew that they could always find this principal in her office every Saturday from nine-to-noon. There was no press for teachers to be in school on Saturdays, but everyone knew that this principal was always available and ready to talk either on the phone or in person. She enabled. No secretaries, no students, no guidance counselors, no other administrators, just the principal was there every Saturday. Leading by example was evident; her standards for her own behavior were higher than those she held for her teachers, and teachers respected her for it (Hoy and Sweetland, 2001).[3]

Research in schools (Hoy and Sweetland, 2000, 2002; Hoy, 2003; Sinden, Hoy, and Sweetland, 2003; Sinden, Hoy, and Sweetland, in press) is beginning to show that there are significant differences in the structures of schools, and not surprisingly, enabling structures usually enhance the administration and operation of schools. The picture that emerges from this research is that enabling school structure is imbued with trust—faculty trust in the principal, in colleagues, and faculty commitment to their school. Principals and teachers are open and authentic with each other. On the other hand, a hindering structure is characterized by teacher sense of powerlessness, role conflict, and dependence on rules and the hierarchy. Teachers in hindering structures avoid conflict and play it safe by hiding behind rules and demonstrating unflagging obedience to principals. Moreover, when teachers are confronted with coercive rules they likely defend their actions by spinning the truth in ways to satisfy their superiors and avoid conflict and punishment.

In sum, enabling and hindering school structures as experienced by teachers have different features, develop through different processes, and have different consequences for the teaching-learning context (see Table 3.4). Furthermore, this conceptual refinement of structure provides a potential explanation for the conflicting findings regarding the impact of bureaucracy on participants—namely, that it is the *kind (hindering structure)* and *not the amount* of structure that explains the negative effects of bureaucracy. Enabling school structures produce positive outcomes; hindering ones yield negative outcomes. In other words, enabling structures are functional; coercive ones are dysfunctional.[4]

Mintzberg on Structure

Henry Mintzberg (1979, 1980, 1981, 1983a, 1983b, 1989) provides another, more comprehensive conceptual framework for examining organizational structure. He describes structure simply as the ways in which an organization divides its labor into tasks and then achieves coordination among them. Five basic **coordinating mechanisms** are the fundamental means organizations use to monitor and control work: mutual adjustment, direct supervision, standardization of work processes, standardization of outputs, and standardization of worker skills. These mechanisms glue the organization together.

TABLE 3.4

Two Types of School Structure: Enabling and Hindering

	Enabling Structure	Hindering Structure
Formalization	Promotes flexible rules and procedures	Enforces rigid rules and procedures
	Views problems as learning opportunities	Views problems as constraints
	Values differences	Demands consensus
	Encourages initiative	Punishes mistakes
	Fosters trust	Fosters suspicion
Centralization	Facilitates problem solving	Demands compliance
	Promotes cooperation	Embraces control
	Encourages openness	Fosters mistrust
	Protects teachers	Punishes teachers
	Encourages innovation	Discourages change
	Seeks collaboration	Rules autocratically
Processes	Participate decision making	Unilateral decision making
	Problem solving	Enforcement
Context	Teacher trust	Teacher distrust
	Truthfulness and authenticity	Truth spinning and deception
	Cohesiveness	Conflict
	Teacher sense of power	Teacher sense of powerlessness

Coordinating Mechanisms

Mutual adjustment is coordination through the simple process of informal communication. Workers coordinate their efforts by informal discussion and adjustment. Mutual adjustment is direct and basic; it is necessary not only in the simplest organization, but also in the most complicated.

Direct supervision is coordination through personal command. One individual has the responsibility for monitoring and controlling the work of others. As the size of an organization increases, the more likely it is that mutual adjustment will become less effective and direct supervision more necessary. As work activities become more and more complicated, however, neither mutual adjustment nor direct supervision is sufficient. Hence, the work is standardized; coordination of parts is achieved by incorporating them in a carefully planned program for the work. There are three basic ways to obtain standardization in organizations: standardize the work processes, the outputs, or the skills.

Standardization of work is achieved by specifying or programming the contents of the work. The written directions to develop a lesson plan are an example. The process of developing the plan is described carefully in step-by-step directions.

Standardization of output is attained by specifying the results of the work; the fundamental dimensions of the product or of the performance are enumerated. Taxicab drivers, for example, are not usually given a route; they are merely told the destination. Similarly, teachers may simply be told that the student should be able to perform at a basic level in a given area; the means to achieve that level may be left to the teacher. The outcomes of the work are described carefully and employees are expected to achieve the standard.

Standardization of skills is a coordination mechanism that provides indirect control of work. Here specifying the kind of training required to do the work standardizes skills and knowledge. Training supplies workers with patterns of work to be performed as well as the bases of coordination. Mintzberg observes that when an anesthesiologist and a surgeon meet in the operating room, typically little communication occurs; by virtue of their respective training, each knows precisely what to expect. Their standardized skills provide most of the coordination.

TIP: THEORY INTO PRACTICE

Think of your school. Give a specific example of the following coordination mechanisms: mutual adjustment, direct supervision, standardization of work, standardization of output, and standardization of skills. Which of these means of coordination is most prevalent in your school? Are any absent? Evaluate the overall practices of coordination. What would you change if you could? Why?

Key Parts

Although most organizations of any size use all five means of coordination, each organization specializes in one, a fact that has important consequences for the basic structure of the organization. Mintzberg also identifies five key parts of the organization (see Figure 3.4). These are the significant aspects of the structure, each with a critical function to perform.

The **operating core** comprises those who perform the basic work—activities directly related to the production of products and services. The core is the heart of the organization; it produces the essential output. In schools, teachers are the operating core and teaching and learning are the outcomes.

The administrative component of the organization has three parts. First, the **strategic apex** consists of the top administrators (superintendent and assistants) who are charged with the responsibility of ensuring that the organization effectively serves its mission. Those administrators who connect the apex with the operating core through the formal authority structure constitute the **middle line.** In school systems, principals are the middle managers. Any organization that relies primarily on direct supervision for control and coordination is bound to have a large middle line. The **technostructure** is the administrative component charged with the responsibility of planning. It is composed of analysts who standardize the work of others and apply their analytic techniques to help the organization adapt to its environment. These analysts design, plan, and train, but they do not directly manage. Curriculum coordinators and instructional supervisors are often members of the school technostructure; their role is to help teachers design

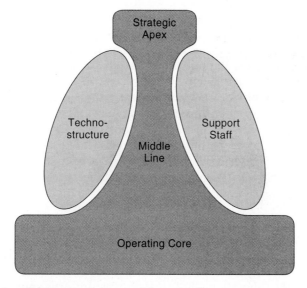

FIGURE 3.4   *The Five Basic Parts of Organization*
SOURCE: Henry Mintzberg. *The Structing of Organizations* (Englewood Cliffs, NJ: Prentice Hall, 1979), p. 20.

and plan instruction and to provide in-service opportunities for professional growth and development.

Finally, a fifth component—the **support staff**—is composed of specialized units that exist to provide support for the organization outside the operating workflow. In schools, for example, we find a building and grounds department, a maintenance department, a cafeteria, and a payroll department. None of these units is part of the operating core, but each exists to provide indirect support for the school.

These five key parts of the organization and the five coordination mechanisms that hold them together serve as the basis for five configurations:

- *Simple structure:* The strategic apex is the key part and direct supervision is the central coordinating device.
- *Machine bureaucracy:* The technostructure is the key part and standardization of work processes is the central coordinating device.
- *Professional bureaucracy:* The operating core is the key part and standardization of skills is the central coordinating device.
- *Divisionalized form:* The middle line is the key part and standardization of outputs is the central coordinating device.
- *Adhocracy:* The support staff is the key part and mutual adjustment is the central coordinating device.[5]

Our discussion will focus on the forms most likely to be found in schools.

Mintzberg's Perspective Applied to Schools

The configurations that Mintzberg describes are abstract ideals, yet these simplifications of more complex structures do come to life in the analysis of schools. Schools experience the basic forces that underlay these configurations: the pull to centralize by top management, the pull to formalize by the technostructure, and the pull to professionalize by teachers.[6] Where one pull dominates, then the school will likely be organized close to one of Mintzberg's ideal configurations; that is, the pull to formalize moves the organization toward machine bureaucracy; the pull to centralize yields a simple structure; and the pull to professionalize leads to professional bureaucracy. With the passage of No Child Left Behind legislation, however, there is a national pull to centralize, formalize, and standardize schools. Clearly one pull does not always dominate and the basic processes may have to coexist in balance. We turn to structural configurations expected in many schools.

Simple Structure   An organization that is coordinated by a high degree of direct supervision, that has a small strategic apex with virtually no middle line, and that is highly centralized is a **simple structure.** In such an organization there is little elaboration—little technostructure, little support staff, little division of labor and specialization, and a small administrative hierarchy.

Because power over important decisions tends to be centralized in the hands of the top administrator, the strategic apex is the key part of the organization. Standardization in a simple structure is unnecessary because things are worked out as they arise; there are loose, informal working relations among participants. Thus, communication flows informally, but most of it is between the top administrator and everyone else. The name tells it all—the structure is simple.

New organizations usually begin simply and elaborate their administrative structures as they grow. Many small organizations, however, retain a simple structure. Informal communications remain effective and a one-person strategic apex attends to coordination. The simple structure can vary. For example, the *autocratic organization* is a simple structure where the top administrator hoards power and rules by fiat; and the *charismatic organization* is a variant where the leader has the same power not because it is hoarded but because the followers lavish it upon the leader. The major strength of the simple structure is its flexibility; only one person must act.

The simple structure is of interest because many schools, particularly small elementary school districts, have such a structure. Autocratic and sometimes charismatic principals who rule with an iron hand administer them. Although some teachers enjoy working in a small, intimate school, where its charismatic principal leads the way, others perceive the simple structure as highly restrictive and autocratic. Such structures are highly dependent upon the expertise, imagination, and energy of the chief executive. As the executive goes, so goes the organization. These are highly centralized structures in which the top administrator makes all major decisions and formal authority flows in one direction—top-down. Schools with simple structures face especially difficult problems in executive succession and as growth renders direct supervision inadequate. A simple structure can be relatively enduring or only a phase in the development and maturing of an organization. Mintzberg (1979, 1989) defines organizational structures that rely on any form of standardization for coordination as bureaucratic. Of the common school configurations derived from Mintzberg's formulation, the simple structure is the only one that is nonbureaucratic; its structure is organic.

Machine Bureaucracy   An organization that is fine-tuned and standardized to run as an integrated, regulated machine is called a **machine bureaucracy.** The work processes in this kind of structure are routine and standard. Indeed, standardization of work is the prime coordinating mechanism and the technostructure is the key part of the structure because it contains the analysts who do the standardizing. In these organizations, a high degree of centralization is supported by considerable formalization: rules and regulations permeate the structure; formal communication predominates at all levels; and decision making follows the hierarchical chain of authority.

This is the Weberian structure of bureaucracy—standardized responsibilities, technical qualifications, formal communication channels, rules and regulations, and hierarchy of authority. It is a structure geared for precision, speed, clarity, continuity, unity, subordination, and efficiency. Machine bureaucracy is obsessed with control; a control mentality develops from top to bottom. As Mintzberg (1979: 321) cogently notes, "The problem in the Machine Bureaucracy is not to develop an open atmosphere where people can talk the conflicts out, but to enforce a closed, tightly controlled one where the work can get done despite them."

Considerable power rests with the administrators of the strategic apex; in fact, the only others to share much power with the top administrators are the analysts of the technostructure because their role is standardizing the work processes of the organization. Machine structures work best when the work is routine—that is, when an integrated set of simple, repetitive, tasks must be performed precisely and consistently by people (Mintzberg, 1979).

A few schools or school districts are machine bureaucracies; they are usually large districts where an elaborate technostructure attempts to standardize the work or in states with elaborate statewide technostructures. Behavior is formalized by an extensive set of rules, procedures, and job descriptions. Moreover, power tends to be highly centralized in the apex of the structure; authority flows downward. Although many schools have the trappings, most are not machine bureaucracies in the pure sense because typically they lack an elaborate administrative structure, a large middle line, and an elaborate technostructure. In fact, the structure of many public schools is a cross between the simple structure and the machine bureaucracy—what Mintzberg calls a simple bureaucracy.

Professional Bureaucracy   Bureaucratic structure can be defined in terms of "the extent to which behavior is predetermined or predictable, in effect, standardized" (Mintzberg, 1979: 86). Thus, organizations can be bureaucratic without being centralized. A **professional bureaucracy** is a structure that permits both decentralization and standardization at the same time. These organizations use standardization of skills as the prime coordinating mechanism; the operating core is the key organizational part; and professionalization is the crucial process. All such structures rely on the skills and knowledge of their operating professionals to function effectively.

The professional bureaucracy receives its coordination indirectly by relying on the standardization of skills that professionals have acquired in their training; hence, it is not surprising to find relationships in these organizations to be much more loosely coupled than in machine or simple bureaucracies. Yet teamwork and collaboration among school professionals seem essential if our schools are to be productive (Tschannen-Moran et al., 2000; Marks and Printy, 2003). The structural looseness of the school supports a professional basis of organization; however, the demand for uniformity in product, the need for movement of students from grade to grade and school to school in an orderly process, and the long period over which students are schooled require a standardization of activities and hence, a bureaucratic basis of school organization (Mintzberg, 1979).

The administrative structure of the professional bureaucracy is relatively flat. It does not need an elaborate hierarchy to control and coordinate or a technostructure to design work standards. Professionals control themselves and, in a sense, develop their own work standards. The standards of the professional bureaucracy originate largely from outside its structure, in self-governing associations to which the professionals belong. These associations set general standards that are taught by the universities and are used by all organizations of the profession. As we have noted before, two sources generate organizational authority. Machine and simple bureaucracies rely on the authority of the position or office, and professional bureaucracies are built on the authority of knowledge and expertise.

Professional bureaucracy is decentralized; a great deal of power rests with the professionals in the operating core. The work is too complex to be supervised directly by managers or standardized by analysts; hence, professionals have a great deal to say about what they do and how they do it. Professionals have close working relations with clients and loose ones with colleagues. It makes more sense to think in terms of a personal strategy for each professional rather than an integrated organizational strategy. Some schools have the characteristics of the professional bureaucracy—a skilled operating core, standardized work skills, professional norms and autonomy, professional associations, structural looseness, and a flat administrative structure. Such schools are staffed by highly competent and well-trained teachers who control their own work and who seek collective control over decisions that affect them.

We have suggested that some small elementary schools are simple structures; they are centralized, but informal structures. The chief administrator provides strong (often autocratic) direction in an informal atmosphere unfettered with rules and regulations. A few schools are machine bureaucracies; they are usually found in large districts where an elaborate technostructure attempts to standardize the work or in states with elaborate statewide technostructures. Behavior is formalized by an extensive set of rules, procedures, and job descriptions. Moreover, power tends to be highly centralized in the apex of the structure; authority flows downward. A few schools are also professional bureaucracies. They are staffed by highly competent and well-trained teachers who monitor their own work and engage in teamwork, collaboration, and shared instructional leadership with their colleagues (Tschannen-Moran et al., 2000; Marks and Printy, 2003). The structure is decentralized and democratic among the professionals. Although some schools fit into one of these three configurations, most schools are hybrid variants of the three "ideal types" that have been described.

Simple Bureaucracy   The **simple bureaucracy** has the basic characteristics of both a simple structure and a machine bureaucracy: it is highly centralized and highly bureaucratic, but it has a relatively flat administrative structure. Nonetheless, control remains a major obsession; hence such organizations are confronted by most of the dysfunctional characteristics of bureaucracy already discussed in our analysis of the Weberian model. As long as control, accountability, standardized educational outcomes, and inexpensive services are demanded by society for schools, simple bureaucratic structures will be a common configuration for schools.

Although there is high centralization and formalization in simple bureaucracies, there is limited specialization. Firestone and Herriott (1981, 1982) refer to such school structures as rational bureaucracies, and their research suggests that a large number of elementary schools, perhaps most, are simple bureaucracies in which a single set of agreed-upon goals guides internal behavior. The power and authority of the principal is dominant. Instruction and curriculum are standardized and teachers are supervised directly by the principal. Teachers' activities are for the most part controlled by the principal and coordinated by an elaborate system of fixed rules, standard procedures, and administrative schedules.

Political Organization   The **political organization** has to do with power, not structure. Politics is usually overlaid on all conventional organizations, but at times it becomes so powerful that it creates its own configuration. In effect, it captures the organization and becomes its dominating process. In such situations, power is exercised in illegitimate ways. There is no primary method of coordination, no single dominant part of the organization, no clear form of decentralization; everything depends on informal power and politics, marshaled to win individual issues (Mintzberg, 1989).

When power becomes so pervasive that it dominates, coordination as well as the formal structure become irrelevant; in fact, politics acts to the detriment of coordination by producing disorder. Negotiation, coalition formation, and political games are the keys to understanding life in such structures. Indeed, political activity is a substitute for the legitimate systems of influence found in conventional configurations. Power and politics will be discussed in detail in Chapter 6.

Conflict is usually high in the political organization; thus, there is pressure for negotiation and alliance formation. The political organization, however, is a dysfunctional configuration for schools because it hinders learning and teaching. Too much energy and activity are diverted to game playing, negotiations, and political machinations. Teaching and learning become secondary considerations. Schools are politicized from time to time and occasionally develop into political organizations, but such structures in schools are usually short-lived because of their ineffectiveness.

Of these structural configurations, our own long-term predilection for schools is for the professional model, but the evidence (Firestone and Herriott, 1981, 1982; Hoy, Blazovsky, and Newland, 1983) suggests that most schools are not professional organizations. Moreover, it is unlikely that schools will move dramatically to the configuration that Mintzberg calls a professional bureaucracy; however, movement toward semiprofessional or professional bureaucracies not only seems possible but highly desirable, especially if schools and teaching are to become more fully professional.

A number of elements in the situation influence the particular configuration of schools. For instance, the age and size of a school are likely to influence its structure. As schools age and grow, informal relations and direct supervision are likely to be replaced by formalization and bureaucratic control. When the technical system is defined as complex (i.e., teaching is viewed as a complex process requiring individualization and multiple and changing strategies), then a highly professional workforce is needed and decentralization of decision making is required. When, on the other hand, the technical system is defined as routine (i.e., teaching is viewed as a routine process of providing standard and simple minimum skills), then the technical system can be regulated through bureaucratic procedures. Moreover, the more organizations are controlled externally, the more centralized and bureaucratic they tend to become. Again consider the impact of the No Child Left Behind legislation. Mintzberg argues that the two most effective means to control an organization from the outside are to hold its most powerful decision maker responsible and to impose specific standards, usually in the form of rules and regulations.

As school districts are increasingly faced with demands for accountability, minimum basic skills, tests for graduation, and myriad other performance targets from state departments of education, the pulls are for more formalization, more centralization, less professionalization, and a more well-developed state technostructure to regulate and control schools. On the other hand, school reformers continue to lament the negative impact of bureaucratic control and call for redesigning school structures to make them more hospitable to competent and skilled teachers (Darling-Hammond, 1985; Darling-Hammond and Wise, 1985; McNeil, 1986, 1988a, 1988b; Elmore, 1988; Wise, 1988; Prestine, 1991; Ouchi, 2003); here the pull is away from formalization and toward more decentralization and increased professionalization.

LOOSE COUPLING PERSPECTIVE

A body of theory and research challenges some of the notions of the school as a bureaucratic structure. Investigators are questioning rationalistic assumptions about the relationship of structure and process to organizational goals. Terrence E. Deal and Lynn E. Celotti (1980) argue that the formal organization and the administration of the school do not significantly affect methods of classroom instruction. In similar fashion, James G. March and Johan P. Olsen (1976) refer to educational organizations as "organized anarchies." Karl E. Weick (1976) and Howard E. Aldrich (1979) propose that elements or subsystems in organizations are often tied together loosely and argue that educational institutions are good examples of loosely coupled systems. Finally,

John Meyer and associates (Meyer and Rowan, 1977, 1978; Rowan, 1982; Meyer and Scott, 1983) propose an institutional explanation to describe loose coupling in schools as they assert that bureaucratic structure and instruction are disconnected (see Chapter 7). In brief, schools are seen as organizations with ambiguous goals, unclear technologies, fluid participation, uncoordinated activities, loosely connected structural elements, and structures that have little effect on outcomes. Analyses such as these are of the **loose coupling perspective** and are useful additions to standard bureaucratic theory.

Almost four decades ago Charles Bidwell (1965) analyzed structural looseness in school organizations. He noted that in order to deal with the problem of variability in student abilities on a day-to-day basis, teachers need to have freedom to make professional judgments. Professional autonomy seems undeniable in schools. Teachers work alone in their classrooms, are relatively unobserved by colleagues and administrators, and possess broad discretionary authority over their students. The result is a structural looseness *within* the school. Similarly, structural looseness exists *among* the school units in the system. Administrators and teachers of each school enjoy broad discretionary powers with respect to curriculum, teaching methods, and teacher selection. For example, even though the system recruits teachers, they typically are not assigned to a particular school without the principal's approval.

The structural looseness of the school supports a professional basis of organization; however, the demand for uniformity in product, the need for movement of students from grade to grade and school to school in an orderly process, and the long period of time over which students are schooled require a routinization of activities and, hence, a bureaucratic basis of school organization. Bidwell (1965), therefore, depicts the school as a distinctive combination of bureaucracy and structural looseness.

Loose coupling theorists (Weick, 1976; Aldrich, 1979) and institutional theorists (Meyer, 1978; Meyer and Rowan, 1977, 1978; Rowan, 1982) focus on the disconnectedness of behavior and outcomes in organizations. Weick (1976) develops probably the most thorough analysis of the concept of loose coupling. By **loose coupling,** he conveys "the image that coupled events are responsive, but that each event also preserves its own identity and some evidence of its physical or logical separateness" (Weick, 1976: 5). Loose coupling connotes weak or infrequent ties between elements that are minimally interdependent; hence, the phrase is invoked to refer to a variety of situations.

Most organizations are concerned with who does the work and how well it is performed. Weick (1976) suggests that in schools there is loose control over how well the work is done. Inspection of the instructional activities is infrequent, and even when evaluation of teaching does occur, it is usually perfunctory. Under these conditions, tight organizational controls over who does the work—through such activities as hiring, certifying, and scheduling—are exerted.

Meyer and Rowan (1977, 1978) expand Weick's thesis. They claim that educators typically "decouple" their organizational structure from instructional activities and outcomes and resort to a **logic of confidence.** Their argument is that schools are basically personnel-certifying agencies of society. Standardized curricula and certified teachers produce standardized types of graduates, who are then given their appropriate place in the economic and stratification system on the basis of their certified educational backgrounds. Ritual classifications such as elementary teacher, English teacher, principal, fourth grader, or college prep student provide the basis for tightly structured educational organizations. Schools gain community support and legitimacy by conforming to the legal and normative standards of the wider society. Much less control is exerted over teaching activities because close supervision and rigorous evaluation might uncover basic flaws in the instructional program and produce uncertainties. It is much easier to demonstrate conformity to abstract ritual classifications than to evaluate the effectiveness of the teaching-learning process. Therefore, schools decouple their ritual structure from instructional activities and buttress the decoupling by embracing an assumption of good faith (Okeafor and Teddlie, 1989). The community has confidence in members of the board of education, who in turn have confidence in the teachers. These multiple exchanges of confidences are supported by an abiding faith in the process by which school officials have been certified as professionals.

Empirical evidence to support the existence, extent, and patterns of loose couplings in schools is mixed. On the one hand, a number of studies depict the school as a highly centralized and formalized organization; in fact, one of the most salient features of secondary schools in New Jersey is the apparent rigid hierarchy of authority (Hoy, Newland, and Blazovsky, 1977; Hoy, Blazovsky, and Newland, 1980, 1983). High school teachers maintain that they must ask permission and get approval before they do "almost anything"; even small matters have to be referred to a superior for a final answer (Hoy, Newland, and Blazovsky, 1977).

On the other hand, the picture of schools presented by Meyer and Rowan (1978), and others (Abramowitz and Tenenbaum, 1978; Deal and Celotti, 1980; Meyer, 1978) is quite different. These investigators paint schools as loosely coupled systems where instructional work is basically removed from the control of the organizational structure. Perhaps when teachers claim that they must ask permission and get approval before they do almost anything they are excluding instructional activity. Although it seems hard to believe that teachers make such a distinction, professional discretion of teachers may be so broad and their autonomy so great concerning classroom instruction that questions of supervision are considered by teachers only within a framework of routine school and classroom management practices.

Several studies on the images of school organizations by William Firestone and his colleagues (Firestone and Herriott, 1981, 1982; Firestone and Wilson, 1985; Herriott and Firestone, 1984) specifically examine contrasting school structures. Their work suggests that schools can be grouped into two clusters: rational bureaucracy and anarchy, or loosely coupled systems. Elementary schools were much more likely to be rational bureaucracies characterized by goal consensus, hierarchy of authority, centralization, formalization, and limited teacher autonomy. Secondary schools, in contrast, were more loosely coupled systems with more teacher autonomy but with little goal consensus and much less centralization.

The crude distinction between bureaucracy and loosely coupled systems can be misleading (Boyd, 2002; Corwin and Borman, 1988; Meyer, 2002; Orton and Weick, 1990; Rowan, 2002) and counterproductive. Most elementary schools are more tightly structured than secondary schools, but it is a matter of degree. Routine tasks and functions are bureaucratically organized in secondary schools. In fact, a comparative analysis of public secondary schools and social welfare agencies by Hoy and his colleagues (Hoy, Blazovsky, and Newland, 1983) found schools to be dramatically more formalized and centralized than the welfare agencies. Not one welfare agency had as much hierarchical control or rule enforcement as the *least* centralized or least formalized high school. In a comprehensive review of the loose coupling literature, R. M. Ingersoll (1993: 108) concludes "that the loose coupling perspective has offered an incomplete and faulty view of the organization of schools." From a Weberian bureaucratic perspective, the recurring surprise is that organizations routinely exhibit structural looseness whereas from a Weickian coupling perspective, the recurring surprise is that organizations routinely exhibit tight couplings (Orton and Weick, 1990). The point is, of course, that schools are complex organizations with both tight and loose structural connections.

Our analysis leads us to the conclusion that in schools there are probably at least two basic organizational domains: a bureaucratic one consisting of the institutional and managerial functions of mediating between the school and community, implementing the law, administering internal affairs, procuring and allocating necessary resources, and mediating between students and teachers; and a professional one involved with the actual technical processes of teaching and learning.[7] The bureaucratic domain is typically a tightly linked and cohesive structure, at times too rigid, preventing adaptation and producing alienation among teachers. The professional sphere is much more loosely structured; teachers have broad discretion to make professional judgments about the teaching-learning process; at times, too much independence produces conflict, confusion, and coordination problems, reducing productivity and hindering efficiency.[8] Schools are affected by their environments; they are open systems. As forces in society change, pressures to tighten and loosen organization linkages also vary. Clearly, administrators need to know the organization and be aware of and sensitive to the negative consequences of *both* tight and loose coupling. In general, the public school is a distinctive combination of bureaucratic and professional elements, a theme we will now explore in more detail.

PROFESSIONAL AND BUREAUCRATIC CONFLICT

Professionals and semiprofessionals employed in formal organizations bring into focus a basic conflict between professional values and bureaucratic ex-

> **TABLE 3.5**
>
> ### Basic Characteristics of Professional and Bureaucratic Orientations: Similarities and Differences
>
> | Professional Orientation | Bureaucratic Orientation |
> | --- | --- |
> | Technical expertise | Technical expertise |
> | Objective perspective | Objective perspective |
> | Impersonal and impartial approach | Impersonal and impartial approach |
> | Service to clients | Service to clients |
> | **Major Sources of Conflict** | |
> | Colleague-oriented reference group | Hierarchical orientation |
> | Autonomy in decision making | Disciplined compliance |
> | Self-imposed standards of control | Subordinated to the organization |

pectations. Although many similarities exist between professional and bureaucratic principles, the potential for conflict remains because differences do exist (Blau and Scott, 2003). The major similarities and differences are summarized in Table 3.5.

Both bureaucrats and professionals are expected to have technical expertise in specialized areas, to maintain an objective perspective, and to act impersonally and impartially. Professionals, however, are expected to act in the best interests of their clients, whereas bureaucrats are expected to act in the best interests of the organization. This apparent conflict between the interests of clients and the organization poses a problem for many formal organizations, but for service organizations such as schools, social work agencies, and hospitals it may not be a major dilemma. Unlike business concerns, the prime beneficiary of service organizations is the client. For service organizations, then, the prime objective of both the bureaucrat and the professional is the same—service to clients.

A fundamental source of **professional-bureaucratic conflict** does emerge from the system of social control used by bureaucracies and the professions. Professionals attempt to control work decisions. They have been taught to internalize a code of ethics that guides their activities, and colleagues support this code of behavior. Professionals are basically responsible to their profession, and at times their colleagues may censure them. On the other hand, control in bureaucratic organizations is not in the hands of the colleague group; discipline stems from one major line of authority. As Blau and Scott (2003: 63) explain, "Performance is controlled by directives received from one's superiors rather than by self-imposed standards and peer-group surveillance, as is the case among professionals."

Considerable variation exists, however, among various professional groups and in the scope of their professional domains. For example, elementary and secondary schoolteachers may have a relatively narrow scope, whereas physicians and scientists typically have broad authority (Scott, 1981). The ultimate basis for a professional act is professional knowledge; however, the ultimate justification of a bureaucratic act is its consistency with the organizational rules and regulations and approval by a superior. Therein lies the major source of conflict between the organization and the profession—conflict between "professional expertise and autonomy" and "bureaucratic discipline and control."

Nevertheless, Scott (1981, 1987b, 1992) argues that, although some conflict exists between professional and bureaucratic principles, the two arrangements are not incompatible in all respects. Both represent alternative paths to the rationalization of a field of action—and at a general level, the two orientations are compatible. But the interaction between bureaucrats and professionals can be strained. Teachers resent interference and directives from the administration and call for shared governance in schools. Of course, different ways are used to resolve the conflicts. In some organizations major structural changes have been made. In others, many professionals have developed orientations that are compatible with the demands of their bureaucratic organizations.

Professional and Bureaucratic Orientations in Schools

Whether or not teaching is a full-fledged profession is debatable. However, few would argue either that teachers are closer to the professional end of an occupational continuum than blue-collar and white-collar workers, or that they are further from the professional pole than physicians or lawyers. Nonetheless, the growth of theory and knowledge in teaching, the increased requirements for teacher education, teachers' sense of responsibility for student welfare, strong professional associations, and increased claims for teacher autonomy provide the basis for considering teaching a profession. Behind the drive to professionalize teaching is the desire for increased status and more control over work—in order to gain not only more responsibility but also more authority or power. For many years, teachers believed that they had professional obligations, such as staying after school to help students with their work; now they are demanding professional rights as well, such as selecting their own colleagues.

As we have already discussed, the characteristics of bureaucratic organizations are not totally compatible with a professional work group. Findings that many conflicts in schools derive from more general conflict between bureaucratic and professional principles should not be surprising. For example, Ronald G. Corwin (1965) studied teacher conflict in schools and found that almost half the conflict incidents involved teachers in opposition to administrators. The higher the level of professional orientation, the greater the number of conflicts. Similarly, DiPaola and Hoy (1994) found in a study of teachers that professional orientation was related to teacher militancy.

Few teachers escape the oral or written exhortations on "professionalism." Some administrators use the term "professionalism" as a cry to rally support for the school or for a given decision. For example, a decision to initiate a merit salary program in one school subsequently resulted in a confidential note to all teachers notifying them of their salaries plus the following addendum: "Salary is a confidential and personal matter. It is your professional obligation not to discuss your salary with other teachers." A safe prediction is that many educational administrators have a conception of a "professional" teacher as one who is loyal to the administration and the organization—that is, one who has a bureaucratic orientation.

Given the bureaucratization of schools and the growing professionalization of teachers, continued conflict seems likely. In teaching, the immediate issues of conflict revolve around the amount of control teachers should have over the selection of textbooks, teaching procedures and methods, and curriculum reform and development; however, the underlying issue is neither peculiar to teaching nor to school organizations. The conflict is between professional expertise and autonomy and bureaucratic discipline and control.

As long as the basic bureaucratic structure of the school tends to be authoritarian, teacher authority will continue to be a major source of tension. If the organizational structure of the school becomes more professional, then the chances for ameliorating the conflict and tension will be greatly improved. In fact, a dual orientation (local-cosmopolitan) of teachers might be the rule rather than the exception. In professional organizational structures, teachers might increasingly have high commitments both to the organization and to the profession. Some research supports the notion that bureaucratic orientation and professional attitudes of teachers need not be in conflict if schools increase the professional autonomy of teachers (Marjoribanks, 1977; DiPaola and Hoy, 1994).

Several other studies of teacher orientations are relevant. Edward Kuhlman and Wayne K. Hoy (1974) studied the bureaucratic socialization of new schoolteachers. They were interested in the extent to which the professional and bureaucratic orientations of beginning teachers were changed as a result of initial socialization attempts by the school organization. They theorized that a dual-role orientation might emerge among new teachers as they were socialized. New teachers, however, did not become both more professional and more bureaucratic in orientation during the first year of teaching. On the contrary, secondary teachers became significantly more bureaucratic and less professional during the first year. The orientations of beginning elementary teachers remained relatively constant, although as a group they were significantly more bureaucratic than secondary teachers. The hypothesis was not supported that a dual orientation would evolve during the initial experience of teaching and would enhance the effectiveness of both the professional and the organization. Furthermore, Harold Wilensky's (1964) contention regarding an interpenetration of bureaucratic and professional cultures in many organizations was not supported by the findings in secondary schools.

The forces of bureaucratic socialization in a majority of secondary schools seem strong. Most schools begin almost immediately to mold neophytes into roles devised to maintain stability, to encourage subordination, and to promote loyalty to the organization; in fact, the socialization process begins with the student-teaching experience. Student teachers, as a result of their practice teaching experience, appear to become significantly more bureaucratic in orientation (Hoy and Rees, 1977). Similar socialization forces and outcomes have been reported for other aspiring professions, especially for social work (Enoch, 1989).

In sum, research portrays the school as a service organization staffed predominantly with professionals and semiprofessionals. The structure of the school organization is basically bureaucratic, with authoritarian trappings. Teachers as a group are becoming somewhat more professional and more militant; yet the bureaucratic structure, especially at the secondary level, seems quite effective at socializing new members to the appropriate bureaucratic stance, often at the expense of professional considerations. Hence, the school milieu comprises a number of countervailing forces. One hopes that administrators and teachers alike will strive to make school organizations more professional and less authoritarian. In such organizations a dual orientation seems likely to become increasingly prevalent, with teachers who are highly committed to both the profession and the school.[9]

A CASE FOR LEADERSHIP

Problems at West High

You have been appointed the new principal at West High School. The school has 1,150 students, 85 teachers, an assistant principal, 4 secretaries, and 2 guidance counselors. West High is one of two high schools in a midsized school system on the East Coast. The school district is average in terms of support for education, falling about at the 48th percentile on statewide per pupil expenditures. You had been a high school teacher and assistant principal in a district 75 miles to the north. When the opportunity presented itself, you applied, were hired, and are eager to do well in your first job as principal of your own school. The job is a promotion and a significant step up in salary. Moreover, it is conveniently located at the site of the state university, where you are completing your doctoral study—albeit at a slower pace for a while.

Your predecessor at West High was a very popular principal who retired after 30 years on the job. Most of the veteran faculty members liked his unobtrusive style; in fact, his style might more aptly be described as indulgent. He permitted teachers to do just about anything they wanted as long as it caused no problems in the community and, for the most part, the community was apathetic. Occasionally an angry citizen would call asking why one of the teachers was at the bank or in the coffee shop when school was in session. Good "Old Bob," as his teachers fondly called him, always covered for them. "They were on school business." Old Bob had been around so long that many of the parents of the community had been students at the high school when he was a beginning principal, and his nickname then was "Mellow Bob." Although he had been a fixture at West High, few saw him as a leader, but most were satisfied. Why rock the boat was the common refrain when talk turned to change. Old Bob just sailed along blissfully in his role as high school principal. He had an assistant principal, Pete Marshall, who ran interference for him if he needed it and a loyal faculty who knew a good deal when they experienced it.

(Continued)

A CASE FOR LEADERSHIP *(Continued)*

But things were changing. Statewide testing was revealing inadequacies in the instructional program. Students were getting into more trouble both in and out of school. Indeed, students were getting out of control—class cutting, fights, absenteeism, and dropouts were on the rise. Parents were beginning to request that their kids be sent to East High, the other high school in the district. Students of East High did better academically, and socially, and the school was cleaner and had a more orderly environment. The administration at East High was directive and sometimes harsh with both students and faculty, but many parents wanted the strong discipline of East High rather than the laid-back approach at West High. As long as there were no crises, however, Old Bob was happy and so were most of his teachers.

Two years ago the school district had hired a new superintendent, Rebecca Goldberg, and the winds of change had been blowing ever since. Rebecca and Old Bob became antagonists almost immediately. Rebecca had a vision for the district, one of better schools, higher statewide test scores, more parental involvement, new curricular programs, and fewer dropouts. Well, two years of interference were more than Old Bob could take. At the early age of 62, he retired and said farewell to his friends. He steadfastly refused to "buckle under" to the new superintendent. Old Bob's teachers were loyal, and they were shocked and a little anxious when he decided to call it a career and retire. After all, he was very teacher-friendly. He opposed bureaucratic rules and regulations because they constrained the activities of his professional faculty. He rewarded his loyal teachers with a hands-off policy. He never threw his position or title around—he was just "one of the boys," a saying that irritated some of the younger women teachers. Yet none said or did anything to offend Old Bob because he was benign. Any time they did need a favor, they could count on him. He had had a great relationship with the previous superintendent; they had been friends for 20 years and it had been about that long that Old Bob had engaged in a pattern of indulgency and benign neglect

with his teachers. No one remembered the time when a new teacher did not get tenure; in fact, the way you got hired at West High was to know someone who knew Old Bob. Bob hired and the appointment was always approved by the superintendent and board—until two years ago. The new superintendent had different ideas; the board had hired Rebecca Goldberg with the goal of changing and improving the district. Some say Old Bob was just forced out; whatever the dynamics, Old Bob is gone and he left behind a faculty that he had handpicked.

Pete Marshall, Bob's 10-year assistant, had been personally groomed by Old Bob to take over the reins—so it was a bombshell when the school board decided to go outside to hire a successor. The board selected you because of your vision of a school with high academic standards, but one that was nurturing as well as rigorous. The Board of Education wanted you as principal because they liked your progressive ideas and energy and both the board and superintendent had given you a mandate for change. You arrived at West High just a month before school opened and now you have been on the job for nearly two months. You really believe that you can turn things around, but it is not going to be as easy as you originally thought. You have inherited a loyal faculty; unfortunately they are loyal to Old Bob and his assistant principal. It seems that you are being opposed on every issue. There are virtually no operating procedures in this school; teachers do what they want to do and the result is near chaos. When you question a teacher on anything, the response is always the same—"That's the way we always did it." When you suggest that perhaps a change could improve things, the common response is "That's not the way Old Bob did it."

Pete, your assistant principal, is distant and not particularly helpful: in fact, you get the idea that he is working to undermine you. Just last week you passed his office and overheard him remarking to a parent on the phone that you were

(Continued)

A CASE FOR LEADERSHIP *(Concluded)*

never around and it made things difficult. You are trying to be supportive of Pete and work with him because you know he is disappointed that he did not get the job. Perhaps you should have taken up the superintendent on the offer to transfer Pete Marshall to East High. You have enough problems with teachers and students without having to watch your back with your assistant. This is a close-knit school and unfortunately, you are an outsider. The board and superintendent expect results and change, but you are getting blocked everywhere you turn. The faculty resents the professional development meetings you have scheduled as part of an upcoming in-service. The faculty resists any attempt to change. You cannot count on your assistant for support; you just don't trust him. Even your secretary (Old Bob's secretary) cannot be depended upon. She too is always idealizing Old Bob. You are sick and tired of hearing about how great Old Bob was; you know that was not the case. You suspect the degree of talk about your predecessor is simply an index of resistance to your leadership. You are frustrated and feel the need to make some drastic changes. The school year is only a month old, but you must do something. You are in charge. You have the support of the board and superintendent right now. You must act, but you need help and you need a plan. Today is the beginning of change at West High, you vow, as you pick up the phone to schedule an appointment with the superintendent. You figure you have a little time to sketch a plan of action, and you believe the superintendent is sympathetic to your plight.

- Should you ask that Pete Marshall be transferred?
- How can you get a supportive secretary?
- How can you use the authority of your office for change?
- Is it time for some unilateral changes in your school? Top-down changes?
- Is it time to institute a system of rules, regulations, and procedures? How?
- Is it time for a dramatic restructuring?
- Is democracy in this situation an unrealistic dream?

These are just some of the questions you must answer before you propose a plan for change to the superintendent. You are the principal; you have the support of your superiors but not your subordinates; your superiors expect improvement; the school needs change; and you need a plan.

SUMMARY AND SUGGESTED READINGS

Virtually all organizations have the distinctive characteristics of bureaucracy—division of labor, specialization, impersonality, hierarchy of authority, rules and regulations, and career orientation—described by Max Weber in his theory of bureaucracy. Weber's model has been criticized because it pays insufficient attention to possible dysfunctional consequences of each component, neglects the significance of the informal organization, ignores the conflict between disciplined compliance and expertise, is gender biased, and has some inherent pathologies. Furthermore, postmodernists challenge the basic structure of the bureaucracy as inappropriate and oppressive. Nevertheless, the Weberian perspective provides a strong conceptual basis for examining school structures because most schools have many of the features of bureaucracy.

We have examined three contemporary views of organizational structure. First, we use Hall's analysis to develop four types of school organizational structures—Weberian, authoritarian, professional, and chaotic—that are quite different and seem to have different consequences for students and teachers. We then use this typology to outline a theory of structural development in schools. Second, Hoy and Sweetland propose an enabling-hindering continuum to examine the structure of schools and suggest that it is the kind of structure rather than the amount of structure that is important in explaining the positive and negative consequences of structure. Finally, Mintzberg provides a comprehensive analysis of the structure of organizations. He describes structure simply as the ways in which an organization divides its labor into tasks and achieves coordination among them. His framework when applied to schools yields a number of contemporary configurations of school structure as well as a political model of schools. The framework provides a basis for synthesizing much of the literature on school structure.

A loose coupling perspective offers a useful addition to bureaucratic and structural theories. The framework challenges many of the assumptions of bureaucratic theory and depicts the school as a distinctive combination of bureaucracy and structural looseness, one in which the institutional structure is decoupled from instructional activities. The natural tendency for bureaucratic and professional elements in school to conflict provides both the school structure and the individual teacher with a challenge to accommodate and change.

We recommend that all students read March and Simon's classic analysis, *Organizations* (1958, 1993). This book is about hierarchical structures and rational decision making. The introduction to the second edition is an intriguing reflection on the world of organizations during the past 35 years by two of the most distinguished organizational theorists of this century. For those students enthralled with the construct of bureaucracy, start with Weber (1947). Mintzberg supplies a readable and extensive contemporary treatment of organizational structure in *Mintzberg on Management* (1989) and Bolman and Deal (2003) provide yet another contemporary analysis of organizational structure. No one who is a student of organization should miss Ferguson's *The Feminist Case against Bureaucracy* (1984). Those interested in an intriguing postmodern analysis should read Hirschhorn's *Reworking Authority: Leading and Following in the Post-Modern Organization* (1997). Finally, the research on Catholic schools (Coleman, 1990; Bryk, Lee, and Holland, 1993) is beginning to provide some strong evidence of how organizational structures influence a school's ability to achieve its goals.

KEY ASSUMPTIONS AND PRINCIPLES

1. Virtually all organizations, including schools, have hierarchical structures.

2. Division of labor promotes specialization, which in turn produces expertise.

3. Informal organization is the other side of formal; in every formal organization there is informal structure, which emerges spontaneously.
4. Organizational structure has both positive and negative consequences; the administrative challenge is to achieve the positive and avoid the negative.
5. The kind of organizational structure (enabling or hindering, tight or loose coupling) is just as important as the amount of structure (tall or flat, centralized or decentralized).
6. There is no one best structure; appropriate structure depends upon the people, task, goals, technology, and context.
7. Organizations are faced with the problems of control and coordination as well those of creativity and change.
8. Tight coupling improves organizational efficiency and accountability, but loose coupling promotes creativity and professionalism.
9. All organizations are faced with the dilemma of order and freedom; there is no final solution but rather a continuous effort to get the right balance.
10. A structural perspective rests on the belief in rationality and confidence that appropriate structural arrangements minimize problems.

NOTES

1. The intended and unintended results of using rules to gain control has been described as Gouldner's model, and it is discussed in more detail in March and Simon (1993).
2. The Aston studies done by D. S. Pugh and his associates (1968, 1969, 1976) at the University of Aston in Birmingham, England, is a comprehensive set of studies of bureaucracy using interview inventories to assess the structure of work organizations rather than questionnaires. The technique has been used by Canadian researchers (Newberry, 1971; Kelsey, 1973; Holdaway et al., 1975; Sackney, 1976) at the University of Alberta and by U.S. researchers (Sousa and Hoy, 1981; Guidette, 1982; Haymond, 1982) at Rutgers University to study educational organizations. Regardless of research strategy, the results of the study of bureaucratic structures in schools are quite consistent.
3. For other specific examples of enabling rules and enabling structure, see Hoy (2003).
4. A note of caution: Enabling school structures can enable the wrong goals just as some parents enable their children to engage in destructive behavior. Enabling structure is neither a panacea nor a substitute for appropriate goals, technology, and expertise. See Hoy (2003).
5. To these five original configurations, Mintzberg (1989) has added two additional ones—the missionary organization and the political organization. Sometimes either ideology or politics becomes so pervasive that it overrides the standard configurations and creates its own configuration. If the organization's ideology (culture) becomes so strong that its entire structure is built around it, Mintzberg labels the configuration a missionary organization. If the politics becomes so strong that it captures the organization, the configuration is labeled

a political organization. But typically, politics (Chapter 6) and ideology (Chapter 5) are components of the standard forms; they are overlays on the five conventional configurations.

6. Mintzberg (1979) also identifies the pull to Balkanize by managers of the middle line and the pull to collaborate by the support staff, which are less pronounced in schools and found predominately in divisional structures and adhocracies.

7. Parsons (1967) details the institutional, managerial, and technical functions in schools.

8. For an insightful discussion of the separate zones of control of principals and teachers, see Lortie (1969).

9. Carlson (1962) provides an intriguing research analysis of local-cosmopolitan orientations for superintendents as they affect administrator behavior, and Hoy and Aho (1973) and Ganz and Hoy (1977) do the same thing for secondary and elementary principals, respectively. See Gouldner (1958) for the classic study of local-cosmopolitan orientations.

CHAPTER 4

INDIVIDUALS IN SCHOOLS

Among the mechanisms of agency, none is more central or pervasive than beliefs of personal efficacy. Unless people believe they can produce desired effects by their actions, they have little incentive to act.

Albert Bandura
Self-Efficacy: The Exercise of Control

It ain't hard to learn what you want to know.

Anonymous Urban Student
Washington, DC

PREVIEW

1. Individuals in schools are motivated by their needs, goals, and beliefs.

2. Maslow's hierarchy of needs theory postulates five basic categories of needs arranged in a hierarchy of prepotency: physiological, safety, belongingness, esteem, and self-actualization needs.

3. Herzberg's hygiene-motivator theory postulates two distinct sets of needs leading to satisfaction and dissatisfaction.

4. Achievement and autonomy needs are also strong motivating forces for many individuals.

5. Goal-setting theory suggests that when an individual accepts specific, realistic, and challenging goals, motivation will be strong, especially if feedback about progress is forthcoming.

6. Attribution theory explains that motivation will be strong when causes of outcomes are perceived

to be internal, amenable to change, and controllable.

7. Equity theory maintains that individuals will work hard when they believe that they have been treated fairly—that is, that they have received appropriate rewards, that allocations of rewards are fair, and that they have been treated with respect.

8. Expectancy theory suggests that individuals will work hard if that extra effort will improve their performance, good performance will be noticed and rewarded, and they value the rewards.

9. Self-efficacy contributes to motivation by determining what goals individuals set for themselves, how much effort they expend, how long they persevere in the face of difficulties, and their resilience to failures.

10. Intrinsic and extrinsic motivation are two different strategies for motivating individuals.

When administrators analyze their organizations, sometimes they focus on structure to the detriment of the individual. But organizations exist to serve human needs as much as to attain organizational goals. To neglect either the structural or individual element of the school social system is shortsighted and incomplete. As we saw earlier (see Chapter 1), students, teachers, and administrators bring with them needs and develop their own personal orientations and cognitive understanding of their roles. What facets of the individual are most instrumental in determining work and other behaviors in schools? What characteristics of the individual motivate behavior in school? Responses to such questions can be framed in many ways because individuals are so complex and because insights regarding human behavior are rooted in many perspectives and disciplines. We believe that a powerful way to gain insights about students, teachers, and administrators as individuals in the school social system is to examine their needs, goals, beliefs, and motivations.

NEEDS

Although people occupy roles and positions in schools, they are not merely actors devoid of unique needs; in fact, human needs and motivations are key elements in determining how individuals behave in organizations. Individuals working in organizations are always concerned about fulfilling their needs in the course of doing their jobs. Parents are concerned about the needs of their children, politicians are attuned to the needs of their constituencies, teachers try to meet the needs of their students, and most principals are sensitive to the needs of their teachers. There is little doubt that individual needs are important in organizations. People have different personal needs that shape their behavior. As far as possible, most individuals try to personalize their roles in an organization; that is, stamp their own brand of behavior on expected roles, behavior that is consistent with their needs. One reason why people who occupy the same roles behave so differently is that each has his or her own style. Teachers have different styles and so do students and administrators.

Edwin A. Locke (1991) observes that needs are used loosely in everyday conversation, but in their biological context, needs are requirements for an organism's survival and well-being. More formally, **needs** are internal states of disequilibrium that cause individuals to pursue certain courses of action in order to regain internal equilibrium (Steers and Porter, 1991). Or as Christopher Hodgkinson (1991: 94) states, "The idea behind need is that of a discrepancy or undesirable imbalance in a state of affairs. Needs imply tension and disequilibrium and provide a dynamic for rectifying action." Consequently, the ultimate objective of goal-directed action is need fulfillment or the reduction of disequilibrium. The concept of need explains at a most basic level why living organisms behave and is the standard to judge whether a specific action is healthy or not.

Hierarchy of Needs

The humanistic psychologist Abraham Maslow (1970) developed a fascinating theory of human needs; in fact, his need hierarchy model has become one of the most widely discussed and influential perspectives of human motivation. The model was derived primarily from Maslow's experience as a clinical psychologist and not from systematic research (Campbell and Pritchard, 1976; Steers and Porter, 1983). His theory posits a **need hierarchy**—a basic innate or inborn set of human needs arranged in a hierarchical order (Kanfer, 1990).

Five basic categories of needs, arranged in hierarchical levels (identified and described in Figure 4.1) constitute the foundation of Maslow's (1970) model:

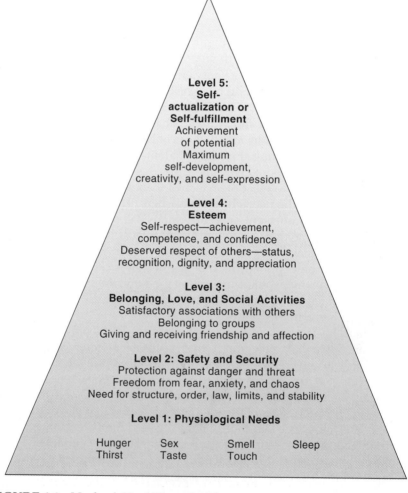

Level 5:
Self-
actualization or
Self-fulfillment
Achievement
of potential
Maximum
self-development,
creativity, and self-expression

Level 4:
Esteem
Self-respect—achievement,
competence, and confidence
Deserved respect of others—status,
recognition, dignity, and appreciation

Level 3:
Belonging, Love, and Social Activities
Satisfactory associations with others
Belonging to groups
Giving and receiving friendship and affection

Level 2: Safety and Security
Protection against danger and threat
Freedom from fear, anxiety, and chaos
Need for structure, order, law, limits, and stability

Level 1: Physiological Needs

| Hunger | Sex | Smell | Sleep |
| Thirst | Taste | Touch | |

FIGURE 4.1 *Maslow's Need Hierarchy Theory*

- At the first level of the hierarchy are *physiological needs,* which consist of such fundamental biological functions as hunger and thirst.
- *Safety and security needs,* the second level, derive from the desire for a peaceful, smoothly running, stable society.
- On the third level, *belonging, love, and social needs* are extremely important in modern society. Maslow contends that maladjustment stems from frustration of these needs. He believes that some proportion of youth rebellion, for example, is motivated by the profound need to belong to a group.
- *Esteem needs,* at the fourth level, reflect the desire to be highly regarded by others. Achievement, competence, status, and recognition satisfy esteem needs.
- Finally, Maslow maintains that discontent and restlessness develop unless individuals do what they are best suited to do—that is, unless they meet their need for *self-actualization,* the fifth level. The meaning of self-actualization is a subject of much discussion. A succinct and simple definition of **self-actualization** is that it is the need to be what an individual wants to be, to achieve fulfillment of life goals, and to realize the potential of his or her personality (Campbell and Pritchard, 1976). Maslow viewed self-actualization as a process, not an end state. Individuals are continually in the process of becoming more and more of what they are uniquely capable of becoming (Cherrington, 1991).

Maslow's needs are related to one another and are arranged in a hierarchy of prepotency, or urgency for survival, of the individual. The more prepotent a need is, the more it precedes other needs in human consciousness and demands to be satisfied. This observation leads to the fundamental postulate of Maslow's theory: *higher-level needs become activated as lower-level needs become satisfied.* Thus, Maslow suggests that a person lives by bread alone—when there is no bread. But when there is plenty of bread, other and higher needs emerge. They, in turn, dominate the person and, as they become satisfied, are displaced by new needs. The sequence—increased satisfaction, decreased importance, increased importance of next higher need level—repeats itself until the highest level of the hierarchy is reached. Therefore, individual behavior is motivated by an attempt to satisfy the need that is most important at that time (Lawler, 1973).

The successive emergence of higher needs is limited because lower-level needs are never completely satisfied; moreover, if an individual cannot satisfy needs at a given level for any period of time, those needs again become potent motivators. A completely satisfied need is not an effective motivator. Hence, the concept of gratification is as important as that of deprivation. Maslow reasons that gratification releases the person from the domination of one need, allowing for the emergence of a higher-level need. Conversely, if a lower-order need is left unsatisfied, it reemerges and dominates behavior.

A common misconception about Maslow's theory is that one need must be entirely satisfied before the next level of needs emerges. Maslow asserts that normal individuals are usually only partially satisfied in all their basic needs. A more realistic description of the need structure is that the percentage of satisfaction decreases as one goes up the hierarchy of prepotency. Maslow argues that for the majority of people, needs at the first three levels are regularly satisfied and no longer have much motivational effect; however, satisfaction of esteem and self-actualization needs is rarely complete. The higher-level needs continually motivate. In other words, most behavior is motivated by needs from more than one level of the hierarchy and new need states do not emerge in a crisp, all or nothing lockstep fashion (Pinder, 1984).

Several observations about work in educational organizations can be made using Maslow's theory. First, although physiological needs seem reasonably well met for educators, some students are deprived of even the most basic needs and therefore present a potent motivational problem. Moreover, the needs for safety and security, the second hierarchical level, certainly can become motivating factors for school employees and students alike. Violence to and from school and within the school has increasingly become a way of life for many students. It is difficult to concentrate on studying or teaching when you are frightened. Administrative actions that arouse uncertainty with respect to continued employment, or discrimination, can affect every individual from custodian to superintendent. Furthermore, Maslow theorizes that broader aspects of the attempt to seek safety and security are seen in the preference many people have for familiar rather than unfamiliar things, for the known rather than the unknown. In schools, those people who have high safety needs may resist change and desire job security, injury-compensation plans, and retirement programs to satisfy those needs.

The need to belong causes an individual to seek relationships with co-workers, peers, superiors, and subordinates. For educators, friendship ties, informal work groups, professional memberships, and school memberships satisfy this need. The need for esteem and status, the fourth hierarchical level, causes an educator to seek control, autonomy, respect from and for others, and professional competence. Finally, the need for self-actualization motivates educators to be the best people they are capable of being. This need is less frequently apparent than others, however, because many individuals are still concerned with lower-level needs. Nevertheless, Maslow (1965) clearly advocates that organizations such as schools should provide the highest level of need satisfaction that is possible because self-actualizing students, teachers, and administrators are the best performers.

Maslow's need hierarchy theory, then, is based on three fundamental postulates (Cherrington, 1991):

- Individual needs are universal and arranged in a hierarchy.
- Unfilled needs lead individuals to focus exclusively on those needs.
- Lower-level needs must be largely satisfied before higher-level needs can be felt and pursued.

One of the reasons that Maslow's theory is so popular is because it is intuitively appealing, but research designed to test it has yielded mixed results (Baron, 1998). There is no clear evidence showing that human needs are classified into five distinct categories, or that these categories are structured in any special hierarchy. In fact, the findings of a number of studies do not support the fundamental assumption of a hierarchy of prepotency; other studies have found modest support (Miner, 1980; Steers and Porter, 1983; Landy and Becker, 1987; Cherrington, 1991). Of three studies published since 1980, one strongly challenges the theory (Rauschenberger, Schmitt, and Hunter, 1980); and two show only modest support (Betz, 1984; Lefkowitz, Somers, and Weinberg, 1984).

In educational settings, an early study by Frances M. Trusty and Thomas J. Sergiovanni (1966) reports that the largest deficiencies for professional educators were satisfying esteem and self-actualization needs. In a more recent investigation, Mary Beth G. Anderson and Edward F. Iwanicki's (1984) findings support Trusty and Sergiovanni. However, the later study indicated a relatively large increase in the deficiency for security needs. Trusty and Sergiovanni also found that administrators, when compared to teachers, have fewer esteem need deficiencies and more self-actualization need deficiencies. The authors conclude that teachers' lack of self-esteem represents the largest source of need deficiency for them. Similarly, a study by Grace B. Chisolm and her colleagues (1980) shows that administrators exhibit fewer need deficiencies than teachers on all five subscales—security, social, esteem, autonomy, and self-actualization.

In brief, this appealing analysis of human needs should be viewed as an intriguing but unverified perspective for examining and explaining behavior. This does not mean the theory is wrong, but merely that it has not been supported at this time (Miner, 2002).

Needs and Worker Satisfaction

Frederick Herzberg and his colleagues (Herzberg, Mausner, and Snyderman, 1959) developed a theory of motivation and job satisfaction based on the findings from their now famous study of engineers and accountants. The results led them to conclude that factors leading to positive job attitudes (motivators) do so because of their potential to satisfy the individual's need for self-actualization, or in Herzberg's terms, promote psychological growth. Conversely, a separate set of factors, hygiene factors, is related to physiological, safety, and social needs. Maslow focuses on general human needs of the psychological person, while Herzberg (1982) concentrates on the psychological person in terms of how the job affects basic needs.

The theory, which has been called motivation-hygiene theory, two-factor theory, dual-factor theory, and simply Herzberg's theory, has been widely accepted by administrators and policy makers. Herzberg and his colleagues found that positive events were dominated by references to achievement, recognition (for achievement), the work itself (challenging), responsibility, and advancement (promotion). Negative events were dominated by references to interpersonal relations with superiors and peers, technical supervision, company policy and administration, working conditions, salary, and personal life. They concluded that the presence of certain factors in the job act to increase an individual's job satisfaction, but absence of these same factors does not necessarily produce job dissatisfaction. The theory has several basic assumptions:

- There are two separate sets of factors in explaining work satisfaction and dissatisfaction.
- Motivators tend to produce satisfaction, and hygiene factors tend to produce dissatisfaction.
- Work satisfaction and dissatisfaction are not opposites, but rather separate and distinct dimensions.

Hence, motivation-hygiene theory postulates that the gratification of certain needs, called **motivators** (i.e., achievement, recognition, work itself, responsibility, and advancement), increases satisfaction, but when the motivators are not gratified, only minimal dissatisfaction results. On the other hand, when factors called **hygienes** (i.e., interpersonal relations, supervision, policy and administration, working conditions, salary, and personal life) are not gratified, negative attitudes are created, producing job dissatisfaction. Gratification of hygienes leads only to minimal job satisfaction. For example, being restricted in your ability to copy exams on the school's copy machine is likely to cause dissatisfaction, but the availability of such service is unlikely to promote high job satisfaction. Job satisfaction is more likely to come from autonomy, responsibility, and the challenge of the job itself. In brief, motivators tend to produce job satisfaction, whereas hygiene factors tend to produce job dissatisfaction. Why the name "hygienes" for factors that produce dissatisfaction and are relatively unimportant in promoting satisfaction? It's a medical metaphor: Although hygiene is very important in preventing serious infection, hygiene alone typically does not produce a cure just as hygiene factors alone cannot produce high levels of satisfaction.

Miner (2002) observes that the five motivator factors are both conceptually and empirically related. When these elements are present in work, the individual's basic needs of personal growth and self-actualization will be satisfied; positive feelings and improved performance will also result. The hygiene factors, when provided appropriately, can serve to remove dissatisfaction and improve performance up to a point. But hygiene elements do not produce as positive feelings or as high performance levels as are potentially possible.

Although Herzberg's theory became quite controversial, it has had a major impact on the field of work motivation and job design. Steers and Porter (1991) argue that Herzberg deserves a great deal of credit. By calling attention to the need for improved understanding of the role played by motivation in work organizations, he filled a void in the late 1950s. His approach is systematic and his language understandable. He advanced a theory that is simple to grasp, based on empirical data, and offers specific action recommendations to administrators. Pinder (1984) offers an even stronger defense for the model. He argues that substantial evidence exists that Herzberg's ideas concerning the design of jobs have considerable validity and practical utility.

In brief, administrators should be aware of both sets of factors as they attempt to design and enrich teaching jobs to make them inherently challenging and interesting as well as to eliminate those aspects of the job that are most likely to produce dissatisfaction. Both hygiene and motivator factors are important but for different reasons. See Table 4.1. One caveat: the two sets of factors are not as separate as theory implies; for example, salary is not just a dissatisfier but also acts as a motivator for some people (Miner, 2002). Yet it is useful to remember that things that encourage dissatisfaction often are different from those that promote satisfaction.

Need for Achievement

David C. McClelland's (1961, 1965, 1985) **achievement motivation theory** is commonly called need achievement or *n*-achievement theory.[1] The need to accomplish hard tasks, to overcome difficulties and obstructions, and to excel is the need for achievement. Individuals who strive for excellence in any field for the sake of achievement, not some other rewards, are considered to have a high need for achievement. In contrast to Maslow's fixed hierarchy and innate needs, McClelland's framework asserts that motives are learned; they become arranged in a hierarchy of potential for influencing behavior;

TABLE 4.1	
Herzberg's Motivation-Hygiene Theory	
Hygienes	**Motivators**
• Interpersonal relations (with subordinates)	• Achievement
• Interpersonal relations (with peers)	• Recognition
• Supervision (technical)	• Work itself
• Policy and administration	• Responsibility
• Working conditions	• Advancement
• Personal life	
• Job security and salary	

Dissatisfaction   Satisfaction

and they vary from person to person. As people develop, they learn to associate positive and negative feelings with certain things that happen to and around them. Accordingly, the achievement value is learned when opportunities for competing with standards of excellence become associated with positive outcomes (Pinder, 1984). For an individual, achievement is directed toward the top of the motive hierarchy and it takes only minimal achievement cues to activate the expectation of pleasure. Thus, the likelihood of achievement striving is increased. Under such circumstances weaker motives will probably give way to the achievement and assume a distinct secondary role in influencing behavior (Miner, 1980).

McClelland (1961, 1985) hypothesized that individuals who are high in achievement motivation have three key characteristics:

- First, they have a *strong desire to assume personal responsibility* for performing a task or solving a problem. Consequently, they tend to work alone rather than with others. If the job requires others, they tend to choose co-workers on the basis of their competence rather than their friendship. Individuals with high achievement needs prefer situations that allow them to take personal responsibility and get personal credit for the outcomes (Miner, 1980). For example, persons with high achievement motivation compared to those with low motives are more attracted to reward for performance systems (Turban and Keon, 1993).
- Second, those with high achievement needs tend to *set moderately difficult goals* and take intermediate levels of risk. Where tasks are too hard, the chance of succeeding and probability of satisfaction are low. Easy tasks represent things that anyone can do; thus little satisfaction will be gained in accomplishing them. High achievers tend to calculate the risks and select situations in which they anticipate feeling slightly overextended by the challenges, but not too overextended (Miner, 1980, 2002).
- Third, people with high achievement needs have a *strong desire for performance feedback.* These individuals want to know how well they have done and are anxious to receive information about results, regardless of whether they have succeeded or failed (Cherrington, 1991). There is little opportunity for achievement satisfaction when a person cannot tell success from failure.

Individuals with high achievement needs are characterized by their single-minded absorption with task accomplishment (Cherrington, 1991). Consequently, the need for achievement is an important motive in schools because students, teachers, and administrators who have a single-minded preoccupation are often successful. McClelland concluded from his research that the achievement motivation is apparently learned at an early age and largely influenced by child-rearing practices and other influences of parents. Children who see that their actions have an impact on their success and who are taught how to recognize good performance are more likely to grow up with the desire to excel (Schunk, 2000).

Other theorists, however, view achievement motivation as a set of conscious beliefs and values that are shaped by recent experiences with success and failure and by such factors in the immediate situation as the difficulty of the task and available incentives. Thus a teacher may have high motivation with her algebra class because she is doing well with the class but low motivation with her geometry class because the class is disinterested and struggling (Stipek, 1993).

Harnessing an existing need for achievement in teachers or students is one thing, but developing the achievement need in those without it is quite a different challenge. McClelland (1965) provides some evidence that training programs that focus on developing achievement needs can produce entrepreneurial behavior among adults where it previously did not exist; hence, one general strategy for changing motives is through education and training (Katzell and Thompson, 1990). Attempts to instill achievement motivation should likely be characterized by:

- Establishing situations in which individuals can succeed.
- Placing emphasis on setting reasonable and achievable goals.
- Accepting personal responsibility for performance.
- Providing clear feedback on performance.

Achievement motivation can be strengthened in schools and other settings through training, with favorable consequences for future success. The need for achievement, rather than being satisfied with accomplishment, seems to grow as it is attained rather than diminish (Wood and Wood, 1999). One caveat: Most of McClelland's research evidence pertains to boys and men, so his theory is currently limited to males; in fact, attempts to generalize it to females have been less successful (Pinder, 1984).

Need for Autonomy

The need for autonomy or self-determination is the desire to have choice in what we do and how we do it. In other words, it is the desire to act independently, rather than to have external pressures and rewards determine our actions (Deci and Ryan, 1985; Deci, Vallerand, Pelletier, and Ryan, 1991; Ryan and Deci, 2000). People seek to be in charge of their own behavior. In fact, Porter (1961) has argued that the need for independent thought and action, autonomy, is a basic need. People resist and struggle against pressure from external forces such as rules, regulations, orders, and deadlines imposed by others because it interferes with their need for autonomy. Sometimes a person even rejects help to remain in control (deCharms, 1976, 1983).

Richard deCharms (1976, 1983) used the metaphor of individuals as "origins" and "pawns" to capture the difference between people with self-determination and those with other-determination. Origins perceive of themselves as the origin or source of their intentions to act. Pawns see themselves in a game controlled by others and powerless to determine their actions. When people are pawns, play becomes work, leisure becomes obligation, and intrinsic motivation becomes extrinsic motivation (Lepper and Greene, 1978). For example, you may have had the experience as a principal of deciding to involve teachers in decision making only to have your motivation dampened by a superintendent who insists on a well-defined program of site-based management. Your chance to be an origin is spoiled by a hierarchical attempt to control you. You have little appetite for site-based management that has been dictated from above because your sense of self-determination has been stolen; indeed, teachers are likely to feel the same way about top-down efforts by principals (Woolfolk, 1998, 2004).

DeCharms' work with students led him to conclude that students are too little controlled by their own intrinsic motivation and too powerless to control their own actions. They are too often pawns rather than origins. It seems likely that teachers and administrators will suffer the same, perhaps stronger, consequences when they find themselves as pawns rather then origins—they become passive and take little responsibility for their work. Individual autonomy can be developed by activities and programs that emphasize setting realistic goals, personal planning of goals, accepting personal responsibility for actions, and developing self-confidence (Woolfolk, 1998, 2004). Results of some studies show that when individuals feel more like origins than pawns, they have higher self-esteem, feel more competent, and perform at higher levels of accomplishment (deCharms, 1976; Ryan and Grolnick, 1986). Needs for autonomy and self-determination can be enhanced by encouraging individuals to make their own choices, plan their own courses of action, and accept responsibility for the consequences of their choices. It seems likely that as we grow, develop, and mature, the need for autonomy becomes increasingly more important.

The needs for achievement, autonomy, social relations, self-esteem, and self-actualization are some of the key needs that motivate teachers and administrators and influence their perceptions and intellectual understandings of their organizational roles. Another driving force in influencing individual behavior is goals.

TIP: THEORY INTO PRACTICE

We have talked about the needs that employees have for security, respect, self-actualization, autonomy, satisfaction, and achievement. In your school, give some examples of which of these needs are most important. Explain why that is the case in your school, and discuss ways a principal might help teachers fulfill these needs and help teachers be more productive.

GOALS

A **goal** is a future state that an individual is striving to attain. Suppose you are getting ready for a big exam. Do you tell yourself that you will not stop studying until you have read so many pages, memorized your notes completely, done so many problems, and completed several practice exams? If you are a serious student, the chances are that you have set a series of similar goals to get ready for that important event. Most people set concrete goals for themselves because goals help eliminate the discrepancy between "where you are" and "where you want to be." Goal setting works for me. One reason that I have been successful in writing this book is that I set realistic writing goals for myself. For example, I write at least one page a day. I stick to it and you are reading the result.

Goals are aims or outcomes that an individual would like to achieve. They define for the individual an acceptable level of performance or direction of action. In terms of individual motivation, goals are always within the person, although they are often constructed from contextual information (Ford, 1992). For example, teachers will commonly adopt goals shared by other teachers or developed by the school. Locke and Latham (1990) suggest two key dimensions to goals—their content and intensity.

Goal content is the object or result being sought and varies from specific to abstract. Examples of concrete or specific goal content include losing 10 pounds in the next two months, earning an A on the next test, implementing a new curriculum, or using an improved set of teaching skills. Examples of more abstract content might include high achievement or better self-esteem. Goal content varies for individuals not only in specificity, but also in time perspective (short term or long term), difficulty (easy or hard), and number (few or many).

Goal intensity is the effort required to form the goal, the importance a person assigns the goal, and the commitment to the goal. Commitment is the degree to which the individual considers it important, is determined to reach it, and keeps it in the face of setbacks and obstacles. Factors that enhance commitment are ones that convince people that achieving the goal is possible and important or appropriate (Latham and Locke, 1991). Commitment influences and regulates goal striving because important goals are more likely to be accepted, to elicit intense involvement, and to foster persistent actions (Miner, 1980, 2002). It is virtually axiomatic that if there is no commitment to goals, then they do not work (Locke, Latham, and Erez, 1988; Latham, Winters, and Locke, 1994).

Goal-Setting Theory

Although the historical origins of goals as important aspects of motivation date to the early 20th century, Edwin A. Locke and his associate Gary P. Latham (Locke, 1968; Locke and Latham, 1984, 1990; Latham, 2000) are generally recognized for the development of contemporary goal-setting theory. Actually, **goal-setting theory** did not begin as a theory, but was one of those cases in which an interesting research triggered the search for an explanation, and hence the significance of goal-setting theory (Baron, 1998). The research finding was simple, clear, and impressive. Let's examine the details of the serendipitous study that begged for theoretical explanation.

Latham and Baldes (1975) studied lumber camp crews who hauled logs to a nearby sawmill. Before the study began, the crews loaded the large lumber trucks to about 60 percent capacity, which was wasteful because mileage for the huge trucks was horrendous—gallons per mile, not miles per gallon. To improve the situation, Latham and Baldes engaged the workers in a discussion of the problem. Together, they set a specific goal: to load all trucks to 94 percent capacity before transporting the logs to the sawmill. What happened? The performance levels improved dramatically and the increased performance persisted; in fact, in a follow-up study seven years later, crews were still loading the trucks to near capacity because the goal had become accepted and was now a regular part of the job (Baron, 1998).

Why do goals often improve our performance? Locke and Latham (1990) propose that successful goal performance meet four conditions:

- First, goals must be *specific.*
- Second, goals must be *challenging.*
- Third, goals must be *attainable.*
- Finally, individuals must be *committed* to the goals.

Research findings (Mento, Locke, and Klein, 1992; Wright et al., 1994; Latham, 2000; Locke and Latham, 2002) have demonstrated that when these four conditions are met, goal setting is an effective way of increasing motivation and performance.

What explains why goal setting is so effective? The basic postulate of the theory is that the intention to achieve a goal is a primary motivating force for behavior. Goals direct both mental and physical actions of individuals. Locke and Latham (1990) use four goal mechanisms to explain the positive effect of goals on action. First, goals *increase attention* to the immediate task; that is, they affect choice by helping individuals focus. Second, goals *increase the effort expended* on activities; they help people take action on goal-relevant activities while ignoring others. Third, goals *increase persistence* because there is less temptation to quit once a goal has been clearly established. Once a person decides on a goal, these three mechanisms become relatively automatic. Finally, goal setting increases motivation and performance by encouraging the *development of specific task strategies,* that is, ways of performing the task. Task strategies are conscious and deliberate plans the individual develops to achieve the goals. So whereas attention, effort, and persistence are fairly automatic consequences of goal setting, developing task strategies has conscious, deliberative, and creative consequences.

Feedback is also important in making goal setting an effective motivating force. In order to be motivated, the individual needs an accurate sense of the discrepancy between "where one is" and "the desired state." Feedback helps individuals evaluate their progress. If they have fallen short, then they can exert more effort or even try another strategy. When the feedback highlights accomplishment, the tendency is for the individual's self-confidence, analytic thinking, and performance to improve (Bandura, 1993).

Support for Locke's ideas came from a series of well-controlled laboratory experiments. Most of these studies used college students who performed relatively simple tasks for short periods of time. Because the theory originally relied on evidence from sheltered and contrived situations, the theory's proponents next attempted to respond to the following question: Can a practice so deceptively simple as setting specific, difficult goals increase the performance of employees in natural organizational settings where experimental effects are absent and goal acceptance is not easily obtained? Yes, the evidence from field studies indicates that goal-setting theory is valid for improving employee behavior in organizations such as schools (Latham and Yukl, 1975; Locke and Latham, 1990; Pinder, 1998).

In particular, three generalizations from goal theory continue to enjoy substantial research support (Locke and Latham, 1990). First, *difficult goals, if accepted, result in higher levels of performance than easy ones.* An explanation of the goal-difficulty effect is that hard goals lead to greater effort and persistence than do easy goals, assuming they are accepted. Similarly, hard goals make self-satisfaction contingent on a higher level of performance than do easy goals.

Second, *specific goals produce higher levels of performance than such vague goals as "do your best" or no goals at all.* General goals are inherently ambiguous and people give themselves the benefit of the doubt in evaluating their performance; they assume that they have met the "do your best" criterion. From the standpoint of goal-setting theory, however, a specific hard goal clarifies for the person what constitutes effective performance, and the person is no longer able to interpret a wide range of performance levels as indicative of excellent performance (Latham and Locke, 1991). A recent study of teaching aids for elementary school students (Audia et al., 1996) underscores the significance of quantitative rather than qualitative goals. Quantity goals (make five products in a specific time) but not quality goals (make products without any defects) increased participants' tendencies to use task strategies that increased production. Again we see that specific goals work more effectively than general ones.

A third and controversial generalization deals with the source of goals, commitment, and performance. Goals can be set in three ways: individuals can choose their own goals, they can be set jointly, or others can assign them. Because of the contradictory research findings, Locke and Latham (1990) helped design an elaborate set of research projects to test the effects of participation in goal settings on commitment and performance. The results suggested that the motivational effects of assigned goals can be as powerful as jointly set goals in generating high goal commitment and subsequent performance. Likewise, self-set goals are not consistently more effective in bringing about goal commitment or an increase in performance than other methods of goal setting. *The key to effective motivation seems to be whether the goals are embraced by individuals regardless of their origin.* People are generally more likely to accept and embrace goals if they are realistic, reasonably difficult, and meaningful (Erez and Zidon, 1984).

In sum, goal-setting theory suggests that specific and challenging but attainable goals can and often do increase motivation because such goals lead to increased focus, effort, and persistence as well as the development of specific task strategies to accomplish the goal. Feedback about progress toward achieving goals reinforces attention, effort, and persistence, or provides information for refining and altering the strategy to make it more effective (see Figure 4.2). The evidence of the effectiveness of goal-setting theory is overwhelming (Locke and Latham, 1990; Baron, 1998; Pinder, 1998; Latham, 2000; Locke and Latham, 2002). Next we turn to how beliefs motivate and influence behavior.

TIP: THEORY INTO PRACTICE

You have just been hired as a new principal of a small school with 20 teachers. This is your first job as principal and you want to succeed. What goals would you establish for yourself? Write two short-term goals (to be accomplished in the first month on the job) and two long-term goals (to be accomplished during the first year). Describe *why* you selected those goals and your commitment to them. Make sure the goals are specific, realistic, challenging, and attainable. How will you get feedback to assess your progress?

BELIEFS

Individuals also act on their beliefs. **Beliefs** are general understandings or generalizations about the world; they are what individuals hold to be true. Beliefs are typically assertions of the existence of things such as intelligence or cause; they also often are associated with an ideal image that contrasts with the existing state; they are frequently associated with evaluations of what should be, for example, the fairness of school rules and regulations; and they are often linked to remembered episodes or events, for instance, the unfairness of school rules and regulations might be traced to an unfortunate episode in school (Nespor, 1987).

FIGURE 4.2   *Goal-Setting Theory*

Beliefs play a pivotal role in motivating individuals to act. Individual beliefs about causality, fairness, intelligence, the consequences of our actions, and our ability to control our own destiny are a few of the pivotal beliefs that influence behavior. We turn to explanations of motivation that are anchored in beliefs.

Beliefs about Causality: Attribution Theory

As individuals see things happen to themselves and others, they ask why and then make inferences or attributions about causes. For example, students ask: Why did I fail the final examination? Was it because of a lack of effort? Or am I not smart enough to understand the material? Based on such observations and questions, Bernard Weiner (1972, 1985, 1986, 1992, 1994a, 1994b) uses the notion of attribution to create a model of motivation. In essence, **attribution theory** deals with causal explanations that individuals make about past behaviors, especially in regard to achievement efforts and expectancies. Attribution theorists assume that individuals naturally search for understanding about why events happen, especially when the outcome is important or unexpected (Stipek, 1993). People attribute successes and failures to such factors as ability, luck, effort, mood, interest, and unfair procedures. When people make causal attributions, they are essentially seeking or creating beliefs about what happened and why. Once they create the explanation, individuals can often use it to better manage themselves and their environments.

Dimensions of Causality
Weiner (1985, 1986, 1992, 1994a, 1994b, 2000) argues that most of the causes to which individuals attribute their successes and failures can be characterized in terms of three **dimensions of causality**—locus, stability, and responsibility.

- *Locus* (internal versus external) defines the location of the cause. Ability and effort are the most common internal factors on the locus dimension. Task difficulty and luck are common external determinants of outcomes.
- *Stability* (stable versus unstable) designates causes as constant or varying over time. Ability is stable because an individual's aptitude for a task is thought to be relatively fixed, whereas effort is unstable because people can vary their labor from one situation to another.
- *Responsibility* (controllable versus uncontrollable) refers to personal responsibility, that is, whether the person can control the cause. Effort is controllable because individuals are thought to be responsible for how hard they try. In contrast, ability and luck are generally believed to be beyond personal control (Weiner, 1986, 2000; Kanfer, 1990; Graham, 1991).

Each of these three dimensions has important implications for motivation because they tend to generate emotional reactions to success and failure. For example, internal-external locus seems to be closely related to self-esteem. If success or failure is attributed to internal factors, then success typically produces pride, whereas failure diminishes self-esteem. The stability dimension is linked to emotions that implicate future expectations. For instance, stable causes for failure produce hopelessness, apathy, and resignation. The responsibility dimension is linked to a set of social emotions that includes guilt, shame, pity, and anger. We feel guilty when the causes of personal failure are due to factors under our control such as lack of effort and deciding not to take responsibility for action; we are proud if we succeed. Shame or anger is more likely if personal failures are due to uncontrollable factors such as ability or the difficulty of the task, whereas succeeding leads to feeling lucky or just grateful. Also, feeling in control of your own destiny seems related to choosing more difficult tasks, working harder, and persisting longer (Schunk, 2000; Weiner, 1994a, 2000).

By attaching emotional reactions to the three attributional dimensions, outcomes may be perceived to have internal and unstable causes yet fall within an individual's responsibility and choice (Kanfer, 1990). For example, if new teachers perceive their failure to engage students in a class project as caused by a lack of preparation, then they will suffer low self-esteem and guilt for their poor performance. Their perception of the cause as being internal, unstable, and controllable—that is, within their power to change—enables them to be optimistic for future success. However, highly experienced teachers who have repeatedly failed to engage students in classroom projects are likely to attribute the cause of their failure to a lack of ability—that is, the cause is internal, stable, and uncontrollable. These teachers expect repeated failures, hopelessness, low self-esteem, and shame. They have low motivation to perform in the classroom. The reasons attributed to failure are varied and depend on combinations of the three dimensions.

Weiner (1994a) summarizes the sequence of motivation when failure is attributed to lack of ability as follows:

Lack of   **Not**   **Performance**
Failure → **Ability** → **Uncontrollable** → **Responsible** → **Embarrassment** → **Declines**

However, when failure is attributed to lack of effort, the sequence is as follows:

Lack of   **Performance**
Failure → **Effort** → **Controllable** → **Responsible** → **Guilt** → **Engagement** → **Improves**

Some criticize attribution theory as no more than common sense (Graham, 1991). For example, we pity the handicapped but feel anger toward the lazy who are unwilling to work, or we expect to repeat our successes when we have high ability. Some might contend that such causal attributions are part of our shared ways of thinking about our social world and not scientific knowledge. Attribution theorists argue, however, that an important goal is to systematize what we know to be common sense and place it in a conceptual framework that accounts for a wide array of social phenomena. The research shows consistent support for the attribution mechanisms and effects of expectancy for future performance (Miner, 1980, 2002; Weiner, 1986, 1994a, 1994b, 2000; Kanfer, 1990).

The central ingredients of attribution theory can be summarized with a series of questions:

- The causal question: What are the causes of the outcome?
- The locus question: Is the cause internal (ability, effort) or external (task difficulty, luck)?
- The stability question: Are causes fixed or changing?
- The responsibility or controllability question: Can I control the causes?

Students, teachers, and administrators will be highly motivated when they know the causes of the outcomes, the causes are internal, the causes are amenable to change, and the causes are under their control.

Beliefs about Ability

Some of the most powerful attributions that affect motivation and behavior are beliefs about ability. If we examine those beliefs, we can begin to understand why people set inappropriate and unmotivating goals, why some teachers give up, and why students sometimes adopt self-defeating strategies.

Adults have two general views of ability—stable and incremental (Dweck, 1999, 2000). A **stable view** (sometimes called an entity view) **of ability** assumes that ability is a stable and uncontrollable trait, that is, a characteristic of an individual that cannot be changed (Dweck and Bempechat, 1983). Accordingly, some people have more ability than others and the ability level is fixed. An **incremental view of ability,** on the other hand, assumes that ability is unstable and controllable—an expanding reservoir of knowledge and skills. Thus, people with an incremental view believe that by hard work, persistence, study, and practice knowledge can be increased and ability can be improved.

Young children hold almost an exclusively incremental view of ability (Nicholls and Miller, 1984). In the early grades in elementary school, for example, most students believe that effort is the same as intelligence. Smart people try hard and trying hard makes you smarter. So if you don't do well, you are not smart because you did not try hard enough. If you do well, you must be a smart, hard worker (Stipek, 1993, 2002). About the age of 12, however, students begin to differentiate between effort and ability. Students begin to realize that some people achieve without working hard and these are smart people. At this point, beliefs about ability begin to influence motivation (Anderman and Maehr, 1994).

People who hold a stable view of intelligence tend to set performance goals. They seek situations where they will look good and protect their self-esteem. They often continue to do what they can do well without expending too much effort or without risking failure because either working hard or failing suggests to them low ability. Moreover, to work hard and fail is a devastating blow to confidence and sense of ability. Such individuals would rather not try than fail; in fact, if you don't try, no one can accuse you of being dumb. When you fail, the reason is obvious—you just didn't prepare or try hard. So not trying or preparing becomes a strategy for protecting oneself from failure and looking dumb. We have all had experiences with students who are content with a C or just passing. Sometimes "just getting by" is a protective strategy for not looking bad. The student who tries for an A and gets a C risks feeling inadequate—so why try and risk humiliation when it is safe to just get by. Such strategies do protect one's self-esteem, but they do not enhance learning.

Individuals with an incremental view of intelligence, in contrast, tend to set learning goals and seek situations in which they can learn and progress because improvement means increasing their ability. To such people, children or adults, failure is not devastating; it merely suggests that more work is needed to improve. Ability is not threatened by failure; in fact, often failure is accepted as a challenge to work harder (Woolfolk, 1998, 2004). People with an incremental view of ability are most likely to set challenging, but realistic goals, and as we have seen, such goals are effective motivators.

In brief, one's beliefs about ability play an important role in motivation and performance in students, teachers, or administrators. Those individuals who believe that they can improve their ability are more likely to set learning goals that are moderately difficult and challenging and are concerned with mastering the task at hand. On the contrary, those who hold a stable, fixed view of ability are more likely to set performance goals that are either very easy or very difficult because they are concerned with self in the eyes of others; they want to look good and avoid anything that would threaten that image. Indeed they often equate high effort with low capabilities.

Beliefs about Fairness: Equity Theory and Procedural Justice

Students, teachers, and administrators, like most individuals in our society, are concerned about matters of basic fairness. We all know of teachers who barely do the minimum on their jobs. They often arrive late, give few tests, never volunteer for anything, leave promptly at the end of the school day, avoid all the meetings they can, and delegate their work to others. Imagine the chagrin of young, new teachers who work long hours, go the extra mile to help students after school, prepare hard for each class, and assist with extracurricular activities when they find that their malingering colleague is making twice the salary and doing half the work.

This basic unfairness in the workplace is what some theorists (Greenberg, 1993a; Tyler, 1994) call an inequity, and it brings us to yet another perspective on motivation called **equity theory**, which focuses on perceived fairness—individuals' beliefs about whether they are being treated fairly or not. The perceived fairness of the procedures used to allocate resources is called *procedural justice* (Greenberg, 1997, 2000) and is the key concept in equity theory. How do individuals decide whether they are being treated unfairly? Equity theory suggests that the key mechanism for such decisions is social comparison; we compare ourselves and our own plight with others. In more technical terms, we compare our ratio of inputs (everything we contribute) to outputs (everything we receive) to the input/output ratio of others (Kulik and Ambrose, 1992). We don't choose just anyone for such comparisons, but rather we select those that are similar to us in various ways. In the example above, young teachers compare themselves with an older teacher. Two points seem worth making. Both young and old teachers were performing the same role, yet the older teacher had more seniority. The inequity would have been viewed as even greater if the teacher comparison had been among those with similar experience and age (see Figure 4.3). In the example above, some rationalization of the difference might occur because of the greater experience of the older teacher.

Equity theory explains that if the input/output ratios are about the same for those with whom we compare ourselves, then we view our treatment as fair. If, however, the ratios are not roughly equal, we believe that we have not been treated fairly and a sense of inequity develops. Inequities are annoying and we try to eliminate them. One of the potential consequences of feelings of inequity is reduced motivation. Baron (1998) explains that feelings of inequity interfere with work motivation and individuals attempt to reduce such feelings in three ways:

- They try to increase their outcomes—they seek increased benefits such as a raise or other reward.
- They try to leave—they quit and find another job.
- They reduce their inputs—they expend less effort on the job.

The latter tactic seems quite common for individuals who conclude that they are being underrewarded, that is, are receiving less than they merit.

Note the Inequities in These Two Ratios

My Inputs

Relatively Large
(long hours,
extra committees,
teaching the most difficult
students, five different
class preparations)

Other Teacher's Inputs

Much Smaller
(shorter hours, few
committees, teaching
the best students, only
one class preparation)

My Outcomes

Relatively Small
(e.g., minimum salary)

Other Teacher's Outputs

Much Larger
(bigger salary,
nicer room,
better schedule,
more free periods)

FIGURE 4.3   *Inequity Example*

They often reduce their efforts relative to those they believe are being treated fairly (Harder, 1992). Reduced performance is not the only demonstration of lowered motivation. For example, some workers attempt to balance things out by engaging in secret actions that yield extra benefits including theft (Greenberg and Scott, 1995; Greenberg, 1993b).

Three more issues should be noted about the theory. First, individual judgments about fairness are subjective; they are in the eye of the beholder. The individual does the comparing and makes the judgment about equity. Second, individuals are more sensitive to receiving less than they deserve rather than more (Greenberg, 1993a). It is easier to rationalize receipt of more rather than less than one deserves. Third, equity and justice are important motivating forces to many individuals. In brief, when students, teachers, or administrators conclude that they are being treated unfairly, their performance motivation often declines dramatically, and they may even plan to "even the score" by cheating or engaging in other questionable practices. Thus, there are important practical, as well as ethical, reasons for ensuring that fairness is the standard operating procedure in schools and other work organizations (Baron, 1998). In fact, Greenberg (2000) concludes that fair procedures and practices enhance the acceptance of organizational performance.

Beliefs about Outcomes: Expectancy Theory

One of the most reliable and valid explanations of what motivates people to work is expectancy theory. Although expectancy models have a long history in psychology, the approach was popularized and modified specifically for work settings during the 1960s by Victor Vroom (1964) and others (Graen, 1963; Galbraith and Cummings, 1967; Porter and Lawler, 1968). In fact, Vroom (1964) sparked an explosion of research with his formulation of expectancy theory. His model was developed to predict choices among jobs, tasks, and effort levels that yield the highest perceived benefits (Kanfer, 1990). During the late 1960s through the early 1980s, the prevalence of expectancy theory in the literature clearly indicates its centrality to the research on motivation in organizations. Although the frequency of publication has declined, its use has continued (Miller and Grush, 1988). Expectancy theory presents a complex view of individuals in organizations. The basic assumptions, concepts, and generalizations of expectancy theory, however, are easily identified and explained.

Expectancy theory rests on two fundamental premises. First, individuals make decisions about their own behavior in organizations using their abilities to think, reason, and anticipate future events. Motivation is a conscious and cognitive process. People subjectively evaluate the expected value on outcomes or personal payoffs resulting from their actions, and then they choose how to behave. Second, individual values and attitudes interact with environmental components, such as role expectations and school culture, to influence behavior. This second assumption is not unique to expectancy theory, and in fact, it was posed in Chapter 1 as a generalization from social systems theory.

Expectancy theory builds on these assumptions with three fundamental concepts—expectancy, instrumentality, and valence.

Expectancy is the extent to which an individual believes that hard work will lead to improved performance. The expectancy question is: If I work hard, will I be successful? For example, if teachers think that a high probability exists of improving student achievement by increasing their own efforts, then they have a high expectancy level. If students strongly believe that they can design and implement a project in science, then the students have high expectancy levels.

Instrumentality is the perceived probability that good performance will be noticed and rewarded. Instrumentality is high when individuals perceive a strong association between performance and being rewarded. The instrumentality question is: If I succeed, what will I receive in return? If teachers think that high student achievement in their classrooms is likely to result in public recognition of their teaching ability, then instrumentality is high. Similarly, if the students perceive that successfully designing and implementing a science project will increase their knowledge about science, then their instrumentalities are high.

Valence is the perceived value or attractiveness of a reward. The concept of valence is similar to the concept of values—that is, what people consider or believe beneficial to their welfare or important in its own right. It is the strength of a person's desire for a particular reward. The valence question is: How do I feel about the rewards of my efforts? Feelings of competence, autonomy, recognition, accomplishment, and creativity, for example, represent valued work outcomes for educators and produce high levels of satisfaction.

In general, motivation to behave in a certain way is greatest when the individual believes that:

- He or she has the ability to perform at the desired level (high expectancy).
- The behavior will lead to anticipated outcomes and rewards (high instrumentality).
- These outcomes have positive personal values (high valence).

When faced with choices about behavior, the individual goes through a process of considering three questions:

- The expectancy question: Can I perform the task if I work hard?
- The instrumentality question: If I perform at the desired level, what are the outcomes?
- The valence question: How do I like these outcomes?

The individual then decides to behave in the way that appears to have the best chance of producing the desired outcomes (Nadler and Lawler, 1977). In other words, individuals consider alternatives, weigh costs and benefits, and select courses of action of maximum utility (Landy and Becker, 1987).

Expectancy theory is summarized in Figure 4.4. Note that the strength of motivation is a function of the interaction of the expectancy, instrumentality, and valence. The interaction suggests that the motivation will not be strong if any of the three elements is near zero. For example, if I believe there is no possibility of improving my performance even if I work hard, then my motivation will be low regardless of how much I desire the outcome and its rewards. Similarly, even if I believe I can accomplish my goal through hard work, but I believe that either my performance will not be rewarded or that the rewards are insignificant, the strength of my motivation will remain low. Let's take a specific example. To motivate your teachers to commit to a new curricular program, you must first convince them that with extra effort the program can be implemented. Further, they have to believe that the consequences of the new program will be noticed and recognized and, finally, that the rewards are worthwhile—in this case that their students will do significantly better on standardized tests.

Several authors (Heneman and Schwab, 1972; Mitchell, 1974; Campbell and Pritchard, 1976) have systematically reviewed the research literature on expectancy motivation theory and their conclusions are similar. The force of motivation in an expectancy model is positively correlated with job satisfac-

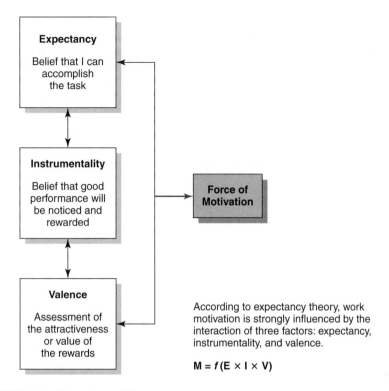

FIGURE 4.4 *Expectancy Theory*

tion, effort, and performance in a variety of settings. Although the relationships between force of motivation and independent ratings of effort and performance have been significant statistically on a consistent basis, the
associations have not been as strong as originally anticipated. In other words,
expectancy motivation is an important factor in effort and performance, but
other factors in the environment also are important contributors. In fact,
stronger support for expectancy theory has been shown for predictions of job
choice than for task effort or job performance (Kanfer, 1990). More recent
studies also continue to confirm the theory (Tubbs, Boehne, and Dahl, 1993;
Van Erde and Thierry, 1996).

Investigations conducted on educational organizations on the basis of
expectancy theory show similar results. Richard T. Mowday (1978) found that
school principals with higher expectancy motivation are more active in attempting to influence district decisions than those with low expectancy motivation. In a study examining the relationship between school structure and
teacher motivation, H. Scott Herrick (1973) found strong negative correla-
tions between expectancy motivational force and centralization and stratification. Thus, schools that were highly centralized and stratified were staffed
with teachers having low forces of expectancy motivation.

In a study of secondary schools teachers, Cecil Miskel, JoAnn DeFrain, and Kay Wilcox (1980) related the force of motivation to job satisfaction and perceived job performance. The force of motivation was significantly related to job satisfaction and perceived performance for both groups. Similarly, Miskel and his colleagues David McDonald and Susan Bloom (1983) found that expectancy motivation of teachers was consistently related to teacher job satisfaction, student attitudes toward school, and perceived school effectiveness. Robert Kottkamp and John A. Mulhern (1987) found that expectancy is positively related to both the openness of school climate and humanism in pupil control ideology. Linda L. Graham (1980) found that expectancy theory predicted the satisfaction, participation in activities, and achievement of college students.

In sum, expectancy theory has generated a large number of investigations in educational as well as business settings. The results are generally supportive. Pinder (1984, 1998) concludes that there are grounds for optimism that the theory is a reasonably valid model of the causes of work behavior. The following conclusions are warranted from the literature:

- Expectancy theory is an excellent predictor of job satisfaction.
- Expectancy theory predicts performance but not as well as it predicts satisfaction.
- Expectancy theory demonstrates that people work hard when they think that working hard is likely to lead to desirable outcomes.

Beliefs about Capabilities: Self-Efficacy Theory

Among all the aspects of self-knowledge and self-regulation, personal efficacy is probably the most influential in everyday life. **Self-efficacy** is *a person's judgment about his or her capability to organize and execute a course of action that is required to attain a certain level of performance* (Bandura, 1986, 1991, 1997). In other words, it is an individual's overall judgment of his or her perceived capacity for performing a task. For example, the belief of a mathematics teacher that he or she can successfully teach calculus to a class of 12th-grade students is an efficacy judgment. Similarly, principals with high self-efficacy might believe that they can have a positive effect on student achievement or they might increase the emphasis on academic learning in schools. Note that, in contrast to causal attributions where the focus is on the past, perceptions of self-efficacy represent future expectations of being able to attain certain levels of performance.

Self-efficacy beliefs contribute to motivation by determining the goals that individuals set for themselves, how much effort they expend, how long they persevere in the face of difficulties, and their resilience to failures (Wood and Bandura, 1989; Bandura, 1993, 2000). The stronger people believe in their capabilities, the greater and more persistent are their efforts. People tend to avoid tasks and situations that exceed their capacity; they seek activities they judge themselves capable of handling. The consequences of high self-efficacy—

willingness to approach and persist on tasks, selection of task and situation, a focus on problem-solving strategies, reduced fear and anxiety, positive emotional experiences—affect achievement outcomes (Stipek, 1993). Hence, people who have the same skills but different levels of personal efficacy may perform at different levels because of the way they use, combine, and sequence their skills in a changing context (Gist and Mitchell, 1992).

Development of Self-Efficacy

Self-efficacy expectations develop from a variety of sources, including performance feedback, previous history, and social influence. However, four primary sources of experience—mastery experiences, modeling, verbal persuasion, and physiological arousal—are postulated for self-efficacy.

Mastery experience is the single most important source of self-efficacy. Performance successes and failures (i.e., actual experiences) in completing tasks have strong effects on self-efficacy. Recurrent successes raise efficacy perceptions; regular failures produce self-doubts and reduce self-efficacy, especially if failure occurs early in a task sequence and does not reflect a lack of effort or opposing external influences. Efficacy is facilitated as gradual accomplishments build skills, coping abilities, and exposure needed for task performance.

Modeling and vicarious experience affect self-perceptions of efficacy through two processes. First, it provides knowledge. Watching an expert complete a task conveys effective strategies for managing similar tasks in different situations. Second, people partly judge their capabilities using social comparisons. Seeing or visualizing people similar to oneself successfully perform a task can raise one's own beliefs about self-efficacy. By observing people modeling certain behaviors, individuals convince themselves that if others can do it, they can at least achieve some improvement in their own performance. Modeling experiences are most influential for individuals in situations in which they have limited personal experience with the task.

Verbal persuasion is widely used to try to talk people into believing that they have the capacity to achieve what they want to accomplish. Social persuasion alone has limited power to create lasting increases in self-efficacy, but it can contribute to successful performance if the heightened appraisal is within realistic bounds. To the extent that verbal persuasion boosts self-efficacy and people try hard to succeed, verbal persuasion can promote the development of skills (Bandura, 1986; Gist, 1987; Wood and Bandura, 1989).

People also rely partly on information from their *physiological* and *affective states* to judge their capability. Individuals make judgments about anticipated performance based on positive arousal such as excitement and enthusiasm and on negative factors such as fear, fatigue, stress, and anxiety. General physical condition, personality factors (Type A), and mood can all induce arousal (Gist, 1987). Hence, another way to modify beliefs of self-efficacy is for individuals to enhance their physical well-being and to reduce their stress (Wood and Bandura, 1989).

Gist and Mitchell (1992) propose that the relationships between the four types of experience and self-efficacy are mediated by analyses of the task situation and causal attributions. On the basis of experience, several situational factors might be considered. An analysis of the situation in terms of task requirements, human resources, and the school organization produces inferences about what it will take to perform successfully. In preparing to teach calculus to twelfth graders, for example, a teacher would determine the mathematical ability and motivational levels of the students; availability of instructional resources such as books, outside tutors, and computer support; and the environmental emphasis on student achievement. An analysis of causal attributions from previous experience in similar situations is likely to affect efficacy judgments. What produced earlier success? In the example of teaching calculus to twelfth graders, the actual experiences of the teacher in previous years, new modeling experiences, persuasion by the principal and colleagues, and his or her physical state will be filtered through the dimensions of locus, stability, and controllability. Gist and Mitchell believe that these analysis processes of the situation and attributions yield summary-level judgments that define self-efficacy.

In the general organization and management literature, empirical studies of self-efficacy have produced consistent results. Self-efficacy is associated with such work-related performance as productivity, coping with difficult tasks, career choice, learning and achievement, and adaptability to new technology (Gist and Mitchell, 1992). Similar results are evident in educational settings. Self-efficacy research in schools tends to focus on one of two areas or approaches. The first group of studies tests for the effects of student and teacher self-efficacy on various motivational and achievement indicators. The general finding is that self-efficacy is positively related to student achievement (Armor et al., 1976), course grades (Pintrich and Garcia, 1991), student motivation (Midgley, Feldlaufer, and Eccles, 1989), teacher adoption of innovations (Berman et al., 1977; Smylie, 1988), superintendents' rating of teachers' competence (Trentham, Silvern, and Brogdon, 1985), and classroom management strategies of teachers (Ashton and Webb, 1986). Moreover, experimental studies have consistently found that changing self-efficacy beliefs can lead to better use of cognitive strategies and higher levels of academic achievement for mathematics, reading, and writing tasks (Schunk, 1991).

To summarize, self-efficacy is an important motivational factor that influences a number of behavioral and performance outcomes. Self-efficacy is learned through a variety of experiences and is dynamic; it can change over time as new information and experiences are acquired. Issues that remain unresolved include the extent to which self-efficacy and performance can be raised and the overall elasticity of self-efficacy (Gist and Mitchell, 1992). Four conclusions are warranted:

- Individuals who have stronger beliefs about their capabilities are more successful and persistent in their efforts.

- Individuals tend to avoid tasks and situations that exceed their capacity.
- Individuals seek activities they judge themselves capable of handling.
- Individuals develop self-efficacy through mastery experiences, modeling, persuasion, and physiological arousal.

Self-Efficacy of Teachers

Over the past 20 years, the construct of teacher efficacy has evolved from J. B. Rotter's (1966) locus of control theory and Albert Bandura's (1977, 1986, 1997) social cognitive theory. The meaning of teacher efficacy, however, has produced considerable debate and some confusion among scholars and researchers (Ashton et al., 1982; Gibson and Dembo, 1984; Guskey, 1987; Guskey and Passaro, 1994; Pajares, 1996, 1997; Tschannen-Moran, Woolfolk Hoy, and Hoy, 1998).

Using the theoretical perspectives of Rotter (1966), researchers at the Rand Corporation studying the effectiveness of reading instruction first viewed teacher efficacy as the extent to which teachers believed that they could control the reinforcement of their actions. Teachers who believed that they could influence student achievement and motivation (internal locus) were more effective than those who thought the external forces could not be overcome. A second, more recent and useful conceptual strand of theory and research has evolved from the work of Bandura (1977). He defined teacher efficacy as a type of self-efficacy—the outcome of a cognitive process in which people construct beliefs about their capacity to perform well. These self-efficacy beliefs affect how much effort people expend, how long they will persist in the face of difficulties, their resilience in dealing with failures, and the stress they experience in coping with demanding situations (Bandura, 1997). The existence of the two separate but intertwined conceptual strands emerging from two theoretical perspectives has contributed some confusion about the nature of teacher efficacy; however, perceived self-efficacy is a much stronger predictor of behavior than locus of control (Bandura, 1997; Tschannen-Moran, Woolfolk Hoy, and Hoy, 1998).

A Model of Perceived Efficacy for Teaching

In response to the conceptual confusion surrounding teacher efficacy and in keeping with the substantial body of research, Megan Tschannen-Moran, Anita Woolfolk Hoy, and Wayne K. Hoy (1998) developed an integrated model of teacher efficacy. **Teacher efficacy** is the *teacher's belief in his or her capability to organize and execute courses of action required to successfully accomplish a specific teaching task in a particular context.* Consistent with social cognitive theory (Bandura, 1986, 1997), the major influences on efficacy beliefs are the attributional analysis and interpretation of the four sources of information about efficacy—mastery experience, vicarious experience (modeling), verbal persuasion, and physiological arousal. All four of these sources are important in the interpretation and cognitive processing of information.

Teacher efficacy is context-specific; teachers do not feel equally efficacious for all teaching situations. Teachers feel efficacious for teaching particular subjects to certain students in specific settings, but often feel more or less efficacious under different circumstances. Even from one class period to another, teachers' levels of efficacy may change (Ross, Cousins, and Gadalla, 1996; Raudenbush, Rowen, and Cheong, 1992). Therefore, in making an efficacy judgment, consideration of the teaching task and its context are required as well as an assessment of one's strengths and weaknesses *in relation* to the requirements of the task at hand.

In analyzing the *teaching task and its context,* the relative importance of factors that make teaching difficult or act as constraints are weighed against an assessment of the resources available that facilitate learning. In assessing *self-perceptions of teaching competence,* the teacher judges personal capabilities such as skills, knowledge, strategies, or personality traits balanced against personal weaknesses or liabilities in this particular teaching context. The interaction of these two components leads to judgments about self-efficacy for the teaching task at hand. The model is summarized in Figure 4.5.

One of the things that makes teacher efficacy so powerful is its cyclical nature. As noted in Figure 4.5, the proficiency of a performance creates a new mastery experience, which provides new information (feedback) that will be processed to shape future efficacy beliefs. Greater efficacy leads to greater effort and persistence, which leads to better performance, which in turn leads to greater efficacy. The reverse is also true. Lower efficacy leads to less effort

FIGURE 4.5 *A Model of Teachers' Perceived Efficacy*

SOURCE: Adapted from Tschannen-Moran, Woolfolk Hoy, and Hoy (1998).

and giving up easily, which leads to poor teaching outcomes, which then produce decreased efficacy. Thus, a teaching performance accomplished with a level of effort and persistence influenced by the performer's sense of efficacy, when completed, becomes a source of future efficacy beliefs. Over time this process stabilizes into a relatively enduring set of efficacy beliefs.

There are both theoretical and practical implications for the teacher-efficacy model. Both self-perception of teaching competence (including an assessment of internal resources and constraints) and beliefs about the task requirements in a particular teaching situation (including an assessment of resources and constraints external to the teacher) contribute to teacher efficacy and to the consequences that stem from efficacy beliefs. Once stabilized, beliefs about both the task of teaching and assessment of personal teaching competence are likely to remain unchanged unless "compelling evidence" intrudes and causes them to be reevaluated (Bandura, 1997). Consequently, helping teachers develop strong efficacy beliefs early in their careers will pay lasting dividends.

During the past two decades, researchers have consistently established strong connections between teacher efficacy and teacher behaviors that foster student achievement (Allinder, 1994; Ashton and Webb, 1986; Gibson ˆ Dembo, 1984; Hoy and Woolfolk, 1990; Hoy and Woolfolk, 1993; T˙ Moran, Woolfolk Hoy, and Hoy, 1998; Woolfolk and Hoy Rosoff, and Hoy, 1990). Teaching success, effort, an˙ the extent to which a teacher believes he or she ˙ and execute teaching that will lead to s˙ tion. Thus, there are two key effi˙

- *Teaching Task* ˙ and can ˙
- *Tea*˙ hav˙

Positive answ˙ for a summary far, see Table 4.2

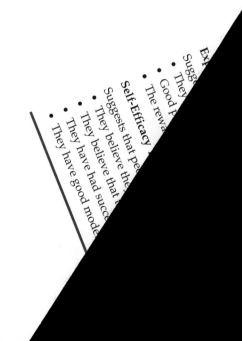

A teacher's strong se˙ ˙ers. Bandura sugg˙ experiences, modeling, ˙ states. Assume you are a ˙ young teacher. Her problem˙ her capability to get kids to˙ teacher's sense of self-efficacy.˙ expect to succeed in working ˙

TABLE 4.2

Summary of How Needs, Goals, and Beliefs Motivate

Needs Theory

Suggests that people work hard when
- Lower-order needs are met—physiological, safety, and belongingness needs.
- Higher-order needs present the challenge—esteem and self-actualization needs.

Motivation-Hygiene Theory

Suggests that
- Unmet lower-level needs produce dissatisfaction with the job.
- Gratified higher-level needs produce job satisfaction.

Goal-Setting Theory

Suggests that people work hard when
- They have realistic, specific, and challenging goals.
- They are committed to the goals.
- They receive feedback about progress toward the goals.

Attribution Theory

Suggests that people work hard when they believe that causes for success are
- Internal—due to ability and effort.
- Not fixed—effort, for example, can vary from one situation to another.
- Controllable—causes can be controlled by hard work, using proper strategy, etc.

Equity Theory

Suggests that people work hard when they have been fairly treated and
- They have been given the rewards they deserve.
- The rewards have been allocated fairly.
- They have been treated with respect and courtesy.

Expectancy Theory

Suggests that people work hard when
- believe extra effort will improve performance.
- performance will be noticed and rewarded.
- rds are valued.

Theory

ple work hard when
- y have the capabilities to be successful.
- he task is not too difficult.
- ss at completing similar tasks.
- ls of success.

INTRINSIC AND EXTRINSIC MOTIVATION

We have seen how needs, beliefs, and goals are important aspects of motivation. **Motivation** is generally defined as an internal state that stimulates, directs, and maintains behavior. Psychologists who study motivation have focused on five basic aspects: choices, initiation, intensity, persistence, and reaction (Graham and Weiner, 1996). We now turn to two important distinctions in examining theories of motivation—intrinsic and extrinsic. We all know what it feels like to be motivated—to energetically tackle a task. We also know how it feels to work hard even though the task is not all that intriguing. What energizes and directs our behavior? Some explanations argue that motivation is personal and internal and relies on needs, interests, curiosity, and enjoyment. Other explanations are linked to external and environmental factors such as incentives, rewards, pressure, punishment, and so on. We are concerned with **work motivation,** "a set of energetic forces that originate both within as well as beyond an individual's being, to initiate work-related behavior, and to determine its form, direction, intensity, and duration" (Pinder, 1984: 8). The challenge for administrators is to develop motivated teachers who are actively engaged in teaching and learning, open to new ideas and approaches, and committed to students and who change over the lifetime of their teaching careers.

Motivation that comes from factors such as interest and curiosity is called **intrinsic motivation** (Woolfolk, 1998, 2004). Intrinsic motivation is the natural tendency to seek and accept challenges as we pursue personal interests and exercise capabilities (Deci and Ryan, 1985; Reeve, 1996). Punishment and rewards are not needed because *the activity itself is rewarding.* Simply put, intrinsic motivation is what stimulates us to do something when we don't have to do anything (Raffini, 1996). **Extrinsic motivation,** in contrast, is based on rewards and punishment. We act to earn a good grade or to get a merit increase or to get promoted or to avoid a grievance. We are not interested in the activity for its own sake, but rather for what the activity will bring us. Extrinsic motivation is a behavioral perspective on motivation because it explains motivation and behavior in terms of rewards and punishment. Extrinsic motivation stimulates us to act with incentives and disincentives.

The key difference between intrinsic and extrinsic motivation is the individual's reason for acting. Is the locus for action internal (intrinsic) or external (extrinsic)? If one freely chooses to act on the basis of personal preferences, the cause is internal and the motivation is intrinsic. The dichotomy between intrinsic and extrinsic is a bit too simple because many actions have traces of both kinds of motivation. For example, what starts out as extrinsic motivation, studying to get a good grade, may become intrinsic when curiosity takes over. Moreover, some individuals may choose to work hard on things that they don't particularly enjoy because they know that the activities are important in achieving a valued goal such as earning a superintendent's certificate. In the latter case, the person has internalized an external cause and the motivation is "in-between," that is, the person has freely chosen to respond to an external cause. Notwithstanding the blending of the two kinds of motivation in some cases (the dichotomy becomes a continuum), the distinction between intrinsic and extrinsic is useful and helps us understand the bases for motivation schemes in schools. Table 4.3 summarizes the variety of elements of motivation that seem critical if teachers and administrators are to be highly motivated in their work.

TABLE 4.3

Summary of Key Elements in Opitimizing Work Motivation

	Optimum Characteristics of Work Motivation	Characteristics That Diminish Strong Work Motivation
Needs	Work satisfies high-level needs Specific	Work satisfies low-level needs General
Type of Goal	Realistic, challenging goals	Very difficult or very easy goals
Attributions	Successes and failures attributed to controllable effort and ability	Successes and failures attributed to uncontrollable causes
Achievement Motivation	Motivation by achievement	Motivation to avoid failure
Type of Involvement	Task-involved: Concerned with mastering the job	Ego-involved: Concerned with self in eyes of others
Beliefs about Equity	Fair and courteous treatment	Unfair and disrespectful treatment
Beliefs about Ability	Incremental view: Belief that ability can be improved with hard work and added knowledge and skills	Stable view: Belief that ability is stable, an inherent trait
Self-Efficacy	High self-efficacy	Low self-efficacy
Source of Motivation	Intrinsic: The nature of the job itself is challenging, interesting, and enjoyable	Extrinsic: Environmental factors such as rewards, social pressures, and punishment

A CASE FOR LEADERSHIP

Reverse the Decline

This is your second year as principal at Samuel Dewitt Proctor Elementary School, an inner-city school (K–5) with 25 teachers—6 men and 19 women. The school is a diverse one with a student body that is about 60 percent African American, 15 percent Hispanic, and about 25 percent white. Each year the white population shrinks as more Hispanic students come into the school. The composition of the teaching staff is also shifting to a younger faculty; in fact, only eight of the teachers are over 55. That is not to say that this faculty is inexperienced. Most of the teachers have at least five years of teaching experience.

You have spent your first year hiring new teachers and building rapport with your current faculty and staff. You have been successful hiring four new teachers, all of whom are young, enthusiastic, and talented. Your assistant principal, Nikke Jabar, is your right arm; she takes care of discipline, parent conferences, and professional development and she does it well. You make a great team.

Teaching at Proctor Elementary is not easy. Too many students come from single-parent homes and poverty is a problem. Student absenteeism is high and parent participation in school activities is low. Many students just do not want to be at school; they would rather be watching TV or playing video games or just hanging out. Once the students are in school, it also is a challenge to motivate them. The school has an early morning breakfast program for students who arrive a half hour before the start of school, but only about 30 students show up for their "free breakfast" each day.

Most teachers at Proctor Elementary are committed to teaching. Some would argue that they work too hard because the work is taking its toll. Five of the "old timers" are burned out. Although not at retirement age, they talk about retiring nearly every day. They find it difficult to get ready for another day of "teaching and losing" as they put it. A few even complain of trouble getting up each morning and getting ready for school; it is pure drudgery. You are sympathetic with these teachers, but you are concerned that their attitude not spread to the younger teachers. All in all, your teachers get along together quite well, and there is a growing feeling that they are doing the best they can for their students in spite of the fact that achievement levels are not high.

You neither believe nor accept the conclusion that the school is doing as well as it can. Yesterday the state proficiency test results were released and the fourth-grade proficiency test scores at Proctor were down for the fourth straight year. Only 33 percent of the students are performing at an acceptable level compared to 35 percent the year before. The decline has been slow but steady. There is increasing pressure from the state, from the central office, and from the community to do better, and you and Nikke both believe that the school can and will do better. You do not need to attend the districtwide meeting of administrators to be held next week to know that the challenge is to reverse the decline in scores. How can you motivate, support, and encourage your four new teachers? How do you deal with your burned-out teachers? How can you breathe new life into your free breakfast program? You need a plan to motivate your teachers and students. Consider the following possibilities:

- Develop a plan to increase teacher efficacy in your school. Who should be involved? How would you use the four sources of efficacy to develop a plan?
- Can you use goal-setting theory to motivate your teachers and students? What reasonable goals can be set? Who should set them and how should they be set? What support can you supply to help your teachers achieve these goals?
- Develop a plan to deal with your burned-out teachers. How can you change their work environment to make it more interesting? Are extrinsic rewards a good idea?
- What are the students' and teachers' need for safety, security, social interaction, and

(Continued)

A CASE FOR LEADERSHIP *(Concluded)*

self-esteem? How can you answer these questions and take action to improve things?
- Is there any way to analyze the test results so they are informational rather than punitive? Can you use the testing results to target strategies for dealing with weaknesses and developing interventions?

With your assistant principal develop a realistic plan to motivate students and teachers at Proctor Elementary. Don't try to do everything at once. Pick one or two theories of motivation from this chapter and explain how you would apply and implement them in the next three months. Consider which theories are most useful in this case and why.

SUMMARY AND SUGGESTED READINGS

The individual is a key element of all social systems. Students, teachers, and administrators bring with them individual needs, goals, and beliefs and develop their own personal orientations and intellectual understanding of their roles. Just as structure helps shape behavior in schools so too do the needs, goals, and beliefs of individuals. Maslow describes a hierarchy of basic needs that motivate behavior ranging from biological to self-actualization needs, and Herzberg distinguishes between needs that produce worker satisfaction and those that cause dissatisfaction. The need for achievement and the need for autonomy are two other powerful motivating forces within individuals.

Individual goals and goal setting are also key ingredients of personal motivation, especially when the goals are embraced by the individual and are specific, challenging, and attainable. Similarly, beliefs are important motivational forces. Administrators, teachers, and students are likely to work hard if they believe that success is primarily due to their ability and effort, that causes of outcomes are under their control, that extra effort will improve performance, that good performance will be noticed and rewarded, that the rewards are valued, and that they have been treated fairly and with respect by their superiors. Moreover, effective performance is closely related to self-efficacy, the belief that one has the capability to organize and execute a course of action that is required to attain the desired level of performance. Motivation that comes from the interest and challenge of the activity itself is intrinsic, whereas extrinsic motivation is based on rewards and punishment. Although both can motivate, intrinsic motivation is typically more effective.

A classic work on motivation is Maslow's (1970) *Motivation and Personality*. For a more contemporary analysis of theory and research on motivation, see Kanfer's (1990) thorough and integrative review and critique. Also see Locke's latest edited book of readings on motivation and organizational behavior (Locke, 2000). The collection of readings by Steers and Porter (1991) is also instructive and provides a wide range of competing models. Finally, two books are must readings for all students of motivation: Locke and Latham's *A Theory of Goal Setting and Task Performance* (1990) and Bandura's *Self-Efficacy: The Exercise of Control* (1997). Locke and Latham provide the details of goal-setting theory as well as an extensive review of the literature. Bandura's book is a tour de force that summarizes two decades of research and theory on self-efficacy. Arguably, goal-setting theory and self-efficacy theory are the most important contemporary approaches to motivation. Check the *Journal of Applied Psychology* and the *Academy of Management Review*, which frequently publish articles on work motivation.

KEY ASSUMPTIONS AND PRINCIPLES

1. Individuals work hard when their lower-level needs of safety and security are met while higher-level needs are challenged by the task.
2. If individuals have the requisite knowledge and skills to perform a task, then their embrace of specific, challenging, and attainable goals produces success.
3. Difficult goals, if accepted, produce higher levels of performance than easy goals.
4. Individuals work hard when they believe that causes for success are under their control.
5. Procedural justice enhances the acceptance of organizational outcomes.
6. Individuals are highly motivated when they believe extra effort will be rewarded by outcomes that they desire.
7. Self-efficacy beliefs determine what goal challenges to undertake, how much effort to exert, and how long to persist; thus, a strong sense of capability to perform a task promotes success.
8. Motivation to avoid failure is usually counterproductive to success, whereas motivation to achieve is powerful impetus to success.
9. Anxiety improves performance on simple tasks, but hinders performance on complex tasks.
10. People will work hard to solve problems that have personal meaning, that is, problems that are intriguing, challenging, and enjoyable.

NOTES

1. According to Campbell, Dunnette, Lawler, and Weick (1970), McClelland sought to refine and investigate a subset of motives from a longer list developed by H. A. Murray. Three motives received the most attention—need for achievement, need for power, and need for affiliation. Achievement motivation has received the most attention and was formalized into a theory of expectancy achievement motivation. For present purposes, we limit our discussion to the value portion of the theory.

2. Studies providing support include Oldham and Miller (1979); Orpen (1979); Bhagat and Chassie (1980); Kiggundu (1980); Johns, Xie, and Fang (1992). Investigations providing partial support include Evans, Kiggundu, and House (1979) and Griffeth (1985); ones showing little or no support include Arnold and House (1980); Adler, Skov, and Salvemini (1985); and Tiegs, Tetrick, and Fried (1992).

3. See, for example, Gorsuch (1977), Pastor and Erlandson (1982), Mennuti and Kottkamp (1986), and Barnabe and Burns (1994).

CULTURE AND CLIMATE IN SCHOOLS

The behavior of a group cannot be predicted solely from an understanding of the personality of each of its members. Various social processes intervene . . . the group develops a "mood," an "atmosphere." In the context of the organization, we talk about a "style," a "culture," a "character."

Henry Mintzberg
Power In and Around Organizations

PREVIEW

1. Organizational culture and organizational climate are two contemporary perspectives for examining the distinctive character of schools; they are partly competing, partly complementary.

2. Organizational culture is manifested in norms, shared values, and basic assumptions, each occurring at a different level of abstraction.

3. Strong organizational cultures can improve or hinder the effectiveness of an organization; different cultures are effective depending on environmental constraints.

4. School cultures can be interpreted by analyzing their symbols, artifacts, rites, ceremonies, icons, heroes, myths, rituals, and legends.

5. Often the most important thing about events in organizations is not what happened but what the events mean.

6. Schools have distinctive cultures of efficacy, trust, and control.

7. School cultures of efficacy and trust promote student achievement, whereas a culture of humanistic control supports the socioemotional development of students.

8. Organizational climate is a relatively enduring quality of a school that is manifested in teachers' collective perceptions of organizational behavior.

9. The climate of schools can be viewed from a variety of vantage points; two useful perspectives are the openness of behavior and the health of interpersonal relations.

10. Each of these climate perspectives can be reliably measured using the appropriate survey instrument.

11. The openness and health of a school are related to a number of important organizational outcomes including perceptions of school effectiveness and student achievement.

12. There is no quick and simple way to change the culture or climate of schools, but long-term planning is more likely to produce change than will short-term fads.

13. Three complementary strategies for organizational change are a clinical view, a growth-centered approach, and a norm-changing plan.

Behavior in organizations is not simply a function of formal expectations and individual needs and motivation. The relationships among these elements are dynamic. Participants bring to the workplace a host of unique values, needs, goals, and beliefs. These individual characteristics mediate the rational aspects of organizational life. Moreover, a collective sense of identity emerges that transforms a simple aggregate of individuals into a distinctive workplace "personality."

This indigenous feel of the workplace has been analyzed and studied under a variety of labels, including "organizational character," "milieu," "atmosphere," "ideology," "climate," "culture," "emergent system," and "informal organization." Our analysis of the internal workplace environment will focus on two related concepts—organizational culture and organizational climate. Each of these notions suggests a natural, spontaneous, and human side to the organization; each suggests that the organizational whole is greater than the sum of its parts; and each attempts to uncover the shared meanings and unwritten rules that guide organizational behavior.[1]

ORGANIZATIONAL CULTURE

Concern for the culture of the work group is not new. As we have seen, in the 1930s and 1940s, both Elton Mayo (1945) and Chester Barnard (1938) were stressing the importance of work-group norms, sentiments, values, and emergent interactions in the workplace as they described the nature and functions of informal organization. Philip Selznick (1957) extended the analysis of organizational life by viewing organizations as institutions rather than merely rational organizations. Institutions, according to Selznick (1957: 14), are "infused with value beyond the technical requirements at hand." This infusion of value produces a *distinctive identity* for the organization; it defines organizational character. Selznick (1957) continues:

> Whenever individuals become attached to an organization or a way of doing things as persons rather than technicians, the result is apprising of the device for its own sake. From the standpoint of the committed person, the organization is changed from an expendable tool into a valued source of personal satisfaction. Where institutionalization is well advanced, distinctive outlooks, habits, and other commitments are unified, coloring all aspects of organizational life and lending it a social integration that goes well beyond formal co-ordination and command. (p. 14)

Indeed, it is Selznick's formulation of organizations as institutions, each with distinctive competence and organizational character, that provides a basis for contemporary analyses of organizations as cultures (Peters and Waterman, 1982).

Organizational culture is an attempt to get at the feel, sense, atmosphere, character, or image of an organization. It encompasses many of the earlier notions of informal organization, norms, values, ideologies, and emergent systems. The popularity of the term "organizational culture" is in part a function of a number of popular books on successful business corporations that emerged in the 1980s (Peters and Waterman, 1982; Deal and Kennedy, 1982; Ouchi, 1981). The basic theme of all these analyses was that effective organizations have strong and distinctive corporate cultures and that a basic function of executive leadership is to shape the culture of the organization.

Definition of Organizational Culture

The notion of culture brings with it conceptual complexity and confusion. No intact definition for culture from anthropology exists; instead, we find numerous, diverse definitions. It should not be surprising, therefore, that there are many definitions of organizational culture. Consider the following:

- William Ouchi (1981: 41) defines organizational culture as "symbols, ceremonies, and myths that communicate the underlying values and beliefs of that organization to its employees."
- Henry Mintzberg (1989: 98) refers to culture as organization ideology, or "the traditions and beliefs of an organization that distinguish it from other organizations and infuse a certain life into the skeleton of its structure."
- Stephen Robbins (1998: 595) defines organizational culture as "a system of shared meaning held by members that distinguishes the organization from other organizations."
- Edgar Schein (1992, 1999), however, argues that the culture should be reserved for a "deeper level of basic assumptions, values, and beliefs" that become shared and taken for granted as the organization continues to be successful.

Our general definition of **organizational culture** is *a system of shared orientations that hold the unit together and give it a distinctive identity.* But substantial disagreement arises about what is shared—norms, values, philosophies, perspectives, beliefs, expectations, attitudes, myths, or ceremonies. Another problem is determining the intensity of shared orientations of organizational members. Do organizations have a basic culture or many cultures? Moreover, there is disagreement on the extent to which organizational culture is conscious and overt or unconscious and covert.

Levels of Organizational Culture

One way to begin to untangle some of the problems of definition is to view culture at different levels. As illustrated in Figure 5.1, culture is manifested in norms, shared values, and basic assumptions, each occurring at different levels of depth and abstraction.

Culture as Shared Norms

A fairly concrete, some would say superficial, perspective on culture emerges when behavioral norms are used as the basic elements of culture (see Figure 5.1). **Norms** are usually unwritten and informal expectations that occur just below the surface of experience. Norms directly influence behavior. They are much more visible than either values or tacit assumptions; consequently, they provide a clear means for helping people understand the cultural aspects of organizational life. Moreover, if we are concerned with changing organizational behavior, then it is important to know and understand the norms of that culture. As Allen and Kraft (1982) cogently note:

> Norms are universal phenomena. They are necessary, tenacious, but also extremely malleable. Because they can change so quickly and easily, they present a tremendous opportunity to people interested in change. Any

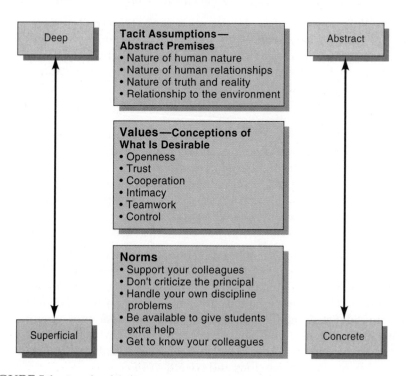

FIGURE 5.1   *Levels of Culture*

group, no matter its size, once it understands itself as a cultural entity, can plan its own norms, creating positive ones that will help it reach its goals and modifying or discarding the negative ones. (pp. 7–8)

Norms are also communicated to participants by stories and ceremonies that provide visible and potent examples of what the organization stands for. Sometimes stories about people are created to reinforce the basic norms of the organization. The principal who stood by the teacher despite overwhelming pressure from parents and superiors becomes a symbol of the cohesiveness and loyalty in a school's culture; it is a story that is retold many times to new teachers. Teachers quickly learn the norms, "don't tell tales out of school," "support your colleagues," and "support your principal." Norms determine the way people dress and talk; the way participants respond to authority, conflict, and pressure; and the way people balance self-interests with organizational interests. Examples of norms include the following: don't rock the boat; don't criticize fellow teachers to students or parents; all men wear neckties; handle your own discipline problems; don't let students out of class before the bell rings; and change the bulletin boards frequently. As noted in Chapter 1, norms are enforced by sanctions; people are rewarded and encouraged when they conform to norms and are confronted, ostracized, or punished when they violate the cultural norms of the group. In brief, the norms of the work group define a major slice of the culture of the organization.

Culture as Shared Beliefs and Values

At a middle level of abstraction, culture is defined as shared beliefs and values. **Values** are beliefs of what is desirable. They are reflections of the underlying assumptions of culture, and lie at the next level of analysis. Values often define what members should do to be successful in the organization. When we ask people to explain why they behave the way they do, we may begin to discover the central values of the organization. Shared values define the basic character of the organization and give the organization a sense of identity. If members know what their organization stands for, if they know what standards they should uphold, they are more likely to make decisions that will support those standards. They are also more likely to feel part of the organization and that organizational life has important meaning.

William Ouchi's (1981) book on the success of Japanese corporations was one of the first contemporary analyses of corporate culture. Ouchi argued that the success of effective corporations in both Japan and America was a function of a distinctive corporate culture, one that was internally consistent and characterized by the shared values of intimacy, trust, cooperation, teamwork, and egalitarianism. Success of these organizations was not as much a matter of technology as it was of managing people. He labeled the American organizations with these values Theory Z cultures.

Theory Z organizations have a number of properties that promote this distinctive culture (see Table 5.1). Long-term employment opportunities create

TABLE 5.1

Theory Z Organization and Culture

Organizational Characteristic	Core Value
1. Long-term employment ⟶	Organizational commitment
2. Slower promotion rates ⟶	Career orientation
3. Participative decision making ⟶	Cooperation and teamwork
4. Individiual responsibility for group decisions ⟶	Trust and group loyalty
5. Holistic orientation ⟶	Egalitarianism

in employees a sense of security and commitment to the organization; participants become invested in the organization. The process of slower rates of promotion creates more opportunities to broaden experiences and diverse career paths as employees perform different functions and occupy different roles. This effectively produces company-specific skills and promotes career development. Participative and consensual decision making demands cooperation and teamwork, values that are openly communicated and reinforced. Individual responsibility for collective decision making demands an atmosphere of trust and mutual support. Finally, concern for the total person is a natural part of the working relationship, which tends to be informal and emphasizes the whole person and not just the individual's work role. This holistic perspective promotes a strong egalitarian atmosphere, a community of equals who work cooperatively on common goals rather than relying on the formal hierarchy. Thus Theory Z organizations are structured and operate to promote the basic values of intimacy, trust, cooperation, and egalitarianism. These **core values** of the culture are the dominant values that most of the organizational members accept and share; they influence virtually every aspect of organizational life.

Other studies (Deal and Kennedy, 1982; Peters and Waterman, 1982) of successful corporations also suggest the pivotal importance of strong organizational cultures in fostering effectiveness. Deal and Kennedy (1982) suggest that successful organizations share some common cultural characteristics. They argue that such organizations have

- A widely shared organizational philosophy.
- Concern for individuals that is more important than formal rules and policies.
- Rituals and ceremonies that build a common identity.
- A well-understood sense of the informal rules and exceptions.
- A belief that what employees do is important to others.

Therefore, sharing information and ideas is encouraged.

In **strong cultures,** beliefs and values are held intensely, shared widely, and guide organizational behavior. It might be tempting to jump to the conclusion that a specific set of values defines excellence in organizations, but that would be unjustified. What promotes excellence yesterday does not necessarily promote it today or tomorrow (Aupperle, Acar, and Booth, 1986; Hitt and Ireland, 1987). In fact, a strong culture can be a liability in times of rapid change because the organization's culture may be so ingrained that it prevents adaptation to new constraints. Hanson (2003) observes that in many ways the link between culture and effectiveness is the same as that between structure and effectiveness. Both culture and structure can undermine outcomes by either stagnating or disrupting the system through rigidities, conflicts, and hidden agendas.

Culture as Tacit Assumptions

At its deepest level, culture is the collective manifestation of tacit assumptions. When members of an organization share a view of the world around them and their place in that world, culture exists. That is, a pattern of basic assumptions has been invented, discovered, or developed by the organization as it learned to cope with its problems of external adaptation and internal integration. This pattern has worked well enough to be considered valid and it is taught to new members as the correct way to perceive, think, and feel in relation to those problems. Because the assumptions have worked repeatedly, they have become so basic that they are taken for granted, tend to be nonconfrontable and nondebatable, and thus are highly resistant to change. From this perspective, the key to understanding organizational culture is to decipher the tacit assumptions members share and to discover how these assumptions fit together into a cultural pattern or paradigm.

Tacit assumptions are abstract premises about the nature of human relationships, human nature, truth, reality, and environment (Dyer, 1985). For example, is human nature basically good, evil, or neutral? How is truth ultimately determined—is it revealed or discovered? What are the assumed relationships among members of the group—primarily hierarchical, cooperative, or individualistic? When organizations develop consistent and articulate patterns of basic assumptions, they have strong cultures.

Consider two strong, but contrasting school cultures. The first school has a strong, distinctive culture based on the following assumptions as suggested by Schein (1985):

- Truth ultimately comes from teachers themselves.
- Teachers are responsible, motivated, and capable of governing themselves and making decisions in the best interests of their students.
- Truth is determined through debate, which often produces conflict and testing of ideas in an open forum.
- Teachers are a family; they accept, respect, and take care of each other.

These core assumptions give rise to such shared values as individualism, autonomy, openness, professionalism, and authority of knowledge.

In contrast, a second school is guided by the following assumptions:

- Truth ultimately comes from experienced teachers and administrators.
- Most teachers are committed and loyal to the school. (They are good "soldiers.")
- Relationships in the school are basically hierarchical.
- Yet, teachers respect and honor each other's autonomy in the classrooms.
- Teachers are family who take care of each other.

In this school the core assumptions produce such values as respect for authority, respect for territory, and conflict avoidance.

There is no simple way to uncover the basic patterns of assumptions that underlie what people value and do. Schein (1992, 1999) develops an elaborate set of procedures to decipher the culture of an organization. It is an approach that combines anthropological and clinical techniques and involves a series of encounters and joint explorations between the investigator and various motivated informants who live in the organization and embody its culture. Joint effort usually involves extensive data-gathering activities that explore the history of the organization, critical events, organizational structure, myths, legends, stories, and ceremonies. Schein (1992, 1999) eschews questionnaires as devices to identify tacit assumptions; at best, he argues, such instruments produce only some of the espoused values of group members. But increasingly researchers (O'Reilly, Chatman, and Caldwell, 1991; Chatman and Jehn, 1994; Cameron and Quinn, 1999) are using quantitative instruments to assess the shared values of culture.

Functions of Culture

Although there may be no one best culture, strong cultures promote cohesiveness, loyalty, and commitment, which in turn reduce the propensity for members to leave the organization (Mowday, Porter, and Steers, 1982). Moreover, Robbins (1991) summarizes a number of important functions performed by the organization's culture:

- Culture has a boundary-defining function; it creates distinctions among organizations.
- Culture provides the organization with a sense of identity.
- Culture facilitates the development of commitment to the group.
- Culture enhances stability in the social system.
- Culture is the social glue that binds the organization together; it provides the appropriate standards for behavior.

Culture serves to guide and shape the attitudes and behavior of organizational members. It is important to remember, however, that a strong culture can be either functional or dysfunctional—that is, it can promote or impede effectiveness.

Common Elements of Culture

At the core on any organizational culture is a set of shared values. A number of studies (O'Reilly, Chatman, and Caldwell, 1991; Chatman and Jehn, 1994) of business corporations suggest that there are seven primary elements that shape the culture of most organizations:

1. *Innovation:* the degree to which employees are expected to be creative and take risks.
2. *Stability:* the degree to which activities focus on the status quo rather than change.
3. *Attention to detail:* the degree to which there is concern for precision and detail.
4. *Outcome orientation:* the degree to which management emphasizes results.
5. *People orientation:* the degree to which management decisions are sensitive to individuals.
6. *Team orientation:* the degree of emphasis on collaboration and teamwork.
7. *Aggressiveness:* the degree to which employees are expected to be competitive rather than easygoing.

The culture of most organizations can be mapped by using these elements to describe the values that are dominant. Schein (1999), however, provides three cautions. First, cultures are deep, not superficial; thus if you assume that you can manipulate it, you are likely to fail. Second, culture is broad because it is formed by beliefs and assumptions about daily life in organizations; hence, deciphering culture is a major challenge that should be focused if it is to be successful. Third, culture is stable because it provides meaning and makes life predictable; consequently, changing it is difficult at best.

School Culture

Although organizational culture has become a fashionable construct for analysis in education, much of the recent discussion about school culture remains analytical, philosophical, and rhetorical rather than empirical (see Cusick, 1987; Marion, 2002). It is not difficult, for example, to use the research results on corporate cultures (Ouchi, 1981; Deal and Kennedy, 1982; Peters and Waterman, 1982) and the effective schools research (Brookover et al., 1978; Rutter et al., 1979; Clark, Lotto, and Astuto, 1984) to develop an ideal description of an effective school culture. For instance, Terrence Deal (1985) proposes that effective schools have strong cultures with the following characteristics:

1. Shared values and a consensus on "how we get things done around here."
2. The principal as a hero or heroine who embodies core values.

3. Distinctive rituals that embody widely shared beliefs.
4. Employees as situational heroes or heroines.
5. Rituals of acculturation and cultural renewal.
6. Significant rituals to celebrate and transform core values.
7. Balance between innovation and tradition and between autonomy and control.
8. Widespread participation in cultural rituals.

What are the core values that transform a school into an effective institution? Schools are for students; experiment with your teaching; teaching and learning are cooperative processes; stay close to your students; strive for academic excellence; demand high, but realistic performance; be open in behavior and communication; trust your colleagues; and be professional. Are these core values or empty slogans? If these beliefs are strongly shared and widely enacted, then these sloganlike themes can define a strong school culture. Unfortunately, there is little systematic research that directly examines the institutional cultures of effective schools.

Anthropological and sociological studies of school cultures are needed. The thick descriptions of qualitative studies are necessary to map the basic assumptions and common values of the cultures of schools. Educational researchers must consider the school as a whole and analyze how its practices, beliefs, and other cultural elements relate to the social structure as well as give meaning to social life. To understand culture one must be immersed in the complex clustering of symbols people use to give meaning to their world. In this vein, Geertz (1973) asserts:

> Believing with Max Weber that man is an animal suspended in webs of significance he himself has spun, I take culture to be those webs, and the analysis of it to be therefore not an experimental science in search of law but an interpretive one in search of meaning. It is explication I am after, construing social expressions on their surface enigmatical. (p. 5)

William Firestone and Bruce Wilson (1985) provide a useful framework for beginning to study the organizational cultures of schools. They suggest that the analysis of school culture can be addressed by studying its content, the expressions of culture, and primary communication patterns.

The symbols through which culture is expressed often help identify important cultural themes. Three symbol systems communicate the contents of a school's culture: stories, icons, and rituals.

- **Stories** are narratives that are based on true events, but they often combine truth and fiction.
- **Myths** are stories that communicate an unquestioned belief that cannot be demonstrated by the facts.
- **Legends** are stories that are retold and elaborated with fictional details.

For example, the principal who stood by her teachers despite overwhelming pressure from parents and superiors becomes a symbol of the cohesiveness and loyalty in the school's culture. It is a story that is retold many times to new teachers, one that takes on special meaning as it is interpreted and embellished. Stories are often about organizational heroes or heroines who epitomize the organization; they provide insight into the core values of the organization. Icons and rituals are also important.

- **Icons** are physical artifacts that are used to communicate culture (logos, mottoes, and trophies).
- **Rituals** are the routine ceremonies and rites that signal what is important in the organization.

Janice Beyer and Harrison Trice (1987) identify rites of passage, degradation, enhancement, and integration as examples of routine ceremonies used to develop and sustain organizational culture. Table 5.2 contains some school examples of these four rites and their likely consequences. Much of the culture of a school can be constructed from artifacts, rites, rituals, and ceremonies related to assemblies, faculty meetings, athletic contests, community activities, cafeteria, report cards, awards and trophies, lesson plans, and the general decor of the school.

An examination of the informal communication system is also important in the cultural analysis of a school. The communication system is a cultural network itself (Bantz, 1993; Mohan, 1993). As Deal and Kennedy (1982) have observed, storytellers, spies, priests, cabals, and whisperers form a hidden hierarchy of power within the school that communicates the basic values

TABLE 5.2

Examples of School Rites, Ceremonies, and Consequences

Type	Examples	Possible Consequences
Rites of Passage	Student teaching Tough class for neophytes Lunch duty Retirement	Facilitate transition to new role; socialization
Rites of Degradation	Negative evaluation Public rebuke	Reduce power; reaffirm appropriate behavior

Rites of Enhancement	Assembly recognition:
	  Teacher of the year
	  Debate team champions
	  Football champions
		Enhance power; reinforce appropriate behavior

Rites of Integration	Holiday party Coffee group Teacher's lounge	Encourage common experiences that bind the group together

of the organization. **Mythmakers** are storytellers who are so effective in informal communication that they create organizational myths. The identification of not only the myths, but also the process of their creation, are important to a full understanding of culture.

Studies of organizational culture often try to capture the essence of culture by using metaphors. For example, consider the use of the following metaphors to describe school cultures:

- *The academy:* The school is a place where learning is dominant and the principal is a master teacher and learner.
- *The prison:* The school is a custodial institution for students in need of control and discipline and the principal is the warden.
- *The club:* The school is a social club where everyone has a good time and the principal is the social director.
- *The community:* The school is a nurturing environment where people learn from and support each other and the principal is the community leader.
- *The factory:* The school is an assembly line producing finely tuned student-machines and the principal is the foreman.

Similarly, Deal and Wise (1983) use the metaphors of factories, jungles, and temples to describe schools with principals as CEOs, lion tamers, and gurus.

Research on School Culture

Good contemporary research on school culture is sparse, a conclusion confirmed by Firestone and Louis (1999) in their review of the literature on school culture. Although there have been numerous analyses of corporate cultures and extrapolations of those findings to public schools, few educational researchers have tested those findings directly in schools. Several important theoretical and practical issues must be addressed in the study of school culture. We have suggested that the conceptual frameworks developed by Firestone and Wilson (1985) and Deal (1985) are useful in the analysis of school cultures. Bates (1987), however, argues that such formulations treat organizational culture as synonymous with managerial culture and are much too narrow to capture the essence of culture. This observation leads to a more general issue of whether most schools have a culture or a variety of subcultures. To expect schools to bear unique and unitary cultures may be more hope than fact, but the issue is ultimately an empirical one.

Whether culture can or should be intentionally managed will be hotly contested. Much of the early literature on school cultures is directed toward change and school improvement and assumes that understanding culture is a prerequisite to making schools more effective (Deal, 1985; Metz, 1986; Rossman, Corbett, and Firestone, 1988; Deal and Peterson, 1990). The success of cultural change and its influence on effectiveness are worthy topics for inquiry. One argument suggests that the level and number of cultures in the organization influence the process of changing culture. A change of norms, for example, is more likely than a change in shared values or tacit assumptions. Others contend that any change is difficult and fraught with ethical dilemmas. For example, Schein (1985) strongly argues that a large part of an organization's culture represents the ways its members have learned to cope with anxiety; therefore, attempts to change culture can be tantamount to asking people to surrender their social defenses. To Schein, the issue of cultural change becomes an ethical question. In a somewhat similar vein, Bates (1987) maintains that advocates of strong organizational cultures are conducting cultural analyses on behalf of managers. What is good for management is not necessarily good for the workers (Hoy, 1990).

The analysis of schools in terms of culture calls attention to the symbolic nature of social interactions in schools (Bolman and Deal, 1997, 2003; Cunningham and Gresso, 1993). In fact, Lee Bolman and Terrence Deal (2003) refer to the culture perspective as the "symbolic frame" for viewing organizations. They argue that the frame is based on the following unconventional assumptions about the nature of organizations and behavior:

- What is most important about events in organizations is *not* what happened, but *what they mean.* Meaning is often more important than fact.
- Events and meanings, however, are often unclear because events have different meanings for different people. Individuals use different schemas to interpret their experiences. Meaning is elusive and sometimes not shared.
- Because events are typically ambiguous or uncertain, it is difficult to know what happened, why it happened, and what will happen next. Explanation is difficult.
- The greater the ambiguity and uncertainty in events, the more difficult it is to use rational approaches in organizational analysis. Rationality clearly has limits.
- Confronted with ambiguity and uncertainty, people create symbols and stories to resolve confusion and provide understanding. Stories create clarity.
- Thus, for many organizational events, importance rests with what they express rather than what is produced; secular myths, rituals, ceremonies, and sagas give people the meanings they seek.

One conclusion from the literature on organizational culture is clear: much of what occurs in schools must be interpreted in the context of the school's culture; often what is said or done is not nearly as important as its symbolic significance.

We finish our analysis of culture by examining three kinds of school culture. Each culture describes the shared beliefs of teachers in the school. Schools with strong cultures of efficacy and trust provide higher levels of student achievement whereas schools with custodial cultures impede the socioemotional development of students.

A Culture of Efficacy

The shared beliefs of capacity and ability of teachers and administrators are an important part of the culture of a school. **Collective teacher efficacy** is the *shared perception of teachers in a school that the efforts of the faculty as a whole will have a positive effect on students.* According to Bandura (1993, 1997), collective teacher efficacy is an important school property from an organizational perspective because it helps explain the differential effect that schools have on student achievement. At the collective level, a culture of efficacy is a set of beliefs or social perceptions that are strengthened rather than depleted through their use and that give the school a distinctive identity.

Sources of Collective Efficacy   Organizations, like individuals, learn (Cohen and Sproull, 1996); in fact, organizations use processes akin to learning in individuals (Cook and Yanon, 1996). Schools act purposefully in pursuit of their educational goals. For example, one school may be working to raise student achievement scores, whereas another works to increase the rate and quality of parental involvement. Organizational functioning depends on the knowledge, vicarious learning, self-reflection, and self-regulation of individual members. For example, a school that responds to declining achievement scores by implementing a curricular reform that was effective in a neighboring district is engaged in a self-regulatory process that is informed by the vicarious learning of its members. Such examples demonstrate the importance of vicarious learning and self-regulation at the organizational level, although we must recognize that it is through individuals that organizations act. As we have seen, the four primary sources of self-efficacy information are mastery experience, vicarious experience, social persuasion, and emotional arousal. Just as these sources are critical for individuals, they are also fundamental in the development of collective teaching efficacy.

Mastery experiences are important for organizations. Teachers as a group experience successes and failures. Successes build strong beliefs in a faculty's sense of collective efficacy; failures undermine it. If success, however, is frequent and too easy, failure is likely to produce discouragement. A resilient sense of collective efficacy requires experience in overcoming difficulties through persistent effort. Indeed, organizations learn by experience and thus are likely to succeed in attaining their goals (Huber, 1996; Levitt and March, 1996).

Direct experience is not the only source of information for teachers about their collective efficacy. Teachers also listen to stories about the accomplishments of their colleagues as well as success stories of other schools. Similarly, the effective schools research describes the characteristics of exemplary schools. So just as *vicarious experience* and *modeling* serve as effective sources of personal teacher efficacy, they also promote collective teacher efficacy. Organizations learn by observing other organizations (Huber, 1996).

Verbal persuasion is another means of strengthening a faculty's conviction that they have the capabilities to achieve what they seek. Teachers can be changed by talks, workshops, professional development activities, and feedback about achievement. In fact, the more cohesive the faculty, the more likely the group as a whole can be persuaded by sound argument. Verbal persuasion alone, however, is not likely to be a powerful change agent, but coupled with models of success and positive direct experience, it can influence the collective efficacy. Persuasion can promote extra effort and persistence, both of which can lead to the solution of problems.

Organizations have *affective states.* Just as individuals react to stress, so do organizations. Efficacious organizations tolerate pressure and crises and continue to function effectively; in fact, they learn how to adapt and cope with disruptive forces. Less efficacious organizations react in dysfunctional ways when confronted by such problems, which often reinforces their basic dispositions toward failure. They misinterpret stimuli—sometimes overreacting and other times underreacting or not reacting at all. The affective state of an organization has much to do with how it interprets challenges.

Formation of Collective Efficacy   Although all four of these sources of information are pivotal in the creation of collective efficacy, processing and interpreting the information is critical. Teachers assess what they will require as they engage in teaching; we call this process the analysis of the teaching task. Such analysis occurs at two levels—the individual and the school. At the school level, the analysis produces inferences about the challenges of teaching in that school, that is, what it would take for the school to be successful. Considerations include the abilities and motivations of students, availability of instructional materials, community constraints, the quality of physical facilities of the school, as well as a general optimism about the capability of the school to deal with negative situations in the students' homes as well as in the school. Teachers analyze the means needed to make the school successful, the barriers or limitations to be overcome, and the resources that are available. Then teachers evaluate the teaching task in conjunction with their assessment of the teaching competency of the faculty; in fact, teachers make explicit judgments of the teaching competence of their colleagues in light of the teaching tasks in their specific school. At the school level, the analysis of teaching competence leads to inferences about the faculty's teaching skills, methods, training, and expertise. Judgments of teaching competence might include faculty beliefs in the ability of all children in their school to succeed. Because the analyses of task and competence occur simultaneously, it is difficult to separate these two domains of collective teaching efficacy. They interact with each other as collective teacher efficacy emerges.

In sum, the major influences on collective teacher efficacy are assumed to be the analysis and interpretation of the four sources of information—mastery experience, vicarious experience, social persuasion, and emotional state. In these processes, the organization focuses its attention on two related domains:

the teaching task and teaching competence. Both domains are assessed in terms of whether the organization has the capacities to succeed in teaching students. The interactions of these assessments shapes collective teacher efficacy in a school. The consequences of high collective teacher efficacy will be the acceptance of challenging goals, strong organizational effort, and a persistence that leads to better performance. Of course, the opposite is also true. Lower collective efficacy leads to less effort, the propensity to give up, and a lower level of performance. The process and components of collective teacher efficacy are similar to those of individual teacher efficacy and are illustrated in Figure 5.2. As the figure shows, the proficiency of performance provides feedback to the organization, which provides new information that will further shape the collective teacher efficacy of the school. Beliefs about both the task of teaching and the teaching competence, however, are likely to remain unchanged unless something dramatic occurs because, once established, a school culture of efficacy is a relatively stable property that requires substantial effort to change. It is relatively easy to map the collective efficacy of a school because Goddard and his colleagues (Goddard, Hoy, and Woolfolk Hoy, 2000; Goddard, 2002a) have developed several valid and reliable instruments to measure it. Information about the Collective Efficacy Scale (CE Scale), its properties, and scoring directions is available at www.coe.ohio.state.edu/whoy.

Collective Efficacy: Some Research Findings

Research support for the model and the importance of collective efficacy in student achievement is limited but continues to grow. In his seminal study of

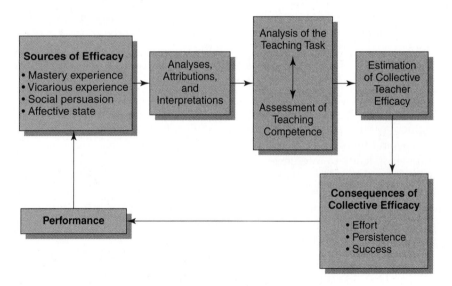

FIGURE 5.2   *A Model of Collective Efficacy*

collective teacher efficacy and student achievement, Bandura (1993) first un-covered two key findings: (1) student achievement (aggregated to the school level) was significantly and positively related to collective efficacy, and (2) collective efficacy had a greater effect on student achievement than did student socioeconomic status (aggregated to the school level). These findings have been supported in subsequent study. Roger Goddard and colleagues (Goddard, Hoy, and Woolfolk Hoy, 2000) also found strong support for the model and again confirmed the significance of collective teacher efficacy in facilitating high student achievement. In subsequent research, the finding that collective efficacy is a positive force in enhancing student achievement, even controlling for the socioeconomic status, has been consistently sup-ported in both elementary and high schools (Goddard, Hoy, and Woolfolk Hoy, 2000; Goddard, Sweetland, and Hoy, 2000; Goddard, 2001; Goddard, 2002b; Hoy, Sweetland, and Smith, 2002; Hoy, Smith, and Sweetland, 2002a; Goddard, Hoy, and LoGerfo, 2003). In brief, strong school culture of efficacy seems to promote high student achievement, in part, because it leads to the acceptance of challenging goals, strong organizational effort, and a persis-tence that leads to better performance. Bandura (1997) observes that because schools present teachers with a host of unique challenges involving such things as public accountability, shared responsibility for student outcomes, and minimal control over work environments, the task of developing high levels of collective teacher efficacy is difficult but possible.

A Culture of Trust

Another view of school culture can be mapped in terms of faculty trust, the collective shared beliefs of teachers. Trust is a little like air; no one thinks much about it until it is needed and it is not there. Yet trust in schools is im-portant because it facilitates cooperation (Tschannen-Moran, 2001); it en-hances openness (Hoffman, Sabo, Bliss, and Hoy, 1994), it promotes group cohesiveness (Zand, 1997), and it improves student achievement (Goddard, Tschannen-Moran, and Hoy, 2001; Hoy, 2002; Bryk and Schneider, 2002). Everyone wants to trust and be trusted. But trust means many things.

Trust relationships are built upon interdependence; that is, the interests of one cannot be achieved without reliance upon another (Rousseau, Sitkin, Burt, and Camerer, 1998). Not surprisingly, the need for trust exists in many social relations in schools because of the high level of interdependence. For example, teachers depend on the principal but the principal is also depend-ent on teachers, and the same can be said for teachers and students and teach-ers and parents. But interdependence in a relationship typically creates vulnerability, which is a common feature of trust (Baier, 1986; Bigley and Pearce, 1998; Coleman, 1990; Mayer, Davis, and Schoorman, 1995; Mishra, 1996). Individuals intuitively know what it is to trust—it means making one-self vulnerable to others with confidence that the others will not act in ways detrimental to you—but trust is complex with many faces.

In addition to vulnerability, there are five other common facets of trust: benevolence, reliability, competence, honesty, and openness (Hoy and Tschannen-Moran, 1999; Hoy and Tschannen-Moran, 2003; Tschannen-Moran and Hoy, 2000). Research on faculty trust in schools (Hoy and Tschannen-Moran, 2003) demonstrates that all these facets of trust vary together and form a coherent notion of trust in schools. In other words, when the faculty has a high level of trust toward the principal, the faculty also believes that the principal is benevolent, reliable, competent, honest, and open in interactions with teachers. Thus, **faculty trust** is *the teachers' willingness to be vulnerable to another party based on the confidence that the latter party is benevolent, reliable, competent, honest, and open.*

Trust is embedded in relationships and specified by its reference to others. Four referents of faculty trust are of particular interest in mapping a culture of organizational trust in schools. The extent to which the faculty trusts its students, its principal, its parents, and each other provides a base for a general picture of trust in schools. Actually, however, teachers do not distinguish between trusting students and trusting parents; to trust the students is the same as trusting the parents and vice versa (Hoy and Tschannen-Moran, 2003). Thus, a culture of trust can be sketched by examining the degree to which faculty trust the students and parents, the principal, and colleagues.

These three referents of trust tend to be moderately and positively related to each other such that trust in one referent spills over to the others, but it is still possible, for example, for teachers to demonstrate high trust in the principal and in colleagues but not in students and parents or to profess strong trust in colleagues but not in the principal. Nonetheless, it is possible to get a good picture of collective trust in the school by examining a profile of faculty trust in the principal, colleagues, and students and parents.

A prototype for a **culture of trust** in schools is one in which faculty trust is high on all three referents. First, teachers trust the principal. They believe that the principal will consistently act in their best interests and is open, honest, and competent. Moreover, the faculty also sees their teacher colleagues as competent, open, honest, and authentic in their interactions with each other; teachers have learned to depend on each other and have confidence that their colleagues, even in difficult situations, will not betray their trust. Finally, the faculty as a whole believes in the students and parents; teachers believe that students are competent learners; they believe what parents and students tell them; they believe they can consistently depend on parents and students; and they believe that parents and students are honest, open, and authentic. In brief, a strong culture of organizational trust in schools is one in which the faculty trusts the principal, faculty members trust each other, and the faculty trusts both students and parents; all groups work together cooperatively.

Faculty trust in a school can be determined by administering the Omnibus T-Scale to the school faculty. The 26-item scale, which can be used at the elementary, middle, or high school levels, measures all three referents of trust and plots—faculty trust in the principal, in colleagues, and in students and parents. Each of the three subtests of the scale measures faculty trust in terms of all the facets of trust discussed above. Further, each measure is highly reliable and has demonstrated construct and predictive validity (Hoy and Tschannen-Moran, 2003). The entire T-Scale can be found on line at www.coe.ohio.state.edu/whoy, and Hoy and Tschannen-Moran (2003) have published technical details about its development and testing.

Faculty Trust: Some Research Evidence

Trust has been found to be an important aspect of relationships in many organizations, including schools. About four decades ago, Rensis Likert (1967) identified trust as a critical element in the interaction-influence process of organizational life. More recently Thomas Sergiovanni (1992) has argued that trust is indispensable to the moral leadership of school principals, and Wayne Hoy and his colleagues (Hoy, Tarter, and Kottkamp, 1991; Hoy and Sabo, 1998; Hoy, Smith, and Sweetland, 2002b) have provided research support for the significance of trust in the leadership efforts of both elementary and secondary principals. Other contemporary organizational scholars (Bennis, 1989; Ouchi, 1981; Zand, 1997) have similarly concluded that trust is a fundamental feature of successful leadership in a variety of organizational settings. How much participants trust their leader determines how much access they will give the leader to their knowledge and commitment (Zand, 1997). One challenge for leaders is clear: to generate the loyalty and trust of your subordinates. If the relationships in schools are to be open and healthy, as we have seen, it seems likely that teachers must trust not only their leaders but also their colleagues as well as students and parents.

Recent evidence (Hoy, Smith, and Sweetland, 2002a; Geist and Hoy, 2003) suggests, however, that factors that enhance faculty trust in the principal are different from those that provide for faculty trust in colleagues, which are different yet from factors that lead to faculty trust in parents and students. Faculty trust in the principal is built by principal behavior that is considerate, supportive, and collegial. Faculty trust in colleagues is built not by principals but by the teachers themselves acting professionally and supportively with colleagues and developing a sense of solidarity and affiliation with each other. Faculty trust in parents and student is more a function of the academic orientation of the school. When the faculty presses for academic excellence and achievement, there is likely a corresponding emphasis on teacher trust in students and the parents. Thus, faculty trust in parents and students seems to be a necessary condition for an academic emphasis in the school, and conversely, an academic emphasis in the school enhances faculty trust in parents and students.

One of the most useful sets of research findings is the strong link between faculty trust in students and parents and student achievement. A number of separate studies have demonstrated this significant relationship between trust and student achievement, even after controlling for the socioeconomic status of the school (Bryk and Schneider, 2002; Goddard, Tschannen-Moran, and Hoy,

2001; Hoy, 2002). Increasingly the evidence is mounting that trusting relations among teachers, parents, and students promote student achievement and improvement. This is an important finding because changing the trust relations among teachers, parents, and students, although not easy, is much more manageable than changing the socioeconomic status of parents.

A Culture of Control

Another way to conceptualize the culture of the school is in terms of dominant beliefs that teachers and principals share about controlling students. Willard Waller (1932), in one of the first systematic studies of the school as a social system, called attention to the importance of pupil control with regard to both structural and normative aspects of the school culture. In fact, most studies that have focused on the school as a social system have described antagonistic student subcultures and attendant conflict and pupil problems (Gordon, 1957; Coleman, 1961; Willower and Jones, 1967). Donald J. Willower and Ronald G. Jones (1967) have described pupil control as the "dominant motif" within the school social system, the integrative theme that gives meaning to patterns of teacher-teacher and teacher-principal relations.

Control is a problem that all organizations face. Richard O. Carlson's (1964) analysis of the relationship of a client to a service organization indicates that public schools are the type of service organization in which control is likely to be the most acute problem. Public schools, along with prisons and public mental hospitals, are service organizations that have no choice in the selection of clients, and the clients must (in the legal sense) participate in the organization. These organizations are confronted with clients who may have little or no desire for the services of the organization, a factor that accentuates the problem of client control. As a strong cautionary note, there are important distinctions to be made when comparing public schools with prisons and public mental hospitals. For example, prisons and public mental hospitals are "total institutions" (Goffman, 1957); schools are not. Moreover, schools normally use much less intense coercive practices. The point is that although control is probably an essential ingredient of all group life it is especially important in service organizations in which clients are unselected and participation is mandatory.

Both empirical and conceptual considerations lead to the same conclusion: Pupil control is a central aspect of school life. Given its saliency, the concept can be used to distinguish school types. The conceptualization of pupil control in research by Donald J. Willower, Terry I. Eidell, and Hoy (1967) at The Pennsylvania State University provides the basis for such a perspective.[2] The Penn State researchers postulated a pupil-control continuum from custodial to humanistic. Prototypes of the two extremes are briefly summarized below.

The model for a **custodial culture** is the traditional school, which provides a rigid and highly controlled setting in which maintenance of order is primary. Students are stereotyped in terms of their appearance, behavior, and parents' social status. Teachers who hold a custodial orientation conceive of the school as an autocratic organization with a rigid pupil-teacher status hierarchy. The flow of power and communication is unilateral and downward; students must accept the decisions of their teachers without question. Teachers do not attempt to understand student behavior but instead view misbehavior as a personal affront. They perceive students as irresponsible and undisciplined persons who must be controlled through punitive sanctions. Impersonality, cynicism, and watchful mistrust pervade the atmosphere of the custodial school.

The model for the **humanistic culture** is the school conceived of as an educational community in which students learn through cooperative interaction and experience. This model views learning and behavior in psychological and sociological terms. It substitutes self-discipline for strict teacher control. A humanistic orientation leads to a democratic atmosphere with two-way communication between pupils and teachers and increased self-determination. The term "humanistic orientation" is used in the sociopsychological sense suggested by Erich Fromm (1948); it stresses both the importance of the individual and the creation of an atmosphere that meets student needs.

In order to measure the pupil-control orientation of schools along the custodial-humanistic continuum, Willower, Eidell, and Hoy (1967: 47–48) developed the Pupil-Control Ideology (PCI) form. The scale provides five response categories for each of twenty items, ranging from strongly disagree to strongly agree. Reliability and validity of the PCI have been supported in numerous studies (Hoy, 1967, 1968, 2002; Hoy and Woolfolk, 1989, 1990). The pupil-control orientation can be measured by pooling the individual orientations of the professional staff of the school; this represents an estimate of the modal orientation of the school and provides an index of the culture of custodialism (or humanism) in pupil-control orientation of the school. For a copy of the PCI and scoring directions, see www.coe.ohio.state.edu/whoy.

Pupil Control: Some Research Findings

Dominant teacher beliefs provide another view of the school culture, one that focuses on shared beliefs about controlling students and that has proved to be a powerful predictor of the tone or feeling of the school and the actions of students (Hoy, 2002).

Appleberry and Hoy (1969) and Hoy and Clover (1986) found that humanism in the pupil-control orientation of schools and the openness of the organizational climate of schools are strongly correlated. Hoy and Appleberry (1970) compared the most humanistic schools and the most custodial schools in terms of their climate profiles. Schools with a custodial pupil-control orientation had significantly greater teacher disengagement, lower levels of morale, and more close supervision by the principal than those with a humanistic, pupil-control orientation. The pupil-control orientation of a school is related to many important aspects of school life.

Consider the following general picture of the school's character that emerges from the research. Custodial schools have more alienated students than humanistic ones (Hoy, 1972), whereas humanistic schools provide healthy social climates that lead to the development of more mature self-images for the students (Diebert and Hoy, 1977). Moreover, students' perceptions of a humanistic school climate are positively related to their motivation, problem solving, and seriousness to learn (Lunenburg, 1983) as well as their positive perceptions of the quality of school life (Lunenburg and Schmidt, 1989). The more custodial the climate of the school, the greater the student vandalism, the more violent incidents, the more suspensions (Finkelstein, 1998), and the more hindering the school structure tends to be (Hoy, 2001).

The evidence suggests a need for public schools that are less custodial and more humanistic because such schools have less alienated, more satisfied, and more productive students. Changes in the humanistic direction, however, are more easily described than made, and inevitably they are slow in coming and often unsuccessful; nevertheless, the effort should be made.

TIP: THEORY INTO PRACTICE

Interview about six or more teachers in your school to try to determine the culture of your school in terms of the core values most teachers share. Describe the shared values and beliefs of the faculty in terms of innovation, stability, attention to detail, outcome orientation, people orientation, team orientation, aggressiveness, trust, control and any other key values and beliefs. Describe the rites of passage and rites of integration for new teachers. Evaluate the school culture in terms of strengths and weaknesses. How functional is the school culture in terms of student achievement and development?

ORGANIZATIONAL CLIMATE

Although the term "organizational culture" is currently in vogue, the concept of organizational climate has generated much more research and until recently was used by most organizational theorists to capture the general feel or atmosphere of schools. Unlike culture, from the beginning, organizational climate has been tied to the process of developing measuring instruments (Pace and Stern, 1958; Halpin and Croft, 1963, Denison, 1996; Hoy, 1997). Climate has its historical roots in the disciplines of social psychology and industrial psychology rather than in anthropology or sociology.

Definition of Organizational Climate

Climate was initially conceived as a general concept to express the enduring quality of organizational life. Renato Taguiri (1968: 23) notes that "a particular configuration of enduring characteristics of the ecology, milieu, social system, and culture would constitute a climate, as much as a particular configuration of personal characteristics constitute a personality."

B. H. Gilmer (1966: 57) defines organizational climate as "those characteristics that distinguish the organization from other organizations and that influence the behavior of people in the organizations." George Litwin and Robert Stringer (1968: 1) introduce perception into their definition of climate: "a set of measurable properties of the work environment, based on the collective perceptions of the people who live and work in the environment and demonstrated to influence their behavior." Over the years, there has been some consensus on the basic properties of organizational climate. Marshall Poole (1985) summarizes the agreement as follows:

- Organizational climate is concerned with large units; it characterizes properties of an entire organization or major subunits.
- Organizational climate describes a unit of organization rather than evaluates it or indicates emotional reactions to it.
- Organizational climate arises from routine organizational practices that are important to the organization and its members.
- Organizational climate influences members' behaviors and attitudes.

School climate is a broad term that refers to teachers' perceptions of the general work environment of the school; the formal organization, informal organization, personalities of participants, and organizational leadership influence it. Put simply, the set of internal characteristics that distinguish one school from another and influence the behavior of each school's members is the **organizational climate** of the school. More specifically, **school climate** is a relatively enduring quality of the school environment that is experienced by participants, affects their behavior, and is based on their collective perceptions of behavior in schools. The definition of organizational climate as a set of internal characteristics is similar in some respects to early descriptions of personality. Indeed, the climate of a school may roughly be conceived as the personality of a school—that is, personality is to the individual as climate is to the organization.

Because the atmosphere of a school has a major impact on the organizational behavior, and because administrators can have a significant, positive influence on the development of the "personality" of the school, it is important to describe and analyze school climates. Climate can be conceived from a variety of vantage points (see Anderson, 1982; Miskel and Ogawa, 1988). We turn to two lenses to view school climate: openness and health. Each provides the student and practitioner of administration with a valuable set of conceptual capital and measurement tools to analyze, understand, map, and change the work environment of schools.

A Climate of Organizational Openness

Probably the most well-known conceptualization and measurement of the organizational climate of schools is the pioneering study of elementary schools by Andrew W. Halpin and Don B. Croft (1962). They began mapping the domain of organizational climate of schools because although schools differ markedly in their feel, the concept of morale did not provide an adequate explanation. In a series of factor analytic studies they developed a descriptive questionnaire, the Organizational Climate Description Questionnaire (OCDQ), to measure important aspects of teacher-teacher and teacher-principal interactions. They asked the faculties of schools to describe the behavior of their colleagues and principals by indicating how frequently certain behaviors occurred in their school, such as, "The principal goes out of his way to help teachers," and "Routine jobs interfere with the job of teaching." Table 5.3 presents examples from a contemporary version of the OCDQ.

TABLE 5.3

Sample Items from the OCDQ-RE

DIRECTIONS: THE FOLLOWING ARE STATEMENTS ABOUT YOUR SCHOOL. PLEASE INDICATE THE EXTENT TO WHICH EACH STATEMENT CHARACTERIZES YOUR SCHOOL BY CIRCLING THE APPROPRIATE RESPONSE.

RO = RARELY OCCURS   SO = SOMETIMES OCCURS   O = OFTEN OCCURS   VFO = VERY FREQUENTLY OCCURS

1.	The teachers accomplish their work with vim, vigor, and pleasure	RO	SO	O	VFO
2.	Teachers' closest friends are other faculty members at this school	RO	SO	O	VFO
3.	Faculty meetings are useless	RO	SO	O	VFO
4.	The principal goes out of his/her way to help teachers	RO	SO	O	VFO
5.	The principal rules with an iron fist	RO	SO	O	VFO
6.	Teachers leave school immediately after school is over	RO	SO	O	VFO
7.	Teachers invite faculty members to visit them at home	RO	SO	O	VFO
8.	The principal uses constructive criticism	RO	SO	O	VFO

For the complete instrument and details for scoring, see Hoy and Tarter (1997b) or www.coe.ohio-state.edu/whoy

There are now three contemporary versions of the OCDQ—one for elementary, one for middle, and one for high schools. For example, the OCDQ-RE defines the climate of elementary schools with six dimensions; three describe openness in interactions between the principal and teachers, and three describe openness of interactions among colleagues. Table 5.4 defines the six dimensions measured by the OCDQ-RE. All the climate instruments (elementary, middle, and high school) provide valid and reliable means to map *openness in the behaviors* of teachers and administrators in schools (Hoy, Tarter, and Kottkamp, 1991; Hoy and Tarter, 1997a; Hoy and Tarter, 1997b).[3] The OCDQ instruments, scoring instructions, and interpretations are online for your use at www.coe.ohio-state.edu/whoy.

The **open climate** is marked by cooperation and respect within the faculty and between the faculty and principal. The principal listens and is open to teacher suggestions, gives genuine and frequent praise, and respects the professional competence of the faculty (high supportiveness). Principals also give their teachers freedom to perform without close scrutiny (low directiveness) and provide facilitating leadership behavior devoid of bureaucratic trivia (low restrictiveness). Similarly, teacher behavior supports open and professional interactions (high collegial relations) among the faculty. Teachers know each other well and are close personal friends (high intimacy). They cooperate and are committed to their work (low disengagement). In brief, the behavior of both the principal and the faculty is open and authentic.

The **closed climate** is virtually the antithesis of the open climate. The principal and teachers simply appear to go through the motions, with the

---

TABLE 5.4

The Dimensions of the OCDQ-RE

Supportive Principal Behavior—reflects a basic concern for teachers. The principal listens and is open to teacher suggestions. Praise is given genuinely and frequently and criticism is constructive.

Directive Principal Behavior—requires rigid, close supervision. The principal maintains close and constant control over all teacher and school activities, down to the smallest details.

Restrictive Principal Behavior—hinders rather than facilitates teacher work. The principal burdens teachers with paperwork, committee requirements, routine duties, and busywork.

Collegial Teacher Behavior—supports open and professional interactions among teachers. Teachers are enthusiastic, accepting, and respectful of the professional competence of their colleagues.

Intimate Teacher Behavior—reflects a strong, cohesive network of social support within the faculty. Teachers know each other well, are close personal friends, and socialize together regularly.

Disengaged Teacher Behavior—refers to a lack of meaning and focus to professional activities. Teachers are simply putting in time. Their behavior is negative and critical of their colleagues.

principal stressing routine trivia and unnecessary busywork (high restrictiveness) and the teacher responding minimally and exhibiting little commitment (high disengagement). The principal's ineffective leadership is further seen as controlling and rigid (high directiveness) as well as unsympathetic, unconcerned, and unresponsive (low supportiveness). These misguided tactics are accompanied not only by frustration and apathy, but also by a general suspicion and lack of respect of teachers for each other as either friends or professionals (low intimacy and noncollegial relations). Closed climates have principals who are nonsupportive, inflexible, hindering, and controlling and a faculty that is divisive, intolerant, apathetic, and uncommitted. Figure 5.3 shows the contrasting climate profiles for schools with open and closed organizational climates. Use the appropriate OCDQ to determine the openness of your school climate.

OCDQ: Some Research Findings

The revised versions of the OCDQ for elementary, middle, and secondary schools are relatively recent developments. Nevertheless, a consistent body of research is beginning to emerge. We do know, for example, that the openness index from the original OCDQ is highly correlated with the new and refined subtests that measure openness. Moreover, openness in climate is positively related to open and authentic teacher and principal behavior (Hoy, Hoffman, Sabo, and Bliss, 1994; Hoy and Sweetland, 2001). Thus, it is expected that the new measures will replicate and refine results from earlier studies.

Those earlier OCDQ studies demonstrated that the openness of a school's climate was related to the emotional tone of the school in predictable

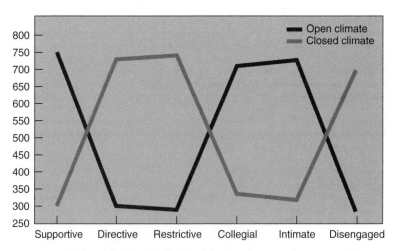

FIGURE 5.3   *Climate Profiles of Open and Closed Elementary Schools*

ways. Schools with open climates have less sense of student alienation toward the school and its personnel than those with closed climates (Hartley and Hoy, 1972). As one might also suspect, studies that examine relationships between characteristics of the principal and the climate of the school often indicate that, in comparison to closed schools, open schools have stronger principals who are more confident, self-secure, cheerful, sociable, and resourceful (Anderson, 1964). Moreover, the teachers who work under principals in open schools express greater confidence in their own and the school's effectiveness (Andrews, 1965). Such principals have more loyal and satisfied teachers (Kanner, 1974).

More recent research (Tarter and Hoy, 1988; Reiss, 1994; Reiss and Hoy, 1998) with the new climate instruments also shows that open school climates are characterized by higher levels of loyalty and trust, faculty trust both in the principal and in colleagues, than closed climates. Principals in open schools also generate more organizational commitment to school—that is, identification and involvement in school—than those in closed climates (Tarter, Hoy, and Kottkamp, 1990). Further, openness of the climate is positively related to teacher participation in decision making (Barnes, 1994) as well as to ratings of school effectiveness (Hoy, Tarter, and Kottkamp, 1991) and, in middle schools, to student achievement in mathematics, reading, and writing as well as to overall effectiveness and quality (Hoy and Sabo, 1998).

In conclusion, the three versions of the OCDQ for elementary, middle, and secondary schools are useful devices for general charting of school climate in terms of teacher-teacher and teacher-principal relationships. The subtests of each instrument seem to be valid and reliable measures of important aspects of school climate; they can provide climate profiles that can be used for research, evaluation, in-service, or self-analysis. In addition, the openness indices provide means of examining schools along an open-closed continuum. Halpin and Croft suggest that openness might be a better criterion of a school's effectiveness than many that have entered the field of educational administration and masquerade as criteria. Openness is likely an important condition in fostering effective organizational change. Similarly, principals who want to improve instructional effectiveness are more likely to be successful if they first develop an open and trusting climate (Hoy and Forsyth, 1987). Although there is much argument about what constitutes school effectiveness (see Chapter 8), there is less doubt that the OCDQ measures provide a useful battery of scales for diagnostic as well as prescriptive purposes.

A Climate of Organizational Health

Another frame for viewing the climate of the school is its **organizational health** (Hoy and Feldman, 1987; Hoy, Tarter, and Kottkamp, 1991; Hoy and Sabo, 1998). The idea of positive health in an organization is not new and calls attention to conditions that facilitate growth and development as well as to those that impede healthy organizational dynamics (Miles, 1969). A school with a healthy organizational climate is one that copes successfully with its environment as it mobilizes its resources and efforts to achieve its goals. The organizational health of secondary schools is defined by seven specific inter-action patterns in schools (Hoy and Feldman, 1987, 1999). These critical components meet the basic needs of the social system and represent the three levels of responsibility and control within the school.

The *institutional* level connects the organization with its environment. It is important for schools to have legitimacy and backing in the community. Administrators and teachers need support to perform their respective functions in a harmonious fashion without undue pressure and interference from individuals and groups outside the school. This level is examined in terms of the school's integrity. That is, institutional integrity is the school's ability to adapt to its environment and cope in ways that maintain the soundness of its educational programs. Schools with integrity are protected from unreasonable community and parental demands.

The *managerial* level mediates and controls the internal efforts of the organization. The administrative process is the managerial function, a process that is qualitatively different from teaching. Principals are the prime administrative officers in schools. They must find ways to develop teacher loyalty and trust, motivate teacher effort, and coordinate the work. Four key aspects of the managerial level must be determined—principal influence, consideration, initiating structure, and resource support. Influence is the ability of the principal to affect the decisions of superiors. Consideration is principal behavior that is open, friendly, and supportive, whereas initiating structure is behavior in which the principal clearly defines the work expectations, standards of performance, and procedures. Finally, resource support is the extent to which the principal provides teachers with all the materials and supplies they need and request.

In schools, the *technical* function is the teaching-learning process, and teachers are directly responsible. Educated students are the product of schools, and the entire technical subsystem revolves around the problems associated with effective learning and teaching. Morale and academic emphasis are the two key elements of the technical level. Morale is the enthusiasm, confidence, and sense of accomplishment that pervade the faculty. Academic emphasis, on the other hand, is the school's press for student achievement. The seven dimensions of organizational health are defined, summarized by level of responsibility, and illustrated in Table 5.5.

Specifically, a **healthy organization** is *one in which the technical, managerial, and institutional levels are in harmony. The organization is both meeting its needs and successfully coping with disruptive outside forces as it directs its energies toward its mission.*

The **healthy school** is protected from unreasonable community and parental pressures. The board successfully resists all narrow efforts of vested interest groups to influence policy. The principal of a healthy school provides dynamic leadership—leadership that is both task oriented and relations oriented. Such behavior is supportive of teachers and yet provides direction

TABLE 5.5

The Dimensions of the OHI-S and Sample Items

Institutional Level

Institutional Integrity—describes a school that is not vulnerable to narrow, vested interests from the community. The school is able to cope well with outside destructive forces.

Sample items: • The school is protected from unreasonable community and parental demands.

• The school is vulnerable to outside pressures.*

Managerial Level

Principal Influence—refers to the principal's ability to affect the action of superiors. The influential principal works successfully with the superintendent for the benefit of teachers.

Sample items: • The principal gets what he or she asks for from superiors.

• The principal is impeded by superiors.*

Consideration—describes behavior by the principal that is friendly, supportive, open, and collegial.

Sample items: • The principal looks out for the personal welfare of faculty members.

• The principal is friendly and approachable.

Initiating Structure—describes behavior by the principal that is task and achievement oriented. The principal makes his expectations clear and maintains standards of performance.

Sample items: • The principal lets faculty members know what is expected of them.

• The principal maintains definite standards of performance.

Resource Support—refers to a situation at the school in which adequate classroom supplies and instructional materials are available and extra materials are easily obtained.

Sample items: • Extra materials are available if requested.

• Teachers are provided with adequate materials for their classrooms.

Technical Level

Morale—refers to a sense of trust, confidence, enthusiasm, and friendliness among teachers. Teachers feel good about each other and, at the same time, feel a sense of accomplishment from their jobs.

Sample items: • Teachers in this school like each other.

• The morale of teachers is high.

Academic Emphasis—refers to the school's press of achievement. High but achievable academic goals are set for students; the learning environment is orderly and serious; teachers believe in the ability of their students to achieve; and students work hard and respect academic achievement.

Sample item: • The school sets high standards for academic performance.

• Students respect others who get good grades.

* Item is scored in reverse.

and maintains high standards of performance. Moreover, the principal has influence with his or her superiors as well as the ability to exercise independent thought and action. Teachers in a healthy school are committed to teaching and learning. They set high, but achievable goals for students; they maintain high standards of performance; and the learning environment is orderly and serious. Furthermore, students work hard on academic matters, are highly motivated, and respect other students who achieve academically. Classroom supplies and instructional materials are accessible. Finally, in a healthy school teachers like each other, trust each other, are enthusiastic about the work, and are proud of their school.

The **unhealthy school** is vulnerable to destructive outside forces. Teachers and administrators are bombarded with unreasonable demands from parental and community groups. The school is buffeted by the whims of the public. The principal does not provide leadership: there is little direction, limited consideration and support for teachers, and virtually no influence with superiors. Morale of teachers is low. Teachers feel good neither about each other nor about their jobs. They act aloof, suspicious, and defensive. Finally, the press for academic excellence is limited. Everyone is simply "putting in time."

The organizational health of a school can be measured using the Organizational Health Index (OHI). For example, the OHI for secondary schools is a 44-item descriptive questionnaire composed of seven subtests to measure each of the basic dimensions as well as the general health of the school. Like the OCDQ, the OHI is administered to the professional staff of the school. Three valid and reliable contemporary versions of the OHI are now available—one for each school level. Health profiles for three schools are graphed in Figure 5.4. School A represents a school with a relatively healthy climate;

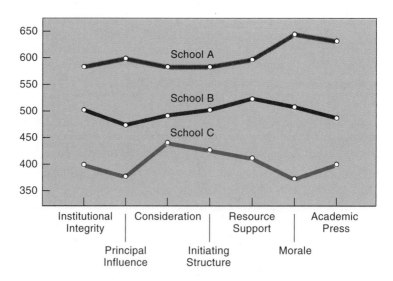

FIGURE 5.4   *Health Profiles of Three Schools*

all dimensions of health are substantially above the mean. School C, in contrast, is below the mean in all aspects of health, and school B is a typical school—about average on all dimensions. All the OHI instruments, scoring instructions, and interpretations are available online for your use.

OHI: Some Research Findings

The OHI is a useful tool for measuring school climate, with three versions—one each for elementary, middle, and high schools. The instruments measure key dimensions of organizational health of schools. Moreover, the conceptual underpinnings are consistent with many of the characteristics of effective schools. In addition, a study of high schools in Taiwan demonstrated stability of the OHI across cultures (Liao, 1994).

Research findings using the OHI continue to be encouraging. As one would expect, the healthier the organizational dynamics, the greater the degree of faculty trust in the principal, in colleagues, and in the organization itself (Tarter and Hoy, 1988; Hoy, Tarter, and Wiskowskie, 1992; Smith, Hoy, and Sweetland, 2001). Not surprisingly, there is a correlation between the openness and the health of schools; healthy schools have high thrust, high esprit, and low disengagement (Hoy and Tarter, 1990). In brief, open schools tend to be healthy and healthy schools tend to be open. Health is also related to the organizational commitment of teachers to their schools; healthy schools have more committed teachers (Tarter, Hoy, and Bliss 1989; Tarter, Hoy, and Kottkamp 1990).

Research findings also show that organizational health is positively related to student performance; in general, the healthier the school climate, the higher the achievement levels on math and reading achievement test scores of high school students (Hoy and Tarter, 1990). More specifically, the stronger the academic emphasis of the climate of middle schools, the higher the student achievement levels on standardized math, reading, and writing tests (Hoy and Hannum, 1997; Hoy, Hannum, and Tschannen-Moran, 1998; Hoy and Sabo, 1998; Goddard, Sweetland, and Hoy, 2000). A study of elementary teachers also demonstrated that a healthy school climate was conducive to the development of teacher efficacy, the belief that they could positively influence student learning (Hoy and Woolfolk, 1993). Our own research continues to demonstrate that school health is related to a host of other important school variables. For example, it is positively related to humanism, teacher participation in decision making, a strong school culture, and a variety of measures of school effectiveness. Finally, it seems likely that a school's health will be significantly related to less student alienation, lower dropout rates, and higher student commitment.

In conclusion, the appropriate OHI instrument can reliably determine the health of a school. Moreover, sound interpersonal dynamics in school life are not only important as ends in themselves but also are predictive of school effectiveness, student achievement, organizational commitment, humanism in teacher attitudes, and faculty trust in colleagues and in the principal.

Healthy schools are likely to have committed teachers who trust each other, who trust the principal, who hold high academic standards, who are open, and who have students who achieve at high levels. In such schools, the improvement of instruction and the continued professional development of teachers and administrators are achievable goals.

TIP: THEORY INTO PRACTICE

Select either a framework of openness (OCDQ) or health (OHI). What do you like about this theoretical perspective? Why do you find it useful? What advantages and disadvantages does this framework have for examining your school climate? Administer the appropriate instrument to five or six teachers in your school who are agreeable. Next score the instrument and develop a climate profile for the school as a chart or graph and explain what the figure means in words. Compare and contrast your school with an average school. How representative do you think the results are for your school? Would your principal agree? Finally, discuss the strengths and weaknesses of your climate. Then read the next section on changing school climate, and develop a plan for improving the climate of your school if you were appointed principal.

CHANGING THE CULTURE AND CLIMATE OF SCHOOLS

We have little information on, let alone answers to, the complex problem of changing the school workplace. Two things are clear, however. There is no quick and simple way to change the culture or climate of schools. Long-term systemic effort is more likely to produce change than short-term fads.

Three general strategies for change follow. Alan Brown (1965) has developed a clinical strategy as well as a growth-centered approach, and Ralph Kilmann (1984) has successfully implemented a procedure for changing the normative culture of organizations. The three strategies are not alternatives to each other; they can be used simultaneously and, indeed, all seem necessary for effective change. The clinical strategy focuses on the nature of the relationships among the school's subgroups; the growth-centered strategy is concerned with the nature of individual development within the school; and the normative procedure is used to change organizational norms. Each of these change strategies offers potential guidelines for the practicing administrator that we will review briefly.

The Clinical Strategy

The manipulation of intergroup and interpersonal interactions can foster change. Such a **clinical strategy** for change can proceed through the following steps.

1. *Gaining knowledge of the organization:* The approach begins with a thorough knowledge of the dynamics of the school organization. Such knowledge, of course, comes through careful observation, analysis, and study. The perceptive principal may have acquired much of this knowledge through experience but, typically, a more systematic analysis is enlightening and valuable. As a prelude to such a study, he or she must understand the salient aspects of organizational life including the basic norms and values of the faculty. The conceptual perspectives provided by such measures as the OCDQ, OHI, and PCI can substantially aid this learning about the school organization.

2. *Diagnosis:* The second step in the process is diagnostic. Here again conceptual capital, from a variety of perspectives, can provide labels for diagnosing potential trouble areas. Poor morale, high disengagement, custodialism, distorted communication, unilateral decision making, and low academic expectations are examples of such conceptual labels. The extent to which these concepts are clearly defined in the mind of the practitioner and fit together in a broader perspective probably mediates the effectiveness of the diagnosis.

3. *Prognosis:* In the third step, the "clinician" judges the seriousness of the situation and develops a set of operational priorities to improve the situation.

4. *Prescription:* The appropriate course of action is often hidden. Suppose we decided that the school's atmosphere is too custodial in pupil-control orientation. How can the situation be remedied? We might replace a number of "custodial" teachers with younger "humanistic" teachers. Research suggests, however, that the pupil-control ideology of beginning teachers becomes significantly more custodial as they become socialized by the teacher subculture (Hoy, 1967, 1968, 1969; Hoy and Woolfolk, 1989), which in this case tends to equate tight control with good teaching. Merely replacing a number of custodial teachers without altering basic teacher norms about pupil control will probably have little or no impact. Altering basic teacher norms calls for a more sophisticated strategy (see below). A first step in such a strategy is to eliminate teacher and administrator ignorance about the PCI—that is, to erase the shared misperceptions of educators with respect to pupil-control ideology. Teachers generally think that principals are much more custodial in pupil-control ideology than they themselves are, and conversely, principals typically believe that teachers are more custodial in pupil-control orientation than they report themselves to be (Packard and Willower, 1972). These common misperceptions need to be swept away if a more humanistic perspective is to be achieved. In other words, developing prescriptions at first seems easy enough, but experience shows that solutions to various school problems are usually oversimplified and often irrelevant. If administrators are going to be successful in changing the school climate and culture, then they must change the

norms and values of the teacher subculture as well as the basic, shared assumptions of the faculty and administration.

5. *Evaluation:* The last step in the clinical strategy is to evaluate the extent to which prescriptions have been implemented and are successful. Because planned change in social systems is often slow, continuous monitoring and evaluation are required.

The Growth-Centered Strategy

A **growth-centered strategy** simply involves the acceptance of a set of assumptions about the development of school personnel and the use of these assumptions as the basis for administrative decision making. The assumptions are the following:

1. *Change is a property of healthy school organizations.* The principal should see organizations, and hence organizational climate, in a constant state of flux.
2. *Change has direction.* Change can be positive or negative, progressive or regressive.
3. *Change should imply progress.* Change should provide movement of the organization toward its goals. Of course not all change represents progress; yet the principal's stance is progress oriented.
4. *Teachers have high potential for the development and implementation of change.* Principals are always ready to provide teachers with more freedom and responsibility in the operation of the school.

These basic assumptions, if acted upon, would allow for a growth policy, which in turn leads to increased opportunities for professional development. From this perspective, administrators would remove obstacles from the path of professional growth and not manipulate people. Finally, the approach should help facilitate a climate of mutual trust and respect among teachers and administrators.

The clinical and growth-centered approaches do not conflict in their assumptions, although they have different focuses—organizational and individual. The astute administrator draws on both strategies to change the climate of the school.

A Norm-Changing Strategy

Most organizational members can list the norms that operate in their work group and even suggest new norms that would be more effective for improving productivity or morale (Kilmann, Saxton, and Serpa, 1985). A number of ways can be used to surface actual norms, but participants are usually reluctant to specify norms *unless* they are confident that the information will not be used against them or the organization. Thus, anonymity and confidentiality of respondents are crucial in identifying the salient norms in an organization.

Kilmann and his associates (1985) have successfully used small groups in workshop settings to elicit norms. He suggests that with just a little prodding and a few illustrations to get the group started, members quickly begin to enumerate many norms; in fact, they revel in being able to articulate what beforehand was not formally stated and rarely discussed.

Prevailing norms map the "way things are" around the organization. Indeed, norm statements often begin with "around here." For example, "Around here, it is all right to admit mistakes, as long as you don't make them again." The key norms of an organization are usually related to such important areas as control, support, innovation, social relations, rewards, conflicts, and standards of excellence. To begin to identify the norms of a school, teachers might be asked to list their views of the school in terms of "around here" statements. For example, they are ask to complete the following statements:

1. At the end of a typical faculty meeting, everyone _____.
2. Around here, the real basis for reward _____.
3. Around here, control of students _____.
4. Around here, decisions are reached through _____.
5. Around here, risk taking _____.
6. Around here, differences in opinion are handled by _____.
7. Around here, achievement standards _____.
8. Around here, we handle problems by _____.

Kilmann (1984) recommends the following five-step procedure as a **norm-changing strategy:**

- *Surface norms.* Teachers, usually in a workshop setting, identify the norms that guide their attitudes and behaviors.
- *Articulate new directions.* Teachers discuss where the school is headed and identify new directions that are necessary for progress.
- *Establish new norms.* Teachers identify a set of new norms that they believe will lead to improvement and organizational success.
- *Identify culture gaps.* Teachers examine the discrepancy between actual norms (step 1) and desired norms (step 3). This discrepancy is a culture gap; the larger the gap, the more probable that the existing norms are dysfunctional.
- *Close the culture gaps.* The act of listing new norms often results in many group members actually adopting the new and desired norms (Kilmann, 1984). But the teachers as a group must also agree that the desired norms will replace the old norms and that the changes will be monitored and enforced. Subsequent teacher meetings can then be used to reinforce the new norms and prevent regression to old norms and practices.

John Miner (1988) notes that this process is especially useful in identifying and changing negative aspects of an organization's culture. For example, negative norms surfaced in step 1 can be replaced by more desirable norms identified in step 3, as follows:

- *From:* Don't rock the boat; don't volunteer to do anything extra; don't share information; don't tell your colleagues or superiors what they don't want to hear.
- *To:* Experiment with new ideas; help others when they need help; communicate openly with your colleagues; persist in identifying problems.

Miner (1988) argues that this group approach to cultural change may be more useful for identifying dysfunctional aspects of the culture than for bringing about real change, and Schein (1985) charges that this process deals at best with the superficial aspects of culture. Nonetheless, Kilmann's five-step process seems a useful vehicle for helping groups of teachers get specific information about the nature of their workplace and for developing a plan for change. The process, together with the clinical and growth-centered approaches, provides teachers and administrators with specific techniques and procedures to change the character of the workplace.

A CASE FOR LEADERSHIP

Surprise at St. Clair Middle School

You have been principal at St. Clair Middle School for more than a year. St. Clair is one of three middle schools in East Hampton, a middle-class community of 30,000 people in the Mid-west. Your middle school (grades 5–8) has 20 teachers and just over 600 students. You believe that you have a good school with good faculty, but there is definitely room for improvement. Since your arrival at St. Clair, you have worked very hard to get to know the teachers. This is your first job as an administrator after teaching seven years in a middle school in Aura, a community similar to East Hampton, but 100 miles to the west. You feel comfortable in your new role and believe that you have been accepted as the new leader at St. Clair.

You believe in collegial administration and share the decision making with teachers; after all, education in your view is a team effort that should involve students, teachers, administrators, and parents. "How am I doing?" you wonder. Things feel good, but are you deceiving yourself? You think not, but decide to get a more objective view of the workplace through the eyes of the teachers.

Your plan is to administer the Organizational Health Inventory (OHI) to your faculty at the next faculty meeting; the anonymous questionnaires should take only 10 minutes to complete and you can score them quickly. You also decide to complete the questionnaire yourself and then compare your perception of the school climate with those of the teachers.

(Continued)

A CASE FOR LEADERSHIP *(Concluded)*

Categories	Teachers' Perceptions	Your Perceptions
Institutional integrity	480 (slightly below average)	600 (high)
Collegial leadership	509 (average)	680 (very high)
Principal influence	520 (above average)	580 (high)
Resource support	600 (high)	720 (very high)
Teacher affiliation	600 (high)	660 (very high)
Academic emphasis	590 (high)	680 (very high)
Overall school health	549 (above average)	653 (very high)

You are right, the teachers seem glad to respond to the OHI; it takes only about 10 minutes, and not even a grumble from teachers. You are, however, quite surprised at the results. Indeed, surprised may be the wrong word; dismayed seems more appropriate. Clearly, your view of the school climate is much more optimistic than the teachers' perspective. The data provide a reality check.

- Do you have a problem here? If so, what is it?

- How should you share the data with your teachers? Or should you?
- Why the major discrepancies between your teachers' and your own perceptions on institutional integrity and collegial leadership?
- What should you do next?
- Should you use a growth-centered strategy? Clinical strategy?
- You need a plan, but what is it?

SUMMARY AND SUGGESTED READINGS

Two related and overlapping perspectives are used to analyze the character of the workplace. Organizational culture and organizational climate both go beyond the formal and individual aspects of organizational life. Each concept deals with the natural, spontaneous, and human side of the organization as attempts are made to uncover shared meanings and unwritten rules that influence behavior.

Organizational culture is the set of shared orientations that holds a unit together and gives it a distinctive identity. Culture can be examined in terms of shared assumptions, shared beliefs and values, or shared norms. We have considered three types of school cultures: a culture of efficacy, a culture of trust, and a culture of control.

Organizational climate denotes members' shared perceptions of behavior rather than beliefs or values; climate is a set of internal behavioral characteristics that distinguishes one school from another and influences the behavior of people in schools. Two conceptualizations of school climate were considered: openness and health. The interaction among teachers can be described along an open-to-closed continuum and can be measured by the appropriate Organizational Climate Description Questionnaire (OCDQ). Another perspective on climate examines the organizational health of schools—that is, the extent to which the school is meeting its basic needs while simultaneously coping with disruptive outside forces as it directs its energies toward its mission. The health of the school can be mapped using the appropriate Organizational Health Inventory (OHI); separate and reliable versions of the OHI exist for elementary, middle, and high schools.

The chapter concludes with three strategies that practitioners can use to change the nature of the school workplace. A clinical strategy deals with the nature of the relationships among the school's subgroups; a growth-centered strategy emphasizes the nature of individual development within the school; and a group procedure offers a strategy to change organizational norms.

Edgar Schein's (1992) book, *Organizational Culture and Leadership,* remains one of the most comprehensive analyses of organizational culture. For a diverse look at culture, a collection of readings, *Reframing Organizational Culture,* provides readers with exemplars of culture research as well as critiques, commentaries, and expositions (Frost et al., 1991). For those interested in corporate cultures, the early works of Peters and Waterman (1982) and Ouchi (1981) are worthwhile and provide a nice backdrop for our discussion of culture.

Students should begin their study of school climate with Andrew Halpin and Don Croft's (1963) pioneering study *The Organizational Climate of Schools.* Two more recent books, *Open Schools/Healthy Schools* (Hoy, Tarter, and Kottkamp, 1991) and *Quality Middle Schools* (Hoy and Sabo, 1998) summarize two decades of research on school climate. The two latter books give researchers six valid and reliable instruments to study school climate and provide practitioners with the tools to diagnose problems and analyze the climate of their schools. The instruments, norms, scoring instructions, and interpretations of results, as well as change strategies, are all carefully illustrated.

KEY ASSUMPTIONS AND PRINCIPLES

1. Schools have distinctive cultures, core values and beliefs, which provide members with a sense of organizational mission and identity.
2. Strong cultures can be good or bad because they can promote or impede effectiveness.
3. Culture calls attention to the symbolic nature of organizations; often what is said or done is not as important as what it symbolizes.

4. Both a school culture of efficacy and a culture of trust promote student achievement.
5. A custodial culture of pupil control impedes the socioemotional development of students.
6. The organizational climate of a school is the set of faculty perceptions of the dominant behaviors of organizational participants.
7. Openness of organizational climate is positively related to loyalty, trust, and commitment of teachers.
8. The health of organizational climate is positively related to openness in member interactions as well as school effectiveness.
9. Strong academic emphasis of the school climate promotes school effectiveness and student achievement.
10. Changing the culture or climate of a school is usually a difficult, continuous, and long-term process.

NOTES

1. Informal organization is another concept that describes the nature of the workplace in terms of the social structure and culture of the work group. You might find it useful to review the discussion of informal organization in Chapter 3.
2. Most of this large body of the research can be found in the Pupil Control Studies Archives, The Pennsylvania State University, Pattee Library, University Park, PA 16802.
3. The specifics for calculating the openness indices are found in Hoy, Tarter, and Kottkamp (1991). We discuss only the elementary version of the OCDQ in the text, but full descriptions of the other versions are available elsewhere. For the secondary school version, see Kottkamp, Mulhern, and Hoy (1987); Hoy, Tarter, and Kottkamp (1991); Hoy and Tarter (1997b). For the middle school version, see Hoy, Hoffman, Sabo, and Bliss (1994); Hoy and Tarter (1997a); Hoy and Sabo (1998).

CHAPTER 6

POWER AND POLITICS
IN SCHOOLS

Political realists see the world as it is: an arena of power politics moved primarily by perceived immediate self-interests, where morality is rhetorical rationale for expedient action and self-interest. It is a world not of angels but of angles, where men speak of moral principles but act on power principles.

Saul Alinsky
Rules for Radicals

Since my intention is to say something that will prove of practical use to the inquirer, I have thought it proper to represent things as they are in real truth, rather than as they are imagined.

Niccolo Machiavelli
The Prince

PREVIEW

1. Power is a broad construct that includes both legitimate and illegitimate methods of ensuring compliance.

2. Power can be classified not only as legitimate or illegitimate but also as formal or informal; hence, four basic kinds of organizational power exist: two forms of legitimate power—formal and informal authority—and two kinds of illegitimate power—coercive and political.

3. Legitimate power is more likely to promote commitment and compliance, whereas illegitimate power produces conflict and alienation.

4. Organizations are political arenas in which power and politics are central.

5. Coalitions of individuals and groups bargain to determine the distribution of power in organizations.

6. The external coalition can be dominated, divided, or passive, and it affects the internal coalition.

7. Internal coalitions can be personalized, bureaucratic, ideologic, professional, or politicized, and they can affect the distribution of power.

8. Power often concerns itself with defining rather than discovering organizational reality.

9. Power and politics are realities of organizational life, and they often undermine rationality.

10. Although the means of politics are illegitimate, the ends need not be; politics can be cruel and destructive or considerate and constructive.

11. Ingratiating, networking, information management, impression management, coalition building, and scapegoating are common political tactics organizational members use to gain advantage.

12. Political games are played to resist authority, to counter the resistance to authority, to build power bases, to defeat rivals, and to produce organizational change.

13. Conflict can be successfully managed by competing, collaborating, accommodating, compromising, or avoiding— depending on the situation.

All social organizations control their participants, but the problem of control is especially important in formal organizations, and the essence of organizational control is power. The classic definition of **power** is the ability to get others to do what you want them to do, or as Weber (1947: 152) defines it, "the probability that one actor within a social relationship will be in a position to carry out his own will despite resistance." Power for our purposes is a general and comprehensive term. It includes control that is starkly coercive as well as control that is based on nonthreatening persuasion and suggestion. Authority has a narrower scope than power. Weber (1947: 324) defines authority as "the probability that certain specific commands (or all commands) from a given source will be obeyed by a given group of persons." Weber is quick to indicate that authority does not include every mode of exercising power or influence over other persons. He suggests that a certain degree of voluntary compliance is associated with legitimate commands.

Organizations are created and controlled by legitimate authorities, who set goals, design structures, hire and manage employees, and monitor activities to ensure behavior is consistent with the goals and objectives of the organization. These official authorities control the legitimate power of the office or positions, but they are only one of many contenders for other forms of power in organizations (Bolman and Deal, 2003). We first examine legitimate forms of power and then turn to illegitimate ones.

SOURCES OF AUTHORITY: LEGITIMATE POWER

Authority relationships are an integral part of life in schools. The basis of many student-teacher, teacher-administrator, or subordinate-superior relations is authority. Unfortunately, many individuals view authority and authoritarianism as synonymous. Because this is not the case, authority as a theoretical concept must be clearly defined.

Contrary to some popular beliefs, the exercise of authority in a school typically does not involve coercion. Herbert A. Simon (1957a: 126–27) proposed that **authority** is distinguished from other kinds of influence or power in that the subordinate "holds in abeyance his own critical faculties for choosing between alternatives and uses the formal criterion of the receipt of a command or signal as his basis of choice." Therefore, two criteria of authority in schools are crucial in superior-subordinate relationships: (1) voluntary compliance to legitimate commands; and (2) suspension of one's own criteria for decision making and acceptance of the organizational command.

Peter Blau and W. Richard Scott (1962, 2003) argue that a third criterion must be added to distinguish authority from other forms of social control. They maintain that a value orientation arises that defines the use of social control as legitimate, and this orientation arises only in a group context. Authority is legitimized by a value that is held in common by the group (Suchman, 1995). Blau and Scott conclude that a basic characteristic of the authority relation is the subordinates' willingness to suspend their own criteria for making decisions and to comply with directives from the superior. This willingness results largely from social constraints exerted by norms of the social collectivity (teachers and students) and not primarily from the power the superior (administrator) brings to bear. Such social constraints are not typical of coercive power and other types of social influence. Authority relations in schools, then, have three primary characteristics: (1) a willingness of subordinates to comply; (2) a suspension of the subordinates' criteria for making a decision prior to a directive; and (3) a power relationship legitimized by the norms of a group.

Authority exists when a common set of beliefs (norms) in a school legitimizes the use of power as "right and proper." Weber (1947) distinguishes three types of authority—charismatic, traditional, and legal—according to the kind of legitimacy typically claimed by each.

Charismatic authority rests on devotion to an extraordinary individual who is leader by virtue of personal trust or exemplary qualities. Charismatic authority tends to be nonrational, affective, or emotional and rests heavily on the leader's personal qualities and characteristics. The authority of the charismatic leader results primarily from the leader's overwhelming personal appeal, and typically a common value orientation emerges within the group to produce an intense normative commitment to and identification with the person. Thus students may obey classroom directives because of a teacher's personal "mystique."

Traditional authority is anchored in an established belief in the sanctity of the status of those exercising authority in the past. Obedience is owed to the traditional sanctioned *position* of authority, and the person who occupies the position inherits the authority established by custom. In a school, for example, students may accept the authority of the position and obey the teacher because their parents and grandparents did so before them.

Legal authority is based on enacted laws that can be changed by formally correct procedures. Obedience is not owed to a person or position per se but to the *laws* that specify to whom and to what extent people owe compliance. Legal authority thus extends only within the scope of the authority vested in the office by law. In schools, obedience is owed to the impersonal principles that govern the operation of the organizations.

Other scholars and organizational theorists have extended these basic concepts of authority. Robert Peabody (1962) distinguishes the bases of formal authority—legitimacy and position—from the bases of functional authority—competence and personal or human relations skills, whereas Blau and Scott (1962, 2003; Scott, 2003) simply describe the authority relation as formal or informal depending on the source of legitimacy for the power.

Formal authority is vested in the organization and is legally established in positions, rules, and regulations. In joining the organization, employees accept the authority relation because they agree, within certain limits, to accept the directives of their supervisors; the organization has the right to command and the employees have the duty to obey (March and Simon, 1958). The basis of formal authority, then, rests with the legally established agreement between the organization and the employees.

Functional authority has a variety of sources, including authority of competence and authority of person. Although Weber treats authority of competence as part of the legal-rational pattern of bureaucracies, competence is not always limited to position. Technical competence can provide the source for legitimate control and directives in a formal organization regardless of the specific position held. This fact poses a dilemma and conflict for professionals.

Informal authority is still another source of legitimate control stemming from personal behavior and attributes of individuals. Regardless of formal position, some organizational members develop norms of allegiance and support from their colleagues. These informal norms buttress and legitimize their power and provide informal authority.

Authority and Administrative Behavior in Schools

Authority is a basic feature of life in schools because it provides the basis for legitimate control of administrators, teachers, and students. A primary source of control is formal authority that is vested in the office or position and not in the particular person who performs the official role (Merton, 1957). When administrators, teachers, and students join a school organization, they accept the formal authority relation. They agree within certain limits to follow directives that officials issue for the school. In short, school members enter into contractual agreements in which they sell their promises to obey commands (Commons, 1924).

Formal authority, anchored and buttressed by formal sanctions, has a somewhat limited scope. The existence of what Chester Barnard (1938) refers to as a bureaucratic "zone of indifference"—in which subordinates, including administrator and teacher professionals, accept orders without question—may be satisfactory for eliciting certain minimum performance levels, but it seems likely that this does not lead to an efficient operation. Formal authority promotes minimal compliance with directives and discipline, but it does

		Formal Authority	
		Yes	No
Informal Authority	Yes	Formal Leader	Informal Leader
	No	Officer	Follower

FIGURE 6.1   *Types of Authority Positions*

not encourage employees to exert effort, to accept responsibility, or to exercise initiative (Blau and Scott, 1962, 2003; Kotter, 1985). Therefore, a basic challenge facing all administrators, and one especially significant for first-level line supervisors such as school principals, is to find methods to extend their influence over their professional staff beyond the narrow limits of formal positional authority.

Hoy and Williams (1971) and Hoy and Rees (1974) have elaborated and empirically examined these ideas. They reasoned that many school administrators have the power and authority of their offices alone. In a sense, they are sterile bureaucrats, not leaders. Barnard (1938) suggests that only when the authority of leadership is combined with the authority of position will superiors be effective in inducing subordinates to comply with directives outside the bureaucratic zone of indifference. Indeed, the possession of both formal and informal authority distinguishes formal leaders from officers and informal leaders. Figure 6.1 illustrates these relationships.

How can school administrators broaden the bases of their authority and enhance their leadership position? The informal organization is an important source of authority that frequently remains untapped. Where legal contracts and position legitimize formal authority, the common values and sentiments that emerge in the work group legitimize informal authority. In particular, informal authority arises from the loyalty that the superior commands from group members (Blau and Scott, 1962, 2003). The significance of subordinate loyalty to superiors is clear. Administrators who command subordinate loyalty seem to have a distinct advantage in enlarging their authority base.

Although authoritarian principal behavior and teacher loyalty to principals are probably incompatible, one strategy some administrators use for extending the scope of formal authority over subordinates is domination (Blau and Scott, 1962, 2003). Authoritarian administrators, for example, attempt to increase control by resorting to formal sanctions or to threats of using those sanctions; however, their prolonged use probably tends to undermine their authority. Subordinates, particularly professionals, resent constant reminders of their dependence on the superior, especially in an egalitarian culture. Given a strategy of domination and close supervision, authoritarian administrators are *unlikely* to command loyalty and support from professionals easily. Blau (1955) neatly called this the *dilemma of bureaucratic authority*. The dilemma depends on the power of sanction, but it is weakened by frequent resort to sanctions. In fact, nonauthoritarian and supportive supervisors seem likely to engage in a contrasting strategy—one of leadership in which they furnish services and assistance to subordinates. Using formal authority to perform special favors, services, and support can create social obligations and build goodwill among subordinates. The result should be enhanced development of subordinate loyalty and informal authority.

The nature of supervision in schools should focus on helping, not directing, teachers to improve their teaching for a number of reasons. Teachers work in closed rooms and are not easily observed. Moreover, teachers frequently make strong claims for professional autonomy, and close supervision seems likely to be seen as an infringement on that autonomy. Finally, teachers attach great importance to authority on the basis of professional competence—much more so than similar professional groups such as social workers (Peabody, 1962). Therefore, it should not be surprising that research consistently demonstrates that authoritarian principals in schools are not successful at generating trust and teacher loyalty, whereas supportive ones are highly successful (Hoy and Rees, 1974; Isaacson, 1983; Mullins, 1983; Hoffman et al., 1994; Reiss, 1994; Reiss and Hoy, 1998). Close, authoritarian control of teachers does not generate informal authority; supportive and helpful supervision does.

Emotional detachment and hierarchical independence are two other important characteristics of principal-teacher relationships. Emotional detachment is the ability of administrators to remain calm, cool, and collected in difficult situations; and hierarchical independence is the extent to which administrators demonstrate their autonomy from superiors as they interact with teachers. Principals stand in the middle—with the higher administration on one side and professional teaching faculty on the other. Their effectiveness depends on the support they receive from both, yet they are likely to be the objects of conflicting pressures from both groups. Consequently, emotional detachment from subordinates and independence from superiors are important in establishing social support from teachers for principals. Indeed, the research has demonstrated the significance of both, but especially emotional detachment, in generating teacher loyalty to principals (Hoy and Williams, 1971; Hoy and Rees, 1974; Isaacson, 1983; Mullins, 1983).

Similarly, hierarchical influence is another attribute of administrators who are likely to tap into the informal teacher groups for authority to lead. Administrators who are able and willing to exert their influences with their superiors on teachers' behalf are respected and valued by teachers, and they earn the confidence, support, and loyalty of their teachers (Isaacson, 1983; Mullins, 1983).

Finally, the authenticity of the principal in dealing with teachers is a critical factor in the administrative process, enabling principals to generate teacher loyalty and informal authority. Leader authenticity is a slippery concept. People glibly talk about genuine, real, and authentic behavior, yet clear definition is another matter. Based on the work of Henderson and Hoy (1983) and Hoy and Henderson (1983), principal authenticity is defined as the extent to which teachers describe their principals as accepting responsibility for their own actions, as being nonmanipulating, and as demonstrating a salience of self over role. In contrast, inauthentic principals are viewed as those who pass the buck, blame others and circumstances for not being successful, manipulate teachers, and hide behind their formal position. As one would expect, leader authenticity is strongly related to commanding trust and teacher loyalty (Hoffman, 1993).

The implications of these empirical studies seem clear. If educational administrators are to be successful in developing informal authority, then they need to behave in ways that foster teacher loyalty. In this regard, authoritarian behavior is doomed to failure. Instead, administrators need to be supportive, independent, and use their influence to help teachers. Furthermore, even in difficult situations, administrative behavior needs to be emotionally tempered, calm, and considerate. Perhaps most important, principals should be authentic in their behavior; they need to show a willingness to share in the blame, to be nonmanipulative of teachers, and to be unfettered by bureaucratic role demands (Blau and Scott, 1962, 2003; Hoffman, 1993; Reiss, 1994; Reiss and Hoy, 1998).

SOURCES OF POWER

Although authority implies legitimacy, not all power is legitimate. Individuals, groups, or organizations can use power. For example, a department or group can have power, which suggests that it has the ability to influence the behavior of other individuals or groups, perhaps in personnel or budgeting decisions. Likewise, an individual can have power, which indicates success in getting others to comply with directives or suggestions. Leaders have power; they get others to comply with their directives. As we have seen, whether a leader or not, most administrators have power simply because as representatives of the organization, they have the power of the organization. But administrators can derive power from personal as well as organizational sources; those who have power influence the behavior of others. One of the first attempts to analyze sources of power was the pioneering work of John R. P. French and Bertram H. Raven (1968). Their focus on the bases of interpersonal power led them to the identification of five kinds of power—reward, coercive, legitimate, referent, and expert. Their typology of interpersonal power has been extended to the organizational level.

Reward power is the administrator's ability to influence subordinates by rewarding their desirable behavior. The strength of this kind of power depends on the attractiveness of the rewards and the extent of certainty that a person can control the rewards. For example, the principal who controls the allocation of teaching assignments or developmental grants for teaching innovations, or who can release teachers from routine housekeeping duties, has reward power over teachers in that school. Teachers may comply with the principal's requests because they expect to be rewarded for compliance. It is important, however, that the rewards be linked to compliance and that the influence attempts are proper and ethical. Philip Cusick (1981) describes one principal's attempt to use reward power by administering the schedule, additional assignments, and unallocated resources. The principal controlled just the things that many teachers desired. The principal could award a department chairperson with a free period, a favorite class, a double lunch period, an honors section, or support for a new activity.

Coercive power is an administrator's ability to influence subordinates by punishing them for undesirable behavior. The strength of coercive power depends on the severity of the punishment and on the likelihood that the punishment cannot be avoided. Punishment can take many forms—official reprimands, undesirable work assignments, closer supervision, stricter enforcement of the rules and regulations, denial of salary increments, or termination. Punishment is not without its negative effects. An official reprimand to a teacher for consistently leaving school early may result in frequent absenteeism, refusal to provide extra help to students unless specified in the contract, and a general tendency to avoid all but the essential aspects of the job. Interestingly, the same relationship can be viewed as one of reward power in one situation but as coercive power in another. For example, if a teacher obeys a principal through fear of punishment, it is coercive power; but if another teacher obeys in anticipation of a future reward, it is reward power.

Legitimate power is the administrator's ability to influence the behavior of subordinates simply because of formal position. Subordinates acknowledge that the administrator has a right to issue directives and they have an obligation to comply. Every administrator is empowered by the organization to make decisions within a specific area of responsibility. This area of responsibility defines the activities over which the administrator has legitimate power. The further removed a directive is from the administrator's area of responsibility, the weaker his or her legitimate power. When directives from an administrator are accepted without question, they fall within the subordinate's "zone of indifference." Such an order lies within an area that was anticipated at the time the employee contracted with the organization and is seen by the employee as a legitimate obligation. For example, teachers expect to compute and turn in grades on time for each marking period. Outside the zone, however, legitimate power fades quickly. It is one thing for the principal to insist that grades be promptly computed and turned in to the office; it is quite another to order teachers to change a grade. The legitimacy of the first request is clear, but not so for the second; hence, compliance with the second request is questionable.

Referent power is an administrator's ability to influence behavior based on subordinates' liking and identification with the administrator. The individual with referent power is admired and respected, and serves as a model to be emulated. The source of referent power rests with the extraordinary personality and interpersonal skills of the individual. For example, young teachers may identify with the principal and seek to imitate the personal demeanor and perhaps the leadership style of the more experienced and well-liked principal. Not only individuals but also groups can have referent power. Members of a positive reference group can also provide a source of referent power. Referent power does not rest simply with the official power holders of an organization. Teachers as well as principals can have referent power; in fact, any highly attractive individual who develops respect, trust, and loyalty among colleagues is likely to develop such power.

Expert power is the administrator's ability to influence subordinates' behavior on the basis of specialized knowledge and skill. Subordinates are influenced because they believe that the information and expertise the administrator holds are relevant, are helpful, and are things they themselves do not have. Like referent power, expert power is a personal characteristic and does not depend on occupying a formal position of power. Expert power is, however, much narrower in scope than referent power. The useful knowledge defines the limits of expert power. New administrators are likely to have a time lag in the acquisition of expert power because it takes time for expertise to become known and accepted by subordinates. New principals must demonstrate that they know how to perform their administrative functions with skill before we willingly accept their attempts to implement new practices and procedures.

These five types of power can be grouped into two broad categories—organizational and personal. Reward, coercive, and legitimate power are bound to the organizational position. The higher the position, the greater the potential for power. In contrast, referent and expert power depend much more on the personal attributes of the administrator, such as personality, leadership style, knowledge, and interpersonal skill. In brief, some sources of power are more amenable to organizational control, whereas others are more dependent on personal characteristics.

ADMINISTRATIVE USES OF POWER

A large portion of any administrator's time is directed at "power-oriented" behavior—that is, "behavior directed primarily at developing or using relationships in which other people are to some degree willing to defer to one's wishes" (Kotter, 1978: 27). Administrators possess varying degrees and combinations of the types of power that have just been discussed. Moreover, the way administrators use one type of power can hinder or facilitate the effectiveness of other kinds (Pfeffer, 1992).

Reward power is likely to produce positive feelings and facilitate the development of referent power, but coercive power has the opposite effect (Huber, 1981). Moreover, subordinates may view administrators who demonstrate expertise as having more legitimate power. In fact, expert power may be the most stable form of power. In one study, changes in the reward structure of an organization increased the perceived use of coercive power and reduced the perceived use of reward, legitimate, and referent power of the administrator, but expert power remained stable (Greene and Podsakoff, 1981).

TABLE 6.1

Probable Subordinate Responses to Power

Type of Power	Probable Subordinate Responses to Power		
	Commitment	Simple Compliance	Resistance
Referent	XXX	XX	X
Expert	XXX	XX	X
Legitimate	XX	XXX	X
Reward	XX	XXX	X
Coercive	X	XX	XXX

XXX—Most likely.
XX—Less likely.
X—Least likely.

Gary Yukl (2002) offers some guidelines to administrators for building and using each of the five kinds of power. The likely consequences of the uses of power are important considerations for administrators. Table 6.1 summarizes the probable outcomes of each form of power in terms of commitment, simple compliance, or resistance. For example, the use of referent power is most likely to promote commitment, next most likely to result in simple compliance, and least likely to create resistance and develop alienation. Commitment is most likely with the use of referent and expert power; legitimate and reward power are most likely to promote a simple compliance; and coercive power will probably produce resistance and eventually alienation. Amitai Etzioni (1975) draws similar conclusions in his analysis of the consequences of using power in organizations.

Referent power depends on personal loyalty to the administrator that grows over a relatively long period of time. The development of loyalty to one's superior is a social exchange process, which is improved when administrators demonstrate concern, trust, and affection for their subordinates. Such acceptance and confidence promote goodwill and identification with superiors, which in turn create strong loyalty and commitment. Referent power is most effective if administrators select subordinates, who are most likely to identify with them, make frequent use of personal appeals, and set examples of appropriate role behavior—that is, lead by example.

Expertise itself is usually not enough to guarantee commitment of subordinates. Successful use of expert power requires that subordinates recognize the administrator's knowledge and perceive the exercise of that expertise to be useful. Thus, administrators must demonstrate their knowledge convincingly by maintaining credibility, keeping informed, acting decisively, recognizing subordinate concerns, and avoiding threats to the self-esteem of subordinates. In short, administrators must promote an image of expertise and then use their knowledge to demonstrate its utility.

Authority is exercised through legitimate power. Legitimate requests may be expressed as orders, commands, directives, or instructions. The outcome of the administrator's request may be committed compliance, simple compliance, resistance, or alienation depending on the nature and manner of the request. There is less likelihood of resistance and alienation if the administrator makes the request politely and clearly, explains the reasons for the request, is responsive to the concerns of subordinates, and routinely uses legitimate authority (Yukl, 2002, 1994).

The use of reward power is a common administrative tactic to achieve compliance with organizational rules or specific leader requests. The rewards may be either explicit or implicit, but it is important that they are contingent on compliance with administrative directives. Compliance is most likely when the request is feasible, the incentive is attractive, the administrator is a credible source of the reward, the request is proper and ethical, and the compliance to the request can be verified. There are some dangers in the use of rewards. Subordinates can perceive reward power as manipulative, a common cause of subordinate resistance and hostility. Moreover, the frequent use of reward power can define the administrative relationship in purely economic terms; thus, subordinate response becomes calculated on the basis of tangible benefits. When rewards are given to express an administrator's personal appreciation for a job well done, however, it can become a source of increased referent power. People who repeatedly provide incentives in an acceptable manner gradually become better liked by the recipients of the rewards (French and Raven, 1968).

Most effective administrators try to avoid the use of coercive power because it typically erodes the use of referent power and creates hostility, alienation, and aggression among subordinates. Absenteeism, sabotage, theft, job actions, and strikes are common responses to excessive coercion. The use of coercion is usually considered when the problem is one of discipline and is most appropriate when used to deter behavior detrimental to the organization—for example, stealing, sabotage, violation of rules, fighting, and direct disobedience to legitimate directives (Yukl, 2002). To be most effective, subordinates need to be informed about the rules and penalties for violations. Coercion is never without the potential to alienate; thus discipline must be administered promptly, consistently, and fairly. The administrator must maintain credibility, stay calm, avoid appearing hostile, and use measured and appropriate punishments. Three guides should be helpful to administrators:

- Avoid the use of coercive power: coercion alienates.
- Use organizational power to develop personal power.
- Use personal power to motivate and create commitment.

Power need not be thought of as a constraining force on subordinates. **Empowerment** is the process by which administrators share power and help others use it in constructive ways to make decisions affecting themselves and their work (Schermerhorn, Hunt, and Osborn, 1994; Hardy and Leiba-

O'Sullivan, 1998; Leuch, Wall, and Jackson, 2003). More than ever before, administrators and reformers are trying to empower teachers (Conley and Bacharach, 1990; Gaziel, 2002; Pugh and Zhau, 2003; Rice and Schneider, 1994; Marks and Louis, 1997, 1999; Rinehart, Short, and Johnson, 1997; Rinehart, Short, Short, and Eckley, 1998). Empowerment gets translated into shared decision making (Hoy and Tarter, 2004), delegation of authority, teamwork (Dee, Henkin, and Duemer, 2003; Lally and Scaife, 1995), and site-based management (see Chapter 9). Rather than viewing power as the domain of administrators, adherents of empowerment increasingly see it as something to be shared by everyone in more collegial organizations (Lugg and Boyd, 1993). When teachers are empowered, principals are less likely to boss and push them around (use coercive power) and more likely to serve as facilitators who guide teams of teachers using their knowledge and expertise (expert power). Principals will increasingly be less able to rely on their position (legitimate power) to direct subordinates; in fact, as teachers are empowered, expertise will become the most significant element in power relationships between teachers and principals. Finally, evidence is beginning to emerge that shows empowering teachers in curricular matters is related to improving student performance (Sweetland and Hoy, 2000a).

MINTZBERG'S PERSPECTIVE ON POWER

Henry Mintzberg (1983a) proposes another way to analyze power in and around organizations. In his view, power in organizations stems from control over a *resource*, a *technical skill*, or a *body of knowledge*. In all cases, however, to serve as a basis for power the resource, skill, or knowledge has to be important to the functioning of the organization; it must be in short supply; and it must not be readily replaceable. In other words, the organization must need something that only a few people can supply. For example, the principal who has primary responsibility for determining tenure for teachers has resource power. The assistant principal who has the interpersonal skills to deal effectively with irate parents, students, and teachers has power, as does the teacher who alone in the school understands the elements of a new curriculum thrust.

A fourth general basis of power derives from *legal prerogatives*, which give some individuals the exclusive right to impose choices. School boards have the legal right to hire and fire administrators and teachers; they are vested with such power through state statute. School administrators in turn are often required by state law to evaluate the competence of nontenured teachers. Moreover, they are delegated the right to issue orders to employees, which are tempered by other legal prerogatives that grant power to teachers and their associations.

Finally, power often comes to those who have *access* to power holders. Many principals' secretaries have power because of their access to and influence with those who wield power. Similarly, friends of the board president or superintendent or principal often change the course of organizational decision making.

Mintzberg also proposes a set of four internal power systems that are the basic sources for controlling organizational life: the system of authority, the system of ideology, the system of expertise, and the system of politics. The system of authority contributes to attainment of the formal goals as the organization defines them; the system of ideology contributes to the achievement of informal objectives that emerge as the organization develops its culture; and the system of expertise controls the behavior of professionals as they subject themselves to the standards of their professional training. These three systems of control typically contribute to the needs of the organization; that is, they are legitimate. But those with power also have personal needs. In the process of striving to accomplish the broader organizational needs, individuals find they have discretion, and discretion opens the way to political power. Thus a system of political power emerges that is not sanctioned by the formal authority, ideology, or certified expertise; in fact, it is typically divisive, parochial, and illegitimate.

The **system of authority** is the formal flow of power through legitimate channels. There are two subsystems of control here, personal and bureaucratic. *Personal control* is wielded by giving orders, setting decision premises, reviewing decisions, and allocating resources. Together these four personal means of controlling give administrators considerable power to orient the decisions and actions of their faculties. *Bureaucratic control,* on the other hand, rests with the imposition of impersonal standards that are established to guide the general behavior of teachers across a whole range of areas—for example, the time they are expected to be at school each day, cafeteria duty, and grading and homework requirements.

The **system of ideology** is the informal agreements among teachers about the school and its relationships to other groups. The character of the work group in terms of climate and culture are the terms we use in this text (see Chapter 5) to capture the essence of the system of ideology. The openness of the climate and the basic values of the school culture provide powerful sources of power and control.

The **system of expertise** is the interplay among experts or professionals to solve critical contingencies that the organization confronts. Faced with the complex tasks of teaching and learning, schools hire specialists (e.g., teachers, counselors, psychologists, and administrators) to achieve their basic goals. The need for autonomy to make professional decisions often conflicts with the system of formal authority, perhaps an inevitable consequence of professionals working in bureaucratic structures (see Chapter 3). As teachers continue to become increasingly professional, the demand for greater autonomy and power seems likely, and the granting of such power will likely be at the expense of the formal authority system.

The **system of politics** is the network of organizational politics, which lacks the legitimacy of the other three systems of power. It is a system that also lacks the consensus and order found in the other systems. There is no sense of unity or pulling together for a common good. This system can be described as a set of political games that power holders play. The games can coexist with the legitimate systems, be antagonistic to the systems, or substitute for the legitimate systems of control.

School administrators must recognize these systems of influence and must know how to tap into and use them. Clearly the system of authority is the beginning point for school administrators. Their positions are vested with power, but the personal and bureaucratic control of the position is not usually sufficient to motivate teachers to expend extra effort or to be creative in their service to the school and students. The danger to the school administrator is exclusive reliance on the system of authority. To do so is to limit commitment to the school and to risk producing resistance and alienation among teachers.

What Mintzberg calls the system of ideology is akin to what others refer to as the culture or climate of the school (see Chapter 5). Organizational ideology can produce a sense of mission among members. First-level administrators, such as principals, are key actors in the development of ideology. The goal is to create a belief among teachers and students that there is something special about their school, that it has a distinctive identity or unique culture. We have already discussed some of the ways that principals can tap into the informal organization, develop loyalty and trust, and enlarge the scope of their authority. Informal authority, however, is another beginning, not an end. Ultimately, the principal must go beyond commanding personal loyalty and generate an organizational commitment in which teachers give loyalty to the school and take pride and identity from it. Of course, the consequence of a strong ideology is to redistribute power; that is, power becomes more evenly distributed among educators.

Although the systems of authority and ideology promote coordination and compliance, they are rarely sufficient. When work is complex, experts or professionals are required, and with them come demands for autonomy to make decisions on the basis of professional considerations, not on the basis of authority or ideology. The power of the administrators needs to be shared with professionals. As teaching becomes more fully professionalized as an occupation, teacher empowerment will likely become a reality rather than merely a slogan, and many more schools will move toward organizational structures that are professional bureaucracies (see Chapter 3).

Our discussion of Mintzberg's systems of power makes one thing clear for school administrators: They must be ready to share power. Those who hoard power are likely to become victims of teacher and student dissatisfaction, alienation, and hostility. Moreover, the inadequacy of their systems of control is likely to open the way in schools for the play of informal power of a more clandestine nature—that is, political power, a topic to which we will return later in this chapter. We summarize this section with four imperatives for effective administrators:

- Extend your system of authority; formal authority is not sufficient for leadership.
- Tap into the system of ideology; organization culture and informal organization are other sources of authority.
- Tap into the system of expertise; share power with your teachers; empower them.
- Know and understand the system of politics; limit it.

A COMPARISON AND SYNTHESIS OF POWER PERSPECTIVES

Our analysis of authority and power has covered a number of conceptual views (see Table 6.2). The perspectives can be compared in terms of the extent to which the power is legitimate or illegitimate and formal or informal. By definition, the three formulations of authority consider only legitimate power. In contrast, the perspectives on power deal with both legitimate and illegitimate control as well as formal and informal power, but none of the

TABLE 6.2

Comparison of Sources of Power and Authority

	Peabody (1962)	Blau and Scott (1962)	Weber (1947)	French and Raven (1968)	Mintzberg (1983a)
Legitimate Formal Power	Formal authority	Formal authority	Bureaucratic authority	Reward power and legitimate power	System of authority
Legitimate Informal Power	Functional authority	Informal authority	Charismatic authority and traditional authority	Referent power and expert power	System of ideology and system of expertise
Illegitimate Formal Power				Coercive power*	
Illegitimate Informal Power					System of politics*

*The power can be legitimate, but it is typically not.

frameworks is so comprehensive as to consider all four combinations of power; hence, we propose a synthesis. The French and Raven (1968) typology provides a classic analysis of interpersonal power, whereas Mintzberg (1983a) focuses his analysis on organizational power, and he develops four systems of influence to explore the power configurations in and around organizations. Only Mintzberg's formulation, however, considers power that is both illegitimate and informal—the system of internal politics. We propose a synthesis of power relations to include formal and informal authority (legitimate power), and coercive and political power (illegitimate). See Figure 6.2.

In analyzing power, a structural perspective calls attention to authority—the legitimate, formal power of the office or position (see Chapter 3). A cultural perspective underscores the legitimate, informal power of the organizational culture (see Chapter 5). An individual perspective emphasizes the legitimate, informal role of expertise and knowledge in generating power (see Chapter 4). But it is the political perspective that calls attention to the illegitimate, informal power that is inherent in organizations.

POWER, RATIONALITY, AND RATIONALIZATION

Power often blurs the difference between rationality and rationalization:

- *Rationality* is the application of evidence and reason to make decisions.
- *Rationalization* is an attempt to make a decision seem rational after it has already been made.

Rationalization masquerading as rationality can be a basic strategy in the exercise of power. Kant (1794) first noted that the possession of power spoils the free use of reason. Many of us have experienced how the view from the top

		Source of Power	
		Formal	Informal
Legitimacy of Power	Legitimate	Formal Authority	Informal Authority
	Illegitimate	Coercive Power*	Political Power*

*The power can be legitimate, but is typically not.

FIGURE 6.2   *Synthesis of Power Relations*

(superintendent, dean, or principal) gets interpreted as the "truth." Power has a way of defining reality because people in power spin the truth to suit their own purposes (Sweetland and Hoy, 2000b). On the basis of an in-depth case study of politics and power, Bent Flyvbjerg (1998) advances a critical theory of power that is instructive to our analysis.

Power often defines reality because superiors specify what counts as knowledge. Those in power interpret and sometimes reinterpret evidence. Nietzsche (1968) said it well: "interpretation is itself a means of becoming master of something and subduing and becoming masters involves a fresh interpretation" (p. 342). When the principal or superintendent explains, teachers are expected to listen and accept. Power is part of rationality because rationality is penetrated by power. Put simply, rationalization and using power are often more forceful tactics than rational argument. Not surprisingly, when powerful participants need support, it is rationalization and not rationality that prevails.

In the world of practice, however, it is difficult to distinguish between rationality and rationalization because rationalization is cloaked in rationality. Although rationality is more legitimate and acceptable, backstage, hidden from public scrutiny, power and rationalization dominate. A rationalized front is not necessarily dishonest because many individuals and organizations believe their own rationalizations. Self-delusion may be part of the will to power (Nietzsche, 1968). Not surprisingly, many administrators are true believers of their own rationalizations; they convince themselves of both the merit and the rationality of their rationalizations.

Machiavelli warns that, "We must distinguish between . . . those who to achieve their purpose can force the issue and those who must use persuasion. In the second case, they always come to grief." (1984: 51–52). These are strong words, but power does enable leaders to define the situation. The greater the power, the less the need to discover the facts because strong leaders can use their power successfully to create the reality they prefer; in fact, a leader's unwillingness to present rational argument or documentation may simply be an indicator of his or her power to act.

Stable power relations are more common in politics and administration than antagonistic confrontations in large part because of the pain and extra effort antagonism demands. Confrontations are actively avoided most of the time, and when they do occur, they are quickly transformed into stable power relations (Flyvbjerg, 1998). Conflict and antagonism get attention because they are not common and they cause organizational excitement, which is fodder for rumor and innuendo. Most administrators, however, prefer harmony and stability to antagonism and instability, and they work to avoid conflict and gain a steady equilibrium of relative harmony.

The use of power is strong and active in all contemporary organizations; power and politics are inevitable. In fact, open, antagonistic confrontation involves little contest. Knowledge and rationality carry little weight; power trumps knowledge. The proverb that "Truth is the first casualty of war" is confirmed in organizations. For example, Flyvbjerg (1998) found that the "use of naked power tends to be more effective than any appeal to objectivity, facts, knowledge, or rationality, even though feigned versions of the latter, that is, rationalization, may be used to legitimate naked power" (p. 232).

Where rational considerations do play a role, they do so in the context of stable power relations. Although stability does not guarantee rationality, rationality is more common in stable power relations because administrators are likely to be more open to rational argument than they are in antagonistic or confrontational ones. School administrators are more likely to listen to reason when relationships with their teachers and the union are not hostile; that is, the power of rationality is most effective and emerges most frequently in the absence of confrontation.

In brief, we cannot escape the fact that much organizational behavior is irrational and that power often undermines rationality. Although Bacon's (1597) famous dictum that "knowledge is power" is true, it is also the case that "power is knowledge." Flyvbjerg's perspective on power and rationality raises a number of intriguing questions, for example:

- Is rationality such a weak form of power that organizations built on rationality will fail?
- Does an emphasis on rationality leave us ignorant about how politics and power work in schools?
- Does a democratic emphasis make school participants more vulnerable to manipulation by those in power?
- Are democracy and rationality insufficient ways to solve problems in schools?

Let us return to Machiavelli's (1984: 91) warning concerning the dangers and reality of power: "A man who neglects what is actually done for what should be done learns the way to self-destruction." We need to see and understand organizational life as it is so that we have some chance to move it toward what we believe it should be; hence, power and politics cannot be neglected.

TIP: THEORY INTO PRACTICE

Describe the people in your school who have power. What is the source of their power? Who are the individuals who have informal power? Why do they have such power? How do the power holders relate to each other? How much confrontation and hostility exist in your school? Evaluate the extent to which rationality and rationalization prevail in your school. Which is dominant and why? Are teachers in your school cynical or optimistic about the distribution of power? Explain.

ORGANIZATIONAL POWER AND POLITICS[1]

Politics is "individual or group behavior that is informal, ostensibly parochial, typically divisive, and above all, in the technical sense, illegitimate—sanctioned neither by formal authority, accepted ideology, nor certified expertise" (Mintzberg, 1983a: 172). Although there are powerful individuals, the political arenas of organizations are composed of **coalitions** of individuals—groups who bargain among themselves to determine the distribution of power (Cyert and March, 1963). Despite all attempts to integrate individual needs in the service of the organization's goals, individuals have their own needs to fulfill. Inevitably, they get caught up in attempts to satisfy their more parochial needs and, in the process, they form coalitions with others who have similar aspirations. These major interest groups are varied and diverse; for example, they represent departmental, professional, gender, and ethnic groups as well as internal and external interests. Moreover, there are enduring differences in values, beliefs, knowledge, and perceptions among the coalitions. These differences are stable, change slowly, and are sources of much tension and conflict. Many of the most important organizational decisions concern allocating scarce resources. Thus a critical question becomes: How does each coalition articulate its preferences and mobilize its power to obtain resources (Bolman and Deal, 2003)?

External Coalitions

Significant outside influencers of schools include a myriad of groups such as teacher associations, unions, parent-teacher associations, taxpayer groups, state departments of education, consortia of colleges and universities, professional organizations, the media, and other organized special interest groups (see Chapter 7). Most of these outside-influence groups are trying to bring their own interests and external power to bear on the activities of the school. Their problem, of course, is figuring out how to achieve the outcomes they desire when they are functioning outside the official decision-making structure of the school. Mintzberg (1983a) notes that the impact of the external coalition on the organization varies dramatically, and he proposes a continuum of three external coalitions—dominated, divided, and passive.

A **dominated external coalition** is composed of one sole, powerful influencer or a set of external influencers acting in concert. In such cases the external coalition is so powerful that it dominates not only the internal coalition but also the board of education and the superintendent. Indeed, the board and superintendent are simply tools for the external coalition. For example, on occasion, a community issue such as "back to basics" can become so popular that a concerted effort by an organized group of external influencers can come to dominate not only curriculum change but, if left unchallenged, the basic policy and activities of the school.

Dominant coalitions do not remain unchallenged; in fact, it seems only a matter of time until other groups and individuals will coalesce and act.

Without a dominant external power coalition, the power system of an organization changes in fundamental ways. When the external coalition is divided among independent and competing external individuals and groups of influencers, the organization is pushed in different directions as it attempts to respond to conflicting pressures.

A **divided external coalition** exists when a few, usually two or three, different sets of influencers emerge such that there is a rough balance of influence among the conflicting groups. For example, in school communities the balance can be between two external coalitions, one conservative and the other progressive. The curriculum and instructional programs often are battle-grounds for control as the coalitions compete. Their power struggles are reflected on the board of education and inevitably spill over into the internal coalitions within the school. In fact, Mintzberg (1983a) claims a divided external coalition often has the effect of politicizing the board as well as the internal coalition.

A **passive external coalition** is reached when the number of outside groups of external influencers continues to increase to the point where the power of each is diffuse and limited. The external coalition becomes passive and power is concentrated within the organization. Apathy becomes the natural strategy for the large, dispersed group (Olsen, 1965, 1968). The external environment is relatively stable and calm as influencers remain dispersed and passive; such an environment is welcomed by many administrators.

Internal Coalitions

Just as the organization can be influenced by external coalitions, it is also affected by internal groups of influencers that band together in common cause—internal coalitions. The external coalition shapes the kind of internal coalitions that emerge. A dominated external coalition tends to weaken internal coalitions; a divided external coalition tends to politicize them; and a passive external coalition gives internal coalitions a chance to flourish. But regardless of the kind of external coalition, it is through the efforts of the internal coalitions that the organization functions. Five dominant types of internal coalitions can develop—personalized, bureaucratic, ideologic, professional, and politicized (Mintzberg, 1983a).

The **personalized internal coalition** is one in which power is concentrated in the hierarchy of authority in the person of the chief executive officer, who rules the internal coalition. The superintendent, for example, controls the critical decisions and functions of the school in such a situation. There is little political game playing by insiders here.

In a **bureaucratic internal coalition,** power is also concentrated in the formal system of authority, but here its focus is on bureaucratic controls—rules, regulations, and procedures. Although bureaucratic controls tend to limit politics, political games arise—for example, between line and staff or among principals as they try to build empires and enlarge their own school budgets, usually at the expense of other schools in the district.

An **ideologic internal coalition** sometimes controls the organization; the system of ideology is so pervasive it dominates. For example, if the culture of a school is sufficiently strong and unified, teachers do not simply accept the goals and objectives; they share them as their very own. The administrator may seem to have great power because he or she embodies the culture, but the fact is that in sharing beliefs everyone shares power. Collegiality and egalitarianism prevail (Sergiovanni, 1992), and internal politics is very limited because of the strong sharing of beliefs.

In a **professional internal coalition,** the system of expertise dominates the organization. Highly trained experts—professionals—surrender a great deal of power to their organizations and the institutions that train them (Mintzberg, 1983a). Here politics is usually substantial because of the conflict between the systems of authority and expertise—what we have discussed as professional-bureaucratic conflict in Chapter 3. The professional internal coalition in this situation is a playing field for a wide assortment of political games, yet politics is held in check by expertise.

In a **politicized internal coalition** power rests on politics. Here antagonistic political games dominate the organization and either substitute for or drive out legitimate power. Whether the organization is politicized or not, however, the game of politics is played in all organizations, and schools are not an exception.

TIP: THEORY INTO PRACTICE

Describe the power coalitions in your school. What groups of teachers have power? Why do these groups have power? Does their power come from the organization, the union, the informal organization, the culture, or expertise? How do they exercise the power? Which is dominant and why? To what extent do external coalitions influence internal ones? Who are the leaders of the internal coalitions in your school? Do the coalitions in the school make organizational life better or worse? Explain.

THE POWER GAME

Power matters; it is an important aspect of what an organization does and it affects what its members do. Hirschman (1970), in his classic book, *Exit, Voice, and Loyalty,* observes that participants in any system have three basic options:

- Leave; find another place—exit.
- Stay and play; try to change the system—voice.
- Stay and contribute as expected; be a loyal member—loyalty.

Those members who leave the organization cease to be influencers; those who are loyal choose not to participate as active influencers; but those who choose to stay and speak out become players in the power game. Access to power itself, however, is not sufficient. Power players must also have the *will* to play, which means they must be willing to expend the energy to be successful, as well as the *skill* to act strategically and tactically when necessary. Power is an elusive blend of negotiating advantages and then willingly and skillfully exploiting those bargaining advantages (Allison, 1971).

Politics is a fact of organization life. Mintzberg (1983a, 1983b) argues that internal politics is typically clandestine and illegitimate because it is designed to benefit the individual or group, usually at the expense of the organization; therefore, the most common consequences of politics are divisiveness and conflict. Conflict is not necessarily bad; in fact, it sometimes calls attention to problems in the legitimate systems of control. Remember, however, that politics is not typically sanctioned by formal authority, ideology, or certified expertise; in fact, it arises because of default, weakness in the other systems of influence, or by design to resist or exploit others in control. Notwithstanding its lack of legitimacy, politics, like all forms of power, can solve important organizational problems (Mintzberg, 1983a):

- Politics ensures that the strongest members of the organization are brought into positions of leadership.
- Politics ensures that all sides of an issue are debated; the systems of authority, ideology, and sometimes even expertise tend to promote only one side.
- Politics are often needed to promote change blocked by the formal organization.
- Politics can ease the execution of decisions; administrators play political games to implement their decisions.

There is no guarantee that those who gain power will use it rationally or justly, but power and politics are not always demeaning and destructive. Politics can be a vehicle for achieving noble purposes (Bolman and Deal, 2003).

Where the formal system is usually a highly organized structure, George Strauss (1964) observes that the political system is a mass of competing power groups, each seeking to influence organizational policy for its own interests, or at least, in terms of its own distorted image of the organization's interest. Successful politics requires organizational members to bargain, negotiate, jockey for position, and engage in a myriad of political games, strategies, and tactics to influence the goals and decisions of their organization. As we have already noted, these politics can coexist with other more legitimate forms of power, array themselves in opposition to the legitimate power, or become substitutes for weak legitimate systems of control. With this view in mind, we turn to three important topics—political tactics, political games, and conflict management.

Political Tactics

All members of an organization can engage in organizational politics. In fact, it seems likely that, regardless of level or position, everyone is a player in the game of politics. Thus, we turn to a set of political tactics that employees at all levels commonly use (Vecchio, 1988).

Ingratiating is a tactic used to gain the goodwill of another through doing favors, being attentive, and giving favors. It is based on what sociologists call the "norm of reciprocity," a pervasive norm in American society. Help a colleague or superior and the person feels obliged to return the favor or repay the positive action. Teachers often attempt to gain the goodwill and obligation of their colleagues and principals by going beyond their duty in helping others. Daniel Griffiths and his colleagues (1965), in a study of teacher mobility in New York City, described how teachers used this tactic to become administrators. A sizable number of teachers volunteered for jobs that most teachers perceived as irritants: teacher in charge of the lunchroom, administrator of the annual field day, school coordinator for student teachers, or trainer of the school track team. None of these jobs was paid, but they earned the teachers the goodwill and attention of superiors and frequently gained them more important positions such as assistant principal or acting chair.

Networking is the process of forming relationships with influential people. Such people may or may not be in important positions, but they often have access to useful information. Teachers who have close, friendly relations with the teachers' union representative or principal usually have access to important information. Likewise, teachers who have contacts with the spouse of the board president or who have an indirect link to the superintendent or who know the union head are also likely to gain valuable inside information.

Information management is a tactic individuals use to control others or build their own status. Although having critical information is useful in itself, the techniques used to spread the information can enhance one's position in both the formal and informal organizations. Releasing information when it has full impact can promote self-interest and defeat the ambitions of others. The key to information management is first to get crucial information (networking) and then to use it skillfully, making things known to others in ways that increase their dependence and build your reputation as one who "really knows" what is happening. Teachers who have networks that garner them important information are typically major actors in the political life of the school, and their careful nurturing and managing of that knowledge usually enhances their roles as important players in the political games of the school.

Impression management is a simple tactic that most everyone uses from time to time to create a favorable image. The tactic includes dressing and behaving appropriately, underscoring one's accomplishments, claiming credit whenever possible, and creating the impression of being important, if not indispensable. The key is to build an image such that others see you as knowledgeable, articulate, sensible, sensitive, and socially adept.

Coalition building is the process of individuals banding together to achieve common goals. Teachers often join forces to oppose a proposed policy, to resist a proposed change, or to initiate change. A change in the curriculum is often successful depending on which teacher coalitions support or oppose it. Individuals alone are much less effective at influencing than groups; and relatively powerless groups become stronger if they can act together in coalition. Those teachers who are effective at organizing internal coalitions are often the political power players in a school.

Scapegoating is blaming and attacking others when things go wrong or badly. Principals often try to blame teachers when their statewide proficiency test scores are not high, and teachers seek to find someone to blame too: the administration, the school board, the parents, or another teacher. Blaming others for shortcomings is common in all organizations and schools are no exception. Finding a scapegoat can allow politically astute individuals an opportunity to shift attention and "get off the hook" by finding someone else to take the fall.

Increasing indispensability is a tactic by which individuals or units make themselves necessary to the organization. Crafty administrators often develop specialized skills or units that make them important and essential in the operation of the organization. For example, they specialize in critical areas that require specialized knowledge such as computers and finance. Thus, their goal is to make the organization dependent upon their knowledge and skill. Further, they are not especially forthcoming in explaining or preparing others to do what they do. Such individuals are increasingly called upon to solve problems, and their successful solutions further enhance their status and value. The common tactics are summarized in Table 6.3.

Some tactics are natural and legitimate; others are devious and illegitimate. When the tactics are based on dishonesty, deceit, and misinformation, they are hard to justify on moral grounds. Robert Vecchio (1988) argues that on the grounds of self-defense, one should be familiar with such devious political

TABLE 6.3

Summary of Political Tactics

Political Tactic	Purpose
Ingratiating	Gain favors by doing favors
Networking	Gain influence by courting influentials
Managing information	Manipulate information to your advantage
Managing impressions	Create a positive image by appearance
Coalition building	Band together with others to achieve goals
Scapegoating	Shift the blame to others for bad outcomes
Increasing indispensability	Make yourself indispensable to the organization

tactics as scapegoating, nurturing conflict by spreading false rumors, excluding rivals from important meetings, and making false promises. Although political tactics are a fact of organizational life, not all are viewed as legitimate (Cox, 1982). Moreover, there are a number of common blunders that are costly political mistakes.

- Violating the chain of command.
- Losing your temper in public.
- Saying no too often to superiors.
- Challenging cherished beliefs (Vecchio, 1988).

Political Games

One way to describe more fully organizational politics is to conceive of it as a set of political games that organizational participants play. The games are complex, with intricate and subtle tactics played according to the rules. Some rules are explicit, others implicit. Some rules are quite clear, others fuzzy. Some are very stable; others are ever-changing. But the collection of rules, in effect, defines the game. First, rules establish position, the paths by which people gain access to positions, the power of each position, and the action channels. Second, rules constrict the range of decisions and actions that are acceptable. Third, rules can sanction such moves as bargaining, coalitions, persuasion, deceit, bluff, and threat while making other moves illegal, immoral, or inappropriate (Allison, 1971).

Mintzberg (1983a) identifies five general kinds of games that organizational members play: games to resist authority, games to counter that resistance, games to build power bases, games to defeat opponents, and games to change the organization. Relying heavily on Mintzberg's work, we will discuss each.

Insurgency games usually are played to resist formal authority. They range from resistance to sabotage to mutiny. When an order is issued, there is typically some discretion in executing it. Because there is no guarantee that the order will be carried out to the letter, the individual who receives the order can manipulate the action to serve his or her ends. For decisions supported, one can go beyond the spirit, if not the letter. For those not supported, Graham Allison (1971: 173) notes that one can "maneuver, to delay implementation, to limit implementation to the letter but not the spirit, and even to have the decision disobeyed."

Participants at the bottom of the structure have little power over the organization; hence, they sometimes attempt control by circumventing, sabotaging, and manipulating the formal structure (Mechanic, 1962). Teacher professionals can and do resist formal actions of the administration. A rule requiring teachers to stay 15 minutes after school each day to help students with their work can easily be undermined by all teachers staying exactly 15 minutes—that is, by meeting the letter but not the spirit of the rule. If the climate of the school (see Chapter 5) is not healthy, then most likely the insurgency is symptomatic of more endemic problems rather than the particular issue itself. Administrators, however, often use more authority to fight re-sistance to authority. For example, when rules are ignored or undermined, a typical administrative response is to develop further rules and buttress their enforcement with close supervision and punishment for those who do not comply. The attempted solution usually fails because it does not deal with the cause of the problem, only the symptom. Thus, if administrators are to suc-cessfully counter insurgency, they must expend a great deal of their own political skill together with the power and authority of their position "to per-suade, cajole, and bargain with operators to get what they want" (Mintzberg 1983a: 193). They end up bargaining and making informal deals with key ac-tors in the system.

Power-building games are used by participants to build a power base. Superiors, peers, or subordinates can be used in the process. The *sponsorship game* is a simple one in which a subordinate attaches himself or herself to a superior and then professes absolute loyalty in return for a piece of the action. For example, the young teacher who would be principal sometimes tries to enlist the sponsorship of an influential vice principal or principal. Rosabeth M. Kanter (1977) notes that such sponsors provide three important services for their protégés. They fight for them and stand up for them in meetings; they enable them to get information and bypass formal channels; and they provide a signal to others, a kind of reflective power. Of course, there are costs in the sponsorship game. When the sponsor falls, the protégé is also in dan-ger, and there is great danger if the young teacher goes against the sponsor or does not show proper deference. Sponsorship is a vulnerable means of power, yet it is a frequent power game many play at virtually all levels in the organization. Principals, assistant principals, teachers, and secretaries all can play if they can find a sponsor and are willing to provide a service in return for a share of the power.

The power-base game is also played among colleagues; here it becomes an *alliance-building game.* Mintzberg (1983a) describes the process in the fol-lowing way: Either an individual develops a concern and seeks supporters, or a group of individuals concerned about an issue seek out an informal leader who can effectively represent their position and around whom they can coalesce. Thus the nucleus of an interest group is formed. Some interest groups disappear as the issue is resolved, but others persist because the play-ers have a number of common issues; they become factions. Interest groups and factions often lack the power to win an issue on their own. Consequently, they enlist the aid of other interest groups or factions to enlarge their power base. Thus alliances are formed. Groups are enticed, threatened, and cajoled to join the alliance. Kanter (1977: 185) notes, "Peer alliances often worked through direct exchange of favors. On lower levels information was traded; on higher levels bargaining and trade often took place around good per-formers and job openings." The alliance continues to grow until no more players are willing to join, or until it dominates or runs into a rival alliance. Over time, issues are won and lost and there is a gradual shifting of mem-bership, but there is a basic stability in the membership of an alliance.

The *empire-building game* is the attempt of an individual, usually in middle management, to enhance his or her power base by collecting subordinates and groups. Empire building is fought over territory. In most school systems, empire building takes place as a budgeting game. Principals want a disproportionate share of the total budget. There is rivalry and feuding among principals as they compete for scarce resources; they want more teachers, more support staff, more computers, more space, more of everything than their competitors have. The goal of the game is simple: Get the largest possible allocation for your school. The strategies are fairly clear: always request more than you need because the request will be cut; highlight all rational arguments that support a large budget and suppress those that do not; and always spend the entire budget for the year, even if some is wasted. In fact, some administrators like to go a "little in the red" to demonstrate that their allocations were inadequate, a risky strategy that may cause scrutiny of expenditures.

Expertise is another base upon which to build power. The *expertise game* is usually played by professionals who really have developed skills and expertise needed by the organization. They play the power game aggressively by exploiting their knowledge to the limit. They emphasize the uniqueness and importance of their talents as well as the inability of the organization to replace them. At the same time, they strive to keep their skills and talents unique by discouraging any attempts to rationalize them. Occasionally a master teacher will develop a reputation in a district as a truly outstanding teacher. Such a teacher has an edge in developing a power base not only on the basis of expertise, but also in terms of playing the alliance and sponsorship games. Moreover, principals who demonstrate rare administrative and leadership skills can use that power as a base to engage in alliance and empire building as well as in sponsorship. Indeed, principals who are successful in building a strong power base become formidable candidates for the superintendency.

The last of the power-building games is *lording*, in which those who have legitimate power "lord it over" those who are their subordinates, thus exploiting them in illegitimate ways. Individuals with limited power are tempted to play the lording game. Kanter (1977: 189) asserts, "When a person's exercise of power is thwarted or blocked, when people are rendered powerless in the larger arena, they tend to concentrate their power needs on those over whom they have even a modicum of authority." Teachers who are frustrated by the full weight of strong bureaucratic control and an authoritarian principal may displace control downward to students, demonstrating that they too can flex their power as they boss their students around. In like fashion, the principal who is ruled with an iron fist by the superintendent may be tempted to lord it over the teachers. Although such behavior may give the players a sense of power over someone, it is no way to build a substantial power base.

Rival games are those to defeat competitors. The *line and staff game* is a classic confrontation between middle-line managers with formal authority and staff advisors with specialized expertise. In schools it often is a conflict between the principal of a school and a districtwide curriculum coordinator. The curriculum coordinator reports directly to the superintendent and so does the principal. In a sense the players are peers. The object of the game is to control behavior in the school. The curriculum coordinator is the expert, but the principal is the formal authority. The game becomes one of the formal authority of the line against the informal authority of expertise. The battles arise over issues of change. Staff is concerned with change and improvement. The curriculum coordinator wants changes in the curriculum. But change often produces conflict and turmoil. Principals as line administrators are responsible for smoothly running organizations; principals have a vested interest in relative stability. The battle lines are drawn. The superintendent will likely get involved, but there is usually no simple solution as each party in the game develops its respective case and mobilizes political allies.

The *rival-camps game* occurs when there are two and only two major alliances facing each other. These are generally vicious games in which all the stops are pulled, and in which there are winners and losers. The game can be between two personalities, between two units, or between forces for stability and change. Proposed changes, for example, can split the organization into two factions—the Old Guard and the New Guard. Normally, the battle is resolved with one group winning and the organization moving ahead with its work. But occasionally no group can win decisively. Schools often have to balance the traditional goals of teaching basic skills with the progressive goals of social and emotional development. So while the balance sometimes shifts one way or the other, the battles continue.

Change games are designed to alter the organization or its practices. The *strategic-candidates game* can be played by anyone in the organization. All it takes is an individual or group to seek a strategic change by using the legitimate system of authority to promote a proposal or project—its "strategic candidate." Those who are successful in initiating an important change gain a large amount of power in the organization. Because many strategic decisions are made in ways that are fundamentally unstructured, they invite political gamesmanship as different alliances and factions champion their cause—that is, their candidates for change (Mintzberg, Raisinghani, and Theoret, 1976). The strategic-candidates game combines the elements of most of the other games. Mintzberg (1983a) describes the process as follows:

> Strategic candidates are often promoted in order to build empires, and they often require alliances; rivalries frequently erupt between line and staff or between rival camps during the game; expertise is exploited in this game and authority is lorded over those without it; insurgencies sometimes occur as byproducts [sic] and are countered; capital budgets often become the vehicles by which strategic candidates are promoted; and sponsorship is often a key to success in this game. (p. 206)

The *whistle-blowing game* has become increasingly more common in all organizations. It is designed to use inside information on particular behavior that an individual believes violates an important norm or perhaps the law. The player blows the whistle by informing an external authority of the foul play. Because the informer is circumventing the legitimate channels of control and is subject to reprisal, the player typically attempts to keep the contact a secret. For example, the story may be published in the newspaper and attributed to an unidentified source. Whistle-blowing is often a dramatic affair that does cause change in the organization, but it is a high-risk game. Whistle-blowers are typically not admired.

Perhaps the most intense of all the games is the *Young Turks game.* The stakes are high; the goal is not simple change or change to counter authority, but rather "to effect a change so fundamental that it throws the legitimate power into question" (Mintzberg, 1983a: 210). The Young Turks challenge the basic thrust of the organization by seeking to overturn its mission, displace a major segment of its expertise, replace its basic ideology, or overthrow its leadership. This is major rebellion and the consequences are severe. Curriculum reform is one area in schools where the Young Turks game is played. Alliances develop and the showdown comes in an intense struggle in which teachers, staff, and administrators find themselves in one of two rival camps, either "for" or "against" the change. If the existing legitimate power yields to the Young Turks, the Old Guard will never have the same authority; indeed, the organization will never be the same because it is quite likely that the Young Turks will take over leadership. If the Young Turks lose, on the other hand, they are permanently weakened. They frequently leave the organization, and sometimes a schism is created within the organization. This is often an all-or-nothing game—win it all or lose it all.

Mintzberg's system of political games is summarized in Table 6.4. There is virtually no research literature that examines the relationships among political games, but there are a number of studies of noneducational organizations that probe into specific commonly played political games (Kanter, 1977; Zald and Berger, 1978). There is little doubt that much game playing occurs in school organizations; however, usually the system of politics coexists with the legitimate means of authority without dominating it. In Mintzberg's (1983a: 217) words, "Here the System of Politics seems to consist of a number of mild political games, some of which exploit the more legitimate systems of influence, and in the process actually strengthen them, others which weaken them, but only to a point, so that politics remains a secondary force."

TIP: THEORY INTO PRACTICE

Describe and explain the political tactics and games that are played in your organization. What are the political tactics that you have successfully used in your school to gain an advantage or to protect yourself? What are the major political games that you have seen unfold in your school? Are you an observer or player? What games or tactics may you engage in to make a difference in your school? In the context of your school, discuss the extent to which politics has been good or bad and explain why. How does your principal view the politics in your school? Is he or she a victim of politics or a skillful player? Explain.

TABLE 6.4

Summary of Political Games

Game	Purpose	Primary Players
Insurgency	Resist authority	Administrators/teachers/staff
Counterinsurgency	Counter resistance to authority	Administrators
Sponsorship	Build power base	Upwardly mobile administrators/teachers
Alliance Building	Build power base	Administrators/teachers
Empire Building	Build power base	Administrators
Budgeting	Build power base	Administrators
Expertise	Build power base	Administrators/teachers
Lording	Build power base	Administrators/teachers
Line versus Staff	Defeat rivals	Administrators/staff
Rival Camps	Defeat rivals	Administrators/teachers
Strategic Candidates	Produce change	Administrators/teachers
Whistle-blowing	Produce change	Administrators/teachers/staff
Young Turks	Produce change	Administrators/teachers

Conflict Management

Because power and organizational politics inevitably produce conflict, we conclude our analysis of power with a brief discussion of conflict and its management. We hasten to add that all conflict is neither bad nor destructive. Conflict can be a source of positive change. Some scholars go so far as to claim that conflict is necessary for authentic involvement, empowerment, and democracy (Tjosvold, 1997). Further, conflict can be used to balance power, to improve communication, and to develop a foundation to manage differences (Putman, 1997). A useful distinction is the type of conflict: cognitive or affective (DeDreu, 1997; DiPaola and Hoy, 2001; Uline, Tschannen-Moran, and Perez, 2003). Cognitive conflict revolves around issues related to the task at hand, policies, and resources whereas affective conflict centers on social-emotional matters, values, and group identity. Research (DeDreu, 1997) has shown that cognitive issues promote more problem solving and less contending behaviors than affective ones. Moreover, contending behaviors often involve affective issues and diminish problem solving. Clearly, affective conflict is fraught with potential negative consequences and is more difficult to manage than its cognitive counterpart. One key to effective conflict management, however, is to promote constructive conflict while avoiding and dampening the destructive variety. That is, conflict resolution can be used as creative

Attempts to Satisfy Individual Needs

FIGURE 6.3   *Conflict-Management Styles*

force for positive change rather than a necessary evil to be controlled. We turn to a useful model for managing conflict in a productive way.

Kenneth Thomas (1976) provides a useful typology for examining five **conflict-management styles.** He identifies two basic dimensions of behavior that can produce conflict: attempting to satisfy one's concerns (organizational demands in the case of administrators), and attempting to satisfy others' concerns (individual needs of the members). Attempting to satisfy organizational demands can be viewed along an assertive-unassertive continuum; attempting to satisfy individual needs can be conceptualized from uncooperative to cooperative. Figure 6.3 shows the five conflict-management styles that are generated.

An *avoiding style* is both unassertive and uncooperative. Here the administrator ignores conflicts, hoping that they will remedy themselves. Problems are simply put on hold. When they are considered, drawn-out procedures are used to stifle the conflict and secrecy is used as a tool to avoid confrontation. Often the administrator will turn to bureaucratic rules to resolve the conflict.

A *compromising style* is a balance between the needs of the organization and those of the individual. The focus of this style is on negotiating, looking for the middle ground, trade-offs, and searching for solutions that are satisfactory or acceptable to both parties.

The use of a *competitive style* creates win–lose situations. The administrator is assertive and uncooperative in attempts to resolve conflict. Invariably, competition produces rivalry, with the objective being to achieve the goals at the expense of others. Power is used to achieve submission—to win.

The *accommodating style* is unassertive and cooperative. The administrator gives in to the demands of the subordinates; it is a submissive and compliant approach.

The *collaborating style* is assertive and cooperative. This is a problem-solving approach. Problems and conflicts are seen as challenges. Differences are confronted and ideas and information are shared. There is a concerted effort to find integrative solutions, those in which everyone wins.

Thomas (1977) proposes that each of the five styles may be effective depending on the situation; in fact, using data collected from a set of chief executives, he matches the five conflict-management styles with the appropriate situations:

Competing

- When quick, decisive action is essential—e.g., emergencies.
- When critical issues require unpopular action—e.g., cost cutting.
- When issues are vital to the welfare of the organization.
- Against individuals who take unfair advantage of others.

Collaborating

- When both sets of concerns are so important that only an integrative solution is acceptable; compromise is unsatisfactory.
- When the goal is to learn.
- To integrate insights from individuals with different perspectives.
- When consensus and commitment are important.
- To break through ill feelings that have hindered relationships.

Compromising

- When the objectives are important, but not worth the potential disruption.
- When there is a "standoff."
- To gain temporary settlements to complex problems.
- To expedite action when time is important.
- When collaboration or competition fails.

Avoiding

- When the issue is trivial.
- When the costs outweigh the benefits of resolution.
- To let the situation "cool down."
- When getting more information is imperative.
- When others can solve the problem more effectively.
- When the problem is a symptom rather than a cause.

Accommodating

- When you find you have made a mistake.
- When the issues are more important to others.
- To build goodwill for more important matters.
- To minimize losses when defeat is inevitable.
- When harmony and stability are particularly important.
- To allow subordinates a chance to learn from their mistakes.

As with so many things, there is no one best way to manage conflict. Rather, successful conflict management is likely by carefully matching the style with the situation, a topic to which we will return in our discussion of leadership (see Chapter 11).

A CASE FOR LEADERSHIP

Conflict at Washington High School[1]

Washington High School had been a peaceful, traditional school for many years. It was located in a bucolic, suburban Midwest community. Citizens were proud of their school and their students excelled academically. That was before a court-ordered busing initiative had brought a substantial population of African American students into the high school. Citizens of the town remember when things were stable and idyllic in this quiet farming community, but that was 15 years ago. Now the community is surrounded by the industrial sprawl of Metro City and forced busing had changed the composition of the student body from virtually an all-white school to one that now had about 25 percent African American students. The change brought with it racial tensions.

Racial tensions peaked at Washington High School (WHS) about the time the United States was sending troops to the Gulf War. The scene was the annual talent show at WHS. Amid high feelings of patriotism and anxiety for the "boys going to the Gulf," seven African American students launched their talent show with a large paper replica of an American flag. They walked through the flag, ripped it apart, crumpled up the pieces, and threw them into the audience. Then the boys unfurled an African National Congress flag and paraded across the stage as they engaged in an original rap piece. The audience went wild. Some got up to leave in protest; others started to argue and yell; some booed while others cheered; it was pandemonium.

[1]This incident is based on an actual case study (Larson, 1997). After you have analyzed what you would do as principal in this case, we urge you to read Professor Larson's sociopolitical analysis of the case and its aftermath.

As the crowd got louder so did the rappers. Things quickly got out of control; indeed, the assistant principal in charge thought there was going to be a riot. Genuinely shaken by the sudden turn of events, an assistant principal had jumped to the stage and announced that the talent show was over. That action was met with more hostility and turmoil. Eventually, order returned and the administrators in charge decided to continue with the rest of the show because "no real harm had occurred."

To the principal of WHS, the talent show performance by the African American students was about a group of students who had broken the school rules and whose misbehavior was punishable by school policy, which clearly stated that no unauthorized acts were permitted. In fact, all students were given a copy of the rules for the talent show before their acts were approved for production. It was clear that the African American students had knowingly violated the rules to stage their protest. Although the principal and his three assistants acknowledged that there were some racial tensions between black and white students in the high school, their view was that this incident was clearly a case of misbehaving students violating school policy and they should be punished. School policy clearly stated that any unauthorized student performance at a school-sponsored event called for "an automatic three-day suspension." Thus, the administrative team (the principal and his three assistants) unanimously concurred that all seven students should be suspended for three days and it was done.

But the incident was far from over. Student protests and racial tensions quickly escalated. The suspensions had exacerbated the racial tensions.

(Continued)

A CASE FOR LEADERSHIP *(Concluded)*

The black and white students segregated themselves into groups and harassed each other. The white students began to wear American flags and the black students African National flags. Students increasingly exchanged racial comments. The captain of the basketball team, a white student, started to collect money to "send black kids back to Africa." Groups of students would walk down the halls and not give students of the opposite race enough room to pass.

The principal and his team knew they were sitting on a powder keg, but they were adamant in their belief that they had made the right decision concerning the student protest at the talent show. It was clear that the students had violated school policy and they had been punished accordingly; yet the repercussions would not go away. Teachers in the school were generally supportive of the administrative action, but a growing number of teachers were having misgivings about the events

of the past few days. The issue had become a political one. Teachers and students were choosing up sides. Now, leaders of the African American community wanted to discuss the talent show protest. A local African American activist pastor demanded a meeting with the principal to "redress the grievances" of the black students.

- What is the immediate problem? The long-term problem?
- Is this a racial problem? Political problem? Social problem?
- How should the principal handle this situation?
- Should the principal schedule a meeting with the African American pastor? If so, what is the agenda?
- Develop a plan of action for the next several weeks. For the next year.

SUMMARY AND SUGGESTED READINGS

Power is a basic element of organizational life. It can be legitimate and willingly accepted by subordinates or it can be coercive, illegitimate, and resisted. Our analysis begins by examining legitimate power—authority. Weber identifies three types of authority based on the source of legitimacy: charisma, tradition, or the law. Peabody extends the notion by distinguishing the bases of formal authority—legitimacy and position—from the bases of functional authority—competence and personal or human relations skills. Finally, Blau and Scott simplify the foundations of legitimate power in organizations by classifying authority as formal or informal.

Next, a general analysis of power is undertaken using French and Raven's bases of interpersonal power—reward, coercion, legitimacy, reference, and expertise—and extending their framework to the organizational level. In another formulation of power, Mintzberg provides another perspective on power and describes four systems of power: authority, ideology, expertise, and politics. His framework makes explicit the importance of organizational politics. In brief, four basic kinds of organizational power exist: two forms of legitimate power—formal and informal authority—and two kinds of illegitimate power—coercive and political.

A critical perspective on power suggests that power defines reality by stating what counts as rationality and knowledge. Those in power reinterpret evidence in ways that are to their advantage. We cannot escape the fact that power is both rational and irrational and that power and politics undermine rationality.

Politics is a fact of organizational life. Although there are powerful individuals, the political arenas of organizations are composed of coalitions of individuals and groups, which bargain among themselves to determine the distribution of resources. External as well as internal coalitions influence organizational politics. Political tactics are the bases of a system of political games played to resist authority, to counter resistance, to build power bases, to defeat opponents, and to change the organization. The system of politics typically coexists with the more legitimate systems of influence without dominating. Because power and politics often generate conflict, our analysis concludes with a model of conflict management.

All students of administration should read Niccolo Machiavelli's classic, *The Prince*. Lee Bolman and Terry Deal (2003) present a nice overview of the political frame of organizations in their book, *Reframing Organizations*. Two comprehensive analyses of power in organizations are Amitai Etzioni's (1975) *A Comparative Analysis of Complex Organizations* and Henry Mintzberg's (1983a) *Power in and around Organizations*. Etzioni uses the concept of power to create a comprehensive theory of organizations. Mintzberg develops a theory of power and politics in organizations. In our view, Mintzberg's treatment of power and politics is the most comprehensive of its kind. No one interested in organizations should miss it. Finally, Rosabeth Moss Kanter (1977) examines organizational politics in her insightful analysis of *Men and Women of the Corporation*, and Bent Flyvbjerg (1998) presents a critical and postmodern approach to power in *Rationality and Power: Democracy in Practice*.

KEY ASSUMPTIONS AND PRINCIPLES

1. Authority is legitimate power that emerges from the formal organization (formal authority), the informal organization (informal authority), expertise (functional authority), and extraordinary personal attributes (charismatic authority).
2. Coercive power tends to alienate subordinates and produces resistance and hostility.
3. Referent and expert power typically create subordinate commitment.
4. Organizational politics is usually dysfunctional because decisions are made on the basis of individual needs rather than organizational ones.
5. Power invariably blurs the distinction between the rationality and rationalization, and rationality is the victim.
6. Organization politics is influenced by both external and internal coalitions.

7. Power and politics in organizations are inevitable, and organization members have three basic choices—they can stay and play (give voice), stay and contribute as expected (be loyal), or leave (exit).
8. Success in the game of organizational politics requires members to negotiate, jockey for position, and engage in a myriad of games, strategies, and tactics.
9. Organizational conflict can be constructive or destructive.
10. There is no one best way to manage conflict; success is dependent on matching the right resolution approach with the situation.

NOTES

1. This section draws heavily on the power analysis of Mintzberg (1983a).

CHAPTER 7

EXTERNAL ENVIRONMENTS
OF SCHOOLS

It becomes evident that the choices of expanding organizations about what units to add are not random but are, rather, partially determined by conditions in the institutional environment.

Brian Rowan
"Organizational Structure and the Institutional Environment: The Case of Public Schools"

PREVIEW

1. Schools are open systems and depend on exchanges with environmental elements to survive.

2. Multiple environmental influences come from different levels of society and affect what happens in schools.

3. Two general perspectives of environment are analyzed—task and institutional.

4. The task perspective includes both the information and the resource-dependency theories, which define task environment as the aspects of the external setting that are potentially relevant for goal setting, effectiveness, and survival.

5. The information perspective treats the external environment as a source of information for decision makers.

6. The resource-dependence perspective views the environment as a place to gain scarce resources

(e.g., fiscal, personnel, information and knowledge, and products and services) to support the technical processes of schools.

7. In contrast to the task perspectives, institutional theory assumes that the environment encourages schools to conform to powerful sets of rules and requirements that the legal, social, professional, and political contexts of organizations impose.

8. Institutional theory asserts that school structures and processes mirror the norms, values, and ideologies institutionalized in society. The essence of the theory is that institutional environments of schools press more for form than for substance.

9. School organizations use both internal and external strategies to minimize the influence of the external environment on their internal elements.

The open-systems concept (see Chapter 1) highlights the vulnerability and interdependence of organizations and their environments. External environments are important because they affect the inputs, internal structures and processes, and outputs of organizations; hence, one is forced to look both inside and outside the organization to explain behavior within school organizations. Indeed, the larger social, cultural, economic, demographic, political, and technological trends all influence the internal operations of schools and districts.

Because school organizations are conceptualized as part of a larger universe or environment, an argument can be made that anything that happens in the larger environment may affect the school and vice versa. For example, the revolutionary developments in computing and information technology created whirls of activity and change in school districts as they tried to find ways to purchase and use the emerging technologies in their administrative and instructional processes. Incidents of extreme violence in schools such as occurred in Littleton, Colorado, a few years ago fixate the media and political leaders, necessitating schools far away from the violent episodes to prepare contingency plans, hire security officers, and install weapon detectors. Similarly, government actions like the No Child Left Behind Act of 2001 require schools to implement new curriculum standards, testing policies, and in some cases, even options for school choice. Even with these vivid examples and a long-standing emphasis on the importance of external environments, educators commonly underestimate the extent to which their organizations are connected to and affected by the larger environment (Scott and Meyer, 1991). In fact, W. Richard Scott (2003) stresses that being open systems, all organizations are incomplete and depend on exchanges with other organizations in the environment as a condition of their survival.

As shown in Figure 7.1, multiple environmental influences come from different levels of society and affect what happens in schools. Technological and informational developments, political structures and patterns of legal norms, social conditions and cultural values, economic and market factors, and population and demographic characteristics influence school structures and processes. Within a specific locality, myriad stakeholder groups play key roles in affecting educational practices—for example, individual parents, taxpayer associations, business groups, legislatures, and accrediting agencies influence school policy.

Administrators tend to focus monitoring and planning processes on local environmental elements and often fail to recognize that environmental factors in the larger society also have the potential to influence not only their schools but local environments as well. Changing demographics—for example, age, sex, race, and ethnicity distributions in the population—will likely bring tremendous pressures for change in virtually all American schools. For example, the increasing percentage of educationally disadvantaged children entering and remaining in the schools has significant implications for educational attainment (Pallas, Natriello, and McDill, 1989). These are the students

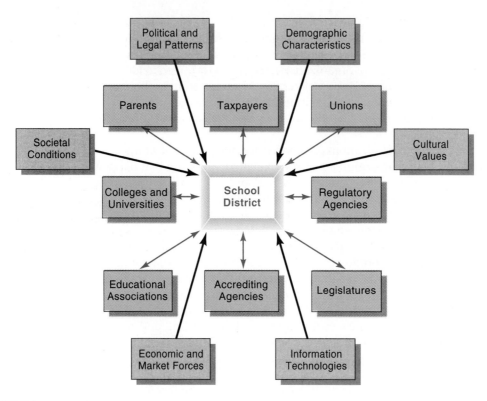

FIGURE 7.1   *Selected External Influences and Constituencies for School Districts*

whose schools have traditionally been unable to serve in highly effective ways. That is, low achievement levels and high absenteeism and dropout rates have characterized the academic careers of the educationally disadvantaged. Without fundamental changes in the ways schools and other organizations educate children, the problems of school effectiveness and the pressures on schools will increase. Thus, demographic trends suggest that external environments of schools are characterized by growing uncertainty and importance.

TASK AND INSTITUTIONAL ENVIRONMENTS

According to William R. Dill (1958), **task environment,** which includes all aspects of the environment that may potentially influence goal setting and achievement, is a useful concept in understanding external influences on organizations. The basic premise of task environments is that organizations are created to perform some function or work in society and to achieve goals. Features in task environments emphasize that organizations such as schools are productive systems—they convert inputs into outputs—and in doing so require material and energy inputs and markets or buyers who will provide resources in exchange for what is produced. Therefore, organizations are not self-sufficient and must enter into exchanges with the external environment to gain the needed information and other resources for survival. Effective school administrators then design efficient work requirements, coordinate technical processes, and ensure adequate resource providers and markets for school outputs (Scott, 2003). Information and resource-dependence perspectives are the best-known examples of task-environment theories.

The institutional perspective offers an alternative approach to understanding external environments. This formulation places limited emphasis on task goals, effectiveness, and efficiency. Instead, the basic premise is that the chances of organizational survival are highest when school structures and processes mirror the norms, values, and ideologies institutionalized in society (Rowan, 1993). The information, resource-dependence, and institutional perspectives will next be reviewed and applied to school settings.

INFORMATION PERSPECTIVE

In the **information perspective,** the external environment is a source of information (e.g., about expected goals and levels of performance) that decision makers use in maintaining or changing the internal structures and processes of their organizations. In this framework, the **external environment** is defined as information about external factors as perceived by organizational participants. Perceptions of information by decision makers link the external environment to actions taken by participants in the organization (Aldrich and Mindlin, 1978). This hypothesis explains organizational changes by variations in perceived information of decision makers about the external environment (Koberg and Ungson, 1987). For instance, how important a superintendent perceives the information from officials in state departments of education to be concerning the need to implement new state curriculum frameworks will partially determine how much effort the district will expend to change its instructional programs.

Although it is true that actions are based on administrator and teacher perceptions of the environment, such perceptions are not likely to be completely idiosyncratic to a particular person or school setting (Aldrich and Pfeffer, 1976). A variety of social processes combine to create similar perceptions. For instance, hiring educators with similar backgrounds, imitating programs from other schools, and following professional norms and governmental regulations promote the development of a common frame of reference for perceiving environmental information.

Environmental Uncertainty

A primary concern of the information perspective is uncertainty. **Environmental uncertainty** exists when decision makers in an organization are unable to make accurate predictions because existing conditions in the external environment prevent them from having adequate information (Milliken, 1987; McCabe and Dutton, 1993). The level of uncertainty is determined by the kind, clarity, and amount of information that organizational decision makers have about trends and changes in environmental conditions. Thus, when uncertainty is high, at least five problematic situations might arise for administrators.

- Lack of knowledge and skills make it difficult to understand the information from the environment.
- Preferences regarding possible outcomes become less clear.
- Alternative courses of action and their outcomes become increasingly unpredictable and risky.
- Strategies and tactics become relatively difficult to communicate and implement.
- Potential outcomes from a decision are not known.

The information framework focuses on decision makers' perceptions of their environments and how they use the information to adjust the internal structures and processes of their organizations. For example, when organizations confront uncertain environments, they are often able to maintain or increase their effectiveness through additional flexibility in their structural configurations (Dill, 1958; Lawrence and Lorch, 1967). In school organizations, educators often attempt to cope with environmental uncertainty by creating special units or programs. As more and diverse groups become interested in education, special units, such as offices of public information, government relations, community involvement, special education, information technology, and business partnerships are created to monitor their activities, report perceived information about their goals and behaviors to key administrators, and engage the groups in information exchanges in an effort to gain their support. The idea is that schools adapt to produce environmental fit—that is, school organizations match their structures and processes to their perceived external environments (Miller, 1992; Pennings, 1992).

In sum, the information perspective emphasizes goal achievement based on perceptions of the external environment as the primary source of information about what schools are expected to produce for society. Based on their perceptions, school administrators then lead efforts to change their school organizations. As the environment becomes more uncertain, organizations become more flexible and organic—that is, less formalized and less centralized.

RESOURCE-DEPENDENCE PERSPECTIVE

In contrast to the information perspective, the **resource-dependence perspective** views the environment as a place to gain scarce resources for the task and technical processes of the organization. Four general types of environmental resources are typically identified—fiscal, personnel (e.g., students, teachers, administrators, school volunteers, and board members), information and knowledge (e.g., outcomes from research, development, and evaluation projects), and products and services (e.g., instructional materials and test scoring services) (Aldrich, 1972; Benson, 1975). Organizations both compete for and share the environmental resources.

Environmental resources are commonly conceptualized on a continuum of **scarcity** to **munificence**—that is, the extent or capacity of the environment to provide resources that support the stability and sustained growth of the organization. The relative abundance of resources in the environment is the ultimate determinant of sufficient input for any organization. When resources are munificent, survival is relatively easy and the pursuit of wide-ranging task goals becomes possible (Castrogiovanni, 1991). For example, school districts in wealthy environments might have high property evaluations that produce relatively large tax revenues with small tax levies. In environments with abundant capacity, school districts would likely offer wide-ranging curricular and extracurricular programs. Under conditions of limited capacity or scarcity, competition for resources among subgroups can take the form of a zero-sum game with each subgroup caring more about its share of finite resources than for the overall welfare of the organization. For example, school districts in impoverished environments would be limited to a basic academic curriculum, and extracurricular programs would compete for what might be left over.

Dependence is defined both by the extent of need for a resource and its availability (i.e., scarcity/munificence) in the environment. For educational settings, dependence is directly related to the school organization's need for resources controlled by other organizations, and inversely related to the resource availability from other organizations. That is, if school organizations cannot accomplish their goals without the resources controlled by other organizations and are unable to secure them elsewhere, they become dependent on the other organizations. Conversely, as resources are provided, the suppliers gain power over the schools. With this power, supplying organizations have two general means of control—deciding whether the schools get the resources they need and determining whether the schools can use the resources the way they want (Froosman, 1999). A major consequence of competition for resources is the development of dependencies among organizations in the environment. Notice that dependence is an attribute of the relationship between the organizations and not an attribute of individual organizations in isolation (Aldrich and Mindlin, 1978; Sutcliffe, 1994). It follows that the greater the resource dependence, the more the organizations communicate with each other (Van de Ven and Ferry, 1980).

Events in school finance illustrate the dependence concept. As fiscal resources from local property taxes and federal grants decline, school districts have an increased need to secure additional appropriations from state legislatures. Because greater percentages of their budgets are supplied by the state, the dependence of school districts on state governments grows dramatically. In a parallel fashion, the power of the state over local school districts expands and state legislatures and offices of education are able to dictate educational reforms to school districts—for example, curriculum standards and testing programs.

As the primary proponent of resource-dependence theory Jeffery Pfeffer (1982, 1997; Pfeffer and Salancik, 1979) asserts that its fundamental proposition is that if organizations are unable internally to generate the resources to maintain themselves, they must enter into exchanges with environmental elements to acquire the needed resources. In exchange for resources, the external organizations may not only consume the organization's outputs but also demand certain actions or changes from the organization. In other words, organizations lose some autonomy and become constrained by a network of interdependencies with other organizations. For example, individuals who have been educated and trained in the schools contribute their efforts to society, and society demands that schools offer particular types of educational programming. Hence, a basic hypothesis is that organizational changes are explained by the abilities of competing organizations to acquire and control critical resources (Koberg and Ungson, 1987). Therefore, as organizations become increasingly dependent on their environments for securing resources, they require and tend to exhibit more flexible and adaptive structures that are more informal, less standardized, and decentralized. Dependence on external elements for resources often leads to interorganizational relationships such as joint programs and cooptation (Aiken and Hage, 1968; Aldrich and Mindlin, 1978).

Because all organizations are dependent on their environments, external control of organizational behavior is possible and constraint inevitable. If they are not responsive to the demands of their environments, organizations cannot thrive and may not survive. Hence, the resource-dependence model emphasizes that organizations adapt to their environments and that they can act to improve their chances of survival (Scott, 2003). But demands often conflict; thus, organizations cannot thrive or even survive by simply responding to every environmental demand. The challenge for school decision makers is to determine the extent to which their schools can and must adapt to various environmental demands and the implications of those responses for their organizations.

In sum, from a resource-dependence framework, school organizations view their external environments as providing a variety of resources for their task structures and processes in exchange for products and services valued in the external environment. As schools become more dependent on their environments, internal control is reduced and external constraints are imposed. As a result schools adapt by becoming more flexible and less bureaucratic. Combining these tenets from resource dependence with the ideas from the information perspective, the essential question for administrators is: "How can environmental uncertainty be reduced without increasing dependence?" (Wood and Gray, 1991: 141).

TIP: THEORY INTO PRACTICE

Applying the Task Environment Perspectives to Schools

Consider the school district or school attendance area in which you are now living.

- How would you characterize the degree of certainty of the information environment? Consider factors such as the stability and diversity of the social, racial, and economic composition of the district or area, the frequency and types of educational issues, the number of interests trying to send messages to the school, and the degree of conflict among the various interest groups.
- How dependent is the school district or school on the local environment? Consider factors such as wealth, sources of funding, governance structures, and market factors (e.g., charter schools, employment opportunities for graduates).
- Does the school or district face high uncertainty and dependence?

Administering Information and Resource Environments

Even in the context of task environments, uncertainty and dependency signify challenging problems for school organizations. Both environmental factors can threaten or constrain educator autonomy and drive changes in the internal structures and operations of school organizations. Therefore, educational administrators often try to minimize external effects and assume key roles in managing the external environments of their school (Pfeffer, 1976). Employing a variety of tactics, educators strive to gain control over resources, to avoid becoming dependent, to make others dependent on them, and to absorb uncertainty. Attempts to reduce environmental uncertainty and dependence can be grouped into internal or interorganizational coping strategies. Both sets of strategies are designed to protect key processes from environmental influences by increasing certainty and gaining additional resources. Before elaborating a number of these tactics, however, we offer two cautions. The external environments for schools remain highly dynamic; and even when a modicum of control is achieved through well-designed and executed strategies, it can easily and quickly be lost (Gross and Etzioni, 1985).

Internal Coping Strategies

Task environments seek to impose technical constraints on organizations such as schools. In response, organizations try to isolate their technical cores and other throughput processes from external influences. Buffering, planning and forecasting, spanning organizational boundaries, and adjusting internal operations are coping strategies widely applicable to school organizations.

Buffering   This strategy of isolation is based on the assumption that efficiency can be maximized only when the technical core, for example, teaching in schools, is not disturbed by external uncertainties and dependencies. **Buffering** uses structures and processes to insulate or surround internal activities and absorb environmental disturbances. Buffering creates a protective layer between the organization and its environment (Miner, Amburgey, and Stearns, 1990; Pennings, 1992). Therefore, schools create specific departments, roles, and processes to deal with uncertainty and dependence from a variety of environmental elements. Purchasing, planning, human resources, curriculum, and facilities departments are created to buffer teachers from factors in the school's environment. These departments transfer materials, services, information, money, and other resources between the environment and school. In addition, principals play key buffering roles in dealing with parental complaints about teachers, and as noted by Janice R. Fauske and Bob Johnson (2002), in protecting the school and themselves from threats in the community. The goal of buffering is to make the technical core as near to a closed system as possible and, thereby, to enhance efficiency (Daft, 1989).

Planning and Forecasting   In environments with high levels of uncertainty and dependence, buffering strategies probably cannot provide adequate protection for the instructional program. Under such conditions, school organizations can attempt to control environmental fluctuations by **planning and forecasting strategies.** These strategies anticipate environmental changes and take actions to soften their adverse effects. Under these circumstances, a separate planning department is frequently established. In uncertain and dependent situations, planners must identify the important environmental elements and analyze potential actions and counteractions by other organizations. Planning must be extensive and forecast a variety of scenarios. As conditions continue to change, the plans must be updated. To the extent that educators can accurately forecast environmental fluctuations, they have an opportunity to reduce uncertainty (Robbins, 1983).

Spanning Organizational Boundaries   **Boundary spanning** creates internal roles to cross organizational boundaries and to link schools with elements in the external environment. This is also an important strategy for coping with environmental uncertainty and dependence. Two classes of functions are typically performed by boundary-spanning roles: detecting information about changes in the external environment and representing the organization to the environment (Aldrich and Herker, 1977).

For the detection function, boundary roles concentrate on the transfer of information between the environment and schools. Boundary personnel scan and monitor events in the environment that can create abrupt changes and long-term trends, and communicate the information to decision makers (Daft, 1989). By identifying new technological developments, curricular innovations, regulations, and funding patterns, boundary personnel provide data that enable schools to make plans and adjust programs. In contrast to buffering personnel, boundary spanners act to keep school organizations open systems in harmony with their environments. A number of individuals in schools—for example, superintendents and principals—play both buffering and boundary-spanning roles. Other school boundary-spanning roles include administrators in public information, government relations and research, evaluation, and development departments.

For the representation function, boundary-spanning personnel send information into the environment from the organization. The idea is to influence other people's perceptions of the organization. Schools often have offices of public information whose express purpose is to communicate information to significant stakeholders. Other district offices also can serve this function. For example, community and adult education programs, which primarily attract tax-paying patrons, can exemplify the quality of instruction that is available to students. Business and legal departments can inform legislators about the school needs or views on political matters. Similarly, the boards of education and school advisory committees link their schools to important constituencies in the environment in highly visible ways to create the impression that interests can be expressed, if not always the opportunity to do so. Thus, women, minority group members, and students are appointed in increasing numbers to a variety of advisory committees (Aldrich and Herker, 1977). Promoting a positive image of the school can reduce uncertainty and dependence on the various elements in the environment. Hence, boundary spanners play key roles in interorganizational relations (Friedman and Podolny, 1992) and can be highly influential with key decision makers in the organization (At-Twajri and Montanari, 1987).

Adjusting Internal Operations   The information and resource-dependence perspectives suggest a structural contingency approach to organizational design (Aldrich and Mindlin, 1978; Pennings, 1992). The way an organization should be designed depends in part on its environment. In other words, no one best way exists to organize schools. Rather, the most effective school structure is one that adjusts to its important environmental elements.

The first researchers to indicate that different types of organizational structure might be effective in different environments were Tom Burns and G. M. Stalker (1961). They found that the types of structure that existed in dynamic environments were different from the types that existed in stable or certain environments. When the external environment was stable, the internal organization was "mechanistic" or highly bureaucratic—that is, characterized by formal rules and regulations, standard operating procedures, and centralized decision making; interpersonal relationships were formal, impersonal, rigid, and clear-cut. Relying heavily on programmed behaviors, mechanistic organizations performed routine tasks effectively and efficiently, but responded relatively slowly to unfamiliar events.

In highly uncertain environments, the internal organization was "organic" or informal—that is, it exhibited few rules, informal agreements about operating procedures, and decentralized decision making; interpersonal relations were informal, personal, flexible, and somewhat ambiguous. Burns and Stalker did not conclude that the mechanistic model was inferior to the organic model, but rather, that the most effective structure is one that adjusts to the requirements of the environment—a mechanistic design in a stable environment and an organic form in an unstable environment. Danny Miller (1992) found considerable support for the contingency or environmental fit model.

Just as the information perspective suggests a structural contingency approach, so does the resource-dependence model. According to resource-dependence theory, the environment does not impose strict requirements for survival. Therefore, a wide range of possible actions and organizational structures are possible; hence, criteria guiding decisions and determining structures become both important and problematic. Internal power differences are important because no single optimal structure or set of actions aligns the organization with its environment. Instead, a range of choices or strategies of alignment are available. The influence of a variety of internal stakeholders may determine, in interaction with the demands of external constituencies, the response of the organization. Resource-dependence theory highlights the importance of environmental factors in promoting and restraining organizational decisions and actions, yet at the same time leaves room for the operation of strategic choice on the part of organizational members as they maneuver through known and unknown contexts. In other words, the resource-dependence model posits that although environmental influences are important, environmental constraints do not reduce the feasible set of structures to only one form. Rather, a variety of internal structures and actions are consistent with the survival of the organization, which means that although the organization may have the goal of survival, survival does not imply only a single or very limited set of structural forms (Aldrich and Pfeffer, 1976).

As a note of caution in applying the findings from contingency research, structural and process variations occur across schools as a result of active alternative generation and search procedures to adapt and change the environment. In fact, Boyd (1976) argues that schools are neither "mirror images" of the communities they serve nor completely insulated bastions dominated by unresponsive and self-serving professional educators. To a considerable extent, school organizations can shape their environments to fit their capabilities.

Interorganizational Coping Strategies

Thus far we have described ways in which school organizations can adapt internally to the external environment. Schools also reach out and change their environments. James G. March (1981) even asserts that, in part, organizations create their environments. Two types of strategies are used to manage the external environment—establishing favorable linkages and shaping environmental elements. A point to be remembered about attempts to control the environment is that it, too, has some organized character and the ability to fight back (Katz and Kahn, 1978).

Establishing Favorable Linkages   A way organizations seek to control their environments is by establishing linkages with other organizations (Gross and Etzioni, 1985). Interorganizational linkages are important because they increase organizational power, reduce uncertainty, increase performance by ensuring a stable flow of critical resources, and protect the organizations from adverse effects of environmental uncertainty and scarcity (Stearns, Hoffman, and Heide, 1987). Moreover, strong ties with other organizations promote adaptation and innovation by increasing communication, sharing information, and learning flexibility strategies (Goes and Park, 1997; Kraatz, 1998). The connections are often in complex networks that try to regularize the flow of information and reduce uncertainty. The primary social process is believed to be some form of social exchange. Organizations create links by exchanging information, personnel, funds, equipment, and other needed items. In short, resources are exchanged in an effort to control the environment.

In business organizations a favorite mechanism to reduce competition and dependence is the merger. If a source of raw material is uncertain, buying the supplier removes the dependence on the external element. Although educational organizations cannot rely on mergers, they do enter into joint ventures with other organizations. School districts form *partnerships* with businesses, foundations, universities, and federal and state governments to share the risks and costs associated with large-scale innovations and research projects. Current examples of joint ventures between business and school organizations include creating and implementing comprehensive school reform with the New American Schools initiative, running a variety of school-to-work programs, and developing and operating charter schools.

The number of joint ventures may be the best predictor of organizational influence on the environment (Boje and Whetten, 1981). Given the recent emphasis on market models of change such as charter schools, public school districts may link with parent groups to create their own charter schools as a way to reduce the number established by non–school district groups.

Cooptation represents another strategy of developing favorable linkages. Cooptation means bringing leaders from important elements in the environment into the policy and decision structures of the school organization. Cooptation occurs when influential citizens are appointed to boards of education or to advisory committees. When cooptation cannot be established directly, Pfeffer (1997) indicates that building favorable linkages with others who in turn can affect influence is sometimes an effective strategy. The evidence is mixed, however, for increasing the influence of organizations through advisory councils. Some research is supportive (Pfeffer, 1972); other studies are not (Boje and Whetten, 1981).

Shaping Environmental Elements   Politicking is a primary method of shaping environmental elements for school districts and other interest groups. Using a relatively large but common set of tools or tactics to promote their interests, school officials and paid lobbyists express their views to local, state, and federal policy makers (Kollman, 1998). As shown in Table 7.1, Baumgartner and Leech (1998) describe 12 types of **influence tactics.** Modern information technologies such as e-mail, Internet search engines and websites, and computerized fax machines enhance both the urgency and pervasiveness of these influence efforts. Using these tactics with the intent of influencing public policy is lobbying.

Rather than trying to control the outcomes of educational policy, educators and other interest groups frequently attempt to influence its formulation using both positive and negative methods (Heinz et al., 1993). **Interest groups** not only promote and advocate new issues or agenda items related to

TABLE 7.1

Influence Tactics of Interest Groups

- Testifying at legislative or agency hearings
- Contacting legislators and other officials directly
- Making informal contacts with legislators and government officials
- Generating constituent influence
- Litigating
- Protesting and demonstrating
- Presenting research results
- Monitoring, influencing appointments, and doing favors for officials
- Drafting legislation and regulations and serving on commissions
- Engaging the mass media
- Electing and endorsing policy allies
- Forming coalitions

their interests, they also work to block unfavorable alternatives. For example, public schools have engaged in extensive efforts to block state and federal support to private schools. They have leveled intense lobbying campaigns against proposals concerning such initiatives as tuition tax credits, schools of choice, and educational vouchers.

Pooling resources is a related strategy to shape the external environment. Educational associations usually have both professional and political missions. Examples include the Parent-Teacher Association, National Education Association, American Federation of Teachers, American Association of School Administrators, Council for American Private Education, Council of Exceptional Children, and Council of Chief State School Officers. A complete list is very long. Moreover, the individual groups do not remain isolated in the policy environment. They actively seek allies for support and leverage of their ideas. By pooling resources, individual educators or educational organizations can afford to pay people to carry out activities such as lobbying legislators, influencing new regulations, promoting educational programs, and presenting public relations campaigns.

Karper and Boyd (1988) describe how the formation of coalitions and lobbying activities increases during periods of increasing uncertainty. Education interest groups in Pennsylvania responded to challenging circumstances during the mid-1980s by increasing the number, specialization, and sophistication of their lobbyists, and by forming a grand coalition to maximize their strength. As the information perspective would suggest, the findings indicate that the groups believed they had to increase the amount of information they had and could share. In turn, the need for information fostered increasing specialization and sophistication within the lobbying groups. The groups increased their research capacity, engaged in policy analysis, and employed higher levels of technology.

Tim L. Mazzoni and Betty Malen (1985) detail a successful attempt to shape educational policy. They analyzed a series of case studies dealing with constituency mobilization to impact state educational policy. In essence, an alliance consisting of the Minnesota Catholic Conference and the Citizens for Educational Freedom wanted the legislature to provide tax concessions for private school parents. Using both electoral and lobbying tactics, the alliance was able to persuade the legislature to endorse a tax concession package. The alliance kept the issue continuously on the legislative agenda, energized sympathetic lawmakers to carry its bills, and, most important, mobilized grassroots constituency pressure to sway votes among legislators. Mazzoni and Malen concluded that the political strategy of constituency mobilization had a significant impact on this policy issue.

The overall implication for practice is that school organizations do not have to be simple, passive instruments of the external environment. Both internal and external coping strategies can be used to buffer environmental influences and actually to change the demands. Structures, programs, and processes can be developed by educational administrators to manage the environments of their school organizations.

TIP: THEORY INTO PRACTICE

Administering Task Environments

A major purpose of the No Child Left Behind Act of 2001 is to strengthen the task environment of schools. It contains many new mandates for local schools, including new curriculum standards, additional testing, fresh requirements for teachers, and provisions for school choice. However, conflicting information from the U.S. Department of Education and protests from many education groups have created considerable uncertainty about the policies and the required practices for local schools. By the time the information arrives at your district through the state office of education, it is even more muddled. Given that your district is dependent on the federal funds in No Child Left Behind, you see a great need to reduce the environmental uncertainty.

- What aspects of the environment are most important to you (e.g., influencing the policies and regulations, clarifying the requirements for local implementation)?
- What strategies would you use to reduce the uncertainty?
- Are there alternative ways of gaining other resources and reducing the dependence on the federal government?

INSTITUTIONAL PERSPECTIVE

Although the important elements of task environments for organizations are material and resource based, the primary factors in institutional environments are symbolic and cultural in nature (Scott, 2003). Moreover, the **institutional perspective** has become a leading approach to understanding organizations and their environments (Mizruchi and Fein, 1999). Brian Rowan (1993) characterizes it as one of the most vital formulations in organizational theory today. The roots of institutional theory are found in the works of Philip Selznick (1949, 1957). His ideas were revitalized and elaborated by Meyer and Rowan (1977) to create a "new" institutional theory. Since the late 1970s institutional theory has generated widespread interest among scholars and provides valuable conceptual and practical insights about schools.

According to Rowan and Miskel (1999), the goal of institutional theory is to explain how socially organized environments arise and how they influence social action. In essence, social actors of all kinds—individuals, administrators, teachers, interest groups, and schools—are seen as embedded in socially organized environments that generate rules, regulations, norms, and definitions of the situation that constrains and shapes behavior and other actions. Institutional arrangements are found at virtually all levels of social systems (e.g., societal, individual organizations, and small groups); have regulative, normative, cognitive roots (Scott, 1995, 2001); and have activities and functions that occur in a stable and recurring fashion.

Institutions can be formal organizations, but they do not have to be. Some institutions are based on formal, written codes of conduct—that is, laws, constitutions, standard operating procedures, and so forth—that are enforced by the coercive power of social agencies. Other institutions endure less formally as norms and values—that is, as strongly felt obligations that have been internalized through socialization. Still others persist as cognitive schema—that is, as relatively tacit, taken for granted, rulelike understandings of a situation. Objects that are commonly thought of as institutions, for example, include marriage, family, voting, the handshake, formal organizations, schools, attending school, teaching, teaching profession, academic tenure, the school principal, labor unions, and schooling (Rowan and Miskel, 1999). To capture this diversity of institutional structures, Peter Abell (1995) defines the **institution** as a more or less agreed-upon set of rules that carry meaning for and determine the actions of some population of actors. More explicitly, Scott (2001: 48) declares that "Institutions are composed of cultural-cognitive, normative, and regulative elements that, together with associated activities and resources, provide stability and meaning to social life."

Jepperson (1991) further observes that all institutions simultaneously empower and control; they are vehicles for activity within constraints. All institutions are frameworks of programs and rules establishing identities and activity schemes for such identities. For instance, a school considered as an institution is a packaged social technology, with accompanying rules and instructions for its incorporation and employment in a social setting. Institutions, then, embody common actions or standardized activities in situations that become taken for granted. Schools as institutions are taken for granted in the sense that they are treated as fixtures in a social environment and are explained as performing a function in that environment.

The **institutional environment,** therefore, is characterized by the elaboration of rules and requirements to which individual organizations must conform if they are to receive support and legitimacy. In modern societies, the environmental requirements (e.g., rules, norms, values, and ideologies) are rational in form, with the chief sources of rationalization being governments and professions. Executive and legislative agencies at the state and federal levels dealing with education like to create policies and bureaucratic arrangements that centralize discretion and allow limited autonomy to local practitioners. Professionals and their associations prefer weaker and more decentralized structures that locate maximum discretion in the hands of local educators. Whatever the source, however, organizations are rewarded for conforming to these institutional rules, beliefs, and ideologies (Meyer and Rowan, 1977; DiMaggio and Powell, 1991; Scott, 1995; Scott and Meyer, 1991).

In fact, rationalized myth is commonly used in discussions of institutions and their environments. Myths are widely held beliefs that cannot be or typically are not objectively tested. They are true because they are believed.

Myths become rationalized when they take the form of bureaucratic or professional rules specifying procedures necessary to accomplish a given end (Scott, 1992). **Rationalized myths,** then, are rules specifying procedures to accomplish an outcome on the basis of beliefs that are assumed to be true or are taken for granted. For example, a rationalized myth is the use of psychological tests and classification systems to place students in special education classes. These diagnostic approaches are rational because they provide procedures for assessing intellectual and emotional processes. They are myths because their use depends heavily on endorsements by professional associations, accrediting bodies, and funding agencies (D'Aunno, Sutton, and Price, 1991).

Conceptual Foundations

Institutional theory is similar to the task-environmental theories. Both institutional and task-environment theories focus on organization-environment relations rather than on internal influences. The task-environment theories, however, concentrate on task or technical environments to gain information and resources from the external environment. In contrast, institutional environments encourage conformity to powerful sets of rules and requirements that the legal, social, professional, and political contexts of organizations impose (Fennell and Alexander, 1987). Both task-environmental and institutional theories promote "rational" organizational forms.

Technical environments emphasize a rationality that incorporates a set of prescriptions for matching means and ends in ways that produce desirable and predictable outcomes. Meyer, Scott, and Deal (1992) conclude that from the technical perspective, schools are peculiarly ineffective organizations. Schools do not have technologies that unequivocally produce desired or measureable outcomes, nor do they control their work processes adequately, particularly those involved in teaching and learning. By comparison, institutional environments press "rationales" as rationality. That is, institutional rationality provides an explanation that makes past actions understandable, acceptable, and seemingly accountable.

Recent versions of institutional theory have moved well beyond the simplistic assertion that institutional rules always conflict with organizational efficiency (Rowan and Miskel, 1999). Hence, task and institutional environments should not be viewed as mutually exclusive factors because they can and do coexist. In other words, technical and institutional factors are not dichotomous, but instead are separate dimensions or continua along which environments can vary. Schools operate in relatively strong institutional and weak technical environments (Powell, 1991; Scott, 2003; Scott and Meyer, 1991). As a consequence, schools tend to be rewarded primarily for their conformity to professional standards and legal requirements rather than for the quality of their outputs. With the current emphasis on linking curriculum frameworks and testing programs, the relative strength of the task environment may be increasing and placing added pressure on schools to meet minimal output criteria (Scott, 2003). Important ideas in institutional theory include conformity, diversity, and stability.

Conformity and Institutional Environments

Institutional theory emphasizes that organizations are open systems, which are strongly influenced by their environments. Moreover, many of the most decisive forces are not rational pressures for more effective performance but social pressures to conform to conventional beliefs (Scott, 1992). Hence, a basic premise of institutional theory is that organizational structures and processes mirror the norms, values, and ideologies institutionalized in society. Accordingly, organizations conform to institutionalized rules and procedures to gain legitimacy—that is, cultural support for the organization. In other words, institutional conformity promotes the apparent success and long-term survival of the organization, independent of any effects that conformity might have on technical productivity. By designing a formal structure that conforms to the prescriptions of the institutional environment, an organization demonstrates that it is acting on collectively valued purposes in a proper and adequate fashion (Meyer and Rowan, 1977; Rowan, 1993). This thesis is particularly salient to educators because organizations lacking clear technologies and not operating in competitive markets—that is, public school systems—are especially likely to adopt institutionalized elements and conform to the institutional environment (DiMaggio, 1988).

Similarly, Paul J. DiMaggio and Walter W. Powell (1983, 1991) contend that organizational change in institutional environments makes organizations more alike without making them more efficient. Organizations within the same institutional environments tend to become homogenized. Public schools within a given country, for example, resemble each other. Their buildings and pedagogies are similar, with classrooms designed for a teacher, a set of students, and similar ways of engaging in teaching and learning processes. DiMaggio and Powell identify three mechanisms that promote institutional conformity.

Coercive conformity stems from political influence and problems of legitimacy. Coercive conformity results when organizations follow the rules and regulations promulgated by government agencies and thereby produce similar structures or processes (Rowan and Miskel, 1999). Common and visible coercive pressures or policy instruments for school change include government mandates and inducements. On the basis of both federal and state regulations, for example, schools now hire special education teachers to serve special-needs children, develop curriculum materials to meet standards or frameworks, and give students achievement tests that conform to government standards. Coercive forces can also be invisible, informal, and subtle, as when a school board member believes that phonics is the only way to teach reading (Hanson, 2001).

A major problem with coercive policy instruments is that they often increase enforcement costs without producing the predicted gains in efficiency and effectiveness. For example, Meyer, Scott, and Strang (1987) reason that school districts have an obvious interest in gaining funds by meeting the federal legal requirements for participation. They found that increments in federal funding produced larger additions to the administrative staffs of school districts than did increments in state or local revenues. Another vivid example of the effects of coercive conformity is school district consolidation (i.e., merging of two or more districts into one). Between 1938 and 1980, consolidation reduced the number of school districts in the United States by over 100,000. David Strang (1987) concluded that, to a substantial extent, these losses were affected by changes in the institutional environment—that is, policy makers' beliefs about the legitimate size and structure of schools changed. Both of these studies illustrate the intended and unintended effects of coercive conformity.

Imitative conformity results from adopting standard responses from other sources to reduce uncertainty. This process is similar to Meyer and Rowan's (1977) concept of rationalized myths, where organizations mimic successful or prestigious organizations. In other words, when organizations such as schools have weak technologies and ambiguous goals, they may model themselves on other organizations that they perceive to be more legitimate and successful. Mark Hanson (2001) observes that mimicry is abetted and supported by educational consultants, professional conferences, and administrators moving from position to position.

Rodney T. Ogawa (1992) offers the following example of an imitative process: A school adopts a new structure to enhance efficiency. If the new structure is perceived to improve performance, others may copy it. Over time, schools may adopt the new structure, not for the technical purpose of improving efficiency but for the institutional purpose of gaining legitimacy with constituents by mimicking a successful organization. A specific instance is the adoption of school-based management by a few urban school districts, an idea designed to deal with a multitude of problems, such as low academic achievement and tight budgets. As word spread of the successes enjoyed by these "innovative" districts, other districts uncritically implemented the innovation, even though they did not share the problems encountered by the original adopters. Betty Malen (1993) similarly concludes that school-based management is tied to a belief that attaches virtue to innovation and helps school districts retain their reputations as progressive systems.

Normative conformity arises when personnel who have been socialized and educated to follow professional standards spread professional codes across organizations (Rowan and Miskel, 1999). Two aspects of professionalism are particularly important in producing conformity in school organizations. The first rests on formal education and cognitive knowledge. Professionals learn standard methods of practice and normative rules about appropriate behavior. The second comes from the growth and elaboration of professional networks and associations that span organizations and allow new models to diffuse rapidly. Associations or labor unions of teachers and administrators, for example, facilitate the exchange of information among professionals and provide policies and practices that can be copied throughout education.

Rowan's (1982) work tracing the incorporation of three occupations into California school district structures illustrates how normative conformity can produce new educational programs. He charted how health, psychological, and curriculum services and occupations were created and institutionalized by the rules and ideologies of state agencies, legislatures, and professional groups, and were then incorporated into the structure of local school districts. As early as 1909, the legislature passed legislation permitting school personnel to make medical inspections of children. The original purpose of the inspections was to combat the spread of infectious diseases. After the legislation passed, crusaders engaged in institution building. The result was that by 1935, the *School Code* mandated yearly medical inspections. Rowan concluded that districts added and subtracted occupations as support for an occupation ebbed and flowed in the institutional environment.

Through these conformity forces, schools produce similar structures and services and begin to resemble each other. Schools tend to look very much alike (Ogawa, 1992). In fact, pressures for conformity probably produce a surprising level of homogeneity within the American public school system. Meyer, Scott, and Deal (1992) found that schools go to great lengths to maintain their legitimate status as schools. They seek accreditation by conforming to a set of rules that are professionally specified or legally mandated. They hire licensed teachers who are assigned carefully defined students. Students are classified in grades that are given standardized meanings throughout the country. Finally, the teachers and students engage a curriculum that in turn is organized in fairly standardized categories of science, English, and mathematics. In other words, individual schools conform to and are constrained by institutional rules of what society defines a school to be; schools are expected to reflect the goals, values, and culture of broader society (Bacharach and Mundell, 1993).

Educational Diversity and Multiple Institutional Environments

While there are strong environmental pressures for conformity, considerable diversity is also evident within the larger K–12 educational sector. In contrast to highly centralized national systems in many countries, the institutional environments of American schools are complex and have many layers. For example, a distinctive characteristic of American education is its decentralized funding and control to state and local levels. The federal government has limited constitutional authority to regulate education and attempts to build such authority have largely been unsuccessful. Although the federal role has expanded, especially with the recent passage of the No Child Left Behind Act, the role remains largely restricted to funding and directing a variety of specific educational programs spread across multiple federal agencies. Consequently, the institutional environment of public education at the federal level involves the centralization of funding without substantive authority; and the linkages at local, state, and national levels tend to be loose, circuitous, and indirect. Meyer (1992) calls this pattern *fragmented centralization*. Consequently, American schools operate amid pressures from parents, community groups, and local governments, many agencies of the federal and state governments, and a wide array of professional and special-interest groups at all levels of society (Meyer, Scott, and Strang, 1987).

Many policy makers, citizens, parents, scholars, and educators probably have not recognized and taken seriously the diversity of the K–12 educational sector. When considering K–12 education in the United States, they see primarily the pervasive public school system. Yet well-developed subsectors of private, vocational, day-care, and alternative approaches also coexist with or within the public subsector of K–12 education. In fact, the persistence and increasing frequency of calls for market approaches to education (e.g., public and private choice, alternative schools, and voucher plans) may signal an increasing interest in private and alternative forms of education. An important point of speculation about this diversity and moves to strengthen the various subsectors is that different institutional environments may not only exist for each subsector of the K–12 system; they may also produce different educational structures and processes.

Rowan (1993) asserts that a strong case can be made that each subsector has a relatively unique institutional environment. He also proposes that by virtue of their institutional location, public schools have had to define a broad mission and are heavily penetrated by rationalizing forces. Conversely, private schools have been able to define narrow missions and are not subject to the kinds of pressures the public schools face. Therefore, a reasonable hypothesis is that in comparison to public schools, private schools have different institutional environments and reflect different structures and processes—for example, smaller size, less bureaucratization, little or no vocational education, fewer curriculum offerings, a communal learning and support environment, and different governance arrangements. Empirical support for this hypothesis is provided by the work of Anthony S. Bryk, Valerie E. Lee, and Peter B. Holland (1993).

Stability and Institutional Environments

In contrast to the common belief that uncertainty is increasing, Meyer and Rowan (1977) theorize that institutional environments tend to stabilize both internal and external relationships. They reason that centralized governments, professional associations, and coalitions among organizations provide for standardized operating procedures and stability. Environmental demands, characteristics of schools' inputs and outputs, and technical processes are brought under the jurisdiction of institutional meanings and control. Support is guaranteed by agreements instead of depending on performance. Regardless of whether schools educate students, for instance, people remain committed to schools and continued funding almost becomes automatic. Moreover, Meyer and Rowan argue that institutional environments buffer organizations from turbulence and allow conformance relationships to remain stable. Changes occur more slowly as the number of agreements increases. In fact, pervasive collective agreements among organizations grant near monopolies and ensure clienteles for organizations such as schools and professional associations. Thus, American school districts are near monopolies and have experienced high stability. The price for this legitimacy has been to conform to ever-widening rules about classifications and credentials of students and teachers, and the official content of the curriculum. In return, school districts are protected by rules that make education, as defined by the institutional classifications, compulsory.

Nonetheless, external environments can promote changes in school organizations. Hanson (2001) posits that environmental shifts, regressions to previous states, and shocks can energize significant change. Significant environmental shifts and even shocks may indeed be occurring. The increased calls by citizens, policy makers, and business representatives for alternative schools and heightened technical performance suggest that previous institutional agreements are being questioned. We will return to this possibility later in this chapter.

Summary Assessments of Institutional Theory

Institutional theory offers a substantially different perspective on the school organization-environment relationships than information and resource-dependence theories do. Schools maintain conformity with institutionalized rules and ideologies and expend little effort in controlling and coordinating instructional processes and outcomes. The image conveyed is form over substance (Ingersoll, 1993).

A criticism of institutional theory is that its broad emphasis on processes of conformity has led to downplaying the role of active agency and resistance in organization-environment relations (Goodstein, 1994). A narrow focus on conformity processes deflects theoretical interest away from explaining the circumstances in which institutionalization is contested or incomplete. Organizations such as schools can exercise some choice in responding to institutional pressures. For example, school districts vary widely in their responses to state policy initiatives (Firestone, Rosenblum, Bader and Massell, 1991). Nonetheless, the criticism of institutional theory, that it portrays organizations as relatively passive actors that simply conform to their environments, does suggest an important area needing additional conceptual development and empirical testing.

A substantial body of research, however, confirms the central insight of institutional theory. Over time, an institutional sector in America and around the world has developed to define and standardize educational organizations (Rowan and Miskel, 1999). In other words, research supports the basic premise of institutional theory that organizational structures respond to trends in the institutional environment. Perhaps the most important contribution of institutional theory, however, has been providing an alternative conceptualization of organizational environments. Meyer and Rowan's (1977) article called attention to a neglected facet of environments: institutionalized or symbolic elements such as beliefs, rules, and roles are capable of affecting organizational forms independent of resource flows and technical requirements.

Administering Institutional Environments

Scott (1992) indicates that there are clear differences in the way organizations respond to technical (i.e., information and resource) and institutional aspects of the environment. Most links with technical environments involve exchanges of information and resources. Although some ties to institutional environments involve exchanges, especially information, the institutional perspective postulates that organizations are constituted by elements drawn from their environments. Because institutional environments are different from technical and resource-dependent environments, and because of the recent development of institutional theory, less is known about how organizations relate to their institutional environments (Scott, 1992). The basic and ubiquitous notion in administering institutional environments is that school organizations will be rewarded for having a legitimate reputation (Elsbach and Sutton, 1992). As with information and resource-dependence models, variations of buffering and boundary-spanning strategies also appear useful in managing institutional environments.

Buffering Strategies

Recall from our earlier discussion that buffers are structures and processes that insulate or surround internal activities and absorb environmental disturbances. Buffering essentially creates a protective layer between the organization and its environment. A major problem to resolve by buffering mechanisms is conflicts between pressures for technical efficiency and institutional rules. From an institutional perspective, decoupling and managing the image are two ways to buffer school organizations from their environments.

Decoupling   Meyer and Rowan (1977) say that organizations designed for efficiency ideally attempt to maintain a close alignment between their structures and their technical activities. Close alignment in institutionalized organizations makes public a record of inefficiency and inconsistency. As a consequence, organizations functioning in institutionalized environments attempt to decouple their institutional structures from their technical structures and activities. **Decoupling** is intentionally neglecting to provide adequate control of work processes (Ingersoll, 1993). Decoupling divides organizations into two parts: one primarily links to the institutional environment and one produces the technical activities. Thus, the technical portion faces inward to its technical core and turns its back on the environment, whereas the institutional part turns its back on the technical core in order to focus on conforming to its institutional environment (Meyer, Scott, and Deal, 1992).

Decoupled school organizations exhibit a number of characteristics. For example, activities are performed beyond the purview of administrators and professionalism is actively encouraged. Goals are made ambiguous and categorical ends are substituted for technical ends—that is, schools produce students, not academic learning (Meyer and Rowan, 1977). Organizations decouple for several reasons. Decoupling masks or buffers inconsistencies, irrationalities, and poor task performance that might undermine public faith in the organization. Moreover, decoupled organizations can incorporate and display structural elements that conform to institutionalized conventions and yet preserve some autonomy of action. In inconsistent or conflicting environments, decoupling represents a particularly useful strategy (Scott, 1992).

Managing the Image   This strategy involves impression management to portray structures and actions in ways that garner endorsement (Elsbach and Sutton, 1992). Impression management makes extensive use of symbolic categories and coding rules. Similar to cognitive schema (see Chapter 4), symbolic categories are created to select, identify, classify, and label the things or people being processed by the organization. Coding rules are the essence of institutional frameworks; they provide the distinctions among things and people that allow standard operating or taken-for-granted procedures to be employed (Scott, 1992). Meyer and Rowan (1977), for instance, state that using cost analysis to justify school projects is an institutional norm that can provide a rationale if a project fails. Administrators whose plans have failed can demonstrate to other administrators, teachers, the board of education, and the public that the procedures were prudent and that their decisions were made rationally. Hence, institutionalized practices and impression management help justify their actions and portray a positive image to constituents. Such symbolic activities can produce shared meanings and value that in turn result in commitments, support, and legitimacy of the school organization (Ogawa, 1992).

Boundary-Spanning Strategies

Earlier in this chapter, boundary spanning, or bridging, was defined as activities that create internal roles to cross organizational boundaries and link the school organization with elements in the external environment. Meyer and Rowan (1977), DiMaggio and Powell (1991), and Scott (1992) propose conformity as the central boundary-spanning strategy in institutional environments. By incorporating institutional rules, beliefs, and ideologies into their own structures, organizations become more homogeneous and gain legitimacy. Scott proposes three types of bridging strategies that can be used to manage institutional environments.

Categorical Conformity   According to Scott (1992), this is a broad and general strategy. Categorical conformity is basically a process whereby institutional rules become distinctions that are taken for granted and provide organizations with a basis to pattern their structures. These distinctions are examples of widely shared cognitive schema. The cognitive structures become built into our language and generally believed. Meyer and Rowan (1978) refer to this as a system of ritual categories. This system has elaborate rules for classifying teachers—for example, elementary or secondary—and each category has its own specifications and credentials. Students, similarly, are categorized by grade level, ability level, and courses completed. Standard categories and ritual classification procedures involve not only educators and students, but also curriculum topics and schools (e.g., alternative and traditional). Schools that incorporate these shared cognitive belief systems—that is, exhibit categorical conformity—enhance their legitimacy and increase their resource capacities.

Structural Conformity   Sometimes institutional environments impose very specific structural requirements on schools as a condition of acceptance and support (Scott, 1992). External mandates cause schools to implement new programs. In the past three decades, many special-education programs—for example, programs for those who are mildly learning disabled to severely and profoundly retarded, and for those who have hearing, visual, and other impairments—have been incorporated into educational organizations to meet various legislative laws, administrative rules, and parental beliefs. Using various arrangements, schools have developed structures to conform to the special-need categories designated in the institutional environments. Administrators know the score—success comes with meeting the demands for institutional conformity rather than with instructional efficiency (Rowan, 1981). As mentioned earlier, schools often borrow or imitate successful structural forms when they confront uncertainty. Thus, by choice and coercion, schools frequently use structural conformity as a mechanism for adapting to the environment (Scott, 1992).

Procedural Conformity   Meyer and Rowan (1977) observe that despite the lack of coordination and control of the technical activities, schools are not anarchies. Day-to-day activities occur in an orderly fashion. In fact, institutional environments pressure schools to carry out activities in specified ways. School organizations can respond with rational myths that detail the steps to be followed in carrying out certain types of procedures. For example, schools tightly control such processes as hiring teachers with proper credentials, assigning students to classes, and scheduling events (Meyer and Rowan, 1978). Adherence to procedural specifications is a method by which stable school forms can be created and legitimated to work in institutional environments. By using socially acceptable procedures to execute controversial activities, schools can maintain the impression that they are rational and legitimate (Scott, 1992).

In sum, practical methods for administering the institutional environments of schools remain somewhat undeveloped. The foregoing sets of buffering and bridging strategies appear to offer substantial insights for developing specific tactics to manage the institutional environments of schools.

TIP: THEORY INTO PRACTICE

Administering Institutional Environments

While a major purpose of the No Child Left Behind Act of 2001 is to strengthen the task environment of schools, its many new rules and regulations will also enrich the institutional environment. Consider the possible requirements for curriculum standards, additional testing, fresh requirements for teachers, and provisions for school choice and respond to the following items.

- In terms of coercive, imitative, and normative conformity, how will the act likely affect elementary and secondary schools?
- What effects do you anticipate the law having on environmental diversity and stability for K–12 education?
- Assume you are a school superintendent. What administrative strategies would you likely use to handle the needed changes in your district?
- Which type of environment—task or institutional—has the act strengthened the most?

Policy Making and the Changing Environments for Education

The multiple levels of government rules, norms of professional associations, and ideological consensus of the public about what schools look like and do have been woven into a relatively stable institutional environment for public K–12 education. Since the early 1980s, however, the prevailing institutional assumptions, decoupled structures and processes, and rationalized myths have been strongly and persistently challenged. Worried about factors such as economic competitiveness in world markets and achievement gaps among racial and socioeconomic groups, policy makers, businesspeople, and many citizens have been demanding that schools emphasize teaching, learning, and academic achievement. The longevity, intensity, and diversity of calls for educational reform may indicate that the public consensus is declining and destabilizing the institutional environment. In particular, initiatives to implement programs of systemic reform and competitive markets in K–12 education may reflect a shift in school environments from primarily institutional to task or technical.

Systemic reform (see Chapter 8 for an extensive discussion of this concept) is a comprehensive change program designed to modify schools in an integrated, coordinated, and coherent fashion to achieve clearly stated educational outcomes (Fuhrman, Elmore, and Massell, 1993). The basic priority of systemic reform is to define ambitious curriculum content and achievement standards in core academic subjects and to tightly couple the goals with an assessment program. The alignment of curriculum content and achievement standards with assessment procedures creates an accountability system for monitoring the efficiency and effectiveness of K–12 schools. From the perspective of environmental theory, a likely result of systemic reform of K–12 education is to increase the influence of task and decrease the influence of institutional environments.

As Ogawa's (1994, 2002, 2003) findings with school-based management and standards-based curriculum indicate, a crucial point in systemic reform is whether the current initiatives promote technical efficiency and effectiveness or societal arguments, further governmental standardization, and professional control. If the goals of systemic reformers are to be achieved, technical environments must become the dominant form for schools and tight linkages must develop for accountability, efficiency, and effectiveness. If the switch to technical environments does not occur, the systemic reform efforts may produce a new, thicker web of rationalized myths and further institutionalize the environments of public K–12 education. Alternatively, further reliance on rationalized myths in the face of intense public calls for reform might force a break in the near monopoly of public education and produce a competitive market for K–12 education.

John E. Chubb and Terry M. Moe (1990) have been particularly articulate in arguing that the best way to improve American schools is to set them free in a competitive marketplace. **Competitive market** means that people choose the school and type of education that they think best meet their educational needs. Free-market proponents believe that competitive forces produce better educational services than do monopolized responses and unleash strong incentives for school reform. In a competitive market, it is reasoned that parents and students will opt for the public or private schools they think are most efficient and effective. If consumers are not satisfied with the outcomes, they can just walk away and thereby send clear signals to educators about the level of school performance. Without such feedback, stimuli for improvement remain weak and monopolistic indifference reigns (Boyd and Walberg, 1990). Methods commonly proposed to produce a competitive educational market include establishing parental choice and alternative schools in both public and private settings, creating charter schools, and offering government-issued tuition vouchers or scholarships that can be used to pay for the students' cost of schooling.

Christopher Lubienski (2003: 401) concludes that "there is a substantial, broad, and voluminous consensus on the potential of choice and competition to induce innovation in education." Of the market alternatives, a legion of supporters widely touts the possible contributions of charter schools. For example, using "charter schools" with the Google search engine in late 2003 produced nearly 3 million hits. Similar to other market-based initiatives, the basic idea of charter schools is that by freeing the schools from onerous regulations, educators will have the freedom and impetus to experiment with new organizational designs and instructional strategies. These innovations will then enhance achievement, provide positive options to parents, and offer new ways of educating students, especially the educationally disadvantaged. Two recent and thorough reviews of the research on charter schools raise doubts about the efficacy of these basic assertions. Although charter schools are making innovations in organizational and governance structures, they are making virtually no innovations in curricular and instructional practices (Lubienski, 2003). In regard to enhancing academic achievement, the results are mixed—charter-school achievement outcomes are not dramatically higher or lower on average than those of conventional public schools. In contrast, parents with children in charter schools express substantially higher satisfaction levels than parents with children in public schools (Gill, Timpane, Ross, and Brewer, 2001). Based on these studies, limited support exists for the hypothesis that market forces will spawn educational innovation and enhance achievement, but the situation could well change. The charter school movement is in its early stages and its many ardent and energetic supporters will likely keep it going.

As is the case with systemic reform, the rationale for competitive-market strategies is to place technical environments ahead of institutional environments. Competitive-market supporters are hypothesizing that parents and students will choose schools with ambitious academic goals, excellent teachers and administrators, motivating instructional materials, high efficiency and effectiveness, and strong accountability systems. Even if market-driven schools are established on a relatively widespread basis, however, forces in the institutional environment will likely counter the drive to enhance their technical environments. For example, market-driven schools already evidence imitative conformity, and they will likely develop their own rationalized myths, operate in environments institutionalized by government agencies and professional associations, and be strongly resisted by the current holders of the K–12 education monopoly.

In sum, we agree with Rowan and Miskel's (1999) conclusion. Concerted institution building over the past three decades by professional associations, government agencies, and private sector organizations is increasing the intensity of technical environments for schooling. This enhanced technical environment includes a model of educational productivity and the technical capacity to inspect educational outcomes of schools. Consequently, schools are facing stronger demands for technical performance than they have in the past, but without also encountering a decline in demands for institutional conformity. Hence, shifting the environment from primarily institutional to both institutional and technical represents fundamental change and will likely have profound effects on how schools operate.

A CASE FOR LEADERSHIP

A Reading War

You have been principal at Goodlion Elementary for nearly seven years. The school has 720 students in grades K–5. Your staff includes 32 teachers, 6 teacher aides, an assistant principal, and 2 secretaries. With expenditures at the 75th percentile on a statewide per pupil basis, Goodlion is one of six elementary schools in a middle-class suburban school system in the Southwest. The parents tend to be upwardly mobile and place a high priority on their children's achievement. You had been a fifth grade teacher for 10 years and an assistant principal in the district for 1 year prior to taking the job at Goodlion. During your service as a teacher and assistant principal, you completed a master's degree and other advanced graduate study in educational administration, curriculum, and philosophy. You especially liked the ideas of John Dewey. As a teacher and graduate student, you prided yourself on being a successful and progressive educator. You employed project-based methods and other constructivist approaches in your teaching and classroom. Your principal, fellow teachers, district administrators, and parents recognized you as an exemplary teacher. When the opportunity presented itself, you applied and were hired as principal of Goodlion Elementary. You were eager to work with the teachers to establish a school where the best constructivist practices of teaching and learning were used.

After four years, Goodlion's early reading program had all of the best features of whole language approaches. You are particularly proud that your school has a literacy rich environment that is characterized by bountiful amounts of reading aloud to children, oral discussions about authentic topics, immersion in individual reading and writing projects, invented spelling, and reading selected books. In this environment, children can learn to read naturally. The program places minimal reliance on basal readers and achievement tests. Phonics instruction is implicit and embedded in the authentic rich literature. From your observations and reports from the teachers, the children are highly motivated

to read, although some students seem to be having some difficulty learning to read. From your perspective, you have successfully realigned the relations between the students, teachers, and yourself. The children have been empowered to direct their own learning; the teachers have been empowered to direct teaching without interference from you or basal readers. From your perspective and that of the teachers, the new approach to reading is working and its continuation and refinement could more or less be taken for granted.

As this new reading program was being developed, ominous clouds were boiling up in the state political environment, however. A moderately conservative governor had been elected. A central campaign plank had been a return to basic education through a model of systemic reform. The primary components of the governor's program are high standards and high-stakes tests. In the fall of your seventh year as principal and three years after the reading program was fully implemented, the new state test was given in all the public schools of the state. The test result for Goodlion Elementary placed it at the 50th percentile.

Given your view that standardized tests are not valid indicators of student learning and school performance, you were not particularly concerned about the results. You assured yourself that your qualitative assessments had found that the students were motivated to read, enjoyed their reading in school, and had attained levels of comprehension not measured by the quantitative test. Your positive conclusions were reinforced by teacher expressions of satisfaction and support for the whole language program.

You are somewhat taken aback when you see a front-page story in the metropolitan newspaper about the test results and find that the test scores for all the schools in the area are listed and ranked within districts. Moreover, the governor's website contains a complete statewide listing of the scores in a report card format. Goodlion ranked fifth of

(Continued)

A CASE FOR LEADERSHIP *(Concluded)*

the six elementary schools in the district and is given a C grade by the governor. You brace yourself for calls from parents demanding an explanation for the low scores. You are surprised when you are accused by some of the parents of harming the children through the whole-language program. Abetted by the local chamber of commerce and the realtors' association, the parents quickly organize and petition the superintendent and board of education to change Goodlion's reading program to emphasize the following principles: teach phonemic awareness directly in kindergarten; teach each sound-spelling relationship systematically; show children exactly how to sound out words; balance but do not mix comprehension and decoding instruction. If you agree to these principles, your progressive program in reading will be destroyed.

- How did this problem arise without your being aware of the potential problem?
- Who are the constituents or stakeholders of Goodlion Elementary?

- In what respects has the environmental uncertainty for Goodlion Elementary increased? Or has it?
- Can the information perspective be used to understand how this set of events arose?
- What resources might you gain/lose by meeting/ignoring the demands of the parents?
- What tactics might be used to limit the influence of the parents?
- What tactics might be used to minimize the effects on the teachers?
- Can institutional theory be used to understand this controversy?
- Is it time to reevaluate your reading program?
- Is it time to deinstitutionalize the reading program? Was it ever institutionalized?

SUMMARY AND SUGGESTED READINGS

Open-systems theory highlights the vulnerability and interdependence of school organizations and their environments. External environment is important because it affects the internal structures and processes of organizations. In this chapter, three perspectives of the environment have been presented. The first two—information and resource-dependence theory—are primarily concerned with the task or technical elements of the external environment that are potentially relevant to goal setting, goal achievement, effectiveness, and survival. These models emphasize that schools are created to perform some type of work and to achieve goals. The information perspective assumes that the environment is a source of information that organizational decision makers can use. The resource-dependence approach assumes that organizations cannot generate internally the needed resources and that resources must come from the environment. In contrast, the third perspective—institutional theory—assumes that environments encourage schools to conform to powerful sets of rules and requirements that are imposed by the legal, social, professional, and political contexts of organizations. The essence of institutional theory is that the environment of schools presses more for form than substance. Nevertheless, technical and institutional environments do coexist; schools now function in relatively strong institutional but weak technical environments. Current drives for systemic reform and competitive markets suggest that worried businesspeople and policy makers may be seeking to place a heightened emphasis on task environments. A shift from primarily institutional to technical environments would shatter the rationalized myths and lead to fundamental changes in schools, a shift that will be bitterly fought by current institutional forces.

Because external environments can threaten organizational autonomy and effectiveness, administrators often try to minimize external effects on internal school operations. Their responses can be classified as either internal or interorganizational coping strategies. Internal coping strategies include buffering the technical core, planning and forecasting, adjusting internal processes, conforming to environmental expectations, and spanning organizational boundaries. Interorganization coping strategies include establishing favorable linkages with important external constituencies and shaping environmental elements through political action. By using the coping strategies, administrators can, to some degree, manage the environments of their schools.

To explore the information perspective in greater depth, a number of classic sources should be consulted, for example, Emery and Trist (1965), Thompson (1967), Lawrence and Lorsch (1967), and Terreberry (1968). To understand resource-dependence theory, one must read the work of Pfeffer (1972, 1981, 1982). Probably the most widely cited source for this perspective is by Pfeffer and Salancik (1978). To enter the literature on interest groups and influence processes, we recommend Baumgartner and Leech (1998) and Kollman (1998). Excellent sources for institutional theory are anthologies by Meyer and Scott (1983) and Powell and DiMaggio (1991). The latter collection includes the classic article by Meyer and Rowan (1977) and an updated version of a classic by DiMaggio and Powell (1983). Scott (2001) provides a comprehensive consideration. In education, works by Rowan (1981, 1982, 1993), Rowan and Miskel (1999), Ogawa (1994), Hanson (2001), and Malen (1993) are particularly useful. Although scholarly work is evident for all three models, theoretical development and research seem most active for institutional theory. Sources for competitive markets and charter schools include Chubb and Moe (1990), Wang and Walberg (2001), and Lubienski (2003).

KEY ASSUMPTIONS AND PRINCIPLES

1. When school organizations are confronted with uncertain environments or become increasingly dependent, additional flexibility in their structural configurations helps maintain or increase the quality and quantity of their outputs.

2. To minimize uncertainty, enhance resources, and gain legitimacy, school organizations attempt to adapt their structures and processes to correspond with factors in their environments.

3. Because school organizations are unable internally to generate the necessary resources to maintain themselves, they must enter into exchanges with environmental elements to acquire the needed resources.

4. Administrators must manage the external environments as well as the internal structures and processes of their schools.

5. In institutional environments, school organizations tend to be rewarded primarily for their conformity to professional standards and legal requirements rather than for the quality of their outputs.

6. Task and institutional environments represent separate continua, operating simultaneously and perhaps competing for dominance.

7. Public and private schools have different institutional environments, as reflected in their varying sizes, levels of bureaucratization, breadths of curricula, and types of governance.

8. In terms of influencing internal processes and outcomes, task environments seem to be becoming more dominant than institutional environments.

SCHOOL EFFECTIVENESS, ACCOUNTABILITY, AND IMPROVEMENT

The work of schools is becoming more complex and demanding while the organization of schools remains, for the most part, static and rigid. . . . The immediate cause of this situation is a simple, powerful idea dominating policy discourse about schools: That students should be held to high, common standards for academic performance and that schools and the people who work in them should be held accountable for ensuring that students—all students—are able to meet those standards.

Richard F. Elmore
Bridging the Gap between Standards and Achievement

PREVIEW

1. An open social-systems model provides the guiding framework for considering the effectiveness, accountability, and improvement of schools.

2. To create effective schools, educators have to surmount an array of ever-changing challenges.

3. During the 1980s calls for higher levels of school effectiveness (especially in terms of student achievement) and for stronger accountability intensified greatly and continue to influence educational policy and practice today.

4. As desired states that an organization is trying to attain, goals provide direction and motivation, reduce uncertainty for participants, and represent standards for assessment.

5. Performance outcomes constitute both the quality of each output and the quantity of the school's services and products for students, educators, and other constituents.

6. Input-output, or production-function, studies examine how educational resources or inputs are changed into educational outcomes.

7. Input-throughput-output research or effective-schools research relates an array of inputs and internal transformational processes to a variety of outputs, including student achievement on standardized tests.

8. During the 1990s, school accountability systems with standards, tests, and consequences as basic components became pervasive.

9. To improve organizational effectiveness and to meet accountability demands, educators are using a number of standards-based and comprehensive school reform approaches.

In Chapter 1, we proposed an open social-systems framework of school organization using input, transformation, and output components. The guiding framework first presented as Figure 1.5 is used extensively in this chapter and is reproduced as Figure 8.1. In Chapters 2 through 6, we make detailed analyses of five internal transformation elements—learning and teaching, school structure, individuals, culture and climate, and power and politics. Moreover, school outputs constitute the performance outcomes of students, teachers, and administrators and can be assessed for both their quantity and quality. In Chapter 7 we posit that important constituents in the

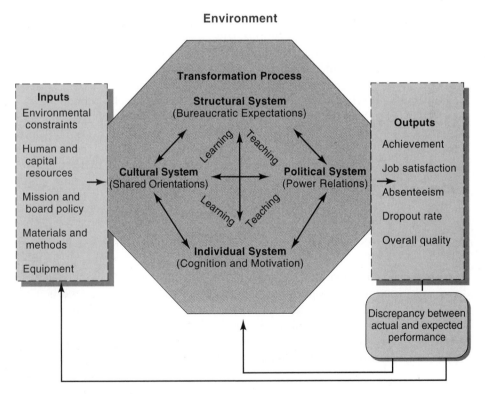

FIGURE 8.1 *Social System Model for Schools*

external environment of schools are calling for added emphasis on task accomplishment. As an overall generalization of open-systems theory, outputs of schools are a function of the interaction of five internal transformation elements as shaped and constrained by environmental forces. We further specified this generalization with a congruence hypothesis that other things being equal, the greater the harmony among the transformation elements, the more effective the system. Clearly, organizational effectiveness constitutes a key and integrating concept in open-systems theory and poses increasingly difficult practical tests for school leaders.

SCHOOL EFFECTIVENESS—CHALLENGING ADMINISTRATIVE PRACTICES

School administrators have long recognized that issues of organizational effectiveness represent enduring and fundamental challenges to their practice. Both educators and the public, for instance, acknowledge that different schools achieve different levels of success, even with similar student populations. Based on information of varying accuracy and completeness, parents decide, for example, to locate in a given area because they know that Lynn Cheney Elementary emphasizes basic skills and has high academic expectations and standards, whereas John Dewey Elementary uses high-quality motivational and hands-on teaching methods. With their differing perceptions and choices, constituents often question educators about the effectiveness of their schools. Administrators have responded to this challenge by offering a variety of information to show that their schools are effective and by implication that they personally are performing effectively. School officials report results to the public that educators believe represent their accomplishments and innovative practices. To illustrate quality and productivity, they also invite patrons to art shows, music performances, science fairs, and athletic events.

A second important challenge is that definitions of what constitutes organizational effectiveness do not remain constant. As preferences of constituencies change, constraints and expectations evolve to define school effectiveness in new ways. During the 1970s, for example, schools emphasized social and emotional growth and equity for all students, but with the reform reports of the early 1980s, the public started demanding an emphasis on efficiency, academic achievement, and employment skills (Cuban, 1990; Wimpelberg, Teddlie, and Stringfield, 1989). During the 1990s the focus continued on academic achievement with a strong thrust for ways to ensure accountability. Hence, as preferences change, performance that is judged effective today may be considered ineffective tomorrow (Cameron, 1984). For school administrators, then, the goal of creating effective schools is continually to *become* effective rather than to *be* effective (Zammuto, 1982).

A third complicating factor for administrators grappling with school effectiveness is that multiple stakeholders, such as parents, administrators, students, teachers, school board members, businesspeople, policy makers, news media, and taxpayers, prefer different effectiveness criteria. Administrators and board of education members, for instance, like to emphasize input resources and structural indicators of effectiveness such as available facilities and their use, amount of financial resources, and personnel practices. These are important in part because they are factors under administrative control. In contrast, teachers prefer to emphasize throughput processes. They argue that effectiveness must be conceived in terms of the quality and appropriateness of their instructional methods, positive classroom climates, and relationships with and among students. Students, taxpayers, and politicians, however, tend to favor outcome and efficiency measures. They evaluate schools in terms of academic achievement and cost per student.

In sum, school administrators face three basic challenges:

- How to demonstrate their system is effective.
- How to continually demonstrate effectiveness as definitions change.
- How to please multiple stakeholders with different definitions of effectiveness.

Despite extensive efforts by school administrators to demonstrate that their schools are performing at high levels, the interest in school effectiveness and accountability intensified significantly during the 1980s. The report, *A Nation at Risk* (National Commission on Excellence in Education, 1983), crystallized the performance problems of schools in the minds of Americans, especially business officials and policy makers. The public came to the clear belief that the world economy had become intensely competitive, interdependent, and knowledge driven; that academic achievement levels in America's schools were not competitive internationally; and that societal demographics for the United States were changing in fundamental ways—for example, the population is aging and a multicultural citizenry is emerging. Jacob E. Adams and Michael W. Kirst (1999) contend that the National Commission on Excellence in Education expanded the definition of excellence for schools and the public. To reduce the nation's risk, schools needed to set high expectations and goals for *all* learners and help their students achieve them, and the public needed to provide adequate support and stability for schools to change. In other words, the commission called for higher levels of effectiveness, especially student achievement, and for stronger accountability by holding "educators and elected officials responsible for providing the leadership necessary to achieve these reforms" (p. 32).

A Nation at Risk set off an explosion of state-level reform activity. In attempts to follow the commission's recommendations, for example, many states changed their high school graduation requirements, extended the school day and year, established new career paths for teachers, created competency tests for graduation, and instituted various types of diplomas to recognize different levels of student performance. This burst of activity during the 1980s became known as the "first wave" of educational reform. During the late 1980s, the substance of the reform movement changed (Vinovskis, 1999) and a second wave of reform activity started. The National Governors'

Association and then President George H. Bush met at the Charlottesville Education Summit in 1989. An important outcome of the meeting was the establishment of six national education goals, which were later expanded to eight for the Goals 2000 program established by the Educate America Act of 1994 (P.L. 103-227). Table 8.1 lists the eight goals.

The reform efforts of the 1980s did focus the public's attention on academic learning, but new policies came under intense criticism as being fragmented, lacking coherence, doing little to change the content and methods of instruction, failing to involve teachers, and slighting factors directly related to learning and achievement (Fuhrman, Elmore, and Massell, 1993; Smith and O'Day, 1991; Vinovskis, 1999). In reaction to such shortcomings, a so-

---

TABLE 8.1

National Education Goals

Goal 1: Ready to Learn—All children in America will start school ready to learn.

Goal 2: School Completion—The high school graduation rate will increase to at least 90 percent.

Goal 3: Student Achievement and Citizenship—All students will leave grades 4, 8, and 12 having demonstrated competency over challenging subject matter including English, mathematics, science, foreign languages, civics and government, economics, the arts, history, and geography, and every school in America will ensure that all students learn to use their minds well, so they may be prepared for responsible citizenship, further learning, and productive employment in our nation's modern economy.

Goal 4: Teacher Education and Professional Development—The nation's teaching force will have access to programs for the continued improvement of their professional skills and the opportunity to acquire the knowledge and skills needed to instruct and prepare all American students for the next century.

Goal 5: Mathematics and Science—United States students will be first in the world in mathematics and science achievement.

Goal 6: Adult Literacy and Lifelong Learning—Every adult American will be literate and will possess the knowledge and skills necessary to compete in a global economy and exercise the rights and responsibilities of citizenship.

Goal 7: Safe, Disciplined, and Alcohol- and Drug-Free Schools—Every school in the United States will be free of drugs, violence, and the unauthorized presence of firearms and alcohol and will offer a disciplined environment conducive to learning.

Goal 8: Parental Participation—Every school will promote partnerships that will increase parental involvement and participation in promoting the social, emotional, and academic growth of children.

called third wave of school reform became firmly established during the 1990s. Known as "systemic reform," this approach attempts to unite the earlier waves of activity with two dominating themes: comprehensive change of many school elements simultaneously and policy integrations and coherence around a set of clear outcomes (Fuhrman, Elmore, and Massell, 1993). Under the push of the third wave of school reform, the concentration on school performance increased substantially, and the heightened concern continues today. Terms such as "accountability," "academic achievement," "performance standards," "assessments," "high-stakes tests," "teacher quality," and "student dropout rates" infused conversations among educators, policy makers, business leaders, and the public. Moreover, systemic and whole-school reform came to dominate the language of school improvement. All of these ideas are compatible with a social-systems framework, which we will use to present major conceptions and relevant research for organizational and school effectiveness.

TIP: THEORY INTO PRACTICE

Using the ideas portrayed in Figure 8.1, consider the school system in which you are currently working or a school district you have knowledge of. How is the effectiveness of your system determined? How dynamic is the notion of school effectiveness; that is, to what extent has the definition of school effectiveness changed during the past 10 years? How does your school system convince the public that it is doing a good job? How does your district measure up to others? What is the evidence? If you were the superintendent in the district, describe a five-step program that you would develop to inform the public of the quality of your district and/or the steps that are being taken to improve the effectiveness of your system.

SOCIAL SYSTEMS AND SCHOOL EFFECTIVENESS

To ask global questions about whether a school is effective or ineffective is of limited value. Effectiveness is not one thing. For instance, effectiveness indicators can be derived for each phase of the open-systems cycle—inputs (human and financial resources), transformations (internal processes and structures), and outputs (performance outcomes). At one time or another, virtually every input, transformation, or outcome variable has been used as an indicator of organizational effectiveness. Consequently, the social-system model can serve as a theoretical guide to advance our understanding of school effectiveness and to assess the actions necessary to promote school effectiveness. This point is illustrated by considering each phase of the open-systems cycle as a category of effectiveness indicators.

Input Criteria

Inputs (see Figure 8.1) for schools include environmental components that influence organizational effectiveness. Inputs can be both monetary and nonmonetary. Monetary resources commonly refer to taxable wealth, money, or things that money buys (Cohen, Raudenbush, and Ball, 2003). Examples include formal qualifications of the faculty and administration, books, libraries, instructional technology, and physical facilities. Nonmonetary inputs are elements such as state and local educational policies and standards, political structures, organizational arrangements, parental support, and abilities of students. The input criteria indicate neither the amount nor the quality of the work performed, but rather set the limits or capacity for the transformation processes and performance outcomes of the system. In other words input criteria strongly influence the school's beginning capacity and potential for effective performance. Until recently, school accreditation models relied heavily on input indicators; that is, good schools had high percentages of experienced teachers holding advanced degrees, plentiful support staff, low student-teacher ratios, great libraries with many books, and well-equipped beautiful modern buildings.

Performance Outcomes

Traditionally organizational effectiveness has been defined relative to the degree of goal attainment. Similar to the definition of individual goals in Chapter 4, organizational goals can be defined simply as the desired states that the organization is trying to attain. Goals provide direction and motivation, and they reduce uncertainty for participants and represent standards for assessing the organization. As Scott (2003) posits, "goals are used to evaluate organizational activities as well as to motivate and direct them" (p. 353). Goals and their relative accomplishment are essential in defining the criteria for organizational effectiveness.

In the current policy environment of education, goals are reflected in the standards for judging the quality and quantity of performance outcomes schools produce. Performance outcomes constitute the quantity of the school's services and products for students, educators, and other constituents and the quality of each output. From a social-system perspective, important outputs include, for students, academic achievement, creativity, self-confidence, aspirations, expectations, and attendance, graduation, and dropout rates; for teachers, job satisfaction, absenteeism, and turnover; for administrators, job satisfaction, balanced budgets, and commitment to school; and for society, perceptions of school effectiveness. From a goal or performance outcome perspective, a school is effective if the outcomes of its activities meet or exceed its goals.

A frequently overlooked factor in goal or outcome models, however, is that complex organizations such as schools have multiple and conflicting goals (Hall, 2002). On the surface, the goal of expecting educators to maintain secure and orderly environments in schools is incompatible with the goal of developing the values of trust, group loyalty, and caring among students. Similarly, the mounting emphasis on standards and high-stakes achievement tests clashes with maintaining educator job satisfaction, an outcome that continues to attract substantial interest. Utilitarian, humanitarian, and organizational effectiveness rationales support the importance of job satisfaction as a component of organizational effectiveness (Spector, 1997). Early human relations proponents held that happy workers behave positively and are productive. During the 1960s and 1970s, a general concern for the quality of working life emerged with the proposition that people deserve to be treated fairly and with respect (U.S. Department of Health, Education and Welfare, 1973). At least partially, job satisfaction is an indicator of good treatment and can reflect how well the school organization is functioning.

Schools contribute much more than the academic achievement of students, and focusing on such a narrow outcome fails to account for the wide range of things that comprise positive school performance. Nonetheless, many parents and other citizens, policy makers, and scholars more and more define the desired performance outcomes for schools narrowly; they equate school effectiveness with the level of academic achievement as measured by standardized tests. These important educational constituencies see test scores as having intrinsic value. Schools with high test scores are seen as being effective. Moreover, achievement growth as a value-added outcome is being added to the definition of school effectiveness (Heck, 2000). Using a value-added line of reasoning, Peter Mortimore (1998) maintains that effective schools are ones in which students score higher on achievement tests than might be expected from their characteristics at entry. Consequently, an emerging definition of school effectiveness includes both the level and change in academic achievement. In other words, for schools to be judged effective, they have to demonstrate high achievement test scores and show substantial gains for all their students. As evidence of its popularity, policy makers are including the value-added criterion in their policy initiatives. For example, schools receiving funds under the recently passed No Child Left Behind Act of 2001 (P.L. 107-110) must show that their students are making "adequate yearly progress or AYP"; that is, making specified gains in academic achievement during a school year. In addition, policy makers seemingly have been relying on input-output approaches to predict and compare the performance outcomes of schools.

Input-Output Research

Input-output, or production-function, studies examine how educational resources or inputs are changed into educational outcomes (Rice, 2002). Production function research assumes that the performance outcomes of schools are related directly to inputs such as per pupil expenditures, teacher characteristics, teacher-student ratios, and student and family characteristics, whereas the outcomes are scores on achievement tests (Monk and Plecki, 1999). In other words, the purpose of production-function research is to predict an outcome such as test scores rather than to explain how the result was produced. Consequently, production-function research ignores the system's internal transformational processes and uses only inputs to predict outputs.

Production-function research gained popularity in the mid-1960s when James S. Coleman and his associates (1966) conducted a highly influential study reflecting this approach, *Equality of Educational Opportunity*. Popularly known as the Coleman Report, it remains the largest survey of American public education ever undertaken. The most surprising finding was that when home background variables were controlled, school inputs or capacity indicators showed limited relationships to test scores. Differences among school libraries, education and experience of teachers, expenditure levels, laboratories, gymnasiums, and other conventional resources had weak relationships with differences in student achievement (Cohen, Raudenbush, and Ball, 2003). In contrast, students' home backgrounds before entering school mattered more than the capacity characteristics of schools. Based on the recent findings of Brian Rowan, Richard Correnti, and Robert J. Miller (2002), this conclusion needs to be tempered. They found that when students enter kindergarten, their levels of achievement are moderately correlated to such factors in their home environments as family size, family structure, and socioeconomic status. These home conditions evidently produce differential opportunities to learn prior to attending school. Once students enter elementary school, however, the effects of home background apparently fade and achievement growth can largely be explained by the effects of instructional differences among schools and classrooms. In other words, differences in family backgrounds are more strongly correlated to initial levels of student achievement in elementary school than their year-to-year achievement gains. Nonetheless, learning in the home is extremely important.

Since the Coleman Report, a large number of additional production-function studies have been conducted. As a strong proponent of the approach, Eric A. Hanushek (1981; 1989; 1997) concludes that production-function research in education has produced startlingly consistent results—variations in school expenditures are not systematically related to variations in student performance. Furthermore, schools are inefficient organizations because there is no strong or consistent relationship between variations in school resources and student performance. Recently, Hanushek (2003) has become even more adamant in stating: "Class sizes have fallen, qualifications of teachers have risen, and expenditures have increased. Unfortunately, little evidence exists to suggest that any significant changes in student outcomes have accompanied this growth in resources devoted to schools" (p. F67). In sum, Hanushek maintains that production-function research generally finds little evidence to support the idea that spending additional money on current schools will improve student learning.

Scholars such as David H. Monk and Margaret L. Plecki (1999) criticize production-function research for lacking a driving theoretical framework that predicts, describes, and explains the findings. Others such as Alan B. Krueger (2003) and Larry V. Hedges, Richard Laine, and Rob Greenwald

(1994) strongly dispute the methods, findings, and implications of this approach. After reanalyzing Hanushek's data, Hedges and his colleagues (1994) found that the influence of school inputs on student performance outcomes are considerably more consistent and positive than Hanushek alleged. In a follow-up study, Greenwald, Hedges, and Laine (1996) assessed the effects on student achievement of three sets of inputs—expenditures (per pupil costs, teacher salaries), teacher background characteristics or quality indicators (ability, education, experience), and size (class, school, district). They concluded that in general, school inputs are systematically related to academic achievement and that the magnitudes of the relationships are large enough to be important. In particular, higher achievement is associated with higher per pupil expenditures, smaller classes and schools, and the quality of teachers. J. D. Finn and Charles M. Achilles (1999) provide substantial support for the conclusion about class size. Their findings from Tennessee's Project STAR (Student/Teacher Achievement Ratio study) show that students, especially minority and inner-city children, in small classes in kindergarten through the third grade performed better than those in regular classes. Hanushek (2003) responds that actual gains in achievement were small and that one limited and flawed experiment is not adequate to advance policy changes that will cost billions of dollars annually.

Even proponents of production-function research such as Hanushek (2003) acknowledge that differences among schools and teachers produce important and differential changes in academic achievement. Schools are not homogeneous in their effects on students; schools differ in the effectiveness of their efforts to influence performance outcomes. Steven T. Bossert (1988) maintains that input-output studies typically do not consider how students actually use available school resources or how schools deliver instructional services to their students. On the basis of reasoning similar to Bossert's, a new line of inquiry (input-throughput-output research) emerged that was designed to explain how home, school, and internal-system factors influence the performance outcomes of schools.

Transformational Criteria

Transformational criteria are the quantity, quality, and consistency of the internal processes and structures that transform the inputs to outcomes (see Figure 8.1). Examples of transformational criteria are the structure and content of the curriculum, health of the interpersonal climate, motivation levels of students and teachers, teacher and administrator leadership, quality and quantity of instruction, and quality-control procedures such as the number of tests given, evaluation of teaching, use of instructional technologies, and personnel evaluations.

The importance of synchronizing the transformational components is shown by the congruence hypothesis that harmony among the throughput structures and processes improves performance. In other words, to maximize school effectiveness, the internal elements of teaching and learning, bureaucratic expectations, group culture, political expectations, and individual needs must work harmoniously to produce the desired performance goals. Congruence among the internal elements enhances the system's ability to secure needed resources from the environment (Yuchtman and Seashore, 1967), to build the capacity of the transformational elements, and ultimately, to survive. This reasoning logically links the quality of internal structures and processes and performance outputs in schools, as in all organizations.

Educational administrators, therefore, place great importance on maintaining harmony because conflict impedes the system's ability to attain the resources needed to support internal actions and ultimately its goals. If Hanushek's conclusions from production-function research are accepted, however, building a case for additional resources to provide more teachers, better facilities, new curricula, and staff development becomes exceedingly difficult. Reacting to this realization and wanting to improve academic achievement, especially in low-income, largely minority schools, researchers developed input-throughput-output research during the mid-1970s (Cuban, 1984; Reynolds and Teddlie, 2000).

Input-Throughput-Output Research

Using a systems perspective, input-throughput-output research not only considers inputs but relates such transformational processes as classroom practices (instructional methods, classroom organization, opportunities to learn, time to learn), school climate or culture, organizational operations, and political relationships to a variety of outputs, including student achievement on standardized tests. This general approach has been called various names, including process-product research, systems research, and organizational research, but the most commonly used designation is effective-schools research.

Job Satisfaction Input and transformational variables that have been related to job satisfaction include centralization; climate and culture; job autonomy; pay and other benefits; challenge and variety; and employee age, gender, education, motivation, ability, age, and predisposition to be happy. For example, when specific structural or bureaucratic aspects of schools are related to job satisfaction, a complex picture emerges. Structural factors that enhance status differences among the professionals, such as the hierarchy of authority and centralization, produce low satisfaction levels. But factors that clarify the job and yield equal applications of school policy promote high levels of satisfaction (Miskel, Fevurly, and Stewart, 1979). However, role conflict and role ambiguity are the strongest—and negative—predictors of educator job satisfaction (Thompson, McNamara, and Hoyle, 1997). In terms of educator work, five job characteristics—autonomy, feedback, skill variety, task identity, and task significance—are positively related to job satisfaction (Hackman and Oldham, 1980). Work motivation is also consistently correlated with job satisfaction (Miskel, DeFrain, and Wilcox, 1980; Miskel, McDonald, and Bloom, 1983). Similarly, as the organizational climates of schools become more open or participative, the level of teacher satisfaction increases (Miskel, Fevurly, and Stewart, 1979). However, only limited relationships seem to exist between personal variables such as age and gender and job satisfaction (Thompson, McNamara, and Hoyle, 1997). In sum, the interest in job satisfaction has been high with widely applicable findings available to guide research and to inform administrative practice.

Academic Achievement   When specifically considering student achievement as the outcome, process-product research, usually designated effective-schools research, has identified a few critical school factors for enhancing scores on standardized tests. As popularized by Ronald Edmonds (1979), the five-factor effective-schools formula has become familiar to most educators. It includes

- Strong leadership by the principal, especially in instructional matters.
- High expectations by teachers for student achievement.
- An emphasis on basic skills.
- An orderly environment.
- Frequent, systematic evaluations of students.

A number of scholars have derived similar lists from the research. As shown in Table 8.2, Jaap Scheerens and Roel Bosker (1997) and S. C. Purkey and Marshall S. Smith (1983) suggest a larger number of school factors than

---

TABLE 8.2

Two Sets of Factors in the Effective-Schools Formula

Smith and Purkey	Scheerens and Bosker
• Instructional leadership	• Educational leadership
• Planned and purposeful curriculum	• Curriculum quality/ opportunity to learn
• Clear goals and high expectations	• Achievement orientation
• Time on task	• Effective learning time
• Recognition of academic success	• Feedback and reinforcement
• Orderly climate	• Classroom climate
• Sense of community	• School climate
• Parental support and involvement	• Parental involvement
• School site management	• Independent learning
• Staff development	• Evaluative potential
• Staff stability	• Consensus and cohesion
• Collegial and collaborative planning	• Structured instruction
• Direct support	• Adaptive instruction

Edmonds. All three lists show significant degrees of overlap in the transformational elements—for example, instructional leadership, high expectations, orderly climates, curricula, teaching, and assessment procedures. Extracting the common ideas from this research, effective schools exhibit characteristics such as consensus about a high-quality curriculum; experienced, motivated, knowledgeable and collegial teachers; clear goals and high achievement expectations; a healthy school climate that encourages teaching and learning; a staff development program; rewards for success; involved parents; and strong instructional leadership by the principal and teachers.

Effective-schools research had a tremendous impact on school practice during the 1980s. Good and Brophy (1986) and Stedman (1987) provide summaries of a number of the school improvement programs—for example, Project RISE in Milwaukee and the School Improvement Project in New York City—that are based on this body of research. Other programs were initiated in Atlanta, Chicago, Minneapolis, Pittsburgh, San Diego, St. Louis, Washington, D.C., and many, many other smaller school districts (Cuban, 1984). Nevertheless, the efforts produced mixed results. According to Good and Brophy, Project RISE achieved some success. Student scores on the achievement tests did improve to an extent, especially in some schools and in the area of mathematics. Stedman takes a more critical stance. Although some schools did improve their math scores, most RISE schools continued to do poorly in reading. Moreover, those schools that achieved success often did so by teaching to the test. In a similar vein, Cuban (1983, 1984) cautioned that rushing to implement the changes called for by the effective-schools advocates would produce significant problems and unanticipated consequences.

During the 1990s, Charles Teddlie and David Reynolds (2000) note that substantial conceptual and empirical progress was made in understanding and explaining effective schools. The emergent theoretical models add specificity about inputs and transformational processes, how they interact in schools, and how their relationships with outcomes vary across different settings or contexts. Moreover, the concept of context has been broadened. Instead of considering only urban inner-city school settings, the contexts of effective-schools research now include public and private elementary, middle, and secondary schools from communities with all social classes in rural, urban, and suburban settings and with various levels of support. The current effective-school models and research not only focus on schools serving all types of students in all types of contexts, but also emphasize growth in achievement and school improvement across all contexts.

Indeed, school effectiveness is starting to be conceptualized as sets of interacting variables. Scheerens and Bosker (1997) review a number of such models. For example, we know that schools serve students who differ enormously on factors such as initial educational attainments, family structure, and social and economic status. As discussed above, Mortimore (1998) contends that effectiveness models and research must account fully for these initial differences when comparing the effects of individual schools on the achievement gains and development of their students. In a study testing value-added models, Ronald H. Heck (2000) found that schools with higher-quality educational environments (principal leadership, high expectations, frequent monitoring of student progress and climate) produced higher than expected achievement gains. Similarly, Rowan and his colleagues (2002) identified a variety of school transformational factors related to changes in academic achievement. They found, for instance, that the classrooms to which students are assigned affect achievement growth; teacher effectiveness varies by academic subject (reading or mathematics); and elementary schools assign students to more and less effective teachers on a random rather than systematic basis. In regard to teaching processes, they found modest positive associations between achievement gains and both active teaching in whole-class settings and the content covered.

Transformational processes also have been elaborated to explain how they can promote learning. For example, schools' instructional or teaching quality depends on factors such as teacher expectations for achievement and how well knowledge (e.g., subject matter, curriculum, pedagogy) and skills (e.g., presentational, classroom management, assessment) are used in the classrooms. David K. Cohen, Steven W. Raudenbush, and Deborah L. Ball (2003) posit that key factors in instruction are the interaction of teachers and students over academic content and the interdependency that develops between them. In hypothesizing a reciprocal relationship, they predict that teacher effectiveness depends partly on how well they use the ideas and initiatives of students, and student effectiveness depends partially on how well they can employ the tasks and feedback their teachers provide.

Wayne Hoy and his colleagues have also focused their analyses on transformational properties of schools that explain academic achievement. That is, what internal characteristics of schools—beyond socioeconomic status—explain high student achievement? Their research suggests three school properties of culture and climate that make a difference: a culture of faculty trust in parents (Goddard, Tschannen-Moran, and Hoy, 2001), a climate that emphasizes academics (Goddard, Sweetland, and Hoy, 2000), and a culture of collective efficacy (Goddard, Hoy, and LoGerfo, 2003). Note that these studies attempt to control socioeconomic status (an input factor) and then link culture and climate (transformation factors) to student achievement (an output performance factor). Although very important, the effects of strong, positive leadership by principals on school effectiveness are not as direct as early writers such as Edmonds (1979) have portrayed them.

Principal and Teacher Effects

A commonly heard contention is that principals are the key to school effectiveness. However, the links between principals and student achievement are not as clear as some proponents of the effective-schools programs claim.

For instance, Good and Brophy (1986) conclude that nearly all studies of effective schools support the importance of principal leadership, but limited accord exists on the behaviors and practices that characterize leadership for enhanced academic achievement. In an even stronger statement, Bossert (1988) maintains that effective-schools studies have tried to resurrect the bureaucratic ideal by stating that strong principal leadership is necessary to structure schools for effectiveness. However, the research is silent on which processes must be structured and which structures need to be created to produce success. Bossert did identify four characteristics that are typically associated with principals who administer effective schools: goals and production emphasis, power and strong decision making, effective management, and strong human relations skills. Similarly, Philip Hallinger and Heck (1996; 1998; Heck, 2000) found that principal leadership has measurable influence on student achievement, but that the effects are indirect and occur when principals manipulate internal school structures, processes, and visions that are directly connected to student learning. Nonetheless, Hallinger and Heck insist that just because the effects of principals are mediated by other school factors does not diminish the importance of their contributions to school effectiveness.

William L. Sanders (1998) contends that "the single largest factor affecting academic growth . . . of students is differences in effectiveness of individual classroom teachers" (p. 27). Jennifer King Rice (2003) agrees with Sanders's contention (1998). Based on her recent review of the literature, Rice declares that "Teacher quality matters. In fact, it is the most important school-related factor influencing student achievement" (p. v). Heck (2000) found schools with higher than expected student achievement are staffed by teachers rated high for creating classroom environments that emphasize academics and for holding strong expectations for student learning. In contrast to principals and as would be expected, teachers directly influence student learning through a variety of classroom activities.

From the foregoing reviews of the many conceptual and research approaches to organizational effectiveness, it seems clear that educational scholars, practitioners, and policy makers have a body of knowledge that they can use to design methods for enhancing school effectiveness. We agree with Rowan, Correnti, and Miller (2002) that a promising way to school improvement is through instructional interventions that diminish differences among classrooms and create positive instructional contexts. During the 1990s, policy makers and educators started to develop policies and practices that reflect the foregoing ideas. The policy initiatives included complex accountability approaches to school effectiveness and systemic and whole-school models of educational reform. As a relatively contemporary set of ideas, educational accountability incorporates more applied and systematic approaches to the success and improvement of schools than the relatively abstract concepts found in goal and resource models of organizational effectiveness.

TIP: THEORY INTO PRACTICE

You have just been appointed principal of your school. How would you go about determining the effectiveness of your school? What criteria would you use? Consider at least three sets of criteria: input, transformation, and performance. Which set of criteria would you emphasize and why? After you have decided on your effectiveness criteria, prepare a brief PowerPoint presentation in which you discuss school effectiveness, the criteria you selected to demonstrate your school's level of effectiveness, and how you will measure each criterion. You will make the presentation at your faculty meeting with the superintendent present.

ACCOUNTABILITY AND EDUCATIONAL REFORM

Recognizing that the flood of reforms during the 1980s were having limited effects on performance outcomes, Smith and O'Day (1991) decried the fragmented, complex, and multilayered features of the policy system that prevented the development and maintenance of successful schools. To loosen the constraints and improve school effectiveness, they called for a coherent systemic approach to educational reform. In their influential essay, "Systemic School Reform," they make a well-reasoned argument for establishing systems of school accountability and improvement using a set of critical environmental, input, transformational, and performance outcome variables. The critical components of the model include a unifying vision with supporting goals and an instructional guidance scheme consisting of curriculum frameworks and standards aligned with high-quality assessment instruments. Through strong leadership by states and restructured governance structures for local flexibility, accountability systems are augmented by aligning or coordinating school-level curricula and instructional materials, in-service professional development, and preservice teacher education with state standards and assessments. For some advocates, accountability systems also can be strengthened by charter schools and vouchers. In essence, the drive for accountability is based on three underlying principles:

- Schools should be held accountable for higher standards of performance.
- Schools should be provided assistance to build their capacities for delivering improved education.
- Schools must increase the quality and quantity of their performance outcomes, especially student achievement.

Building on ideas such as those proposed by Smith and O'Day, policy makers and educators have developed and widely applied what they call systemic or standards-based approaches to educational accountability and change.

Accountability

Changing from accountability rooted in community and parental control through local school boards (Carnoy and Loeb, 2002), virtually all 50 states developed standards-based accountability systems for schools and districts during the 1990s. Elmore (2002a) believes that this pervasive drive for accountability comes from a basic societal belief that schools should demonstrate both their contributions to student learning and how they are improving their internal transformational processes. The driving force and theory behind educational accountability are straightforward, but its practice is highly technical, legalistic, and political. Consequently, many different types of accountability have emerged. For example, Adams and Kirst (1999) describe six accountability models: bureaucratic, legal, professional, political, moral, and marker. For current purposes, however, we rely on what Elmore (2002a) calls the dominant form of educational accountability—a system that holds students, schools, and districts responsible for academic achievement.

Evolving primarily at the state level during the 1990s, accountability systems focus on performance outcomes with data collected and reported school by school (Fuhrman, 1999). Accountability plans generally include three components:

- Standards to identify the subject matter knowledge and skills to be learned.
- Tests aligned with the standards.
- Consequences to recognize the differing levels of goal attainment.

Accountability advocates claim that aligning these and other elements of the educational process provides the coherence and direction necessary for improving the quality and quantity of school outputs. Martin Carnoy and Susanna Loeb (2002) provide support for this hypothesis. They found that states with stronger accountability systems experienced larger gains in student performance on the mathematics portion of the National Assessment of Educational Progress examination. In addition, Helen F. Ladd and Arnaldo Zelli (2002) found considerable support among principals for North Carolina's accountability program. Sixty percent of the principals held overall positive views of the program; 80 percent agreed that school-level performance standards were desirable, and over 70 percent thought that aligning the standards and tests and using value-added measures of school performance were good ideas. In contrast, the principals did not view the state tests as being a good measure of student mastery of the curriculum nor did they like the sanction of removing principals from low-performing schools. The principals also reported that the accountability program had substantially changed their behavior. For example, they placed added emphasis on preparing for testing sessions by encouraging the teaching of test-taking skills, allocating additional funds to mathematics and reading, and spending additional time with teachers.

The federal No Child Left Behind Act of 2001 adds considerable impetus to the accountability movement. It mandates that states develop and implement standards in reading/language arts, mathematics, and science; administer annual assessments connected to the standards; and provide sanctions for continued poor performance. Even when these three sets of actions are in place, however, many other complex jobs must be completed for standards-based approaches to influence classroom instruction and student learning substantially. For instance, accountability proponents call on states to create new instructional frameworks, curricula, and assessments and demand that educators make teaching more demanding and coherent (Cohen, 1996). For Jane G. Coggshall (2004), the tasks include enabling large numbers of people at multiple levels of the education system to acquire new knowledge, improving or even creating the technical capacity to track changes in student performance, transferring useful practices within and across schools, and coordinating task-based practices in uncertain technical environments. To more fully understand standards, tests, and sanctions and their complexities in the emerging accountability systems, we will now consider each component separately.

Standards   As a specific form of goal statement, standards detail what is expected. Outcome standards specify what students should know and be able to do and are used to gauge student achievement. In other words, standards describe the knowledge, skills, and other learning that schools should teach and define the levels of competence students must attain. Advocates maintain that standards provide schools with a common sequence of goals and supply students, teachers, and principals with a consistent and coherent guide for selecting content, developing teaching and learning strategies, and assessing whether the goals have been met. When standards are defined and used, they are highly popular. In 2002 all states except Iowa had developed content standards in the core academic subjects, particularly English/language arts and mathematics (Doherty and Skinner, 2003).

   To generate content standards for a given state, developers detail all the possible elements in a subject area and select a subset of what they consider the most important to represent the whole. States typically have built on and adapted standards from frameworks produced by various disciplinary associations. The first and probably most influential professional organization to develop standards was the National Council of Teachers of Mathematics (NCTM). NCTM first published its standards in 1989, and in 2000 the organization released a revised set, *Principles and Standards for School Mathematics*. Similarly, under the auspices of the National Research Council, several societies developed standards for science education. Heather C. Hill (2001) indicates that once states have new standards, they then urge districts to adapt the standards to their local contexts, which in turn stimulate their application at the school and classroom levels.

The creation of standards is fraught with difficulty (Hanushek and Raymond, 2002). Terry Moe (2003) asserts that creating standards is hardly an objective process, even for relatively well-defined subjects like mathematics and science. In fields such as reading and social studies, conflicts constantly break out over what content is important, what it means, and how to teach it. For example, skirmishes commonly break out in the so-called reading war between proponents of phonics and those of whole-language instruction.

Developing standards at the state level is tricky, but translating and implementing the standards at the district and school levels are even more problematic. In their study of developing district-level standards, Rodney T. Ogawa and his colleagues (2003) found that local educators did not have a clear instructional philosophy or vision to guide their work. As a consequence, they relied on a variety of standards and corresponding criterion-referenced tests to derive a set of locally generated standards. The overall results were not good. The new standards fell below state and national criteria, narrowed the curriculum and teaching strategies, and provided little guidance for professional development and instructional supervision activities. With similar findings, Hill (2001) observes that communicating the intent of the standards from the state to the local level is especially challenging. Hill explains that state standards are typically written by reformers who want to improve schools through challenging content, innovative teaching techniques, and higher-order learning. Not knowing the reformist language, members of local curriculum committees and classroom teachers apply conventional definitions to words that reformers intended to describe unconventional practices. Accordingly, local standards are crafted to suit local interests rather than systemic reform. Nonetheless, even with the difficult issues of development, implementation, and alignment, the drive remains strong for accountability systems using standards and assessments.

Assessments   All 50 states have some type of testing program, and 18 use additional information such as dropout rates in their accountability systems (Doherty and Skinner, 2003). Focusing on reading and mathematics, a majority of states test students once during elementary, middle, and high schools, or three times in total (Goertz and Duffy, 2001). Both the range of content and the frequency of testing will be changing dramatically, however, because the No Child Left Behind Act requires that students be tested in three subjects annually in grades 3 through 8 and at least once in high school.

Traditionally, educators have largely used tests to divide students into academic tracks, to diagnose learning problems, and to make general judgments about school success (Carnoy and Loeb, 2002). When employing tests for such purposes, the linkages are quite loose between accountability and tests. In the new accountability systems, however, the primary purposes of testing are to monitor improvement trends and to find out whether interventions such as new standards, curricula, and staff development programs are influencing student performance positively (Barton, 2001). Accountability systems are now tightening the link or alignment between standards and assessments significantly by prescribing that student learning outcomes become the content of the tests.

Using tests in accountability systems to determine whether the standards have been met and to evaluate school improvement initiatives generates considerable controversy. Conflicts arise about the procedures and adequacy of testing programs. Intense arguments are generated when stakeholders start responding to questions such as the following:

- Who should be tested (e.g., all students, random samples, special needs children)?
- What content should be assessed?
- What types of measures should be used (e.g., norm- or criterion-referenced, portfolios)?
- How often should the examinations be administered?
- Are the assessments valid?
- What level or cut score indicates the standard has been met?

Concerns also occur about how much importance to assign to testing. Paul E. Barton (2001) contends that standards-based reform is perilously close to becoming simply a testing movement. Similarly, Elmore (2002b) harshly criticizes the No Child Left Behind law for grossly overemphasizing testing, calling it an "unwarranted intrusion." Moreover, Audrey L. Amrein-Beardsley and David C. Berliner (2002, 2003) conclude that high-stakes testing policies are not working. They assert that such testing programs do not improve academic achievement much and any increases are explained by teaching to the test, drilling students on items similar to those on the test, excluding students from the testing process, and increasing the dropout rates of students. Other researchers strongly dispute these findings and inferences. For example, Raymond and Hanushek (2003) discount Amrein-Beardsley and Berliner's study, saying that the data analysis is rife with errors. Similarly, Jay P. Greene, Marcus A. Winters, and Greg Forester (2003) contend that accountability systems can be designed with high-stakes tests that produce credible results, do not distort teaching or manipulate the testing procedures, and provide a basis to reward or sanction schools.

Rewards, Sanctions, and Interventions   The third leg of most accountability systems is a scheme of consequences attached to performance outcomes. The supposition undergirding this component is that rewarding successful schools, educators, and students will reinforce good performance and enhance motivation; and conversely, penalizing those not meeting expectations will alter their behavior and subsequently improve poor performance.

While rewards and sanctions most commonly apply to school organizations, some accrue directly to individuals. Educators and students can be granted monetary payments (e.g., cash, scholarships) and symbolic rewards (e.g., pendants, special commendations) when their schools attain particular levels of performance or improve their performance by a given amount. Individuals can also receive sanctions. For example, teachers and administrators can be transferred or terminated; student promotion to the next grade or high school graduation can be contingent on passing an examination. Many educators favor the use of positive incentives (Ladd and Zelli, 2002). However, states are finding it very hard to enforce penalties by holding children in the same grade, denying diplomas, or removing teachers and principals (Finn, 2003).

Fixing incentives and punishment for educators to student performance raises the issue of fairness because accountability systems generally are not designed to motivate students (Fuhrman, 1999; Goertz and Duffy, 2001). Because academic achievement is coproduced by teachers and students, teacher success depends on student effort in school and on tests. Ignoring student consequences is unfair to teachers because teachers can be penalized if their students fail to exert the needed energy; yet few incentives exist to motivate students to do well on the tests. Recognizing this issue, policy makers in a majority of states have enacted rules that prevent students from progressing to the next grade or graduating from high school if they do not meet district or state performance standards.

In contrast to the relatively limited number of alternatives for individuals, states use an impressive array of inducements to hold schools accountable for student performance (Goertz and Duffy, 2001). After surveying accountability models, Ronald C. Brady (2003) identified 20 different types of sanctions and interventions that he characterized as being mild, moderate, or strong.

For mild sanctions and interventions, current teachers and administrators are required to acknowledge the low performance of their schools and to implement new programs within the existing school structures. Mild interventions include identifying low-performing schools, publishing report cards with rankings and comparisons to other schools or districts, requiring technical assistance for the schools, and mandating professional development for the staff. Mild sanctions are pervasive features of accountability systems. For example, all states require public reporting (Goertz and Duffy, 2001); 47 issue report cards detailing student achievement and other information; and 29 states rate schools or at least identify low-performing ones (Doherty and Skinner, 2003).

Moderate interventions raise the stakes and often involve substantial material and nonmaterial costs. These programs normally continue with the same educators, but require the staff to make substantial alterations in basic school structures and processes (Brady, 2003). Existing school staff typically initiate the modifications and do them voluntarily. Returning to our model of social systems (see Figure 8.1), changes can focus on improving school governance and organization, climate, motivation, decision making, personnel assignments, teaching practices, and leadership. For example, moderate interventions often include decentralizing decision making and allowing added principal, teacher, and parent participation; altering staff assignments to create nondepartmentalized schools within a school where teachers stay with students for a longer portion of the day and teach them multiple subjects; or having teachers remain with the same students across two or more grades. In sum, educators can draw on a vast array of moderate interventions to boost student achievement, including prepackaged whole-school reform models (see below).

Strong sanctions and interventions are truly high-stakes measures, causing significant personnel turnover and extensive changes in the transformational structures and processes of schools. Brady (2003) indicates that strong interventions are rarely tried because they are controversial, difficult to mount, and carry significant political costs. Strong interventions include reconstituting schools, taking over or closing schools and districts, providing school choice options, and withholding funds. Although research on strong sanctions is limited, Betty Malen, Robert Croninger, Donna Muncey, and Donna Redmond-Jones (2002) concluded that reconstitution interventions in a large metropolitan district failed to produce the promised results. They found that the replacement teachers and administrators were less competent and dedicated than the ones they replaced; the reconstituted staffs could not restore familiar routines and near chaos pervaded the schools; the reconstituted schools were not redesigned; and student achievement gains were not apparent. Malen and her colleagues' findings reinforce the reasons why strong sanctions are applied so sparingly.

Primarily using a behavioral perspective (see Chapter 2), a host of positive and negative consequences for individuals and schools have been incorporated into standards-based accountability systems. Combined with standards and assessments, the rewards, sanctions, and interventions are influencing the behaviors and attitudes of students, teachers, and administrators, especially in regard to performance outcomes.

Accountability and Institutional Theory

As strong as the drive seems at the moment, knowledge of institutional theory (see Chapter 7) should trigger some caution when projecting the likely long-term effects of standards-based accountability on educational practice. Schools operate in highly institutionalized environments but with a growing emphasis on technical accomplishments, a situation conducive to high levels of conflict and exploitation. The emphasis on standards-based accountability is clearly an example of policy makers attempting to reinforce the technical environment of schools without necessarily decreasing the institutional demands for conformity. Nonetheless, educators have shown themselves to be quite wily in resisting external pressures for fundamental changes. During this period of foment, institutional theory predicts that a host of initiatives will likely arise that appear to show compliance with the tenets of accountability while not actually improving or affecting the work of the technical core very much (Coggshall, 2004; Coggshall et al., 2003). On the other hand, by systematically implementing standards and assessments and showing sustained accountability over the long term, schools can increase their institutional legitimacy and maintain or even gain additional support from their environments (Elmore, 2002a). That is, for schools to gain in legitimacy and support in this age of standards-based accountability, they will have to change in fundamental ways. Questions about how educators and schools will balance the institutional and task demands from their environments and incorporate accountability measures into their operations remain both pressing and open.

TIP: THEORY INTO PRACTICE

What educational accountability system is used in your school or one with which you are knowledgeable? What are the main features of the accountability system (e.g., standards, tests, rewards, sanctions, and interventions)? Describe the primary components and indicate how they manifest themselves in the school. How does the accountability system affect the attitudes and behaviors of educators and students in the school? Since starting the accountability system, have the performance indicators changed?

Improving School Effectiveness and Accountability

The emerging accountability systems call for numerous, simultaneous, and systemic changes in organizing, teaching, and administering schools. But as Elmore (2002a) maintains, educators are neither prepared nor hired to make systematic, continuous improvements in their schools' transformational processes and to measure their success by narrow performance outcomes. Making such transformations and gauging success on state tests is difficult for all educators, but achieving the changes and outcomes is particularly problematic in schools serving children from unstable, poverty-ridden families who are living in unsafe communities. To meet these challenges, a plethora of initiatives have been launched. Two with particular promise are professional development and whole-school reform.

Professional Development   For standards-based reform to be successful in advancing student achievement, early reformers recognized that educators would require many and varied professional development opportunities (Fuhrman, 1994). For example, teachers and administrators would have to gain an understanding of the accountability requirements, deepen their content and pedagogical knowledge, and learn how to use new teaching practices. To accomplish these goals, the standard one-shot in-service workshops delivering prepackaged information simply are not adequate.

Considerable agreement seems to have emerged about the main features of effective professional development programs. The National Staff Development Council (2001) has established 12 context, process, and content standards to guide practice. The standards call for professional development programs to be rooted in practice, research-based, collaborative, long-term, aimed at instructional improvement, and aligned with standards and assessments. Similar to Elmore's (2002a) conception, this type of professional development is a set of ongoing activities that increases the capacity or knowledge and skills of teachers and administrators to improve their practices and performance. The basic premise is that student learning can be increased by enhancing the skill and knowledge of educators.

Drawing on research and best practices, Laura M. Desimone and her colleagues (2002) identify six key features of professional development programs. The three structural components are reform type, duration, and collective participation, and the three substantive aspects are active learning, coherence, and content focus. They obtained two important findings. First, professional development is more effective in changing the classroom practices of teachers when a cohort or collective of teachers from a school, department, or grade are involved as a unit. Second, change is advanced through active learning opportunities such as reviewing student work and receiving feedback on teaching.

Overall, well-conceived and well-executed professional development programs offer considerable promise in reforming schools. Yet, acquiring resources for intensive, long-term efforts linking what teachers know to what students are expected to learn and do is a difficult task. As Fuhrman, Elmore, and Massell (1993) explain, many policy makers and citizens see professional development as an expensive fringe benefit for teachers and administrators rather than as a powerful way to improve schools. Nevertheless, the new accountability models require educators to develop new knowledge, skills, and beliefs, and they maintain that the most direct path to upgrading classroom instruction and improving student learning is through systematic programs of professional development. Additionally, developers of whole-school reform models recognize the importance of professional development and commonly incorporated it into their models.

Comprehensive School Reform   These initiatives commonly offer unified freestanding packages of reforms with their own goals and standard protocols for adoption and use. Offering a wide array of thematic emphases and promising substantial improvements, whole-school reform models have become extremely popular. Thousands of schools across the United States are implementing over 100 different models of comprehensive school reform, and the numbers are growing at unprecedented rates (Datnow et al., 2003). Among the plethora of options, models receiving widespread recognition include Accelerated Schools, Coalition of Essential Schools, Core Knowledge, Direct Instruction, School Development Program, and Success for All. In addition, the efforts of New American Schools, a business-oriented, private nonprofit corporation, to establish "break the mold" school designs produced seven models, including Audrey Cohen College, CoNECT, Expeditionary Learning Outward Bound, Modern Red School House, and Roots & Wings.

Based on the ideas expressed by the National Clearinghouse on Comprehensive School Reform and Murphy and Datnow (2003), these initiatives consistently call for five sets of actions:

- Changing multiple aspects of schools, such as teaching and instruction, professional development, school organization and administration, and culture, in systematic ways.
- Enabling all students to learn demanding academic subject matter and to meet performance standards.
- Providing a unified plan of change with an explicit focus on academic achievement.
- Promoting long-term collaborative efforts by educators and parents.
- Tightening the linkages among all aspects (inputs, throughputs, and outcomes) of the school.

When considering these ideas, it is important to recognize that the comprehensive school reform models have been developed by a wide variety of entrepreneurs, and that the different models exhibit substantial variation in which of the basic actions they emphasize. For example, Success for All and Accelerated Schools represent more and less scripted approaches to teaching respectively. Moreover, implementation at the local school level requires adjustments for a wide range of contexts. In practice, therefore, variations can be expected in how the same model manifests itself across schools.

The program developers and implementers generally claim that their models advance systemic reform. In accordance with Smith and O'Day's (1991) formulation, however, the comprehensive school reform initiatives are systemic only if they promote coherence and reduce fragmentation, align with the standards and assessments of the state accountability system, and focus on improving academic achievement. Obviously, not all the models meet the criteria set by Smith and O'Day.

Because whole-school reform is a recent and evolving phenomenon, high-quality research is quite limited in addressing questions about whether whole-school reform models actually improve school effectiveness and if so, which ones produce the greatest gains. Geoffery D. Borman and his colleagues (2002) have provided preliminary evidence. They conclude that comprehensive school reform programs are having a statistically significant and meaningful effect on student achievement. Moreover, the effects appear to be larger than the effects of other intervention programs such as traditional Title I. Interestingly, the differences in effectiveness levels are not explained by the aspects that proponents typically tout as leading to higher achievement, such as professional development, measurable goals for student learning, faculty votes on whether the school should adopt the model, and innovative curriculum materials and instructional practices. The amount of technical assistance from the developers of the intervention and the cost of the program show only limited positive effects, and active parental and community involvement tends to display negative associations with performance outcomes. The effects of the models on student achievement did vary. The Direct

Instruction, School Development Program, and Success for All initiatives have the strongest evidence of effectiveness. Finally, the largest effects occur after the programs have been operating for six or more years, making a long-term commitment necessary to reap the maximum rewards.

While comprehensive school reform packages show significant promise in raising student achievement, Mark Berends, Susan Bodilly, and Sheila Nataray Kirby (2002) caution that changing whole schools is a complex and difficult task because so many people are involved and so many aspects have to be aligned. In their study of the New American Schools designs, they found that implementation is most successful in elementary schools and when teachers have high expectations for student learning and support the change, the schools are smaller and led by strong principals, the external consultants can communicate clearly and provide useful assistance, and stable financial and district leadership support are available.

Selecting and implementing comprehensive school reform models may be further complicated because the reform entrepreneurs and educators make different assumptions about school organizations. Larry Cuban (1998) posits that reform entrepreneurs assume that schools should be more rational and tightly coupled organizations with behavior driven by the intervention requirements and goals. In contrast, educators assume that schools should be less rational and tightly linked with behavior shaped by characteristics of the individuals within the organization. These differing assumptions led Cuban to postulate that reform entrepreneurs and educators choose different standards for assessing potential interventions. The creators of the systemic or comprehensive school reform models value three criteria: effectiveness in achieving the program goals, fidelity (the program in use reflects the original design), and popularity (how many schools adopt the model). In contrast, teachers prize adaptability or the opposite of fidelity and longevity. Using these five criteria to examine the effective schools movement, Cuban concludes that adaptability and longevity are more important than effectiveness and fidelity. The schools changed the effective schools innovation. With the popularity of the systemic reform movement, we may be witnessing another struggle between the organizational assumptions and preferred standards of the reformers and educators.

A CASE FOR LEADERSHIP

A Mandate for Higher Accountability

You have recently been appointed as the principal of New Central High School (NCHS), which is to open next fall. This new school is located in the inner corridor of a large urban city in the northeast. The new building was awarded a prize for its architectural design and is equipped with the latest instructional and security technology. The school is projected to have 2,500 students who have been

(Continued)

A CASE FOR LEADERSHIP *(Concluded)*

attending two nearby schools—East and West High Schools. Both are being closed at the end of the academic year. The students come primarily from low-income, minority families. Both schools have been experiencing declining enrollments, high dropout rates, and low scores on state-mandated tests. NCHS will open with a professional staff of 150. You have been able to select your administrative staff and to influence the selection of the teachers. However, the contract with the teachers' union specifies that many of the teachers would be assigned to NCHS on the basis of seniority. The state has instituted an aligned standards-based accountability system with a range of sanctions. The low test scores and high dropout rates of East and West High Schools place them in the low-performing category on the state report card. Given the large investment in the new facility with its state-of-the-art equipment, the parents and other stakeholders expect NCHS to overcome the

performance problems of its predecessors. Obviously, the pressure is on you to produce a highly effective and accountable school.

- What criteria will you advance for determining the effectiveness of the new school? Will your criteria be the same as the state accountability system?
- Who should be involved in establishing the importance of the effectiveness outcomes?
- Which context factors will likely have the most effects on the performance outcomes? Which ones can you influence?
- Given your analysis of the outcome and context factors, which throughput or transformational characteristics should be given the highest priority? What actions on your part might promote the effectiveness of these processes?

SUMMARY AND SUGGESTED READINGS

Organizational effectiveness now plays such a central role in the theory and practice of education that a thorough understanding of the concept is essential. From a social-system perspective, effectiveness is not one thing but is comprised of indicators from inputs or resources from the environment, harmony among and quality of the school organization's transformational components, and the relative attainment of feasible standards that can be exchanged for other resources and incentives. This complex view means that defining school effectiveness in terms of performance outcomes, while extremely important, is insufficient. This conclusion comes as no surprise to those who use a systems approach to understand organizational behavior. Outcomes are only one part of the system. The inputs as well as the transformational processes of the system are equal partners in determining both the quality and the effectiveness of schools.

Accountability systems for schools typically include standards to identify the subject matter knowledge and skills to be learned; tests aligned with the standards to determine whether the standards have been met and to evaluate school improvement initiatives; and a set of consequences to recognize the current levels of goal attainment and to motivate future efforts. By aligning these and other elements of the educational process, schools will exhibit the coherence and direction necessary for improving the quality and quantity of school outcomes. However, caution should be exercised when projecting the long-term effects of standards-based accountability on educational practice. Educators and schools will find many ways to balance the institutional and task demands from their environments as they incorporate accountability measures into their operations.

To meet the challenges posed by these accountability programs, educators are seeking ways to improve the performance outcomes of their schools. Some schools are abandoning the traditional one-shot in-service workshops and launching intensive long-term professional development programs. Other schools are adopting and implementing ambitious comprehensive school reform models that promise to change multiple school components, enable all students to learn, focus on academic achievement, promote collaboration, and tighten the couplings among the inputs, throughputs, and outcomes of the school. Preliminary evidence suggests that these approaches, although difficult to implement, offer considerable promise in enhancing the academic achievement of students.

The open-systems perspective also places great value on optimizing such administrative processes as deciding, communicating, motivating, and leading people. All of these ideas are congruent with contemporary models of school improvement such as systemic and whole-school reform. School leaders can improve the quality and effectiveness of schools by using a number of other critical processes—decision making, communication, and leadership. These are administrative processes that educators must employ effectively if they are to help develop quality schools. Thus, Chapters 9 to 11 provide in-depth examinations of the theory, research, and practice in these areas.

Several sources are recommended to further your exploration of effectiveness, accountability, and whole-school reform. Cameron and Whetten's (1983) *Organizational Effectiveness* provides an excellent analysis of the theoretical underpinnings of organizational effectiveness. S. C. Purkey and Marshall Smith's (1983) review of the literature remains a "must read" for students interested in school effectiveness. Reports by Scheerens and Bosker (1997) and Mortimore (1998) are first-rate sources as well. With its comprehensive, in-depth, and comparative review of the school effectiveness literature, the handbook by Teddlie and Reynolds (2000) merits special recommendation. Smith and O'Day (1991) is an essential source for understanding the roots of systemic reform. Adams and Kirst (1999) provide an insightful conceptualization of accountability systems. For an exemplary study of school interventions, we recommend the work by Malen and her colleagues (2002). Elmore (2002a) nicely describes and analyzes the roles of professional development programs in standards-based reform models. For extensive discussions of whole-school reform models, we recommend the work by Murphy and Datnow (2003) and the National Clearinghouse for Comprehensive School Reform website at www.goodschools.gwu.edu.

KEY ASSUMPTIONS AND PRINCIPLES

1. A social-systems perspective on school effectiveness has three important dimensions: acquiring resources from the environment (input), harmonious operation of the school's internal components (transformation/throughput), and goal achievement (output performance).
2. Congruence among the internal elements enhances the system's ability to secure needed resources from the environment, to build the capacity of the transformational elements, and to effectively achieve its goals.
3. School effectiveness is a dynamic concept that has multiple dimensions, multiple stakeholders, and multiple environmental constraints.
4. Student learning in the home is extremely important. Differences in socioeconomic background are highly related to student achievement, but show limited relationships to gains in year-to-year achievement.
5. Socioeconomic status is not a factor that school leaders can control, but they can directly influence the transformation process within the school.
6. Principal leadership has an indirect rather than a direct effect on student achievement.
7. The principal's basic impact on student achievement is through the development of effective transformation processes (teaching and learning, structure, individual motivation, culture, and politics).
8. Educational accountability systems that align standards, assessments, rewards, and sanctions of the educational process provide the coherence and direction necessary for improving the quality and quantity of school outputs.
9. The accountability systems are changing the behaviors and attitudes of students, teachers, and administrators, especially in regard to performance outcomes.
10. Comprehensive school reform models are systemic when they promote coherence, reduce fragmentation, align the state accountability system, and focus on improving academic achievement.

CHAPTER 9

DECISION MAKING IN SCHOOLS

The task of "deciding" pervades the entire administrative organization. . . . A general theory of administration must include principles of organization that will insure correct decision making, just as it must include principles that will insure effective action.

Herbert A. Simon
Administrative Behavior

PREVIEW

1. Administrative decision making is a dynamic process that solves some organizational problems and, in the process, often creates others.

2. Decision making is a general pattern of action found in the rational administration of all functional and task areas in organizations.

3. Values are an integral part of decision making.

4. The classical decision-making model uses a strategy of optimizing to maximize the achievement of goals, but the model is an ideal rather than an actual description of practice.

5. Satisficing is a pragmatic decision-making strategy that some administrators use to solve the problems of practice.

6. Most administrators probably use an incremental model of deciding; they muddle through.

7. An adaptive strategy of deciding unites the rationalism and comprehensiveness of satisficing with the flexibility and utility of the incremental model.

8. Like most complex processes, however, there is no single best way to decide; the best approach is the one that best fits the circumstances. Thus a contingency approach is proposed.

9. Not all organizational decisions are rational; the garbage can model helps explain nonrational decision making.

10. Irrationality in decision making is often produced by stress; the Janis-Mann conflict model describes the pitfalls of defective decision making.

11. Sometimes participation improves the quality of decisions; sometimes it does not. The Hoy-Tarter model suggests when and how to involve subordinates in decision making.

12. One of the dangers of group decision making is groupthink, shared illusions about the correctness and invulnerability of the group.

13. Groupthink can be avoided by understanding its causes and by appropriately structuring group decision making.

Decision making is a major responsibility of all administrators, but until decisions are converted into action they are only good intentions. Deciding is a sine qua non of educational administration because the school, like all formal organizations, is basically a decision-making structure. Our analysis begins with an examination of classical decision making.

THE CLASSICAL MODEL: AN OPTIMIZING STRATEGY

Classical decision theory assumes that decisions should be completely rational; it employs an **optimizing** strategy by seeking the best possible alternative to maximize the achievement of goals and objectives. According to the classical model, the decision-making process is a series of sequential steps:

1. A problem is identified.
2. Goals and objectives are established.
3. *All* the possible alternatives are generated.
4. The consequences of each alternative are considered.
5. All the alternatives are evaluated in terms of the goals and objectives.
6. The *best* alternative is selected—that is, the one that maximizes the goals and objectives.
7. Finally, the decision is implemented and evaluated.

The **classical model** is an ideal (a normative model), rather than a description of how most decision makers function (a descriptive model). Most scholars, in fact, consider the classical model an unrealistic ideal, if not naive. Decision makers virtually never have access to all the relevant information. Moreover, generating all the possible alternatives and their consequences is impossible. Unfortunately, the model assumes information-processing capacities, rationality, and knowledge that decision makers simply do not possess; consequently, it is not very useful to practicing administrators.

THE ADMINISTRATIVE MODEL: A SATISFICING STRATEGY

Given the severe limitations of the classical model, it should not be surprising that more realistic conceptual approaches to decision making in organizations have evolved. The complexity of most organizational problems and the limited capacity of the human mind make it virtually impossible to use an optimizing strategy on all but the simplest problems. Herbert Simon (1947) was the first to introduce the **administrative model** of decision making to provide a more accurate description of the way administrators both do and should make organizational decisions.[1] The basic approach is **satisficing**—that is, finding a satisfactory solution rather than the best one. Before analyzing the satisficing strategy in detail, we examine the basic assumptions upon which the model rests.

Some Basic Assumptions

Assumption 1: *Administrative decision making is a dynamic process that solves some organizational problems and creates others.*

Specific decisions that foster the achievement of the organization's purposes frequently interfere with other conditions that are also important. Peter M. Blau and W. Richard Scott (2003: 250–51) explain that the process of decision making is dialectical: "problems appear, and while the process of solving them tends to give rise to new problems, learning has occurred which influences how the new challenges are met." Thus at best, decision making by thoughtful and skillful executives and their staffs should lead to more rational decisions, but the complex nature of organization life usually precludes final decisions.

Assumption 2: *Complete rationality in decision making is impossible; therefore, administrators seek to satisfice because they have neither the ability nor the cognitive capacity to optimize the decision-making process.*

Effective administration requires rational decision making. Decisions are rational when they are appropriate for accomplishing specific goals, and people typically try to make rational decisions (Tversky, 1969; Payne, Bettman, and Johnson, 1988). Administrative decisions are often extremely complex, and rationality is limited or bounded for a number of reasons:

- All the alternatives cannot be considered because there are too many options that do not come to mind.
- All the probable consequences for each alternative cannot be anticipated because future events are exceedingly difficult to predict and evaluate.
- Finally, rationality is limited not only by the administrators' information-processing capacities, but also by their unconscious skills, habits, and reflexes as well as their values and conceptions of purpose that may deviate from the organization's goals (Simon, 1947, 1991).

Because individuals are not capable of making completely rational decisions on complex matters, they are concerned with the selection and implementation of satisfactory alternatives rather than optimal ones. To use Simon's words, administrators "satisfice" rather than "optimize." Administrators look for solutions that are "good enough." They recognize that their perception of the world is a drastically simplified model of the complex interacting forces that constitute the real world. They are content with this oversimplification because they believe that most real-world facts are not important to the particular problem(s) they face and that most significant chains of cause and effect are short and simple. Consequently, they ignore many aspects of the situation and make choices using a simplified picture of reality that accounts for only a few of the factors that they consider most relevant and important (Simon, 1947). That is, they operate in a world of

bounded rationality by limiting the scope of their decisions so that rationality can be approached (Gigerenzer, 2004; Simon, 1947, 1955, 1956).

Assumption 3: *Decision making is a general pattern of action found in the rational administration of all major tasks and functional areas in organizations.*

In deciding, those with the responsibility generally go through a general pattern of action that includes the following:

- Recognizing and defining the problem or issue.
- Analyzing the difficulties in the situation.
- Establishing criteria for a satisfactory solution.
- Developing a strategy for action.
- Initiating a plan of action.
- Evaluating the outcomes.

Although the process is conceptualized as a sequential pattern because each step serves as a logical basis for the next, the process is also cyclical. Thus, decision making may be entered into at any stage. Moreover, the steps are taken again and again in the process of administering organizations. The cyclical evolution of rational, deliberate, purposeful action—beginning with the development of a decision strategy and moving through implementation and appraisal of results—occurs in all types of organizations (Litchfield, 1956).

The structure of the decision-making process is the same regardless of the kind of organization (military, educational, or industrial) and whether the task at hand is formulating policy, allocating resources, developing curriculum, or making financial decisions. The universality of rational decision making calls attention to the fact that essentially it is the same regardless of specific context or task. Educational organizations are different from industrial organizations in a great many important ways, but the decision-making process is not.

Assumption 4: *Values are an integral part of decision making.*

Decisions are not value free. Values and moral choice are critical in systematic and deliberate decision making. When administrators pursue actions that they believe will attain a valued outcome, they are making judgments of value between competing goods or the lesser of evils.[2] But action requires more than good intention. For example, educational administrators often must weigh compassion for students against the judgments of teachers. Teachers may be threatened by students and react strongly to reestablish their authority. In the process, students may be punished for infractions that challenge the teacher's position. Most administrators value the welfare of both teachers and students, and yet administrators often must make decisions that favor one over the other. Judgments of value are inextricably tied to judgments of fact. The same kind of scanning and assessing used by decision makers to consider their options can abet moral choices (Willower, 1991; Willower and Licata, 1997).

Neither science and rationality nor ethics and practice should be sharply separated (Dewey, 1938; Evers and Lakomski, 1991; Willower, 1993, 1999). One goes through the same process to make an ethical judgment or a rational decision; that is, the reflective examination of alternative courses of action and their consequences is necessary. The practice of administrative decision making is a continuing exercise in both rationality and valuation; it is both a rational and ethical activity. To separate the activities is foolhardy and impossible. Values and rationality are symbiotic not antithetical.

Decision-Making Process: An Action Cycle

The specific sequence of steps in the decision-making process has already been outlined. The action cycle of that process is illustrated in Figure 9.1. Many decision-making action cycles may be occurring simultaneously. One elaborate cycle, regarding fundamental goals and objectives (strategic planning), may be proceeding at the level of the board of education, whereas smaller and related sequential cycles, regarding curriculum and instruction, pupil personnel services, finance and business management, and facilities planning, may be progressing at the district level.

Let us turn to a more detailed analysis of each step in the action cycle.[3]

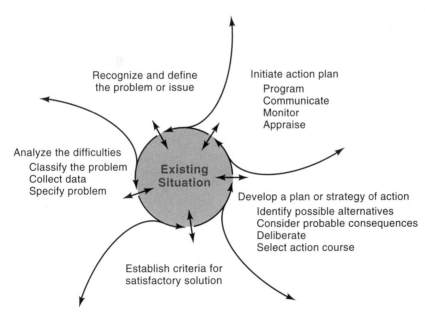

FIGURE 9.1 *Decision-Making Action Cycle*

Step 1. Recognize and Define the Problem or Issue

The recognition of a difficulty or disharmony in the system is the first step in the decision-making process. Effective administrators are sensitive to organizational actions and attitudes that do not measure up to the prescribed standards. The common retort, "We don't have problems; we have answers," is symptomatic of insensitive administrators who are headed for trouble. Although it may be possible for them to maintain equilibrium in the organization over the short run, the likelihood of organizational chaos over the long run seems great.

The recognition and definition of a problem are crucial to deciding and often do not receive adequate attention. The way a problem is conceptualized is important to subsequent analysis and solution. Not only are sensitivity and perceptual acuteness in the administrator necessary, but a rich conceptual background and a thorough understanding of formal and informal organizations are desirable in framing the problem. Too often administrators define problems quickly and narrowly and, in so doing, restrict their options. They treat only the symptoms of the problems, not the problem itself. For example, the response to a request from a teacher group for more autonomy in selecting curricular materials can be seen by a principal as an attempt to undermine administrative authority. The problem so conceived yields a set of alternatives that likely will be unduly narrow and restrictive. Such a teacher request, however, can open up a host of positive, creative possibilities for long-range curriculum development. This example, coincidentally, underscores the importance of security and confidence; the secure and confident administrator is unlikely to view such a teacher request as a threat to his or her authority.

During this first stage in the process, it is important to place the problem in perspective. If the problem is complex, its definition likewise will be complicated, perhaps multidimensional. The problem may need to be broken down into subproblems, with each subproblem cycled through the decision-making process. Furthermore, the problem may require several solutions. For instance, the problem of districting in a school system, where large numbers of parents want their children in school X rather than Y, may be settled in the short run by a policy statement indicating that a child will be assigned to a school solely on the basis of geographic location. The long-run solution, however, might well involve equalizing educational opportunities and improving the program of instruction in one or more schools.[4] There are two guides for defining the problem:

- First, define the immediate problem.
- Then, define the long-term problem.

Step 2. Analyze the Difficulties in the Existing Situation

This stage of the decision-making process is directly related to the first stage; in fact, some writers prefer to combine definition and analysis. However, analysis calls for the classification of the problem. Is the problem unique? Or is it a new manifestation of a typical difficulty for which a pattern of action has already been developed?

Peter F. Drucker (1966) proposed two basic kinds of decisions—generic or unique. **Generic decisions** arise from established principles, policies, or rules. Indeed, recurring problems are routinely solved by formulaic rules and regulations. A great many decisions that confront school principals are generic. That is, the organization has established mechanisms and procedures for dealing with problems. This does not mean, however, that they are unimportant; it simply means that they belong to a general group of organizational problems that frequently occur and that the organization wants to be prepared to deal with. Such decisions are needed when a principal implements policy mandated by the board, monitors absenteeism among teachers, mediates student-teacher conflicts, and interprets disciplinary procedures. All these generic decisions can be intermediary or appellate decisions (originating from above or below the principal in the hierarchy). In most cases the principal should be able to handle the situation by applying the appropriate rule, principle, or policy to the concrete circumstances of the case.

Unique decisions, however, are probably creative decisions that require going beyond established procedures for a solution; in fact, they may require a modification of the organizational structure. Here the decision maker deals with an exceptional problem that is not adequately answered by a general principle or rule. Creative decisions quite often change the basic thrust or direction of an organization. In order to seek a creative solution, decision makers explore all ideas that are relevant to the problem.

A unique decision might arise when principal and staff work to resolve a curricular issue where there are no established guidelines. The superintendent may specifically request an innovative solution. Completely unique events are rare; nevertheless, the distinction between problems that are routine and those that are unique is an important one in terms of deciding. Two common mistakes administrators need to guard against are:

- Treating a routine situation as if it were a series of unique events.
- Treating a new event as if it were just another old problem to which old procedures should be applied.

Once the problem has been classified as generic or unique, the administrator is in a position to address a number of other questions. How important is the problem? Can the problem be more fully specified? What information is needed to specify the problem? The original definition of a problem is usually global and general. After classifying and determining the importance of the problem, the decision maker begins to define more precisely the problem and issues involved. This entails the need for information. The amount of information that should be collected depends on a number of factors, including the importance of the problem, time constraints, and the existing procedures and structure for data collection. The more important the problem, the more information the decision maker gathers. Time, of course, is almost always a constraint. Finally, the existing procedures for data collection may facilitate or prohibit the search for relevant information.

In brief, decision makers need relevant facts. What is involved? Why is it involved? Where is it involved? When? To what extent? Answers to these questions provide information to map the parameters of the problem. Such information can be collected in formal, sophisticated ways, making use of operations research and computer facilities, as well as in informal ways, through personal contacts, by telephone, or in conversations.

Step 3. Establish Criteria for a Satisfactory Solution

After the problem has been analyzed and specified, the decision maker must decide what constitutes an acceptable solution. What are the minimum objectives that are to be achieved? What are the musts compared to the wants? It is not unusual for the perfect solution in terms of outcomes to be unfeasible. What is good enough? Answers to such questions help the decision maker establish his or her aspiration level. That is, what are the criteria for a satisfactory decision? At this point, sometimes the decision maker will rank possible outcomes along a continuum from minimally satisfying to maximally satisfying; a completely satisfactory outcome usually does not remain after compromise, adaptation, and concession. It is also useful to consider what is satisfactory in both the short and long term.

Criteria of adequacy need to be specified early so that the decision maker knows that a "right" decision is being made and not just one that will be accepted. In general, the criteria used to judge the decision should be consistent with the organization's mission. What we have referred to as criteria of adequacy, scientists often refer to as **boundary conditions**—the limits that the decision maker must meet if the decision is to be judged satisfactory.

Step 4. Develop a Plan or Strategy of Action

This is the central step in the process. After recognizing the problem, collecting data, and specifying the problem and its boundary conditions, decision makers develop a systematic and reflective plan of action. The process involves at least the following steps:

- Specify alternatives.
- Predict the consequences of each alternative.
- Deliberate.
- Select a plan of action.

Before we proceed to analyze each of these steps, several limitations need to be reiterated. Administrators base their plans of action on simplified pictures of reality; they choose the factors that they regard as most relevant and crucial; and thus they are able to come to some general conclusions and take actions without becoming paralyzed by the facts that "could be" indirectly related to the immediate problems. In describing the art of administrative decision making, Barnard (1938) warns:

- Do not decide questions that are not pertinent.
- Do not decide prematurely.
- Do not make decisions that cannot be effective.
- Do not make decisions that others should make.

The search for alternatives to solve a particular organizational problem is called **problemistic search.** It is distinguished from random curiosity and from the search for understanding per se (Cyert and March, 1963; Bass, 1985b). Problemistic search is straightforward, usually reflecting simplified notions of causality, and based on two simple rules:

- Search in the area of the problem symptom(s).
- Search in the area of the current alternative(s).

When these two rules do not produce enough reasonable alternatives, expand the search. Problemistic search probably is the dominant style of administrators; hence, most decision making is reactive.

But deciding need not be reactive. James D. Thompson (1967) has suggested that it is possible to develop behavior-monitoring procedures to search the environment for opportunities that are not activated by a problem. He calls this process **opportunistic surveillance;** it is the organizational counterpart of curiosity in the individual. Obviously, a decision-making structure that encourages opportunistic surveillance is more desirable than one that allows for only problemistic search.

Specifying Alternatives   A preliminary step in formulating an intention to act is to list possible alternatives. In actuality, only some of the options are specified because, as we have noted earlier, people do not have the information-processing capacity to think of all alternatives. With few exceptions, advancing a greater number of choices increases the likelihood of finding satisfactory alternatives that meet the already-specified conditions. One such exception is the expert with much experience in the decision context (Klein, 1997; Sales and Klein, 2001). For example, expert chess players (Klein et al., 1995) make high-quality decisions based on the first option they consider, as do experienced fighter pilots (Klein, 1997). Hence, experts in a situation often limit their search for options without undermining decision quality.

Creative decision makers are able to develop unique, viable alternatives, an often time-consuming task. Unfortunately, too many administrators do not take the time to develop a comprehensive set of possible options; they see the solution as a simple dichotomy—it is either this or that. Don't be overly impressed with speed in deciding; it is often a symptom of sloppy thinking. The impact of a solution is much more important than the technique. Educational organizations need sound decisions, not clever techniques.

Time is necessary to develop a comprehensive set of alternatives, yet time is limited. Consider as your first alternative doing nothing. Once in a great while, such an alternative turns out to solve the problem; things work themselves out. Unfortunately, most problems do not just work themselves out, but the decision not to decide should always be reflectively considered. Even if "doing nothing" does not solve the problem, sometimes it buys time for further thinking and information gathering, that is, it becomes a short-term strategy. In fact, it is useful to consider other temporary alternatives that do not really solve the problem but that provide more time for deliberation. Temporary alternatives, once refined and more completely thought through, are often the basis for more elaborate proposals. The key in developing preliminary and temporary alternatives is that, if successful, they buy time without creating hostility. There is always the danger that options that buy time will be seen as stalling; hence, buying time should be used sparingly and adroitly.

Routine decisions often can be handled quickly and effectively. Unique decisions demand more thoughtful and creative decision making. Creative thinking is of particular value in generating options. To think creatively, individuals must be able to reduce external inhibitions on the thinking process, to make relativistic and nondogmatic distinctions, to be willing not only to consider but also to express irrational impulses, and to be secure and amenable to brainstorming. Of course, the climate and culture (see Chapter 5) of the organization can either inhibit or facilitate creative thinking.

In brief, the development of effective solutions typically requires the following:

- A willingness to make fewer black-and-white distinctions.
- The use of divergent and creative thinking patterns.
- Time to develop reasonable alternatives.

Predicting Consequences   For each alternative that is developed, probable consequences should be proposed. Although for analytic purposes we have treated specifying alternatives and predicting consequences as separate operations, they usually occur simultaneously. The formulation of alternatives and probable consequences is a good place to use groups—pooling brainpower and experience to make predictions as accurately as possible. By and large, predicting consequences to proposed alternatives is hazardous. On some issues—for example, those involving financial costs—accurate predictions of consequences can be made; however, when trying to anticipate the reactions of individuals or groups, the results typically are much more problematic.

Predicting consequences underscores the need for a good management-information system, and those school structures that have built-in capacities to collect, codify, store, and retrieve information have a distinct advantage in the decision-making process. In addition, consulting with a number of individuals who are in a position to know improves one's predictive power. For each decision alternative, the consequences can be predicted only in terms of probable rather than certain outcomes.

Deliberating on and Selecting the Course of Action The final phase of developing a strategy for action involves a reflective analysis of the alternatives and consequences. Sometimes it is helpful to list all the alternatives with their accompanying probable consequences. Prior to selecting the appropriate alternatives, decision makers carefully weigh the probable consequences of each alternative in light of the criteria for a satisfactory solution. After such reflection, they choose the "best" alternative or select a series of alternatives that are linked in some sequential order, which provides a strategy and plan of action; the more problematic the issue, the more likely a complex course of action.

To illustrate the planning of strategy, let us simplify the procedure. It may be possible to set up a strategy several moves in advance, just as a good chess player does. Alternative A may result in a positive and acceptable solution; however, if it does not, the decision maker goes to alternative B and, if need be, to alternative C, and so on, provided the probable consequences are still satisfactory. Of course, unanticipated consequences may require a rethinking of viable alternatives. Occasionally decision makers cannot find an acceptable alternative. A reduction in the aspiration level may be necessary; that is, the criteria for a satisfactory solution are reconsidered (return to step 3). A new set of objectives, new alternatives, new data, and a new and more feasible strategy may have to be formulated.

In the process of searching for satisfactory alternatives, decision makers seek to keep the activity manageable by using simplified decision rules called **heuristics**—simple rules of thumb that guide the decision making and enable us to make decisions in a rapid and efficient manner.[5] For example, rules about when to take a "hit" in blackjack ("hit on 16, stick on 17") or how to play chess (dominate the center of the board) are heuristics. Some heuristics are useful, but others can be misleading (Gigerenzer, 2000; Gigerenzer, Todd, and ABC Research Group, 1999).

The **recognition heuristic** is the tendency to infer a higher value (e.g., stronger, faster, higher) to that which is familiar. The recognition heuristic for a two-object problem is simply stated:

> If one of two objects is recognized and the other is not, then infer that the recognized object has a higher value (Gigerenzer, Todd, and ABC Research Group, 1999).

For example, "Which city has a larger population: Munich or Dortmund?" The person who has not heard of Dortmund would infer Munich to be larger and would be correct. The recognition heuristic should only be applied when one of the objects is not recognized, but in such cases research demonstrates that the recognition rule of thumb is quite powerful (Gigerenzer, Todd, and ABC Research Group, 1999).

The **availability heuristic** is the tendency for decision makers to base their judgments on information already available to them (Abelson and Levi, 1985). Although such a strategy is quick and efficient, it is limited by what is known and what first comes to mind. Moreover, this heuristic can cause people to make errors (Tversky and Kahneman, 1974) and to overestimate the frequencies of events. In short, what is available in the decision maker's memory is often inadequate and sometimes misleading.

The **representative heuristic** is the tendency to view others as the typical stereotype that they represent; for example, an accountant is seen as bright, mild-mannered, and precise (Tversky and Kahneman, 1974; Greenberg and Baron, 1997). The representative heuristic applies to events and objects as well as people—the more closely an item represents the most typical occurrence, the more likely it will be judged to be that prototype. Even though such quick judgments are incomplete and prone to error, they are quite common in decision making (Tversky and Kahneman, 1974, 1981).

The **anchoring-and-adjustment heuristic** is a mental rule of thumb in which existing information is accepted as a reference point for decision making but is adjusted as new information becomes available (Baron, 1998). For example, a principal may evaluate teacher performance during an observation as satisfactory, but when confronted with new information from the teacher may make an adjustment on the rating. Such a process is more likely if the principal does not have a good basis for judging the quality.

The influence of heuristics on decision making is strong and often occurs unconsciously; in fact, recent evidence suggests that arbitrary numbers can anchor people's judgments even when the numbers are irrelevant to the decision (Wilson et al., 1996). The bad news is that the potential sources of errors of some heuristics are strong; but the good news is that such errors can be reduced by experience and expertise (Frederick and Libby, 1986; Northcraft and Neale, 1987; Smith and Kida, 1991).

Obviously, a large number of factors mediate the choice of a preferred alternative or alternatives. The values of the administrator, the cultural context in which the decision is made and implemented, the perceptions of those involved, the importance of the situation, the pressure on the decision maker, heuristics, and the importance of the goal—all of these and other factors intervene in the selection of a final course of action. Nonetheless, deliberate, rational, and reflective decisions generally result from following a systematic sequence of steps.

Step 5. Initiate the Plan of Action

Once the decision has been made and a plan of action formulated, the decision needs to be implemented—the final element in the decision-making cycle. The initiation of the plan of action requires at least four steps: programming, communicating, monitoring, and appraising.

Programming   Decisions must be translated and interpreted into specific programs—that is, the mechanics and specific details for implementing the plan must be specified. For example, the plan to change the system of grading elementary school students contains a specific and detailed set of operations that require answers to a number of questions. Who has to have information about the plan? What actions need to be taken and by whom? What preparation is needed so that those who have to take action can do so? The action that is to be programmed must be appropriate to the abilities of the people involved. In brief, the program must be realistic and capable of implementation.

Communicating   Once the plan has been programmed, it is necessary that each involved individual become aware of his or her responsibilities. Channels of communication among the individuals as well as opportunities for communicating both horizontally and vertically must be given careful attention. For a program to be successful, individuals need to know clearly not only what their own roles are, but also the roles of others as they relate to the total plan. Otherwise, efforts may be duplicated, counterproductive, or ineffective. The communication system developed to implement the plan in large part can and should be a crucial mechanism to initiate action and to enhance coordination of the program. Communicating is discussed in detail in Chapter 10.

Monitoring   The process of overseeing the implementation of the plan of action is monitoring. Evaluation and reporting must be built into the action cycle to provide continuous assessment of actual outcomes as compared to expected ones. Monitoring is a control process using systematic feedback. Standards of performance, once they are set, need to be enforced. Enforcement does not necessarily mean coercive control. There are many techniques of control such as rewards and incentives, persuasion, and identification with organizational goals. Different modes of control and enforcement are more or less effective depending on the situation and the individuals involved. Continuous feedback is necessary to evaluate the progress of implementing the plan of action.

Appraising   Once the decision has been programmed, communicated, and monitored, the outcomes still need to be appraised to determine how successful the decision has been. Has the decision been a satisfactory one? What new issues or problems have arisen? Decisions commonly are made in situations where probabilities, not certainties, are weighed. Even the most carefully conceived and executed decisions can fail or become obsolete. Organizational decisions are made in a context of change—facts, values, and circumstances change. Therefore, a fully articulated decision—one that has been reflectively made, programmed, communicated, and monitored—in itself brings about sufficient change to necessitate its own further reevaluation and appraisal (Litchfield, 1956). Hence, the appraisal stage is both an end and a new beginning in the action cycle of decision making. Clearly, there are no ultimate solutions—only satisfactory decisions and solutions for the moment.

THE INCREMENTAL MODEL: A STRATEGY OF SUCCESSIVE LIMITED COMPARISONS

Although the satisficing strategy that we have just described in detail is well suited to dealing with many problems in educational administration, occasionally some situations require an incremental strategy. When relevant alternatives are difficult to discern or the consequences of each alternative are so complicated as to elude prediction, even satisficing does not work well (Grandori, 1984). For example, to what new activities should a school administrator allocate more resources? The answer to this question is probably more adequately addressed by considering only alternatives that differ marginally from existing conditions. The underlying assumption of the strategy is that small incremental changes will not produce major unanticipated negative consequences for the organization.

Charles Lindblom (1959, 1965, 1968, 1980; Braybrook and Lindblom 1963; Lindblom and Cohen, 1979) first introduced and formalized the incremental strategy. He characterizes this method of deciding as the science of **muddling through** and argues that it may be the only feasible approach to systematic decision making when the issues are complex, uncertain, and riddled with conflict. The process is best described as a method of successive limited comparisons. Deciding does not require objectives, exhaustive analysis of alternatives and consequences, or a priori determination of either optimum or satisfactory outcomes. Instead only a small and limited set of alternatives, similar to the existing situation, is considered by successively comparing their consequences until decision makers come to some agreement on a course of action.

This incremental approach has a number of important features. First, the setting of objectives and the generation of alternatives are not separate activities. Goals and objectives are not established prior to decision analysis. Rather, a feasible course of action emerges as alternatives and consequences of action are explored. The more complex the problems, the more likely objectives will change as the decision evolves. Thus, the marginal differences in value among alternative courses of action rather than any prior objectives serve as the basis for deciding.

The **incremental model** also greatly reduces the number of alternatives. The strategy considers only alternatives that are very similar to the existing situation, analyzes only differences between the current state and proposed outcomes, and ignores all outcomes that are outside the decision maker's narrow range of interest. With this approach, the complexity of the decision making is dramatically reduced and made manageable. Lindblom (1959) argues that this simplification of analysis, achieved by concentrating on alternatives that differ only slightly, is not capricious; simplifying by limiting the focus to small variations from existing situations merely makes the most of available knowledge. Administrators who limit themselves to a reasonable set of alternatives on the basis of their experiences can make predictions of consequences with accuracy and confidence. Moreover, by emphasizing only differences among alternatives, time and energy are conserved. The narrow focus on outcomes avoids possible paralysis caused by attempts to predict and analyze all possible outcomes of a specific course of action.

Finally, successive comparison is often an alternative to theory. In both the classical and the administrative models, theory is viewed as a useful way to bring relevant knowledge to bear on specific problems. As problems become increasingly complex, however, the inadequacies of our theories to guide decisions become more prevalent. The strategy of successive limited comparisons suggests that, in such complex situations, decision makers make more progress if they successively compare concrete practical alternatives rather than emphasize more abstract, theoretical analyses.

In brief, the incremental approach has the following distinctive features:

- Means-end analysis is inappropriate because setting objectives and generating alternatives occur simultaneously.
- Good solutions are those upon which decision makers agree regardless of objectives.
- Alternatives and outcomes are drastically reduced by considering only options similar to the current state of affairs.
- Analysis is restricted to differences between the existing situation and proposed alternatives.
- The incremental method eschews theory in favor of successive comparisons of concrete, practical alternatives.

TIP: THEORY INTO PRACTICE

Describe a recent administrative problem in your school. How did the administration respond? What decision strategy was used? Did the administration choose a satisficing model or an incremental model? How open was the decision-making process? What were the consequences of the administrative action? Assess the success of the action.

THE MIXED-SCANNING MODEL: AN ADAPTIVE STRATEGY

Although widely used, muddling through has its limitations: It is conservative and aimless (Hoy and Tarter, 2003). Yet most administrators make decisions with only partial information and under the press of time. Amitai Etzioni (1967, 1986, 1989) offers a model of decision making that is a pragmatic approach to complexity and uncertainty. His adaptive model, or **mixed-scanning model,** is a synthesis of the administrative and incremental models that we have just described (Thomas, 1984; Wiseman, 1979a, 1979b).

Mixed scanning involves two questions:

- What is the organization's mission and policy?
- What decisions will move the organization toward its mission and policy?

Mixed scanning seeks to use partial information to make satisfactory decisions without either getting bogged down examining all the information or proceeding blindly with little or no information.[6] This **adaptive strategy** is "a mixture of shallow and deep examination of data—generalized consideration of a broad range of facts and choices followed by detailed examination of a focused subset of facts and choices" (Etzioni, 1989: 124). Higher-order, fundamental decision making (mission or policy decisions) is combined with lower-order, incremental decisions that work out the higher-order ones (Etzioni, 1986; Goldberg, 1975; Haynes, 1974). Mixed scanning unites the rationalism and comprehensiveness of the administrative model with the flexibility and utility of the incremental model.

As we have suggested, there are times when alternatives are difficult to discern and when consequences are hard to predict. In these situations, administrators often muddle through. Their incremental decisions are tentative or remedial—small steps taken in directions not far afield from the existing state. Such decision making has its downside, however; it is patently conservative and often without direction. That is, unless decision makers evaluate these incremental decisions in terms of some broad, fundamental policy, drift is likely. Broad guidelines, however, are not incrementally formulated; in fact, they have all the trappings of grand, a priori, decisions, which incrementalism seeks to avoid (Etzioni, 1989).

The mixed-scanning model has its roots in medicine. It is the way effective physicians make decisions. Unlike incrementalists, doctors know what they are trying to achieve and on which parts of the organism to focus attention. Moreover, unlike decision makers who seek to optimize, they do not engage all their resources on the basis of an initial diagnosis, or wait for every conceivable bit of personal history and scientific data before beginning treatment. Doctors survey the symptoms of a patient, analyze the difficulty, initiate a tentative treatment, and, if it fails, they try something else (Etzioni, 1989).

The principles for mixed scanning are straightforward; in fact, Etzioni (1989) advances seven basic rules for a mixed-scanning strategy, which Wayne Hoy and John Tarter (2003) have summarized as follows:

1. *Use focused trial and error.* First, search for reasonable alternatives; then select, implement, and test them; and finally, adjust and modify as the outcomes become clear. Focused trial and error assumes that, despite the fact that important information is missing, the administrator must act. Thus decisions are made with partial information and then carefully monitored and modified in light of new data.

2. *Be tentative; proceed with caution.* Be ready to modify a course of action as necessary. It is important that administrators view each decision as experimental, expecting to revise it.

3. *If uncertain, procrastinate.* Waiting is not always bad. When the situation is ambiguous, delay as long as possible so that more information can be collected and analyzed before taking action. Complexity and uncertainty frequently justify delay.

4. *Stagger your decisions.* Commit to a decision in stages, evaluating the outcomes of each phase before proceeding to the next phase.

5. *If uncertain, fractionalize decisions.* Staggered decisions can be tested in parts. Do not invest all your resources to implement a decision, but instead use partial resources until the consequences are satisfactory.

6. *Hedge your bets.* Implement several competing alternatives, provided that each has satisfactory outcomes. Then make adjustments on the basis of the results.

7. *Be prepared to reverse your decision.* Try to keep decisions tentative and experimental. Reversible decisions avoid overcommitment to a course of action when only partial information is available.

Educational administrators can skillfully employ all of these adaptive techniques; all illustrate flexibility, caution, and a capacity to proceed with partial knowledge.

In sum, the mixed-scanning model has the following distinctive features:

- Broad, organizational policy gives direction to tentative incremental decisions.
- Good decisions have satisfactory outcomes that are consistent wit organizational policy and mission.
- The search for alternatives is limited to those close to the prob
- Analysis is based on the assumption that important informa missing but action is imperative.
- Theory, experience, and successive comparisons are use

The major differences in the four models of decision making ministrative, incremental, and mixed scanning—are compa

A Contingency Approach: The Right Stra for the Situation

We have proposed four decision-making models way to decide? There is no best way to decide j organize, to teach, to do research, or to do a m complex tasks, the correct approach is t circumstances—a contingency approach.

The decision strategies can be ord deal with complexity and conditions o

TABLE 9.1

Comparison of the Classical, Administrative, Incremental, and Mixed-Scanning Models of Decision Making

Classical	Administrative	Incremental	Mixed Scanning
Objectives are set prior to generating ᵗᵗᵉʳnatives	Objectives are usually set prior to generating alternatives.	Setting objectives and generating alternatives are intertwined.	Broad policy guidelines are set prior to generating alternatives.
	Decision making is ᵗⁱⁱⁱically means- ˡᵥsis;	Because means and ends are not separable, means-ends analysis is inappropriate.	Decision making is focused on broad ends and tentative means.

The test of a good decision
is that it can be shown to
ᵉsult in a satisfactory
ᵗcision that is
ᵗsistent with the
ⁿization's policy.

tisficing)

ᵗ and
ᵉrnatives
ᵗroblem, but
ᵗtative
ᵗs in terms of
ᵗicy. More
ᵗensive than
ᵗentalism.

ᵗ, experience, and
ᵗcessive comparisons
ᵗed together.

(Grandori, 1984). When decisions are simple, information complete and certain, and a collective preference (no conflict) exists, then an optimizing strategy is most appropriate. As we have already noted, however, organizational problems are almost never simple, certain, and without conflict in preferences; thus, optimizing is not really a choice.

When uncertainty and conflict prevail, as is typically the case in administrative decision making, a satisficing strategy becomes appropriate. The administrative model is flexible and heuristic. Decisions are based on comparisons among consequences of alternatives and the decision maker's aspiration level. Only a partial exploration of the alternatives is performed until a satisfactory course of action is discovered. If satisfactory solutions are not found, then the aspiration level is lowered. Lack of time, of course, may truncate the process by forcing the consideration of fewer options.

When alternatives are difficult if not impossible to discern or consequences are so complicated as to elude prediction, even a satisficing strategy has its limits. In such situations, a muddling or incremental strategy may be appropriate because such an approach deals with both uncertainty and conflict of interest by assuming that small changes will not produce large negative consequences for the organization (Grandori, 1984). Thus, when the organization is in turmoil and without direction, muddling through may be the appropriate *short-run* strategy.

Some students of organization (Starkie, 1984; Etzioni, 1989), however, argue that even when the decisions are complex and outcomes are difficult to predict, incrementalism is too conservative and self-defeating. Small, incremental decisions made without guidelines lead to drift—to action without direction. Instead, mixed scanning or adaptive decision making is recommended to deal with exceedingly complex decisions. Mixed scanning combines the best of both the satisficing and the incremental models; a strategy of satisficing is combined with incremental decisions guided by broad policy. Full scanning is replaced by partial scanning of a set of satisfactory options, and tentative and reversible decisions are emphasized in an incremental process that calls for caution as well as a clear sense of destination. Time again may limit the number of possibilities considered before action.

In sum, the appropriate decision strategy depends on the information, complexity of the situation, time, and importance of the decision. We propose a simplified approach for selecting the appropriate decision model based on three questions:

- Is there sufficient information to define a satisfactory outcome?
- Is there time to engage in a comprehensive search?
- How important is the decision?

If there is sufficient information to define a satisfactory outcome, then satisficing is the model of choice. But depending on time and importance of the decision, the satisficing strategy can be truncated and adapted. If, however, there is insufficient information, then adaptive satisficing is the

preferred strategy. But again depending on time and importance of the decision, adaptive satisficing may be truncated or moderated by muddling
through. The eight possibilities and strategies are mapped in the contingency tree in Figure 9.2.

THE GARBAGE CAN MODEL: NONRATIONAL DECISION MAKING

Individuals and institutions sometimes need ways of doing things for which
there are no good reasons. Not always, not even usually, but occasionally
people need to act before they think (March, 1982, 1994). The so-called
garbage can model describes this tendency, which is most likely to occur in

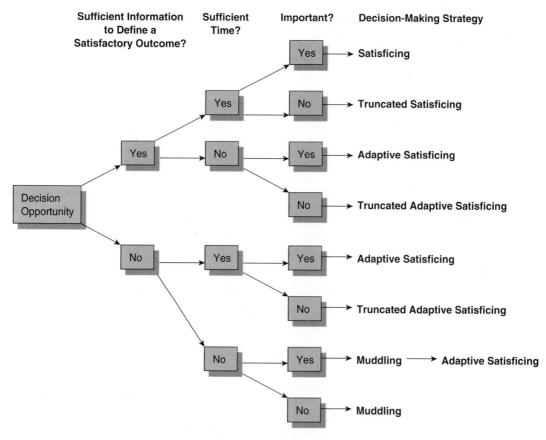

FIGURE 9.2   *Contingency Tree: A Simplified Approach to Match Decision-Making Strategy and Situation*

organizations that experience extremely high uncertainty. Michael Cohen, James March, and Johan Olsen (1972), the originators of the model, call such organizations organized anarchies. These organizations are characterized by *problematic preferences, unclear technology, and fluid participation.* That is, ambiguity accompanies each step of the decision process; cause-and-effect relationships within the organization are virtually impossible to determine; there is a rapid turnover in participants; and time is limited for any one problem or decision. Although no organization fits this extremely organic and loosely coupled system all the time, the model is often useful for *understanding* the pattern of decisions for situations of organized anarchy.

The basic feature of the garbage can model is that the decision process does not begin with a problem and end with a solution; rather, decisions are a product of independent streams of events in the organization (Cohen, March, and Olsen, 1972; Cohen and March, 1974; March, 1982; Estler, 1988; Daft, 1989; Tarter and Hoy, 1998; Slater and Boyd, 1999). The following four streams are particularly relevant for organizational decision making in organized anarchies:

- *Problems* are points of dissatisfaction that need attention; however, problems are distinct from solutions and choices. A problem may or may not lead to a solution and problems may or may not be solved when a solution is adopted.
- *Solutions* are ideas proposed for adoption, but they can exist independently of problems. In fact, the attractiveness of an idea can produce a search for a problem to justify the idea. Cohen and colleagues (1972: 3) argue, "Despite the dictum that you cannot find the answer until you have formulated the question well, you often do not know what the question is in organizational problem solving until you know the answer."
- *Participants* are organizational members who come and go. Because personnel are fluid, problems and solutions can change quickly.
- *Choice opportunities* are occasions when organizations are expected to make decisions—for example, contracts must be signed, people hired and fired, money spent, and resources allocated.

Within these four streams of events, the overall pattern of organizational decision making takes on a quality of randomness. Organizational decision makers do not perceive that something is occurring about which a decision is necessary until the problem matches one with which they already have had some experience (Hall, 1987). When problems and solutions happen to match, a decision may occur. An administrator who has a good idea may suddenly find a problem to solve. When a problem, solution, and participant just happen to connect at one point, a decision may be made and the problem may be solved, but it will not be solved if the solution does not fit the problem. In the garbage can model, organizations are viewed as a set of choices looking for problems, issues and feelings looking for decision arenas in which they might be aired, solutions looking for questions to which they might be answers, and decision makers looking for work (Cohen, March, and Olsen, 1972).

The garbage can model helps explain why solutions may be proposed to problems that don't exist; why choices are made without solving problems; why problems persist without being solved; and why few problems are solved. Events may be so poorly defined and complex that problems, solutions, participants, and choice opportunities act as independent events. When they mesh, some problems are solved, but in this chaotic decision process many problems are not solved—they simply persist (Daft, 1989). Undoubtedly the garbage can metaphor contains elements of truth, and it appears to be an apt description of the way decisions are reached in some situations but not in others. The model has received support in a number of studies of different kinds of organizations (Sproull, Weiner, and Wolf, 1978; Bromily, 1985; Levitt and Nass, 1989), but other recent research has questioned its utility as a *general* model of decision making, even in organizations of complexity, uncertainty, discontinuity, and power politics (Janis and Mann, 1977; Padgett, 1980; Hickson et al., 1986; Pinfield, 1986; Heller et al., 1988).

In brief, the garbage can model has the following distinctive features:

- Organizational objectives emerge spontaneously; they are not set beforehand.
- Means and ends exist independently; chance or happenstance connects them.
- A good decision occurs when a problem matches a solution.
- The decision relies more on chance than rationality.
- Administrators scan existing solutions, problems, participants, and opportunities looking for matches.

The garbage can metaphor is a description of how decisions sometimes occur; it is not a suggestion for action.

JANIS-MANN CONFLICT THEORY: STRESS AND IRRATIONALITY IN DECISION MAKING

Regardless of which decision-making strategy is employed, the pressures of the situation and the decision-making process itself often produce stress. Irving Janis and Leon Mann (1977) have developed an insightful model of conflict that answers the following two questions:

- Under what conditions does stress have unfavorable effects on the quality of decision making?
- Under what conditions will individuals use sound decision-making procedures to avoid choices that they would quickly regret?[7]

People handle psychological stress in different ways as they make vital decisions. The main sources of such stress are the fear of failure, worry about unknown consequences, concern about making a public fool of oneself, and losing self-esteem if the decision is disastrous (Janis, 1985). Critical decisions also usually involve conflicting values. People face the unsettling dilemma that any choice they make will require sacrificing other valued objectives; hence, the decision makers' anxiety, shame, and guilt rise, which increases the level of stress (Janis, 1985).

There is no question that errors in decision making are a result of a myriad of causes, including poor analysis, ignorance, bias, impulsiveness, time constraints, and organizational policies. But another major reason for many poorly conceived and implemented decisions is related to the motivational consequences of conflict—in particular, attempts to overcome stress produced by extremely difficult choices of vital decisions. Thus people employ a variety of defensive mechanisms. Some people ignore information about risks and forge ahead (unconflicted adherence). Others simply accept the most popular course of action (unconflicted change), and still others procrastinate and avoid action (defensive advoidance). At the other extreme, some decision makers panic and become hypervigilant as they search frantically for a solution, rapidly vacillating back and forth between alternatives, and then impulsively seize upon a hastily contrived solution that promises immediate relief. All of these actions are dysfunctional and typically lead to defective decisions.

Better decisions are likely if the decision makers are vigilant; that is, they search carefully for relevant information, assimilate the information in an unbiased manner, and then evaluate the alternatives before making a reflective choice. The vigilant decision maker is most effective because he or she avoids many of the traps of the other four patterns (Janis and Mann, 1977). But even when decision makers are vigilant, they sometimes make mistakes by taking cognitive shortcuts. All kinds of people, including scientists and statisticians, make cognitive errors such as overestimating the likelihood that events can be easily imagined, giving too much weight to information about representativeness, relying too much on small samples, and failing to discount biased information (Tversky and Kahneman, 1973; Nisbet and Ross, 1980; Janis, 1985). Moreover, these kinds of errors probably increase when decision makers are under psychological stress. The bottom line is that stress often has negative consequences on decision making.

What are the conditions that foster and hinder vigilance? When confronted with a decision, typically decision makers either consciously or unconsciously consider four issues (Janis and Mann, 1977):

Question 1: *Are the risks serious if I don't change?* If the answer is no, then change is unlikely. But if the answer is yes, then a second question is asked.

Question 2: *Are the risks serious if I do change?* If the anticipated losses of changing are minimal, then the risks are not serious and the decision maker is predicted to accept uncritically the first reasonable alternative. If the answer to the second question is yes, then stress builds because there are serious risks in both changing and not changing. The anxiety typically produces another question.

Question 3: *Is it realistic to hope to find a better solution?* If the decision maker believes there is no realistic hope of finding a better solution, then the result is a state of defensive avoidance. In order to escape from the conflict and reduce the stress, the individual avoids making the decision by either passing the buck or rationalizing the current situation. However, if there is hope for a better solution, another question emerges.

Question 4: *Is there sufficient time to search and deliberate?* If no, then a state of hypervigilance may occur. Panic sets in and the individual seizes upon a hastily contrived solution that promises immediate relief. If time is ample, then the decision maker is much more likely to engage in vigilant information processing, a process that enhances the effectiveness of the decision making through careful search, appraisal, and contingency planning. The path to vigilance is sketched in Figure 9.3.

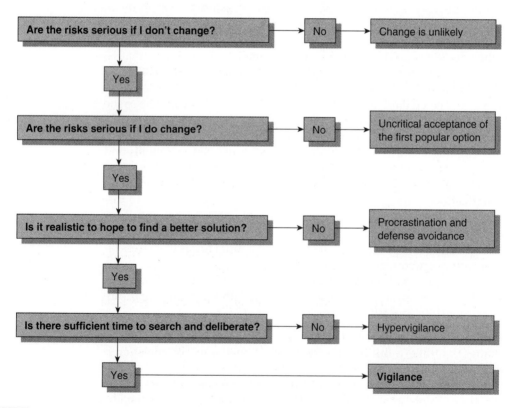

FIGURE 9.3   *The Path to Vigilance in Decision Making*

Clearly, administrators should seek vigilance in decision making; however, the forces of labor, time, and stress often operate against vigilance. Knowing the dangers and when they are most likely to occur should help avoid the pitfalls. Vigilant decision making usually requires risk taking, determination, and finding or making time to engage in reflection and contingency planning.

PARTICIPATION IN DECISION MAKING

In 1948 Lester Coch and John R. P. French conducted a classic study on the effects of participation in decision making, using a series of field experiments at the Harwood Manufacturing Corporation. The results were clear and conclusive: employee participation in decision making improved productivity. Other studies also have supported the desirability and influence of participation in decision making, both in business and in educational organizations.[8] The following generalizations summarize much of the research and theoretical literature on teacher participation in decision making.

- The opportunity to share in formulating policies is an important factor in the morale of teachers and in their enthusiasm for the school.
- Participation in decision making is positively related to the individual teacher's satisfaction with the profession of teaching.
- Teachers prefer principals who involve them in decision making.
- Decisions fail because of poor quality or because they are not accepted by subordinates.
- Teachers neither expect nor want to be involved in every decision; in fact, too much involvement can be as detrimental as too little.
- The roles and functions of both teachers and administrators in decision making need to be varied according to the nature of the problem.

Should teachers be involved in decision making and policy formulation? Wrong question! Sometimes they should. Other times they should not. Involvement can produce either positive or negative consequences. The appropriate questions are: Under what conditions should subordinates be involved in decision making? To what extent? How?

A number of models of shared decision making are useful in answering these questions. The most well-known model is one originally developed by Victor Vroom and Phillip Yetton (1973) and refined by Vroom and Jago (1988). The Vroom-Jago model matches participation in decision making with the nature of the problem and situation. From the extant research, a set of eight rules has been developed to improve the quality and acceptance of a decision. In addition, the constraints of time and development have been formulated as two additional rules. In brief, these 10 rules provide a complicated model of participation that requires the use of a complex set of decision trees or a computer (Vroom and Jago, 1988). The model has its limitations for practice in that it is initially difficult to learn and then challenging to apply; nonetheless, students of administration would be well advised to examine the formulation in some depth (Vroom and Jago, 1988; Hoy and Tarter, 2003). We focus our attention on a simplified model of shared decision making developed by Hoy and Tarter (1992, 1993a, 1993b, 2003).

Hoy-Tarter Model of Shared Decision Making

Subordinates accept some decisions without question because they are indifferent to them. As Barnard (1938: 167) explains, there is a **zone of indifference** "in each individual within which orders are accepted without conscious questioning of their authority." Simon prefers the more positive term, **zone of acceptance,** but the terms are used interchangeably in the literature. The subordinates' zone of acceptance is critical in deciding under what conditions to involve or not involve subordinates in decision making.

Zone of Acceptance: Its Significance and Determination

Drawing on the work of Barnard (1938), Simon (1947), and Chase (1951), Edwin M. Bridges (1967) advances two propositions about shared decision making:

1. As subordinates are involved in making decisions located within their zone of acceptance, participation will be less effective.
2. As subordinates are involved in making decisions located outside their zone of acceptance, participation will be more effective.

The problem for the administrator is to determine which decisions fall inside and which outside the zone. Bridges suggests two tests to answer this question:

- *The test of relevance:* Do the subordinates have a personal stake in the decision outcomes?
- *The test of expertise:* Do subordinates have the expertise to make a useful contribution to the decision?

The answers to these two questions define the four situations pictured in Figure 9.4. When subordinates have both expertise and a personal stake in the outcomes, then the decision is clearly outside their zone of acceptance. But if subordinates have neither expertise nor a personal stake, then the decision is inside the zone. There are, however, two marginal conditions, each with different decisional constraints. When subordinates have expertise but no personal stake, or have a personal stake but no particular expertise, the conditions are more problematic. Hoy and Tarter (1995) propose two additional theoretical propositions for guidance:

		Do Subordinates Have a Personal Stake?	
		Yes	No
Do Subordinates Have Expertise?	Yes	Outside Zone of Acceptance (Probably Include)	Marginal with Expertise (Occasionally Include)
	No	Marginal with Relevance (Occasionally Include)	Inside Zone of Acceptance (Definitely Exclude)

FIGURE 9.4   *The Zone of Acceptance and Involvement*

3. As subordinates are involved in making decisions for which they have marginal expertise, their participation will be marginally effective.
4. As subordinates are involved in making decisions for which they have marginal interest, their participation will be marginally effective.

Trust and Situations

One more consideration is useful if we are to be successful in applying the model to actual problems. Trust of subordinates should sometimes moderate their degree of involvement.[9] When subordinates' personal goals conflict with organizational ones, it is ill-advised to delegate decisions to them because of the high risk that decisions will be made on personal bases at the expense of the overall welfare of the school.[10] Thus subordinate trust is important, and to gauge trust, we propose a final test.

- *The test of trust:* Are subordinates committed to the mission of the organization? And can they be trusted to make decisions in the best interests of the organization?

If the decision is outside the zone of acceptance and if subordinates can be trusted to make decisions in the best interest of the organization, then participation should be extensive. We call this a *democratic situation* because the only issue is whether the decision should be made by consensus or majority rule. But if the decision is outside the zone and there is little trust in the subordinate, then we have a *conflictual situation* and participation should be restricted. To do otherwise invites moving in directions inconsistent with the overall welfare of the organization.

If the decision issue is not relevant to subordinates and they have no expertise, however, then the decision clearly falls within their zone of acceptance and involvement should be avoided; this is a *noncollaborative situation.*

Indeed, participation in such cases will likely produce resentment because subordinates typically are not interested.

When subordinates have a personal stake in the issue but little expertise, we have a *stakeholder situation* and subordinate participation should be limited and only occasional. To do otherwise courts trouble. If subordinates have nothing substantive to contribute, the decision ultimately will be made by those with the expertise (not subordinates), and a sense of frustration and hostility may be generated. Subordinates, in fact, may perceive the experience as an empty exercise in which the decisions have "already been made." Daniel L. Duke, Beverly K. Showers, and Michael Imber (1980) conclude from their research that shared decision making is often viewed by teachers as a formality or attempt to create the illusion of teacher influence. On the other hand, occasionally it may be useful to involve teachers in a limited way. When involvement is sought under these circumstances, it must be done skillfully. Its major objectives should be to open communication with subordinates, to educate them, and to gain support for the decision.

Finally, there is an *expert situation*—when subordinates have no personal stake in the outcomes but do have the knowledge to make a useful contribution. Should subordinates be involved? Only occasionally! To involve them indiscriminately in decisions of this type is to increase the likelihood of alienation. Although involvement under these circumstances increases the administrator's chances of reaching a higher-quality decision, subordinates too often are likely to wonder aloud "what the administrator gets paid for." These decision situations and appropriate responses are summarized in Figure 9.5.

Decision-Making Structures

Once the administrator has determined that subordinates should be involved in deciding, the next question becomes how the process should proceed. Hoy and Tarter (2003) suggest five decision-making structures:

1. *Group consensus:* The administrator involves participants in the decision making, then the group decides. All group members share equally as they generate and evaluate a decision, but total consensus is required before a decision can be made.
2. *Group majority:* The administrator involves participants in the decision making, then the group decides by majority rule.
3. *Group advisory:* The administrator solicits the opinions of the entire group, discusses the implications of group suggestions, then makes a decision that may or may not reflect subordinates' desires.

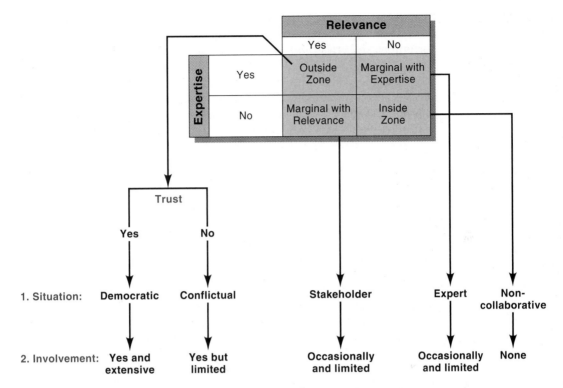

FIGURE 9.5   *Decision Situation and Subordinate Involvement*

4. *Individual advisory:* The administrator consults with subordinates individually who have expertise to inform the decision, then makes a decision that may or may not reflect their opinions.
5. *Unilateral decision:* The administrator makes the decision without consulting or involving subordinates in the decision.

Leader Roles

Thus far we have focused on subordinates in shared decision making. Now we turn to the administrator and define five leadership roles: integrator, parliamentarian, educator, solicitor, and director. The *integrator* brings subordinates together for consensus decision making. Here the task is to reconcile divergent opinions and positions. The *parliamentarian* facilitates open communication by protecting the opinions of the minority and leads participants through a democratic process to a group decision. The *educator* reduces resistance to change by explaining and discussing with group members the opportunities and constraints of the decisional issues. The *solicitor* seeks advice from subordinate-experts. The quality of decisions is improved as the administrator guides the generation of relevant information. The *director* makes unilateral decisions in those instances where the subordinates have no expertise or personal stake. Here the goal is efficiency. The function and aim of each role is summarized in Table 9.2.

Putting It Together: A Model for Shared Decision Making

Administrators are too often exhorted to involve teachers in all decisions. The more appropriate stance is to reflect upon the question: When should others be involved in decision making and how? We have proposed a model that answers this question.

The key concept in the model, drawn from Barnard (1938) and Simon (1947), is the zone of acceptance. There are some decisions that subordinates simply accept and, therefore, in which they need not be involved. The administrator identifies those situations by asking two questions:

1. *Relevance question:* Do the subordinates have a personal stake in the outcome?
2. *Expertise question:* Can subordinates contribute expertise to the solution?

If the answer to both these questions is yes, the subordinates have both a personal stake in the outcome and the expertise to contribute, then the situation is outside the zone of acceptance. Subordinates will want to be in-

TABLE 9.2

Administrative Roles for Shared Decision Making

Role	Function	Aim
Integrator	Integrates divergent positions	To gain consensus
Parliamentarian	Promotes open discussion	To support reflective group deliberation
Educator	Explains and discusses issues	To seek acceptance of decisions
Solicitor	Solicits advice	To improve quality of decisions
Director	Makes unilateral decisions	To achieve efficiency

volved, and their involvement should improve the decision. However, one must next evaluate their commitment to the organization by asking the following question:

3. *Trust question:* Can subordinates be trusted to make a decision in the best interests of the organization?

If they are committed, their involvement should be extensive as the group tries to develop the "best" decision. In the process, the role of the administrator is to act either as an integrator (if consensus is essential) or as a parliamentarian (if a group majority is sufficient). If subordinates are not committed (conflictual situation), their involvement should be limited. In this situation the administrator acts as an educator, and the group serves to advise and identify pockets of resistance.

If, however, subordinates have only a personal stake in the decision but no expertise (stakeholder situation), their involvement should be occasional and limited. Subordinates are interested in the outcome, but they have little knowledge to bring to bear on the decision. The reason for occasional involvement in this situation is to lower resistance and educate participants. If the involvement is more than occasional, the danger is alienation as teachers feel manipulated because their wishes are not met. At the outset, all parties should know that the group is clearly advisory to the leader. The administrator's role is to decide and educate.

If subordinates have expertise but no personal stake (expert situation), their involvement should also be occasional and limited as the administrator attempts to improve the decision by tapping the expertise of significant individuals who are not normally involved in this kind of action. At first blush, one might think that expertise should always be consulted in a decision, but if workers have no personal stake in the outcomes, their enthusiasm will quickly wane. They may well grumble, "This isn't my job."

In noncollaborative situations the teachers have neither the interest nor the expertise to contribute to the decision. Yet there is such a strong norm about involving teachers in all sorts of decisions that school administrators often feel constrained to involve teachers regardless of their knowledge or interest. Such ritual is dysfunctional and illogical. Why would you involve someone in a decision when that person doesn't care and can't help? The model suggests that administrators make direct unilateral decisions when the issue is within the zone of acceptance of subordinates. The entire model is summarized in Figure 9.6.

This model for shared decision making is not a panacea. It is not a substitute for sensitive and reflective administrative thought and action; it simply provides some guidelines for determining when and how teachers and principals should be involved in joint decision making. The effectiveness of decisions is determined by both the quality of the decision and the acceptance and commitment of subordinates to implement the decision.

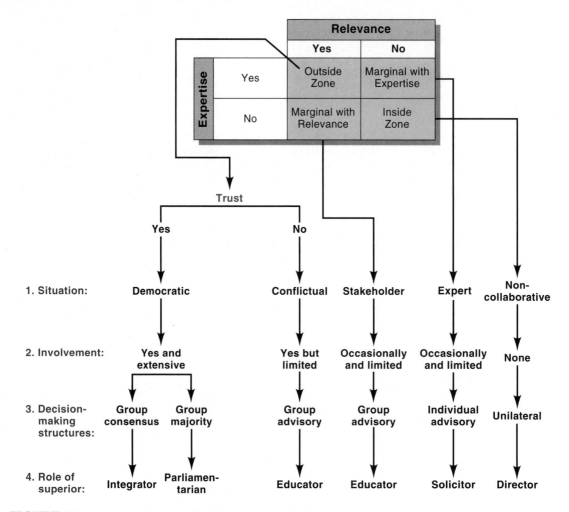

FIGURE 9.6   *A Normative Model for Participative Decision Making*

TIP: THEORY INTO PRACTICE

You are the principal of a high school, and your school has just won the state football championship. Although the basketball coach also promises a successful season, he is stopping short of predicting another state title. The community and students are high with success, and your teachers are also rightly proud of the school's athletic accomplishments. But make no mistake, students and teachers generally respect academic pursuits as well as athletic ones. Your school has more than its fair share of graduates accepting admissions to outstanding colleges and universities. There is a nice balance between curricular and extracurricular activities, but academic accomplishment is clearly valued by the school and community.

(Continued)

TIP: THEORY INTO PRACTICE *(Concluded)*

You have been disturbed by the complaints of several science teachers that they are tired of excusing athletes from class early. Apparently, what had been an occasional request from the coaching staff to excuse athletes from their last period class five minutes early on game days has precipitated some conflict among the faculty. Most teachers have no problem with an occasional early dismissal, but some of the science teachers and a few of the math teachers have been making a point to say no to such requests, and tension and conflict among teachers and between teachers and coaches is on the rise. Two science teachers have demanded that you stop the policy of early dismissals of players on game day; they are tired of being the "bad guys."

Clearly you have the authority to establish a policy that would end the practice of student-athletes leaving classes early. But you have also earned the reputation of involving your teachers in important decisions and they have responded well. Use the model of shared decision making to analyze this case and to develop a strategy of action. Is this a matter for shared decision making or is quick unilateral action most appropriate? Why?

A Caution on Group Decision Making: Groupthink

There is little question that group decision making can be an effective process, but there are some dangers even when the conditions call for a group decision. Time is always a potential constraint on participation in decision making, and group decisions typically require more time than individual ones. Participation involves discussion, debate, and often conflict; in fact, as the number of actors increases in the process, coordination becomes more important and difficult. Speed and efficiency are not basic advantages of group decision making.

Although participation in decision making can produce rampant conflict in the group, success in group problem solving often produces a strong cohesiveness, especially among members of smaller "in" groups. Too much cohesiveness can be as dangerous as conflict. Conflict prevents action; strong cohesiveness promotes uniformity within the group. The problem with uniformity is that it can produce a like-mindedness that is uncritical. Janis (1985) highlights this concurrence-seeking tendency among highly cohesive groups. When the tendency is dominant, the members use their collective cognitive resources to develop rationalizations consistent with the shared illusion about the invulnerability of their organization; that is, they display the **groupthink** syndrome.

Janis (1985) provides a comprehensive analysis of the conditions that encourage groupthink. One of the most potent conditions for groupthink is insulation from contact with others in the same organization who are not members of the "in group" of policy makers. Lack of impartial leadership also encourages concurrence seeking, especially when the leader is charismatic and followers seek to please. Knowing a leader's initial preferences colors and channels their thinking. Moreover, lack of norms requiring systematic analysis as well as homogeneity of members' social background and ideology contribute to like-mindedness.

Similarly, the situational context may nurture groupthink. High stress from external threats combined with little hope that the leader will advance a better solution pushes the group toward uncritical consensus. Furthermore, low self-esteem of the group, temporarily induced by recent failures, excessive difficulties, and moral dilemmas, fosters groupthink. All these antecedent conditions promote a tendency toward groupthink, which in turn produces the consequences of groupthink—overestimation, closed mindedness, and pressure for unanimity. Such behavior undermines vigilance and ultimately produces defective decision making and likely failure. See Figure 9.7 for a summary of the groupthink process.

Put plainly, when smart people think in unison, poor decisions are likely to follow. Groupthink remains a contemporary problem that has been around a long time; just consider the decisions of the Bay of Pigs invasion, the escalation of the Vietnam War, and the NASA Challenger tragedy. It is easy for cohesive groups under pressure to choose unanimity over their motivation to assess realistic alternative courses of action. For example, when a particular

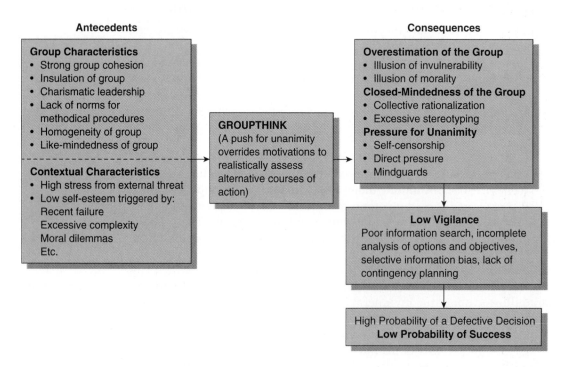

FIGURE 9.7 *Janus Groupthink Model*

faculty member rises to speak, you can almost hear a general groan because the faculty and principal know there is going to be a complaint. Such faculty members are valuable to the school because they serve as a foil and potential check on administrative mistakes. Nurturing the complaining faculty member may seem odd, but it is one antidote to groupthink. Giving dissenting voices greater influence in decision making is tricky when time pressures are great and stakes are high, but guarding against groupthink by preventing a premature rush to consensus is needed to avoid defective decisions.

A CASE FOR LEADERSHIP

The Teachers Council[11]

Few would deny that Superintendent Beverly Edison had the best of intentions in setting up a Teachers Council elected by teacher-representatives of every public school faculty in this large industrial city. Widely acknowledged to be an educator of the highest professional standing, Dr. Edison was a woman of impeccable integrity. She frequently assured large groups of her teachers that she wanted them to regard her as their "colleague with special responsibility." Her office was open to teachers who had problems of any kind. She routinely consulted teachers on proposed policies and rule changes before her recommendations were submitted to the Board of Education for adoption. It is true that teacher suggestions were not always adopted, but enough were accepted to give teachers both individually and collectively the feeling that their superintendent meant what she said in the matter of wanting a democratic school system.

In 1992, after six years of service in Metro City, Superintendent Edison announced a plan for setting up the Teachers Council to give the superintendent a vehicle to meet and communicate with rank-and-file teachers. She wanted a direct connection with the teachers to assess their reaction to her and the policies and conditions in the schools. The teachers' union (American Federation of Teachers—AFT), the exclusive bargaining agent for the teachers with a membership of 8,000, wrote to the superintendent, after due consideration and vote by the union's executive committee, that the proposed council would simply duplicate functions now performed by the union and other existing organizations. Dr. Edison responded that it was not her plan to have the Teachers Council vote or advise her on matters pertaining to teachers' benefits or welfare. She promised the union that she had no intention of having the council usurp the functions of the union. "All I want," she wrote, "is to have an opportunity to meet with teachers so that I can interpret our policies and to have the teachers advise me about educational issues in our schools. The council will not concern itself with issues of teacher welfare and benefits." Despite some protest from the union, Dr. Edison proceeded to set up the council.

Since approximately 80 percent of teachers were union members, the union adopted a circumspect strategy to deal with the council threat. Union members would be elected to serve on the council to keep the deliberations under control. The union, working quietly through its membership and under the procedures instituted by Dr. Edison, was successful in electing union members to 90 percent of the council seats for an initial one-year term.

Trouble was not long in coming. Written minutes of the council's monthly meetings with the superintendent revealed detailed accounts of the deliberations, and the union viewed with alarm the fact that questions of teacher welfare were raised and discussed at the meetings. Was the council already beginning to usurp the union's authority?

(Continued)

A CASE FOR LEADERSHIP *(Continued)*

Vincent Riley, a long-term union leader, was outraged by the turn of events. He felt betrayed and undermined by Dr. Edison. After consulting with the executive board of the union, he officially notified Superintendent Edison that the union regarded the Teachers Council as inappropriate, counterproductive, and illegitimate; Riley wanted to abolish the council. He reminded the superintendent that the union was the exclusive bargaining agent for the teachers and that discussing questions of teacher welfare violated the contract.

Dr. Edison was surprised by this turn of events. She replied that the council's meetings were informal and that no votes or formal actions were taken. The council was merely an informal source of communication and advice. It enabled her to take the pulse of the teachers in this large district. Nevertheless, she yielded to the union. In light of the union's opposition, she would submit to the council the union proposal that it be dissolved. The council promptly responded by voting unanimously to continue its existence. Union leaders were caught flat-footed by their members' show of independence.

The union represented only 80 percent of the teachers. It had come into prominence at a time when Metro City teachers were not being paid very well and the state and local teacher associations were seen as inactive and controlled by the administration. Teacher pay and working conditions steadily deteriorated until Vincent Riley and a handful of union teachers waged a "war" to break the tyrannical hold of the former superintendent and board of education on the school system and its employees. The union swept into power by first winning the right to be the teachers' exclusive bargaining agent, and then negotiating "the best contract teachers had had for more than a decade." Many in the community, including most teachers, believed that the union had freed the school system from a despotic administration. Decisions were now made on the basis of merit rather than political influence, and the union was seen as an agent of responsible change. Unfortunately the dishonesty and repression of the former

administration left scars that had not healed. It was probably this history of distrust and manipulation that colored the union's reaction to Dr. Edison's proposal for the Teachers Council. Despite the fact that during her six-year tenure, Dr. Edison demonstrated a democratic and impartial leadership style, the union was not entirely trustful of any administrator.

Metro City is a blue-collar city. Trouble with one union could be trouble with all the unions in the city. The school system could be paralyzed completely by a strike of its nonprofessional workers as well as its teachers. Union members across the city would observe picket lines around the schools. Unionized truck drivers would not make deliveries.

Many teachers, however, felt peculiar about being considered union members rather than professionals, and Dr. Edison sensed a need to go beyond simple labels. She had argued often with Vincent Riley over the union's assertion that it represented everybody. In point of fact, 2,000 teachers were not represented by the union. Many of these teachers had strong ties with the state educational association affiliated with the National Education Association (NEA). Dr. Edison contended that through the Teachers Council she could meet with the representatives of all the teachers.

The union, although well-disposed toward Dr. Edison, was concerned that a future administration might resort to the "old ways" and use the council to destroy the union. Because the union represented most of the teachers, it did not share her concern for the minority that it did not represent; in fact, it viewed this group as "freeloaders." Dr. Edison was concerned that the majority could completely disregard the wishes of the minority.

A superintendent faces many conflicting pressures. There is a constant push and pull of forces. No doubt pressures were operating to get Dr. Edison to reduce its strength, if not eliminate the union. Representatives of large industrial and business establishments as well as taxpayer groups did not

(Continued)

A CASE FOR LEADERSHIP *(Concluded)*

want labor-oriented groups to dominate the schools. However, union leaders did not believe that Dr. Edison would appease these groups by destroying the union because of the progress that had occurred and the good relationships that had developed during the past six years. Dr. Edison was far too worthy a professional to succumb to such pressure. In fact, she was on record as describing the Metro City Teachers' Union as one of the most highly professional and responsible organizations she had ever dealt with. She, in turn, was held in high regard. She welcomed the union's generous financial support of the Self-Help School Alliance, a federation of voluntary community associations providing opportunities for disadvantaged children in the school system. She approved of the union's lobbying of the legislature to increase state support for urban schools. In spite of her strong support of the union, she was unwilling to give in to its demand to abolish the Teachers Council. She believed that she had a right—no, an obligation—to consult with all the teachers, not merely union members.

In her last meeting with Vincent Riley, Riley had said, "This most recent audit of our finances shows that out of a total of 10,000 teachers, we have 7,953 paid memberships."

"You don't represent all the teachers," rejoined Dr. Edison. "I want to know how all my teachers feel about our programs and policies. I need information about educational issues, not union matters. It is curriculum and instructional matters that provide the salient topics for the Teachers Council. I need the professional advice of all the teachers if this district is to prosper and develop."

Riley paused momentarily; then responded, "Maybe you should spend less time in your office. I realize it is hard for a lady to go into some of these rougher schools. But, I am in the schools every day, and I can tell you that the professionals are union teachers. Furthermore, if you submit the question of whether the Teachers Council should be contin-

ued to a vote of all teachers, I have no doubt that a majority would vote to abolish the council."

Dr. Edison could feel her face redden, and she fought back the urge to respond to his insensitive, if not sexist, comment. Finally, she said, "The council didn't vote that way, and many of your people are council members."

When Vincent Riley reported the result of this meeting to the union executive board, they agreed that Dr. Edison should be given a chance to explain her actions to the committee before any formal grievance was initiated. The board hoped the grievance committee could convince Dr. Edison of the threat the council posed to good management-labor relations.

The executive board conceded the good intentions of the superintendent, recognizing Dr. Edison's desire to democratize the school system. Despite good intentions, however, the union was worried about the turn of events. It saw itself as the guardian of the teachers' interests and the integrity of the schools. It needed to act decisively.

Dr. Edison received a letter on Metro City Federation of Teachers stationery, over the signature of Donald Strickland, executive committee chairman (Strickland is a full-time employee of the union; he is not a teacher), requesting an appointment for the committee and Vincent Riley to discuss the advisability of continuing the Teachers council.

- Assume you are Dr. Edison. What are your next steps?
- What are the long-term and short-term problems?
- Is the council worth the aggravation? How important is the council?
- If you give in to the union, what are the consequences?
- If you resist the union, what are the consequences?
- Select the appropriate decision model and formulate a plan of action.

SUMMARY AND SUGGESTED READINGS

An understanding of the decision-making process is vital to successful administration. This chapter identifies and describes four basic strategies of managerial decision making. The optimizing strategy of the classical model is found not to be useful to administrators because it assumes perfect information, rationality, and human capacity not found in the actual world of administration.

Although completely rational decision making is impossible, administrators need a systematic process to enhance the selection of satisfactory solutions. Thus, a strategy of satisficing is central to decision making in the administrative model. In this strategy, decision making is a cycle of activity that includes recognition and definition of the problem, analysis of difficulties, establishment of criteria for a satisfactory resolution, development of a plan of action, and initiation of the plan. Because of its cyclical nature, the decision-making action cycle may be entered at different stages and the stages may be again and again in the process of administration.

The satisficing strategy is well suited for dealing with many problems in educational administration; however, when the set of alternatives is indefinable or the consequences of each alternative are unpredictable, then an incremental strategy may seem more appropriate. This process is a method of successive limited comparisons; only a limited set of alternatives, similar to the existing situation, is considered by successively comparing their consequences until agreement is reached on a course of action. It is assumed that small changes are not likely to produce large negative consequences for the organization.

Incrementalism, however, can be too conservative and self-defeating. Incremental decisions made without fundamental guidelines can lead to action without direction. Thus, the mixed-scanning model of decision making is proposed for complex decisions. Mixed scanning unites the best of both the administrative and the incremental models. A strategy of satisficing is used in combination with incremental decision making guided by broad policy. Full scanning is replaced by partial scanning and tentative decisions are made incrementally in a process that is guided by a clear sense of destination.

As in most complex tasks, however, there is no single best approach to deciding; the best strategy is the one that best matches the circumstances. We have proposed a set of guidelines that matches the right strategy with the situation.

The garbage can model of organizational decision making is useful for understanding nonrational decisions. In this model, the decision does not begin with a problem and end with a solution; rather, organizations are viewed as sets of choices looking for problems, issues and feelings seeking opportunities, solutions searching for problems, and administrators looking for work. Problems, solutions, participants, and choice opportunities act as independent events. When they mesh, some problems are solved, but in this chaotic decision process many problems are not solved—they simply persist.

The model explains why solutions may be proposed to problems that do not exist and why irrelevant choices are made.

Regardless of the strategy, decision making often causes stress, which produces irrationality. The conditions under which stress has unfavorable effects on the quality of decision making are discussed, and five coping mechanisms that decision makers are most likely to use in stressful situations are analyzed.

It is not always beneficial for administrators to involve subordinates in decision making. A simplified model of shared decision making is proposed to help administrators determine under what conditions subordinates should and should not participate in the decision-making process. The framework uses the tests of relevance, expertise, and commitment as guides for participation. Administrators, depending on the circumstances, use the roles of integrator, parliamentarian, educator, solicitor, and director. Finally, the conditions that foster groupthink are analyzed, and suggestions are proposed for avoiding them.

Decision making is a complex process. Ideas and theories are drawn from such diverse disciplines as cognitive science, economics, political science, psychology, and sociology. Several supplementary books are useful for beginning students. James G. March (1994) provides a primer on decision making; his book is concerned with how decisions actually happen rather they how they should happen, as is an edited selection by Eduardo Salas and Gary Klein (2001). Amitai Etzioni (1988) reminds us of the moral dimension of decision making and the centrality of moral issues in economic thought. Two edited selections are worth perusing: Mary Zey's (1992) collection pursues alternatives to the rational-choice models, and the March (1988) selections examine decision making under ambiguity. For those students who want a sophisticated treatment of participation in decision making, Victor Vroom and Arthur Jago (1988) provide an excellent and comprehensive model. Hoy and Tarter (2003) use case studies to link decision theory to problems of practice; they demonstrate the utility of good theory in solving actual administrative problems in schools. Finally, Willower and Licata (1997) discuss values and valuation in educational decision making and demonstrate the use of "consequence analysis" to solve the problems of practice.

KEY ASSUMPTIONS AND PRINCIPLES

1. Administrators use a satisficing model of decision making because they have neither the ability nor capacity to optimize the decision-making process.
2. Decision making is a general pattern of action found in the rational administration of tasks and functions in organizations.
3. An incremental model of decision making is a popular but limited framework for organizational decision making.

4. A mixed scanning perspective of decision making combines the best of the incremental and satisficing models.
5. The appropriate decision strategy depends upon the information, complexity of the situation, sufficient time, and importance of the decision.
6. Psychological stress increases poorly conceived and implemented decisions.
7. Better decisions are likely if decision makers are vigilant but not hypervigilant.
8. The roles and functions of teachers and administrators in making important decisions need to be varied according to the nature of the problem.
9. If subordinates have a personal stake in the outcome and expertise to contribute to the decision, and if they can be trusted to make a decision in the best interests of the organization, then subordinate involvement in the decision-making process should be maximized.
10. Groupthink is detrimental to effective decision making because the rush to consensus short-circuits the systematic assessment of options.

NOTES

1. Research suggests that many administrators ignore normative methods prescribed by scholars for effective decision making and persist in questionable decision tactics. See Nutt (1984).
2. For an excellent discussion and application of values and valuation in the practice of educational administration, see Willower and Licata (1997).
3. Iterations of this cycle occur frequently in the organizational literature. For example, see Griffiths (1959) and Daft (1989).
4. The problem is much more complex, however, if it also involves the integration of minority students into segregated schools.
5. A group of cognitive psychologists called the *prospect school* have made a critical and interesting analysis of heuristics. Their main thesis is that individuals cope with their limited cognitive abilities by using heuristic devices to solve complex problems. Although the heuristics help, they themselves sometimes introduce systematic biases that may subvert decision making. For example, see Nisbett and Ross (1980), Kahneman, Solvic, and Tversky (1982), Kahneman and Tversky (1996), and Gigerenzer (2004).
6. Etzioni (1967) reports that 50 articles and Ph.D. dissertations have been written on mixed scanning since his original article. For his synthesis, see Etzioni (1986).
7. This section draws heavily on the work of Janis (1985) and Janis and Mann (1977).
8. For studies that support the desirability of participation in decision making, see Sharma (1955); Guest (1960); Vroom (1960, 1976); Belasco and Allutto (1972);

Allutto and Belasco (1973); Conwa, (1976); Hoy, Newland, and Blazovsky (1977); Driscoll (1978); Mohrman, Cooke, and Mohrman (1978); Moon (1983). For a comprehensive and somewhat critical review of participation in decision making, see Locke and Schweiger (1979). Likewise, for a review of participative decision making in education, see Conway (1984). The effects of subordinate participation in decision making, however, are neither simple nor unambiguous; for example see Imber (1983); Conway (1984); Imber and Duke (1984); Vroom and Jago (1988); Conley, Bower, and Bacharach (1989); Bacharach, Bamberger, Conley, and Bauer (1990); Conley (1990).

9. In earlier versions of this model, this third test was called commitment; we believe "trust" is a better word to capture the meaning of the test.

10. For a useful distinction between shared decision making and delegation of decision making, see Hoy and Sousa (1984), and for a critical analysis on participation in schools, see Keith (1996).

11. From Wayne K. Hoy, and C. J. Tarter, *Administrators Solving the Problems of Practice* © 1995. Published by Allyn & Bacon, Boston, MA. Copyright © 1995 by Pearson Education. Reprint by permission of the publisher.

CHAPTER 10

COMMUNICATION IN SCHOOLS

Humans live by communication, and many of the practices that we think define us as human are a direct outgrowth of the ways in which we communicate: our language, our reasoning, our morality, and our social organization.

Nicholas C. Burbules
Dialogue in Teaching

PREVIEW

1. Communication pervades virtually all aspects of school life. It does not, however, provide all the answers to the problems confronting educational administrators.

2. As a relational process, communication involves initiating messages using symbols, signs, and contextual cues to express meaning and create similar understandings.

3. One-way communication is unilateral, initiated by a speaker, and terminated at a listener.

4. Two-way communication is a reciprocal, interactive process with all participants in the process initiating and receiving messages; it has no necessary beginning or ending.

5. Conversation, inquiry, debate, and instruction are four types of two-way communication.

6. Communication competence can be enhanced by improving individual sending, listening, and feedback skills.

7. Humans use two major symbol systems in their efforts to communicate—verbal and nonverbal.

8. Each new communication technology imposes its own special requirements on how messages are composed. Technology also governs the speed and convenience of sending messages and influences the ways receivers reconstruct meaning.

9. Formal channels are communication networks sanctioned by the organization and directed toward organizational goals.

10. Individuals bypass formal channels of communication by using informal networks or "grapevines."

Communication is complex, subtle, ubiquitous, and important; it permeates every aspect of school life. Teachers instruct, using oral, written, and other media such as videotapes, computers, and art forms. Students demonstrate their learning through similar media. And superintendents and principals spend the majority of their time communicating. Given this importance, educational administrators simply must understand communication because it underlies or infuses the interpersonal, organizational, and administrative processes and structures of schools. Communication skills, therefore, are essential tools for an effective administrator. However, before concluding that communication provides all the answers to the problems confronting educational administrators, four caveats must be observed:

- Communication is difficult to isolate from such other administrative processes as deciding, motivating, and leading.
- Not all school problems involve unsuccessful communication. Problems commonly attributed to poor interactions may reflect breakdowns in other fundamental components of school life.
- Communication reveals and hides as well as eliminates problems (Katz and Kahn, 1978). It can surface conflicts in values among teachers, students, and administrators that may otherwise go unnoticed, and it also may obscure existing problems by glossing over issues with empty rhetoric, or "spinning" the truth.
- Communication is a process that evokes action, but it is far from being the substance of good administration. It is no substitute for faulty ideas and misguided educational programs.

Even though these cautions are limitations, communication does serve several pervasive and integrative functions in schools. At a minimum, for instance, communication should provide accurate information with a fitting affective tone to all participants needing the content (Hall, 2002). To claim that communication is either the universal problem or problem solver oversimplifies and limits both the analysis and the solution of educational problems. In this chapter, we will discuss a variety of conceptual approaches while attempting to keep both the important functions and the cautionary guides in proper perspective.

INDIVIDUAL APPROACHES TO COMMUNICATION

In everyday usage, communication is the process that people use to exchange significant messages and share meaning about their ideas and feelings with one another (Porter and Roberts, 1976; Manning, 1992). **Communication,** in other words, is sharing information, ideas, or attitudes in ways that produce a degree of understanding between two or more people (Lewis, 1975). Using face-to-face or technological media, individuals interact and influence each other through communication (Craig, 1999). Practically all conceptions of communication contain explicit or implicit notions that involve meaningful interactions between at least two people. For example, educators do not communicate in a vacuum but with other educators, citizens, and students; and successful exchange does not occur unless both parties develop shared interpretations of the information.

Kathleen J. Krone, Fredric M. Jablin, and Linda L. Putnam (1987) observe that virtually all perspectives dealing with communication processes recognize and use the same concepts. Although each term varies somewhat across different theoretical perspectives, we agree with the definitions summarized by Krone and her colleagues:

- **Message** is typically the verbal or nonverbal cues or symbols that each communicator conveys. It is the idea or information that an individual hopes to communicate.
- **Channel** is the vehicle, medium, or form in which a message travels. Form can range from light waves of nonverbal cues to sound waves of talking face-to-face, to electronic signals in telephones and e-mail.
- **Sender** is the person or a generalized source (e.g., office of the superintendent) sending a message; **receiver** marks the destination of the message or the individual who deciphers it.
- **Transmission** is the actual sending and receiving of messages through designated channels or media.
- **Encoding** and **decoding** involve cognitive structures and processes to create, transform, and decipher messages. Encoding is converting the intended message to symbolic form by the sender. Decoding is retranslating the message by the receiver. Through encoding and decoding processes, individuals compose **meanings** by interpreting or making sense of the message.
- **Feedback** is the message sent in response to the initial message or, as defined in Chapter 1, it is information that enables corrections to be made. Using feedback facilitates interpretation of a message.
- **Communication effects** are the outcomes or general results of the message exchange process—for example, new knowledge, different attitudes, culture, and satisfaction.

Hence, a more elaborate definition is that human communication is a relational process during which source individuals initiate messages using symbols, signs, and contextual cues to express meaning by transmitting information in ways so that similar understandings are constructed by the receiving individual(s) (DeFleur, Kearney, and Plax, 1993). This definition incorporates the concepts defined above and produces the general model shown in Figure 10.1.

A sender encodes a message with certain intentions and transmits it by some channel to a receiver who then decodes the message and provides feedback to the original sender (see Figure 10.1). Both the source and the receivers

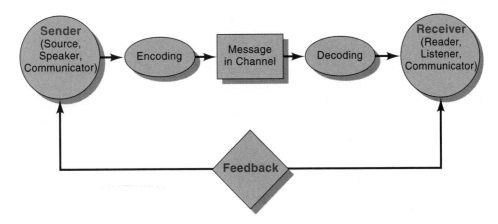

FIGURE 10.1   *A General Model of the Communication Process*

are communicators in this process. Note the process is interactive and trans-actional (Adler and Rodman, 1991); it flows back and forth, often going both ways simultaneously as both talk or as one talks and the other listens and gives feedback through nonverbal cues. Thus Thomas E. Harris (1993) con-cludes that the process is complex, dynamic, and with no necessary begin-ning or end. In fact, designating participants as senders and receivers is a subjective but sometimes useful decision.

Components of a General Model of the Communication Process

Michele Tolela Myers and Gail E. Myers (1982) posit that communication can be viewed as a transactional process where people construct meaning and de-velop expectations about what is happening around them through the ex-change of symbols. In constructing meanings, people use **symbols** (i.e., objects or words that stand for ideas, feelings, intentions, and other objects) to describe their experiences and develop a common symbol system or lan-guage for sharing their experiences with others. Learning symbols or a lan-guage and associating learning symbols with experiences come about by interacting with people and observing what they do when they use symbols. As a result of these interactions and observations, individuals not only learn to construct meanings that are reasonably similar to those of people around them, but also develop expectations or make predictions about what people will do and think. Every day individuals in schools exchange symbols using several different verbal and nonverbal forms (e.g., lecturing, exhorting, ex-plaining, visiting, arguing, negotiating, discussing, dressing, making visual displays). These transactions to gain shared meanings can be conceptualized as a continuum from one-way to two-way communication.

One-Way Communication

As shown in Figure 10.2, **one-way communication** occurs when one person tells another person something. This type of communication is unilateral; it is initiated by a speaker and terminated at a listener (Schmuck and Runkel, 1985). Lectures in classrooms about subject matter or exhortations in the principal's office about appropriate demeanor represent widespread applications of one-way communication in schools. Other examples include announcements over the public address system in a school or during meetings. A metaphor for one-way communication as shown in Figure 10.2 is the hypodermic needle approach of injecting information into another person (Broms and Gahmberg, 1983). Like a nurse, the speaker is trying to inject a message into the receiver (Clampitt, 2001).

The advantages of one-way communication are twofold (Clampitt, 2001). First, it emphasizes the skills of the message sender and encourages administrators and teachers to think through their ideas, accurately articulate them, and provide specificity in their instructions, explanations, and descriptions. Second, one-way strategies typically imply strong linkages between communication behavior and action. Teachers and administrators who use one-way communication discourage idle chatter, discussions of personal problems, and unnecessary information sharing. In other words, it conveys a strong emphasis on efficiency and goal achievement.

Given the need for shared understandings in schools, one-way communication many times is inadequate. For instance, Philip G. Clampitt (2001) asserts that the basic flaw in one-way communication lies in the belief that effective expression equals effective communication. Even if the message sender effectively articulates an idea, it does not necessarily guarantee that it will be understood as intended. Clampitt believes that two faulty assumptions explain the continued reliance on one-way communication. First, receivers are seen as passive information processors. Instead of being passive processing machines, however, people actively reconstruct messages and create their own meanings. Second, words are seen as containers of meaning. Language works against this assumption. For example, meaning depends on how the words are used, the context in which the statement is made, and the people involved. Words do not serve so much as containers of meaning as stimulators of meaning. Therefore, the need for understanding in schools

FIGURE 10.2   *Model of One-Way Communication*

suggests that additional or other forms of communication are required for goal achievement, change, and social purposes.

Two-Way Communication

By **two-way communication** we mean a reciprocal, interactive process; all participants in the process initiate and receive messages. In contrast to the one-way approach, two-way communication requires continuous exchanges and transactions. As shown in Figure 10.3, this means that each participant initiates messages and that each message affects the next one. Such interactive exchanges can improve the communication process by reducing the chance of major disparities between the information or idea received and the one intended.

Two-way communication takes a number of forms. For example, Nicholas C. Burbules (1993) describes four types of individual dialogue— conversation, inquiry, debate, and instruction. With relatively modest changes, these forms of dialogue can be viewed as methods of two-way communication in school organizations.

Conversation is distinguished by two qualities: a generally cooperative, tolerant spirit and direction toward mutual understanding. This form is used when individuals are interested in understanding each other's perspectives and experiences. An example would be two students talking about how they spent their summer vacations and what they learned as a result.

Inquiry involves two or more people cooperating to answer a question, resolve a disagreement, or formulate a compromise that is agreeable to all. Dialogue of this nature typically investigates alternatives and examines

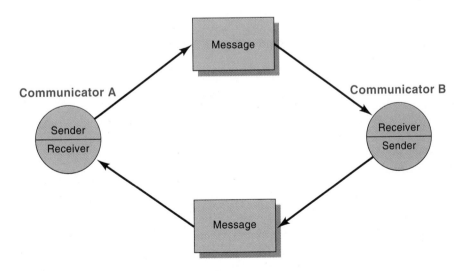

FIGURE 10.3   *Model of Two-Way Communication*

possible answers within a structure that encourages a range of perspectives and approaches to the problem. An example would be a group of science teachers exploring why some students are thriving in classes using a new project-based curriculum whereas others are failing.

Debate exhibits sharp questioning, a skeptical spirit, and no necessary need for agreement among the participants. The potential benefit of debate is that the participants see that their alternative ideas and opinions receive the most intense challenge possible. The aim is to clarify and strengthen alternative perspectives. An example would be conservative and liberal policy makers arguing the relative merits of providing vouchers to support private schools.

Instruction, as two-way communication, involves an intentional process in which a teacher leads students to certain answers or understandings. It generally uses critical questions and other statements to move a discussion to a definite conclusion. The exemplar of this type of two-way communication is the *Socratic Method*. A good example of instruction as dialogue is reciprocal teaching. In reciprocal teaching, teachers and students engage in a highly interactive process in which participants take turns assuming the role of teacher (Palincsar, 1986).

Feedback

In all types of communication environments, there is a significant probability that what we say will be ambiguous and misinterpreted. For example, "I'll be there in a minute" and "Call me later and we'll talk about it" make vague references to time. How long a "minute" or "later" is varies greatly across individuals and cultures. Through the use of feedback (see Figure 10.1), however, even unclear statements can become part of specific effective communications (Alessandra and Hunsaker, 1993).

Feedback is a response from a person who has received a message. It provides knowledge about the meaning and impact of the message for the receiver and an opportunity for the sender to correct any problems. Hence, if a dialogue is to continue for any length of time and still have meaning, feedback is important. This process provides at least two benefits. First, it supplies clues about the success of the communication and improves the accuracy and clarity of a message. Second, the knowledge of results forms a basis for correcting or modifying future communications (Ashford, 1986). The point is clear—feedback increases the accuracy and clarity of communication.

In work settings, we usually think of feedback as involving information about task performance or how others perceive and evaluate an individual's behavior (Ashford, 1986; Cusella, 1987). Two types of feedback are possible. When feedback reinforces, accentuates, or adds to the direction the person or school is taking, it is positive. Feedback is negative when it corrects a deviation (Harris, 1993). It can be communicated either verbally or nonverbally, consciously or unconsciously. For example, a student who falls asleep during a class lecture may provide as much feedback to the teacher as the student who responds to examination questions.

By employing a variety of communication strategies, school administrators should be able to advance mutual understandings, shared meanings, and new learning among their colleagues, students, and other constituents. While individuals vary in their abilities to use the different types of one- and two-way communication effectively, everyone can enhance their communication competence.

Improving Individual Communication Competence

Communication competence is a set of abilities or resources that a communicator has available for use. Individual resources include both strategic knowledge about such things as communication rules and norms, and communication capacities such as traits and abilities for encoding and decoding skills (Jablin and Sias, 2001). Hence, individuals can build their communication resources by gaining knowledge from communication theory and research and by developing and enhancing sending, listening, and feedback skills.

Sending skills are the abilities to make oneself understood. As a key to effective communication, educators' sending skills can be enhanced through the following five methods. First, educators should use appropriate, direct language, avoiding educational jargon and complex concepts when simpler words will do. However, to establish credibility, the language must demonstrate that the sender is knowledgeable about educational issues. Second, they should provide clear, complete information to the listener, which is needed to build or reorganize the listener's cognitive schemas. Third, educators should minimize noise from the physical and psychological environments. During parent conferences, for example, they must take steps to eliminate telephone interruptions and to reduce stereotypes that either they or the parent may hold. Fourth, they should employ multiple and appropriate channels of media. For instance, a one-way speech can be augmented by audiovisual presentations and systematic opportunities for two-way exchanges. Being skillful in matching richness of media to situational and communication needs may be a key factor in administrator performance (Alexander, Penley, and Jernigan, 1991). Fifth, educators should use face-to-face communication and redundancy when communicating complex or equivocal messages. Richness, repetition, and feedback enhance the likelihood that the intended effect of gaining a shared meaning for the message will occur.

Listening skills are the abilities of individuals to understand others. Listening is a form of behavior in which individuals attempt to comprehend what others are communicating to them through the use of words, actions, and things (DeFleur, Kearney, and Plax, 1993). In active listening, a listener reflects back to the speaker what he or she has heard—content, feeling, and meaning—from the speaker's perspective (Elmes and Costello, 1992). Listening skills are required for relatively accurate, two-way exchanges. Listening to a person shows respect, interest, and concern for one's fellow communicator. When it is an active effort, listening can encourage others to develop and express their own points of view (Burbules, 1993).

Developing important listening skills, however, is frequently neglected. How many times have you been asked a question by someone only to get disturbing nonverbal cues that the questioner is not really interested or, worse, not listening to your response? How often are your responses not truly heard or misinterpreted? Allen Ivey and Mary Ivey (1999) suggest a number of critical elements in effective listening skills: attending, questioning, encouraging, paraphrasing, reflecting feeling, and summarizing.

Attending is the process of being attentive to the conversation. It involves appropriate eye contact, receptive body language, and staying focused and on task. Making eye contact and looking at the person doing the talking communicates interest and attentiveness just as looking away communicates disinterest. Leaning forward, maintaining an open posture, smiling, and looking pleasant are the kinds of nonverbal cues that communicate interest. Finally the effective listener stays with the other person; that is, the listener pays attention and does not zone out. Effective listening demands attention.

Questioning is often essential to understanding the message. The message may not be as clear as the communicator thinks; some messages are vague. They require questions for clarification. Some factual questions are direct, clear, and simple and are answered by a yes or no. Other questions are more open and call for speculation and development, for example, "Why do you think the conflict occurred?" Skillful questions clarify and elaborate and are a natural part of careful listening.

Encouraging is also part of skillful listening. A few minimal "encouragers" can facilitate communication (Morse and Ivey, 1996). Silence is a powerful, nonverbal message. Saying nothing but remaining interested suggests to the communicator that you want to hear more. Empathic acknowledgement also adds communication. Verbal cues such as "yes," "um-hum," and "I see" encourage, especially when they are linked to such nonverbal cues of nodding and smiling. A number of short sentence encouragers can also stimulate communication, such as "Tell me more," "Give me an example," and "Say a little more about that."

Paraphrasing is another way to show that you are paying attention and understanding what is being said. It helps the listener respond effectively to people, and it provides feedback to the speaker that you understand the essence of the message. Paraphrasing also provides feedback and serves as a correction mechanism. Skillful listeners paraphrase and make sure they have the correct message.

Reflecting feeling is a positive way to embrace the speaker. The listener should be attentive to the feelings and emotions of the communicator. Acknowledging feelings is a good place to begin the reflecting process because it paces the other individual's emotional state but does not get the listener overly involved (Morse and Ivey, 1996). Acknowledging feelings focuses on labeling the feeling and communicating it back to the speaker, and often tempers the emotion and controls it. Statements such as "You feel that way because . . ." and "I sense you are disappointed," reflect emotion and create empathy. Also, using the person's name from time to time is helpful. Skillful listeners sort out facts from emotions and acknowledge and reflect feelings.

Summarizing is quite similar to paraphrasing except that the summary covers a longer period of time and it typically comes near the end of the conversation. The goal of summary is to organize the facts and feelings into a coherent, accurate, and brief synopsis.

Feedback skills are sending and receiving skills that convey knowledge of results or the effects of previous communications and behaviors. Asking questions, describing behavior, and paraphrasing what the speaker has said are forms of verbal feedback. Providing feedback consists of both verbal and nonverbal messages, which are sometimes sent inadvertently. For example, people sometimes speak loudest with their feet (i.e., they walk away to avoid contact). In planning to give feedback, the information should be helpful to the recipient, specific rather than general, recent rather than old, directed toward behavior that the person could change, and timely—the more immediate, the better (Anderson, 1976; Harris, 1993).

Even with these guidelines, neutral or positive feedback is easier to give than negative assessments; people are reluctant both to give and receive negative feedback. Most of us are fairly adept at sending back messages that do not really represent our true reactions. Some people rationalize such behavior as tact, human relations, or survival. Consequently, both personal skill and preparation are critical to give and receive helpful feedback (Rockey, 1984). Acceptance of both positive and negative feedback can be increased by expressing a goal of being helpful, using descriptive rather than evaluative information, timing the session appropriately (Anderson, 1976), and building trust within the group through frequent communication (Becerra and Gupta, 2003).

Similarly, feedback-seeking behavior involves consciously striving to determine the correctness and adequacy of communication and behavior. Individuals should develop feedback-seeking skills because such actions will help them adapt and be successful (Ashford, 1986). Two strategies for seeking feedback can be suggested. The first is monitoring the environment by observing naturally occurring informational cues, other individuals, and how others respond. In other words, monitoring involves receiving feedback vicariously through watching how people respond to and reinforce others. The second strategy is to inquire directly about how others perceive and evaluate your behavior. Feedback must be pursued vigorously because people do not always give it voluntarily. As a caution, however, feedback-seeking actions can be hard on an individual's self-esteem because it potentially increases the chances of hearing information that one would rather not know or confront. In fact, individuals who suspect that they are performing poorly tend to use feedback-seeking strategies that minimize the amount of negative information they receive (Larson, 1989). In many situations, individuals would rather risk doing the task incorrectly than ask for clarification.

When considering communication from an individual perspective (see Figures 10.1, 10.2, and 10.3) then, one-way and two-way communication can take many forms and employ an array of skills, channels, and media. As an interactive process, effective communication involves listening as well as speaking. Blocking out external distractions, attending to verbal and nonverbal cues, probing and encouraging, differentiating between the intellectual and emotional content of a message, and summarizing and making inferences about the speaker's meaning and feelings are critical to effective communication (Woolfolk, 2000). An administrator who is a competent communicator will have a repertoire of communication strategies from which to draw and can be creative and flexible in moving from one approach to another as people, situations, and content change (Burbules and Bruce, 2000).

TIP: THEORY INTO PRACTICE

Find a colleague and engage in the following communication activities. Both should prepare a two- to three-minute presentation on a problem currently confronting school administrators, such as curriculum standards, testing, privatization, educator job satisfaction, student behavior, teaching innovation, and the like. One individual makes the initial presentation, relying primarily on one-way communication using at least two types of media. The other person should be attentive and encouraging during the presentation. When the presentation ends, the listener should summarize what has been presented.

The original listener now becomes the sender and should now make a presentation relying primarily on two-way communication methods. The new listener should not only be attentive and encouraging but also should paraphrase portions, ask questions, and finally offer a summary of what has been presented.

After the presentations, both should share their feelings about the content, efficiency, and effectiveness of the presentations. Then each participant should provide feedback to the other participant that describes the other's behavior during the sessions. Both positive and negative information should be provided about how to improve the presentations.

What personal communication skills do you need to develop further?

Channels of Communication: Methods of Exchanging Symbols

In their efforts to communicate, humans use two major symbol systems—verbal and nonverbal (Dahnke and Clatterbuck, 1990). Verbal symbols include:

- Human speech—direct, face-to-face conversation or electronic exchanges via telephone, radio, television, computer conferences, and instant messages.
- Written media—memos, letters, faxes, electronic mail and bulletin boards, and newspapers.

Nonverbal symbols include:

- Body language or gestures—facial expressions, posture, and arm movements.
- Physical items or artifacts with symbolic value—office furnishings, clothing, and jewelry.
- Space—territoriality and personal space.
- Touch—hugging.
- Time.
- Other nonverbal symbols—intonation, accents, pitch, intensity of the voice, and rate of speech.

Hence, messages can be communicated in a variety of channels, ways, forms, or media.

Verbal Channels   Richard L. Daft and Robert H. Lengel (1984, 1986) hypothesize that media determine the richness of communication, where **richness** is the medium's potential to carry information and resolve ambiguity. Four criteria define media richness: speed of feedback, variety of communication channels, personalness of source, and richness of language. Rich media combine multiple cues, rapid or timely feedback, tailoring the messages to personal circumstances, and a variety of language (Huber and Daft, 1987). Rich media are characterized by high touch and qualitative data; they are best for lessening ambiguity. Lean media are suitable for technology-based, high-volume data exchanges and are best for conveying quantitative data with precision and accuracy to large audiences (Daft, Bettenhausen, and Tyler, 1993). Using these four criteria, Daft and his colleagues place communication media and richness on the parallel continua as shown in Figure 10.4.

Face-to-face communication has the highest carrying capacity and the best potential for transmitting rich information (Barry and Crant, 2000). It is the richest form because the face-to-face medium provides immediate feedback through verbal and visual cues. Although verbal feedback is rapid, the telephone medium is less rich than face-to-face because the visual cues are absent. Written communication is described as being moderate or low in richness because feedback is slow and only written information is conveyed. Addressed correspondence is personal in character and somewhat richer than general memos and bulletins, which are anonymous and impersonal. Formal numeric documents—for example, computer printouts containing quantitative data such as achievement test scores—convey the least-rich information because numbers do not have the information-carrying capacity of natural language. Electronic messaging can be placed between telephone and written personal media on the richness continuum (Steinfield and Fulk, 1986).

FIGURE 10.4   *Continua for Communication Media and Richness*

The basic hypothesis is that as the content of communication becomes more ambiguous or uncertain, richer media will be selected to improve communication performance. A number of studies have tested the hypothesis with the number supporting and not supporting being about equal (Schmitz and Fulk, 1991). Studies by Daft and his colleagues (Trevino, Lengel, and Daft, 1987; Russ, Daft, and Lengel, 1990) are generally supportive of the basic richness hypothesis. Other studies (Steinfield and Fulk, 1986; Rice, 1992) have found weak or mixed support. Overall, the results are more supportive of the media richness hypothesis when applied to traditional (e.g., face-to-face) rather than newer media (e.g., computers and other electronic devices) (Fulk and Boyd, 1991).

As might be expected from the discussion of richness, when the effects of written and oral media are compared, the communicator faces a problem (Porter and Roberts, 1976). Comprehension is higher when information is presented in written form. However, opinion change or persuasiveness is greater in face-to-face interactions. The appropriate medium thus depends on the purpose—that is, understanding or persuading.

Redundancy in media increases both the richness of the information and the accuracy of message transmission (Redding, 1972). Generally, the most effective and accurate communication efforts use a combination of written and oral media; the next most effective is oral alone; and the least powerful is written (Level, 1972). The combination of written and oral media is seldom inappropriate. Written communication alone can be effective in two situations—where information requires future action or where it is general. The oral medium by itself also can be effective in two situations demanding immediate feedback: for administering reprimands and settling disputes.

Nonverbal Channels of Communication Although redundancy in media usually leads to better understanding, vocal and written media carry only a portion of the information that administrators convey when they interact with others. At least as important as verbal signals are the less fully understood nonverbal symbols. **Nonverbal communication** is all behavior of communicative value done in the presence of another that does not use words. The raised eyebrow, the firm handshake, and the impatient tapping of the fingers are well-known actions of nonverbal media that convey meaning. Even silence and rigid inactivity may signal anger, annoyance, depression, or fear. Although this definition of nonverbal communication suggests a rather all-inclusive domain, a gray area still exists between verbal and nonverbal forms. Paralanguage is vocal but not strictly oral. It includes stress, inflection, and speed of speech, as well as nonword vocalizations such as grunts, laughter, sighs, and coughs (Knapp, 1972; Wietz, 1974).

Research on nonverbal communication often explores the meanings of paralanguage, body motion, and spatial cues. For example, a combination of five types of nonverbal behaviors consistently exerts the strongest positive influence on one individual's attempts to build rapport with another person: smiling, touching, affirmative head nods, immediacy behavior (e.g., leaning forward), and eye behavior. These behaviors are essential in communicating a sense of warmth, enthusiasm, and interest (Heintzman, Leathers, Parrot, and Cairns, 1993).

The face is the most obvious nonverbal conveyor of feelings (McCaskey, 1979). Most feeling is communicated through facial expression. Without formal training, observers of facial expression can distinguish a variety of human emotions such as excitement, humiliation, and fear (Harris, 1993). Eye-to-eye contact is one of the most direct and powerful ways people communicate nonverbally. In mainstream American culture, the social rules indicate that in most situations eye contact for a short period is appropriate. Direct eye contact is also seen as an indication of honesty and credibility. Prolonged eye contact is usually taken to be either threatening or, in another context, a sign of romantic interest. Speakers know that a way to enhance the impact of their presentations is to look directly at individual members of the audience and establish eye contact.

In regard to workspace, Michael B. McCaskey (1979) notes that an office represents personal territory, which separates what belongs to one person from what belongs to others. Where a meeting is held may intimate the purpose of the meeting. To conduct an adversarial discussion, to emphasize hierarchy and authority, or to give directions, McCaskey advises the supervisor to hold the meeting in his or her own office. The office arrangement itself might communicate the intended nature of the interactions. For example, many administrators arrange their offices with two different areas. In one, the administrator talks across the desk to a person seated at the other side. This layout emphasizes the administrator's authority and position. In the second area, chairs are in a circle at a round table. Because the arrangement signals a willingness to downplay hierarchical differences, freer exchanges are encouraged. Hence, an office arrangement with a center for informal conversations, a display of personal memorabilia and decorations, and a relatively close distance between the chairs and desk represents nonverbal symbols that transmit powerful messages of welcome to visitors. James M. Lipham and Donald C. Francke (1966) confirmed these propositions in schools.

Congruence of Verbal and Nonverbal Messages   Verbal and nonverbal messages must be consistent for effective understanding. An illustration of this generalization usually occurs when a new administrator meets with the staff. A typical verbal statement is, "If you have any questions or problems, please come by my office, and we'll discuss the situation. My door is always open." When a staff member interprets the words literally and does visit the principal, the nonverbal messages probably will determine the meaning of the verbal message. If the person is met at the door, ushered to a chair, and a productive conference results, the verbal message is reinforced and the meaning is understood. If, however, the administrator remains in the chair behind the desk, leaves the staff member standing or seats him or her across the room, and continues to write, the verbal message is contradicted. When verbal and nonverbal message conflict, a problem of meaning results.

TIP: THEORY INTO PRACTICE

As an elementary principal, you are being encouraged by officials in the central office to implement a new math program in your school. What channels would you use to communicate this possible initiative to the teachers? Would you use different channels to communicate the potential changes to the parents of students in your school? Outline samples of memoranda and presentations that you might use to communicate the proposed changes to the teachers and parents. How might you gain feedback through nonverbal channels?

Sources in the Communication Process: Senders and Receivers

The source of a message does not have to be a person. It can be organizations, supervisors, co-workers, or the task itself (Northcraft and Earley, 1989; Bantz,

1993). In considering the source, credibility and cognitive capacities are important factors.

Credibility   The credibility or believability (Adler and Rodman, 1991) of the sender influences the effectiveness of a message. Two characteristics that influence credibility are expertness and trustworthiness (Shelby, 1986; Becker and Klimoski, 1989). Credibility consists of the trust and confidence that the receiver has in the words and actions of the sender. The level of credibility, in turn, influences the reactions of the receiver to the words and actions of the communicator (Gibson, Ivancevich, and Donnelly, 1976). In some cases the identity and reputation of the sender, far from authenticating the message, lead instead to the receiver distorting the information or ignoring the message completely (Bowers, 1976). For example, faculty members who view the principal as less than competent, dishonest, or both probably will distort all communications from him or her.

Being prepared to speak can show expertise. It starts by organizing the idea into a series of symbols such as words or pictures that will communicate the intended meaning. These symbols are arranged for rationality, coherence, and compatibility with the methods of delivery, or media. An e-mail message, for instance, usually is worded differently from a formal letter of reprimand, and both are different from face-to-face conversation. In other words, a message that is well researched, organized, written, or presented will greatly increase the receiver's assessment of the sender's competence and hence credibility.

Cognitive Capacities   Psychological characteristics limit an individual's ability to communicate. Information-processing capacity (e.g., communication skills and knowledge of the subject) and personality and motivation factors (e.g., attitudes, values, interests, and expectations) combine to limit and filter the content and the quality of the message (Berlo, 1970). For example, the assistant superintendent for instruction, when communicating with principals, screens out information that he or she thinks is not pertinent to building administrators; principals filter information to the assistant superintendent that might reflect negatively on their performance.

Cognitive structures and processes also influence the recipient's ability to understand or decode the message. If the listener is effective, cooperative, and knowledgeable, he or she attempts to interpret the message as intended by the sender. However, as is the case with the sender, the receiver has communication capacities, knowledge of the subject, interests, values, and motivational characteristics that combine to limit qualitatively what is decoded. Consequently, the meaning the receiver applies is not exactly what the sender intended. Meanings may, of course, be relatively comparable, but they are never identical. Based on experience as represented by cognitive structures and processes, the receiver selects how to act or respond to the message. The actions serve as feedback to the sender (see Figures 10.1 and 10.3).

Communicating in Context

Communication among people also depends on a combination of contextual, cultural, or environmental factors. The process is clouded by contextual factors that are typically called *noise* or *barriers*. **Noise** is any distraction that interferes with the communication process. Noise can be so intense that it becomes more important than the content of the message itself (Reilly and DiAngelo, 1990).

In schools, noise resulting from social and personal factors can produce more troublesome problems than physical interference. For example, closed organizational climates, punishment-centered bureaucratic structures, cultural and gender differences, and authoritarian leaders create distortions in the communication processes. In such cases, group membership becomes important. Militant teachers cannot hear arbitrary administrators and vice versa; bureaucratic educators do not pay attention to demanding parents.

Prejudices toward age, gender, race, social class, and ethnic group differences constitute barriers in the communication process that distort messages. In a multicultural society, demographic attributes such as race, occupation, and gender provide surrogate indicators for the common experiences and background attributes that shape language development and communication abilities (Zenger and Lawrence, 1989). For example, a man who believes that his particular work can be done effectively only by a man is predisposed to deny facts, information, and messages that suggest that a woman can do the work equally well or better. Every message is filtered through barriers, predispositions, or cognitive schemas (Reilly and DiAngelo, 1990).

Hence, context noise of all types—for example, physical, social, and personal—may produce language disparities that constrain communication within schools even further. Given the growing diversity and other changes of school contexts (e.g., in economic wealth, ethnicity, gender in administrative positions, and with at-risk children), the challenge of communicating accurately and clearly will surely increase. As shown in Figure 10.1, creating shared meaning through the communication process depends on individual skills and motivation (MacGeorge and colleagues, 2003), content of the message, methods used, and context. Succinctly stated, the relationship is shown with the following formula:

Meaning = Information + Communicators + Media + Context

The essence of the formula and approach can be understood by considering the following questions:

- Who is speaking to whom and what roles do they occupy? Administrators? Administrator and teacher? Teachers? Men and women? Teacher and student? Administrator and parent?
- Is the language or set of symbols able to convey the information so both the sender and receiver can understand it?

- What is the content and effect of the communication? Positive or negative? Relevant or irrelevant?
- What methods or media are being used?
- What is the context in which the communication is taking place?
- What factors are creating noise that might block or distort the message?

As a general conclusion, the lack of two-way communication, the use of conflicting media and messages, and the existence of situational noise constitute the serious problems for understanding in educational organizations.

ORGANIZATIONAL PERSPECTIVES OF COMMUNICATION

Organizations are information-processing systems (Hall, 2002). Information flows through organizations and influences virtually all structures and processes. Moreover, organizations are processing an increasing volume of data and the preferred media are becoming face-to-face discussion and group participation (Daft, Bettenhausen, and Tyler, 1993). Consequently, the escalating volume and change to richer media make understanding organizational communication in schools even more important than previously thought. In sum, communication offers an additional way to conceptualize, describe, and explain organizations such as schools (Deetz, 2001).

Organizational Communication

The earlier general definition can be adapted to define **organizational communication** as the sending of messages through both formal and informal networks that results in the construction of meaning and influences both individuals and groups (DeFleur, Kearney, and Plax, 1993). In other words, organizational communication is a collective and interactive process that creates and interprets messages. Coordinated activities and relationships among participants within and outside the organization produce networks of understanding (Stohl, 1995). For example, staff development activities are held for teachers and administrators across a school district to communicate information about new curriculum standards.

Purposes of Communication in School Organizations

Communication in organizations such as schools serves a number of key purposes—for example, production and regulation, innovation, and individual socialization and maintenance (Myers and Myers, 1982). Production and regulation purposes include activities aimed at doing the primary work of the organization, such as teaching and learning in schools. They include setting goals and standards, transmitting facts and information, making decisions, leading and influencing others, and assessing outcomes. Innovation purposes include messages about generating new ideas and changing programs, structures, and procedures in the school. Finally, socialization and maintenance purposes of communication affect the participants' self-esteem, interpersonal relationships, and motivation to integrate their individual goals with the school's objectives. The capacity of a school to maintain such complex, highly interdependent patterns of activity is limited by its ability to handle communication for these purposes.

To serve the multiple purposes of production, regulation, innovation, socialization, and maintenance in schools, communication must promote high levels of shared understandings. Human action is needed to accomplish goals in schools. Goal-directed behavior is elicited through communication; hence, the greater the clarity and understanding of the message, the more likely the administrator, teacher, and student actions will proceed in fruitful, goal-oriented directions. Within an effectively operating school, for example, administrators, teachers, and students want to understand and accept each other's ideas and to act on them. School goals and guidelines for their accomplishment are developed through extensive dialogue. One innovative goal might be to implement a project-based approach to instruction. The accompanying guidelines to accomplish the goal would include the development of new curricula, new interactive instructional strategies, socialization and training for teachers, portfolio-assessment procedures, and plans for maintaining the programs. As group leaders, the principal, teachers, parents, and students emphasize the validity of the goal, stress the usefulness of the new procedures, promote shared understandings, encourage collective actions to implement the program, and assist in implementation and continuation. The extent and success of the actions depend in large measure on how effectively communication about the goal and accompanying procedures are initiated and maintained by networks in the school organization.

Communication Networks

Communication networks are patterns of formal and informal contacts established between communicators that are created by sending and exchanging messages through time and space (Monge and Contractor, 2001). **Formal channels** are methods sanctioned by the organization and are related to such organizational goals as regulation and innovation. When individuals communicate through **informal channels** and networks, they are using **grapevines** (Harris, 1993). These forms of communication are part of the organizational structure of schools, even though they are not shown on the hierarchical chart (Lewis, 1975). The direction of formal and informal channels can be vertical (up and down) and horizontal as well as one- or two-way. Hence, networks and channels are simply methods, vehicles, or forms a message travels in organizations such as schools; they are lines of communication.

The general notions of networks and channels are familiar because we all have had extensive experience with physical networks and channels, such as rivers, streets and highways, telephone lines, and sewer pipes (Monge, 1987). In contrast, communication networks in organizations are more difficult to identify because they comprise abstract human behaviors over time rather than physical materials such as pavement, streams, and pipes. Nevertheless, communication networks are regular patterns of person-to-person contacts that can be identified as people exchange information in schools. By observing the communication behavior over time, inferences can be made about which individuals are connected to other individuals through the exchange of information.

As shown in Figure 10.5, the members within communication networks assume a variety of roles. The communication role that a person serves within a communication network is important because it can influence the person's attitudes and behaviors. A **star role** is where a large number of people communicate with an individual. The star is a nexus within the network. Having a central role, the star is potentially powerful because he or she has greater access to and possible control over group resources (McElroy and Shrader, 1986; Yamagishi, Gillmore, and Cook, 1988). Hence, a star can be thought of as a leader in the network.

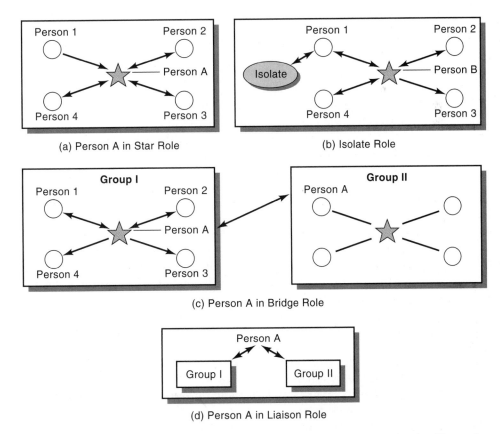

FIGURE 10.5   *Examples of Star, Isolate, Bridge, and Liaison Roles in Communication Networks*

In contrast, an **isolate role** is one where individuals are involved in communication with others only infrequently (see Figure 10.5). Isolates are loosely coupled or even decoupled from the network—that is, removed from the regular flow of communication and out of touch with the rest of the network. Isolates are a concern because their lack of communication activity is often accompanied by feelings of alienation, low job satisfaction, little commitment to the work organization, and low performance. Active participation in communication networks seems to produce positive outcomes, whereas isolation is associated with disaffection (Harris, 1993). However, programs designed to lessen educator isolation in schools may produce a situation in which the individuals who should benefit the most will resist and benefit little (Bakkenes, de Brabander, and Imants, 1999).

Patrick Forsyth and Wayne Hoy (1978) found that, without exception, being isolated in one instance carries over to other instances. The results of a subsequent study were similar, except that isolation from friends was not related to isolation from formal authority (Zielinski and Hoy, 1983). In other words, communication isolates in schools tend to be separated from perceived control, respected co-workers, the school's control structure, and sometimes friends. The potentially destructive aspect of this isolation is alienation. To counteract this negative effect, administrators must devise alternative communication processes because the isolates are not reachable by existing channels.

Exchanges occur across networks through individuals who fill special roles as bridges and liaisons. For example, people who belong to more than one group are called **bridges.** By belonging to a district curriculum committee and the department within a school, an English teacher serves in a bridging role for the two groups and will likely pass information between them (see Figure 10.5). **Liaisons** are individuals who link groups to which they do not belong. Liaisons serve as intermediaries among various groups within schools. In other words, they perform the vital function of keeping groups informed about each other's activities. Interactions among liaisons and group members do not occur with great frequency or formality, but when communication occurs regularly, the members usually know what the others are doing. As described in Chapter 3, these important linkages are weak ties or loose couplings. Liaisons many times are formally assigned by the organization to link different departments or committees and ensure accurate communication among them. By supervising the English curriculum committees in two schools, for example, the assistant superintendent for curriculum and instruction is a liaison for the two groups. There are formal as well as informal liaisons. Cynthia Stohl (1995) concludes that highly effective groups have more links with other groups in the organization or the external environment than less effective groups. However, the most cohesive and highly satisfied groups interact infrequently with outside constituents.

Formal Communication Networks in Schools

According to Scott (2003) one explanation of why organizations develop is their superior capacity to manage flows of information. The hierarchal structure of schools (see Chapter 3) incorporates several features, such as status and power differences among positions, but among the most important is a centralized communication system. Communication is embedded in all school structures. Richard H. Hall (2002) emphatically declares that, "The very establishment of an organizational structure is a sign that communications are supposed to follow a particular path" (p. 164).

Formal communication channels, or networks, traverse the organization through the hierarchy of authority. Barnard (1938) calls these formal networks "the communication system." According to Barnard, several factors must be considered when developing and using the formal communication system:

- The channels of communication must be known.
- The channels must link every member of the organization.
- Lines of communication must be as direct and as short as possible.
- The complete network of communication should typically be used.
- Every communication must be authenticated as being from the correct person occupying the position and within his or her authority to issue the message.

Figure 10.6 illustrates a school district's formal communication network using Barnard's descriptive statements. Note that the chart delineates the formal communication channels and that every member reports to someone. The directors report to the assistant superintendent for instruction, who, with the assistant superintendent for finance, report to the superintendent. The line of communication from the superintendent to the teachers goes through five hierarchical levels. This is reasonably short and direct for a large school district. Adding specific names and the bureaucratic rules and regulations that define the jobs places this system in compliance with Barnard's suggestions.

Within all organizations, formal restrictions on the communication process are apparent. "Making certain to go through proper channels" and "following the chain of command" are two common expressions that reflect a demand for control and structure of communication in organizations (Harris, 1993). Three characteristics of school bureaucracies seem particularly critical to the formal system of communication. They are centralization in the hierarchy, the organization's shape or configuration, and the level of information technology.

Centralization—the degree to which authority is not delegated but concentrated in a single source in the organization—is important to the effectiveness of communication systems (Porter and Roberts, 1976). In centralized schools, a few positions in the structure have most of the information-obtaining

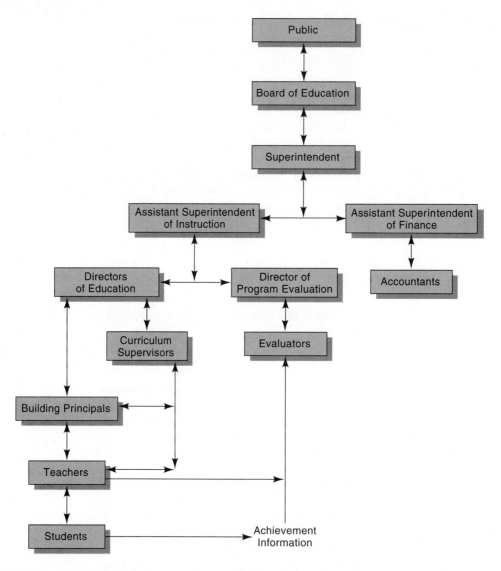

FIGURE 10.6 *Formal Communication Channels for Program Implementation in a School District*

ability. For example, the superintendent and two assistant superintendents pictured in Figure 10.6 would gather most of the information for the formal system of communication. If the district is decentralized or loosely coupled (see Chapter 3), however, the information-obtaining potential is more or less spread across all of the positions. Research examining the different information-obtaining abilities supports the finding that centralized structures are more efficient communicators when the problems and tasks are relatively simple and straightforward. When the problems and tasks become more complex, however, decentralized hierarchies appear to be more efficient (Argote, Turner, and Fichman, 1989). Similarly, centralized schools tend to rely on less-rich media, such as memos and employee manuals, than decentralized schools (Jablin and Sias, 2001).

Shape—the number of hierarchical levels or tallness versus flatness of the school organization—also affects the communication processes. Hierarchical levels and size are structural characteristics that are commonly associated with shape. A school district with five levels, such as the one depicted in Figure 10.6, differs from systems with more or fewer levels in its ability to communicate across levels and from top to bottom. The number of levels can be seen as the distance a message must travel. As the distance increases, the chance for message distortion increases and the satisfaction with the quality and quantity of communication decreases (Clampitt, 1991; Zahn, 1991). Teachers will generally express less satisfaction with messages from superintendents than from principals. In addition, organizational size is negatively related to communication quality; as the district becomes larger, communication becomes more impersonal or formal and quality declines (Jablin, 1987).

Technology also appears to have significant effects on organizational communication, though *the exact* effects remain somewhat speculative. As we noted in Chapter 3, writers subscribing to the position that schools are loosely coupled systems argue that educational organizations have a relatively low level of technology. However, as communication technology becomes more sophisticated in schools, its use will dramatically alter the communication that takes place in both the formal and informal networks (Jablin and Sias, 2001).

We are living in a creative and dynamic era that is producing fundamental changes, as is apparent in such advances as computer networks, the Internet, the World Wide Web, electronic mail, computer conferences, communication satellites, and data-handling devices. Until recently, electronic information exchange has largely been adapted to convey voice, vision, text, and graphics as distinct and separate types of communication. Now, simultaneous and instantaneous transmission of voice, vision, text, and graphics to many locations is becoming common. Even while imagining the tremendous changes yet to come, the usual descriptions of the forthcoming power of electronic technologies together with the geographic distribution of participants do not adequately capture the differences between these and traditional media. Consequently, the potential influence of such technologies on all aspects of communication in schools—administrative, instructional, and social—is probably underestimated.

TIP: THEORY INTO PRACTICE

Assessing and Improving Communication in the Formal Organization

Improving school communication requires a planned program that assesses existing conditions and planning new mechanisms. Consider a school district, division, or building and complete following tasks:

- Assess the organizational design of the communication system against the criteria suggested earlier in this chapter by Barnard.
- If implemented, what mechanisms would likely facilitate the process for improving the formal system? Possibilities include modifying the organizational structure, creating convenient sites for formal and informal interaction, using new technologies, forming a committee system to accomplish tasks and make decisions, establishing information storage and retrieval systems, selecting personnel with good communication skills, and developing professional development programs to improve communication skills.

Informal Communication Networks in Schools

Informal networks or grapevines exist in all organizations regardless of how elaborate the formal communication system happens to be. One generalization that researchers and participants in organizations have observed repeatedly is that people who are in groups, cliques, or gangs tend to reach an understanding on things or issues very quickly. They communicate easily and well among themselves. Facts, opinions, attitudes, suspicions, gossip, rumors, and even directives flow freely and rapidly through the grapevine. Built around social relationships among the school members, informal channels develop for such simple reasons as common office areas, similar duties, shared coffee breaks, carpools, and friendships. Social relationships and communication channels arise at all organizational levels of the school. Returning to Figure 10.6, informal communication patterns exist at the central office. One central office group might include some of the directors, an assistant superintendent, some supervisors, an evaluator, and an accountant. Certainly, informal communication channels thrive among school principals and within teacher groups and the student body.

The communication patterns among principals in elementary and secondary schools are quite different (Licata and Hack, 1980). Secondary school principals form informal groups that are guildlike. That is, the communication patterns are based on common professional interests and the need for mutual aid and protection. In contrast, elementary principals cluster into clanlike groups in which their communications revolve around social ties with mentors, friends, neighbors, and relatives. In brief, secondary principals structure the grapevine around professional survival and development, whereas elementary principals communicate informally about social matters.

Although a major disadvantage of grapevines is the spread of rumors, informal networks serve a number of purposes in formal school organization. First, they reflect the quality of activities in a school. Communication through informal sources provides vital feedback to administrators and other school leaders. Moreover, active informal networks are indicative of a school's culture and leaders can learn a great deal by listening to them. Second, informal channels may satisfy social or affiliation needs not met by formal channels. Third, grapevines fill an information void by carrying a great deal of information. No matter how elaborate, formal communication networks simply cannot carry all of the information required in contemporary schools. Informal networks provide outlets when formal channels are clogged. Informal channels are particularly helpful during periods of change, when the information is new, and when face-to-face or electronic communication is relatively easy. Fourth, informal networks provide meaning for activities within the school. As messages travel through informal networks, the messages are translated with surprising accuracy into terms that make sense to the participants. The accuracy is 75 to 90 percent for noncontroversial information. When distortions occur, they generally reflect an incorrect emphasis that is based on incomplete information. A problem is that even a small distortion or error can have dramatic consequences (Clampitt, 1991; Harris, 1993).

TIP: THEORY INTO PRACTICE

Informal Communication Groups

Think of a school that you have attended or in which you have worked. Focus on students and teachers and respond to the following statements:

- Quickly identify informal groups or networks of students and teachers that you have observed. Do they have particular names?
- For the informal groups that you identified, what are some typical values and norms that guide their behavior?
- What formal school aspects might contribute to the groups' development?
- Do status structures exist within the groups? Do they exist between the groups? If yes, describe.
- Are there isolated individuals who do not belong to any group?
- Does the principal belong to any of these groups? If not what is the principal's relationship to the groups?
- Provide any other observations.

Complementary Networks:
Formal and Informal Communication

As we have noted, formal and informal communication networks exist in all educational organizations. The results from research studying networks across a variety of settings indicate that communication patterns in organizations are extraordinarily complex. Within schools, there is not a single unitary network, but rather a series of overlapping and interrelated networks (Jablin, 1980). A large majority of all participants interact consistently with many other individuals and in far greater numbers than formal organizational charts suggest. Although the task network is larger and better developed than the social network, both are closely related to each other and critical to the organization (O'Reilly and Pondy, 1979). Generally, communication groups form along task-focused lines. Task structures of work groups act to improve or detract from the accuracy and openness of the transmitted message. Groups with specialized skills and high status are more open in information exchanges than other groups (O'Reilly and Roberts, 1977). Further, accuracy and openness have a positive impact on performance, but the frequency of communication among educators is not high (Miskel, McDonald, and Bloom, 1983). In sum, both the substance and the direction of communication can make the two systems complementary.

Substance

In terms of content, communication can be thought of as instrumental or expressive (Etzioni, 1960). Instrumental communication distributes information and knowledge that affect cognitive structures and processes. Administrative directives, policies, curricular objectives and materials, and attendance data are typical examples. The purpose of instrumental communication is to develop consensus about methods and procedures. Expressive communication, on the other hand, attempts to change or reinforce attitudes, norms, and values. Appropriate affective orientations toward students, militancy, discipline, and organizational rewards are typical examples of the substance of expressive communication.

Formal communication channels carry both instrumental and expressive content. The informal network can enhance both. For example, the grapevine serves as a barometer of opinion and sentiment. School administrators can often tap the informal flow for information about the morale of students, teachers, and other administrators. They also can float trial balloons to test receptivity to a new procedure or program. For instance, an administrator may want to introduce a new professional development program for teacher preparation. Before making a final decision, the hypothetical possibilities are discussed informally with some staff members. As the information flows through the grapevine, the sentiment can be monitored. Depending on the reaction, the administrator uses the formal communication system to announce plans for the new program, allows the program to remain hypothetical, or formally quashes the rumor. Barnard (1938) suggests that this type of communication flows without interruption in the informal networks, but would be either inconvenient or raise issues calling for premature decisions in the formal channels. Hence, informal can complement formal instrumental communication by serving as a testing ground for possible courses of action. In terms of expressive communication, the informal network can be a positive vehicle for personal expression by allowing participants to communicate and interact socially. Informal networks then provide gratification of the social needs of many school members at little financial cost to the district.

Direction

Messages do not sit around waiting to be discovered, nor do they float around randomly to be picked up by some lucky accident (Myers and Myers, 1982). Communication in organizations flows directionally through the formal and informal networks. The direction of information flow also demonstrates the possible complementary nature of formal and informal communication networks. Information flows vertically and horizontally in both networks.

Vertical flow refers to the upward and downward direction of communication through the different levels of the school's hierarchy. Information is passed down or up the line of authority through memos, directions, policies, and programs of action. An important point about the vertical flow of organizational communication is that messages moving in the formal network are extremely important to the people who send them and those who receive them. The jobs of individuals can depend on the messages they receive about such matters as directives, assessments, requests, and instructions (DeFleur, Kearney, and Plax, 1993).

In formal downward communication, information passes through the chain of command—that is, through the hierarchical status structure. These messages typically reaffirm the chain of command and reinforce control (Harris, 1993). Five types of communications from superior to subordinate include (Katz and Kahn, 1978):

- Instructions about specific tasks.
- Rationale about why the task needs to be done and how it relates to other tasks.
- Information about organizational procedures and practices.
- Feedback about the performance levels of individuals.
- Information regarding the organization's goals.

Downward communication is relatively easy to send, but subordinates often may misunderstand the message. To ensure that the intended meanings are understood, administrators must develop two-way communication channels and use extensive feedback processes up and down the hierarchy.

Communication from the lower levels of the hierarchy to the upper levels is upward communication. Upward communication provides four types of messages (Katz and Kahn, 1978; DeFleur, Kearney, and Plax, 1993):

- Routine operational messages.
- Reports on problems.
- Suggestions for improvement.
- Information on how subordinates feel about each other and the job.

Upward communication is one means by which subordinates are made accountable to superiors. Such communication is often viewed as an instrument of administrative control. Consequently, subordinates have a tendency to emphasize positive information, withhold negative data, and communicate what they think the "boss wants to hear." Because many decisions are made at the top of the hierarchy, the quality of the decisions will depend on the accuracy and timeliness of the communication that moves through the formal system. In general, the more tangible and the more objective the information, the more likely that subordinates will communicate accurately with their superiors. Frequent two-way exchanges also improve accuracy (Porter and Roberts, 1976).

A well-developed informal network can help administrators gain timely information and assess the accuracy of formal upward communication. In exchange for the information, however, teachers influence administrator behavior. Some teachers gain influence and power because they have information about how to get things accomplished or who can resolve specific problems. Similarly, department chairs, committee members, and teachers with specialized skills possess valued information. As a result of their knowledge and positions in the communication network, they can exert considerable influence on administrator decisions (Barnett, 1984).

Horizontal flow indicates that communication moves across organizational members at the same hierarchical level. A principal, for instance, may provide information to another principal, who in turn, passes it to still other principals. Such communication is the strongest and most easily understood (Lewis, 1975). Horizontal communication can be either formal or informal. In Figure 10.6, the lateral communication link between the two assistant superintendents would be formal when they are working on ways to finance the introduction of a new curriculum. Another common example is teachers talking with each other in a lounge or planning room during class periods when they are not teaching. The major purposes of horizontal communication are coordinating tasks, solving problems, sharing information with colleagues, resolving conflicts, and building rapport (Harris, 1993). For example, principals communicate so that their activities or curriculum emphases will be similar in different schools, and to share information about content, avoid potential conflicts, and build friendly relationships with peers. The direction affects the ease, content, and accuracy of organizational communication.

In studying horizontal communication, W. W. Charters, Jr. (1967), found substantial differences between elementary and high schools. Elementary schools exhibited a much larger volume, with most teachers in direct contact with one another. In contrast, only 15 percent of the high school staff interacted regularly. This difference in communication volume is partially explained by staff size. The average number of contacts per staff member declined with increasing faculty size. Larger facilities and physical dispersion, along with specialized personnel (guidance counselors or special teachers) who are not in the main flow of classroom instruction, help explain the impact of size on communication volume. Charters did note, however, that size alone does not account for the entire difference. Elementary school staffs communicate more than high school staffs. Finally, Charters found that stability in the communication patterns is related to the division of labor and physical proximity. Teachers in the same subject specialty and, to a lesser extent, those in closer physical proximity form enduring communication networks. Thus, three factors—level and size of school, specialization, and proximity—affect the horizontal communication patterns in schools.

In sum, communication plays such a central role in schools that the key issue is not whether administrators, teachers, and students engage in communication but whether they communicate effectively. People must exchange information in schools, but to develop shared meanings requires communication competence at both the individual and organizational levels.

A CASE FOR LEADERSHIP

Scandal at Placido High: Coincidence or Conspiracy?

Placido is a small bedroom community with a population of nearly 12,000. Its public schools enjoy a fine reputation. Parents are interested and involved in the education of their children. Last week, during the high school graduation ceremonies, the president of the board of education spoke proudly of the recognition the district has received for high student scores at all grade levels on statewide tests.

The superintendent of schools, Debra Bass, has just completed her third year in Placido. The members of the community have been very pleased with her performance and members of the board of education recently renewed her contract. Dr. Bass is a student-centered educator who has at-

tempted to heighten the sensitivity of the professional staff to the needs of all students. She had just concluded a regular Monday meeting with her administrative team when she received a phone call from a representative of the National Testing Corporation (NTC).

Robert Bender, the NTC representative, informed Superintendent Bass that he had received a letter from three recent graduates of Placido High School. In their letter, the students claimed to have had an unfair advantage over the thousands of students in other high schools all over the country who were administered a university placement exam on May 13. They noted that they had received prior knowledge of four of the five reading passages on the interpretative section of the exam and two of the three passages on the translation

(Continued)

section several days prior to the exam from their teacher, Mr. Will Johnson. The students enclosed photocopies of the passages in question with their letter. They explained that they waited until after graduation to reveal the impropriety for fear of jeopardizing final course grades and their graduation, even though they did nothing wrong or dishonest.

Dr. Bass requested a meeting with Mr. Bender to discuss the situation and to determine jointly how the investigation of the allegations would proceed. Mr. Bender politely informed Dr. Bass that NTC had an established procedure to investigate these situations, but he would be pleased to meet with her to discuss how NTC planned to proceed. He made it clear to the superintendent that NTC would safeguard the identity of the graduates who sent the letter and assured her that no other contacts would be made until after their meeting, scheduled for the next morning.

The superintendent immediately called Hal Curry, the high school principal. Principal Curry was appointed principal January 1, upon the retirement of his predecessor. He served as assistant principal for 12 years prior to the appointment and he knew the faculty, students, and community well. The superintendent arranged to meet Principal Curry in 30 minutes to brief him and to plan a course of action.

Dr. Bass knew that the director of student services, Lorna Leonard, was responsible for both test security and test administration. NTE is an independent organization that contracts with school districts to have their exams administered during normal school hours by school employees. Exam packets are delivered to each site by courier to the designated test coordinator, who has the responsibility to keep them secure until their administration on a specified day and time.

Lorna, the designated coordinator for Placido, has been in the district for 28 years and was currently on vacation and not due to return for 10 days. Will Johnson, the teacher of that particular university placement course, already had

departed for summer break with the rest of the nonadministrative professional staff. Superintendent Bass placed a phone call to the president of the board to inform him of the situation and promised to report back after she had met the NTC representative the next day.

Principal Curry was visibly shaken as the superintendent conveyed the allegations. He felt responsible for the actions of his staff and often reminded staff members that, "the buck stopped at his desk." The possibility that innocent students would suffer negative consequences as a result of inappropriate behavior by one of their teachers really upset both the principal and superintendent.

A search of the records revealed that 15 students, 9 seniors and 6 juniors, were administered the exam at the high school in May. Superintendent Bass reminded the principal that it was important to conduct a thorough investigation while safeguarding the privacy and rights of all parties. They agreed that Principal Curry would call the 15 students who took the exam to request a private meeting with each student and his/her parents. He also would attempt to contact Will Johnson, the teacher, and Lorna Leonard, director of student services, immediately.

By late afternoon, the principal had made contact with six of the students. He provided his home phone number and requested that each have a parent call him later that evening. He left a message for Lorna Leonard at her vacation home. There was no response to the call to Will Johnson's home. A check of the teacher's contact card revealed a summer address in a resort community several hours away by auto, but no other phone number. The principal planned to make calls from his home that night with hopes of contacting Will Johnson and all involved students.

During their meeting the following morning, Robert Bender gave the superintendent a copy of the letter with names removed, and copies of the passages that he received. Although the students

(Continued)

A CASE FOR LEADERSHIP *(Continued)*

never saw a copy of the exam prior to its administration, they claimed that during the review process, Mr. Johnson specifically reviewed and focused on four reading passages and two translation passages, which comprised the vast majority of the exam. Mr. Bender described the procedures that the NTC would follow in the investigation. He explained that all the individual tests of the students from Placido had been analyzed and that none of their scores would be reported. Students would be given an opportunity to retake another form of the exam at no cost, as soon as a mutually convenient time could be arranged. Superintendent Bass was surprised by the hasty decision, but offered complete cooperation and expressed the desire of the district to get to the truth.

She suggested that NTC use offices in the school to meet with students and any staff members they wished to interview. Mr. Bender thanked the superintendent and informed her that his staff would begin contacting the students immediately. He asked the superintendent to arrange interviews with the high school principal, guidance counselors, Lorna Leonard, and Will Johnson. Dr. Bass explained that some of the individuals were on vacation, but she would attempt to contact them and make arrangements for the interviews as soon as possible.

The superintendent was upset. She knew that it was just a matter of time before the local newspaper got wind of the "scandal." Parents of innocent students would be outraged that their children were being required to retake the exam. To make matters worse, the high school principal was not able to make contact with the teacher. Lorna Leonard had returned the principal's call last evening and promised to return to Placido by the beginning of next week. Principal Curry had made appointments to meet with 11 of the students beginning that evening, determined that two were on vacation for the week, and left a message for the other two students.

A call to the board president only generated questions. Were the testing materials secured?

Who had access to the keys to the storage area? Was it possible that the allegations were untrue? What should be done about the public relations nightmare that was emerging? All these questions had run through the superintendent's mind, along with dozens of others. The president of the board agreed to brief all other board members and instructed the superintendent to have a special board meeting advertised for next Monday evening.

Superintendent Bass prepared a press release and called the editor of the local paper and arranged to meet. She drafted a letter to Will Johnson and sent a copy to his home and vacation addresses via Express Mail. The teacher has been the instructor of the university placement course every year since its inception at Placido High. He attended annual summer training sessions and boasted that his students always performed well. However, Will Johnson's performance in his other classes was not stellar. The superintendent really needed to speak with him.

During the meetings that followed, the principal assured each of the students and their parents that he expected them to tell the truth. No matter what they revealed to him or during interviews with NTC, there would be no reprisals. The principal assured them that everyone wanted to know what happened and that he would deal with anyone, student or faculty member, who had done anything dishonest or inappropriate.

Wednesday morning brought the anticipated headline "Honest Students Report Unfair Advantage" as well as dozens of calls from concerned parents and community members. It also brought some very disturbing information conveyed to the principal during meetings with two of the students.

One of the students, a junior, claimed to have received an exam packet that was torn open. At that time, he verbally expressed that fact loud enough for others in the room to hear. The student noted that Ms. Leonard did not respond to his statement, continued to give test instructions, and

(Continued)

A CASE FOR LEADERSHIP *(Concluded)*

reminded the students that they were on a tight schedule. The other student reported that within a day of the exam, she and at least five other students had gone to a teacher "they trusted," Mrs. Anne Bishop, to express their concern that they "knew more than they should" when they took the exam.

The phone rang. The president of the board of education asked for a report on findings. He also expressed the collective opinion of several board members, including his own, that the teacher should be dismissed. The scandal was the talk of the community. Honest students were being punished by having to take another exam because of Johnson's actions. Will Johnson had gone too far and perhaps he had not acted alone. The superintendent's requests "not to jump to conclusions" had fallen on deaf ears. She urged the board president to be patient and give her the opportunity to get to the facts of the incident.

As Dr. Bass hung up, her secretary gave her a message from the local newspaper editor requesting a return call as soon as possible. She placed the call and much to her chagrin was asked to verify the charge that, during the test administration, one of the students had been given an examination packet that had previously been opened.

Things were really spinning out of control. Priorities must be established and decisions must be made! Assume that you are the superintendent:

- Do circumstances suggest a conspiracy? How can the principal and superintendent find out? What are key communication channels?
- What happens to communication within the organization during the summer when

schools are closed for vacation? How can some of the impediments to effective communication be overcome?
- What should the superintendent communicate to the board? How? When?
- Discuss the superintendent's public relations strategy. Is public relations the same as communication?
- What other groups should be involved in the communication process? When? How?
- What are the political ramifications of the incident? How can the negative consequences be anticipated and controlled?
- Develop two scenarios, one in which the teacher is innocent of the charges and one in which he is not. If true, are the charges grounds for dismissal of a tenured teacher?
- What should the superintendent do if she finds that all the evidence is circumstantial and the teacher and director deny any wrongdoing?
- What is the appropriate stance with the media?
- How can such a situation be avoided in the future? Are new district policies and procedures about testing required?

The author of this case, Michael F. DiPaola, Ed.D., is a former high school principal and district superintendent. He is currently an associate professor in the Educational Policy, Planning and Leadership Program of the School of Education at the College of William and Mary in Virginia. This case is from DiPaola (1999). "Scandal at Placido High: Coincidence or Conspiracy?" *Journal of Cases in Educational Leadership* [online].2(3).

SUMMARY AND SUGGESTED READINGS

Communication is so pervasive in schools that it is a fundamental and integrative process in educational administration. Communication means sharing messages, ideas, or attitudes to produce understanding or shared meanings among people. Four conclusions seem clear. First, to be a good communicator is to know the various types of communication, their particular characteristics, how to choose among them, and how to apply them skillfully. Second, individuals exchange symbols with other persons when interacting in social situations; the people who interpret them in a given situation construct the meanings of those symbols. This means that direct transmission of an intended meaning is not always straightforward. Third, messages traverse formal and informal channels, using a variety of verbal and nonverbal media. Although the formal network is usually larger and better developed than the informal, they are closely related, can be complementary, and are critical to the organization. Fourth, to ensure a high level of shared understanding, feedback is essential. Although perfection is impossible, several techniques are available to measure and improve the communication process at both the individual and organizational levels.

Chester Barnard (1938) proposed an early and still important set of ideas about individual and organizational communication. This is an excellent source to consult on communication and other concepts. Two excellent general sources dealing with the communication literature are the textbooks by DeFleur, Kearney, and Plax (1993) and Harris (1993). They provide relatively comprehensive and in-depth coverage of the various theories and applications in the communication field. Clampitt's (2001) book is useful because he presents the models of communication in a context of administrative applications, myths, and tactics. For extensive reviews of the literature and suggestions for further research on communication, we suggest consulting Jablin and Putnam (2001).

KEY ASSUMPTIONS AND PRINCIPLES

1. Using multiple communication strategies increases the probability of shared understandings and new learning.
2. Administrators who are competent communicators will have larger repertoires of communication strategies than less-competent communicators.
3. When communicating ambiguous information, using richer media and redundancy improves communication performance.
4. For effective understanding, verbal and nonverbal messages must convey the same meaning.
5. The meaning of a message depends on the information to be conveyed, skills and traits of the communicators, type of media employed, and the level of noise in the communication context.
6. The communication systems of highly centralized, tall (with many hierarchical layers) school organizations are characterized by using less-rich media, while less-centralized, flatter school organizations are typified by employing richer media.
7. Formal communication networks are usually larger and better developed than informal networks, but they are closely related, can be complementary, and are critical to the school organization.

LEADERSHIP IN SCHOOLS

Who can say that government is not about charismatic leadership after watching Ronald Reagan. It is important to build consensus but leadership must first be bold and have a direction.

Jesse Jackson, 1990

The effective functioning of social systems from the local PTA to the United States of America is assumed to be dependent on the quality of their leadership.

Victor H. Vroom
"Leadership"

PREVIEW

1. Leaders and leadership are important because they serve as anchors, provide guidance in times of change, and are responsible for the effectiveness of organizations.

2. Leadership is a social influence process that is comprised of both rational and emotional elements.

3. "Leader" and "administrator" refer to individuals who occupy positions in which they are expected to exert leadership.

4. The work of leaders exhibits similar patterns across different countries and organizational settings.

5. Personality, motivation, and skill factors appear to be systematically related to leadership in schools.

6. Critical situational factors in educational leadership are environment, leader roles, nature of subordinates, and characteristics of the organization.

7. Task-oriented, relations-oriented, and change-oriented behaviors are fundamental classes of leader behavior.

8. Leader effectiveness can be conceptualized as having three dimensions—personal, organizational, and individual.

9. Contingency models attempt to explain the relationships among traits, situations, behaviors, and effectiveness.

10. Visionary and change-oriented ideas emerged to drive the "new leadership" theories and gave a new impetus to the field during the 1980s and 1990s.

11. Transformational leaders use idealized influence, inspirational motivation, intellectual stimulation, and individualized consideration to change their schools.

12. Distributed leadership is emerging as an important framework for school leaders.

Leadership evokes highly romanticized, emotional, and courageous images for many of us. When we think of specific leaders, names such as Gandhi, Churchill, Kennedy, King, Mandela, Mao Zedong, Meir, Napoleon, Reagan, Roosevelt, and Thatcher come to mind. According to Gary Yukl (2002), the term itself projects images of powerful, dynamic individuals who command victorious armies, build wealthy and influential empires, or alter the course of nations. Stated succinctly, people commonly believe that leaders make a difference and want to understand why. Indeed, leadership is often regarded as the single most important factor in the success or failure of institutions (Bass, 1990).

The foregoing views also hold for educational organizations. In fact, a wide, diverse, and growing set of stakeholders assume that leaders are largely responsible for school performance (Ogawa and Scribner, 2002). Many of these stakeholders, both within and outside of education, see the growing and changing demands on schools as further elevating the importance of educational leadership. As a result school leaders are under intense scrutiny, with many critics concluding that the current cadre is highly deficient. While some allege that school leaders are to blame for inadequate academic achievement, the main concern is that current leaders are not up to the task of bringing about needed changes. The critics contend that school leaders, for example, are not responding adequately to standards-based accountability, guiding and directing instructional improvement, incorporating revolutionary new information technologies in their schools, modernizing outmoded administrative structures, and providing needed services to all children (see for example Elmore, 2000; Finn, 2003; Hess, 2003). Such criticisms and challenges make understanding school leadership all the more important. We will address these issues by building on the premise that leaders are essential to educational organizations and by presenting useful theoretical perspectives from an extensive and growing knowledge base for leadership.

DEFINING LEADERSHIP

As a word from our everyday language, **leadership** has been incorporated into the technical vocabulary of organizational studies without being precisely redefined (Yukl, 2002). Therefore, it is not surprising that definitions of the concept are almost as numerous as the scholars engaged in its study. Bennis (1989), for example, opined that leadership is like beauty—it is hard to define, but you know it when you see it. Martin M. Chemers (1997: 1) offers the following typical definition: "leadership is a process of social influence in which one person is able to enlist the aid and support of others in the accomplishment of a common task." The only assumption shared by this and most definitions is that leadership involves a social influence process in which one individual exerts intentional influence over others to structure activities and relationships in a group or organization. Disputes about definitions remain, however, over whether leadership is a specialized role or social influence process; over the kind, basis, and purpose of influence attempts; and over leadership versus management (Yukl, 2002).

One view is that all groups have a specialized leadership role that includes some responsibilities and functions that cannot be shared without jeopardizing the effectiveness of the group (Yukl, 2002). The individual who has the most influence and who is expected to carry out the leadership role is the leader; other members are followers. An alternative concept is that leadership is a social process that occurs naturally within a social system and is shared among its members. Leadership, then, is a process or property of the organization rather than of the individual. Rodney T. Ogawa and Steven T. Bossert (1995) contend that leadership is a quality of school organizations, which flows broadly through social networks and roles. Mark A. Smylie and Ann W. Hart (1999) note empirical support for leadership as an organizational property of schools. Similarly, James P. Spillane, Richard Halverson, and John B. Diamond (2003) maintain that leadership is distributed across leaders, followers, and their situation. Katz and Kahn (1978) identify three major components of leadership that clarify the controversy: (1) an attribute of an office or position, (2) a characteristic of a person, and (3) a category of actual behavior. Hence, both views can be useful—leadership can profitably be examined as a property of individuals or as roles and processes of the social system.

A second set of controversies involves how much to circumscribe the kind, basis, and purpose of influence attempts. Yukl (2002) delineates dichotomous perspectives on these issues. In regard to the type and outcome of influence processes used by leaders, some theorists include only strategies that produce willing commitment by followers and exclude those that result in neutral or reluctant conformity. Other scholars contend that this is too restrictive because the same kind of influence attempts can produce different results across different situations. Similarly, some theorists restrict influence processes of leaders to those related to task goals and group maintenance; that is, to what is ethical and favorable to the organization and its people. Others place no restrictions on the definition and include all attempts to influence followers, regardless of the intended purpose or actual beneficiary, because acts of leadership frequently have multiple motives. Finally, traditional definitions of leadership tend to emphasize rational processes in which leaders influence followers to believe that it is in their best interest to cooperate and achieve shared task goals. Recent formulations of charismatic and transformational leadership use definitions that recognize the importance of emotions as a basis of influence. In other words, leaders inspire their followers to sacrifice their selfish interests for a larger cause.

Another debate involves distinctions between leaders and administrators and what and how they try to influence (Yukl, 1994). Obviously, individuals can be leaders without being administrators (e.g., an informal leader); conversely, individuals can be administrators without being leaders.

Some argue that leadership and administration are fundamentally different concepts. The basis of the dispute appears to be that **administrators** emphasize stability and efficiency, whereas **leaders** stress adaptive change and getting people to agree about what needs to be accomplished. For example, administrators plan and budget, organize and staff, and control and solve problems; leaders establish direction, align people, and motivate and inspire (Kotter, 1990). In school settings, Kenneth Leithwood and Daniel Duke (1999) conclude that justifying a conceptual distinction between leadership and management is difficult. Although no one suggests that administering or managing and leading schools are equivalent, the degree of overlap is disputed. Rather than argue about the specific amount of overlap, we will use both terms to refer to individuals (e.g., administrators, teachers, school board members, parents, students) who occupy positions in which they are expected to exert leadership for subordinates or followers, but without the assumption that they actually do so.

Thus, we agree with Yukl (2002). Leadership should be defined broadly as a social process in which a member or members of a group or organization influence the interpretation of internal and external events, the choice of goals or desired outcomes, organization of work activities, individual motivation and abilities, power relations, and shared orientations. Moreover, as a specialized role and social influence process, leadership is comprised of both rational and emotional elements with no assumptions about the purpose or outcome of the influence efforts. Employing such a broad definition opens an abundance of useful conceptual and empirical capital for both practitioners and scholars of school administration and leadership.

THE NATURE OF ADMINISTRATIVE WORK

Given the intense and long-standing interest in leaders and leadership, what is it that leaders do that is so intriguing? Can describing the nature of leaders' work advance our understanding of leadership? Certainly, partial responses to these questions can be gained by observing leaders as they administer and lead their organizations. A number of studies have used a structured observation approach to describe what managers, administrators, and leaders do in their everyday jobs.[1] These studies provide detailed and vivid pictures of what business managers and school administrators do in their jobs, and with whom and where they spend their time. Given the regularities in the research, Kyung Ae Chung and Cecil Miskel (1989) summarize the major findings.

- Administering schools is feverish and consuming; school administrators work long hours at an unrelenting, physically exhausting pace.
- School leaders rely on verbal media; they spend a great deal of time walking around the building and talking to individuals and groups.

- Administrator activities vary widely; hence, administrators constantly change gears and tasks.
- Managerial work is fragmented; for school administrators, the pace is rapid and frenzied, discontinuity prevalent, and the span of concentration short.

Overall, the descriptions of administrative work are similar across different countries and organizational settings. Administrators work primarily in their offices or school buildings. Their jobs are characterized by long hours and brief verbal encounters across a wide range of issues with diverse individuals and groups. Structured observation studies are useful because they respond descriptively and clearly to the question, What do school administrators and leaders do in their jobs? Nevertheless, it is not clear how individuals engaged in work characterized as consuming, reactive, and fragmented can actually provide leadership to their organizations. Moreover, technological advances, demands for increased achievement and standards-based accountability, and environmental competition from new forms of schools are changing the nature of work for school administrators. Although the results from these studies are important and interesting, they largely fail to answer the key question, How do we understand the nature of this work in terms of leading schools? To respond to this question, we will summarize the dominant theoretical approaches to understanding leadership.

Traits, Skills, and Leadership

Many individuals still believe, as Aristotle did centuries ago, that from the hour of birth, some are marked for subjection, others for rule. Aristotle thought that individuals are born with characteristics that would make them leaders. The conception that the key factors in determining leadership are inherited produced the so-called **trait approach of leadership.** Bass (1990) observes that early in this century, leaders were generally regarded as superior individuals who, because of fortunate inheritance or social circumstance, possessed qualities and abilities that differentiated them from people in general. Until the 1950s investigations to find the traits that determine who will be leaders dominated the study of leadership. Researchers attempted to isolate unique traits or characteristics of leaders that differentiated them from their followers. Frequently studied traits included physical characteristics (height, weight), a host of personality factors, needs, values, energy and activity levels, task and interpersonal competence, intelligence, and charisma. Over time, recognition grew that traits can generally be affected by inheritance, learning, and environmental factors.

Early Trait Research

Pure trait approaches—that is, the view that only traits determine leadership capacity—were all but put to rest with the publication of literature reviews during the 1940s and 1950s. In particular, Ralph M. Stogdill (1948) reviewed 124 trait studies of leadership that were completed between 1904 and 1947. He classified the personal factors associated with leadership into the following five general categories:

- Capacity—intelligence, alertness, verbal facility, originality, judgment.
- Achievement—scholarship, knowledge, athletic accomplishments.
- Responsibility—dependability, initiative, persistence, aggressiveness, self-confidence, desire to excel.
- Participation—activity, sociability, cooperation, adaptability, humor.
- Status—socioeconomic position, popularity.

Although Stogdill found a number of traits (e.g., above-average intelligence, dependability, participation, and status) that consistently differentiated leaders from nonleaders, he concluded that the trait approach *by itself* had yielded negligible and confusing results. He asserted that a person does not become a leader by virtue of the possession of some combination of traits because the impact of traits varies widely from situation to situation. As a consequence, Stogdill added a sixth factor associated with leadership—situational components (e.g., characteristics of followers and goals to be achieved). R. D. Mann's (1959) later review produced similar conclusions.

Recent Perspectives on Leadership Traits and Skills

Notwithstanding the lack of success in identifying general leadership traits, research persisted. More recent trait studies, however, use a wider variety of improved measurement procedures, including projective tests and assessment centers, and they focus on managers and administrators rather than other kinds of leaders. Yukl (1981, 2002) explains that although Stogdill's 1948 literature review greatly discouraged many researchers from studying leader traits, industrial psychologists interested in improving managerial selection continued to conduct trait research. Their emphasis on selection focused trait research on the relationship between leader traits and leader effectiveness, rather than on the comparison of leaders and nonleaders. This distinction is a significant one. Predicting who will become leaders and predicting who will be more effective are quite different tasks. Hence, the so-called trait studies continue, but they now tend to explore the relationship between traits and leadership effectiveness of administrators in particular types of organizations and settings.

This second generation of studies has produced a more consistent set of findings; in fact, in 1970, after reviewing another 163 new trait studies, Stogdill (1981) concluded that a leader is characterized by the following traits: a strong drive for responsibility and task completion, vigor and persistence in pursuit of goals, venturousness and originality in problem solving, drive to exercise initiative in social situations, self-confidence and sense of personal identity, willingness to accept consequences of decision and action, readiness to absorb interpersonal stress, willingness to tolerate frustration and delay, ability to influence other persons' behavior, and capacity to structure interaction systems to the purpose at hand. Similarly, Glenn L. Immegart (1988) concluded that the traits of intelligence, dominance, self-confidence, and high energy or activity level are commonly associated with leaders. Nevertheless, the evidence does support the conclusion that the possession of certain traits increases the likelihood that a leader will be effective (Yukl, 2002), but it does not represent a return to the original trait assumption that "leaders are born, not made." Rather, it is a more sensible and balanced view, one that acknowledges the influence of both traits and situations.

Given the plethora of concepts and for ease of discussion, we will classify the trait and skill variables that currently are associated with effective leadership into one of three groups. The categories are: personality, motivation, and skills (see Table 11.1). We will discuss selected traits within each group.[2]

Personality Traits   According to Yukl (2002), **personality traits** are relatively stable dispositions to behave in a particular way. The list of personality factors associated with effective leadership is quite long. Four seem particularly important.

- Self-confident leaders are more likely to set high goals for themselves and their followers, to attempt difficult tasks, and to persist in the face of problems and defeats.
- Stress-tolerant leaders are likely to make good decisions, to stay calm, and to provide decisive direction to subordinates in difficult situations. As shown by the structured observation studies, the pace, long hours, fragmentation, and demands for decisions place leaders under intense pressure that can best be addressed by stress-tolerant individuals.
- Emotionally mature leaders tend to have an accurate awareness of their strengths and weaknesses and to be oriented toward self-

TABLE 11.1

Traits and Skills Associated with Effective Leadership

Personality	Motivation	Skills
Self-confidence	Task and interpersonal needs	Technical
Stress tolerance	Achievement orientation	Interpersonal
Emotional maturity	Power needs	Conceptual
Integrity	Expectations	

improvement; they do not deny their shortcomings or fantasize about success. Consequently, emotionally mature administrators can maintain cooperative relationships with subordinates, peers, and supervisors.

- Integrity means that the behaviors of leaders are consistent with their stated values and that they are honest, ethical, responsible, and trustworthy. Yukl believes that integrity is an essential element in building and retaining loyalty and obtaining cooperation and support of others.

Hence, self-confidence, stress tolerance, emotional maturity, and integrity are personality traits associated with leader effectiveness.

Motivational Traits   Motivation is a set of energetic forces that originate both within as well as beyond an individual to initiate work-related behavior and to determine its form, direction, intensity, and duration. A basic postulate is that motivation factors play key roles in explaining both the choice of action and its degree of success. Generally, highly motivated leaders are likely to be more effective than individuals with low expectations, modest goals and limited self-efficacy. Drawing from the works of several scholars (e.g., Fiedler, 1967; McClelland, 1985; Yukl, 2002), four **motivational traits** are especially critical for leaders.

- Task and interpersonal needs are two underlying dispositions that motivate effective leaders. Effective leaders are characterized by their drive for the task and their concern for people.
- Power needs refer to motives of individuals to seek positions of authority and to exercise influence over others.
- Achievement orientation includes a need to achieve, desire to excel, drive to succeed, willingness to assume responsibility, and a concern for task objectives.
- High expectations for success of school administrators refers to their belief that they can do the job and will receive valued outcomes for their efforts.

In addition to these motivation traits, the physical traits of energy and activity levels allow individuals to exhibit competence through active engagement with others.

In sum, approaching leadership from a trait perspective has a long and productive track record. A number of traits have shown clear and consistent relationships with leader effectiveness. The basic rationale for trait studies is that some personality and motivation traits increase the likelihood that individuals can and will engage in efforts to influence others in regard to factors such as defining appropriate school outcomes, organizing teaching and learning activities, and building a cooperative culture. From a practical standpoint, Northouse (2004) shows how both individuals and organizations can use the trait perspective. Individuals assess their strengths and weaknesses and then take actions to develop their leadership abilities. School organizations seek to identify individuals with particular traits and skills who will fit within and help lead their organizations.

Skills   An important but often neglected component of educational leadership is the skills to complete a job. If one compiled a list of the skills leaders need to solve problems and advance their organizations, it would be a long one. However, a variety of schemes classify the plethora of skills into a small number of groups. A recent model posits that problem-solving skills, social judgment skills, and knowledge make effective leadership possible (Mumford et al., 2000). Similarly, both Yukl (2002) and Northouse (2004) discuss three particularly important categories of skills associated with leader effectiveness: technical, interpersonal, and conceptual.

- Technical skills mean having specialized knowledge about and being adept at a specific type of work, activity, procedure, or technique to accomplish the task. For educational leaders, examples of technical skills are being familiar with school facts (e.g., rules, regulations, enrollment and staffing levels, programs, and demographics), managing budgets, knowing how to implement standards-based accountability, interpreting test results, supervising and coordinating improvements in teaching and learning, evaluating personnel, and maintaining student discipline.
- Interpersonal skills encompass an understanding of feelings and attitudes of others and knowing how to work with people in individual and cooperative work relationships. To be effective, educational leaders display social or human skills naturally, unconsciously, and consistently. Examples of interpersonal skills include communicating clearly through written and oral media, establishing and maintaining cooperative and collaborative relationships, being sociable, and showing sensitivity, empathy, consideration, and tact.
- Conceptual or cognitive skills involve the abilities to form and work with concepts, to think logically, and to reason analytically, deductively, and inductively. In other words, conceptual skills help leaders develop and use ideas to analyze, organize, and solve complex problems; to generate creative alternatives; and to recognize emergent trends, opportunities, and problems. Specific conceptual skills include understanding the interacting structures and processes of school organizations and how change ripples through the component parts; monitoring the external environment and predicting how societal trends will impact schools; and formulating and communicating a vision for the educational organization.

The underlying principle of a skills approach is that leadership requires the mastery of task-relevant knowledge and abilities to formulate and implement solutions to complex social and technical problems and to accomplish goals in an effective fashion (Mumford et al. 2000).

All three skills are required of effective leaders, but the relative priority of each likely depends on the level of administration (Yukl, 2002). Technical skill is especially important for administrators at the lower hierarchical levels, such as assistant principals for instruction or curriculum coordinators, because they work with highly skilled teachers. When leaders move into mid-level positions such as the principalship, they need high degrees of expertise in all three skills. For top-level administrators in the superintendent's office, conceptual skills are particularly important in contributing to leader effectiveness. In comparison to lower-level leaders, upper-level administrators deal with more novel problems, face a wider scope of complex, ambiguous activities, and interact with larger and more diverse groups of constituents. Consequently, as leaders progress in their careers, they must acquire an ever increasing number of skills to solve the new problems that they will confront.

As summarized in Table 11.1, we have identified three sets of characteristics—personality, motivational, and skills—that are related to leadership effectiveness. Although traits are relatively more stable or fixed than skills, both can be assessed, learned, and enhanced through a variety of methods. For example, administrators commonly assert that experience is the best teacher. By learning the job and applying skills in high-stakes situations, experience does have powerful effects. Other less risky or even traumatic alternatives offer ways to make sound judgments about the desirability of becoming an administrator and learning the requisite skills. Good options include assessment centers, personality and skill inventories, internships, job rotations, workshops, and graduate programs in educational leadership and administration. However, the traits and skills associated with effective leadership are many and complex and developing them requires a long process, maybe 10 or more years (Mumford et al., 2000). Nonetheless, whether you are a prospective or practicing administrator, it is fundamentally important to know your strengths and weaknesses, to learn new skills and continue developing old ones, to enhance deficiencies, and to compensate for weaknesses (Yukl, 2002).

Situations and Leadership

Reaction, or perhaps more appropriately overreaction, to the trait approach was so intense during the late 1940s and 1950s that for a time it seemed scholars had substituted a strictly situational analysis for the then-questionable trait approach. The view that leaders are born was rejected (Bass, 1990). Researchers sought to identify distinctive characteristics of the setting to which the leader's success could be attributed; they attempted to isolate specific properties of the **leadership situation** that had relevance for leader behavior

TIP: THEORY INTO PRACTICE

Assessing Your Leadership Potential

Organizations such as schools attempt to select people with traits and skills associated with effective leadership and subsequently try to provide needed professional development activities for further personal growth. Individuals also should be active agents in consciously assessing their strengths and weaknesses for assuming leadership positions. To start the process, we recommend using the traits and skills listed in Table 11.1 and engaging in the following activities:

- As objectively as possible, think about how strongly you like to influence other people and events, especially when doing so calls for exhibiting the traits and skills shown in Table 11.1.
- Find and complete a number of assessment instruments. Northouse (2004), for example, provides relatively simple self-assessment guides for both traits and skills. Northouse's book also is a source for other measures, including a variety of personality, skill, and behavior instruments such as the Least Preferred Co-Worker (LPC) scale and the Multifactor Leadership Questionnaire (MLQ). Many other leadership assessment devices can be found through Internet searches.
- Talk to about five people who know you. Ask them specific questions about how they rate you on variables such as self-confidence, stress tolerance, interpersonal skills, and achievement orientation. You should also request that they describe you using one or more of the leadership assessment instruments.
- Using the information that you have gained in the previous steps, develop a list of your strengths and weaknesses.
- Outline a plan for gaining a leadership position that takes advantage of your strengths, changes or compensates for deficient traits, improves existing skills, and develops new ones.

and performance (Campbell et al., 1970; Lawler, 1985; Vecchio, 1993). As shown throughout this book and summarized in Table 11.2, a number of variables have been postulated to influence behavior in schools and, hence, can be viewed as situational determinants of leadership. A few general examples follow:

- Structural properties of the organization—size, hierarchical structure, formalization, technology.
- Role characteristics—type and difficulty of task, procedural rules, content and performance expectations, power.
- Subordinate characteristics—education, age, knowledge and experience, tolerance for ambiguity, responsibility, power.

TABLE 11.2

Situational Factors of Educational Leadership

Subordinate	Organizational	Internal Environment	External Environment
Personality	Size	Climate	Social
Motivation	Hierarchy	Culture	Economic
Abilities	Formalization		
	Leader role		

- Internal environment—climate, culture, openness, participation levels, group atmosphere, values, and norms.
- External environment—complexity, stability, uncertainty, resource dependency, institutionalization.

Situational factors are particularly important during periods of leader succession. Changing leaders produces naturally occurring instabilities in the organization and offers challenging opportunities for individuals. The replacement of principals or superintendents is disruptive because it changes the lines of communication, realigns relationships of power, affects decision making, and generally disturbs the equilibrium of normal activities. Administrative succession also substantially raises the level of consciousness among organizational participants about the importance of school leaders (Hart, 1993). Those who appoint new leaders, individuals who work with them, and those who may be affected by their actions watch for signs that change will occur. In other words, new leaders face high performance expectations to maintain or improve existing levels of organizational effectiveness (Miskel and Cosgrove, 1985). Critical situational phenomena occur for both the prospective leaders and the school organization before new administrators arrive on the scene and shortly after their arrival. Consequently, candidates for administrator positions who know about key situational factors (for example, how the selection process worked, reasons for the succession, mandates for action, and instability during the succession) can use the knowledge to enhance their success in getting and keeping a leadership position.

John P. Campbell and his colleagues (1970) came to an interesting conclusion about the situational phase of leadership study. Everyone believed that the need for research was great, but actual empirical activity was scarce. Consequently, the jump from "leaders are born, not made" to "leaders are made by the situation, not born," was short-lived. Bass (1990) maintains that the situational view overemphasized the situational and underemphasized the personal nature of leadership. Personal and situational factors have strong reciprocal associations. Leaders exert influence through the situation; the situation supports and limits leader influence. To restrict the study of leadership to either traits or situations, therefore, is unduly narrow and counterproductive.

Behaviors and Leadership

Early conceptualizations of leadership typically relied on two distinct categories of **leader behavior**—one concerned with people, interpersonal relations, and group maintenance, and the other with production, task completion, and goal achievement (Cartwright and Zander, 1953). Similar findings were reflected in other early studies of leadership. We now turn to a description of an early program of research and a more recent perspective on leader behavior.

The Ohio State and Related Leadership Studies

To students of educational administration, probably the most well-known leader research inquiries are the leader behavior description questionnaire (LBDQ) studies started at Ohio State University in the 1940s. Originally developed there by John K. Hemphill and Alvin Coons (1950), the LBDQ was later refined by Andrew Halpin and B. J. Winer (1952). It measures two basic dimensions of leader behavior—initiating structure and consideration.

Initiating structure includes any leader behavior that delineates the relationship between the leader and subordinates and, at the same time, establishes defined patterns of organization, channels of communication, and methods of procedure. **Consideration** includes leader behavior that indicates friendship, trust, warmth, interest, and respect in the relationship between the leader and members of the work group (Halpin, 1966). Using the LBDQ, subordinates, superiors, or the individuals themselves can describe the leader behavior of themselves and each other.

Four major findings emerged from the Ohio State University LBDQ studies (Halpin, 1966).

- Initiating structure and consideration are fundamental dimensions of leader behavior.
- Effective leader behavior tends most often to be associated with frequent behaviors on both dimensions.
- Superiors and subordinates tend to evaluate the contributions of the leader behavior dimensions oppositely in assessing effectiveness. Superiors tend to emphasize initiating structure; subordinates are more concerned with consideration.
- Only a slight relationship exists between how leaders say they should behave and how subordinates describe that they do behave.

The findings of Kunz and Hoy (1976) and Leverette (1984) support the conclusions made by other scholars (Vroom, 1976; House and Baetz, 1979; Mitchell, 1979). Consideration is typically related to subordinate satisfaction with work and with the leader. While the evidence is somewhat mixed, initiating structure has been identified as a source of subordinate performance. However, situational variables apparently affect the relationship between consideration and initiating structure and affect the criteria of organizational effectiveness as well. Consideration has its most positive effect on the satisfaction of subordinates who work in structured situations or who work on stressful, frustrating, or dissatisfying tasks. In contrast, initiating structure has the greatest impact on group performance when subordinates' tasks are ill defined.

The implications of these findings are fairly clear to us. To neglect initiation of structure limits the leader's impact on the school; to ignore consideration reduces the satisfaction of the subordinates. Certainly, leader behavior that integrates strength on both initiating structure and consideration into a consistent pattern is desirable. Nevertheless, the converse also seems likely; there are situations especially favorable to considerate leadership style that are characterized by strong consideration and limited initiating structure. Matching leadership style with the appropriate situation in order to maximize effectiveness is a knotty problem to which we will return throughout this chapter.

A Recent Perspective on Leader Behavior

Yukl (2002) also cautions not to interpret the results of the early studies as universal theories of effective leader behavior. In other words, concluding that the same style of leader behavior is optimal across all situations is not warranted. Blake and Mouton's (1985) managerial grid is a well-known universal theory. Its basic hypothesis is that the most effective leaders are high on both production and people concerns. Production and people concerns are similar to terms in the earlier models such as "task" or "initiating structure" and "relationship" or "consideration." Yukl notes that Blake and Mouton suggest a situational aspect with the idea that the behaviors must be relevant to the situation to be effective. However, they never actually state specific generalizations linking appropriate behaviors to different situations. As we have shown in our discussion of the earlier studies, situational factors do affect the effectiveness of leader behavior, even when an individual is high on both people and task dimensions.

Although we have limited our discussion to structured observations and the Ohio State studies, many listings of leader behavior are found in the literature. To integrate the many typologies and taxonomies, Yukl (2002) developed a three-category framework of leader behavior. His categories and brief descriptions follow.

- Task-oriented behaviors encompass clarifying roles, planning and organizing operations, and monitoring organizational functions.

These actions emphasize accomplishing tasks, using personnel and resources efficiently, maintaining stable and reliable processes, and making incremental improvements.

- Relations-oriented behaviors include supporting, developing, recognizing, consulting, and managing conflict. These activities focus on improving relationships and helping people, increasing cooperation and teamwork, and building commitment to the organization.
- Change-oriented behaviors consist of scanning and interpreting external events, articulating an attractive vision, proposing innovative programs, appealing for change, and creating a coalition to support and implement changes. These acts concentrate on adapting to change in the environment, making major changes in goals, policies, procedures and programs, and gaining commitment to the changes.

Task-oriented and relations-oriented behaviors are similar to initiating structure and consideration, respectively, but are defined more broadly.

Leaders typically engage in all three types of behaviors. Yukl (2002) believes, however, that the external environment plays a particularly important role in determining the appropriate mix for leader effectiveness. In stable environments, task-oriented behavior should be used more frequently than change-oriented behavior. For example, when a school's programs are appropriate to its stable community, the emphasis needs to be such task-oriented behaviors as increasing efficiency and maintaining stable operations. Some change-oriented behaviors are needed in monitoring the environment and diffusing new knowledge. Similarly, relations-oriented behaviors are more feasible in simple stable environments than in complex unstable environments. In uncertain environments, change-oriented behavior is likely to be the most effective. In sum, appropriately applying or balancing different types of behaviors for varying situations is fundamental to enhancing leader performance.

Leadership Effectiveness

The final set of concepts in a contingency model is the criteria used to judge leadership effectiveness. To both practicing administrators and scholars, effectiveness is a complicated, multifaceted, and subtle topic. Three types of effectiveness outcomes are suggested in Table 11.3:

- Personal—other perceptions of reputation and self-assessments.
- Individual member satisfaction.
- Organizational goal attainment.

Perceived evaluations of performance are important: subjective judgments of the leader by himself or herself, subordinates, peers, and superiors within the school and by members of the public outside the school yield measures of effectiveness. In schools, the opinions—for example, respect, ad-

TABLE 11.3		
Effectiveness Indicators for Educational Leaders		
Personal	**Organizational**	**Individual**
Perceived reputation	Goal attainment	Satisfaction
Self-assessment		Performance

miration, and commitment—held by students, teachers, administrators, and patrons are highly significant. However, these groups may view the performance levels quite differently. A second indicator of leadership effectiveness is the satisfaction of organizational participants. Finally, the relative levels of school goal achievement also define the effectiveness of educational leaders (see Chapter 8). **Leadership effectiveness,** then, can be defined as having a more objective dimension—accomplishment of organizational goals—and two subjective dimensions—perceptual evaluations of significant reference groups and overall job satisfaction of subordinates.

Contingency Models of Leadership

Hitting their zenith in the 1970s, contingency approaches such as the general model shown in Figure 11.1 were the most influential models of leadership into the 1980s. At their best, **contingency approaches** include the four sets of concepts that we have just considered—traits of leaders, characteristics of the situation, behaviors of the leader, and effectiveness of the leader. Two basic hypotheses are shown in Figure 11.1. First, traits and skills of the leaders and characteristics of the situation combine to produce leader behavior and

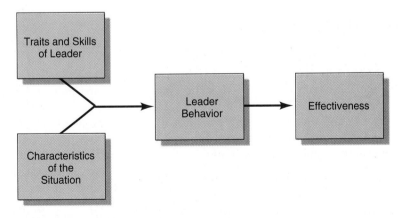

FIGURE 11.1   *A Contingency Schema for Understanding Leadership*

effectiveness. Second, situational factors directly impact effectiveness. For example, the motivation and ability levels of teachers and students are related to the goal attainment of schools. Moreover, the socioeconomic status of individuals attending a school is strongly related to student achievement on standardized tests. From a short-range perspective, at least, the situational characteristics of the school may have a greater influence on leader effectiveness than a leader's own behavior. Contingency approaches also seek to specify the conditions or situational variables that moderate the relationship among leader traits, behaviors, and performance criteria (Bryman, 1996). The evidence indicates that in one set of circumstances, one type of leader is effective; under another set of circumstances, a different type of leader is effective.

Bossert, David C. Dwyer, Rowan, and Ginny V. Lee (1982) developed a specific contingency model to describe and explain instructional leadership of principals. Their model hypothesizes that personal, district, and external environment characteristics influence the management behaviors of principals, which in turn affect school climate and instructional organization. School climate and instructional organization then shape teachers' behavior and students' learning experiences that produce student learning. Ronald Heck, Terry J. Larsen, and George A. Marcoulides (1990) empirically tested the model and found substantial support for its basic hypothesis. Principals influence student achievement indirectly by creating instructional organizations in their schools through participative actions and by building school climates and cultures characterized by clearly communicated goals and high expectations for academic achievement and social behavior.

We will briefly review three general contingency models for leadership: least preferred co-worker, substitutes for leadership, and path-goal theories. Each theory has received considerable attention across a wide range of organizations.

Least Preferred Co-worker Theory

Fiedler (1967) constructed the first major theory to propose specific contingency relationships in the study of leadership. Lacking a behavior component, the least preferred co-worker model uses leader style as a trait, three indicators of situational control, and effectiveness.

Leadership style is determined by the motivational system of the leader, that is, the underlying needs structure that motivates behavior in various interpersonal situations. The least preferred co-worker (LPC) scale is used to measure this trait. Using the LPC, a respondent selects the person with whom he or she works least well (least preferred co-worker) and then describes that individual on the scale. A person scoring high on the LPC describes the least preferred co-worker positively as being pleasant, loyal, warm, kind, efficient, and so forth. In contrast, the individual scoring low on the LPC describes the least preferred co-worker negatively as being unpleasant, backbiting, cold, unkind, inefficient, and so forth. The LPC score indicates the extent to which the individual sets a higher priority or value on task accomplishment (task-motivated) or on maintaining good interpersonal relations (relationship-motivated) (Fiedler and Garcia, 1987).

Situational control is the degree of power and influence that leaders have to implement plans, decisions, and action strategies (Fiedler and Garcia, 1987). Situational control is determined by three factors. First, *position power* is the power that the organization confers on the leader for the purpose of getting the job done. Examples include the extent to which a leader can reward and punish members and whether the group can depose the leader. Second, *task structure* is the extent to which the task has clearly specified goals, methods, and standards of performance. The more structured the task, the more control the leader has in directing the group. Third, *leader-member relations* is the extent to which the leader is accepted and respected by group members. Two factors are important with respect to leader-member relations: the quality of interpersonal relations between the leader and subordinates, and the level of informal authority granted to the leader. The quality of leader-member relations is the most important factor in determining the leader's influence over group members, followed by task structure and position power. Fiedler formed eight situations by dichotomizing the three factors—that is, good or bad leader-member relations, structured or unstructured tasks, and high or low position power. The eight combinations or octants map the range of situations from high control to low control. The basic contention is that the leader has more control and influence when the group is supportive, the leader knows exactly what to do and how to do it, and the organization gives the leader means to reward and punish the group members.

Fiedler, Chemers, and Mahar (1976) proposed that administrators such as principals can be trained to modify aspects of their situation. They developed a program to teach leaders how to analyze their situations in terms of leader-member relations, task structure, and position power, and based on the analysis, to change the conditions that will improve group performance.

Effectiveness in the least preferred co-worker theory is straightforward—namely, the extent to which the group accomplishes its primary task. In many of Fiedler's studies, objective measures of group effectiveness are used—net profit, cost per unit, percentage of wins, number of problems solved. If a reliable objective measure of group performance is not available, then performance ratings by the supervisor of the leader or group are used. But in all cases, leader effectiveness is determined by the degree to which the task is judged to be achieved.

From data collected before 1962, Fiedler developed three propositions for his contingency theory:

- In high-control situations, task-oriented leaders are more effective than relationship-oriented leaders.
- In moderate-control situations, relationship-oriented leaders are more effective than task-oriented leaders.
- In low-control situations, task-oriented leaders are more effective than relationship-oriented leaders.

Two studies provide rigorous and complete tests of the model—that is, investigations that meet Fiedler's criteria and include leaders from all eight situations. One study was supportive (Chemers and Skrzypek, 1972); one was not (Vecchio, 1977). Moreover, three meta-analyses (Strube and Garcia, 1981; Peters, Hartke, and Pohlman, 1985; Crehan, 1985) of research testing the contingency model provide some support, but not for all octants and not as strongly for field studies as for laboratory studies. In school settings, findings from a number of studies also partially test and support Fiedler's theory (McNamara and Enns, 1966; Williams and Hoy, 1973; Martin, Isherwood, and Lavery, 1976).

The LPC theory has been subjected to several criticisms. Probably the most persistent objection is that the definition has changed over the years concerning what the LPC measures. At first, it was seen simply as a measure of an emotional reaction to individuals with whom the leader found it difficult to work; then it was thought to differentiate between individuals who had a task orientation as opposed to an interpersonal one; later the LPC score was interpreted as an indicator of a leader's motivational hierarchy. Overall, Fiedler's theory represents an ambitious and laudable effort to build a powerful contingency theory of leadership. Although interest has waned, the model demonstrates that a combination of situational and individual characteristics partly explains the leadership phenomenon. Like most pioneering efforts, it undoubtedly is incorrect in detail if not in substance. Yet Fiedler's contingency model was the first and, to date, the longest-lasting attempt to answer the question, What particular style in what special situation?

Substitutes for Leadership Model

An assumption of contingency models other than this one is that some kind of formal leadership is needed and important in organizations such as schools (Howell, 1997). Steven Kerr and John M. Jermier (1978) questioned this assumption and created the **substitutes for leadership model.** The primary concepts of this contingency model are supportive and instrumental leader behaviors, situational variables that act as substitutes and neutralizers for leadership, and outcome variables. *Substitutes* are persons or things that make person-oriented or task-oriented behavior unnecessary and redundant. In other words, substitutes are situational aspects that replace or reduce a leader's ability to influence the attitudes, perceptions, or behaviors of followers. In contrast, *neutralizers* do not replace leader behaviors but are situational factors that prevent a leader from acting in a particular way or that nullify the effects of the leader's actions. For example, a principal's lack of authority to reward a teacher's effective performance is situational constraint on the leader behavior, whereas the teacher's lack of interest in an incentive offered by the principal is a condition that makes the behavior pointless (Yukl, 1998).

Kerr and Jermier (1978) identify three categories of situational variables that have the potential to act as leader substitutes. First, characteristics of subordinates include their abilities, training, experience and knowledge, professional orientation, and indifference toward rewards. Second, task characteristics comprise structured routine tasks, intrinsically satisfying tasks, and feedback provided by the task. Third, organizational characteristics consist of such things as formalization of roles and procedures, flexibility of rules and policies, work group cohesiveness, and spatial distance between the administrator and followers. The substitutes for leaders model sees performance as dependent on subordinate, task, and organizational characteristics rather than on those of the leader. For example, when the subordinates have high ability, are experienced and knowledgeable, or the task is unambiguous and routine, task-oriented leadership is not needed. Similarly, when the task is intrinsically satisfying or the work group is closely knit and cohesive, relationship or supportive leadership is of limited usefulness.

Philip M. Podsakoff and his colleagues (1993) conclude that the theory has generated substantial interest because it helps explain why leader behaviors have significant effects in some situations and may have no effects in others. Although results from recent attempts to test the model have not been particularly supportive, Podsakoff and his colleagues conclude that it is necessary to consider both leader behaviors and substitutes to understand how employee attitudes, behaviors, and role perceptions are determined. In sum, they believe that the leadership substitutes model should receive additional attention.

Reformulated Path-Goal Theory

House (1971, 1973) initially developed the path-goal theory of leadership, and House and Mitchell (1974) refined it. With 40 to 50 studies lending mixed support for the model, House (1996) made a major overhaul of the theory. For example, he expanded the number of leader behaviors and outcome variables, modernized the situational concepts, and formulated 26 specific propositions or hypotheses. The major concepts—leader behavior, situational factors, and effectiveness—comprising the reformulated path-goal theory are shown in Table 11.4.

TABLE 11.4

Concepts in the Reformulated Path-Goal Theory of Leadership

Leader Behaviors		Situation	Outcomes
Path-goal clarifying	Group decision process	Subordinate motivation	Subordinate satisfaction
Achievement oriented	Representation		Subordinate empowerment
Work facilitation	Networking	Subordinate abilities	Subordinate effectiveness
Supportive	Value based		
Interaction facilitation	Shared	Task demands	Work unit effectiveness

Based in expectancy motivation theory, the model's core assumption is that followers will be motivated if they believe they are capable of doing the work, that their efforts will produce desired outcomes, and that the rewards for doing the work will be worthwhile (Northouse, 2004). Its overall proposition is that subordinate satisfaction and individual and work unit effectiveness increase as leaders engage in behaviors that complement the task environments and subordinates' abilities and compensate for deficiencies. To illustrate the specific propositions of this complex theory, five leader behaviors will be defined and then related to the situational and outcome variables through five specific propositions.

First, under certain conditions, a leader's **path-goal clarifying behaviors** are capable of making subordinates' needs and preferences contingent on effective performance. These include clarifying performance goals, means to carry out the tasks, standards of performance, expectations of others, and rewards and punishments for subordinates. This leads to the proposition that when task demands of subordinates are satisfying but ambiguous, path-goal clarifying behaviors by superiors will be a source of clarification and subordinate satisfaction will be motivational.

Second, **achievement-oriented leader behavior** is behavior that encourages excellent performance, sets challenging goals, seeks improvement, and shows confidence that subordinates will attain high performance standards. More than merely emphasizing performance or goals, it depends on the motivational orientations of the subordinates. Hence, House (1996) proposes that achievement-oriented leader behavior will be effective when performed by superiors who administer subordinates who have individual responsibility and control over their work.

Third, **supportive leader behavior** displays a concern for subordinates' welfare, creates a friendly and psychologically supportive work environment, and takes into account subordinates' needs and preferences. Such behavior is particularly needed when the situation is dangerous, monotonous, stressful, or frustrating. Conversely, House (1996) proposes that when tasks are intrinsically satisfying or the situation is not stressful, supportive leader behavior will have limited effect on follower satisfaction, motivation, or performance.

Fourth, **value-based leader behavior** appeals to followers' treasured values, enhances their self-efficacy and sense of consistency, and makes their self-worth contingent on contributing to the leaders' mission. Behaviors include articulating a vision or ideological goal for a better future for the followers, displaying passion for the vision, and using symbolic behaviors to emphasize the values contained in collective vision. Because ideological visions often challenge the status quo, their expression is often suppressed. Hence, when the values inherent in the vision of a value-based leader are in conflict with the dominant coalition or prevailing culture of the organization, value-based leadership will induce substantial intergroup conflict.

Finally, **shared leadership** occurs when the formally appointed leader shares the leader behaviors with members of the work group. Following research that found peer leadership to be more strongly related to effectiveness than leadership exercised by formal administrators, House (1996) offers the following proposition: When the work is interdependent within the work unit, encouragement by the leader of collaborative shared responsibility for performing leader behaviors will enhance work unit cohesiveness and performance.

Any given leader is unlikely to have the ability to engage in all or even most of the 10 sets of behavior. On the basis of their personalities and inventories of abilities, House (1996) contends that effective leaders will select the behaviors with which they are most comfortable. In addition, some of the behaviors are probably substitutable for each other. For example, articulating a vision coupled with modeling appropriate behaviors may substitute for path-goal clarifying behaviors. Some of the moderating variables may substitute for each other. Task-relevant knowledge may substitute for task structure.

Although the reformulated path-goal theory of leadership has not yet been tested empirically, House (1996) maintains that it is consistent with and integrates the predictions from other current leadership theories and empirical generalizations. It is limited, however, in not dealing with emergent informal leadership, political behavior of leaders, leadership as it affects several levels of administrators or subordinates in organizations, or leadership for change.

Changing Leadership Perspectives

In presenting the trait, behavior, situational, and contingency approaches, we have tended to follow a historical sequence of knowledge development for leadership. Most of the theory development and research on these traditional models occurred before 1980. The accumulated knowledge from these approaches is substantial and provides significant insights about leadership. Nevertheless, James G. Hunt (1999) describes the development of a sense of "doom and gloom" about the study of leadership during the 1970s. A number of scholars questioned the usefulness of the leadership concept (e.g., Lieberson and O'Connor, 1972; Salancik and Pfeffer, 1977; McCall and Lombardo, 1978; Kerr and Jermier, 1978). Scholars saw little new conceptual capital being created and thought the massive number of leadership studies had produced a field that was rigorous, boring, and static. Most important, the research examined more and more the inconsequential questions and provided little new knowledge.

Amid cries of catastrophe, a bright spot—transformational leadership—appeared to save the day (Hunt, 1999). With new ideas of visionary and change-oriented leadership, the doom and gloom atmosphere was transformed during the 1980s to a burst of enthusiasm for the "new leadership."

A MODEL OF TRANSFORMATIONAL LEADERSHIP

James MacGregor Burns (1978) is commonly credited with formulating the ideas of transactional and transformational leadership and applying them in the political arena. Building on Burns's ideas, Bass (1985a) constructed a wide-ranging and highly influential model for leaders in social organizations. The basic framework of transformational leadership can be conceptualized using a continuum, which Bass (1998) calls a "full range leadership model." As shown in Table 11.5, Bass identifies three major types of leadership: laissez-faire, transactional, and transformational. While the three types of leadership have remained constant, the number of factors or components comprising the three types has varied (Avolio, Bass, and Jung, 1999). The formulation shown in Table 11.5 uses the nine factors—one for laissez-faire, three for transactional, and five for transformational (Antonakis, Avolio, and Sivasubramaniam, 2003).

Three Types of Leadership

Laissez-Faire Leadership

Bass (1998) characterizes this type of leadership as the absence of transactions with followers. For instance, laissez-faire leaders avoid expressing their views or taking action on important issues, fail to make or at least delay decisions, ignore responsibilities, provide no feedback, and allow authority to remain dormant. It essentially is the avoidance or absence of leadership, and consequently is the most passive and least effective. An example would be a principal who stays in the office, engages faculty and students as little as possible, shows minimal concern for the learning and development of students or needs of the teachers, and allows school structures and processes to continue in the same way.

Transactional Leadership

Transactional leaders motivate followers by exchanging rewards for services rendered—for example, a principal provides new instructional materials or increased planning time to teachers so they can institute a new curricular program. When subordinates are doing their work in organizations such as schools, transactional leaders recognize what followers want from work and try to provide them with what they want. They exchange rewards and promises of reward for effort and respond to followers' immediate self-interests. Transactional leaders pursue a cost-benefit, economic exchange to meet followers' current material and psychological needs in return for contracted services rendered by the subordinate (Bass, 1985a).

As shown in Table 11.5, transactional leadership is posited to have three components (Antonakis, Avolio, and Sivasubramaniam, 2003). **Contingent reward leadership** refers to leader behaviors that focus on clarifying role and task requirements and provide followers with rewards contingent on the fol-

---

TABLE 11.5

A Full-Range Leadership Continuum

Full-Range Leadership Continuum

Laissez-Faire Leadership	Transactional Leadership	Transformational Leadership
1. Nontransactional	2. Contingent reward leadership	5. Idealized influence-attributed
	3. Management-by-exception-active	6. Idealized influence-behavior
	4. Management-by-exception-passive	7. Inspirational motivation
		8. Intellectual stimulation
		9. Individualized consideration

---

lower's performance. In other words, this subtype of leadership behavior gives followers things they want in exchange for things leaders want (Kuhnert and Lewis, 1987). **Active management-by-exception** means that leaders maintain high levels of vigilance to ensure that standards are met. That is, leaders actively monitor performance and take corrective action as problems become apparent. **Passive management-by-exception** means that leaders fail to intervene until problems become serious. These leaders wait to take action until after mistakes or other performance problems have happened and are called to their attention.

Transformational Leadership

Bass views transformational leadership as an expansion of transactional leadership that goes beyond simple exchanges and agreements. Transformational leaders are proactive, raise the awareness levels of followers about inspirational collective interests, and help followers achieve unusually high performance outcomes. The theory posits that four I's comprise transformational leadership: *i*dealized influence, *i*nspirational motivation, *i*ntellectual stimulation, and *i*ndividualized consideration (Antonakis, Avolio, and Sivasubramaniam, 2003).

Idealized influence builds trust and respect in followers and provides the basis for accepting radical and fundamental changes in the ways individuals and organizations do their work. These leaders display conviction about important issues; exhibit high standards of ethical and moral conduct, sharing risks with followers in setting and attaining goals; consider the needs of others over their own; and use power to move individuals or groups toward accomplishing their mission, vision, and cause, but never for personal gain. As a result, transformational leaders are admired, respected, and trusted. Followers identify with their leaders and want to emulate them. Without such trust and commitment to the leaders, attempts to change and redirect the organization's mission are likely to be met with extreme resistance (Avolio, 1994). Idealized influence results from transformational leaders behaving as role models for their followers.

In recent formulations of the model, idealized influence has been divided into two subtypes. **Attributed idealized influence** is the extent to which followers *perceive* leaders as being charismatic, confident, powerful, and focused on higher-order ideals and ethics. In contrast, **idealized influence as behavior** is charismatic actions of leaders that focus on values, beliefs, and a sense of mission (Antonakis, Avolio, and Sivasubramaniam, 2003).

Inspirational motivation changes the expectations of group members to believe that the organization's problems can be solved (Atwater and Bass, 1994). It also plays a central role in developing an appealing vision that guides the development of organizational goals and operating procedures (Avolio, 1994). Inspirational motivation comes primarily from leader behaviors that provide meaning and challenge for followers. Transformational leaders energize people by projecting an attractive and optimistic future, emphasizing ambitious goals, and creating idealized visions for the organization and clearly communicating to followers that the vision is attainable. Hence, team spirit, enthusiasm, optimism, goal commitment, and a shared vision arise and coalesce within the work group or organization (Bass and Avolio, 1994).

Intellectual stimulation addresses the problem of creativity (Atwater and Bass, 1994). Transformational leaders stimulate followers to be innovative and creative by questioning old assumptions, traditions, and beliefs; reframing problems; and approaching old situations in new ways. Transformational leaders challenge followers to think creatively, design new procedures and programs, and solve difficult problems; foster unlearning and eliminate the fixation on old ways of doing things; and refrain from publicly criticizing individual members for mistakes (Bass and Avolio, 1994). Leaders insist on constant open examination of everything and total receptivity to change (Avolio, 1994). In turn, followers stimulate their leaders to reconsider their own perspectives and assumptions. Nothing is too good, too fixed, too political, or too bureaucratic that it cannot be contested, changed, or cleared out (Avolio, 1999).

Individualized consideration means that transformational leaders pay particular attention to each individual's needs for achievement and growth. The purpose of individualized consideration is to determine the needs and strengths of others (Atwater and Bass, 1994). Using this knowledge and acting as mentors, transformational leaders help followers and colleagues develop to successively higher levels of potential and to take responsibility for their own development (Avolio, 1994). Creating new learning opportunities in a supportive climate, recognizing and accepting individual differences in needs and values, using two-way communication, and interacting with others in a personalized fashion are necessary behaviors to accomplish individualized consideration. The individually considerate leader listens actively and effectively.

Most research studies measuring the primary factors and testing transformational leadership theory have used the multifactor leadership questionnaire (MLQ). Early versions of MLQ were severely criticized (Sashkin and Burke, 1990). Since its introduction, the content of the MLQ has changed and been refined to increase the items describing observable leader behaviors. A recent evaluation of the MLQ found support for the nine-factor model shown in Table 11.5 (Antonakis, Avolio, and Sivasubramaniam, 2003).

Theory and Research about Transformational Leadership

Bass (1998) and Avolio (1999) contend that transactional leadership forms the basis of a sustainable leadership system. For instance, if leaders stand by their many transactions with followers, over time the people come to trust their leaders. It is this higher level of trust and identification that transformational leaders use as a foundation for achieving exemplary performance. Transformational leadership does not replace transactional leadership but does augment or expand its effects on follower motivation, satisfaction, and performance. Hence, these types of leadership can be represented as points on the same leadership continuum as shown in Table 11.5.

However, transformational leadership goes well beyond exchanging inducements for desired performance (Bennis and Nanus, 1985; Tichy and Devanna, 1986; Howell and Frost, 1989; Howell and Avolio, 1993). Transformational leaders build commitment to the organization's objectives and empower followers to achieve these objectives (Yukl, 2002). As illustrated above in the descriptions of the four I's, transformational leaders are expected to define the need for change, create new visions and muster commitment to the visions, concentrate on long-term goals, inspire followers to transcend their own interests to pursue higher-order goals, change the organization to accommodate their vision rather than work within the existing one, and mentor followers to take greater responsibility for their own development and that of others. Followers become leaders and leaders become change agents and ultimately transform the organization.

The source of transformational leadership is in the personal values and beliefs of leaders. By expressing their personal standards, transformational leaders are able to both unite followers and change their goals and beliefs in ways that produce higher levels of performance than previously thought possible (Kuhnert and Lewis, 1987). Indeed, Thomas J. Sergiovanni (1994) argues that the heart of leadership talk is conceptions, values, and ideas. House (1988) further maintains that transformational leadership depends on leaders effectively expressing their need for power by using metaphors and other imagery to represent socially desirable examples of change and outcomes.

Similarly, Bass (1985a, 1998) observes that transformational leadership is seen when leaders stimulate others to view their work from new perspectives, generate an awareness of the mission or vision of the organization, develop colleagues and followers to higher levels of ability and potential, and motivate them to look beyond their own interests toward those that will benefit the group. Transformational leaders set more challenging goals and typically achieve higher performances than transactional leaders.

In an overall assessment of the theory, Yukl (1999) concludes that transformational leadership seems to be making important contributions to the explanation of leadership processes and outcomes. In particular, it relies on important symbolic aspects and is more than just the technical and interpersonal aspects of efficient management. It rests upon meanings as well as actions, and leaders make meanings. However, Yukl contends that additional emphasis on situational variables that both limit and facilitate transformational leadership is needed, even though the model has wide applicability.

Situational Factors

Proponents of transformational leadership theory tend to deemphasize the importance of the setting or context. Bass (1997), for example, argues that the transformational leadership model is valid across situations and cultures. Bass (1998) does recognize crisis situations as being highly important. He asserts that for leaders to be effective in crisis conditions, they must be transformational and rise above what their followers see as their immediate needs and appropriate responses. Only transformational leaders can arouse their followers to see the threats and their lack of preparedness and provide goals to transcend self-interests and to provide confident direction. Bass (1998) further acknowledges that a number of situational conditions (e.g., environment, organization, task and goals, and distribution of power between the leaders and followers) will likely influence the emergence and success of both transactional and transformational leadership. Three contextual factors that were found to be important are follower gender, level of environmental risk, and leader hierarchical level (Antonakis, Avolio, and Sivasubramaniam, 2003).

Research

Since the introduction of transformational leadership in the mid-1980s, a vast research literature about it has developed. According to Avolio (1999), research findings support a number of generalizations dealing with the factors forming transactional leadership. For example, idealized influence and inspirational leadership are the most effective and satisfying; intellectual stimulation and individualized consideration have somewhat less effect. All are more effective than transactional leadership. Overall, then, transformational leadership is close to what people have in mind when they describe their ideal leader. Practically, it means that leaders develop in their followers an expectation of high performance rather than merely spending time in transactional activities. In other words, the leader must be a developer of people and a builder of teams (Bass, 1990).

In regard to the overall theory, findings from studies using the MLQ indicate that transformational leaders receive higher ratings, are perceived as leading more effective organizations, and have subordinates who exert greater effort than transactional leaders (Yukl, 1999). Likewise, Bass (1998) concludes that research evidence clearly demonstrates that transformational leadership can move followers to exceed expected performance. In comparison to transactional leadership, he believes that transformational leadership generates greater subordinate effort, commitment, and satisfaction. Other scholars tend to be positive about the model as well.

In educational settings, the best-known work has been conducted by Keith Leithwood. In a four-year study of schools making a variety of structural changes, Leithwood (1994) assessed the effects of seven dimensions of transformational leadership. His conceptual framework is based on two assertions. First, transformational leadership in schools directly affects such school outcomes as teacher perceptions of student goal achievement and student grades. Second, transformational leadership indirectly affects these outcomes by influencing three critical psychological characteristics of staff—perceptions of school characteristics, teacher commitment to change, and organizational learning—which in turn affect the outcomes. From his research, Leithwood draws the following generalizations:

- Transformational leadership depends on attending to all aspects of leadership—for example, in Bass's terms, idealized influence, inspirational motivation, intellectual stimulation, and individualized consideration.
- School organizations may require unique formulations of transformational leadership with its base being individualized consideration.
- Except for expert thinking, transformational leadership represents a contingency approach.
- Distinctions between management and leadership cannot be made in terms of observed behavior.

Leithwood concludes that reasonably robust support exists for the claim that transformational forms of leadership are of significant value in restructuring schools. Similarly, H. C. Silins (1992) found that transformational leaders have greater positive effects on schools than transactional leaders. Recently, Helen M. Marks and Susan M. Printy (2003) examined the effects of two forms of leadership—transformation and instruction—on the quality of pedagogy and student achievement. They found that when two types of leadership are coupled throughout schools, high-quality pedagogy and high levels of student performance are also evident.

Overall, transformational leadership theory is being used widely and is generally supported by numerous research studies. Consequently, a model of transformational leadership can provide intellectual capital for educational leaders as they confront the challenges of modernizing their school organizations. As has been made clear throughout this book, making fundamental changes in any of the major components of schools is typically fraught with ambiguity and resistance. Transformational leadership offers some promise in overcoming these difficulties. To lead transformational initiatives, however, requires a range of abilities, skills, and behaviors that, according to Bass (1998), can be developed, taught, and learned. Some evidence does uphold the hypothesis that transformational leadership can be enhanced through formal training (Dvir, Eden, Avolio, and Shamir, 2002). Hence, current and prospective leaders ought to consider whether a training program would elevate their capacity to transform schools.

TIP: THEORY INTO PRACTICE

Analysis of Transformational Leadership

Study the nine factors of transformational leadership shown in Table 11.5, the narrative in this chapter, and if possible, the MLQ's measurement of leadership. Sources for obtaining the MLQ include Northouse (2004, pp. 194–197) and Mind Garden, Inc. (www.mindgarden.com).

- As an individual or in a small group, think of a principal or other leader with whom you have worked. Describe the individual using the nine factors in Table 11.5. The description should be as explicit as possible, including examples of behavior the individual displayed and how the followers reacted.
- Think of yourself in an actual or imagined leadership situation and repeat the foregoing analysis.

DISTRIBUTED LEADERSHIP

Scholars in education have recently become quite enthused about building and applying frameworks for organizational or distributed leadership. In contrast to approaches that emphasize or in some cases romanticize leadership by individuals such as principals as being "the key" to school effectiveness, distributed models embrace leadership by teams, groups, and organizational characteristics. Practically, these approaches challenge the common assumption that one person has to be in charge to make change happen (Heller and Firestone, 1995).

The basic idea of distributed leadership is straightforward (Elmore, 2000)—it means relying on multiple sources of leadership across the organization to guide and complete numerous tasks that vary in size, complexity, and scope. These include recurring and routine tasks, such as budget hearings, staff meetings, and annual evaluations, and unanticipated tasks such as emergencies and highly salient problems (Gronn, 2002), as well as change functions such as sustaining a vision for change, encouraging others, modifying existing procedures, monitoring progress, and handling disturbances (Heller and Firestone, 1995). Proponents claim that distributed leadership is necessary because school organizations are so complex and the tasks so wide-ranging that no single person has the energy and skill to handle all of the leadership functions. As a consequence, the responsibility for leading these tasks is distributed across multiple individuals and roles, for example, central office administrators, principals, assistant principals, teachers, other staff members, external consultants, parents, and students.

It seems pretty obvious that distributed or organizational leadership is not a new phenomenon. Schools and other organizations have always practiced a division of labor for leadership responsibilities (Gronn, 2002), but conceptions of individual, heroic, or solo leadership have dominated both the popular and scholarly literatures. Educational reformers and policy makers, according to Eric Camburn, Brian Rowan, and James Taylor (2003), expanded their focus during the 1980s to recognize the importance of both individual and distributed leadership. For example, site-based management and career ladders for teachers represent policy initiatives that attempted to incorporate additional leadership roles into schools. Educational scholars intensified their efforts to develop frameworks and conduct research on distributed leadership during the 1990s, although Peter Gronn (2002: 424) recently concludes that "there is a dearth of extended, analytical discussions of the concept." Keeping Gronn's caution in mind, two early formulations will be considered.

Ogawa and Bossert (1995) conceive leadership as an organizational quality. They argue that all members of the organization can lead and that leadership goes beyond distributing the functions across individuals in the organization. Leadership also flows through the network of roles that comprise school organizations and influences individuals, structures, cultures, and how work is produced and coordinated. Furthermore, the amount of leadership varies over time and across schools. Extending these ideas, Diana G. Pounder, Ogawa, and E. Ann Adams (1995) hypothesize that several groups contribute to school leadership and the total amount of leadership is positively related to school performance. They found general support for the hypothesis and speculated that efforts to implement shared decision making (see Chapter 9) and other forms of distributed leadership have the potential to improve school effectiveness.

James Spillane and his colleagues (Spillane, Halverson, and Diamond, 2001; 2003; Spillane, Hallett, and Diamond, 2003) offer a model of distributed leadership that is focused rather narrowly on leading the technical core of schools, especially practices directed toward improving teaching and learning in reading, mathematics, and science. School leadership is defined as "the identification, acquisition, allocation, coordination, and use of social, material, cultural resources necessary to establish the conditions for the possibility of teaching and learning" (Spillane, Halverson, and Diamond, 2001: 24). Reasoning that principals and superintendents cannot succeed alone, multiple formal and informal leaders and their followers are mobilized to guide and do the tasks necessary to transform or make major changes in their schools. Spillane and his associates further postulate that leadership is stretched over two or more leaders, their followers, and the material and symbolic artifacts in the situation. In this perspective, the situation is a defining element because as tasks are carried out, leadership practice emerges in and through the interaction of leaders, followers, and situation. For example, the distribution and quantity of leadership vary by subject area. Mathematics instruction appears to have fewer leaders than language arts and science even fewer. In sum, distributed school leadership is more than what individual leaders know and do; it is constructed through the dynamic interaction of multiple leaders, followers, and their situation as particular leadership tasks are enacted (Spillane, Halverson, and Diamond, 2001).

Many comprehensive school reform initiatives call for shared or distributed leadership and offer excellent sites to research the phenomenon. For instance, Camburn, Rowan, and Taylor (2003), found that schools implementing Accelerated Schools, America's Choice, and Success for All programs had about 1.5 more leadership positions than comparison schools and that the effects of staff development significantly increased the likelihood that the new leaders would actually engage in instructional leadership. Similarly, Amanda Datnow and Marisa Eileen Castellano (2001) examined the shared leadership roles of principal and teacher facilitator roles in schools implementing Success for All programs. They found that both roles were critical for successful implementation. Principal leadership was especially important in selecting the Success for All initiative. However, when the facilitators started defining their roles and relationships with principals and teachers, they experienced significant ambiguity and tension, and had to expend considerable effort in negotiating their place in the reform effort. As would be expected, when a new leadership model is introduced into traditional school structures and cultures, the participants (for example, principals, teachers, and facilitators) have to reconcile their various conceptions of leadership and improve their skills at collaboration and reform leadership.

Our early assessment of the distributed leadership theory is that it has excellent potential for adding to our knowledge of educational leadership. To fulfill its potential requires extensive conceptual development and empirical testing. Without such advances, distributed leadership could easily become idealized, oversimplified, and romanticized. As has been the case with many highly popular ideas (for example, democratic administration during the mid-20th century and total quality management—TQM—during the 1990s), "distributed leadership theory" could become very long on rhetoric and woefully short on research and practice (Campbell, 1971). Moreover, widely held conceptions of good administrative practice require that one or a few individuals be held responsible for the overall leadership and performance of the organization. Nonetheless, distributed leadership is a pervasive, important, and underrecognized phenomenon in the administration of schools. Hence, our conclusion is that individual and distributed leadership approaches certainly do not negate or even lessen the significance of the other, but offer complementary perspectives on leading schools.

TIP: THEORY INTO PRACTICE

Analysis of Distributed Leadership

According to the models of distributed leadership, schools rely on a variety of individuals and roles to accomplish leadership tasks. Consider a school in which you have worked or of which you have knowledge and list the individual leaders by name and organizational role. What leadership functions did they fulfill? How harmonious and effective was your leadership team? Why? How applicable are distributed leadership models to practice?

Finally, leadership in schools is a complex and ambiguous process, which includes balancing technical and symbolic demands (Deal and Peterson, 1994). It involves more than mastering a set of skills, finding the right situation, exhibiting a certain style of behavior, combining these factors in a contingency approach, or even deciding to become a transformational leader. Matching the appropriate leader traits and behaviors with a specific situation is important, but so too are the human, symbolic and cultural sides of leadership. The issue is not one of choosing between leadership as an instrumental and behavioral activity and leadership as a symbolic and cultural one; it is clearly both and more. Hence, we strongly maintain that while simple formulations of leadership, such as offering five exemplary practices and 10 commitments (Kouzes and Posner, 2002) or universal level five leadership (Collins, 2001), may have palliative effects on harried administrators, they deliver few productive effects on performance outcomes. Instead, we believe that building effective capacity for leading educational organizations demands using the best ideas from existing models, building new theories and empirically testing them, and employing the knowledge to create intensive professional development programs for current and prospective leaders of our schools.

A CASE FOR LEADERSHIP

District Leadership and Systemic Reform

For the past five years, you have been the superintendent of Camargo Unified School District. Located in the Southwest, the school district enrolls about 5,000 students. As a consolidated district, the students come from the surrounding rural areas and from city neighborhoods. The average expenditure per student is about $7,000 per year. Other than the typical variations in family income and rural-city attendance area, the district is rather homogeneous. About 15 percent of the students are Hispanic and about 2 percent are Native American. During your tenure, you have worked energetically to establish trust with many constituencies, including the board of education, other administrators, teachers, business leaders, and parents from the rural and city areas. In a real sense, you have become a respected member of the community. As superintendent, you have set high expectations for school improvement and performance. The other educators and students have responded positively and Camargo School District now is seen as high achieving and well managed. In a front-page story, the local newspaper recently asserted that the district had been transformed under your leadership.

During the fall of your fifth year at Camargo, the president of a national search firm approached you about applying for the position of superintendent of the Willow Tree School District. This relatively affluent district of about 15,000 students is located in a large metropolitan area in the upper Midwest. Being ambitious and wanting to try new challenges, you investigate the district by visiting Willow Tree School District's website and other websites for area businesses, governments, and media outlets. You find that the district has 20 elementary, 6 middle, 3 comprehensive high schools and 3 other special and alternative schools. The

teaching staff is highly qualified with about 75 percent of them holding master's degrees and above. In addition, the average expenditure is about $9,000 per student. Although the district appears rather homogeneous and wealthy, you note that minority students, mostly African American and Hispanic, comprise about 15 percent of the enrollment. By consulting the school report card at the governor's website, you find the district's scores on the state achievement test to be relatively high at about the 65 percentile and stable over the past five years.

With encouragement from the search firm and the tremendous professional opportunity for you, you apply for the position in Willow Tree and are invited for an interview, along with four other candidates. The interview process is a whirlwind. During the formal interview sessions and in follow-up meetings and discussions, you meet individually and collectively with the seven school board members, several members of the administration, teachers and their union representatives, parents and members of the public. It seems that the overriding concern is student achievement. First, parents in this relatively affluent school district hold high ambitions for their children and business leaders see high test scores as essential for the area's continued economic development. The school board clearly wants rapid improvements on the state test scores. Moreover, they seem committed to a systemic reform approach that is based on aligning the district's curriculum with the state standards and testing program. Second, there is an achievement gap between minority and majority students. In a variety of interview settings, parents of minority children and five school board members, two of whom are African American and one of whom is Hispanic, asked repeated questions about what actions you would propose to close the achievement gap.

(Continued)

A CASE FOR LEADERSHIP *(Concluded)*

After returning to Camargo and reflecting on the prospects, you start asking yourself questions about whether the Willow Tree job is for you.

- What are my strengths and weaknesses as a leader? Self-confidence? Preferred behaviors? Communication abilities? Values and beliefs?
- What are the situational constraints and facilitators in Willow Tree? How strong and clear is the situation for a new superintendent?

- How do my strengths and weaknesses match the situation? Are there substitutes to help with my weaknesses?
- Can the situation be changed or engineered to fit my strengths?
- How will the board's likely mandates for implementing systemic reform and closing the achievement gap affect my ability to transform the district?
- Can I be successful in Willow Tree?

SUMMARY AND SUGGESTED READINGS

Leadership remains an important topic for students of educational administration. Given the fact that leadership is an extremely complex and elusive concept, some conceptual confusion and empirical shortcomings are to be expected. Nevertheless, substantial progress has been made in building a solid body of knowledge about leadership. General agreement exists that leadership involves a social influence process in which an individual exerts intentional influence over others to structure activities and relationships in a group or organization. To explain the influence process, a number of leadership models have been proposed and tested. Contingency theories reached their peak popularity in the 1970s. The approach has been illustrated by Fiedler's postulate that leadership effectiveness is contingent upon matching leadership style with the appropriate situation. As interest in contingency theory waned, an exciting new model became dominant during the 1980s. Transformational leadership has been receiving extensive attention from scholars and practitioners. It incorporates emotional responses of followers and visionary, change-oriented behaviors. Transformational leadership has four critical elements—idealized influence, inspirational motivation, intellectual stimulation, and individualized consideration. While still needing extensive development and empirical testing, distributed leadership has been receiving extensive attention in educational settings and potentially offers an excellent complement to individually based leadership models. It is our conclusion that all of these developments attest to an enhanced understanding of the leadership phenomenon.

The leadership literature is huge with over 5,000 published studies, and the number continues to increase by the hundreds each year (Yukl, 1994).

Within this expansive body of knowledge, rich sources of theories, empirical studies, and practical applications of leadership can be found in Yukl's book, *Leadership in Organizations.* Northouse's (2004), recent work, *Leadership: Theory and Practice,* provides excellent summaries and analyses as well as many assessment instruments and other applications. Probably the most complete review of the leadership literature is found in *Bass and Stogdill's Handbook of Leadership* (Bass, 1990). The journal *Leadership Quarterly* publishes only papers focusing on leadership. For those interested in transformational leadership, the following sources are recommended: Bass and Avolio (1994), Leithwood (1994), Avolio (1999), and Bass (1998). Many other worthy publications could have been given as examples, but our recommendation to individuals interested in exploring leadership in detail is to review this chapter, consult the references we cite, and then plunge yourself into a very deep pool of literature.

KEY ASSUMPTIONS AND PRINCIPLES

1. A number of personality and motivation traits increase the likelihood that individuals can and will engage in effective leadership efforts to influence others.

2. Leadership skills help individuals formulate and implement solutions to complex social and technical problems and to accomplish goals in an effective fashion.

3. Leadership and situational factors display strong reciprocal relationships. Leaders exercise influence through situational variables while situational variables support and limit leader influence.

4. Neglecting task behaviors limits leader influence on performance outcomes, while discounting interpersonal relations reduces the satisfaction of followers.

5. A general proposition of contingency models of leadership is that leader traits and skills combine with characteristics of the situation to produce leader behaviors, which in turn impact performance outcomes.

6. Transformational leaders expand on transactional relationships to manage meaning, to emphasize the importance of the followers' emotional responses, and to achieve unusually high performance outcomes.

7. Distributed leadership theory postulates that schools rely on multiple sources of leadership to complete numerous tasks, especially during periods of transformation and in implementing comprehensive school reforms.

8. Leading includes not only instrumental and behavioral activity, but symbolic and cultural action as well.

NOTES

1. Structured observation techniques typically observe and question leaders intensively as they perform their work. Mintzberg (1973) and Kotter (1982) conducted two of the best-known investigations in business organizations. A number of investigations using structured observation procedures also have been conducted in school settings across a number of countries on superintendents (O'Dempsey, 1976; Friesen and Duignan, 1980; Duignan, 1980; Pitner and Ogawa, 1981); on principals (Peterson, 1977–78; Willis, 1980; Martin and Willower, 1981; Morris and his associates, 1981; Kmetz and Willower, 1982; Phillips and Thomas, 1982; Chung, 1987; Chung and Miskel, 1989); and on educational innovators (Sproull, 1981). In addition to providing a fascinating glimpse of their work, the findings are important because the behaviors of school administrators have been described systematically and found to be consistent across organizational types—businesses and schools—across organizational roles—superintendents, supervisors, and principals—and across countries—Australia, Canada, and the United States.

2. For readers interested in a detailed consideration of the traits associated with effective leadership, a comprehensive treatment can be found in Bass (1990). Although less extensive, Yukl (2002) provides an insightful discussion of traits and leader effectiveness.

CHAPTER 12

ONE LAST TIME:
A REVIEW OF THE SCHOOL
AS A SOCIAL SYSTEM

Systems thinking is the fifth discipline. It is the discipline that integrates the disciplines, fusing them into a coherent body of theory and practice. . . . It continually reminds us that the whole can exceed the sum of its parts.

Peter M. Senge
The Fifth Discipline

The preceding chapters present a substantial body of knowledge that constitutes a strong argument for the value of an open social-systems approach to educational administration. In this chapter, we review the social-systems model that serves as a theoretical guide to the ideas developed in our work. Intrinsic dilemmas of the model will then be considered.

A MODEL OF SYNTHESIS

Open-systems theory is organic rather than mechanical. As a conceptual language, it is useful in describing the recurring structures and dynamic processes in educational organizations to make their full patterns clearer and to help us change successfully. According to the social-systems model for schools, organizational performance is determined by at least four sets of key elements—structure, the individual, culture and climate, and power and politics—as they interact with the teaching-learning process. These elements take inputs from the environment and transform them. The elements and their interactions form the transformation system, which is constrained by the opportunities and demands from the environment. In addition, internal and external feedback mechanisms enable the system to evaluate the quality of all its systems and inputs. As discrepancies between actual and expected performance are detected, feedback enables the system to adjust.

In brief, the model in Figure 12.1 (first developed in Chapter 1) summarizes the major external and internal features of organizations conceived as open social systems. Of course, the figure cannot capture the dynamic movement of a system as it responds to its environment through internal processes and as it produces such products as student learning or employee

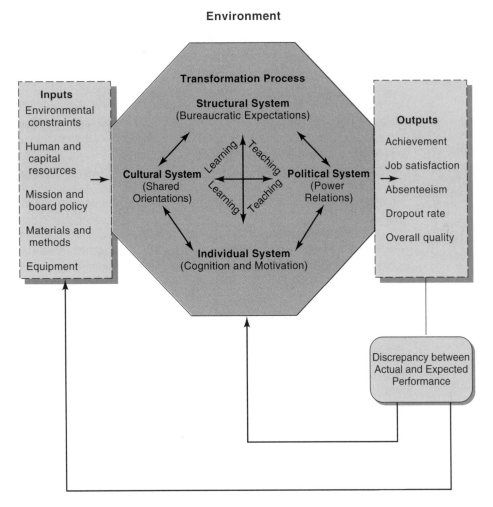

FIGURE 12.1   *Social System Model for Schools*

satisfaction. Although we examine the parts of the system, do not lose sight of the fact that the system is a working whole.

Structure in Schools

Bureaucratic structure (see Chapter 3) is the formal organization specifically established to achieve explicit goals and carry out administrative tasks. Whatever the organizational goals, such structural properties as rules, regulations, hierarchy, and division of labor are consciously designed to attain those goals. In Weber's analysis of ideal types, bureaucracy employs authority through these means to achieve rational decision making and maximize efficiency.

Division of labor and specialization produce impersonal experts who make technically correct, rational decisions based on fact. Once these decisions have been made, the hierarchy of authority implements a disciplined, coordinated compliance to directives through rules and regulations. Career-oriented employees have an incentive to be loyal and productive.

Although probably the best known, Weber's is not the only theory of organizational structure. Henry Mintzberg provides another framework for examining bureaucratic structure. He describes structure simply as the ways in which an organization divides its labor into tasks and then achieves coordination among them. Mutual adjustment, direct supervision, and standardization are basic coordinating mechanisms—the glue that holds the organization together. His analysis yields five ideal types. Mintzberg describes organizations as structures that are influenced by their environments—that is, open systems.

Contemporary research on school structures suggests that it is not so much the amount of structure but the *kind* of structure that determines whether it will have positive or negative consequences for the effectiveness and efficiency of the school.

Individuals in Schools

The fact that an organization has been formally established does not mean that all its activities and interactions conform to structural requirements. The individual is also a key element of all social systems. Students, teachers, and administrators bring with them individual (Chapter 4) needs, goals, and beliefs and develop their own personal orientations and intellectual understanding of their roles. Just as structure helps shape behavior in schools so too do the needs, goals, and beliefs of individuals.

Maslow describes a hierarchy of basic needs that motivate behavior ranging from biological to self-actualization needs, and Herzberg distinguishes between needs that produce worker satisfaction and those that cause dissatisfaction. The need for achievement and the need for autonomy are two other powerful motivating forces within individuals, which moderate teacher and administrator behavior in schools.

Work motivation is a set of energetic forces that originate both within as well as beyond an individual's being. Individual goals and goal setting are key ingredients of personal motivation, especially when the goals are embraced by the individual and are specific, challenging, and attainable. These forces initiate work-related behavior and determine the form, direction, intensity, and duration of motivation. Similarly, beliefs are important motivational forces. Administrators, teachers, and students are likely to work hard if they believe that success is primarily due to their ability and effort, that causes of outcomes are under their control, that extra effort will improve performance, that good performance will be noticed and rewarded, that the rewards are valued, and that they have been treated fairly and with respect by their superiors. Moreover, effective performance is closely related to self-efficacy, the belief that one has the capability to organize and execute a course of action that is required to attain the desired level of performance. Finally, motivation that comes from the interest and challenge of the activity itself is intrinsic, whereas extrinsic motivation is based on rewards and punishment. Although both can motivate, intrinsic motivation is typically more effective.

Culture and Climate in Schools

Our analysis of the internal atmosphere of schools focused on two related concepts—culture and climate (see Chapter 5). Each of these notions goes beyond the formal and individual aspects of organizational life. Each suggests a natural, spontaneous, and human side to organization; each suggests that the whole is greater than the sum of its parts; and each deals with shared meanings and unwritten rules that guide organizational behavior.

Organizational culture is the set of shared orientations that holds a unit together and gives it a distinctive identity. Although climate tends to focus on shared perceptions, culture is defined in terms of shared assumptions, values, and norms. These three levels of culture—assumptions, values, and norms—are explored as alternative ways of describing and analyzing schools. Research on business organizations suggests that effective systems have strong corporate cultures: cultures characterized by intimacy, trust, cooperation, egalitarianism, a bias for action, and orientations that stress quality, innovation, and people. Yet, in many respects, culture is like structure; both can improve or impede the effective functioning of the school depending on the mission and environmental conditions.

Organizational climate is a relatively enduring quality of the school environment that is experienced by teachers, affects their behavior, and is based on their collective perceptions of behavior in schools. A climate emerges through the interaction of members and exchange of sentiments among them. The climate of a school is its "personality." Two different conceptualizations of climate were described and analyzed.

When schools have an open climate, we find that principals and faculty are acting authentically, but when the climate is closed, everyone simply goes through the motions of education without dedication and commitment. As might be expected, research has shown that such affective characteristics as positive student and faculty attitudes are related to openness of climate.

The climate of schools can also be examined in terms of organizational health. A healthy school is one that is meeting both its instrumental and its expressive needs, while successfully coping with disruptive outside forces as it directs its energies toward its mission. The healthier the organizational dynamics of a school, the greater are the trust and openness in member relations and the greater the student achievement. Changing the climate or culture of a school is a long-term objective; there are no simple, quick fixes.

Power and Politics in Schools

Even before joining an organization, individuals grant the use of formal authority to the system when they voluntarily agree to comply with legitimate commands. Once in the organization, however, power relations expand; in fact, power becomes a central aspect of relations within the system.

Power is a broad construct that includes both legitimate and illegitimate and formal and informal methods of ensuring compliance (see Chapter 6). Hence, four basic kinds of organizational power exist: two forms are legitimate—formal and informal authority—and two kinds are illegitimate—coercive and political power.

The legitimate system of authority promotes coordination and compliance and contributes to attainment of the formal goals. Legitimate power comes from the formal organization by virtue of position, from informal norms and values of the culture, and from the expertise of individuals in the system. These three systems of control typically contribute to the needs of the organization; that is, they are legitimate. But those with power also have personal needs. In the process of striving to accomplish the broader organizational needs, individuals find they have discretion, and discretion opens the way to political power. Thus a system of political power emerges that is not sanctioned by the formal authority, culture, or certified expertise; in fact, it is typically divisive, parochial, and illegitimate. Politics is illegitimate because it is a means to serve personal ends at the expense of the overall organization. That does not mean that politics never produces positive results. To the contrary, politics can promote change blocked by the formal organization, can ensure that strong members acquire leadership roles, can encourage debate among diverse positions, and can help in the execution of decisions.

Politics is a fact of organizational life. Although there are powerful individuals, the political arenas of organizations are composed of coalitions of individuals and groups, which bargain among themselves to determine the distribution of resources. External as well as internal coalitions influence organizational politics. Political tactics are the bases of a system of political games played to resist authority, to counter resistance, to build power bases, to defeat opponents, and to change the organization. The system of politics typically coexists with the more legitimate systems of influence without dominating them, but power and politics generate conflict. Thus, conflict management is a useful administrative tool.

Teaching and Learning in Schools

The teaching-learning process is the technical core of the school (Chapter 2). Other activities are secondary to the basic mission of teaching and learning; in fact, the process shapes many of the administrative decisions that must be made in schools. Indeed, teaching and learning provide a crucial set of internal opportunities and constraints.

Both teaching and learning are elaborate processes that need careful attention. Learning occurs when there is a stable change in an individual's knowledge or behavior. Although most experts on learning would agree with this general definition of learning, some would emphasize behavior and others, knowledge. Learning is a complex cognitive process and there is no one best explanation of learning. Different theories of learning offer more or less useful explanations depending on what is to be explained. We examined three general theories of learning—behavioral, cognitive, and constructivist—each with a different focus.

Behavioral theories of learning stress observable changes in behaviors, skills, and habits. The focus of this perspective is clearly on behavior. Learning is defined as a change in behavior brought about by experience with virtually no concern for the mental or internal processes of thinking. Behavior is simply what a person does in a given situation. The intellectual underpinnings of this perspective rest with Skinner's (1950) operant conditioning. Learning objectives, mastery learning, direct instruction, and basic skills are teaching strategies that evolve from this perspective. When specific skills and behaviors need to be learned, teaching approaches consistent with behavioral learning theory are quite effective.

Cognitive theories of learning focus on thinking, remembering, creating, and problem solving. How information is remembered and processed as well as how individuals use their own knowledge to monitor and regulate their cognitive processes are critical in this perspective. Some of the most important teaching applications of cognitive theories are teaching students how to learn and remember by using learning tactics such as note taking, mnemonics, and use of visuals. Teaching strategies based on cognitive views of learning, particularly information processing, highlight the importance of attention, organization, practice, and elaboration in learning and provide ways to give students more control over their own learning by developing and improving their own self-regulated learning strategies. The emphasis of the cognitive approach is on what is happening "inside the head" of the learner.

Constructivist theories of learning are concerned with how individuals make meaning of events and activities; hence, learning is seen as the construction of knowledge. In general, constructivism assumes that people create and construct knowledge rather than internalize it from the external environment, but there are a variety of different approaches to constructivism. Some constructivist views emphasize the shared and social construction of knowledge, whereas others see social forces as less important. Constructivist perspectives on learning and teaching, which are increasingly influential today, are grounded in the research of Piaget, Brunner, Dewey, and Vygotsky. Inquiry and problem-based learning, cooperative learning, and cognitive apprenticeships are typical teaching strategies that are grounded in the constructivist approach. The essence of the constructivist approach is that it places the students' own efforts at the center of the educational process.

External Environments of Schools

Schools are open systems, which must adapt to changing environmental conditions to be effective and, in the long term, to survive. The environments of schools (see Chapter 7) affect their internal structures and processes. Social, economic, political, and technological trends influence the internal operations of schools, as do more specific aspects such as unions, taxpayer associations, and state legislatures.

Environments are complex and difficult to analyze, but two general perspectives are useful—task and institutional. The task perspective includes both information and resource-dependency theories, which define the task environment as all aspects of the external setting that are potentially relevant for goal setting, goal achievement, effectiveness, and survival.

The information model treats the external environment as a source of information for decision makers. Perceived organizational uncertainty affects the flexibility and bureaucratic configuration of organizations. Like all organizations, schools strive for certainty because they are under pressure to demonstrate rationality.

The resource-dependency approach assumes that organizations cannot generate internally the needed resources; resources must come from the environment. Thus, schools must enter into exchanges and competition with environmental units to obtain the requisite products and services. Scarcity produces competition with other organizations for resources.

Because environmental uncertainty and scarcity of resources threaten organizational autonomy and effectiveness, administrators often attempt to develop strategies to gain more control over the environment. Internal coping strategies include buffering the technical core, planning or forecasting, adjusting internal operations on the basis of contingency theory, and spanning organizational boundaries. Interorganizational coping strategies include establishing favorable linkages with important external constituencies and shaping environmental elements through political actions. Combining the ideas from the resource and information perspectives, the essential question for administrators is, "How can environmental uncertainty be reduced without increasing dependency?"

In contrast to the task perspectives, institutional theory assumes that the environment encourages schools to conform to powerful sets of rules and requirements that the legal, social, professional, and political institutions impose. The theory asserts that school structures and processes mirror the norms, values, and ideologies institutionalized in society. The essence of the theory is that the environment of schools presses more for form than for substance.

Nevertheless, technical and institutional environments do coexist; schools function in relatively strong institutional but weak technical environments. Current drives for systemic reform and competitive markets suggest that worried businesspeople and policy makers may be seeking to place heightened emphasis on task environments. A shift from primarily institutional to technical environments would shatter the rationalized myths and lead to fundamental changes in schools, a shift that will be bitterly fought by current institutional forces.

School Effectiveness, Accountability, and Improvement

Outputs of schools are a function of the interaction of structure, individuals, culture, and politics as constrained by environmental forces. Issues of organizational effectiveness represent fundamental challenges to school administration (Chapter 8). In our open-systems model, school outputs are the performances of students, teachers, and administrators. All can be used as indicators of organizational effectiveness and can be assessed for their quality. As an overall generalization of open-systems theory, outputs of schools are a function of the interaction of five internal transformation elements as shaped and constrained by environmental forces. We further specified this generalization with a congruence hypothesis that other things being equal, the greater the harmony among the transformation elements, the more effective the system.

We have proposed a social-systems model of school performance. The perspective underscores the importance of all the aspects of a social system, especially the quality of inputs, transformation processes, and outcomes. Each of these system phases needs to be assessed over the short term as well as the long term, using a variety of such constituencies as students, teachers, and administrators. Teacher quality, internal harmony, effort, student achievement, job satisfaction, and overall performance are examples of indicators of organizational effectiveness.

Building on ideas such as those proposed by Smith and O'Day (1991), policy makers and educators have developed and widely applied systemic or standards-based approaches to educational accountability and change. The accountability systems focus on performance outcomes as determined from data collected and reported school by school (Fuhrman, 1999) and generally include three components: standards to identify the subject matter knowledge and skills to be learned; tests aligned with the standards; and consequences to recognize the differing levels of goal attainment. Advocates hypothesize that aligning these and other elements of the educational process provides the coherence and direction necessary for improving the quality and quantity of school outputs.

The emerging accountability systems call for numerous, simultaneous, and systemic changes in organizing, teaching, and administering schools. But as Elmore (2002a) maintains, educators are neither prepared nor hired to make systematic, continuous improvements in their schools' transformational processes and to measure their success by narrow performance outcomes. Making such transformations and gauging success on state tests is difficult for all educators, but achieving the changes and outcomes is particularly problematic in schools serving children from unstable, poverty-ridden families who are living in unsafe communities. To meet these challenges, a plethora of initiatives have been launched. Two with particular promise are professional development and comprehensive school reform.

Feedback Loops

The knowledge of the outcomes enters two different types of feedback loops. Internally, the relative level of goal achievement serves as an indicator of the need to adjust one or more of the elements of the transformation process. Externally, different constituencies in the community evaluate the school's products. This assessment provides information that also influences the structural, cultural, individual, and political subsystems.

Put bluntly, administrators are responsible for school effectiveness and quality of student learning and teaching. On the one hand, they must respond to the expectations and information carried in the feedback loops; on the other hand, they must maintain or increase goal-directed behavior of teachers, students, and other employees. One of the major administrative problems—control of performance—requires not only the allocation of resources, but also the integration of the basic organizational dimensions (structure, culture, individuals, and politics). Fulfillment of administrative functions requires deciding, motivating, communicating, and leading.

Decision Making in Schools

Deciding means selecting and implementing a course of action from among alternatives (see Chapter 9). This behavior affects the total organization, including the system phases of inputs, throughputs, and outputs.

Although completely rational decision making is impossible, administrators need systematic ways to enhance the selection of satisfactory solutions; hence, a strategy of satisficing is central to administrative decision making. The process is conceptualized as being cyclical with distinct phases: recognition and definition of a problem, analysis of difficulties, establishment of criteria of success, development of an action plan, and initiation and appraisal of the plan. Owing to its cyclical nature, administrators go through the stages repeatedly.

This administrative strategy is well suited to dealing with most problems. Occasionally, however, the set of alternatives is undefinable or the consequences of each alternative are unpredictable with respect to a given aspiration level; here an incremental strategy is more appropriate. This process is a method of successive limited comparisons; only a limited set of alternatives, similar to the existing situation, is considered by successively comparing their consequences until agreement is reached on a course of action. Incrementalism, however, can be too conservative and self-defeating. Incremental decisions made without fundamental guidelines can lead to action without direction. Thus, the mixed-scanning model of decision making is proposed for complex decisions. Mixed scanning unites the best of both the administrative and the incremental models. It uses a strategy of satisficing in combination with incremental decision making guided by broad policy.

Research suggests that the quality of administrative action can be judged by the amount of preparation for implementing a course of action and by the amount of work done in making the decision. Effective decision makers engage in substantial preliminary work; they seek more information, differentiate between fact and opinion, and frequently encourage subordinate participation in the process. Sometimes participation improves the quality of decisions; sometimes it does not. We have proposed a model that suggests when and how to involve subordinates in decision making. In complex organizations, motivation, communication, and leadership are necessary to translate the decisions into concrete action.

Communication in Schools

Verbal and nonverbal interactions pervade virtually all aspects of school life. Good communication does not, however, provide all the answers to the problems confronting educational administrators. Nearly all current conceptions of information exchange rely on the notion that communication involves meaningful exchanges of symbols between at least two people (see Chapter 10). The process is dynamic because it continually influences the transformation and environmental elements of the social system.

One-way communication is unilateral, initiated by a speaker and terminated at a listener. In contrast, two-way communication is reciprocal and interactive with all participants initiating and receiving messages. It has no necessary beginning or ending. Messages flow through formal and informal channels of the school. Although the formal network is usually larger and better developed than the informal, they are closely related, can be complementary, and are critical to the organization.

Leadership in Schools

Leaders are important because they serve as anchors, provide guidance in times of change, and are responsible for the effectiveness of organizations (see Chapter 11). General agreement exists that leadership involves a social influence process. The leader exerts intentional influence over others to structure activities and relationships in a group or organization. A number of personality, motivation, and skill characteristics increase the likelihood that individuals can and will engage in effective leadership efforts to influence others. Into the 1980s, however, the most influential theories of leadership were contingency models, which explain the interrelationships among traits, situations, behaviors, and effectiveness. We developed a schema to categorize and link together these four sets of concepts. Contingency theory poses two basic hypotheses. First, traits of the leaders and characteristics of the situation combine to produce leader behavior and effectiveness. Second, situational factors have direct impacts on effectiveness. We briefly reviewed four contingency models for leadership: instructional leadership, least preferred co-worker, substitutes for leadership, and path-goal theories.

Two relatively new approaches to leadership are now receiving considerable attention. First, transformational leadership is currently receiving extensive attention from scholars and practitioners. It has four critical elements: idealized influence, inspirational motivation, intellectual stimulation, and individualized consideration. Transformational leaders expand on transactional relationships to manage meaning, emphasize the importance of the followers' emotional responses, and achieve unusually high performance outcomes. Second, in education, scholars have become enthused about building and applying frameworks for organizational or distributed leadership. Distributed leadership theory postulates that schools rely on multiple sources of leadership to complete numerous tasks, especially during periods of transformation and in implementing comprehensive school reforms.

Leadership in schools is a complex process. It involves more than mastering a set of leadership skills or matching the appropriate leader behavior with a specific situation. Useful methods to improve school leadership are selecting and educating leaders, assuming new leadership positions, engineering the situation, and transforming schools. Leadership is not only an instrumental and behavioral activity, but also a symbolic and cultural one.

Administrative Behavior

We have been arguing that administrative behavior in the context of teaching and learning should be analyzed in relation to the primary elements of the school social system. Structure, individuals, culture, and politics represent "leverage points" that can be used to influence the performance of organizational members. A number of observations are important and bear repeating. First, deciding, communicating, and leading are key processes that modify school performance. If a leader consciously manipulates one dimension of the system, a "ripple effect" is created; the other dimensions are affected, and a new combination of expectations and behaviors results. Second, a variety of means are available to reach desired goals: there is no one best way to organize, lead, decide, motivate, or teach. Rather, the means to achieve goals depend on many factors including the community, complexity, and culture as well as opportunities and constraints in the situation. Administration is a complex process that requires careful reflection and continuous vigilance to changing conditions. Finally, complexity and connectedness in schools require "systems thinking"—recognition of the importance of the whole rather than a focus on parts; the school is a social system in which the whole is always greater than the sum of its parts. We conclude our examination of schools as social systems by looking at some of the continuing dilemmas that teachers and administrators must face.

ORGANIZATIONAL DILEMMAS

Both change and dilemmas will always be with us, but dilemmas, unlike change, need not accelerate. Peter M. Blau and W. Richard Scott (1962) maintain that the concept of dilemma contributes to our understanding of internal pressures for change. A dilemma arises when one is confronted by decision alternatives in which any choice sacrifices some valued objectives in the interest of other objectives. Daniel Katz and Robert L. Kahn (1978) have elaborated on this definition by distinguishing between problems and dilemmas. Problems are difficulties that can be solved by past precedents or by the application of existing theory or policy. Dilemmas are unsolvable within the existing framework. Solutions and perfect adjustments are impossible. Because dilemmas are endemic to organizations, they serve as perpetual sources of change.

The fundamental dilemma facing formal organizations is order versus freedom. Both order and freedom are desirable and necessary conditions for high levels of effectiveness, but increasing one decreases the other. The tension between order and freedom is manifested in at least four operational dilemmas in schools: coordination and communication, bureaucratic discipline and professional expertise, administrative planning and individual initiative, and learning as behavior and cognition.

Coordination and Communication

Based on the work of Blau and Scott (1962), two-way communication with unrestricted exchange of ideas, criticism, and advice contributes to effective problem solving in at least three ways: it furnishes social support to individual participants; it provides an error-correcting mechanism; and it fosters a healthy competition for respect.

Problem-solving situations often produce stress and anxiety for individual participants and lead to mental blocks that interfere with effective development of their thinking. However, when individuals communicate openly, good ideas are likely to receive the approval of others (thus reducing anxiety) and to promote further participation, development, and refinement of ideas; hence, the social support derived from an unrestricted exchange of ideas aids in problem solving.

It is not easy for a person to detect mistakes in his or her own thinking. An individual takes a set framework to the problem-solving situation that makes it difficult to see the problem from a different perspective. Open and free-flowing communication brings a variety of perspectives, experiences, and information to bear on the common task; hence, it increases the chances of identifying an error in thinking. Other members of the group are more prone to spot inconsistencies and blind spots than the individual; therefore, two-way communication facilitates error correction. Finally, open, two-way communication motivates members of a group to make expert suggestions in order to win the respect and esteem of fellow participants.

Whereas the free flow of information improves problem solving, it also impedes coordination. Unrestricted communication may drown effective action in a sea of conflicting ideas. True, information helps in the selection of good ideas, but too many ideas hinder agreement, and coordination requires agreement on a single master plan.

Coordination in organizations is accomplished primarily through hierarchical differentiation, but such structure impedes decision making because it interferes with the free flow of information (see Chapter 3). In fact, differentiation, centralized direction, and restricted communication appear essential for effective coordination. In brief, those very things that enhance the coordination process also hinder the free flow of communication. Organizations require both effective coordination and effective problem solving. But the hierarchical structure in organizations that facilitates efficient coordination also impedes communication and problem solving. The dilemma seems inherent in the conflicting requirements of coordination and problem solving because they have simultaneous needs for restricted and unrestricted communication. The conflict, which causes adaptation and change, cannot be readily resolved and needs continuing attention.

Bureaucratic Discipline and Professional Expertise

The similarities and differences in the characteristics of professional and bureaucratic orientations (see Chapter 3) lead to a second dilemma. Although both orientations stress technical competence, objectivity, impersonality, and service, the unique structure of the professions is a basic source of conflict. Professionals attempt to control themselves through self-imposed standards and group surveillance. In contrast, bureaucratic employees are expected to adhere to rules and regulations and to subordinate themselves to the hierarchy. The ultimate basis for a professional act is the professional's knowledge; the ultimate justification of a bureaucratic act is its consistency with organizational rules and regulations and approval by a superior. The conflict is between professional expertise and autonomy, and bureaucratic discipline and control. The significance of the discord is brought into sharp focus when we examine employees who are subject to both forms of social control: professionals working in bureaucracies.

The strain created by the merger of these two institutional means of control can be resolved in different ways. In some organizations, major structural changes have been instituted through the development of two separate authority lines—one professional and one administrative. Nonetheless, when professional considerations conflict with bureaucratic ones, dividing authority seems to be a partial solution at best. Without organizational change some individuals attempt to accommodate themselves to the conflict by developing role orientations that are compatible with the bureaucracy or the profession, and some adopt orientations that are compatible with both. Although accommodation is made, the conflict remains a continuing dilemma and thus a fundamental issue.

Professional expertise and bureaucratic discipline are alternative modes of coping with uncertainty. Discipline restricts its scope, whereas expertise provides knowledge and social support to cope with uncertainty. Blau and Scott held that the struggle will remain as long as professionals are employed in bureaucratic organizations. It seems likely that the professional-bureaucratic dilemma will become an even more significant internal one in schools as teachers and administrators become more professionalized and continue to function in school organizations that are essentially bureaucratic in nature.

Administrative Planning and Individual Initiative

A third manifestation of the tension between order and freedom is the need for both administrative planning and individual initiative. The disharmony between them poses a major difficulty in the administrative process, which includes not only the development of plans to solve problems but their subsequent implementation and appraisal. Organizational decision making takes place within the setting of the organization as a collectivity. The exercise of any independent judgment must be compatible with the thrust of the formal organization. The formal organization exerts continuous pressure through its elaborate bureaucratic machinery to subordinate individual initiative to organizational directives. The organization is, of course, interested in creative, individual efforts, but only when they do not conflict with formal plans.

How can the organization encourage individual initiative without confounding administrative planning? We have suggested a number of organizational responses. A model for shared decision making has been introduced that delineates under what conditions the individual should be involved in the decision-making process (see Chapter 9). The arrangement calls for empowering teachers and harnessing the creative initiative of individuals in a constructive way that is beneficial to both the organization and the person. We have sketched the characteristics of a professional organizational structure that emphasizes shared decision making rather than autocratic bureaucracy (see Chapter 3). Further, we described organizational climates—open and healthy—that would tend to lessen the conflict between compliance and initiative (see Chapter 5).

In brief, organizations can be structured and organizational climates and cultures can be developed to minimize the conflict between administrative planning and individual initiative. This is not to suggest that the dilemma can be resolved. The best that we can probably hope for is a healthy balance between compliance and initiative, a balance continually disrupted by the conflicting needs for order and freedom.

Learning as Behavior and Cognition

Finally, the tension between behaviorism and cognitive approaches to teaching and learning ripple through virtually all administrative decisions in schools. On the one hand, there is strong research to support using principles of reinforcement in teaching and classroom management. Learning objectives, mastery learning, and direct instruction are examples of teaching applications that are effective in certain situations. On the other hand, cognitive theories, especially constructivism, put the student at the center of the teaching-learning and the teacher in the indirect role of assistant and coach. Inquiry and problem-based learning are critical aspects of teaching in this approach. Constructivists and most cognitive approaches eschew the research and practice of the behaviorists. Indeed, many of the contemporary conflicts about teaching are manifestations of the behavior-cognitive dilemma; for example, "phonics" versus "whole reading," "basic skills" versus "critical thinking," "direct instruction" versus "discovery," and "core knowledge" versus "authentic knowledge."

How can school administrators encourage the use of cognitive and constructivist approaches without denigrating or eliminating behaviorist approaches? We argue that first, administrators and teachers must understand the basic theory and research that undergird each approach (see Chapter 2). Understanding is essential if we are to avoid the negative consequences of choosing sides in the most current educational controversy. For example, when the goal is to learn new behaviors or explicit information or when learning is sequential or factual, a behavioral approach to teaching and learning is usually quite effective. If, however, the goal is problem solving or critical thinking, then a cognitive approach is a more effective teaching-learning strategy, one, for example, that uses scaffolding and coaching and stresses meaning rather than memory. The point is that the kind of outcome is related to the kind of teaching that is most effective. There is no one best way to teach because teaching and learning depend on the goal of instruction. Effective teachers and administrators need to incorporate sound behavioral as well as cognitive principles in their practice.

Balance and knowledge are the keys to coping successfully with this dilemma. We do not suggest that the behavioral and cognitive learning dilemma can ever be finally resolved, but rather that success rests with knowing when and how to use each approach. An "either-or" approach to teaching and learning is bound to be counterproductive. A learning environment that encourages freedom while tempering it with order is likely to be most successful in schools. The balance between freedom and order, however, is dynamic. Continuous assessment and change are necessary.

CONCLUSION

The position that we have held throughout this book embodies two related perspectives: what Peter F. Drucker (1968) calls "reality" and what Peter M. Senge (1990) calls "systems thinking." Knowledge has become a central resource. The systematic acquisition of knowledge—that is, organized formal education—

must supplement experience as the foundation for increasing productive capacity and improving performance. But knowledge and experience themselves are not enough. Events must be seen as a whole pattern of change, not isolated snapshots. Increasingly, successful performance will depend on the ability to use concepts and theories as well as skills acquired through experience to make the full patterns clearer and help us to cope with them.

The dilemmas we have explored demand basic changes in administrators. They require new training, knowledge, policies, and a readiness to shed deeply entrenched practices. The practice of administration can become one of deepened dilemmas or of heightened achievements. We hold that a path to the latter is through reflective leadership anchored in sound theory and research in educational organizations. We recommend that students continue to apply the administrative principles developed in this text by analyzing actual cases found in "A Collection of Cases for Educational Leadership."

A COLLECTION OF CASES
FOR EDUCATIONAL LEADERSHIP

CASE 1

Anonymous Letter

Jack Garner is principal of Dewey Elementary School. Dewey is one of five elementary schools in Pleasantville, a community of 30,000 in a middle Atlantic state.

Pleasantville is an interesting cross-section of America. It is a working-class community in transition to a different kind of workforce. The old work of farms, mills, and mines has given way to newer occupations in a small aircraft plant and in the emergence of the state college (recently renamed the State University at Pleasantville). The paper mill, a carpet factory, a chemical plant, a small steel mill, and a coal mine were formerly the major employers of the townspeople. But recently, much to the dismay of the working people in Pleasantville, most of the factories and mills were in decline. Unemployment is up to 13 percent and not getting better. The people blamed the government. In the old days, there had been no

EPA and no environmentalists and no interference from the state and federal bureaucrats. In those days, people worked hard and made a decent living.

With the advent of environmental-protection regulations and changes in the marketplace, the steel mill employed only half of what it had employed 15 years ago. So too with the paper mill and the coal mine. The chemical plant was on the verge of bankruptcy as newer dyes were imported from abroad and expensive chemical cleanup projects plagued the plant for the past three years. In fact, there seemed to be only one major industry that was thriving in Pleasantville—the state university. It was growing, from an enrollment of 2,000 ten years ago to nearly 10,000 students today. Although construction of the expanding campus had produced many jobs during the past five years, it did not offset the decline of the old industries. Moreover, many of the jobs that were produced by the state university were professional positions that required employment of outsiders rather than townspeople.

Some people resented the intrusion from the outside and harkened back to the halcyon days of the past. Others in the community, especially businesspeople, welcomed the expansion of the school and were proud of the fact that Pleasantville was becoming sophisticated.

Jack Garner is no stranger to Pleasantville. At 35, his entire life had been spent in and around Pleasantville. He had gone to elementary school, junior high, and high school in town. Upon graduation, he went to the local state college and majored in education. His first job was as science teacher at Pleasantville High. During his first year of teaching, Jack Garner decided that he wanted an expanded role in education down the road. He began taking curriculum classes in the summers at the main campus of the state university, sixty-five miles from Pleasantville.

Taking courses at the main campus was Garner's first real exposure to life outside of Pleasantville. A chronic bad knee had kept him out of the service, and perhaps just as well. Thinking back, Garner judged the experience at the main campus to be an eye-opener for a country boy, as he sometimes referred to himself. Ten years later, he had completed his doctorate in educational curriculum, served as district-wide elementary science curriculum coordinator, and as a result of his success in working with people and his genuine good sense, he was promoted to principal of the new Dewey Elementary School. Some might think that Dewey was a progressive school, but the Dewey this elementary school was named after was Thomas, the former governor of New York, not the educator. Therein lay a substantial difference. Dewey Elementary School was not a place hospitable to change. Students had grown up in the system and sent their children to Dewey. They want the same good education they had received—no frills, no life adjustment, no multiculturalism, no debates on right to life or the nature of families, just basic learning in reading, math, science, writing, and history.

There is no question that the surrounding neighborhood of Dewey was conservative, but it was slowly changing as more and more college professors bought houses in Dewey Heights. In fact, the Dewey neighborhood was becoming a choice residential area for young professionals in the community.

As a curriculum person and skillful adminis-

trator, Garner had been able to initiate a strong elementary school curriculum. He had combined many of the elements of cooperative learning and mastery education to engage students individually and collectively in the pursuit of math, science, and reading. His whole-language approach to the teaching of English and composition was a model that was frequently observed by students from the local college. (Garner had a hard time thinking of his undergraduate school as a state university; he still thought of it as his college.) Five years as curriculum coordinator and five years as principal had produced a school of which he was proud. The elementary school students continued to do well and parents were generally supportive of his initiatives, even though some complained that he was getting away from the basics.

It is Monday morning. As Jack reviews his mail, he is shocked at the third letter that he opens and reads.

May 11
Dear Dr. Garner:

You should know that your science curriculum supervisor is a homo. He lives with another man and I have seen them fondling each other in the tavern in Greenville. I don't care what people do in their private lives, but teachers are different. I don't want my son endangered by this guy. Of course, there is always the question of AIDS, and I don't want him abusing my child. There is a rumor that Jenkins has not been well. Frankly, we're worried for the safety of our children.

We know that you are with us on this issue. After all, you are one of us. Why don't you do something about this? Everyone is talking about it. And if you don't do something, I can't be responsible for what some hotheads might do. Jenkins is in some danger.

I am not going to sign this letter because I don't want to be involved in this, but I think you ought to know about the situation. Someone is going to get hurt. Do something before it becomes a police matter.
Sincerely,
A Concerned Parent

Matt Jenkins had been Garner's new elementary science supervisor for the past three years. Although Garner had not hired Jenkins directly, the former superintendent, who had thought highly of Jenkins, consulted him. Garner had called one of his former professors in curriculum at the state university and the professor had said, "He is a little peculiar but without question he is one of the brightest and most creative students I have known. He will be an asset to your program." Without much further ado, Jenkins was hired, even though he was an outsider and a segment of the community was opposed to hiring from outside.

There is no question in Garner's mind that Jenkins had shown strong leadership in improving the science curriculum at Dewey. Other teachers like him because he is low-key, supportive, sensitive, and nurturing. He has a few odd mannerisms, but they don't seem to bother anyone. He stays to himself and lives ten miles outside of the city, in a small suburb of Pleasantville called Greenville. No one seems to know much about Jenkins or his personal life. Rumor has it that Jenkins spends a lot of his time at University Station, the main campus of the state university. Many of the townspeople take a dim view of the liberal goings-on in University Station, but it is a world away. Only one time could Garner remember any negative comments about Jenkins. One of the parents had complained that he was always touching her son. Garner had discreetly looked into this matter and found nothing substantial. Rather, he found that Jenkins had grabbed the student in question a number of times to correct his aggressive behavior with the other children. The student in question was a little on the wild side.

Garner was a bit surprised to discover that Jenkins lived with a new high school English teacher, Brad Korbus. Garner had been instrumental in the recruitment and selection of Korbus, and now they were roommates in Greenville. Garner is inclined to feel that whatever people did privately is their own business. His policy for dealing with anonymous letters was to file them in the circular file. Yet the implied threat of this letter troubled him.

He felt constrained to do something, but what? He thought about turning the matter over to the local police. Should he talk to his superintendent? Was this a crank letter from an isolated individual? Did he have a right to make inquiries—even if done discreetly? Should he talk to Jenkins? What would he say, if he did? Supposing Jenkins was gay and living with another man, would it matter? Is there a problem? A potential problem? Is this a time for preventive action? Or will any action simply exacerbate the situation? Is it time for the district to develop a policy on private behavior or alternate lifestyles?

Assume the role of principal.

- What are the short-term and long-term problems in this case?
- Is this a case for satisficing, muddling through, or adaptive scanning?
- What are your immediate and long-term plans?
- Who should be involved in this decision and how?
- No matter what your eventual strategy, make sure it includes a plan to address the dysfunctional consequences of your actions.

CASE 2

Snubbing Creationists?

You are the principal of Canterbury High School, a suburban high school in the southeast. The school has the reputation of being one of the best in the state; its motto, emblazoned on the wall of the foyer, is "An Odyssey of Excellence." People move into the community for the schools, and for the most part they are not disappointed. The district has only one high school with 1,500 students evenly divided into the 10th, 11th, and 12th grades. Each year approxi-

mately 75 percent of the students go on to higher education and a significant number apply to the best colleges and universities in the country. Admission to the Ivy League is a goal of a substantial number of students because their parents are successful professionals, many of who have graduated from prestigious schools themselves.

The teachers in your school are consummate professionals. They are well-educated, hard working, and they care about their students. Four teachers have Ph.D.'s in their disciplines and every teacher has at least a master's degree. You are proud of your school and the students, teachers, and community. In many ways, the job of being principal is delightful but it is also challenging. Parents are demanding; they expect their children to get the very best education possible. They pay a hefty tax bill to be part of this district, which often means that they speak out and question any school policy or event that might be an impediment to the success of their children.

At this very moment you are in the midst of a problem involving one of your biology teachers and a group of parents. Dr. Henry Washington is a veteran biology teacher of 15 years, who teaches the AP biology class at Canterbury High. Hank is a popular teacher and students compete to get into AP class; only the brightest and the best succeed. Two days ago you received a phone call from a lawyer representing the Legal Institute for Freedom, a group of Christian lawyers. The lawyer was concerned in general about Dr. Washington's Web page where he posted the following statement:

The central unifying principle of biology is the theory of evolution. Students in this class are expected to show mastery of the theory and be able to defend it against rival explanations of the origin of species.

But the particular issue that was troubling to the lawyer was Dr. Washington's adamant stand that he would not write a college letter of recommendation for Michael Hayes, a student in the AP class, because Hayes, who described himself as a devout Christian, did not subscribe to the theory of evolution; in fact, the student was an avid believer in creationism and the role of God in science.

This was the first time Washington had encountered such a student, and although he was tolerant of other ideas and explanations, he did not believe that he could in good conscience write letters of recommendation for students who did not accept the theory of evolution as a convincing explanation of the origin of the species. After all, exclaimed Washington, "I am a biologist teaching biology. Evolution is the tool that brought us about. To deny the theory of evolution is like denying the law of gravity. In science, a theory is about as close to a fact as you can get." He added, "My stance is not discriminatory toward anyone else's beliefs, but rather to ensure that anyone that I write a letter of recommendation for is

on the road to becoming a first-rate scientist. Science and religion address different questions, and they don't overlap."

You have kept your superintendent abreast of the evolving situation, and she is supportive and has expressed confidence in your leadership and problem-solving ability. The district has no policy on letters of recommendation because the board prefers to leave such matters to the teachers themselves. You would like to nip this problem in the bud. You don't want to see the school involved in a protracted legal suit, but the legal institute is pushing hard as they represent the student. The student, Michael Hayes, wants his teacher, Dr. Washington, to write him two letters, one to Stanford and the other to Princeton, where he hopes to major in biology in preparation for his eventual admission to medical school. Dr. Washington insists that he cannot and will not write any letter for this student or any other with similar beliefs. He maintains that this is a matter of academic freedom and personal freedom. The student, his parents, and his lawyers see it as a matter of religious freedom. They assert that the student is being punished for his religious beliefs. Moreover, they insist that a letter from the AP biology teacher is especially important because the student wants to be a medical doctor.

You have another appointment to speak with Dr. Washington after school today and an appointment to speak with the lawyer representing the student tomorrow morning. You feel caught in the middle. You need a plan. Is compromise possible? Or is legal action inevitable?

- What kind of decision-making model is appropriate? Satisficing? Mixed scanning? Other?
- Who should be involved in the decision making? The superintendent? Board? Teachers?
- Define the long-term and short-term problems.
- Can the school force a teacher to write a letter of recommendation? If so, can it specify what the teacher should say?
- Does the teacher have an obligation to write letters of recommendation for students who get an A in the course, who they know well, and who demonstrate a knowledge of evolutionary theory?
- As principal, develop a strategy to deal with the problem in a way that seeks resolution without legal action.

CASE 3

Crossing the Line or Only a Crush?[1]

Superintendent Henry Chalmers, eyeing the flashing light on his phone, sat heavily in his seat and swiveled away from his desk to view the expanse of football and soccer fields beyond his window. Ordinarily, his job was gratifying. Superintendent of a large, prestigious public high school in an affluent suburb of a large Midwestern city, Chalmers was used to the spotlight—his school seemed to be a lightning rod for the local media. When fans of Midtown Heights behaved badly at the state basketball tournament, reporters were there. When famous alums in government and show business returned to speak at the school, reporters were there. When state test scores annually revealed that MHHS had once again dominated all subject areas, the school's achievements were duly noted in the area's two major metropolitan newspapers. Midtown Heights had even enjoyed some national press as two weekly news magazines had, in recent years, featured the school as a model of excellence in public education. Media contact, even when the press was not so good, was an area of relative expertise for Chalmers, and he secretly enjoyed it. The light on his phone, blinking ominously, suggested that this was all about to change. He was almost certain the call would be about one of his teachers; in fact, the only question was who was calling—the media, the parents, the teacher, the union, or an attorney.

In September, the parents of a junior girl, Elizabeth Sanders, had become concerned about their daughter's increasingly intense relationship with her former teacher, Hal Franklin. Like many students in Hal's honors freshman World History class, Elizabeth greatly admired her charismatic teacher, and spoke reverently of his intellectual honesty, depth, and sincerity. She and her classmates appreciated his informal style—he allowed them to call him by his first name, and sat comfortably on his desk during wide-ranging, open discussions about society, humanity, and existence. In Hal's class, students were fond of saying, they talked about meaningful issues and didn't have to worry about performance. Some-

[1]*Written for this text by Eileen McMahon.*

thing of an iconoclast, Hal had done away with the constraints of regular assessments, lesson plans, and tests, declaring in notably heated department meetings that such trivia interfered with a more "organic" process of learning. Conceding, after a spirited exchange with his department chair, the necessity of quarterly and semester grades, Hal nevertheless represented intellectual freedom to his young devotees, who appreciated that they were, for once, "being treated like adults."

Indeed, treating their daughter like an adult was exactly what alarmed Elizabeth's parents about Hal. They were happy that their daughter was having a good experience and recalled that their older son had also admired this same teacher, even though they did have slight concerns about the lack of structure in his class. Throughout Elizabeth's sophomore year, she maintained a relationship with her favorite teacher, and became intensely involved in Amnesty International, which Hal sponsored. As the spring passed and Elizabeth talked of little else, the Sanders looked forward to the summer break and the distance it would impose. They supposed Elizabeth had developed a pretty typical crush, and that her activities and friends at summer camp, where she was going to be a counselor, would soon supplant her teacher as the foremost concern in her mind. Knowing that Hal was reportedly happily married, with three kids close to their own in age, the Sanderses never imagined that their daughter's feelings for her teacher might be reciprocated, or that the two would correspond throughout the summer via e-mail.

As they became less and less confident that their daughter's fixation on her former teacher was harmless, they remained confident in his judgment and decided to make him aware of their concerns. Elizabeth's mother called the social studies office one afternoon and spoke pleasantly with Hal, somewhat nervously explaining that they were worried that Elizabeth was devoting more of her attention to Amnesty International than to anything else, and that they were hoping he might help guide her to a more balanced approach. He reassured her that Elizabeth seemed to be handling all of her responsibilities pretty well, and that he would keep an eye on her for them. He seemed to understand why they would want her to branch out a bit, so the subject of the crush never came up explicitly. Mrs. Sanders assumed Mr. Franklin, as an experienced teacher, must have dealt with situations like this before, and knew to handle the matter delicately.

But Elizabeth never seemed to distribute her attention to anything but Hal Franklin; if anything, she seemed to spend even more time meeting with him, sometimes off-campus in coffee shops in a neighboring town, all under the pretext of Amnesty International activity. As parent conferences approached in November, the Sanderses thought that they might as well try again to talk with Mr. Franklin, this time together, and address their real concerns a little more directly. They made an appointment to see him during conferences, even though it had been two years since Elizabeth had actually been in his class.

The meeting did not satisfy them in the least. Although Hal recalled their earlier conversation pleasantly enough, he and Mrs. Sanders had clearly not been on the same page. So far from reassuring them that he would establish some distance from Elizabeth, he asserted his attachment to her as "a friend and very important person" in his life, and gave no indication that he would see less of her or reduce the familiarity that he and Elizabeth so obviously enjoyed. Holding his frustration in check, Mr. Sanders decided to be blunt. "Look," he enjoined. "It's pretty clear she has a crush on you, and we're worried about where it's headed. We know you're not doing anything to encourage her, and we're sorry if it's an embarrassing situation, but surely you've dealt with things like this before. It's just that we think if she continues to indulge it, it's just going to be that much harder for her to get over it."

To their dismay, Hal still refused to stop meeting with Elizabeth or to reduce their level of contact in any way. Cordially, he told them that he appreciated their concerns, but felt that their daughter was "old enough to make these kinds of decisions for herself." He hardly felt that it was appropriate for them to tell her with whom she could spend her time if she were pursuing activities that were constructive. He felt they should "give her some space," and let her make her own choices. Of course, as parents, they could be as restrictive as they chose, but he certainly wasn't going to cooperate with them if they did choose to "put her in lockdown or something." As the next family was waiting for their appointment, he led them to the door, thanked them for coming, and wished them a pleasant evening.

Somewhat shocked, they stood in the hallway and tried to think what to do next. They decided that getting angry would only make things worse, so they tried to calm down and proceed thoughtfully. Down the hall, they spotted the social studies department office, so they made their way to find the department chair and appeal to her for advice. Not exactly a Hal Franklin fan, she listened to their story with increasing anger. Clearly, she thought, here was a man who felt himself completely beyond the rules. She had tangled with him over the curriculum in his class, over the necessity of grades and attendance, and over the general direction of the department's course of study. He had fomented a certain amount of dissension in her department, she felt, and she for one believed that behind his "intellectual honesty" hid a guy who was actually pretty lazy. He accused his colleagues of "marching in lockstep" because they actually planned lessons and gave tests, but he did manage, she noticed, to leave the office every day at 3:30 and make his way down to the gym to play pick-up basketball with students, or to meet his Amnesty International "groupies" off-campus. Thanking the Sanderses for coming to her, she assured them that she would look into the matter and get back to them promptly, and then hurried off to track down the principal.

Over the next few weeks, the principal presided over meetings with the Sanderses, the department chair, the union president, and Hal Franklin himself. Superintendent Chalmers was kept informed, but saw no need to involve himself directly since the situation, while difficult, was nonetheless well in hand. Hal was instructed to immediately stop his practice of meeting off-campus with students. All Amnesty International meetings were to be held on-campus, in accordance with the club's charter. In addition, he was told he must honor the parents' request that he limit his contact with their daughter to official club activities. He must also begin submitting weekly lesson plans to his department chair, accounting for planned assessments and grading policies. He reluctantly agreed to follow these directives, to the satisfaction of both the department chair and the Sanders family, who had decided, in the interests of peace at home, to allow Elizabeth to continue her work in Amnesty International, so long as the stipulated conditions were met.

One day after agreeing to these conditions, Hal walked into his morning classes and announced that he was being persecuted by an administration that felt threatened by his popularity. "They don't like that I challenge the way things are done around here," he said. "So I have to watch my ass." He handed out copies of his lesson plan for the week, and announced an upcoming test. Students protested vocally, but he quieted them. "Look, they'd love the chance to get rid of me, so I can't give them any opportunities," he said. "Much as I hate to say it, we're just going to have to compromise. I'm going to play by their rules. My hands are tied. I guess freedom and intellectualism are dangerous around here." As students denounced the principal loudly, Hal murmured, "I know, I know . . . people in power. What are you gonna do?" The students continued to grumble throughout the week. A few of Hal's friends on the faculty joined them.

But Hal didn't play by the rules; at least, not with respect to Elizabeth. He arranged for another faculty member, an English teacher with whom he had team-taught Elizabeth's class, to deliver notes to the girl. Two and a half weeks after receiving the school's assurances that the relationship was under control, the Sanderses found e-mails in the trash on their computer that Elizabeth had obviously meant to destroy. The messages, all dated after the meetings at school, contained a diatribe or two against the administration and the Sanderses themselves. Enraged at how flagrantly Franklin was ignoring the rules, they called Superintendent Chalmers, whose son had played soccer with their son, at home.

By the next morning, Hal had been placed on indefinite administrative leave, and a substitute teacher appeared in his classes. Primed by their teacher's accounts of what the administration was trying to do, students were militant in their support of Franklin and relentless in their abuse of the substitute, who had just finished student-teaching and was trying to get her bearings in a course that had no text and no plans for the semester. They put up signs in the cafeteria and sent around a petition to have their teacher reinstated. A group of seniors in Hal's sociology class requested a meeting with the principal, who met with them but refused to give any information about Franklin's specific circumstances. Meanwhile, after two more meetings with Franklin and the union president, during which he

was given an ultimatum by the superintendent to cease contact entirely or lose his job, Hal returned to school, 10 days after having left. Students gave him a standing ovation, and some faculty congratulated him on having survived his persecution. None had any inkling that the suspension involved anything other than his philosophical differences with the administration.

He lasted two days before the Sanderses again called Superintendent Chalmers, this time with the news that they had hired a lawyer. They had been suspicious of two phone calls Elizabeth had received on her cell from a number within the school. When they confronted her, she admitted that they had been from Franklin, who had called twice from a coach's locker room. She also admitted to having met with him in a little-used equipment room off one of the gyms. Confused and upset, she told them that she and Franklin planned to marry one day, when she had graduated from high school and he had left his wife. She denied that they had had any physical contact, but she insisted that their romantic attachment was a lasting one, and she had faith in their long-term plans to be together. That night the Sanderses made three calls: to a lawyer, to the superintendent, and to a therapist for their daughter.

Upon finding the substitute in their room again the following morning, students went up for grabs. Some refused to do any work at all or to cooperate in any way with the new teacher. Some walked out. They restarted both the petition and the systematic abuse of the substitute, who Xeroxed readings and made plans for the rest of the semester. Under the threat of poor grades, the honors freshmen settled down, but the seniors continued to cause major disruptions until the Dean of Students positioned himself in the back of the class. The student newspaper was flooded with letters protesting the draconian treatment of Franklin, and the principal's secretary was flooded with calls from irate parents who demanded the reinstatement of their children's favorite teacher. Some of Hal's colleagues berated the union president and the department chair for allowing him to be "railroaded like that," and the English teacher who had team-taught with Hal wrote a passionate letter to the local paper defending his value as an educator. Only the principal, the department chair, the union president, and Elizabeth's advisor, to whom the Sanderses had turned for help in managing their daughter's fragile emotions, knew that issues other than teaching style were in play.

Mercifully, the winter break interrupted the simmering resentment, and Superintendent Chalmers believed that with the start of a new semester, tensions would soon dissipate. This prediction looked to be correct, until he received his most recent phone call from Mr. Sanders who claimed that the teacher still was contacting their daughter. Mr. Sanders was on the verge of losing any semblance of control as he concluded the phone conversation with the threat, "Either you get rid of that son-of-a-bitch or I will."

- What do you think of Superintendent Chalmers' decision to let the building administrators handle the Franklin situation early on?

- What would have been the appropriate level of involvement for the superintendent in a situation like this?
- Put yourself in the role of the superintendent as this case comes to a conclusion—what do you do next?
- What obligations, if any, does the superintendent have to the parents? To the teacher?
- Is the parent's threat cause for concern?
- What does the case tell you about school culture at Midtown Heights High School?
- Does the case give you any insights into cultural norms that school leadership might want to address?

CASE 4

Leading to Change, Changing to Lead[1]

As you prepared for another meeting with your staff, you think back several months to the day that set everything in motion. The superintendent had called a meeting of administrators and teachers' union leaders to look at the district's achievement data. Because of the No Child Left Behind legislation, achievement data had been disaggregated for the first time. Seeing it had been a shock; page after page of evidence showed that students in your district and your school were falling through the academic cracks. There were large achievement gaps between Caucasian, African American, Hispanic, and non–English-speaking students; socioeconomic differences caused equivalent achievement gaps with students in the lower economic bandwidths failing to make gains on state-mandated tests; nearly a fourth of your ninth-graders failed to achieve enough credits in one year to reach sophomore status; and your school's cherished graduation rate appeared to be more illusion than reality—even though the graduation rate in the past few senior classes had gone up, more students were dropping out at earlier ages. You had always been

proud of your district's high achievement rating but now it appeared that high achievement only held true for the dominant group—economically comfortable white kids. The superintendent, administrators, and teachers' union leadership all agreed that the data sounded a clarion call for educational change. After all, who could argue against change in the face of such clear evidence?

Several months of discussion followed that initial meeting. Committees formed to talk about changing class schedules, instructional delivery, and curriculum. Other groups met to discuss better ways of meeting the emotional needs of students. Teachers from all buildings were involved and, in time, recommendations were presented, your school should move to block scheduling and develop smaller learning communities. That's when things went awry.

A handful of vocal teachers in your building mounted a teacher-to-teacher campaign to scuttle the recommendations. Some based their concerns on educational grounds, as overheard in a math teacher's comments to English department colleagues. "You must consider the pedagogy of mathematics. Students in math courses need consistent, year-long courses. Block scheduling is a failure when it comes to mathematics." Others, particularly those who taught music, art, and higher-level foreign languages worried that, "These recommendations will destroy

[1]*Written for this text by Nancy Nestor-Baker.*

our electives. Teachers will lose their jobs and high achieving students will lose opportunities." Aghast, you saw the web of support developed through months of committee work begin to unravel.

It wasn't long before some parents were up in arms, complaining that the proposed changes would harm their children's education. The parent group, while small, was made up of white, well-connected, higher-income residents. They did not want any changes to be made to the traditional education program—and they knew how to apply pressure and generate support for their views. As one father said, "The school worked for me and it's working just fine for my son. Why tinker around with a school that works well?" Others proclaimed loudly that any changes were a "taxpayer boondoggle" without any "proof of need or chance of success." Most of the parents of children who stood to gain the most from change were silent. The few who spoke up were ridiculed and accused of "less than effective parenting." While no overt racial comments were made, you sensed racial undertones in some of the parent group's comments.

The data had not changed; the evidence of underperformance was still clear. But the data flew in the face of dearly held assumptions and values. You were frustrated by the e-mails and phone messages you received from parents and the conversations you held with faculty members. You thumbed through a list of the most recent negative comments:

- "Why all this push to get those kind of kids to do well? Maybe you should be more realistic about their chances. Somebody has to flip burgers and clean bathrooms."
- "Some students are going to fail. Simple knowledge of the bell curve tells you that."
- "We pay high taxes to go to this school. The parents have spoken but you are not listening to what the people want."

- "I see no reason to change what I have done for 20 years."
- "Student achievement is not my responsibility. It is the student's responsibility. If they choose to fail, it's their problem and they need to learn from that."
- "What's so wrong with our traditional school, anyway?"

You now understand that people have very different ideas about education and about who should be educated. You also understand that tradition can be more important than success. In your more cynical moments, you have begun to feel that the class system can matter more than the individual students. Picking up your sheaf of data, you head for the media center to meet with your teachers. As your footsteps echo in the hall, you wonder where to go from this point. How can educational practice be moved forward in your building? What more can be done to help faculty and parents see the need for change? What agendas are at work among those who oppose change? Is it possible that you are wrong to try to restructure? How much say should various groups have in deciding how education should be delivered? As you face your teachers, your thoughts begin to gel and you begin to speak. . . .

Assume you are the principal of this school.

- What is your diagnosis of the problem(s)?
- What is your plan of action for the short term? Longer term?
- Outline what you are going to say to the teachers as you now face them in a faculty meeting.
- Try to anticipate the negative as well as the positive consequences of your speech to the teachers and your action plan.
- Do you think the principal here can lead effectively? Why?

Motivational Challenge: The Superintendent Is Watching

You have just started as the new principal of Martin Luther King Elementary School. This is your first job as principal. After serving in a nearby elementary school, first as a teacher for five years and then as the assistant principal for one year, the opportunity opened for you to become the principal of your own school. Martin Luther King Elementary (K–4) is a relatively small school with only 15 teachers. The school is an urban one with a diverse student population—approximately 30 percent of the students are African American, 30 percent are Hispanic, 30 percent are white, and the remainder are of Asian descent. The school scores on statewide proficiency tests are slightly below average, falling at the 42nd percentile.

The first two months of school have passed quickly for everyone—especially for you as you spend most of the time getting to know your students and teachers and making sure that the school is running smoothly. You feel good about how things have gone thus far. There are always the routine problems with student discipline, complaining parents, teacher tensions, PTA initiatives, and bureaucratic directives, but you feel good about things on that front. Most would agree that your school was well administered.

But you have a nagging feeling about what is going on in the classrooms and how much progress students are making in the basic skill areas of reading, writing, and mathematics. Nothing specific leaps to mind except your final conversation with the superintendent, Dr. Rosa Young, the night you were hired. She was very direct in her message. On the one hand, she proclaimed confidence in your ability to improve student performance at Martin Luther King, but on the other hand, she was clear that you had two years to raise the proficiency test scores or else she would mandate new reading and math programs that she believed would make a difference. You embraced the challenge that evening and your words keep coming back. "No problem!" you had exclaimed as you shook hands with Dr. Young. You were surprised a month later when she sent you a personal memo encouraging you to "make a difference." Moreover, she was offering you monetary support for professional development of teachers in your school. "No problem, make a difference," you keep thinking.

Now the reality of the challenge keeps flashing through your thoughts. "No problem, make a difference." It is time to move from maintaining the organization to initiating action that will have a positive impact on the teachers and students of your school. As you consider the teachers in your school, there are three groups. One group is composed of five teachers who are either second-year or third-year teachers plus two new teachers you helped select. All seven of these teachers are eager, enthusiastic and easy to work with. Five other teachers are good teachers, but they seem rather indifferent to any new ideas or innovative programs; they just do their jobs. Finally, like most schools, you have three teachers who are "Old Guard." These three account for 73 years of teaching experience, most of it in the same building stretching back to when the school was simply the Fourth Ward Elementary with a predominantly white population. The Old Guard is a negative group. No matter what comes up, they say, "It won't make any difference. We've been there and done that." The indifferent group usually just shrugs, whereas the new group tries to come up with some different ways of doing things.

At the last faculty meeting, you suggested that each grade level set goals to improve reading performance. Resistance had met your suggestion. "We tried that eight years ago and it made no difference," was the first response from the leader of the Old Guard, Sam Horton. What ensued for the next 30 minutes was general carping about the low ability and indifference of the students, lack of student and parent motivation, not enough time, not enough extra materials, not enough teaching aids, and on and on. The meeting was a fiasco. The Old Guard led the "do nothing" charge; the indifferents followed; and the new group said little and appeared to acquiesce. This was not what you had in mind, but you could see a pattern of apathy, indifference, and opposition to change emerging. The new group of seven is able and willing to move forward, but you are afraid that they will be influenced by the more experienced teachers into a mode of pessimistic rather than optimistic thinking.

You need a plan to motivate the teachers to do their best. The reading and mathematics instructional programs appear more than adequate. Each teacher has at least a part-time teaching aid. Class size is reasonable. Instructional materials are plentiful; teachers get what they need. All in all, the materials and curriculum are fine. What is lacking, in your judgment, is strong motivation on the part of some of your teachers. You decide that you have to encourage and protect the new teachers, stimulate the indifferents to commit to some new goals and procedures, and isolate the Old Guard while working one-on-one with each of them to improve the performance of their students. You have the resources that you need to engage in professional development with your teachers, that is, you have professional development days and money. What to do? Should you engage in different motivational strategies for each of the groups—new teachers, indifferents, and Old Guard? You consider the following options to motivate students and teachers at Martin Luther King Elementary School.

- Develop a strategy to enhance a high degree of collective efficacy among the new teachers and indifferents. What mastery experiences are needed and how will you get them for your teachers? What kinds of models or other vicarious experiences should your teachers have and where will they get them? What kind of activities will be useful to persuade teachers that they can improve the proficiency of their students? What kind of affective state is needed in your school to develop the collective efficacy that you need? How will you achieve that state?
- Develop a strategy to have your teachers set some realistic performance goals for their students. Make sure the goals are specific, challenging, and attainable. Also find ways to have teachers commit to the goals.
- Design a strategy to develop a high degree of teacher efficacy in selected teachers. How can you help develop in the teachers a belief that they have the capability to organize and execute the courses of action required to successfully improve the reading performance

of their students? How can you make their task attainable? What kinds of skills and knowledge do they need?

- Develop a strategy to motivate the Old Guard teachers. What kind of motivation is mostly likely to work—intrinsic or extrinsic? What are your alternatives in each area? How much time should you invest in these teachers? Should you just forget about these teachers and focus all your energy on the others? But what about their students?

Suddenly a buzzing phone interrupts your thoughts, and your secretary informs you that Superintendent Young is on the line. You are surprised. Actually, it is not Dr. Young on the phone but her assistant who wants you to know that the superintendent's office is ready to do what it can to help you raise reading test scores for next year. The conversation that pursues is friendly and supportive, but there is an edge. The unspoken message is that if scores don't go up, the superintendent's office may well mandate changes. There is no question that you need a plan to motivate your teachers and their students to improve. You have just begun to consider what motivational strategies you will use. With whom should you consult? What motivation perspectives are most useful? What are your first steps? Your job is clear: ***Develop a plan and implementation strategy to motivate your teachers to improve the reading performance of their students.*** Just do it.

CASE 6

Parental Demand[1]

Judy Claxton was hired as building principal at Oak Street Elementary, one of three primary schools serving an affluent bedroom community 20 miles north of a booming metropolitan area. Housing nearly 400 K–3 students, 22 certified staff, and 12 support staff, Oak Street Elementary was by far the oldest building in the district. In fact, not more than a decade ago it was the only elementary school in the district ser-

[1]*Written for this text by Thomas Reed.*

ving all children in grades K–6 for the previous quarter of a century. While students living in the luxurious homes at the town's perimeter attended the two new state-of-the-art primary buildings, Oak Street was the most diverse of the three schools. Its enrollment was mostly comprised of students whose families had lived in the community for generations, and many in the community were growing increasingly uncomfortable with the influx of "new money." While many "Oak Streeters" too were from wealthy, professional households, the school did have a small number of displaced students from lower and middle socioeconomic conditions.

This was Judy's first principalship. Beginning her career as a sixth grade science teacher, she most recently served as elementary curriculum director in a rural county district on the opposite side of the state. Desperately missing daily interaction with students, she knew she wanted to be a building principal and embarked on a statewide search to find a position. Following the Board of Education's official action to employ her the second Monday in August, she had scarcely two weeks to move her belongings, get into her school, introduce herself to her teaching and support staff, and prepare for the 400 primary children who would be arriving at the end of the month.

To say she was surprised to get the job was an understatement. After all, she knew from a long-time friend who happened to teach at the high school that Daniel Baines also applied for the position. Baines was a third grade teacher who had served in that building in the same classroom for 24 years. He was well respected and liked by the rest of the staff, and numerous letters of support from colleagues seemed to make him the clear favorite from the start. Why the search committee didn't select him was a mystery, but his feelings for being passed over weren't. He was bitter, and he would never forgive those responsible.

Early one morning, as teachers readied their classrooms in the oppressive August heat, Judy Claxton found Mr. Baines inventorying textbooks. "Good morning, Dan," she said. He raised his head only a moment until he realized who had spoken to him. "Is there anything I can do to assist? Are you finding everything you need?" she asked politely.

Baines worked on, counting textbooks, carefully checking the condition of each one. Judy struggled to find something else to say. "Please don't hesitate to call on me if there is anything I can do for you. I want you to know my door is open."

"Look," snapped Baines. "That was MY job! I don't know who you had pulling strings for you, and I don't know how you got it, but I am quite certain there is nothing you can do for me except leave me alone."

Stunned, Judy Claxton turned and retreated to her office. This was not the way she hoped her first meeting with Mr. Baines would go. She knew of no one in central office who had pulled any strings. She didn't KNOW anyone in central office. No one owed her any favors. She was certain that her selection was based on her performance as a classroom teacher and administrator, her vision for school leadership, and her dedication to the profession. For the time being, she would give Dan Baines the distance he asked for although she knew sooner or later, she would need to confront him again.

Though hectic and sometimes overwhelming, the opening of school went well for Ms. Claxton, that is until one evening a couple of weeks into the first grading period. She received a call at home from a parent, Dr. Marcy Davis, expressing concern about an incident at school involving her son, Hunter, and his teacher. Dr. Davis advised the principal that she and her husband, John, a lawyer from a prominent family in town, would be at the principal's office promptly at 8:00 AM to air a formal complaint. Before Principal Claxton had a chance to respond, the phone line went dead. She sat disoriented.

Certain to get to school early the next morning, Principal Claxton arrived at 7:15 and headed straight for the student files. Leafing through them, she found a thin one tabbed "Hunter Scott Davis." She opened it and found little evidence of any trouble. In fact, the only hint of difficulty was Hunter's classroom assignment for this year—Third Grade, Mr. Baines. The principal had not spoken to Baines since his terse rebuke of her a few weeks prior, but she instinctively knew that this parent conference would likely lead to a confrontation with him.

At 7:30, Mr. Baines unlocked his classroom door just as he had done every morning for 26 years. This time, standing behind him was his principal.

"Dan, I received a call at home last night from Hunter Davis's mother." Baines looked irritated. "She was upset over an incident that happened at school yesterday, but didn't give me any details. She and her husband are coming in at 8:00 to meet with me. Is there anything I should know?"

"I don't have any idea what she is talking about," Mr. Baines said coldly. "Nothing happened. But I'm sure whatever the Davis's want, they will get. They always do." His voiced trailed off as he walked into his classroom leaving Principal Claxton standing alone in the hallway.

Just before 8:00, the principal's secretary, Nancy Drummond, arrived. Principal Claxton immediately called her into her office. "I have an 8:00 meeting with Marcy and John Davis about their son Hunter. Do you know anything about these people?"

Nancy's eyes lit up, "Oh," she gasped, "they are wonderful! They always support the school and the teachers. Volunteers . . . big donors . . . alumni . . . they graduated from here about 15 years ago. You won't have any trouble."

"What about their son, Hunter?" Judy probed.

"Well, you know how boys can be sometimes," Nancy replied in a dismissive tone. "Trouble just seems to find him. But nothing serious, he's just a little ornery—a lot like his father was." She chuckled a reflective laugh, sighed and exited.

A short time later, the principal heard her secretary enthusiastically welcoming the Davises in the outer office. Principal Claxton emerged and greeted the parents with a confident smile and a handshake. Then she invited them into her office, closed the door, and began, "Tell me about your concerns."

Pointedly, Dr. Davis explained that Mr. Baines wrongfully accused Hunter of bullying some other third graders and ordered him to stand on the wall. Innocent, Hunter tried to explain his side of the story. That was when the teacher grabbed for him, knocked him down, and then dragged Hunter by one arm to the farthest point on the wall where he stood in blazing sun without water or shade for 20 minutes. "Hunter was extremely upset when I picked him up from latchkey. So I contacted his friends' parents who confirmed his version of the story. His friends saw the whole thing."

Judy respectfully interjected, "Have you spoken with Mr. Baines about this?"

"No!" the parents replied in unison. "We're afraid if we say something, he'll take it out on Hunter. That is the way he is. We've had other parents warn us about him."

"I think it would be best if I called Mr. Baines down here and we could hear his explanation," Judy offered. The parents refused, going on to demand that Hunter be moved to a different third grade classroom.

"You should know, Ms. Claxton," the mother stood, "the board president and superintendent are close friends and neighbors of ours. They have already assured me that Mr. Baines will be punished swiftly and severely. We are keeping Hunter home today and expect you will have a new classroom assignment for him by tomorrow morning." She turned away and exited defiantly. Her husband followed, stopping only to add, "I really don't think we can afford to have teachers like Baines in the classroom."

Judy Claxton removed her glasses, eased back in her chair, rubbed her eyes and drew a deep breath. She had a strong feeling that things could quickly escalate and get out of control.

- What are Judy Claxton's immediate problems?
- What is her long-term problem?
- Should she move swiftly to protect the child or cautiously to protect the rights of the teacher?
- Should she involve the students who claim to have witnessed the incident?
- How can she buy more time without jeopardizing the safety of the child or neglecting the request of the parents?
- What are the positive and negative consequences of honoring the parents' request to move the child to a new classroom?
- Should the superintendent be consulted?
- Put yourself in the principal's role and develop a strategy to deal with the difficulty.

CASE 7

Dilemma at Urban High[1]

Urban High is one of more than 100 high schools in a major metropolitan center. From the outside Urban High looks forbidding. It is a five-story brick building built in part by the grandparents and great-grandparents of its current students. The equally old

[1]Written for this text by John Tarter.

and imposing Catholic Church a few blocks away was built almost entirely by the labor of then recent immigrants. The neighborhood is a model of stability, and local shops carry a flavor of Italy. Indeed, the common language is Italian and some bakeries and restaurants have a reputation throughout the region for their excellence.

The other side of the stability is an insularity that keeps residents, both young and old, focused inwardly and narrowly. The people in this community do not engage the greater city of which their neighborhood is a part. In many respects the community is a throwback to earlier times of ethnic segregation, and this context plays out in the schools surprisingly.

A substantial number of the high school students are unprepared to speak formal English. They come from Italian-speaking homes in which Italian is the first language. They have learned enough English to get by local grade school programs, but faced by the challenges of secondary education they find reading difficult and the consequence is often failure. Make no mistake about it, these students have the talent but, unfortunately, that ability has not translated into a fundamental grasp and use of Standard English.

Principal Dante Lavelli has roots in the neighborhood. By stint of hard work and an enlightened mother, he made a success of the public secondary and city university system. After he graduated from the city university with a doctorate in educational leadership, he was able to fulfill his desire to return to a school where he had been a student and a teacher some years ago. In the intervening years, while continuing his studies, he worked as an assistant principal and, finally, principal of another large urban high school. But there was something special about returning to Sorrento Heights, the old neighborhood.

Dr. Lavelli understands the predicament of many of these young people who have difficulty with English through no fault of their own. Determined to do something about the problem, he was successful in developing a grant to help students who didn't have the language skills to keep pace in the regular English program. Although the program was not exclusively for Italian-speaking students from Sorrento Heights, they comprised a little over half of the enrollment. The remainder of these Limited English Proficiency enrollees were students transferring to Urban High from other parts of the city or recent immigrants.

Lavelli's program was successful. Guided by relevant research, the reading program has no classes larger that 20 students; in fact, 15 was the average. Teachers provided independent tutorials for students and each student progressed at his or her own pace. The program was individualized and intensive. Typically in a year students were able to join their classmates in the regular program and do well. It seemed too good to be true.

Alas, after only two years, hard times came to the city and to Urban High. There were no funds available to continue the successful program. The granting agencies had no resources and the city resources were needed for programs of higher priority. Everyone was genuinely sorry to see the resources dry up and the program end, but such is life in the big city.

Lavelli was committed to the children and the program, but he was blocked at every turn in his quest for funding. His superiors told him that "We understand your dilemma, and we sympathize, but our hands are tied." Lavelli was determined to move forward and address the needs of his students. What could he do?

- To whom could Lavelli turn?
- What is the immediate problem? The long-term problem?
- Is this issue worth the time and effort that it will likely take to make a difference?
- Is this a political problem? With a political solution?
- Can he mobilize the community?
- Develop short- and long-term strategies of action.

CASE 8

Litigation, Religion, and Politics[1]

The Washington School District is a K–12 system with 4,500 students, which was formed as a result of a lengthy desegregation law case. The Commissioner of Education ordered the forced merger of the wealthy and white Washington Township school system with the heavily minority Washington City schools. The case was triggered by the K–8 Washington Township attempt to withdraw its high school–age population from Washington High School and build its own high school. The consequence would have been an increase in Washington

[1]This case was written for this text by Dr. Harry Galinski, Paramus, NJ.

High School's minority population from 20 to 70 percent. The commissioner of education not only denied Washington Township's withdrawal request but also determined that the best interests of the children would be served by merging both school systems into one desegregated K–12 school system, a decision upheld by the state supreme court.

The first reactions from many of the parents and from the board of education of Washington Township were anger and threats to boycott the new school system. In fact over 20 percent of the parents did withdraw their children and enrolled them in private or parochial schools. Because the students in the Washington Township schools were almost all white, a state desegregation plan was implemented that created four elementary school zones, each with four public and four Catholic elementary schools.

New Superintendent

Dr. Lawrence Epstein had just been appointed the superintendent of the merged district following the retirement of the former superintendent, who had been instrumental in the creation of the new district. Although this is Dr. Epstein's first superintendency, he came to Washington with a strong background having served as a teacher, guidance director, principal, and assistant superintendent; in fact, he has both urban and suburban school experience during his 21 years as a public school teacher and administrator.

The Board of Education

Because this is a merged school district, the composition of the board is determined by the percentage of students who attend the district from either Washington Township or Washington City. Superintendent Epstein inherited a board with five members from Washington Township and the other four from the city. The merger is now 10 years old and many of the fears that caused parents to pull their children from the then new school district never materialized, and the reputation of the school district has improved significantly. Washington High School is considered one of the best in the state and is proud of its ethnic and racial diversity. The board members are also proud of their schools and pleased with their selection of the new superintendent. Board members no longer vote to represent where they live, but they see their responsibility to the entire district. Al-

though they are a diverse group, they are all college educated, successful in their careers, and have or have had children in the merged school district. They function well together and present a united front to the public and staff.

The Problem

Three months after Dr. Epstein took over the reins as superintendent, he received a telephone call from an irate parochial school parent protesting a notice from the district's transportation coordinator that his children would no longer be entitled to receive "courtesy busing." The state's requirement for busing students is primarily based on a minimum distance of two miles from a student's home to the assigned elementary school. Many of the students attending the elementary schools live less than two miles from their schools, but they are transported under the board of education policy called "courtesy busing." When a board of education decides to provide transportation for students who live less than two miles from their schools, the district does not receive any financial reimbursement from the state for these students. "Courtesy busing" is further complicated by a series of decisions by commissioners of education in this state that ordered public boards of education to provide transportation to private and parochial students on the same basis as they do to their public school students.

The superintendent listened patiently to the parent's complaint and promised that he would investigate the case and get back to him. Superintendent Epstein called Marilyn Ricco, his transportation coordinator, to his office to provide him with the rationale or policy that supported the decision to remove this parent's children from the eligible list of students provided transportation. Marilyn Ricco explained that Jim Ryan, the parent who was protesting the decision, was no longer eligible for courtesy busing. Mr. Ryan had removed his children from one parochial school and enrolled them in another one because of a dispute with the parochial school principal. The decision by the parent to remove his children from the parochial school in one of the elementary school districts created by the desegregation plan and enroll them in another parochial school resulted in forfeiting his right to "courtesy busing." The explanation seemed reasonable to the superintendent, particularly when Ricco indicated that all similar cases were handled the same way, and this was strong past practice in the district.

Armed with this information, Superintendent Epstein called Jim Ryan back to tell him why he was supporting the decision by his transportation coordinator. Ryan exploded and angrily threatened a lawsuit because he claimed that he had evidence that there were a number of parochial school students being transported under similar circumstances. Dr. Epstein tried to calm the situation by suggesting that if names and addresses of these other students were produced, then he would consider reversing his decision. The parent, however, refused to inform on his friends. "Just take my word," he said. The conversation ended congenially with both agreeing to keep an open mind.

Dr. Epstein immediately and discreetly launched an investigation into the facts, and what he found, he didn't like. First, it was true that there were many such cases; the parent was correct. Second, the parent was influential in the community and was mobilizing a parental action group. Third, Marilyn Ricco, his transportation coordinator, had not been fair in her administration of the busing policy. When confronted with more than a dozen cases of parochial school students who had been receiving transportation in violation of board policy, she admitted the variance but tried to justify her decision. Finally, this case proved to be only the tip of the iceberg. More than 130 students were subsequently identified who were not eligible for transportation; yet they had been receiving it at a substantial cost to the district.

Faced with this information, the superintendent asked the board president to call a special closed session of the board. The session was closed because of the potential of litigation. The board members expressed their dismay about a practice that has been going on for many years and unanimously agreed that the 100+ parochial students who were not eligible for transportation should be removed from the buses. The board directed the superintendent to do two things: take disciplinary action with Marilyn Ricco and inform the parents of these parochial students that "courtesy busing" for their children would stop.

The superintendent sensed a major challenge that, if not handled effectively, would undermine his leadership. He called a meeting of all the parochial school principals to give them advance notice of the board's intentions and listened carefully to their reactions and suggestions. Although the meeting was cordial, he understood that litigation was inevitable. He alerted both the board attorney and members about the outcome of the meeting. The attorney advised the board that the history of these cases suggested that the board's position might not be upheld; however, he promised to review the state Supreme Court's prior decisions in similar cases and report at the next board meeting. Meanwhile the superintendent was directed to notify the parents by letter that in the following school year busing would not be provided.

It took only a week after the letters were sent for the board of education to receive notice that the parents of the affected students had retained an attorney and litigation to reverse the board's decision was being filed. The reaction came as no surprise, but the report of the board's attorney was intriguing. He advised the board that his research had convinced him that not only would the board prevail in the impending litigation but that "courtesy busing" for any private or parochial student was not a requirement. He indicated that all the transportation being provided for all private and parochial students was not required except for those who attend schools more than two miles from their homes.

His findings were a surprise because the board thought that the issue had been settled in the state by a number of decisions from the commissioner of education and state board of education. The attorney informed the board that the issue of "courtesy busing" for private and parochial students had never been appealed to the state's supreme court, and he was convinced that the board would be successful if they determined to proceed with the case. Board members were elated because a saving of over $600,000 a year was a possibility if the attorney were correct in his assessment. Some of the board members were enthused for other reasons beyond the financial reward. They believed that the board would gain widespread support from other boards that would now have the opportunity to save significant money without negatively affecting their programs. The Washington District and its board of education would again gain statewide attention as it did when the district was the first and only one to be formed to resolve the desegregation dilemma.

Superintendent Epstein pondered the prospect of spending the next year or two preparing for litigation as well as dealing with the daily impact of the negative reactions that were sure to come from the parochial schools and churches as well as parents and teachers in the district. He knew that both he and the board members would be the targets of ugly rhetoric and vicious attacks. The board turned to him for his recommendations as they sought the safety of a superintendent's advice. Because he and four board members were not Catholic, they would be special targets during the next few months. He also was concerned that the board members who were Catholic would be pressured in church and by many of their friends. Would they buckle under the impending assault? He knew that he and the board had to make a momentous decision and soon. Oh yes, and then there was his transportation coordinator, Marilyn Ricco; he was under pressure to fire her. He needed a plan and a timetable to act. Assume you are the superintendent.

- Is there a way to prevent this issue from polarizing the community?
- Is litigation inevitable? If not, how can it be avoided?
- What kind of external coalition is likely? What are the consequences?
- Is this issue likely to spill into the school and affect students and teachers? How?
- What kind of political games and tactics are likely to get played out?
- What kind of conflict management styles are needed? Why?
- How should you deal with Marilyn Ricco?
- Formulate a thoughtful plan of action. What are your short-term goals? Long-term goals?

BIBLIOGRAPHY

AASA. (1991). *An Introduction to Total Quality Management: A Collection of Articles on the Concepts of Total Quality Management and W. Edwards Deming.* Arlington, VA: American Association of School Administrators.

Abbott, M. (1965a). Hierarchical Impediments to Innovation in Educational Organizations. In M. Abbott and J. Lovell (Eds.), *Change Perspectives in Educational Administration* (pp. 40–53). Auburn, AL: Auburn University.

Abbott, M. (1965b). Intervening Variables in Organizational Behavior. *Educational Administration Quarterly, 1,* 1–14.

Abbott, M., and Caracheo, F. (1988). Power, Authority, and Bureaucracy. In N. J. Boyan (Ed.), *Handbook of Research on Educational Administration* (pp. 239–57). New York: Longman.

Abelson, R. P., and Levi, A. (1985). Decision-Making and Decision Theory. In G. Lindzey and E. Aronson (Eds.), *Handbook of Social Psychology* (3rd ed., Vol. 1, pp. 231–309). Reading, MA: Addison-Wesley.

Abell, P. (1995). The New Institutionalism and Rational Choice Theory. In W. R. Scott and T. Christiansen (Eds.), *The Institutional Construction of Organizations: International and Longitudinal Studies* (pp. 3–14). Thousand Oaks, CA: Sage.

Abramowitz, S., and Tenenbaum, E. (1978). *High School '77.* Washington, DC: National Institute for Education.

Adams, J. E., and Kirst, M. W. (1999). New Demands and Concepts for Educational Accountability: Striving for Results in an Era of Excellence. In J. Murphy and K. S. Louis (Eds.), *Handbook of Research on Educational Administration* (2nd ed., pp. 463–89). San Francisco: Jossey-Bass.

Adler, P. S., and Borys, B. (1996). Two Types of Bureaucracy: Enabling and Coercive. *Administrative Science Quarterly, 41,* 61–89.

Adler, R. B., and Rodman, G. (1991). *Understanding Human Communication.* Fort Worth, TX: Holt, Rinehart and Winston.

Adler, S., Skov, R. B., and Salvemini, N. J. (1985). Job Characteristics and Job Satisfaction: When Cause Becomes Consequence. *Organizational Behavior and Human Decision Processes, 35,* 266–78.

Agho, A. O., Mueller, C. W., and Price, J. L. (1993). Determinants of Employee Job Satisfaction: An Empirical Test of a Causal Model. *Human Relations, 46(8),* 1007–27.

Aiken, M., and Hage, J. (1968). Organizational Interdependence and Intra-Organizational Structure. *American Sociological Review, 33,* 912–30.

Albanese, M. A., and Mitchell, S. A. (1993). Problem-Based Learning: A Review of Literature on Its Outcomes and Implementation Issues. *Academic Medicine, 68,* 52–81.

Aldrich, H. E. (1972). An Organization-Environment Perspective on Cooperation and Conflict between Organizations in the Manpower Training System. In A. R. Negandi (Ed.), *Conflict and Power in Complex Organizations* (pp. 11–37). Kent, OH: Center for Business and Economic Research, Kent State University.

Aldrich, H. E. (1979). *Organizations and Environment.* Englewood Cliffs, NJ: Prentice Hall.

Aldrich, H. E., and Herker, D. (1977). Boundary-Spanning Roles and Organization Structure. *Academy of Management Review, 2,* 217–30.

Aldrich, H. E., and Mindlin, S. (1978). Uncertainty and Dependence: Two Perspectives on

Environment. In L. Karpik (Ed.), *Organization and Environment: Theory, Issues and Reality* (pp. 149–70). Beverly Hills, CA: Sage.

Aldrich, H. E., and Pfeffer, J. (1976). Environments of Organizations. *Annual Review of Sociology, 2,* 79–105.

Alessandra, T., and Hunsaker, P. (1993). *Communicating at Work.* New York: Simon & Schuster.

Alexander, E. R., Penley, L. E., and Jernigan, I. E. (1991).The Effect of Individual Differences on Managerial Media Choice. *Management Communication Quarterly, 5*(2), 155–73.

Alexander, P. A. (1996). The Past, Present, and Future of Knowledge Research: A Reexamination of the Role of Knowledge in Learning and Instruction. *Educational Psychologist, 31,* 89–92.

Alinsky, S. (1971). *Rules for Radicals.* New York: Random House.

Allen, R. F., and Kraft, C. (1982). *The Organizational Unconscious: How to Create the Corporate Culture You Want and Need.* Englewood Cliffs, NJ: Prentice Hall.

Allinder, R. M. (1994). The Relationship between Efficacy and the Instructional Practices of Special Education Teachers and Consultants. *Teacher Education and Special Education, 17,* 86–95.

Allison, G. T. (1971). *Essence of Decision: Explaining the Cuban Missile Crisis.* Boston: Little, Brown.

Allutto, J. A., and Belasco, J. A. (1973). Patterns of Teacher Participation in School System Decision Making. *Educational Administration Quarterly, 9,* 27–41.

Amrein, A. L., and Berliner, D. C. (2002). High-Stakes Testing, Uncertainty, and Student Learning. *Education Policy Analysis Archives, 10* (18). Retrieved April 10, 2003 from http://epaa.asu.edu/epaa/v10n18/.

Amrein-Beardsley, A. L., and Berliner, D. C. (2003). Re-analysis of NAEP Math and Reading Scores in States with and without High-stakes Tests: Response to Rosenshine. *Education Policy Analysis Archives, 11* (25). Retrieved August 10, 2003 from http://epaa.asu.edu/epaa/v11n25/.

Anderman, E. M., and Maehr, M. L. (1994). Motivation and Schooling in the Middle Grades. *Review of Educational Research, 64,* 287–310.

Anderson, B. (1971). Socioeconomic Status of Students and Schools Bureaucratization. *Educational Administration Quarterly, 7,* 12–24.

Anderson, C. S. (1982). The Search for School Climate: A Review of the Research. *Review of Educational Research, 52,* 368–420.

Anderson, D. P. (1964). *Organizational Climate of Elementary Schools.* Minneapolis: Educational Research and Development Council.

Anderson, J. (1976). Giving and Receiving Feedback. In P. R. Lawrence, L. B. Barnes, and J. W. Lorsch (Eds.), *Organizational Behavior and Administration* (pp. 103–11). Homewood, IL: Irwin.

Anderson, J. C., Rungtusanatham, M., and Schroeder, R. G. (1994). A Theory of Quality Management Underlying the Deming Management. *Academy of Management Review, 19* (3), 472–509.

Anderson, J. R. (1990). *Cognitive Psychology and Its Implications* (3rd ed.). New York: Freeman.

Anderson, J. R. (1993). Problem Solving and Learning. *American Psychologist, 48,* 35–44.

Anderson, J. R. (1995). *Cognitive Psychology and Its Implications* (4th ed.). New York: Freeman.

Anderson, J. R., Reder, L. M., and Simon, H. A. (1996). Applications and misapplication of cognitive psychology to mathematics education. Unpublished manuscript (accessible at http://www.psy. cmu.edu/~mm4b/ misapplied.html).

Anderson, L. M. (1989a). Learners and Learning. In M. Reynolds (Ed.), *Knowledge Base for Beginning Teachers* (pp. 85–100). New York: Pergamon.

Anderson, M. B. G., and Iwanicki, E. F. (1984). Teacher Motivation and Its Relationship to Burnout. *Educational Administration Quarterly, 20,* 109–32.

Andrews, J. H. M. (1965). School Organizational Climate: Some Validity Studies. *Canadian Education and Research Digest, 5,* 317–34.

Antonakis, J., Avolio, B. J., and Sivasubramaniam, N. (2003). Context and Leadership: An Examination of the Nine-Factor Full-Range Leadership Theory Using the Multifactor Leadership Questionnaire. *Leadership Quarterly, 14,* 261–95.

Appleberry, J. B., and Hoy, W. K. (1969). The Pupil Control Ideology of Professional Personnel in

"Open" and "Closed" Elementary Schools. *Educational Administration Quarterly, 5,* 74–85.

Arches, J. (1991). Social Structure, Burnout, and Job Satisfaction. *Social Work, 36*(3), 202–6.

Arends, R. I. (2000). *Learning to Teach* (5th ed.). New York: McGraw-Hill.

Argote, L., Turner, M. E., and Fichman, M. (1989). To Centralize or Not to Centralize: The Effects of Uncertainty and Threat on Group Structure and Performance. *Organizational Behavior and Human Performance, 43,* 58–74.

Aristotle (1883). *Politics.* Book I, Chapter 5. London: Macmillan.

Armbruster, B. B., and Anderson, T. H. (1981). Research Synthesis on Study Skills. *Educational Leadership, 39,* 154–56.

Armor, D., Conry-Oseguera, P., Cox, M., King, N., McDonnell, L., Pascal, A., Pauly, E., and Zellman, G. (1976). *Analysis of the School Preferred Reading Program in Selected Los Angeles Minority Schools* (No. R-2007-LAUSD). Santa Monica, CA: Rand.

Arnold, H. J., and House, R. J. (1980). Methodological and Substantive Extensions to the Job Characteristics Model of Motivation. *Organizational Behavior and Human Performances, 25,* 161–83.

Ashcraft, M. H. (2002). *Cognition* (3rd ed.). Upper Saddle River, NJ: Prentice Hall.

Ashford, S. J. (1986). Feedback-Seeking in Individual Adaptation: A Resource Perspective. *Academy of Management Journal, 29,* 465–87.

Ashforth, B. E. (1985). Climate Formations: Issues and Extensions. *Academy of Management Review, 10,* 837–47.

Ashton, P. T., Olejnik, S., Crocker, L., and McAuliffe, M. (1982, April). *Measurement Problems in the Study of Teachers' Sense of Efficacy.* Paper presented at the annual meeting of the American Educational Research Association, New York.

Ashton, P. T., and Webb, R. B. (1986). *Making a Difference: Teachers' Sense of Efficacy.* New York: Longman.

Astuto, T. A., and Clark, D. L. (1985a). *Merit Pay for Teachers.* Bloomington: School of Education, University of Indiana.

Astuto, T. A., and Clark, D. L. (1985b). Strength of Organizational Coupling in the Instructionally Effective School. *Urban Education, 19,* 331–56.

At-Twaijri, M. I. A., and Montanari, J. R. (1987). The Impact of Context and Choice on the Boundary-Spanning Process: An Empirical Study. *Human Relations, 40,* 783–98.

Atwater, D. C., and Bass, B. M. (1994). Transformational Leadership in Teams. In B. M. Bass and B. J. Avolio (Eds.), *Improving Organizational Effectiveness through Transformational Leadership* (pp. 48–83). Thousand Oaks, CA: Sage.

Audia, G., Kristof-Brown, A., Brown, K. C., and Locke, E. A. (1996). Relationship of Goals and Microlevel Work Processes to Performance on a Multipath Task. *Journal of Applied Psychology, 81,* 483–97.

Aupperle, K. E., Acar, W., and Booth, D. E. (1986). An Empirical Critique of *In Search of Excellence:* How Excellent Are the Excellent Companies? *Journal of Management, 12,* 499–512.

Ausubel, D. P. (1963). *The Psychology of Meaningful Verbal Learning.* New York: Grune and Stratton.

Averich, H. A., Carroll, S. J., Donaldson, T. S., Kiesling, H. J., and Pincus, J. (1972). *How Effective Is Schooling: A Critical Review and Synthesis of Research Findings.* Santa Monica, CA: Rand.

Avolio, B. J. (1994). The Alliance of Total Quality and the Full Range of Leadership. In B. M. Bass and B. J. Avolio (Eds.), *Improving Organizational Effectiveness through Transformational Leadership* (pp. 121–45). Thousand Oaks, CA: Sage.

Avolio, B. J. (1999). *Full Leadership Development.* Thousand Oaks, CA: Sage.

Avolio, B. J., Bass, B. M., and Jung, D. I. (1999). Re-examining the Components of Transformational and Transactional Leadership Using the Multifactor Leadership Questionnaire. *Journal of Occupational and Organizational Psychology, 72,* 441–62.

Babbie, E. R. (1990). *Survey Research Methods* (2nd ed.). Belmont, CA:Wadsworth.

Bacharach, S. B. (1988). Four Themes of Reform: An Editorial Essay. *Educational Administration Quarterly, 24,* 484–96.

Bacharach, S. B. (1989). Organizational Theories: Some Criteria for Evaluation. *Academy of Management Review, 14,* 496–515.

Bacharach, S. B., Bamberger, P., Conley, S. C., and Bauer, S. (1990). The Dimensionality of Decision

Participation in Educational Organizations: The Value of Multi-Domain Educative Approach. *Educational Administration Quarterly, 26,* 126–67.

Bacharach, S. B., Conley, S., and Shedd, J. (1986). Beyond Career Ladders: Structuring Teacher Career Development Systems. *Teachers College Record, 87,* 565–74.

Bacharach, S. B., and Mundell, B. L. (1993). Organizational Politics in Schools: Micro, Macro, and Logics of Action. *Educational Administration Quarterly, 29*(4), 423–52.

Bacon, F. (1597). *Meditationes Sacrae.*

Baddeley, A. D. (1986). *Working Memory.* Oxford, UK: Claredon Books.

Baker, M. A. (1991). Gender and Verbal Communication in Professional Settings: A Review of Research. *Management Communication Quarterly, 5*(1), 36–63.

Bailyn, L. (1985). Autonomy in the R & D Lab. *Human Resource Management, 24* (2), 129–46.

Bakkenes, I., de Brabander, C., and Imants, J. (1999). Teacher Isolation and Communication Network Analysis. *Educational Administration Quarterly, 35*(2), 166–202.

Baltzell, D. C., and Dentler, R. A. (1983). *Selecting American School Principals: A Sourcebook for Educators.* Cambridge, MA: Abt Associates.

Bandura, A. (1977). Self-Efficacy: Toward a Unifying Theory of Behavioral Change. *Psychological Review, 84,* 191–215.

Bandura, A. (1986). *Social Foundations of Thought and Action.* Englewood Cliffs, NJ: Prentice Hall.

Bandura, A. (1991). Social Cognitive Theory of Self-Regulation. *Organizational Behavior and Human Decision Processes, 50,* 248–87.

Bandura, A. (1993). Perceived Self-Efficacy in Cognitive Development and Functioning. *Educational Psychologist, 28,* 117–48.

Bandura, A. (1997). *Self-Efficacy: The Exercise of Control.* New York: Freeman.

Bandura, A. (2000). Cultivate Self-Efficacy for Personal and Organizational Effectiveness. In E. A. Locke (Ed.) *Handbook of Principles of Organizational Behavior* (pp. 120–36). Malden, MA: Blackwell.

Bantz, C. R. (1993). *Understanding Organizations: Interpreting Organizational Communication Cultures.* Columbia: University of South Carolina Press.

Barnabe, C., and Burns, M. L. (1994). Teachers' Job Characteristics and Motivation. *Educational Research, 36*(2), 171–85.

Barnard, C. I. (1938). *Functions of an Executive.* Cambridge, MA: Harvard University Press.

Barnard, C. I. (1940). Comments on the Job of the Executive. *Harvard Business Review, 18,* 295–308.

Barnes, R. M. (1949). *Motion and Time Study.* New York: Wiley.

Barnes, K. M. (1994). The Organizational Health of Middle Schools, Trust and Decision Participation. Doctoral diss., Rutgers University, New Brunswick.

Barnett, B. G. (1984). Subordinate Teacher Power in School Organizations. *Sociology of Education, 57,* 43–55.

Baron, R. A. (1998). *Psychology* (4th ed.). Boston: Allyn and Bacon.

Barry, B., and Crant, J. M. (2000). Dyadic Communication Relationships in Organizations: An Attribution/Expectancy Approach. *Organization Science, 11*(6), 648–64.

Barton, P. E. (2001). *Facing the Hard Facts in Educational Reform.* Princeton, NJ: Educational Testing Service.

Bass, B. M. (1985a). *Leadership and Performance Beyond Expectation.* New York: Free Press.

Bass, B. M. (1985b). *Organizational Decision Making.* Homewood, IL: Irwin.

Bass, B. M. (1990). *Bass and Stogdill's Handbook of Leadership* (3rd ed.). New York: Free Press.

Bass, B. M. (1997). Does the Transactional-Transformational Paradigm Transcend Organizational and National Boundaries? *American Psychologist, 52,* 130–39.

Bass, B. M. (1998). *Transformational Leadership: Industrial, Military, and Educational Impact.* Mahwah, NJ: Erlbaum.

Bass, B. M., and Avolio, B. J. (1994). Introduction. In B. M. Bass and B. J. Avolio (Eds.), *Improving Organizational Effectiveness through Transformational Leadership* (pp. 1–10). Thousand Oaks, CA: Sage.

Bates, R. (1987). Conceptions of School Culture: An Overview. *Educational Administration Quarterly, 23,* 79–116.

Baumgartner, F. R., and Leech, B. L. (1998). *Basic Interests: The Importance of Groups in Politics and in Political Science*. Princeton, NJ: Princeton University Press.

Baumgartner, F. R., and Walker, J. L. (1989). Educational Policymaking and the Interest Group Structure in France and the United States. *Comparative Politics, 21*, 273–88.

Becerra, M., and Gupta, A. K. (2003). Perceived Trustworthiness Within the Organization: The Moderating Impact of Communication Frequency on Trustor and Trustee Effects. *Organization Science, 14*(1), 32–44.

Becker, T. E., and Klimoski, R. J. (1989). A Field Study of the Relationship Between the Organizational Feedback Environment and Performance. *Personnel Psychology, 42*, 343–58.

Becker, W. C., Engelmann, S., and Thomas, D. R. (1975). *Teaching 1: Classroom Management*. Chicago: Science Research Associates.

Belasco, J. A., and Allutto, J. A. (1972). Decisional Participation and Teacher Satisfaction. *Educational Administration Quarterly, 8*, 44–58.

Ben-Peretz, M., and Schonmann, S. (1998). Informal Learning Communities and Their Effects. In K. Leithwood and K. S. Louis (Eds.), *Organizational Learning in Schools* (pp. 47–66). Lisse: Swets and Zeitlinger.

Bennis, W. G. (1959). Leadership Theory and Administrative Behavior. *Administrative Science Quarterly, 4*, 259–301.

Bennis, W. G. (1966). *Changing Organizations*. New York: McGraw-Hill.

Bennis, W. G. (1989). *On Becoming a Leader*. Reading, MA: Addison-Wesley.

Bennis, W., and Nanus, B. (1985). *Leaders: The Strategies for Taking Charge*. New York: Harper & Row.

Benson, J. K. (1975). The Interorganizational Network as a Political Economy. *Administration Science Quarterly, 20*, 229–49.

Berends, M., Bodilly, S., Kirby, S. N. (2002). *Facing the Challenges of Whole-School Reform: New American Schools After a Decade*. Santa Monica, CA: RAND. www.rand.org/publications/MR/MR1498/

Berg, C. A., and Clough, M. (1991). Hunter Lesson Design: The Wrong One for Science Teaching. *Educational Leadership, 48*(4), 73–78.

Berieter, C. (1997). Situated Cognition and How I Overcome It. In D. Kirshner and J. A. Whitson (Eds.), *Situated Cognition: Social, Semiotic, and Psychological Perspectives* (pp. 281–300). Mahwah, NJ: Erlbaum.

Berlo, D. K. (1970). *The Process of Communication*. New York: Holt, Rinehart & Winston.

Berman, P., McLaughlin, M., Bass, G., Pauly, E., and Zellerman, G. (1977). *Federal Programs Supporting Educational Change: Factors Affecting Implementation and Continuation* (Vol. 7, No. R-1589/7-HEW). Santa Monica, CA: Rand.

Betz, E. L. (1984). Two Tests of Maslow's Theory of Need Fulfillment. *Journal of Vocational Behavior, 24*, 204–20.

Beyer, J. M., and Trice, H. M. (1987). How an Organization's Rites Reveal Its Culture. *Organizational Dynamics, 15*, 4–24.

Bhagat, R. S., and Chassie, M. B. (1980). Effects of Changes in Job Characteristics on Some Theory-Specific Attitudinal Outcomes: Results from a Naturally Occurring Quasi-Experiment. *Human Relations, 33*, 297–313.

Bidwell, C. E. (1965). The School as a Formal Organization. In J. G. March (Ed.), *Handbook of Organization* (pp. 972–1022). Chicago: Rand McNally.

Bimber, B. (1993). *School Decentralization: Lessons from the Study of Bureaucracy*. Santa Monica, CA: Rand.

Birnbaum, R. (1971). Presidential Succession: An Interinstitutional Analysis. *Educational Record, 52*, 133–45.

Blackburn, R., and Rosen, B. (1993). Total Quality and Human Resources Management: Lessons Learned from Baldrige Award-Winning Companies. *Academy of Management Executive, 2*(3), 49–66.

Blake, R. R., and Mouton, J. S. (1985). *The Managerial Grid III*. Houston, TX: Gulf.

Blau, P. M. (1955). *The Dynamics of Bureaucracy*. Chicago: University of Chicago Press.

Blau, P. M. (1956). *Bureaucracy in Modern Society*. New York: Random House.

Blau, P. M., and Scott, W. R. (1962). *Formal Organizations: A Comparative Approach.* San Francisco: Chandler.

Blau, P. M., and Scott, W. R. (2003). *Formal Organizations: A Comparative Approach.* Stanford, CA: Stanford Business Books.

Bloom, B. S. (1968). Learning for Mastery. *Evaluation Comment, 1*(2). Los Angeles: University of California, Center for the Study of Evaluation of Instructional Programs.

Bluedorn, A. C., and Denhardt, R. B. (1988). Time and Organizations. *Journal of Management, 4,* 299–320.

Blumberg, A. (1984). The Craft of School Administration and Some Other Rambling Thoughts. *Educational Administration Quarterly, 20,* 24–40.

Blumberg, A. (1989). *School Administration as a Craft: Foundations of Practice.* Needham Heights, MA: Allyn and Bacon.

Bobbit, F. (1913). Some General Principles of Management Applied to the Problems of City School Systems. *The Supervision of City Schools, Twelfth Yearbook of the National Society for the Study of Education, Part I* (pp. 137–96). Chicago: University of Chicago Press.

Boje, D. M., and Whetten, D. A. (1981). Effects of Organizational Strategies and Contextual Constraints on Centrality and Attributions of Influence in Interorganizational Networks. *Administrative Science Quarterly, 26,* 378–95.

Bok, D. (1993). *The Cost of Talent.* New York: Free Press.

Bolman, L. G., and Deal, T. E. (1997). *Reframing Organizations: Artistry, Choice, and Leadership* (2nd ed.). San Francisco, CA: Jossey-Bass.

Bolman, L. G., and Deal, T. E. (2003). *Reframing Organizations: Artistry, Choice, and Leadership* (3rd ed.). San Francisco: Jossey-Bass.

Bonstingl, J. J. (1992). The Quality Revolution in Education. *Educational Leadership, 50,* 4–9.

Borman, G. D., Hewes, G. M., Overman, L. T., and Brown, S. (2002). Comprehensive School Reform and Student Achievement. Report N. 59. Baltimore, MD: CRESPAR. Available at www.csos.jhu.edu/crespar.

Bose, C., Feldberg, R., and Sokoloff, N. (1987). *Hidden Aspects of Women's Work.* New York: Praeger.

Bossert, S. T. (1988). School Effects. In N. J. Boyan (Ed.), *Handbook of Research on Educational Administration* (pp. 341–52). New York: Longman.

Bossert, S. T., Dwyer, D. C., Rowan, B., and Lee, G. V. (1982). The Instructional Management Role of the Principal. *Educational Administration Quarterly, 18,* 34–64.

Bowditch, J. L., and Buono, A. F. (1985). *A Primer on Organizational Behavior.* New York: Wiley.

Bowers, D. G. (1976). *Systems of Organizations: Management of the Human Resource.* Ann Arbor: University of Michigan Press.

Boyan, N. J. (1951). A study of the formal and informal organization of a school faculty: the identification of the systems of interactions and relationships among the staff members of a school and an analysis of the interplay between these systems. Doctoral diss. Harvard University, Cambridge.

Boyd, W. L. (1976). The Public, the Professional, and Educational Policy Making: Who Governs? *Teachers College Record, 77,* 539–77.

Boyd, W. L., and Walberg, H. J. (1990). Introduction and Overview. In W. L. Boyd and H. J. Walberg (Eds.), *Choice in Education: Potential and Problems* (pp. ix–xiii). Berkeley, CA: McCutchan.

Brady, L. (1985). The "Australian" OCDQ: A Decade Later. *Journal of Educational Administration, 23,* 53–58.

Brady, R. C. (2003). *Can Failing Schools Be Fixed?* Washington, DC: Fordham Foundation.

Braybrook, D., and Lindblom, C. E. (1963). *The Strategy of Decision.* New York: Free Press.

Bredderman, T. (1983). Effects of Activity-Based Elementary Science on Student Outcomes: A Qualitative Synthesis. *Review of Educational Research, 53,* 499–518.

Bredekamp, S., and Copple, C. (1997). *Developmentally Appropriate Practice in Early Childhood Programs.* Washington, DC: National Association for the Education of Young Children.

Bridges, E. M. (1967). A Model for Shared Decision Making in the School Principalship. *Educational Administration Quarterly, 3,* 49–61.

Bromily, P. (1985). Planning Systems in Large Organizations: Garbage Can Approach with Applications to Defense PPBS. In J. G. March and R. Weissinger-Baylon (Eds.), *Ambiguity and Command: Organization Perspectives on Military*

Decision Making (pp. 120–39). Marshfield, MA: Pitman.

Broms, H., and Gahmberg, H. (1983). Communication to Self in Organizational Cultures. *Administrative Science Quarterly, 28*(3), 482–95.

Brookover, W. B., Schweitzer, J. H., Schneider, J. M., Beady, C. H., Flood, P. K., and Wisenbaker, J. M. (1978). Elementary School Social Climate and School Achievement. *American Educational Research Journal, 15,* 301–18.

Brooks, J. G., and Brooks, M. G. (1993). Becoming a Constructivist Teacher. *In Search of Understanding: The Case for Constructivist Classrooms.* Alexandria, VA: The Association for Supervision and Curriculum Development.

Brophy, J. E., and Good, T. L. (1986). Teacher Behavior and Student Achievement. In M. C. Wittrock (Ed.), *Handbook of Research on Teaching* (3rd ed., pp. 328–75). New York: Macmillan.

Brown, A. (1987). Metacognition, Executive Control, Self-Regulation, and Other More Mysterious Mechanisms. In F. Weinert and R. Kluwe (Eds.), *Metacognition, Motivation, and Understanding* (pp. 65–116). Hillside, NJ: Erlbaum.

Brown, A. F. (1965). Two Strategies for Changing Climate. *CAS Bulletin, 4,* 64–80.

Brown, A. L., Bransford, J., Ferrara, R., and Campione, J. (1983). Learning, Remembering, and Understanding. In P. Mussen (Ed.), Handbook of Child Psychology (Vol. 3). New York: Wiley.

Brown, D. (1990). *Decentralization and School-Based Management.* New York: Falmer Press.

Brown, J. S. (1990). Toward a New Epistemology for Learning. In C. Frasson and G. Gauthier (Eds.) *Intelligent Tutoring Systems: At the Crossroads of Artificial Intelligence and Education* (pp. 266–82). Norwood, NJ: Ablex.

Bruner, J. S. (1966). *Toward a Theory of Instruction.* New York: Norton.

Bruner, J. S., Goodnow, J. J., and Austin, G. A. (1956). *A Study of Thinking.* New York: Wiley.

Bruning, R. H., Schraw, G. J., and Ronning, R. R. (1999). *Cognitive Psychology and Instruction* (3rd ed.). Englewood Cliffs, NJ: Merrill.

Bryk, A. S. (1993). Educational Indicator Systems: Observations on Their Structure Interpretation, and Use. *Review of Research in Education, 19,* 451–84.

Bryk, A. S., Lee, V. E., and Holland, P. (1993). *Catholic Schools and the Common Good.* Cambridge, MA: Harvard University Press.

Bryk, A. S., and Schneider, B. (2002). *Trust in Schools: A Core Resource for Improvement.* New York: Russell Sage Foundation.

Bryman, A. (1996). Leadership in Organizations. In S. R. Clegg, C. Hardy, and W. R. Nord (Eds.), *Handbook of Organizational Studies.* Thousand Oaks, CA: Sage.

Burbules, N. C. (1993). *Dialogue in Teaching: Theory and Practice.* New York: Teachers College Press.

Burbules, N. C., and Bruce, B. C. (2000). Theory and Research on Teaching as Dialogue. In V. Richardson (Ed.), *Handbook of Research on Teaching* (4th ed.). Washington, DC: American Educational Research Association.

Burlingame, M. (1979). Some Neglected Dimensions in the Study of Educational Administration. *Educational Administration Quarterly, 15,* 1–18.

Burns, J. M. (1978). *Leadership.* New York: Harper & Row.

Burns, T., and Stalker, G. M. (1961). *The Management of Innovation.* London: Travistock.

Burrell, G., and Morgan, G. (1980). *Sociological Paradigms and Organizational Analysis.* London: Heinemann.

Calas, M. B., and Smircich, L. (1997). *Postmodern Management Theory.* Brookfield, VE: Ashgate Publishing.

Callahan, R. E. (1962). *Education and the Cult of Efficiency.* Chicago: University of Chicago Press.

Camburn, E., Rowan, B., and Taylor, J. (2003, Winter). Distributed Leadership in Schools: The Case of Elementary Schools Adopting Comprehensive School Reform Models. *Educational Evaluation and Policy Analysis, 25,* 347–373.

Cameron, K. S. (1978). Measuring Organizational Effectiveness in Institutions of Higher Education. *Administrative Science Quarterly, 23,* 604–32.

Cameron, K. S. (1984). The Effectiveness of Ineffectiveness. *Research in Organizational Behavior, 6,* 235–85.

Cameron, K. S., and Quinn, R. E. (1999). *Diagnosing and Changing Organizational Climate.* New York: Addison-Wesley.

Cameron, K. S., and Whetten, D. A. (1983). *Organizational Effectiveness: A Comparison of Multiple Models.* New York: Academic.

Cameron, K. S., and Whetten, D. A. (1996). Organizational Effectiveness and Quality: The Second Generation. *Higher Education Handbook of Theory and Research, 11,* 265–306.

Campbell, J. P. (1977). On the Nature of Organizational Effectiveness. In P. S. Goodman and J. M. Pennings (Eds.), *New Perspectives on Organizational Effectiveness* (pp. 13–55). San Francisco: Jossey-Bass.

Campbell, J. P., Dunnette, M. D., Lawler, E. E. III, and Karl E. Weick, J. (1970). *Managerial Behavior, Performance, and Effectiveness.* New York: McGraw-Hill.

Campbell, J. P., and Pritchard, R. D. (1976). Motivation Theory in Industrial and Organizational Psychology. In M. D. Dunnette (Ed.), *Handbook of Industrial and Organizational Psychology* (pp. 63–130). Chicago: Rand McNally.

Campbell, R. (1971). *NCPEA—Then and Now.* National Conference of Professors of Educational Administration Meeting, University of Utah, Salt Lake City.

Campbell, R., Fleming, T., Newell, L. J., and Bennion, J. W. (1987). *A History of Thought and Practice in Educational Administration.* New York: Teachers College Press.

Capper, C. A., and Jamison, M. T. (1993). Let the Buyer Beware: Total Quality Management and Educational Research and Practice. *Educational Researcher, 22*(8), 25–30.

Carey, M. R. (1992). Transformational Leadership and the Fundamental Option for Self-Transcendence. *Leadership Quarterly, 3* (3), 217–36.

Carlson, R. O. (1962). *Executive Succession and Organizational Change.* Chicago: University of Chicago, Midwest Administration Center.

Carlson, R. O. (1964). Environmental Constraints and Organizational Consequences: The Public School and Its Clients. In D. E. Griffiths (Ed.), *Behavioral Science and Educational Administration* (pp. 262–76). Chicago: University of Chicago Press.

Carnegie Task Force on Teaching as a Profession (1986). *A Nation Prepared: Teachers for the 21st Century.* New York: Carnegie Corporation, Carnegie Forum on Education and the Economy.

Carnoy, M., and Loeb, S. (2002). Does External Accountability Affect Student Outcomes? A Cross State Analysis. *Educational Evaluation and Policy Analysis, 24*(4), 305–31.

Carpenter, H. H. (1971). Formal Organizational Structural Factors and Perceived Job Satisfaction of Classroom Teachers. *Administrative Science Quarterly, 16,* 460–65.

Carroll, S. J. (1986). Management by Objectives: Three Decades of Research and Experience. In S. L. Rynes and G. T. Milkovich (Eds.), *Current Issues in Human Resource Management.* Plano, TX: Business Publications.

Cartwright, D., and Zander, A. (1953). *Group Dynamics: Research and Theory.* Evanston, IL: Row, Peterson.

Casner-Lotto, J. (1988). Expanding the Teacher's Role: Hammond's School Improvement Process. *Phi Delta Kappan, 69,* 349–53.

Castrogiovanni, G. J. (1991). Environmental Munificence: A Theoretical Assessment. *Academy of Management Review, 16*(3), 542–65.

Chandler M. (1997). Stumping for Progress in a Post-Modern World. In E. Amsel and K. A. Renninger (Eds.). *Change and Development: Issues of Theory, Method, and Application* (pp. 1–26). Mahwah, NJ: Erlbaum.

Chapman, D. W., and Hutcheson, S. M. (1982). Attrition from Teaching Careers: A Discriminant Analysis. *American Educational Research Journal, 19,* 93–105.

Charters, W. W., Jr. (1967). Stability and Change in the Communication Structure of School Faculties. *Educational Administration Quarterly, 3,* 15–38.

Chase, F. S. (1951). Factors for Satisfaction in Teaching. *Phi Delta Kappan, 33,* 127–32.

Chatman, J. A., and Jehn, K. A. (1994). Assessing the Relationship between Industry Characteristics and Organizational Culture: How Different Can You Be? *Academy of Management Journal, 37* (3), 522–53.

Chemers, M. M. (1997). *An Integrative Theory of Leadership.* Mahwah, NJ: Erlbaum.

Chemers, M. M., and Skrzypek, G. J. (1972). Experimental Test of Contingency Model of Leadership Effectiveness. *Journal of Personality and Social Psychology, 24,* 172–77.

Cherrington, D. J. (1991). Need Theories of Motivation. In R. M. Steers and L. W. Porter (Eds.), *Motivation and Work Behavior* (pp. 31–44). New York: McGraw-Hill.

Chisolm, G. B., Washington, R., and Thibodeaux, M. (1980). Job Motivation and the Need Fulfillment Deficiencies of Educators. Annual Meeting of the American Educational Research Association, Boston.

Choo, C. W. (1998). *The Knowing Organization.* New York: Oxford.

Chubb, J. E., and Moe, T. M. (1990). *Politics, Markets, and America's Schools.* Washington, DC: Brookings Institution.

Chung, K. A. (1987). A Comparative Study of Principals' Work Behavior. Doctoral diss., University of Utah, Salt Lake City.

Chung, K. A., and Miskel, C. (1989). A Comparative Study of Principals' Administrative Behavior. *Journal of Educational Administration, 27,* 45–57.

Clampitt, P. G. (2001). *Communicating for Managerial Effectiveness* (2nd Ed.). Newbury Park, CA: Sage.

Clark, D. L., Astuto, T. A., Foster, W. P., Gaynor, A. K., and Hart, A. W. (1994). Organizational Studies: Taxonomy and Overview. In W. K. Hoy, T. A. Astuto, and P. B. Forsyth (Eds.), *Educational Administration: The UCEA Document Base.* New York: McGraw-Hill Primus.

Clark, D. L., Lotto, L. S., and Astuto, T. A. (1984). Effective Schools and School Improvement: A Comparative Analysis of Two Lines of Inquiry. *Educational Administration Quarterly, 20,* 41–68.

Clark, K. E., and Clark, M. B. (Eds.). (1990). *Measures of Leadership.* West Orange, NJ: Leadership Library of America.

Clune, W. H., and White, J. F. (Eds.). (1990). *Choice and Control in American Education. Volume 2: The Practice of Choice, Decentralization and School Restructuring.* New York: Falmer Press.

Cobb, P., and Bowers, J. (1999). Cognitive and Situated Learning: Perspectives in Theory and Practice. *Educational Researcher, 28* (2), 4–15.

Coch, L., and French, J. R. P., Jr. (1948). Overcoming Resistance to Change. *Human Relations, 1,* 512–32.

Coggshall, J. G. (2004). "Reform Refractions: Organizational Perspectives on Standards-Based Reform." In W. K. Hoy and C. G. Miskel (Eds.), *Educational Administration, Policy, and Reform: Research and Measurement.* Greenwich, CT: Information Age.

Coggshall, J. G. Athan, R. G. DeYoung, D. A., and Miskel, C. G. (2003). *Constructing Legitimacy: Policy Actors' Perspectives of Statewide Standards and Assessments.* Paper presented at the Annual Meeting of the American Educational Research Association, Chicago, IL.

Cognition and Technology Group at Vanderbilt. (1990). Some Thoughts about Constructivism and Instructional Design. *Educational Technology, 31*(5), 16–18.

Cognition and Technology Group at Vanderbilt. (1993). Anchored Instruction and Situated Learning Revisited. *Educational Technology, 33*(3), 52–70.

Cohen, D. K. (1987). Schooling More and Liking It Less: Puzzles of Educational Improvement. *Harvard Educational Review, 57,* 174–77.

Cohen, D. K. (1996). Standards-Based Reform: Policy, Practice, and Performance. In H. F. Ladd (Ed.), *Holding Schools Accountable: Performance-Based Reform in Education* (pp. 99–127). Washington, DC: Brookings Institutions.

Cohen, D. K., Raudenbush, S. W., and Ball, D. L. (2003). Resources, Instruction, and Research. *Educational Evaluation and Policy Analysis, 25*(2), 119–42.

Cohen, D. K., and Spillane, J. P. (1992). Policy and Practice: The Relations between Governance and Instruction. *Review of Research in Education, 18,* 3–49.

Cohen, M. D., and March, J. G. (1974). *Leadership and Ambiguity.* New York: McGraw-Hill.

Cohen, M. D., March, J. G., and Olsen, J. P. (1972). A Garbage Can Model of Organizational Choice. *Administrative Science Quarterly, 17,* 1–25.

Cohen, M. D., and Sproull, L. S. (Eds.). (1996). *Organizational Learning.* Thousand Oaks, CA: Sage.

Coleman, J. S. (1990). *Foundations of Social Theory.* Cambridge, MA: Belknap.

Coleman, J. S. (1961). *The Adolescent Society.* New York: Free Press.

Coleman, J. S. (1974). *Power and Structure of Society.* New York: Norton.

Coleman, J. S., Campbell, E. Q., Hobson, C. J., McPartland, J., Mood, A. M., Weinfeld, F. D., and York, R. L. (1966). *Equality of Educational Opportunity.* Washington, DC: U.S. Government Printing Office.

Collins, A., Brown, J. S., and Holum, A. (1991). Cognitive Apprenticeship: Making Thinking Visible. *American Educator, 15*(3), 38–39.

Collins, A., Brown, J. S., and Newman, S. E. (1989). *Cognitive Apprenticeship: Teaching the Crafts of Reading, Writing, and Mathematics.* In L. B. Resnick (Ed.), Knowing, Learning, and Instruction: Essays in Honor of Robert Galser. Hillsdale, NJ: Erlbaum.

Collins, J. (2001). *Good to Great.* New York: Harper Business.

Commons, J. R. (1924). *Legal Foundations of Capitalism.* New York: Macmillan.

Conant, J. B. (1951). *Science and Common Sense.* New Haven: Yale University Press.

Conger, J. A. (1991). Inspiring Others: The Language of Leadership. *Academy of Management Executive, 5*(1), 31–45.

Conger, J. A. (1999). Charismatic and Transformational Leadership in Organizations: An Insider's Perspective on These Developing Streams of Research. *Leadership Quarterly, 10*(2), 145–79.

Conger, J. A., and Kanungo, R. N. (1988). The Empowerment Process: Integrating Theory and Practice. *Academy of Management Journal, 13,* 471–82.

Conley, S. C. (1990). A Metaphor for Teaching: Beyond the Bureaucratic-Professional Dichotomy. In S. B. Bacharach (Ed.), *Educational Reform: Making Sense of It All* (pp. 313–24). Boston: Allyn and Bacon.

Conley, S. C., and Bacharach, S. B. (1990). From School Site-Management to Participatory Site-Management. *Phi Delta Kappan, 72,* 539–44.

Conley, S. C., Bower, S., and Bacharach, S. B. (1989). The School Work Environment and Teacher Career Satisfaction. *Educational Administration Quarterly, 25,* 58–81.

Conley, S., and Levinson, R. (1993). Teacher Work Redesign and Job Satisfaction. *Educational Administration Quarterly, 29*(4), 453–78.

Connolly, T., Conlon, E. J., and Deutsch, S. J. (1980). Organizational Effectiveness: A Multiple-Constituency Approach. *Academy of Management Review, 5,* 211–17.

Constas, H. (1958). Max Weber's Two Conceptions of Bureaucracy. *American Journal of Sociology, 63,* 400–9.

Conway, J. A. (1976). Test of Linearity between Teachers' Participation in Decision Making and Their Perceptions of Schools as Organizations. *Administrative Science Quarterly, 21,* 130–39.

Conway, J. A. (1984). The Myth, Mystery, and Mastery of Participative Decision Making in Education. *Educational Administration Quarterly, 3,* 11–40.

Cook, S. D., and Yanon, D. (1996). Culture and Organizational Learning. In M. D. Cohen and L. S. Sproull (Eds.). *Organizational Learning* (pp. 430–59). Thousand Oaks, CA: Sage.

Cordery, J. L., and Sevastos, P. P. (1993). Responses to the Original and Revised Job Diagnostic Survey: Is Education a Factor in Responses to Negatively Worded Items? *Journal of Applied Psychology, 78* (1), 141–43.

Corno, L., and Snow, R. E. (1986). Adapting Teaching to Individual Differences in Learners. In M. Wittrock (Ed.), *Handbook of Research on Teaching* (3rd ed.). (pp. 605–29). New York: Macmillan.

Corwin, R. G. (1965). Professional Persons in Public Organizations. *Educational Administration Quarterly, 1,* 1–22.

Corwin, R. G., and Borman, K. M. (1988). School as Workplace: Structural Constraints on Administration. In N. J. Boyan (Ed.), *Handbook of Research on Educational Administration* (pp. 209–37). New York: Longman.

Corwin, R. G., and Herriott, R. E. (1988). Occupational Disputes in Mechanical and Organic Social Systems: An Empirical Study of Elementary and Secondary Schools. *American Sociological Review, 53,* 528–43.

Cosgrove, D. (1985). The Effects of Principal Succession on Elementary Schools. Doctoral diss., University of Utah, Salt Lake City.

Cox, A. (1982). *The Cox Report on the American Corporation.* New York: Delacorte.

Craig, R. T. (1999). Communication Theory as a Field. *Communication Theory, 9*(2), 119–61.

Craig, T. (1995). Achieving Innovation through Bureaucracy. *California Management Review, 38*(10), 8–36.

Craik, F. I. M., and Lockhart, R. S. (1972). Levels of Processing: A Framework for Memory Research. *Journal of Verbal Learning and Verbal Behavior, 11*, 671–84.

Cranny, C. J., Smith, P. C., and Stone, E. F. (1992). *Job Satisfaction.* New York: Lexington.

Crehan, E. P. (1985). A Meta-Analysis of Fiedler's Contingency Model of Leadership Effectiveness. Doctoral diss., University of British Columbia, Vancouver.

CTGV (*see* Cognition and Technology Group at Vanderbilt)

Cuban, L. (1983). Effective Schools: A Friendly but Cautionary Note. *Phi Delta Kappan, 64*, 695–96.

Cuban, L. (1984). Transforming the Frog into a Prince: Effective Schools Research, Policy, and Practice at the District Level. *Harvard Educational Review, 54*, 129–51.

Cuban, L. (1990). Cycles of History: Equity versus Excellence. In S. B. Bacharach (Ed.), *Education Reform: Making Sense of It All* (pp. 135–40). Needham Heights, MA: Allyn and Bacon.

Cuban, L. (1998). How Schools Change Reforms: Redefining Reform Success and Failure. *Teachers College Record, 99*(3), 453–77.

Cunningham, W. G., and Gresso, D. W. (1993). *Cultural Leadership.* Boston: Allyn and Bacon.

Cusella, L. P. (1987). Feedback, Motivation, and Performance. In F. M. Jablin, L. L. Putnam, K. Roberts, and L. W. Porter (Eds.), *Handbook of Organizational Communication: An Interdisciplinary Perspective* (pp. 624–78). Newbury Park, CA: Sage.

Cusick, P. A. (1981). A Study of Networks among Professional Staffs in Secondary Schools. *Educational Administration Quarterly, 17*, 114–38.

Cusick, P. A. (1987). Organizational Culture and Schools. *Educational Administration Quarterly, 23*, 3–117.

Cyert, R. M., and March, J. G. (1963). *A Behavioral Theory of the Firm.* Englewood Cliffs, NJ: Prentice Hall.

D'Aunno, T., Sutton, R. L., and Price, R. H. (1991). Isomorphism and External Support in Conflicting Institutional Environments: A Study of Drug Abuse Treatment Units. *Academy of Management Journal, 34*(3), 636–61.

Daft, R. L. (1989). *Organization Theory and Design* (3rd ed.). St. Paul, MN: West.

Daft, R. L. (1994). *Organizational Theory and Design.* St. Paul, MN: West.

Daft, R. L., Bettenhausen, K. R., and Tyler, B. B. (1993). Implications of Top Managers' Communication Choices for Strategic Decisions. In G. P. Huber and W. H. Glick (Eds.), *Organizational Change and Redesign.* New York: Oxford University Press.

Daft, R. L., and Lengel, R. H. (1984). Information Richness: A New Approach to Managerial Behavior and Organizational Design. *Research in Organizational Behavior, 6*, 191–233.

Daft, R. L., and Lengel, R. H. (1986). Organizational Information Requirements, Media Richness, and Structural Design. *Management Science, 32*, 554–71.

Dahnke, G. L., and Clatterbuck, G. W. (Eds.). (1990). *Human Communication: Theory and Research.* Belmont, CA: Wadsworth.

Dalton, M. (1959). *Men Who Manage.* New York: Wiley.

Damanpour, F. (1991). Organizational Innovation. *Academy of Management Journal, 34*, 555–91.

Dansereau, D. F. (1985). Learning Strategy Research. In J. Segal, S. Chipman, and R. Glaser (Eds.), *Thinking and Learning Skills. Volume I: Relating Instruction to Research.* Hillsdale, NJ: Erlbaum.

Darling-Hammond, L. (1984). *Beyond the Commission Reports: The Coming Crisis in Teaching.* Santa Monica, CA: Rand.

Darling-Hammond, L. (1985). Valuing Teachers: The Making of a Profession. *Teachers College Record, 87*, 205–18.

Darling-Hammond, L., and Wise, A. (1985). Beyond Standardization: State Standards and School Improvement. *Elementary School Journal, 85*, 315–36.

Datnow, A., Borman, G. D., Stringfield, S., Overman, L. T., and Castellano, M. (2003). Comprehensive School Reform in Culturally and Linguistically Diverse Contexts: Implementation and Outcomes from a Four-Year Study. *Educational Evaluation and Policy Analysis, 25*(2), 143–70.

Datnow, A., and Castellano, M. E. (2001). Managing and Guiding School Reform:

Leadership in Success for All Schools. *Educational Administration Quarterly, 37*(2), 219–49.

David, J. L., Purkey, S., and White, P. (1989). *Restructuring in Progress: Lessons from Pioneering Districts.* Washington, DC: Center for Policy Research, National Governor's Association.

Deal, T. E. (1985). The Symbolism of Effective Schools. *Elementary School Journal, 85,* 601–20.

Deal, T. E., and Celotti, L. D. (1980). How Much Influence Do (and Can) Educational Administrators Have on Classrooms? *Phi Delta Kappan, 61,* 471–73.

Deal, T. E., and Kennedy, A. A. (1982). *Corporate Cultures: The Rites and Rituals of Corporate Life.* Reading, MA: Addison-Wesley.

Deal, T. E., and Peterson, K. D. (1990). *The Principal's Role in Shaping School Culture.* Washington DC: U.S. Government Printing Office.

Deal, T. E., and Peterson, K. D. (1994). *The Leadership Paradox.* San Francisco, CA: Jossey-Bass.

Deal, T., and Wise, M. (1983). Planning, Plotting, and Playing in Education's Era of Decline. In V. Baldridge and T. Deal (Eds.), *The Dynamics of Educational Change.* San Francisco: McCutchan.

Dean, J. W., and Bowen, D. E. (1994). Management Theory and Total Quality. *Academy of Management Review, 19* (3), 392–418.

deCharms, R. (1976). *Enhancing Motivation.* New York: Irvington.

deCharms, R. (1983). Intrinsic Motivation, Peer Tutoring, and Cooperative Learning: Practical Maxims. In J. Levine and M. Wang (Eds.), *Teacher and Student Perceptions: Implications for Learning* (pp. 391–98). Hillsdale, NJ: Erlbaum.

Deci, E. and Ryan, R. M. (1985). *Intrinsic Motivation and Self-Determination in Human Behavior.* New York: Plenum.

Deci, E., Vallerand, R. J., Pelletier, L. G., and Ryan, R. M. (1991). Motivation and Education: The Self-Determination Perspective. *Educational Psychologist, 26,* 325–46.

De Corte, E., Greer, B., and Verschaffel, L. (1996). Mathematics Learning and Teaching. In D. Berliner and R. Calfee (Eds.), *Handbook of Educational Psychology* (pp. 491–549). New York: Macmillan.

DeDreu, C. (1997). Productive Conflict: The Importance of Conflict Management and Conflict Issues. In C. DeDreu and E. Van De Vliert (Eds.), *Using Conflict in Organizations* (pp. 9–22). London: Sage.

Dee, J. R., Henkin, A. B., Deumer, L. (2003). Structural Antecedents, and Psychological Correlates of Teacher Empowerment. *Journal of Educational Administration, 41,* 257–77.

Deetz, S. (2001). Conceptual Foundations. In Jablin, F. M., and Putnam, L. L. (Eds.), *The New Handbook of Organizational Communication* (pp. 3–46). Thousand Oaks, CA: Sage.

DeFleur, M. L., Kearney, P., and Plax, T. G. (1993). *Mastering Communication in Contemporary America.* Mountain View, CA: Mayfield.

Deming, W. E. (1983). *Quality, Productivity, and Competitive Advantage.* Cambridge: Massachusetts Institute of Technology, Center for Advanced Engineering.

Deming, W. E. (1986). *Out of Crisis.* Cambridge: Massachusetts Institute of Technology, Center for Advanced Engineering.

Deming, W. E. (1993). *The New Economics for Economics, Government, Education.* Cambridge: Massachusetts Institute of Technology, Center for Advanced Engineering.

Denhardt, R. B., and Perkins, J. (1976). The Coming Death of Administrative Man. *Women in Public Administration, 36,* 379–84.

Denison, D. R. (1990). *Corporate Culture and Organizational Effectiveness.* New York: Wiley.

Denison, D. R. (1996). What Is the Difference between Organizational Culture and Organizational Climate? A Native's Point of View on a Decade of Paradigm Wars. *The Academy of Management Review, 3,* 619–54.

Derry, S. J. (1989). Putting Learning Strategies to Work. *Educational Leadership, 47*(5) 4–10.

Derry, S. J. (1992). Beyond Symbolic Processing: Expanding Horizons for Educational Psychology. *Journal of Educational Psychology, 84,* 413–19.

Desimone, L. M., Porter, A. C., Garet, M. S., Yoon, K. S., and Briman, B. F. (2002). *Educational Evaluation and Policy Analysis 24*(2), 81–112.

Dewey, J. (1933). *How We Think.* Boston: Heath.

Dewey, J. (1938). *Experience and Education.* New York: Collier Books.

Dickson, P. H., and Weaver, K. M. (1997). Environmental Determinants and Individual-Level Moderators of Alliance Use. *Academy of Management Journal, 40*(2), 404–25.

Diebert, J. P., and Hoy, W. K. (1977). Custodial High Schools and Self-Actualization of Students. *Educational Research Quarterly, 2,* 24–31.

Dill, R. W. (1958). Environment as an Influence on Managerial Autonomy. *Administrative Science Quarterly, 2,* 409–43.

DiMaggio, P. J. (1988). Interest and Agency in Institutional Theory. In L. G. Zucker (Ed.), *Institutional Patterns in Organizations: Culture and Environments* (pp. 3–21). Cambridge, MA: Ballinger.

DiMaggio, P. J. (1995). Comments on "What Theory is Not." *Administrative Science Quarterly, 40,* 391–97.

DiMaggio, P. J., and Powell, W. W. (1983). The Iron Cage Revisited: Institutional Isomorphism and Collective Rationality in Organizational Fields. *American Sociological Review, 48,* 147–60.

DiMaggio, P. J., and Powell, W. W. (1991). The Iron Cage Revisited: Institutional Isomorphism and Collective Rationality. In W. W. Powell and P. J. DiMaggio (Eds.), *The New Institutionalism in Organizational Analysis* (pp. 41–62). Chicago: University of Chicago Press.

DiPaola, M. F. (1999). Scandal at Placido High: Coincidence or Conspiracy? *Journal of Cases in Educational Leadership* [www.ucea.org]. 2 (3).

DiPaola, M. F., and Hoy, W. K. (1994). Teacher Militancy: A Professional Check on Bureaucracy. *The Journal of Research and Development in Education, 27,* 78–82.

DiPaola, M. F., and Hoy W. K. (2001). Formalization, Conflict, and Change: Constructive and Destructive Consequences in Schools. *The International Journal of Educational Management, 15,* 238–44.

Doherty, K. M., and Skinner, R. A. (2003). Quality Counts 2003. Introduction: State of the States. *Education Week.* /www.edweek.org/sreports/qc03/templates/article.cfm?slug=17sos.h22

Donmoyer, R. B. (1999). The Continuing Quest for a Knowledge Base: 1976–1998. In J. Murphy and K. S. Louis (Eds.), *Handbook of Research on Educational Administration* (2nd ed., pp. 25–44). San Francisco: Jossey-Bass.

Donmoyer, R. B., Scheurich, J., and Imber, M. L. (Eds.). (1994). *The Knowledge Base in Educational Administration: Multiple Perspectives.* Albany: SUNY Press.

Downs, C. W. (1977). *Organizational Communicator.* New York: Harper & Row.

Driscoll, J. W. (1978). Trust and Participation in Decision Making as Predictors of Satisfaction. *Academy of Management Journal, 1,* 44–56.

Driscoll, M. P. (1999). *Psychology of Learning for Instruction.* Boston: Allyn and Bacon.

Drucker, P. F. (1954). *The Practice of Management.* New York: Harper & Row.

Drucker, P. F. (1966). *The Effective Executive.* New York: Harper & Row.

Drucker, P. F. (1968). *The Age of Discontinuity.* New York: Harper & Row.

Dubin, R. (1969). *Theory Building.* New York: Free Press.

Duchastel, P. (1979). Learning Objectives and the Organization of Prose. *Journal of Educational Psychology, 71,* 100–6.

Duignan, P. (1980). Administrative Behavior of School Superintendents: A Descriptive Study. *Journal of Educational Administration, 18,* 5–26.

Duke, D. L., Showers, B. K., and Imber, M. (1980). Teachers and Shared Decision Making: The Costs and Benefits of Involvement. *Educational Administration Quarterly, 16,* 93–106.

Duncan, R. B. (1972). Characteristics of Organizational Environments and Perceived Environmental Uncertainty. *Administrative Science Quarterly, 17,* 313–27.

Duncan, R. B. (1979). What Is the Right Organizational Structure? Decision Free Analysis Provides the Answer. *Organizational Dynamics, 7,* 59–80.

Dvir, T., Eden, D., Avolio, B. J., and Shamir, B. (2002). Impact of Transformational Leadership on Follower Development and Performance: A Field Experiment. *Academy of Management Journal, 45*(40), 735–44.

Dweck, C. S. (1999). Self theories: Their role in motivation, personality, and development. Philadelphia: Psychology Press.

Dweck, C. S., and Bempechat, J. (1983). Children's Theories on Intelligence: Consequences for

Learning. In S. Paris, G. Olson, and W. Stevenson (Eds.), *Learning and Motivation in the Classroom* (pp. 239–56). Hillsdale, NJ: Erlbaum.

Dyer, W. G. (1985). The Cycle of Cultural Evolution in Organization. R. H. Kilmann, M. J. Saxton, and R. Serpa (Eds.) *Gaining Control of the Corporate Culture.* (pp. 200–30). San Francisco: Jossey-Bass.

Ebmeier, H., and Hart, A. W. (1992). The Effects of a Career-Ladder Program on School Organizational Process. *Educational Evaluation and Policy Analysis, 14*(3), 261–81.

Edmonds, R. (1979). Some Schools Work and More Can. *Social Policy, 9,* 28–32.

Einstein, A., and Infeld, L. (1938). *The Evolution of Physics.* New York: Simon & Schuster.

Elmes, M. B., and Costello, M. (1992). Mystification and Social Drama: The Hidden Side of Communication Skills Training. *Human Relations, 45*(5), 427–45.

Elmore, R. F. (1988). *Early Experiences in Restructuring Schools: Voices from the Field.* Washington, DC: Center for Policy Research, National Governor's Association.

Elmore, R. F. (2000). *Building a New Structure for School Leadership.* Washington, DC: Albert Shanker Institute. Available at www.shankerinstitute.org/

Elmore, R. F. (2002a). *Bridging the Gap Between Standards and Achievement.* Washington, DC: Albert Shanker Institute.

Elmore, R. F. (2002b). "Unwarranted Intrusion." *Education Next, 2*(1), 31–35.

Elsbach, K. D., and Sutton, R. I. (1992). Acquiring Organizational Legitimacy through Illegitimate Actions: A Marriage of Institutional and Impression Management Theories. *Academy of Management Journal, 35*(4), 699–738.

Emery, F. E., and Trist, E. L. (1965). The Causal Texture of Organization Environments. *Human Relations, 18,* 21–32.

English, F. W. (1994). *Theory in Educational Administration.* New York: HarperCollins.

English, F. W. (1998). The Cupboard Is Bare: The Postmodern Critique of Educational Administration. *Journal of School Leadership, 7,* 4–26.

English, F. W. (2003). *The Postmodern Challenge to the Theory and Practice of Educational Administration.* Springfield, IL: Charles C. Thomas.

Enoch, Y. (1989). Change of Values during Socialization for a Profession: An Application of the Marginal Man Theory. *Human Relations, 42,* 219–39.

Erez, M., and Zidon, I. (1984). Effects of Goal Acceptance on the Relationship of Goal Difficulty to Performance. *Journal of Applied Psychology, 69,* 69–78.

Estler, S. E. (1988). Decision Making. In N. J. Boyan (Ed.), *Handbook of Research on Educational Administration* (pp. 304–20). New York: Longman.

Etzioni, A. (1960). Two Approaches to Organizational Analysis: A Critique and Suggestion. *Administrative Science Quarterly, 5,* 257–78.

Etzioni, A. (1964). *Modern Organizations.* Englewood Cliffs, NJ: Prentice Hall.

Etzioni, A. (1967). Mixed Scanning: A Third Approach to Decision Making. *Public Administration Review, 27,* 385–92.

Etzioni, A. (1975). *A Comparative Analysis of Complex Organizations.* New York: Free Press.

Etzioni, A. (1986). Mixed Scanning Revisited. *Public Administration Review, 46,* 8–14.

Etzioni, A. (1988). *The Moral Dimension: Toward a New Economics.* New York: Free Press.

Etzioni, A. (1989). Humble Decision Making. *Harvard Business Review, 67,* 122–26.

Evans, M. G., Kiggundu, M. N., and House, R. J. (1979). A Partial Test and Extension of the Job Characteristics Model of Motivation. *Organizational Behavior and Human Performance, 24,* 354–81.

Evensen, D. H., Salisbury-Glennon, J. D., and Glenn, J. (2001). A Qualitative Study of Six Medical Students in a Problem-Based Curriculum: Toward a Situated Model of Self-Regulation. *Journal of Educational Psychology, 93,* 659–76.

Evers, C. W., and Lakomski, G. (1991). *Knowing Educational Administration.* Oxford, England: Pergamon Press.

Farnaham-Diggory, S. (1994). Paradigms of Knowledge and Instruction. *Review of Educational Research, 64,* 463–77.

Fauske, J. R., and Johnson, B. L., Jr. (2002). Principals Respond to the School Environment with Fluidity, Alignment, Vigilance, and Fear. In

W. K. Hoy and C. G. Miskel (Eds.), *Theory and Research in Educational Administration* (pp. 91–119). Greenwich, CT: Information Age.

Fennell, M. L., and Alexander, J. A. (1987). Organizational Boundary Spanning in Institutionalized Environments. *Academy of Management Journal, 30*(3), 456–76.

Ferguson, K. E. (1984). *The Feminist Case against Bureaucracy.* Philadelphia: Temple University Press.

Feynman, R. P. (1985). *Surely You're Joking, Mr. Feynman.* New York: Norton.

Fiedler, F. E. (1967). *A Theory of Leadership Effectiveness.* New York: McGraw-Hill.

Fiedler, F. E. (1971). Validation and Extension of the Contingency Model of Leadership Effectiveness: A Review of Empirical Findings. *Psychological Bulletin, 76,* 128–48.

Fiedler, F. E. (1973). The Contingency Model and the Dynamics of the Leadership Process. *Advances in Experimental Social Psychology, 11,* 60–112.

Fiedler, F. E. (1984). *The Contribution of Cognitive Resources and Leader Behavior to Organizational Performance.* Organization Research Technical Report No. 84–4. Seattle: University of Washington.

Fiedler, F. E., and Chemers, M. M. (1974). *Leadership and Effective Management.* Glenview, IL: Scott, Foresman.

Fiedler, F. E., Chemers, M. M., and Mahar, L. (1976). *Improving Leadership Effectiveness: The Leader Match Concept.* New York: Wiley.

Fiedler, F. E., and Garcia, J. E. (1987). *New Approaches to Effective Leadership: Cognitive Resources and Organizational Performance.* New York: Wiley.

Finkelstein, R. (1998). The Effects of Organizational Health and Pupil Control Ideology on the Achievement and Alienation of High School Students. Doctoral diss., St. John's University.

Finn, C. E., Jr. (2003a). Foreword. *Better Leaders for America's Schools: A Manifesto.* Washington, DC: Thomas B. Fordham Institute. Available at www.edexcellence.net/institute/publication/

Finn, C. E. Jr. (2003b, January 9). Reforming Education: The Hard Part Lies Ahead. *Education Gadfly, 3*(1). Available at www.edexcellence.net/foundation/gadfly/index.cfm

Finn, J. D., and Achilles, C. M. (1999). Tennessee's Class Size Study: Findings, Implications, and Misconceptions. *Educational Evaluation and Policy Analysis, 21*(2), 97–109.

Firestone, W. A. (1991). Merit Pay and Job Enlargement as Reforms: Incentives, Implementation, and Teacher Response. *Educational Evaluation and Policy Analysis, 13*(3), 269–88.

Firestone, W. A., and Bader, B. D. (1992). *Redesigning Teaching: Professionalism or Bureaucracy.* Albany, NY: State University of New York Press.

Firestone, W. A., and Herriott, R. E. (1981). Images of Organization and the Promotion of Change. *Research in the Sociology of Education and Socialization, 2,* 221–60.

Firestone, W. A., and Herriott, R. E. (1982). Two Images of Schools as Organizations: An Explication and Illustrative Empirical Test. *Educational Administration Quarterly, 18,* 39–60.

Firestone, W. A., and Louis, K. L. (1999). Schools as Cultures. In Murphy, J. and Louis, K. S. (Eds.), *Handbook on Research of Educational Administration* (pp. 297–322). San Francisco: Jossey-Bass.

Firestone, W. A., and Pennell, J. (1993). Teacher Commitment, Working Conditions, and Differential Incentives. *Review of Educational Research, 63*(4), 489–526.

Firestone, W. A., Rosenblum, S., Bader, B. D., and Massell, D. (1991). *Education Reform from 1983–1990: State Action and District Response.* New Brunswick, NJ: Consortium for Policy Research in Education.

Firestone, W. A., and Wilson, B. L. (1985). Using Bureaucratic and Cultural Linkages to Improve Instruction: The Principal's Contribution. *Educational Administration Quarterly, 21,* 7–31.

Flavell, J. H. (1985). *Cognitive Development* (2nd ed.). Englewood Cliffs, NJ: Prentice Hall.

Flavell, J. H., Friedrichs, A. G., and Hoyt, J. D. (1970). Developmental Changes in Memorization Processes. *Cognitive Psychology, 1,* 324–40.

Flavell, J. H., Green, F. L., and Flavell, E. R. (1995). *Young Children's Knowledge about Thinking.* Monographs of the Society for Research in Child Development, 60(1) (Serial No. 243).

Flyvbjerg, B. (1998). *Personality and Power: Democracy in Practice*. Chicago: University of Chicago Press.

Follett, M. P. (1924). *Creative Experience*. London: Longman and Green.

Ford, M. E. (1992). *Motivating Humans: Goals, Emotions, and Social Agency Beliefs*. Newbury Park, CA: Sage.

Forsyth, P. B., and Hoy, W. K. (1978). Isolation and Alienation in Educational Organizations. *Educational Administration Quarterly, 14*, 80–96.

Foster, W. (1986). *Paradigms and Promises*. Buffalo, NY: Prometheus.

Foucault, M. (1984). Nietzsche, Genealogy, History. In P. Rabinow (Ed.), *The Foucault Reader*. New York: Pantheon.

Fox, S., and Feldman, G. (1988). Attention State and Critical Psychological States as Mediators Between Job Dimensions and Job Outcomes. *Human Relations, 41*, 229–45.

Frase, L. E., and Heck, G. (1992). Restructuring in the Fort McMurray Catholic Schools: A Research-Based Approach. *The Canadian School Executive, 11*(8), 3–9.

Frase, L. E., and Matheson, R. R. (1992). Restructuring: Fine-Tuning the System in Fort McMurray Catholic Schools. *Challenge, 29*(1), 16–22.

Frase, L. E., and Sorenson, L. (1992). Teacher Motivation and Satisfaction: Impact on Participatory Management. *NASSP Bulletin, 76*, 37–43.

Frederick, D., and Libby, R. (1986). Expertise and Auditors' Judgment of Conjunctive Events. *Journal of Accounting Research, 24*, 270–90.

Freeman, J. H. (1979). Going to the Well: School District Administrative Intensity and Environmental Constraint. *Administrative Science Quarterly, 24*, 119–133.

French, J. R. P., and Raven, B. H. (1968). Bases of Social Power. In D. Cartwright and A. Zander (Eds.), *Group Dynamics: Research and Theory* (pp. 259–70). New York: Harper & Row.

Friedman, R. A., and Podolny, J. (1992). Differentiation of Boundary-Spanning Roles: Labor Negotiations and Implications for Role Conflict. *Administrative Science Quarterly, 37*, 28–47.

Friesen, D., and Duignan, P. (1980). How Superintendents Spend Their Working Time. *Canadian Administrator, 19*, 1–5.

Fromm, E. (1948). *Man for Himself*. New York: Farrar & Rinehart.

Froosman, J. (1999). Stakeholder Influence Strategies. *Academy of Management Review, 24*(2), 191–205.

Frost, P. J., Moore, L. F., Louis, M. R., Lundberg, C. C., and Martin, J. (Eds.). (1991). *Reframing Organizational Culture*. Newbury Park, CA: Sage.

Fuhrman, S. H. (1999). *The New Accountability*. CPRE Policy Brief No. RB-27. Philadelphia, PA: University of Pennsylvania, Consortium for Policy Research in Education.

Fuhrman, S. H. (1994). *Challenges in Systemic Education Reform*. CPRE Policy Brief No. RB-14. Philadelphia, PA: University of Pennsylvania, Consortiumn for Policy Research in Education.

Fuhrman, S. H., Elmore, R. F., and Massell, D. (1994). School Reform in the United States: Putting It into Context. In S. L. Jacobson and R. Berne (Eds.), *Reforming Education: The Emerging Systemic Approach* (pp. 3–27). Thousand Oaks, CA: Corwin.

Fulk, J., and Boyd, B. (1991). Emerging Theories of Communication in Organizations. *Journal of Management, 17*(2), 407–46.

Gagné, E. D., Yekovich, C. W., and Yekovich, F. R. (1993). *The Cognitive Psychology of School Learning* (2nd ed.). New York: HarperCollins.

Gagné, R. M. (1985). The Conditions of Learning and Theory of Instruction (4th ed.). New York: Holt, Rinehart & Winston.

Galbraith, J., and Cummings, L. L. (1967). An Empirical Investigation of the Motivational Determinants of Task Performance: Interactive Effects Between Instrumentality-Valence and Motivation-Ability. *Organization Behavior and Human Performance, 2*, 237–57.

Ganz, H. J., and Hoy, W. K. (1977). Patterns of Succession of Elementary Principals and Organizational Change. *Planning and Changing, 8*, 185–96.

Gardner, D. G., and Cummings, L. L. (1988). Activation Theory and Job Design: Review and Reconceptualization. *Research in Organizational Behavior, 10*, 81–122.

Gardner, W. L., and Avolio, B. J. (1998). The Charismatic Relationship: A Dramaturgical Perspective. *Academy of Management Review, 23*(1), 32–58.

Garner, R. (1990). When Children and Adults Do Not Use Learning Strategies: Toward a Theory of Settings. *Review of Educational Psychology, 60,* 517–30.

Garrison, J. (1995). Deweyan Pragmatism and the Epistemology of Contemporary Social Constructivism. *American Educational Research Journal, 32,* 716–41.

Gartner, W. B., and Naughton, M. J. (1988). The Deming Theory of Management. *Academy of Management Review, 17,* 138–42.

Gaziel, H. (2002). Teacher Empowerment Reform and Teacher Perceived Effectiveness: Contradictory or Complimentary? A Theoretical Framework and Some Empirical Evidence. *Education and Society 20,* 79–90.

Geertz, C. (1973). *The Interpretation of Cultures.* New York: Basic.

Geist, J. R., and Hoy, W. K. (2003). Culitivating a Culture of Trust: Enabling School Structure, Teacher Professionalism, and Academic Press. Working Paper, Educational Policy and Leadership, The Ohio State University.

Gergen, K. J. (1997). Constructing Constructivism: Pedagogical Potentials. *Issues in Education: Contributions from Educational Psychology, 3,* 195–202.

Gerhardt, E. (1971). Staff Conflict, Organizational Bureaucracy, and Individual Satisfaction in Selected Kansas School Districts. Doctoral diss., University of Kansas, Lawrence.

Gerth, H. H., and Mills, C. W. (Eds.). (1946). *From Max Weber: Essays in Sociology.* New York: Oxford University Press.

Getzels, J. W., and Guba, E. G. (1957). Social Behavior and the Administrative Process. *School Review, 65,* 423–41.

Getzels, J. W., Lipham, J. M., and Campbell, R. F. (1968). *Educational Administration as a Social Process: Theory, Research, and Practice.* New York: Harper & Row.

Gibson, J. L., Ivancevich, J. M., and Donnelly, J. H. (1976). *Organizations: Behavior, Structure, and Processes* (Rev. ed.). Dallas, TX: Business Publications.

Gibson, S., and Dembo, M. (1984). Teacher Efficacy: A Construct Validation. *Journal of Educational Psychology, 76*(4), 569–82.

Gigerenzer, G. (2000). *Adaptive Thinking: Rationality in the Real World.* New York: Oxford University Press.

Gigerenzer, G. (1996) On Narrow Norms and Vague Heuristics: A Reply to Kahneman and Tversky. *Psychological Review, 103,* 559–69.

Gigerenzer, G. (2004). Striking a Blow for Sanity in Theories of Rationality. In B. Augier and J. G. March (Eds.), *Essays in Honor of Herbert Simon.* Cambridge, MA: MIT Press.

Gigerenzer, G., Todd, P. M., and ABC Research Group. (1999). *Simple Heuristics That Make Us Smart.* New York: Oxford University Press.

Gill, B. P., Timpane, M., Rose, K. E., and Brewer, D. J. (2001). Rhetoric versus Reality: What We Know and We Need to Know about Vouchers and Charter Schools (MR-1118-EDU). Santa Monica, CA: RAND.

Gilligan, C. (1982). *In a Different Voice: Psychological Theory and Women's Development.* Cambridge, MA: Harvard University Press.

Gilmer, B. H. (1966). *Industrial Psychology* (2nd ed.). New York: McGraw-Hill.

Gilovich, T. (1991). *How We Know What Isn't So: The Fallibility of Human Reason in Everyday Life.* New York: Free Press.

Gist, M. E. (1987). Self-Efficacy: Implications for Organizational Behavior and Human Resource Management. *Academy of Management Review, 12* (3), 472–85.

Gist, M. E., and Mitchell, T. R. (1992). Self-Efficacy: A Theoretical Analysis of Its Determinants and Malleability. *Academy of Management Review, 17* (2), 183–211.

Glaub, J. (1990). Made in Japan. *Illinois School Board Journal, 58,* 5–7.

Glisson, C., and Durick, M. (1988). Predictors of Job Satisfaction and Organizational Commitment in Human Service Organizations. *Administrative Science Quarterly, 33,* 61–81.

Goddard, R. D. (2001). Collective Efficacy: A Neglected Construct in the Study of Schools and Students Achievement. *Journal of Educational Psychology, 93*(3), 467–76.

Goddard, R. D. (2002a). A Theoretical and Empirical Analysis of the Measurement of Collective Efficacy: The Development of a Short Form. *Educational and Psychological Measurement, 62*(1), 97–110.

Goddard, R. D. (2002b). Collective Efficacy and School Organization: A Multilevel Analysis of Teacher Influence in Schools. In W. K. Hoy and C. Miskel (eds.) *Theory and Research in Educational Administration* (vol. 1, pp. 169–84). Greenwich, CT: Information Age Publishing.

Goddard, R. D., and Goddard, Y. L. (2001). A Multilevel Analysis of Teacher and Collective Efficacy. *Teaching and Teacher Education, 17,* 807–18.

Goddard, R. D., Hoy, W. K., and LoGerfo, L. (2003, April). *Collective Efficacy and Student Achievement in Public High School: A Path Analysis.* Paper presented at the annual meeting of the American Educational Research Association, Chicago, IL.

Goddard, R. D., Hoy, W. K., and Woolfolk Hoy, A. (2000). Collective Teacher Efficacy: Its Meaning, Measure, and Impact on Student Achievement. *American Educational Research Journal, 37,* 479–508.

Goddard, R. D., Sweetland, S. R., and Hoy, W. K. (2000a). Academic Emphasis and Student Achievement in Urban Elementary Schools. Annual Meeting of the American Educational Association, New Orleans.

Goddard, R. D., Sweetland S. R., and Hoy, W. K. (2000b). Academic Emphasis of Urban Elementary Schools and Student Achievement: A Multi-Level Analysis. *Educational Administration Quarterly, 5,* 683–702.

Goddard, R. D., Tschannen-Moran, M., and Hoy, W. K. (2001). Teacher Trust in Students and Parents: A Multilevel Examination of the Distribution and Effects of Teacher Trust in Urban Elementary Schools. Elementary School Journal, 102, 3–17.

Goertz, M. E., and Duffy, M. C. (2001). *Assessment and Accountability across the 50 States.* CPRE Policy Brief No. RB-33. Philadelphia, PA: University of Pennsylvania, Consortium for Policy Research in Education.

Goes, J. B., and Park, S. O. (1997). Interorganizational Links and Innovation: The Case of Hospital Services. *Academy of Management Journal, 40*(3), 673–96.

Goffman, E. (1957). The Characteristics of Total Institutions. *Symposium on Prevention and Social Psychiatry* (pp. 43–84). Washington, DC: Walter Reed Army Institute of Research.

Goldberg, M. A. (1975). On the Efficiency of Being Efficient. *Environment and Planning, 7,* 921–39.

Goldring, E. B., and Chen, M. (1992). Preparing Empowered Teachers for Leadership. *Planning and Changing, 23,* 3–15.

Good, T. L. (1996). Teaching Effects and Teacher Evaluation. In J. Sikula (Ed.), *Handbook of Research on Teacher Education* (pp. 617–65). New York: Macmillan.

Good, T. L. (1983). Classroom Research: A Decade of Progress. *Educational Psychologist, 18,* 127–44.

Good, T. L., and Brophy, J. E. (1986). School Effects. In M. C. Wittrock (Ed.), *Handbook of Research on Teaching* (pp. 570–602). New York: Macmillan.

Good, T. L., Grouws, D., and Ebmeier, H. (1983). *Active Mathematics Teaching.* New York: Longman.

Goodman, P. S., and Pennings, J. M. (1977). Toward a Workable Framework. In P. S. Goodman and J. M. Pennings (Eds.), *New Perspectives on Organizational Effectiveness* (pp. 147–84). San Francisco: Jossey-Bass.

Goodstein, J. D. (1994). Institutional Pressures and Strategic Responsiveness: Employer Involvement in Work-Family Issues. *Academy of Management Journal, 37*(2), 350–82.

Gordon, C. W. (1957). *The Social System of the High School.* New York: Free Press.

Gordon, G. E., and Rosen, N. (1981). Critical Factors in Leadership Succession. *Organizational Behavior and Human Performance, 27,* 227–54.

Gorsuch, R. A. (1977). An Investigation of the Relationships between Core Job Dimensions, Psychological States, and Personal Work Outcomes among Public School Teachers (Doctoral diss., University of Maryland, 1976). *Dissertation Abstracts International, 38,* 1779A.

Gouldner, A. (1950). *Studies in Leadership.* New York: Harper.

Gouldner, A. (1954). *Patterns of Industrial Bureaucracy.* New York: Free Press.

Gouldner, A. (1958). Cosmopolitans and Locals: Toward an Analysis of Latent Social Roles—II. *Administrative Science Quarterly, 3,* 444–79.

Gouldner, A. (1959). Organizational Analysis. In R. K. Merton, L. Broom, J. Leonard, and S. Cottrell (Eds.), *Sociology Today* (pp. 400–28). New York: Basic Books.

Govindarajan, V. (1988). A Contingency Approach to Strategy Implementation at the Business-Unit Level: Integrating Administrative Mechanisms with Strategy. *Academy of Management Journal, 31,* 828–53.

Grabe, M., and Latta, R. M. (1981). Cumulative Achievement in a Mastery Instructional System: The Impact of Differences in Resultant Achievement Motivation and Persistence. *American Educational Research Journal, 18,* 7–14.

Graen, G. (1963). Instrumentality Theory of Work Motivation: Some Experimental Results and Suggested Modifications. *Journal of Applied Psychology Monograph, 53,* 1–25.

Graham, L. L. (1980). Expectancy Theory as a Predictor of College Student Grade Point Average, Satisfaction, and Participation. Doctoral diss., University of Kansas, Lawrence.

Graham, S. (1991). A Review of Attribution Theory in Achievement Contexts. *Educational Psychology Review, 3* (1), 5–39.

Graham, S., and Weiner, B. (1996). Theories and Principles of Motivation. In D. Berliner and R. Calfee (Eds.), *Handbook of Educational Psychology* (pp. 63–84). New York: Macmillan.

Grandori, A. (1984). A Prescriptive Contingency View of Organizational Decision Making. *Administrative Science Quarterly, 29,* 192–208.

Grassie, M. C., and Carss, B. W. (1973). School Structure, Leadership Quality, Teacher Satisfaction. *Educational Administration Quarterly, 9,* 15–26.

Gray, J. (1992). *Men Are from Mars, Women Are from Venus.* New York: HarperCollins.

Greenberg, J. (1993a). The Social Side of Fairness: Interpersonal and Informational Classes of Organizational Justice. In R. Cropanzano (Ed.), *Justice in the Workplace* (pp. 79–103). Hillsdale, NJ: Erlbaum.

Greenberg, J. (1993b). Stealing in the Name of Justice: Informational and Interpersonal Moderators of Theft Reactions to Underpayment Inequity. *Organizational Behavior and Human Decision Processes, 54,* 81–103.

Greenberg, J. (1997). A Taxonomy of Organizational Justice Theories. *Academy of Management Review, 21,* 9–22.

Greenberg, J. (2000). Promote Procedural Justice to Enhance Acceptance of Work Outcomes. In E. A. Locke (Ed.), *Handbook of Principles of Organizational Behavior* (pp. 181–95). Malden, MA: Blackwell.

Greenberg, J., and Baron, R. A. (1997). *Behavior in Organizations* (6th ed.). Englewood Cliffs, NJ: Prentice Hall.

Greenberg, J., and Scott, K. S. (1995). Why Do Workers Bite the Hands That Feed Them? Employee Theft as a Social Exchange Process. In B. M. Staw and L. L. Cummings (Eds.), *Research in Organizational Behavior* (Vol. 18). Greenwich, CT: JAI Press.

Greene, C. N., and Podsakoff, P. M. (1981). Effects of Withdrawal of a Performance Contingent Reward of Supervisory Influence and Power. *Academy of Management Journal, 24,* 527–42.

Greene, J. P., Winters, M. A., and Forster, G. (2003). *Testing High Stakes Tests: Can We Believe the Results of Accountability Tests?* New York: Manhattan Institute.

Greenfield, T. B., and Ribbins, P. (Eds.). (1993). *Greenfield on Educational Administration: Towards a Human Science.* London: Routledge.

Greeno, J. G., Collins, A. M., and Resnick, L. B. (1996). Cognition and Learning. In D. Berliner and R. Calfee (Eds.), *Handbook of Educational Psychology* (pp. 15–46). New York: Macmillan.

Greenwald, R, Hedges, L. V., and Laine, R. D. (1996). The Effect of School Resources on Student Achievement. *Review of Educational Research, 66*(3), 361–96.

Griffeth, R. W. (1985). Moderation of the Effects of Job Enrichment by Participation: A Longitudinal Field Experiment. *Organizational Behavior and Human Decision Processes, 35,* 73–93.

Griffin, R. W. (1987). Toward an Integrated Theory of Task Design. *Research in Organizational Behavior, 9,* 79–120.

Griffin, R. W. (1991). Effects of Work Redesign on Employee Perceptions, Attitudes, and Behaviors: A Long-Term Investigation. *Academy of Management Journal, 34*(2), 425–35.

Griffiths, D. E. (1959). *Administrative Theory.* New York: Appleton-Century-Crofts.

Griffiths, D. E. (1988). Administrative Theory. In N. Boyan (Ed.), *Handbook of Research on Educational Administration* (pp. 27–51). New York: Longman.

Griffiths, D. E., Goldman, S., and McFarland, W. J. (1965). Teacher Mobility in New York City. *Educational Administration Quarterly, 1,* 15–31.

Griffiths, D. E., Stout, R. T., and Forsyth, P. B. (1988). The Preparation of Educational Administrators. In D. E. Griffiths, R. T. Stout, and P. B. Forsyth (Eds.), *Leaders for America's Schools* (pp. 284–304). Berkeley, CA: McCutchan.

Gronn, P. (2002). Distributed Leadership as a Unit of Analysis. *Leadership Quarterly, 13,* 423–51.

Gross, E., and Etzioni, A. (1985). *Organizations in Society.* Englewood Cliffs, NJ: Prentice Hall.

Grusky, O. (1960). Administrative Succession in Formal Organizations. *Social Forces, 39,* 105–15.

Grusky, O. (1961). Corporate Size, Bureaucratization, and Managerial Succession. *American Journal of Sociology, 67,* 261–69.

Guest, R. H. (1960). *Organizational Change: The Effect of Successful Leadership.* Homewood, IL: Dorsey.

Guidette, M. R. M. (1982). The Relationship between Bureaucracy and Staff Sense of Powerlessness in Secondary Schools. Doctoral diss., Rutgers University, New Brunswick.

Gulick, L. (1937). Notes on the Theory of Organization. In L. Gulick and L. F. Urwick (Eds.), *Papers on the Science of Administration* (pp. 3–45). New York: Institute of Public Administration, Columbia University.

Guskey, T. R. (1987). Context Variables That Affect Measures of Teacher Efficacy. *Journal of Educational Research, 81*(1), 41–47.

Guskey, T. R., and Gates, S. L. (1986). Synthesis of Research on Mastery Learning. *Education Leadership, 43,* 73–81.

Guskey, T. R., and Passaro, P. (1994). Teacher Efficacy: A Study of Construct Dimensions. *American Educational Research Journal, 31,* 627–43.

Hackman, J. R., and Oldham, G. R. (1975). Development of the Job Diagnostic Survey. *Journal of Applied Psychology, 60,* 159–70.

Hackman, J. R., and Oldham, G. R. (1976). Motivation through the Design of Work: A Test

of a Theory. *Organizational Behavior and Human Performance, 16,* 250–79.

Hackman, J. R., and Oldham, G. R. (1980). *Work Redesign.* Reading, MA: Addison-Wesley.

Hackman, J. R., and Suttle, J. L. (1977). *Improving Life at Work.* Santa Monica, CA: Goodyear.

Hackman, J. R., and Wageman, R. (1995). Total Quality Management: Empirical, Conceptual, and Practical Issues. *Administrative Science Quarterly, 40*(2), 309–42.

Hage, J. (1980). *Theories of Organizations.* New York: Wiley.

Hajnal, V. J., and Dibski, D. J. (1993). Compensation Management: Coherence Between Organization Directions and Teacher Needs. *Journal of Educational Administration, 31*(1), 53–69.

Hall, R. H. (1962). The Concept of Bureaucracy: An Empirical Assessment. *American Sociological Review, 27,* 295–308.

Hall, R. H. (1980). Effectiveness Theory and Organizational Effectiveness. *Journal of Applied Behavioral Science, 16,* 536–45.

Hall, R. H. (2002). *Organizations: Structures, Processes, and Outcomes* (8th ed.). Upper Saddle River, NJ: Prentice Hall.

Hallahan, D. P., and Kauffman, J. M. (1997). *Exceptional Learners: Introduction to Special Education* (7th ed.). Boston: Allyn and Bacon.

Haller, E. J., and Monk, D. H. (1988). New Reforms, Old Reforms, and the Consolidation of Small Rural Schools. *Educational Administration Quarterly, 24,* 470–83.

Hallinger, P., and Heck, R. H. (1996). Reassessing the Principal's Role in Effectiveness: A Review of Empirical Research, 1980–1995. *Educational Administration Quarterly, 32*(1), 5–44.

Hallinger, P., and Heck, R. H. (1998). Exploring the Principal's Contribution to School Effectiveness, 1980–1995. *School Effectiveness and School Improvement, 9*(2), 157–91.

Halpin, A. W. (1966). *Theory and Research in Administration.* New York: Macmillan.

Halpin, A. W., and Croft, D. B. (1962). *The Organization Climate of Schools.* Contract #SAE 543–8639. U.S. Office of Education, Research Project.

Halpin, A. W., and Croft, D. B. (1963). *The Organizational Climate of Schools.* Chicago:

Midwest Administration Center of the University of Chicago.

Halpin, A. W., and Winer, B. J. (1952). *The Leadership Behavior of the Airplane Commander.* Washington, DC: Human Resources Research Laboratories, Department of the Air Force.

Hamilton, R. J. (1985). A Framework for the Evaluation of the Effectiveness of Adjunct Questions and Objectives. *Review of Educational Research, 55,* 47–86.

Hamman, D., Berthelot, J., Saia, J., and Crowley, E. (2000). Teachers' Coaching of Learning and Its Relation to Students' Strategic Learning. *Journal of Educational Psychology, 92,* 342–48.

Hannum, J. (1994). The Organizational Climate of Middle Schools, Teacher Efficacy, and Student Achievement. Doctoral diss., Rutgers University, New Brunswick.

Hanson, M. (2001). Institutional Theory and Educational Change. *Educational Administration Quarterly, 37*(5), 637–61.

Hanson, E. M. (2003). *Educational Administration and Organizational Behavior.* Boston: Allyn and Bacon.

Hanushek, E. A. (1981). Throwing Money at Schools. *Journal of Policy Analysis and Management, 1*(1), 19–41.

Hanushek, E. A. (1989). The Impact of Differential Expenditures on School Performance. *Educational Researcher, 18,* 45–51, 62.

Hanushek, E. A. (1997). Assessing the Effects of School Resources on Student Performance: An Update. *Educational Evaluation and Policy Analysis, 19*(2), 141–64.

Hanushek, E. A. (2003). The Failure of Input-Based Schooling Policies. *Economic Journal, 113* (February), F64–F98.

Hanushek, E A., and Raymond, M. E. (2002). Sorting Out Accountability Systems. In W. M. Evers and H. J. Walberg (Eds.), *School Accountability* (pp. 75–104). Palo Alto, CA: Hoover Press.

Harder, J. W. (1992). Play for Pay: Effects of Inequity in Pay-for-Performance Contest. *Administrative Science Quarterly, 37,* 321–35.

Hardy, C., and Leiba-O'Sullivan, S. (1998). The Power Behind Empowerment: Implications for Research and Practice. *Human Relations, 51,* 451–83.

Harris, T. E. (1993). *Applied Organizational Communication.* Hillsdale, NJ: Erlbaum.

Hart, A. W. (1987). A Career Ladder's Effect on Teacher Career and Work Attitudes. *American Educational Research Journal, 24*(4), 479–503.

Hart, A. W. (1990a). Impacts of the School Social Unit on Teacher Authority During Work Redesign. *American Education Research Journal, 27*(3), 503–32.

Hart, A. W. (1990b). Work Redesign: A Review of Literature for Education Reform. *Advances in Research and Theories of School Management, 1,* 31–69.

Hart, A. W. (1993). *Principal Succession: Establishing Leadership in Schools.* Albany, NY: State University of New York Press.

Hart, A. W. (1995). Reconceiving School Leadership: Emergent Views. *The Elementary School Journal, 96,* 9–28.

Hart, A. W., and Murphy, M. J. (1990). New Teachers React to Redesigned Teacher Work. *American Journal of Education, 93*(3), 224–50.

Hart, D. K., and Scott, W. G. (1975). The Organizational Imperative. *Administration and Society, 7,* 259–85.

Hartley, M., and Hoy, W. K. (1972). Openness of School Climate and Alienation of High School Students. *California Journal of Educational Research, 23,* 17–24.

Hatry, H. P., and Greiner, J. M. (1985). *Issues and Case Studies in Teacher Incentive Plans.* Washington, DC: Urban Institute Press.

Hayes, A. E. (1973). A Reappraisal of the Halpin-Croft Model of the Organizational Climate of Schools. Annual Meeting of the American Educational Research Association, New Orleans.

Haymond, J. E. (1982). Bureaucracy, Climate, and Loyalty: an Aston Study in Education. Doctoral diss., Rutgers University, New Brunswick.

Haynes, P. A. (1974). Towards a Concept of Monitoring. *Town Planning Review, 45,* 6–29.

Heck, R. H. (2000). Examining the Impact of School Quality on School Outcomes and Improvement: A Value-Added Approach. *Educational Administration Quarterly, 36*(4), 513–52.

Heck, R. H., Larsen, T. J., and Marcoulides, G. A. (1990). Instructional Leadership and School Achievement: Validation of a Causal Model.

Educational Administration Quarterly, 26(2), 94–125.

Heclo, H. (1978). Issue Networks and the Executive Establishment. In A. King (Ed.), *The New American Political System* (pp. 87–124). Washington, DC: AEI Press.

Hedges, L. V., Laine, R. D., and Greenwald, R. (1994). Does Money Matter? A Meta-Analysis of Studies of the Effects of Differential School Inputs on Student Outcomes. *Educational Researcher, 23*(3), 5–14.

Heinz, J. P., Laumann, E. O., Nelson, R. L., and Salisbury, R. H. (1993). *The Hollow Core: Private Interests in National Policymaking.* Cambridge, MA: Harvard University Press.

Heintzman, M., Leathers, D. G., Parrot, R. L., and Cairns, I. (1993). Nonverbal Rapport-Building Behaviors' Effects on Perceptions of a Supervisor. *Management Communication Quarterly, 7*(2), 181–208.

Heller, F., Drenth, P., Koopman, P., and Rus, V. (1988). *Decisions in Organizations.* Beverly Hills, CA: Sage.

Heller, M. F., and Firestone, W. A. (1995). Who's in Charge Here? Sources of Leadership for Change in Eight Schools. *Elementary School Journal, 96*(1), 65–86.

Hellriegel, D., Slocum, J. W., and Woodman, R. W. (1992). *Organizational Behavior* (6th ed.). St. Paul, MN: West.

Hemphill, J. K., and Coons, A. E. (1950). *Leader Behavior Description Questionnaire.* Columbus: Personnel Research Board, Ohio State University.

Henderson, J. E., and Hoy, W. K. (1983). Leader Authenticity: The Development and Test of an Operational Measure. *Educational and Psychological Research, 2,* 123–30.

Heneman, H. G. I., and Schwab, D. P. (1972). An Evaluation of Research on Expectancy Theory Predictions of Employee Performance. *Psychological Bulletin, 78,* 1–9.

Hernshaw, L. S. (1987). *The Shaping of Modern Psychology: A Historical Introduction from Dawn to Present Day.* London: Routledge and Kegan Paul.

Herrick, H. S. (1973). *The Relationship of Organizational Structure to Teacher Motivation in Multiunit and Non-multiunit Elementary Schools No. 322.* Madison: Wisconsin Research and Development Center for Cognitive Learning, University of Wisconsin.

Herriott, R. F., and Firestone, W. A. (1984). Two Images of Schools as Organizations: A Refinement and Elaboration. *Educational Administration Quarterly, 20,* 41–58.

Hersey, P. W. (1982). *The NASSP Assessment Center: Validation and New Development.* Reston, VA: National Association of Secondary School Principals.

Hershey, P., and Blanchard, K. H. (1977). *The Management of Organizational Behavior* (3rd ed.). Englewood Cliffs, NJ: Prentice Hall.

Herzberg, F. (1982). *The Managerial Choice: To Be Efficient and to Be Human* (Rev. ed.). Salt Lake City, UT: Olympus.

Herzberg, F., Mausner, B., and Snyderman, B. (1959). *The Motivation to Work.* New York: Wiley.

Hess, F. M. (2003). A License to Lead? A New Leadership Agenda for America's Schools. Washington, DC: Progressive Policy Institute. Available at www.ppionline.org/

Hickson, D., Butler, R., Gray, D., Mallory, G., and Wilson, D. (1986). *Top Decisions: Strategic Decision Making in Organizations.* Oxford: Basil Blackwell.

Hill, H. C. (2001). Policy Is Not Enough: Language and the Interpretation of State Standards. *American Educational Research Journal, 38*(2), 289–318.

Hill, P. T., and Bonan, J. (1991). *Decentralization and Accountability in Public Education.* Santa Monica, CA: Rand.

Hill, W. F. (2002). *Learning: A Survey of Psychological Interpretations* (7th ed.). Boston: Allyn & Bacon.

Hirschhorn, L. (1997). *Reworking Authority: Leading and Following in a Post-Modern Organization.* Cambridge, MA: MIT Press.

Hirschman, A. O. (1970). *Exit, Voice, and Loyalty: Responses to the Decline in Firms, Organizations, and States.* Cambridge, MA: Harvard University Press.

Hitt, M. A., and Ireland, R. D. (1987). Peters and Waterman Revisited: The Unended Quest for Excellence. *Academy of Management Executive, 1,* 91–98.

Hodgkinson, C. (1991). *Educational Leadership: The Moral Art*. Albany, NY: State University of New York Press.

Hofer, B. K., and Pintrich, P. R. (1997). The Development of Epistemological Theories: Beliefs about Knowledge and Knowing and Their Relation to Learning. *Review of Educational Research, 67*, 88–140.

Hoffman, A. J. (1999). Institutional Evolution and Change: Environmentalism and the U.S. Chemical Industry. *Academy of Management Journal, 42*(4), 351–71.

Hoffman, J. D. (1993).The Organizational Climate of Middle Schools and Dimensions of Authenticity and Trust. Doctoral diss., Rutgers University, New Brunswick.

Hoffman, J. D., Sabo, D., Bliss, J., and Hoy, W. K. (1994). Building a Culture of Trust. *Journal of School Leadership, 3*, 484–99.

Holdaway, E. A. (1978a). Facet and Overall Satisfaction of Teachers. *Educational Administration Quarterly, 14*, 30–47.

Holdaway, E. A. (1978b). *Job Satisfaction: An Alberta Report*. Edmonton: University of Alberta.

Holdaway, E. A., Newberry, J. F., Hickson, D. J., and Heron, R. P. (1975). Dimensions of Organizations in Complex Societies: The Educational Sector. *Administrative Science Quarterly, 20*, 37–58.

Holmes Group. (1986). *Tomorrow's Teachers*. East Lansing, MI: Holmes Group.

Homans, G. C. (1950). *The Human Group*. New York: Harcourt, Brace and World.

Hoppock, R. (1935). *Job Satisfaction*. New York: Harper.

House, R. J. (1971). A Path-Goal Theory of Leadership Effectiveness. *Administrative Science Quarterly, 16*, 321–38.

House, R. J. (1973). A Path-Goal Theory of Leader Effectiveness. In E. A. Fleishman and J. G. Hunt (Eds.), *Current Developments in the Study of Leadership* (pp. 141–77). Carbondale, IL: Southern Illinois University Press.

House, R. J. (1977). A 1976 Theory of Charismatic Leadership. In J. G. Hunt and L. L. Larson (Eds.), *Leadership: The Cutting Edge* (pp. 189–207). Carbondale, IL: Southern Illinois University Press.

House, R. J. (1988). Leadership Research: Some Forgotten, Ignored, or Overlooked Findings. In J. G. Hunt, B. R. Baliga, H. P. Dachler, and C. A. Schriesheim (Eds.), *Emerging Leadership Vistas* (pp. 245–60). Lexington, MA: Lexington.

House, R. J. (1996). Path-Goal Theory of Leadership: Lessons, Legacy, and a Reformulated Theory. *Leadership Quarterly, 3*(2), 323–52.

House, R. J., and Baetz, M. L. (1979). Leadership: Some Empirical Generalizations and New Research Directions. *Research in Organizational Behavior, 1*, 341–423.

House, R. J., and Howell, J. M. (1992). Personality and Charismatic Leadership. *Leadership Quarterly, 3(2)*, 81–108.

House, R. J., and Mitchell, T. R. (1974). Path-Goal Theory and Leadership. *Journal of Contemporary Business, 3*, 81–97.

House, R. J., Spangler, W. D., and Woycke, J. (1991). Personality and Charisma in the U.S. Presidency: A Psychological Theory of Leader Effectiveness. *Administrative Science Quarterly, 36*, 364–96.

Howell, J. M., and Avolio, B. J. (1993). Transformational Leadership, Transactional Leadership, Locus of Control, and Support of Innovation: Key Predictors of Consolidated Business-Unit Performance. *Journal of Applied Psychology, 78*(6), 891–902.

Howell, J. M., and Frost, P. J. (1989). A Laboratory Study of Charismatic Leadership. *Organizational Behavior and Human Decision Processes, 43*, 243–69.

Howell, J. P. (1997). Substitutes for Leadership: Their Meaning and Measurement—An Historical Assessment. *Leadership Quarterly, 8*(2), 113–16.

Hoy, W. K. (1967). Organizational Socialization: The Student Teacher and Pupil Control Ideology. *Journal of Educational Research, 61*, 153–55.

Hoy, W. K. (1968). Pupil Control and Organizational Socialization: The Influence of Experience on the Beginning Teacher. *School Review, 76*, 312–23.

Hoy, W. K. (1969). Pupil Control Ideology and Organizational Socialization: A Further

Examination of the Influence of Experience on the Beginning Teacher. *School Review, 77,* 257–65.

Hoy, W. K. (1972). Dimensions of Student Alienation and Characteristics of Public High Schools. *Interchange, 3,* 38–51.

Hoy, W. K. (1978). Scientific Research in Educational Administration. *Educational Administration Quarterly, 14,* 1–12.

Hoy, W. K. (1990). Organizational Climate and Culture: A Conceptual Analysis of the School Workplace. *Journal of Educational and Psychological Consultation, 1,* 149–68.

Hoy, W. K (1996). Science and Theory in the Practice of Educational Administration: A Pragmatic Perspective. *Educational Administration Quarterly, 32,* 366–78.

Hoy, W. K. (1997). A Few Quibbles with Denison, *The Academy of Management Review, 22*(1), 13–14.

Hoy, W. K. (2001). The Pupil Control Studies: A Historical, Theoretical, and Empirical Analysis. *Journal of Educational Administration, 39,* 424–41.

Hoy, W. K. (2002). Faculty Trust: A Key to Student Achievement. *Journal of School Public Relations, 23* (2), 88–103.

Hoy, W. K. (2003). An Analysis of Enabling and Mindful School Structures: Some Theoretical, Research, and Practical Considerations. *Journal of Educational Administration, 41,* 87–108.

Hoy, W. K., and Aho, F. (1973). Patterns of Succession of High School Principals and Organizational Change. *Planning and Changing, 2,* 82–88.

Hoy, W. K., and Appleberry, J. B. (1970). Teacher Principal Relationships in "Humanistic" and "Custodial" Elementary Schools. *Journal of Experimental Education, 39,* 27–31.

Hoy, W. K., Astuto, T. A., and Forsyth, P. B. (Eds.). (1994). *Educational Administration: The UCEA Document Base.* New York: McGraw-Hill Primus.

Hoy, W. K., Blazovsky, R., and Newland, W. (1980). Organizational Structure and Alienation from Work. Annual Meeting of the American Educational Research Association, Boston.

Hoy, W. K., Blazovsky, R., and Newland, W. (1983). Bureaucracy and Alienation: A Comparative Analysis. *The Journal of Educational Administration, 21,* 109–21.

Hoy, W. K., and Brown, B. L. (1988). Leadership Behavior of Principals and the Zone of

Acceptance of Elementary Teachers. *Journal of Educational Administration, 26,* 23–39.

Hoy, W. K., and Clover, S. I. R. (1986). Elementary School Climate: A Revision of the OCDQ. *Educational Administration Quarterly, 22,* 93–110.

Hoy, W. K., and Feldman, J. (1987). Organizational Health. The Concept and Its Measure. *Journal of Research and Development in Education, 20,* 30–38.

Hoy, W. K., and Feldman, J. (1999). Organizational Health Profiles for High Schools. In J. Freiberg (Ed.)., *School Climate: Measuring, Sustaining, and Improving.* Philadelphia: Falmer Press.

Hoy, W. K., and Ferguson, J. (1985). A Theoretical Framework and Exploration of Organizational Effectiveness in Schools. *Educational Administration Quarterly, 21,* 117–34.

Hoy, W. K., and Forsyth, P. B. (1986). *Effective Supervision: Theory into Practice.* New York: Random House.

Hoy, W. K., and Forsyth, P. B. (1987). Beyond Clinical Supervision: A Classroom Performance Model. *Planning and Changing, 18,* 210–23.

Hoy, W. K., and Hannum, J. (1997). Middle School Climate: An Empirical Assessment of Organizational Health and Student Achievement. *Educational Administration Quarterly, 33,* 290–311.

Hoy, W. K., Hannum, J., and Tschannen-Moran, M. (1998). Organizational Climate and Student Achievement: A Parsimonious and Longitudinal View. *Journal of School Leadership, 8,* 1–22.

Hoy, W. K., and Henderson, J. E. (1983). Principal Authenticity, School Climate, and Pupil-Control Orientation. *Alberta Journal of Educational Research, 2,* 123–30.

Hoy, W. K., Hoffman, J., Sabo, D., and Bliss, J. (1994). The Organizational Climate of Middle Schools: The Development and Test of the OCDQ-RM. *Journal of Educational Administration, 34,* 41–59.

Hoy, W. K., and Miskel, C. G. (1991). *Educational Administration: Theory, Research, and Practice* (4th ed.). New York: McGraw-Hill.

Hoy, W. K., Newland, W., and Blazovsky, R. (1977). Subordinate Loyalty to Superior, Esprit, and Aspects of Bureaucratic Structure. *Educational Administration Quarterly, 13,* 71–85.

Hoy, W. K., and Rees, R. (1974). Subordinate Loyalty to Immediate Superior: A Neglected Concept in the Study of Educational Administration. *Sociology of Education, 47,* 268–86.

Hoy, W. K., and Rees, R. (1977). The Bureaucratic Socialization of Student Teachers. *Journal of Teacher Education, 28,* 23–26.

Hoy, W. K., and Sabo, D. (1998). *Quality Middle Schools: Open and Healthy.* Thousand Oaks, CA: Corwin Press.

Hoy, W. K., Smith, P. A., and Sweetland, S. R. (2002a). A Test of a Model of School Achievement in Rural Schools: The Significance of Collective Efficacy. In W. K. Hoy and C. Miskel (Eds.). *Theory and Research in Educational Administration,* (pp. 185–202).

Hoy, W, K., Smith, P. A., and Sweetland, S. R. (2002b). The Development of the Organizational Climate Index for High Schools: Its Measure and Relationship to Faculty Trust. *The High School Journal, 86,* 38–49.

Hoy, W. K., and Sousa, D. (1984). Delegation: The Neglected Aspect of Participation in Decision Making. *Alberta Journal of Educational Research, 30,* 320–31.

Hoy, W. K., and Sweetland, S. R. (2000). Bureaucracies that Work: Enabling, Not Coercive. *Journal of School Leadership, 10,* 525–41.

Hoy, W. K., and Sweetland, S. R. (2001). Designing Better Schools: The Meaning and Nature of Enabling School Structure. *Educational Administration Quarterly, 37,* 296–321.

Hoy, W. K., Sweetland, S. R. and Smith, P. A. (2002). Toward an Organizational Model of Achievement in High Schools: The Significance of Collective Efficacy. *Educational Administration Quarterly, 38,* 77–93.

Hoy, W. K., and Tarter, C. J. (1990). Organizational climate school health and student achievement: a comparative analysis. Unpublished paper.

Hoy, W. K., and Tarter, C. J. (1992). Collaborative Decision Making: Empowering Teachers. *Canadian Administration, 32,* 1–9.

Hoy, W. K., and Tarter, C. J. (1993a). A Normative Model of Shared Decision Making. *Journal of Educational Administration, 31,* 4–19.

Hoy, W. K., and Tarter, C. J. (1993b). Crafting Strategies, Not Contriving Solutions: A Response to Downey and Knight's Observations on Shared Decision Making. *Canadian Administration, 32,* 1–6.

Hoy, W. K., and Tarter, C. J. (1997a). *The Road to Open and Healthy Schools: A Handbook for Change, Secondary Edition.* Thousand Oaks, CA: Corwin Press.

Hoy, W. K., and Tarter, C. J. (1997b). *The Road to Open and Healthy Schools: A Handbook for Change, Elementary Edition.* Thousand Oaks, CA: Corwin Press.

Hoy, W. K., and Tarter, C. J. (2003). *Administrators Solving the Problems of Practice: Decision-Making Concepts, Cases, and Consequences.* Boston: Allyn and Bacon.

Hoy, W. K., Tarter, C. J., and Kottkamp, R. (1991). *Open Schools/Healthy Schools: Measuring Organizational Climate.* Beverly Hills, CA: Sage.

Hoy, W. K., Tarter, C. J., and Wiskowskie, L. (1992). Faculty Trust in Colleagues: Linking the Principal with School Effectiveness. *Journal of Research and Development in Education, 26*(1), 38–58.

Hoy, W. K., and Tschannen-Moran, M. (1999). Five Faces of Trust: An Empirical Confirmation in Urban Elementary Schools. *Journal of School. Leadership, 9,* 184–208.

Hoy, W. K., and Tschannen-Moran, M. (2003). The Conceptualization and Measurement of Faculty Trust in Schools. In W. K. Hoy and C. Miskel (Eds.). *Studies in Leading and Organizing Schools* (pp. 181–207).

Hoy, W. K., and Williams, L. B. (1971). Loyalty to Immediate Superior at Alternate Levels in Public Schools. *Educational Administration Quarterly, 7,* 1–11.

Hoy, W. K., and Woolfolk, A. E. (1989). Socialization of Student Teachers. Annual Meeting of the American Educational Research Association, San Francisco.

Hoy, W. K., and Woolfolk, A. E. (1990). Socialization of Student Teachers. *American Educational Research Journal, 27*(2), 279–300.

Hoy, W. K., and Woolfolk, A. E. (1993). Teachers' Sense of Efficacy and the Organizational Health of Schools. *Elementary School Journal, 93*(4), 355–72.

Huber, G. P. (1996). Organizational Learning: The Contributing Processes and Literatures. In Cohen, M. D., and Sproull, L. S. (Eds.). *Organizational Learning* (pp. 124–62). Thousand Oaks, CA: Sage.

Huber, G. P., and Daft, R. L. (1987). The Information Environments of Organizations. In F. M. Jablin, L. L. Putnam, K. Roberts, and L. W. Porter (Eds.), *Handbook of Organizational Communication: An Interdisciplinary Perspective* (pp. 130–64). Newbury Park, CA: Sage.

Huber, V. L. (1981). The Sources, Uses, and Conservation of Managerial Power. *Personnel, 51,* 66–67.

Hunt, J. G. (1991). *Leadership: A New Synthesis.* Newbury Park, CA: Sage.

Hunt, J. G. (1999). Transformational/Charismatic Leadership's Transformation of the Field: An Historical Essay. *Leadership Quarterly, 10*(2), 129–44.

Hunter, M. (1982). *Mastery Teaching.* El Segundo, CA: TIP Publications.

Huseman, R. C., and Miles, E. W. (1988). Organizational Communication in the Information Age: Implications of Computer-Based Systems. *Journal of Management, 14,* 181–204.

Iannaccone, L. (1962). Informal Organization of School Systems. In D. Griffiths, D. L. Clark, R. Wynn, and L. Iannaccone (Eds.), *Organizing Schools for Effective Education* (pp. 227–93). Danville, IL: Interstate.

Imber, M. (1983). Increased Decision Making Involvement for Teachers: Ethical and Practical Considerations. *Journal of Educational Thought, 17,* 36–42.

Imber, M., and Duke, D. L. (1984). Teacher Participation in School Decision Making: A Framework for Research. *Journal of Educational Administration, 22,* 24–34.

Immegart, G. L. (1988). Leadership and Leader Behavior. In N. J. Boyan (Ed.), *Handbook of Research on Educational Administration* (pp. 259–77). New York: Longman.

Ingersoll, R. M. (1993). Loosely Coupled Organizations Revisited. *Research in the Sociology of Organizations, 11,* 81–112.

Irwin, J. W. (1991). *Teaching Reading Comprehension* (2nd ed.). Boston: Allyn and Bacon.

Isaacson, G. (1983). Leadership Behavior and Loyalty. Doctoral diss., Rutgers University, New Brunswick.

Isherwood, G., and Hoy, W. K. (1973). Bureaucracy, Powerlessness, and Teacher Work Values. *Journal of Educational Administration, 9,* 124–38.

Ishikawa, K. (1985). *What Is Total Quality Control? The Japanese Way.* Englewood Cliffs, NJ: Prentice Hall.

Ivey, A. E., and Ivey, M. B. (1999). *Intentional Interviewing and Counseling: Facilitating Client Development in a Multicultural Society.* Pacific Grove, CA: Brooks/Cole Publishing.

Jablin, F. M. (1980). Organizational Communication Theory and Research: An Overview of Communication Climate and Network Research. *Communication Yearbook, 4,* 327–47.

Jablin, F. M. (1987). Formal Organization Structure. In F. M. Jablin, L. L. Putman, K. Roberts, and L. W. Porter (Eds.), *Handbook of Organizational Communication: An Interdisciplinary Perspective* (pp. 389–419). Newbury Park, CA: Sage.

Jablin, F. M., and Putnam, L. L. (Eds.). (2001). *The New Handbook of Organizational Communication.* Thousand Oaks, CA: Sage.

Jablin, F. M., Putnam, L. L., Roberts, K., and Porter, L. W. (Eds.). (1987). *Handbook of Organizational Communication: An Interdisciplinary Perspective.* Newbury Park, CA: Sage.

Jablin, F. M., and Sias, P. M. (2001). Communication Competence. In Jablin, F. M., and Putnam, L. L. (Eds.), *The New Handbook of Organizational Communication* (pp. 819–64). Thousand Oaks, CA: Sage.

Jackson, J. (1990, January 28). Interview with Jesse Jackson. *Parade,* 5.

Jackson, S., and Schuler, R. S. (1985). A Meta-Analysis and Conceptual Critique of Research on Role Ambiguity and Role Conflict in Work Settings. *Organizational Behavior and Human Decision Processes, 36,* 17–78.

James, W. (1983). *Talks to Teachers on Psychology and to Students on Some of Life's Ideals.* Cambridge, MA: Harvard University Press.

Jamison, D., Suppes, P., and Wells, S. (1974). The Effectiveness of Alternative Instructional Media: A Survey. *Review of Educational Research, 44,* 1–67.

Janis, I. L. (1982). *Groupthink: Psychological Studies of Policy Decisions and Fiascoes.* Boston: Houghton Mifflin.

Janis, I. L. (1985). Sources of Error in Strategic Decision Making. In J. M. Pennings (Ed.), *Organizational Strategy and Change* (pp. 157–97). San Francisco: Jossey-Bass.

Janis, I. L., and Mann, L. (1977). *Decision Making: A Psychological Analysis of Conflict, Choice, and Commitment.* New York: Free Press.

Jepperson, R. L. (1991). Institutions, Institutional Effects, and Institutionalism. In W. W. Powell and P. J. DiMaggio (Eds.), *The New Institutionalism in Organizational Analysis* (pp. 164–82). Chicago: University of Chicago Press.

Johns, G., Xie, J. L., and Fang, Y. (1992). Mediating and Moderating Effects in Job Design. *Journal of Management, 18*(4), 657–76.

Johnson, S. M. (1986). Incentives for Teachers: What Motivates, What Matters. *Educational Administration Quarterly, 22,* 54–79.

Jones, M. S., Levin, M. E., Levin, J. R., and Beitzel, B. D. (2000). Can Vocabulary-Learning Strategies and Pair-Learning Formats Be Profitably Combined? *Journal of Educational Psychology, 92,* 256–62.

Juran, J. A. M. (1989). *Juran on Leadership and Quality.* New York: Free Press.

Jurden, F. H. (1995). Individual Differences in Working Memory and Complex Cognition. *Journal of Educational Psychology, 87,* 93–102.

Jurkovich, R. (1974). A Core Typology of Organizational Environments. *Administrative Science Quarterly, 19,* 380–94.

Kagan, S. (1994). *Cooperative Learning.* San Juan Capistrano, CA: Kagan Cooperative Learning.

Kahneman, D., Solvic, P., and Tversky, A. (1982). *Judgment under Uncertainty: Heuristics and Biases.* Cambridge, England: Cambridge University Press.

Kahneman, D., and Tversky, A. (1973). On the Psychology of Prediction. *Psychological Review, 80,* 251–73.

Kahneman, D. K. and Tversky, A. (1996). On the Reality of Cognitive Illusions. *Psychological Review, 103,* 582–91.

Kakabadse, A. (1986). Organizational Alienation and Job Climate. *Small Group Behaviour, 17,* 458–71.

Kanfer, R. (1990). Motivation Theory and Industrial Organizational Psychology. In M. D. Dunnette and L. M. Hough (Eds.), *Handbook of Industrial and Organizational Psychology* (pp. 75–170). Palo Alto, CA: Consulting Psychologists Press.

Kanigel, R. (1997). *The One Best Way.* New York: Viking.

Kanner, L. (1974). Machiavellianism and the Secondary Schools: Teacher-Principal Relations. Doctoral diss., Rutgers University, New Brunswick.

Kant, I. (1794). *Kritik der Reinen Vernunft* [Critique of Pure Reason] (4th ed.). Riga, Latvia: J. R. Hartknoch.

Kanter, R. (1977). *Men and Women of the Corporation.* New York: Basic Books.

Kanter, R., and Brinkerhoff, D. (1981). Organizational Performance: Recent Developments in Measurement. *Annual Review of Sociology, 7,* 321–49.

Karper, J. H., and Boyd, W. L. (1988). Interest Groups and the Changing Environment of State Educational Policymaking: Developments in Pennsylvania. *Educational Administration Quarterly, 24,* 21–54.

Karpov, Y. V., and Haywood, H. C. (1998). Two Ways to Elaborate Vygotsky's Concept of Mediation Implications for Instruction. *American Psychologist, 53,* 27–36

Katz, D., and Kahn, R. L. (1966). *The Social Psychology of Organizations.* New York: Wiley.

Katz, D., and Kahn, R. L. (1978). *The Social Psychology of Organizations* (2nd ed.). New York: Wiley.

Katzell, R. A., and Thompson, D. E. (1990). Work Motivation: Theory and Practice. *American Psychologist, 45*(2), 144–53.

Keeley, M. (1984). Impartiality and Participant-Interest Theories of Organizational Effectiveness. *Administrative Science Quarterly, 29,* 1–25.

Keith, N. V. (1996). A Critical Perspective on Teacher Participation in Urban Schools. *Educational Administration Quarterly, 32,* 45–79.

Kelly, J. (1992). Does Job Re-Design Theory Explain Job Re-Design Outcomes? *Human Relations, 45* (8), 753–74.

Kelsey, J. G. T. (1973). Conceptualization and Instrumentation for the Comparative Study of Secondary School Structure and Operation. Doctoral. diss., University of Alberta, Edmonton.

Kerlinger, F. N. (1986). *Foundations of Behavioral Research* (3rd ed.). New York: Holt, Rinehart & Winston.

Kerr, S., and Jermier, J. M. (1978). Substitutes for Leadership: Their Meaning and Measurement.

Organizational Behavior and Human Performance, 22, 375–403.

Kets de Vries, M. F. R., and Miller, D. (1986). Personality, Culture, and Organization. *Academy Management Review, 11,* 266–79.

Kiewra, K. A. (1985). Investigating Notetaking and Review: A Depth of Processing Alternatives. *Educational Psychologist, 20,* 23–32.

Kiewra, K. A. (1988). Cognitive Aspects of Autonomous Note Taking: Control Processes, Learning Strategies, and Prior Knowledge. *Educational Psychologist, 23,* 39–56.

Kiewra, K. A. (1989). A Review of Note-Taking: The Encoding Storage Paradigm and Beyond. *Educational Psychology Review, 1,* 147–72.

Kiggundu, M. N. (1980). An Empirical Test of the Theory of Job Design Using Multiple Job Ratings. *Human Relations, 33,* 339–51.

Kilmann, R. H. (1984). *Beyond the Quick Fix.* San Francisco: Jossey-Bass.

Kilmann, R. H., and Saxton, M. J. (1983). The *Kilmann-Saxton Culture Gap Survey.* Pittsburgh, PA: Organizational Design Consultant.

Kilmann, R. H., Saxton, M. J., and Serpa, R. (1985). *Gaining Control of the Corporate Culture.* San Francisco: Jossey-Bass.

Kirchhoff, B. A. (1977). Organization Effectiveness Measurement and Policy Research. *Academy of Management Review, 2,* 347–55.

Klein, G. (1997). An Overview of Naturalistic Decision Making Applications. In C. D. Zsambok and G. Klein (Eds.). *Naturalistic Decision Making* (pp. 49–59). Mahwah, NJ: Erlbaum.

Klein G., Wolf, S., Militello, L., and Zsambok, C. (1995). Characteristics of Skilled Option Generation in Chess. *Organizational Behavior and Human Decision Processes.* San Diego, CA: Academic Press.

Kmetz, J. T., and Willower, D. J. (1982). Elementary School Principals' Work Behavior. *Educational Administration Quarterly, 18,* 62–78.

Knapp, M. L. (1972). *Nonverbal Communication in Human Interaction.* New York: Holt, Rinehart, & Winston.

Koberg, C. S., and Ungson, G. R. (1987). The Effects of Environmental Uncertainty and Dependence on Organizational Structure and Performance: A Comparative Study. *Journal of Management, 13,* 725–37.

Kofman, F., and Senge, P. M. (1993). Communities of Commitment: The Heart of Learning Organizations. *Organizational Dynamics, 22,* 5–23.

Kolesar, H. (1967). An Empirical Study of Client Alienation in the Bureaucratic Organization. Doctoral diss., University of Alberta, Edmonton.

Kollman, K. (1998). *Outside Lobbying: Public Opinion and Interest Group Strategies.* Princeton, NJ: Princeton University Press.

Kondrasuk, J. N. (1981). Studies in MBO Effectiveness. *Academy of Management Review, 6,* 419–30.

Kotter, J. P. (1978). Power, Success, and Organizational Effectiveness. *Organizational Dynamics, 6,* 27–40.

Kotter, J. P. (1982). *The General Managers.* New York: Free Press.

Kotter, J. P. (1985). *Power and Influences: Beyond Formal Authority.* New York: Free Press.

Kotter, J. P. (1990). *A Force for Change: How Leadership Differs from Management.* New York: Free Press.

Kottkamp, R. B., and Mulhern, J. A. (1987). Teacher Expectance Motivation, Open to Closed Climate and Pupil Control Ideology in High Schools. *Journal of Research and Development in Education, 20,* 9–18.

Kottkamp, R. B., Mulhern, J., and Hoy, W. K. (1987). Secondary School Climate: A Revision of the OCDQ. *Educational Administration Quarterly, 23,* 31–48.

Kouzes, J. M., and Posner, B. Z. (2002). *The Leadership Challenge.* San Francisco, CA: Jossey-Bass.

Kozulin, A., and Presseisen, B. Z. (1995). Meditated Learning Experience and Psychological Tools: Vygotsky's and Feuerstein's Perspectives in a Study of Student Learning. *Educational Psychologist, 30,* 67–75.

Kraatz, M. S. (1998). Learning by Association? Interorganizational Networks and Adaptation to Environmental Change. *Academy of Management Journal, 41*(6), 621–43.

Krone, K. J., Jablin, F. M., and Putnam, L. L. (1987). Communication Theory and Organizational Communication: Multiple Perspectives. In F. M. Jablin, L. L. Putnam, K. Roberts, and L. W. Porter (Eds.), *Handbook of Organizational*

Communication: An Interdisciplinary Perspective (pp. 18–40). Newbury Park, CA: Sage.

Krueger, A. B. (2003). Economic Considerations and Class Size. *Economic Journal, 113*(February). F34–F63.

Kuhlman, E., and Hoy, W. K. (1974). The Socialization of Professionals into Bureaucracies: The Beginning Teacher in the School. *Journal of Educational Administration, 8*, 18–27.

Kuhnert, K. W., and Lewis, P. (1987). Transactional and Transformational Leadership: A Constructive/Developmental Analysis. *Academy of Management Review, 12*(4), 648–57.

Kulik, C. T., and Ambrose, M. L. (1992). Personal and Situational Determinants of Referent Choice. *Academy Management Review, 17*, 212–37.

Kulik, C. L., Kulik, J. A., and Bangert-Drowns, R. L.(1990). Effectiveness of Mastery Learning Programs: A Meta-analysis. *Review of Educational Research, 60*, 265–99.

Kunz, D., and Hoy, W. K. (1976). Leader Behavior of Principals and the Professional Zone of Acceptance of Teachers. *Educational Administration Quarterly, 12*, 49–64.

Ladd, H. F., and Zelli, A. (2002). School-Based Accountability in North Carolina: The Responses of School Principals. *Educational Administration Quarterly, 38(4)*, 494–529.

Lally, V., and Scaife, J. (1995) Towards a Collaborative Approach to Teacher Empowerment. *Bristish Educational Research Journal, 21*, 323–39.

Landy, F. J., and Becker, W. S. (1987). Motivation Theory Reconsidered. *Research in Organizational Behavior, 9*, 1–38.

Larson, J. R. J. (1989). The Dynamic Interplay between Employee's Feedback-Seeking Strategies and Supervisors' Delivery of Performance Feedback. *Academy of Management Review, 14*, 408–22.

Latham, G. P. (2000). Motivate Employee Performance through Goal-Setting. In E. A. Locke (Ed.), *Handbook of Principles of Organizational Behavior* (pp. 107–19). Malden, MA: Blackwell.

Latham, G., and Baldes, J. (1975). The Practical Significance of Locke's Theory of Goal Setting. *Journal of Applied Psychology, 60*, 122–24.

Latham, G. P., and Locke, E. A. (1991). Self-Regulation through Goal Setting. *Organizational Behavior and Human Decision Processes, 50*, 212–47.

Latham, G. P., Winters, D. C., and Locke, E. G. (1994). Cognitive and Motivational Effects of Participation: A Mediator Study. *Journal of Organizational Behavior, 15*, 49–63.

Latham, G. P., and Yukl, G. A. (1975). A Review of Research on the Application of Goal Setting in Organizations. *Academy of Management Journal, 18*, 824–45.

Lau, L. J. (1978). Education Production Functions. Conference on School Organization and Effects, National Institute of Education, Washington, DC.

Lave, J. (1988). *Cognition in Practice: Mind, Mathematics, and Culture in Everyday Life.* New York: Cambridge University Press.

Lave, J., and Wenger, E. (1991). *Situated Learning: Legitimate Peripheral Participation.* Cambridge, MA: Cambridge University Press.

Lawler, E. E., III. (1973). *Motivation in Work Organizations.* Monterey, CA: Brooks/Cole.

Lawler, E. E., III. (1985). Education, Management Style, and Organizational Effectiveness. *Personnel Psychology, 38*, 1–26.

Lawler, E. E., III. (1992). *The Ultimate Advantage.* San Francisco, CA: Jossey-Bass.

Lawler, E. E., III. (1994). Total Quality Management and Employee Involvement: Are They Compatible? *Academy of Management Executive, 8*(1), 68–76.

Lawrence, P. R., and Lorsch, J. W. (1967). *Organization and Environment: Managing Differentiation and Integration.* Boston: Graduate School of Business Administration, Harvard University.

Leach, D. J., Wall, T. D., and Jackson, P. R. (2003). The Effect of Empowerment on Job Knowledge: An Empirical Test Involving Operators of Complex Technology. *Journal of Occupational and Organizational Psychology, 76*, 27–52.

Leavitt, H. J., Dill, W. R., and Eyring, H. B. (1973). *The Organizational World.* New York: Harcourt Brace Jovanovich.

Lee, V. E., Bryk, A. S., and Smith, J. B. (1993). The Organization of Effective Secondary Schools. *Review of Research in Education, 19*, 171–267.

Lefkowitz, J., Somers, M. J., and Weinberg, K. (1984). The Role of Need Level and/or Need

Salience as Moderators of the Relationship between Need Satisfaction and Work Alienation-Involvement. *Journal of Vocational Behavior, 24,* 142–58.

Leithwood, K. (1994). Leadership for School Restructuring. *Educational Administration Quarterly, 30*(4), 498–518.

Leithwood, K., and Duke, D. L. (1999). A Century's Quest to Understand School Leadership. In J. Murphy and K. S. Louis (Eds.), *Handbook of Research on Educational Administration* (pp. 45–72). San Francisco, CA: Jossey-Bass.

Leithwood, K., Jantzi, D., and Steinbach, R. (1998). Leadership and Other Conditions Which Foster Organizational Learning in Schools. In K. Leithwood and K. S. Louis (Eds.), *Organizational Learning in Schools* (pp. 67–90). Lisse: Swets and Zeitlinger.

Leithwood, K., and Louis, K. S. (1998). *Organizational Learning in Schools.* Lisse: Swets and Zeitlinger.

Leonard, J. F. (1991). Applying Deming's Principles to Our Schools. *South Carolina Business, 11,* 82–87.

Lepper, M. R., and Greene, D. (1978). *The Hidden Costs of Rewards: New Perspectives on the Psychology of Human Motivation.* Hillsdale, NJ: Erlbaum.

Level, D. A., Jr. (1972). Communication Effectiveness: Method and Situation. *Journal of Business Communication, 9,* 19–25.

Leverette, B. B. (1984). Professional Zone of Acceptance: Its Relation to the Leader Behavior of Principals and Socio-Psychological Characteristics of teaching. Doctoral diss., Rutgers University, New Brunswick.

Levin, J. R. (1985). Educational Applications of Mnemonic Pictures: Possibilities beyond Your Wildest Imagination. In A. A. Sheikh (Ed.), *Imagery in the Educational Process.* Farmingdale, NY: Baywood.

Levitt, B. L., and March, J. G. (1996). In Cohen, M. D., and Sproull, L. S. (Eds.), *Organizational Learning* (pp. 516–40). Thousand Oaks, CA: Sage.

Levitt, B. L., and Nass, C. (1989). The Lid on the Garbage Can: Institutional Constraints on Decision Making in the Technical Core of College-Text Publishers. *Administrative Science Quarterly, 34,* 190–207.

Lewis, P. V. (1975). *Organizational Communications: The Essence of Effective Management.* Columbus, OH: Grid.

Liao, Y. M. (1994). School Climate and Effectiveness in Taiwan's Secondary Schools. Doctoral diss., St. John's University, Queens.

Licata, J. W., and Hack, W. G. (1980). School Administrator Grapevine Structure. *Educational Administration Quarterly, 16,* 82–99.

Lieberson, S., and O'Connor, J. F. (1972). Leadership and Organizational Performance: A Study of Large Corporations. *American Sociological Review, 37,* 117–30.

Lindblom, C. E. (1959). The Science of Muddling Through. *Public Administrative Review, 19,* 79–99.

Lindblom, C. E. (1965). *The Intelligence of Democracy: Decision Making through Mutual Adjustment.* New York: Free Press.

Lindblom, C. E. (1968). *The Policy-Making Process.* Englewood Cliffs, NJ: Prentice Hall.

Lindblom, C. E. (1980). *The Policy-Making Process* (2nd ed.). Englewood Cliffs: Prentice Hall.

Lindblom, C. E., and Cohen, D. K. (1979). *Usable Knowledge: Social Science and Social Problem Solving.* New Haven, CT: Yale University Press.

Lipham, J. A. (1988). Getzel's Model in Educational Administration. In N. J. Boyan (Ed.), *Handbook of Research on Educational Administration* (pp. 171–84). New York: Longman.

Lipham, J. A., and Francke, D. C. (1966). Nonverbal Behavior of Administrators. *Educational Administration Quarterly, 2,* 101–9.

Litchfield, E. H. (1956). Notes on a General Theory of Administration. *Administrative Science Quarterly, 1,* 3–29.

Litwin, G. H., and Stringer, R. A., Jr. (1968). *Motivation and Organizational Climate.* Boston: Harvard University Press.

Locke, E. A. (1968). Toward a Theory of Task Motivation and Incentives. *Organizational Behavior and Human Performance, 3,* 157–89.

Locke, E. A. (1976).The Nature and Causes of Job Satisfaction. In M. D. Dunnette (Ed.), *Handbook of Industrial and Organizational Psychology* (pp. 1297–349). Chicago: Rand McNally.

Locke, E. A. (1991). The Motivation Sequence, the Motivation Hub, and the Motivation Core. *Organizational Behavior and Human Decision Processes, 50,* 288–99.

Locke, E. A., and Latham, G. P. (1984). *Goal Setting: A Motivational Technique That Works.* Englewood Cliffs, NJ: Prentice Hall.

Locke, E. A., and Latham, G. P. (1990). *A Theory of Goal Setting and Task Performance.* Englewood Cliffs, NJ: Prentice Hall.

Locke, E. A., and Latham, G. P. (2002). Building a Practically Oriented Theory of Goal Setting and Task Motivation: A 35-Year Odyssey. *American Psychologist, 57,* 705–17.

Locke, E. A., Latham, G. P., and Erez, M. (1988). The Determinants of Goal Commitment. *Academy of Management Review, 13,* 23–39.

Locke, E. A., and Schweiger, D. M. (1979). Participation in Decision Making: One More Look. *Research in Organizational Behavior, 1,* 265–339.

Logan, C. S., Ellet, C. D., and Licata, J. W. (1993). Structural Coupling, Robustness, and Effectiveness of Schools. *Journal of Educational Administration, 31*(1), 19–32.

Lorsch, J. W. (1985). Strategic Myopia: Culture as an Invisible Barrier to Change. In R. H. Kilmann, M. J. Saxton, and R. Serpa (Eds.), *Gaining Control of the Corporate Culture* (pp. 84–102). San Francisco: Jossey-Bass.

Lortie, D. C. (1969). The Balance of Control and Autonomy in Elementary School Teaching. In A. Etzioni (Ed.), *The Semiprofessions and Their Organization* (pp. 1–53). New York: Free Press.

Lortie, D. C. (1975). *Schoolteacher: A Sociological Study.* Chicago: University of Chicago Press.

Louis, K. S., and Kruse, S. D. (1998). Creating Community in Reform: Images of Organizational Learning in Inner-City Schools. In K. Leithwood and K. S. Louis (Eds.), *Organizational Learning in Schools* (pp. 17–45). Lisse: Swets and Zeitlinger.

Lubienski, C. (2003). Innovation in Education Markets: Theory and Evidence on the Impact of Competition and Choice in Charter Schools. *American Educational Research Association, 40*(2), 395–443.

Lugg, C. A., and Boyd, W. L. (1993). Leadership for Collaboration: Reducing Risk and Fostering Resilience. *Phi Delta Kappan, 75,* 252–58.

Lunenburg, F. C. (1983). Pupil Control Ideology and Self-Concept as a Learner. *Educational Research Quarterly, 8,* 33–39.

Lunenburg, F. C., and Schmidt, L. J. (1989). Pupil Control Ideology, Pupil Control Behavior, and Quality of School Life. *Journal of Research and Development in Education, 22,* 35–44.

MacGeorge, E L., Gillihan, S. J., Samter, W., and Clark, R. A. (2003). Skill Deficit or Differential Motivation? *Communication Research, 30*(3), 272–303.

Machiavelli, N. (1984). *The Prince.* Harmondsworth: Penguin.

MacKay, D. (1964). An Empirical Study of Bureaucratic Dimensions and Their Relations to Other Characteristics of School Organization. Doctoral diss., University of Alberta, Edmonton.

MacKensie, D. E. (1983). Research for School Improvement: An Appraisal and Some Recent Trends. *Educational Research, 12,* 5–17.

MacKinnon, J. D., and Brown, M. E. (1994). Inclusion in Secondary Schools: An Analysis of School Structure Based on Teachers' Images of Change. *Educational Administration Quarterly, 30,* 126–52.

Madaus, G. F., Airasian, P. W., and Kellaghan, T. (1980). *School Effectiveness: A Reassessment of the Evidence.* New York: McGraw-Hill.

Maeroff, G. I. (1988). *The Empowerment of Teachers: Overcoming the Crisis of Confidence.* New York: Teachers College Press.

Mager, R. (1975). *Preparing Instructional Objectives* (2nd ed.). Palo Alto, CA: Fearon.

Malen, B. (1993). Enacting Site Based Management: A Political Utilities Analysis. Unpublished paper, College of Education, University of Washington.

Malen, B., Croninger, R., Muncey, D., and Redmond-Jones, D. (2002). Reconstituting Schools: "Testing" the "Theory of Action." *Educational Evaluation and Policy Analysis, 24*(2), 113–32.

Malen, B., Murphy, M. J., and Hart, A. W. (1988). Restructuring Teacher Compensation Systems: An Analysis of Three Incentive Strategies. In K. Alexander and D. H. Monk (Eds.), *Eighth Annual Yearbook of the American Educational Finance Association* (pp. 91–142). Cambridge, MA: Ballinger.

Malen, B., and Ogawa, R. T. (1992). Site-Based Management: Disconcerting Policy Issues,

Critical Policy, and Choices. In J. J. Lane and E. G. Epps (Eds.), *Restructuring the Schools: Problems and Prospects* (pp. 185–206). Berkeley, CA: McCutchan.

Malen, B., Ogawa, R. T., and Kranz, J. (1990). What Do We Know about School-Based Management? A Case Study of the Literature—A Call for Research. In W. H. Clune and J. F. White (Eds.), *Choice and Control in American Education. Volume 2: The Practice of Choice, Decentralization and School Restructuring* (pp. 289–342). New York: Falmer Press.

Mann, R. D. (1959). A Review of the Relationships between Personality and Performance. *Psychological Bulletin, 56,* 241–70.

Manning, P. K. (1992). *Organizational Communication.* New York: Aldine De Gruyer.

March, J. G. (1981). Footnotes to Organizational Change. *Administrative Science Quarterly, 26,* 563–77.

March, J. G. (1982). Emerging Developments in the Study of Higher Education. *Review of Higher Education, 6,* 1–18.

March, J. G. (1988). *Decisions and Organizations.* Oxford: Blackwell.

March, J. G. (1994). *A Primer of Decision Making.* New York: Free Press.

March, J. G., and Olsen, J. P. (1976). *Ambiguity and Choice in Organization.* Bergen, Norway: Universitetsforlaget.

March, J. G., and Simon, H. (1958). *Organizations.* New York: Wiley.

March, J. G., and Simon, H. (1993). *Organizations* (2nd ed.). Cambridge, MA: Blackwell.

Marion, R. (2002). Leadership in Education: Organizational Theory for the Practitioner. Upper Saddle, NJ: Merrill Prentice Hall.

Marjoribanks, K. (1977). Bureaucratic Orientation, Autonomy and Professional Attitudes of Teachers. *Journal of Educational Administration, 15,* 104–13.

Mark, J. H., and Anderson, B. D. (1985). Teacher Survival Rates in St. Louis, 1969–1982. *American Educational Research Journal, 22,* 413–21.

Markman, E. M. (1977). Realizing That You Don't Understand: A Preliminary Investigation. *Child Development, 48,* 986–92.

Markman, E. M. (1979). Realizing That You Don't Understand: Elementary School Children's Awareness of Inconsistencies. *Child Development, 50,* 643–55.

Marks, H. M., and Louis, K. S. (1997). Does Teacher Empowerment Affect the Classroom? The Implications of Teacher Empowerment for Instructional Practice and Student Academic Performance. *Educational Evaluation and Policy Analysis, 19,* 245–75.

Marks, H. M., and Louis, K. S. (1999). Teacher Empowerment and the Capacity for Organizational Learning. *Educational Administration Quarterly, 35,* 707–50.

Marks, H. M., and Printy, S. M. (2003). Principal Leadership and School Performance: An Integration of Transformational and Instructional Leadership. *Educational Administration Quarterly, 39*(3), 370–97.

Marshall, H. (1996). Implications of Differentiating and Understanding Constructivist Approaches. *Journal of Educational Psychology, 31,* 235–40.

Martin, J. (1985). Can Organizational Culture Be Managed? In P. J. Frost, L. F. Moore, M. R. Lousi, C. C. Lundberg, and J. Martin (Eds.), *Organizational Culture* (pp. 95–98). Beverly Hills, CA: Sage.

Martin, J. (1990a). Deconstructing Organizational Taboos: Suppression of Gender Conflict in Organizations. *Organizational Science, 1,* 339–59.

Martin, J. (1990b). Rereading Weber: Searching for Feminist Alternatives to Bureaucracy. Annual Meeting of the Academy of Management, San Francisco.

Martin, J. (1992). *Cultures in Organizations.* New York: Oxford University Press.

Martin, J., and Knopoff, K. (1999). The Gendered Implications of Apparently Gender-Neutral Theory: Rereading Weber, in *Ruffin Lectures Series.* Volume 3: *Business Ethics and Women's Studies,* Eds. E. Freeman and A. Larson. Oxford: Oxford University Press.

Martin, W. J., and Willower, D. J. (1981). The Managerial Behavior of High School Principals. *Educational Administration Quarterly, 17,* 69–90.

Martin, Y. M., Isherwood, G. B., and Lavery, R. G. (1976). Leadership Effectiveness in Teacher Probation Committees. *Educational Administration Quarterly, 12,* 87–99.

Marx, K. (1963). *Karl Marx: Early Writings.* T. Bottomore (Trans. and Ed.). London: Watts.

Maslow, A. H. (1965). *Eupsychian Management.* Homewood, IL: Irwin.

Maslow, A. H. (1970). *Motivation and Personality* (2nd ed.). New York: Harper & Row.

Maxey, S. J. (1995). *Democracy, Chaos, and New School Order.* Thousand Oaks, CA: Corwin Press.

Mayo, E. (1945). *The Social Problems of an Industrial Civilization.* Boston: Graduate School of Business Administration, Harvard University.

Mazzoni, T. L., and Malen, B. (1985). Mobilizing Constituency Pressure to Influence State Education Policy Making. *Educational Administration Quarterly, 21,* 91–116.

McCabe, D. L., and Dutton, J. E. (1993). Making Sense of the Environment: The Role of Perceived Effectiveness. *Human Relations, 46*(5), 623–43.

McCall, M. W., Jr., and Lombardo, M. M. (Eds.). (1978). *Leadership: Where Else Can We Go?* Durham, NC: Duke University Press.

McCaskey, M. B. (1979). The Hidden Messages Managers Send. *Harvard Business Review, 57,* 135–48.

McCaslin, M., and Hickey, D. T. (2001). Self-Regulated Learning and Academic Achievement: A Vygotskian View. In B. Zimmerman and D. Schunk (Eds.). *Self-Regulated Learning and Academic Achievement: Theoretical Perspectives* (2nd ed., pp. 227–52). Mahwah, NJ: Erlbaum.

McClelland, D. C. (1961). *The Achieving Society.* Princeton, NJ: Van Nostrand.

McClelland, D. C. (1965). Toward a Theory of Motive Acquisition. *American Psychologist, 20* (5), 321–33.

McClelland, D. C. (1985). *Human Motivation.* Glenview, IL: Scott, Foresman.

McConkie, M. L. (1979). A Clarification of the Goal Setting and Appraisal Process in MBO. *Academy of Management Review, 4,* 29–40.

McCormick, C. B., and Levin, J. R. (1987). Mnemonic Prose-Learning Strategies. In M. Pressley and M. McDaniel (Eds.), *Imaginary and Related Mnemonic Processes.* New York: Springer-Verlag.

McElroy, J. C., and Schrader, C. B. (1986). Attribution Theories of Leadership and Network Analysis. *Journal of Management, 12,* 351–62.

McFarland, A. S. (1992). Interest Groups and the Policymaking Process: Sources of Countervailing Power in America. In M. P. Petracca (Ed.), *The Politics of Interests* (pp. 58–79). Boulder, CO: Westview.

McNall, S. G., and McNall, S. A. (1992). *Sociology.* Englewood Cliffs, NJ: Prentice Hall.

McNamara, V., and Enns, F. (1966). Directive Leadership and Staff Acceptance of the Principal. *Canadian Administrator, 6,* 5–8.

McNeil, L. M. (1986). *Contradictions of Control: School Structure and School Knowledge.* New York: Routledge & Kegan Paul.

McNeil, L. M. (1988a). Contradictions of Control, Part 1: Administrators and Teachers. *Phi Delta Kappan, 69,* 333–39.

McNeil, L. M. (1988b). Contradictions of Control, Part 2: Administrators and Teachers. *Phi Delta Kappan, 69,* 432–38.

Meany, D. P. (1991). Quest for Quality. *California Technology Project Quarterly, 2,* 8–15.

Mechanic, D. (1962). Sources of Power of Lower Participants in Complex Organizations. *Administrative Science Quarterly, 6,* 349–64.

Meichenbaum, D., Burland, S., Gruson, L., and Cameron, R. (1985). Metacognitive Assessment. In S. Yussen (Ed.), *The Growth of Reflection in Children.* Orlando, FL: Academic Press.

Mendell, P. R. (1971). Retrieval and Representation in Long-Term Memory. *Psychonomic Science, 23,* 295–96.

Mennuti, N., and Kottkamp, R. B. (1986). Motivation through the Design of Work: A Synthesis of the Job Characteristics Model and Expectancy Motivation Tested in Middle and Junior High Schools. Annual Meeting of the American Educational Research Association, San Francisco.

Mento, A. J., Locke, E. A., and Klein, H. J. (1992). Relationship of Goal Level to Valence and Instrumentality. *Journal of Applied Psychology, 77,* 395–405.

Merton, R. (1957). *Social Theory and Social Structure.* New York: Free Press.

Metz, M. H. (1986). *Different by Design: The Context and Character of Three Magnet Schools.* New York: Routledge and Kegan Paul.

Meyer, H. D. (2002a). From "Loose Coupling" to "Tight Management"? Making Sense of the

Changing Landscape in Management and Organizational Theory. *Journal of Educational Administration, 40,* 515–20.

Meyer, H D. (2002b) The New Managerialism in (Higher) Education: Between Corporatization and Organization Learning. *Journal of Educational Administration, 40,* 534–51.

Meyer, J. W. (1992). Centralization of Funding and Control in Educational Governance. In J. W. Meyer and W. R. Scott (Eds.), *Organization Environments: Ritual and Rationality* (pp. 179–97). Newbury Park, CA: Sage.

Meyer, J. W., and Rowan, B. (1977). Institutionalized Organizations: Formal Structure as Myth and Ceremony. *American Journal of Sociology, 83,* 440–63.

Meyer, J. W., and Rowan, B. (1978). The Structure of Educational Organizations. In M. W. Meyer (Ed.), *Environments and Organizations* (pp. 78–109). San Francisco: Jossey-Bass.

Meyer, J. W., and Scott, W. R. (1983). *Organizational Environments: Ritual and Rationality.* Beverly Hills, CA: Sage.

Meyer, J. W., Scott, W. R., and Deal, T. E. (1992). Institutional and Technical Sources of Organizational Structure: Explaining the Structure of Educational Organizations. In J. W. Meyer and W. R. Scott (Eds.), *Organization Environments: Ritual and Rationality* (pp. 45–67). Newbury Park, CA: Sage.

Meyer, J. W., Scott, W. R., and Strang, D. (1987). Centralization, Fragmentation, and School District Complexity. *Administrative Science Quarterly, 32,* 186–201.

Meyer, M. W. (1978). Introduction: Recent Developments in Organizational Research and Theory. In M. W. Meyer (Ed.), *Environments and Organizations* (pp. 1–19). San Francisco: Jossey-Bass.

Michaels, R. E., Cron, W. L., Dubinsky, A. J., and Joachimsthaler, E. A. (1988). Influence of Formalization on the Organizational Commitment and Work Alienation of Salespeople and Industrial Buyers. *Journal of Marketing Research, 25,* 376–83.

Michels, R. (1949). *Political Parties.* E. and C. Paul (Trans.). Glencoe, IL: Free Press (first published in 1915).

Midgley, C., Feldlaufer, H., and Eccles, J. S. (1989). Change in Teacher Efficacy and Student Self- and Task-Related Beliefs in Mathematics during the Transition to Junior High School. *Journal of Educational Psychology, 81*(2), 247–58.

Midgley, C., and Wood, S. (1993). Beyond Site-Based Management: Empowering Teachers to Reform Schools. *Phi Delta Kappan, 75,* 245–52.

Miles, M. B. (1965). Education and Innovation: The Organization in Context. In M. Abbott and J. Lovell (Eds.), *Changing Perspectives in Educational Administration* (pp. 54–72). Auburn, AL: Auburn University Press.

Miles, M. B. (1969). Planned Change and Organizational Health: Figure and Ground. In F. D. Carver and T. J. Sergiovanni (Eds.), *Organizations and Human Behavior* (pp. 375–91). New York: McGraw-Hill.

Milgram, S. (1963). Behavioral Study of Obedience. *Journal of Abnormal and Social Psychology, 17,* 371–78.

Milgram, S. (1973). The Perils of Obedience. *Harper's* (December), 62–66, 75–77.

Milgram, S. (1974). *Obedience to Authority.* New York: Harper & Row.

Miller, D. (1992). Environmental Fit versus Internal Fit. *Organization Science, 3*(2), 159–78.

Miller, G. A. (1956). The Magical Number Seven, Plus or Minus Two: Some Limits on Our Capacity for Processing Information. *Psychological Review, 63,* 81–97.

Miller, G. A., Galanter, E., and Pribram, K. H. (1960). *Plans and the Structure of Behavior.* New York: Holt, Rinehart & Winston.

Miller, L. E., and Grush, J. E. (1988). Improving Predictions in Expectancy Theory Research: Effects of Personality, Expectancies, and Norms. *Academy of Management Journal, 31,* 107–22.

Miller, P. (1993). *Theories of Developmental Psychology.* New York: Freeman.

Miller, P. H. (2002). *Theories of Developmental Psychology* (4th ed.). New York: Worth.

Milliken, F. J. (1987). Three Types of Perceived Uncertainty about the Environment: State, Effect, and Response Uncertainty. *Academy of Management Review, 12,* 133–43.

Mindlin, S. E., and Aldrich, H. (1975). Interorganizational Dependence: A Review of the Concept and a Reexamination of the Findings of the Aston Group. *Administrative Science Quarterly, 20,* 382–92.

Miner, J. B. (1980). *Theories of Organizational Behavior.* Hinsdale, IL: Dryden.

Miner, J. B. (1988). *Organizational Behavior.* New York: Random House.

Miner, J. B. (2002). *Organizational Behavior: Foundations, Theories, and Analyses.* New York; Oxford University Press.

Miner, A. S., Amburgey, T. L., and Stearns, T. M. (1990). Interorganizational Linkages and Population Dynamics: Buffering and Transformational Shields. *Administrative Science Quarterly, 35,* 689–713.

Mintzberg, H. (1973). *The Nature of Managerial Work.* New York: Harper & Row.

Mintzberg, H. (1978). Patterns in Strategy Formulation. *Management Science, 24,* 934–48.

Mintzberg, H. (1979). *The Structuring of Organizations.* Englewood Cliffs, NJ: Prentice Hall.

Mintzberg, H. (1980). Organizational Structure and Alienation from Work. Annual Meeting of the American Educational Research Association, Boston.

Mintzberg, H. (1981). The Manager's Job: Folklore and Fact. *Harvard Business Review, 53*(4), 49–61.

Mintzberg, H. (1983a). *Power in and around Organizations.* Englewood Cliffs, NJ: Prentice Hall.

Mintzberg, H. (1983b). *Structure in Fives.* Englewood Cliffs, NJ: Prentice Hall.

Mintzberg, H. (1989). *Mintzberg on Management.* New York: Free Press.

Mintzberg, H., Raisinghani, D., and Theoret, A. (1976). The Structure of "Unstructured" Decision Processes. *Administrative Science Quarterly, 23,* 246–75.

Miskel, C., and Cosgrove, D. (1985). Leader Succession in School Settings. *Review of Educational Research, 55,* 87–105.

Miskel, C., DeFrain, J., and Wilcox, K. (1980). A Test of Expectancy Work Motivation Theory in Educational Organizations. *Educational Administration Quarterly, 16,* 70–92.

Miskel, C., Fevurly, R., and Stewart, J. (1979). Organizational Structures and Processes,

Perceived School Effectiveness, Loyalty, and Job Satisfaction. *Educational Administration Quarterly, 15,* 97–118.

Miskel, C., McDonald, D., and Bloom, S. (1983). Structural and Expectancy Linkages within Schools and Organizational Effectiveness. *Educational Administration Quarterly, 19,* 49–82.

Miskel, C., and Ogawa, R. (1988). Work Motivation, Job Satisfaction, and Climate. In N. J. Boyan (Ed.), *Handbook of Research on Educational Administration* (pp. 279–304). New York: Longman.

Mitchell, T. R. (1974). Expectancy Models of Job Satisfaction, Occupational Preference, and Effort: A Theoretical, Methodological and Empirical Appraisal. *Psychological Bulletin, 81,* 1053–77.

Mitchell, T. R. (1979). Organization Behavior. *Annual Review of Psychology, 30,* 243–81.

Mitroff, I. I., and Kilmann, R. H. (1978). *Methodological Approaches to Social Science: Integrating Divergent Concepts and Theories.* San Francisco: Jossey-Bass.

Mizruchi, M. S., and Fein, L. C. (1999). The Social Construction of Organizational Knowledge: A Study of the Uses of Coercive, Mimetic, and Normative Isomorphism. *Administrative Science Quarterly, 44*(4), 653–83.

Moe, T. M. (2003). "Politics, Control, and the Future of School Accountability." In P. E. Peterson and M. West (Eds.), *Leave No Child Behind? The Politics and Practices of School Accountability* (pp. 80–106) Washington, DC: Brookings Institution.

Moeller, G. H., and Charters, W. W., Jr. (1966). Relation of Bureaucratization to Sense of Power among Teachers. *Administrative Science Quarterly, 10,* 444–65.

Mohan, M. L. (1993). *Organizational Communication and Cultural Vision.* Albany, NY: State University of New York Press.

Mohrman, A. M., Jr., Cooke, R. A., and Mohrman, S. A. (1978). Participation in Decision Making: A Multidimensional Perspective. *Educational Administration Quarterly, 14,* 13–29.

Monge, P. R. (1987). The Network Level of Analysis. In C. R. Berger and S. H. Chaffee (Eds.), *Handbook of Communication Science* (pp. 239–70). Newbury Park, CA: Sage.

Monge, P. R., and Contractor, N. S. (2001). Emergence of Communication Networks. In Jablin, F. M., and Putnam, L. L. (Eds.), *The New Handbook of Organizational Communication* (pp. 440–502). Thousand Oaks, CA: Sage.

Monk, D. H. (1992). Education Productivity Research: An Update and Assessment of Its Role in Education Finance Reform. *Educational Evaluation and Policy Analysis, 14*(4), 307–32.

Monk, D. H., and Plecki, M. L. (1999). Generating and Managing Resources for School Improvement. In J. Murphy and K. S. Louis (Eds.), *Handbook of Research on Educational Administration* (2nd ed., pp. 491–509). San Francisco: Jossey-Bass.

Moon, N. J. (1983). The Construction of a Conceptual Framework for Teacher Participation in School Decision Making. Doctoral diss., University of Kentucky, Lexington.

Moran, E. T., and Volkwein, J. F. (1992). The Cultural Approach to the Formation of Organizational Climate. *Human Relations, 45*(1), 19–47.

Morgan, G. (1997). *Images of Organizations* (New Ed.). Thousand Oaks, CA: Sage.

Morris, P. F. (1990). Metacognition. In M. W. Eysenck, (Ed.), *The Blackwell Dictionary of Cognitive Psychology* (pp. 225–29). Oxford, UK: Basil Blackwell.

Morris, V. C., Crowson, R. L., Hurwitz, E. Jr., and Porter-Gehrie, C. (1981). *The Urban Principal.* Chicago: College of Education, University of Illinois at Chicago.

Morse, P. S., and Ivey, A. E. (1996). *Face to Face: Communication and Conflict Resolution in Schools.* Thousand Oaks, CA: Sage.

Mortimore, P. (1993). School Effectiveness and the Management of Effective Learning and Teaching. *School Effectiveness and School Improvement, 4*(4), 290–310.

Mortimore, P. (1998). *The Road to Improvement: Reflections on School Effectiveness.* Lisse: Swets and Zeitlinger.

Moshman, D. (1982). Exogenous, Endogenous, and Dialectical Constructivism. *Developmental Review, 2,* 371–84.

Moshman, D. (1997). Pluralist Rational Constructivism. *Issues in Education* (3), 235–44.

Mott, P. E. (1972). *The Characteristics of Effective Organizations.* New York: Harper & Row.

Mowday, R. T. (1978). The Exercise of Upward Influence in Organizations. *Administrative Science Quarterly, 23,* 137–56.

Mowday, R. T., Porter, L. W., and Steers, R. M. (1982). *Employee-Organizational Linkages: The Psychology of Commitment, Absenteeism, and Turnover.* New York: Academic Press.

Mullins, T. (1983). Relationships among Teachers' Perception of the Principal's Style, Teachers' Loyalty to the Principal, and Teachers' Zone of Acceptance. Doctoral diss., Rutgers University, New Brunswick.

Mumford, M. D., Zaccaro, S. J., Harding, F. D., Jacobs, T. O., and Fleishman, E. A. (2000). Leadership Skills for a Changing World: Solving Complex Social Problems. *Leadership Quarterly, 11*(1), 11–35.

Murnane, R. J. (1981). Interpreting the Evidence on School Effectiveness. *Teachers College Record, 83,* 19–35.

Murnane, R. J. (1987). Understanding Teacher Attrition. *Harvard Educational Review, 57,* 177–82.

Murphy, J., and Datnow, A. (Eds.). (2003). *Leadership Lessons from Comprehensive School Reforms.* Thousand Oaks, CA: Corwin.

Murphy, M. J. (1985). Testimony before the California Commission on the Teaching Profession. Sacramento.

Myers, I. B., and Briggs, K. C. (1962). *The Myers-Briggs Type Indicator.* Princeton: NJ: Educational Testing Service.

Myers, M. T., and Myers, G. E. (1982). *Managing by Communication: An Organizational Approach.* New York: McGraw-Hill.

Nadler, D. A., and Lawler, E. E., III. (1977). Motivation: A Diagnostic Approach. In J. R. Hackman, E. E. Lawler III, and L. W. Porter (Eds.), *Perspectives on Behavior in Organizations* (pp. 26–38). New York: McGraw-Hill.

Nadler, D. A., and Tushman, M. L. (1983). A General Diagnostic Model for Organizational Behavior Applying a Congruence Perspective. In J. R. Hackman, E. E. Lawler III, and L. W. Porter (Eds.), *Perspectives on Behavior in Organizations* (pp. 112–24). New York: McGraw-Hill.

Nadler, D. A., and Tushman, M. L. (1989). Organizational Frame Bending: Principles for

Managing Reorientation. *Academy of Management Executive, 3,* 194–203.

National Commission on Excellence in Education. (1983). *A Nation at Risk.* Washington, DC: U.S. Government Printing Office.

National Commission on Excellence in Educational Administration. (1987). *Leaders for America's Schools.* Tempe, AZ: University Council for Educational Administration.

National Council of Teachers of Mathematics (NCTM). (1989). *Curriculum and Evaluation Standards for School Mathematics.* Reston, VA: Author.

National Council of Teachers of Mathematics (NCTM). (2000). *Principles and Standards for School Mathematics.* Reston, VA: Author.

National Staff Development Council. (2001). *Standards for Staff Development* (Rev. Ed.). Oxford, OH: Author. Available at www.nsdc.org/educatorindex.htm.

Needles, M., and Knapp, M. (1994). Teaching Writing to Children Who Are Undeserved. *Journal of Educational Psychology, 86,* 339–49.

Nelson, T. O. (1996). Consciousness and Metacognition. *American Psychologist, 51,* 102–16.

Nespor, J. (1987). The Role of Beliefs in the Practice of Teaching. *Journal of Curriculum Studies, 19,* 317–28.

Newberry, J. F. (1971). A Comparative Analysis of the Organizational Structures of Selected Post-Secondary Educational Institutions. Doctoral diss., University of Alberta, Edmonton.

Nicholls, J. G., and Miller, A. (1984). Conceptions of Ability and Achievement Motivation. In R. Ames & C. Ames (Eds.), *Research on Motivation in Education. Volume 1: Student Motivation* (pp. 39–73). New York: Academic Press.

Nicholson, J. H. (1980). Analysis of Communication Satisfaction in an Urban School System. Doctoral diss., George Peabody College for Teachers of Vanderbilt University, Nashville, TN.

Nietzsche, F. (1968). *The Will to Power.* New York: Vintage Books.

Nietzsche, F. (1968). *Twilight of the Idols.* Harmondsworth: Penguin.

Nietzsche, F. (1969). *Ecce Homo.* New York: Vintage Books.

Nisbett, R. E., and Ross, L. (1980). *Human Interferences: Strategies and Shortcomings in Social Judgments.* Englewood Cliffs, NJ: Prentice Hall.

Northcraft, G. B., and Earley, P. C. (1989). Technology, Credibility, and Feedback Use. *Organizational Behavior and Human Performance, 44,* 83–96.

Northcraft, G. B., and Neale, M. A. (1987). Experts, Amateurs, and Real Estate: An Anchoring-and-Adjustment Perspective on Property Pricing in Decision. *Organizational Behavior and Human Decision Processes, 39,* 84–97.

Northouse, P. G. (2004). *Leadership: Theory and Practice* (3rd ed.). Thousand Oaks, CA: Sage.

Nutt, P. C. (1984). Types of Organizational Decision Processes. *Administrative Science Quarterly, 29,* 414–50.

O'Dempsey, K. (1976). Time Analysis of Activities, Work Patterns and Roles of High School Principals. *Administrator's Bulletin, 7,* 1–4.

Odiorne, G. S. (1979). *MBO II: A System of Managerial Leadership for the 80s.* Belmont, CA: Pitman.

O'Donnell, A. M., and O'Kelly, J. (1994). Learning from Peers: Beyond the Rhetoric of Positive Results. *Educational Psychology Review, 6,* 321–50.

Ogawa, R. T. (1991). Enchantment, Disenchantment, and Accommodation: How a Faculty Made Sense of the Succession of a Principal. *Educational Administration Quarterly, 27*(1), 30–60.

Ogawa, R. T. (1992). Institutional Theory and Examining Leadership in School. *International Journal of Educational Management, 6*(3), 14–21.

Ogawa, R. T. (1994). The Institutional Sources of Educational Reform: The Case of School-Based Management. *American Educational Research Journal, 31*(3), 519–48.

Ogawa, R. T., and Bossert, S. T. (1995). Leadership as an Organizational Property. *Educational Administration Quarterly, 31,* 224–43.

Ogawa, R. T., Sandholtx, H. J., Martinez-Flores, M., and Scribner, S. P. (2003). The Substantive and Symbolic Consequences of a District's Standards-Based Curriculum. *American Educational Research Journal, 40*(1), 147–76.

Ogawa, R. T., and Scribner, S. P. (2002). Leadership: Spanning the Technical and Insitutional Dimensions of Organizations. *Journal of Educational Administration, 40*(6), 576–88.

Okeafor, K. R., and Teddlie, C. (1989). Organizational Factors Related to Administrator's Confidence in Teachers. *Journal of Research and Development in Education, 22,* 28–36.

Oldham, G. R., and Kulik, C. T. (1984). Motivation Enhancement through Work Redesign. In J. L. Bess (Ed.), *College and University Organization* (pp. 85–104). New York: New York University Press.

Oldham, G. R., and Miller, H. E. (1979). The Effect of Significant Other's Job Complexity and Employee Reactions to Work. *Human Relations, 32,* 247–60.

Olsen, M. E. (1965). *The Logic of Collective Action: Public Goods and the Theory of Groups.* Cambridge, MA: Harvard University Press.

Olsen, M. E. (1968). A Theory of Groups and Organizations. In B. M. Russett (Ed.), *Economic Theory of International Politics.* Chicago: Markham.

O'Reilly, C. A. I., Chatman, J. A., and Caldwell, D. (1991). People and Organizational Culture: A Q-sort Approach to Assessing Person-Organization Fit. *Academy of Management Journal, 34*(3), 487–516.

O'Reilly, C. A. I., and Pondy, L. R. (1979). Organizational Communication. In S. Kerr (Ed.), *Organizational Behavior* (pp. 119–50). Columbus, OH: Grid.

O'Reilly, C. A. I., and Roberts, K. H. (1977). Task Group Structure, Communication, and Effectiveness in Three Organizations. *Journal of Applied Psychology, 62,* 674–81.

Orpen, C. (1979). The Effects of Job Enrichment on Employee Satisfaction, Motivation, Involvement, and Performance: A Field Experiment. *Human Relations, 32,* 189–217.

Orton, J. D., and Weick, K. E. (1990) Loosely Coupled Systems: A Reconceptualization. *Academy of Management Review, 15,* 203–23.

Ostroff, C., and Schmitt, N. (1993). Configurations of Organizational Effectiveness and Efficiency. *Academy of Management Journal, 36*(6), 1345–61.

Ouchi, W. (1981). *Theory Z.* Reading, MA: Addison-Wesley.

Ouchi, W. G. (2003). *Making Schools Work.* New York: Simon and Schuster.

Ouchi, W., and Wilkins, A. L. (1985). Organizational Culture. *Annual Review of Sociology, 11,* 457–83.

Pace, C. R., and Stern, G. C. (1958). An Approach to the Measure of Psychological Characteristics of College Environments. *Journal of Educational Psychology, 49,* 269–77.

Packard, J. S. (1988). The Pupil Control Studies. In N. J. Boyan (Ed.), *Handbook of Research on Educational Administration* (pp. 185–207). New York: Longman.

Packard, J. S., and Willower, D. J. (1972). Pluralistic Ignorance and Pupil Control Ideology. *Journal of Educational Administration, 10,* 78–87.

Padgett, J. F. (1980). Managing Garbage Can Hierarchies. *Administrative Science Quarterly, 25,* 583–604.

Page, C. H. (1946). Bureaucracy's Other Face. *Social Forces, 25,* 88–94.

Pajares, F. (1996). Current Directions in Self Research: Self-Efficacy. Paper presented at the annual meeting of the American Educational Research Association, New York.

Pajares, F. (1997). Current Directions in Self-Efficacy Research. In M. L. Maehr and P. R. Pintrich (Eds.), *Advances in Motivation and Achievement* (pp. 1–49). Greenwich, CT: JAI Press.

Palincsar, A. S. (1986). The Role of Dialogue in Providing Scaffolding Instruction. *Educational Psychologist, 21,* 73–98.

Palincsar, A. M. (1998). Social Constructivist Perspectives on Teaching and Learning. In J. T. Spence, J. M. Darley, D. J. Foss (Eds.), *Annual Review of Psychology* (pp. 345–76). Palo Alto, CA: Annual Reviews.

Pallas, A. M., Natriello, G., and McDill, E. L. (1989). The Changing Nature of the Disadvantaged Population: Current Dimension and Future Trends. *Educational Researcher, 18,* 16–22.

Pallas, A. M., and Neumann, A. (1993). Blinded by the Light: The Applicability of Total Management to Educational Organizations. Annual Meeting of the American Educational Research Association, Atlanta, GA.

Paris, S. G., Byrnes, J. P., and Paris, A. H. (2001). Constructing Theories, Identities, and Actions of Self-Regulated Learners. In B. J. Zimmerman and D. H. Schunk (Eds.), *Self-Regulated Learning and Academic Achievement: Theoretical Perspectives* (2nd ed., pp. 253–87). Mahwah, NJ: Erlbaum.

Paris, S. G., and Cunningham, A. E. (1996). Children Becoming Students. In D. Berliner and

R. Calfee, (Eds.), *Handbook of Educational Psychology* (pp. 117–46). New York: Macmillan.

Paris, S. G., Lipson, M. Y., and Wixson, K. K. (1983). Becoming a Strategic Reader. *Contemporary Educational Psychology, 8,* 293–316.

Parsons, T. (1947). Introduction. In Max Weber, *The Theory of Social and Economic Organization* (pp. 3–86). A. M. Henderson and T. Parsons (Trans.). New York: Free Press.

Parsons, T. (1960). *Structure and Process in Modern Societies.* Glencoe, IL: Free Press.

Parsons, T. (1967). *Sociological Theory and Modern Society.* New York: Free Press.

Parsons, T., Bales, R. F., and Shils, E. A. (1953). *Working Papers in the Theory of Action.* New York: Free Press.

Parsons, T., and Shils, E. A. (Eds.). (1951). *Toward a General Theory of Action.* Cambridge, MA: Harvard University Press.

Pasch, M., Sparks-Langer, G., Gardner, T. G., Starko, A. J., and Moody, C. D. (1991). *Teaching as Decision Making: Instructional Practices for the Successful Teacher.* New York: Longman.

Pastor, M. C., and Erlandson, D. A. (1982). A Study of Higher Order Need Strength and Job Satisfaction in Secondary Public School Teachers. *Journal of Educational Administration, 20,* 172–83.

Pawar, B. S., and Eastman, K. K. (1997). The Nature and Implications of Contextual Influences on Transformational Leadership: A Conceptual Examination. *Academy of Management Review, 22*(1), 80–109.

Payne, J. W., Bettman, J. R., and Johnson, E. J. (1988). Adaptive Strategy Selection in Decision Making. *Journal of Experimental Psychology: Learning, Memory, and Cognition, 14,* 534–52.

Peabody, R. L. (1962). Perceptions of Organizational Authority: A Comparative Analysis. *Administrative Science Quarterly, 6,* 463–82.

Penley, L. E., Alexander, E. R., Jernigan, I. E., and Henwood, C. I. (1991). Communication Abilities of Managers: The Relationship to Performance. *Journal of Management, 17*(1), 57–76.

Pennings, J. M. (1985). *Organizational Strategy and Change.* San Francisco: Jossey-Bass.

Pennings, J. M. (1992). Structural Contingency Theory: A Reappraisal. *Research in Organizational Behavior, 14,* 267–309.

Perkins, D. N. (1991, May). Technology Meets Constructivism: Do They Make a Marriage? *Educational Technology, 31,* 18–23.

Perrow, C. (1978). Demystifying Organization. In R. Saari and Y. Hasenfeld (Eds.), *The Management of Human Services* (pp. 105–20). New York: Columbia University Press.

Perrow, C. (1986). *Complex Organizations: A Critical Essay* (3rd ed.). Glencoe, IL: Scott, Foresman.

Peters, L. H., Hartke, D. D., and Pohlmann, J. T. (1985). Fiedler's Contingency Theory of Effectiveness: An Application of the Meta-Analysis Procedures of Schmidt and Hunter. *Psychological Bulletin, 97,* 274–85.

Peters, T. J., and Waterman, R. H., Jr. (1982). *In Search of Excellence.* New York: Harper & Row.

Peterson, K. D. (1977–78). The Principal's Tasks. *Administrator's Notebook, 26,* 1–4.

Peterson, P. E. (1989). The Public Schools: Monopoly or Choice? Conference on Choice and Control in American Education. Robert M. LaFollette Institute of Public Affairs, University of Wisconsin, Madison.

Pfeffer, J. (1972). Size and Composition of Corporate Boards of Directors: The Organization and Its Environment. *Administrative Science Quarterly, 17,* 218–28.

Pfeffer, J. (1976). Beyond Management and the Worker: The Institutional Function of Management. *Academy of Management Review, 1,* 36–46.

Pfeffer, J. (1981). *Power in Organizations.* Boston: Pitman.

Pfeffer, J. (1982). *Organizations and Organization Theory.* Boston: Pitman.

Pfeffer, J. (1992). *Managing with Power: Politics and Influence in Organizations.* Boston: Harvard Business School.

Pfeffer, J. (1997). *New Directions for Organization Theory.* New York: Oxford University Press.

Pfeffer, J., and Leblebici, H. (1973). The Effect of Competition on Some Dimensions of Organizational Structure. *Social Forces, 52,* 268–79.

Pfeffer, J., and Salancik, G. (1978). *The External Control of Organizations: A Resource Dependence Perspective.* New York: Harper & Row.

Phillips, D. C. (1997). How, Why, What, When, and Where: Perspectives on Constructivism and

Education. *Issues in Education: Contributions from Educational Psychology, 3,* 151–94.

Phillips, D. C., and Thomas, A. R. (1982). Principals' Decision Making: Some Observations. In W. S. Simpkins, A. R. Thomas, and E. B. Thomas (Eds.), *Principal and Task: An Australian Perspective* (pp. 74–83). Armidale, NSW, Australia: University of New England.

Piaget, J. (1969). *Science of Education and the Psychology of the Child.* New York: Viking.

Pinder, C. C. (1984). *Work Motivation: Theory, Issues, and Applications.* Dallas: Scott, Foresman.

Pinder, C. C. (1998). *Work Motivation in Organizational Behavior.* Toronto, ON: Prentice Hall.

Pinfield, L. T. (1986). A Field Evaluation of Perspectives on Organizational Decision Making. *Administrative Science Quarterly, 31,* 365–88.

Pintrich, P. R. (1988). A Process-Oriented View of Student Motivation and Cognition. In J. S. Stark and L. A. Mets (Eds.), *Improving Teaching and Learning through Research* (pp. 65–79). San Francisco: Jossey-Bass.

Pintrich, P. R., and Garcia, T. (1991). Student Goal Orientation and Self-Regulation in the College Classroom. In M. Maehr and P. R. Pintrich (Eds.), *Advances in Motivation and Achievement* (pp. 371–402). Greenwich, CT: JAI.

Pintrich, P. R., Marx, R. W., and Boyle, R. A. (1993). Beyond Cold Conceptual Change: The Role of Motivational Beliefs and Classroom Contextual Factors in the Process of Conceptual Change. *Review of Educational Research, 63*(2), 167–99.

Pitner, N., and Ogawa, R. T. (1981). Organizational Leadership: The Case of the Superintendent. *Educational Administration Quarterly, 17,* 45–65.

Podgurski, T. P. (1990). School Effectiveness as it Relates to Group Consensus and Organizational Health of Middle Schools. Doctoral diss., Rutgers University, New Brunswick.

Podsakoff, P. M., Niehoff, B. P., MacKenzie, S. B., and Williams, M. L. (1993). Do Substitutes for Leadership Really Substitute for Leadership? An Empirical Examination of Kerr and Jermier's Situational Leadership Model. *Organizational Behavior and Human Decision Processes, 54,* 1–44.

Poole, M. S. (1985). Communication and Organizational Climates: Review, Critique, and a New Perspective. In R. D. McPhee and P. K. Tompkins (Eds.), *Organizational Communications: Traditional Themes and New Directions* (pp. 79–108). Beverly Hills, CA: Sage.

Popham, W. J. (2002). *Classroom Assessment: What Teachers Need to Know.* Boston, MA: Allyn & Bacon.

Porter, L. W. (1961). A Study of Perceived Need Satisfactions in Bottom and Middle Management Jobs. *Journal of Applied Psychology, 45,* 1–10.

Porter, L. W., and Lawler, E. E., III. (1968). *Managerial Attitudes and Performance.* Homewood, IL: Dorsey.

Porter, L. W., and Roberts, K. H. (1976). Communication in Organizations. In M. D. Dunnette (Ed.), *Handbook of Industrial and Organizational Psychology* (pp. 1533–89). Chicago: Rand McNally.

Pounder, D. G., Ogawa, R. T., and Adams, E. A. (1995). Leadership as an Organization-Wide Phenomena: Its Impact on School Performance. *Educational Administration Quarterly, 31*(4), 564–88.

Powell, T. C. (1995). Total Quality Management as Competitive Advantage: A Review and Empirical Study. *Strategic Management Journal, 16,* 15–37.

Powell, W. W. (1991). Expanding the Scope of Institutional Analysis. In W. W. Powell and P. J. DiMaggio (Eds.), *The New Institutionalism in Organizational Analysis* (pp. 183–203). Chicago: University of Chicago Press.

Powell, W. W., and DiMaggio, P. J. (1991). Introduction. In W. W. Powell and P. J. DiMaggio (Eds.), *The New Institutionalism in Organizational Analysis* (pp. 1–38). Chicago: University of Chicago Press.

Prawat, R. S. (1992). Teachers Beliefs about Teaching and Learning: A Constructivist Perspective. *American Journal of Education, 100,* 354–95.

Pressley, M., Levin, J., and Delaney, H. D. (1982). The Mnemonic Keyword Method. *Review of Research in Education, 52,* 61–91.

Prestine, N. A. (1991). Shared Decision Making in Restructuring Essential Schools: The Role of the Principal. *Planning and Changing, 22,* 160–78.

Pugh, D. S., and Hickson, D. J. (1976). *Organizational Structure in Its Context.* Westmead, Farnborough, Hants., England: Saxon House, D. C. Heath.

Pugh, D. S., Hickson, D. J., and Hinings, C. R. (1968). Dimensions of Organizational Structure. *Administrative Science Quarterly, 13,* 56–105.

Pugh, D. S., Hickson, D. J., Hinings, C. R., and Turner, C. (1969). The Context of Organizational Structure. *Administration Science Quarterly, 14,* 91–114.

Pugh, K., and Zhao, Y. (2003). Stories of Teacher Alienation: A Look at the Unintended Consequences of Efforts to Empower Teachers. *Teaching and Teacher Education, 19,* 187–202.

Purkey, S. C., and Smith, M. S. (1983). Effective Schools: A Review. *Elementary School Journal, 83,* 427–52.

Putman, L. (1997). Productive Conflict: Negotiation as Implicit Coordination. In C. DeDreu and E. Van De Vliert (Eds.), *Using Conflict in Organizations* (pp. 147–60). London: Sage.

Quarstein, V. A., McAfee, R. B., and Glassman, M. (1992). The Situational Occurrences Theory of Job Satisfaction. *Human Relations, 45*(8), 859–72.

Rachlin, H. (1991). *Introduction to Modern Behaviorism* (3rd ed.). New York: Freeman.

Raffini, J. P. (1996). *150 Ways to Increase Intrinsic Motivation in the Classroom.* Boston: Allyn and Bacon.

Ratsoy, E. W. (1973). Participative and Hierarchical Management of Schools: Some Emerging Generalizations. *Journal of Educational Administration, 11,* 161–70.

Raudenbush, S., Rowen, B., and Cheong, Y. (1992). Contextual Effects on the Self-Perceived Efficacy of High School Teachers. *Sociology of Education, 65,* 150–67.

Rauschenberger, J., Schmitt, N., and Hunter, J. E. (1980). A Test of the Need Hierarchy Concept by a Markov Model of Change in Need Strength. *Administrative Science Quarterly, 25,* 654–70.

Raymond, M. E., and Hanushek, E. A. (2003). High-Stakes Research. *Education Next, 3* (Summer), 48–55.

Recht, D. R., and Leslie, L. (1988). Effect of Prior Knowledge on Good and Poor Readers'

Memory of Text. *Journal of Educational Psychology, 80,* 16–20.

Redding, W. C. (1972). *Communication within the Organization.* West Lafayette, IN: Purdue Research Council.

Reder, L. M., and Anderson, J. R. (1980). A Comparison of Texts and Their Summaries: Memorial Consequences. *Journal of Verbal Learning and Verbal Behavior, 19*(2), 121–34.

Reeve, J. (1996). *Motivating Others: Nurturing Inner Motivational Resources.* Boston: Allyn and Bacon.

Reeves, C. A., and Bednar, D. A. (1994). Defining Quality: Alternatives and Implications. *Academy of Management Review, 19*(3), 419–45.

Reilly, B. J., and DiAngelo, J. A. (1990). Communication: A Cultural System of Meaning and Value. *Human Relations, 43*(2), 129–40.

Reiss, F. (1994). Faculty Loyalty in and around the Urban Elementary School. Doctoral diss., Rutgers University, New Brunswick.

Reiss, F., and Hoy, W. K. (1998). Faculty Loyalty: An Important but Neglected Concept in the Study of Schools. *Journal of School Leadership, 8,* 4–21.

Resnick, L. B. (1981). Instructional Psychology. *Annual Review of Psychology, 32,* 659–704.

Reynolds, D., and Teddlie, C. (with Creemers, B., Scheerens, J., and Townsend, T.). (2000). An Introduction to School Effectiveness Research. In C. Teddlie, and D. Reynolds, (Eds.), *The International Handbook on School Effectiveness Research* (pp. 3–25). New York: Falmer.

Reynolds, P. D. (1971). *A Primer in Theory Construction.* Indianapolis, IN: Bobbs-Merrill.

Rhodes, L. A. (1990). Why Quality Is within Our Grasp . . . If We Reach. *The School Administrator, 47*(10), 31–34.

Rice, A. W. (1978). Individual and work variables associated with principal job satisfaction. Doctoral diss., University of Alberta, Edmonton.

Rice, J. K. (2002). Making the Evidence Matter: Implications of the Class Size Research Debate for Policy Makers. In L. Mishel and R. Rothstein (Eds.), *The Class Size Policy Debate* (pp. 89–94). Washington, DC: Economic Policy Institute.

Rice, J. K. (2003). *Teacher Quality: Understanding the Effects of Teacher Attributes.* Washington, DC: Economic Policy Institute.

Rice, M. E., and Schneidner, G. T. (1994). A Decade of Teacher Empowerment: An Empirical Analysis of Teacher Involvement in Decision Making, 1980–1991. *Journal of Educational Administration, 32,* 43–58.

Rice, R. E. (1992). Task Analyzability, Use of New Media, and Effectiveness: A Multi-Site Exploration of Media Richness. *Organization Science, 3*(4), 475–500.

Rinehart, J. S., Short, P. M, and Johnson, P. E. (1997). Empowerment and Conflict at School-Based and Non-School-Based Sites in the United States. *Journal of International Studies in Educational Administration, 25,* 77–87.

Rinehart, J. S., Short, P. M., Short, R. J., and Eckley, M. (1998). Teacher Empowerment and Principal Leadership: Understanding the Influence Process. *Educational Administration Quarterly, 24,* 608–30.

Robbins, S. P. (1983). *The Structure and Design of Organizations.* Englewood Cliffs, NJ: Prentice Hall.

Robbins, S. P. (1998). *Organizational Behavior: Concepts, Controversies, Applications.* Upper Saddle, NJ: Allyn and Bacon.

Roberts, K. H., Hulin, C. L., and Rousseau, D. M. (1978). *Developing an Interdisciplinary Science of Organizations.* San Francisco: Jossey-Bass.

Roberts, N. C., and Bradley, R. T. (1988). Limits of Charisma. In J. A. Conger and R. N. Kanungo (Eds.), *Charismatic Leadership: The Elusive Factor in Organizational Effectiveness* (pp. 253–75). San Francisco, CA: Jossey-Bass.

Robinson, D. H., and Kiewra, K. A. (1995). Visual Argument: Graphic Outlines Are Superior to Outlines in Improving Learning from Text. *Journal of Educational Psychology, 87,* 455–67.

Rockey, E. H. (1984). *Communication in Organizations.* Lanham, MD: University Press of America.

Roethlisberger, F. J., and Dickson, W. J. (1939). *Management and the Worker.* Cambridge: Harvard University Press.

Rogers, R. C., and Hunter, J. E. (1989). The Impact of Management by Objectives on Organizational Productivity. Unpublished paper, School of Public Administration, University of Kentucky, Lexington.

Rogoff, B. (1998). Cognition as a Collaborative Process. In W. Damon (series ed.) and D. Kuhn and R. S. Siegler (volume eds.), *Handbook of Child Psychology: vol. 2* (5th ed., pp. 679–744). New York: Wiley.

Rosenau, P. M. (1992). *Post-Modernism and the Social Sciences: Insights, Inroads, and Intrusions.* Princeton, NJ: Princeton University Press.

Rosenshine, B. (1979). Content, Time, and Direct Instruction. In P. Peterson and H. Walberg (Eds.), *Research on Teaching: Concepts, Findings, and Implications* (pp. 28–56). Berkeley, CA: McCutchan.

Rosenshine, B. (1988). Explicit Teaching. In D. Berliner and B. Rosenshine (Eds.), *Talks to Teachers* (pp. 75–92). New York: Random House.

Rosenshine, B., and Stevens, R. (1986).). Teaching Functions. In M. Wittrock (Ed.) *Teaching Research on Teaching* (3rd ed., pp. 376–91). New York: Macmillan.

Ross, J. A., Cousins, J. B., and Gadalla, T. (1996). Within-Teacher Predictors of Teacher Efficacy. *Teaching and Teacher Education, 12,* 385–400.

Rossman, G. B., Corbett, H. D., and Firestone, W. A. (1988). *Change and Effectiveness in Schools: A Cultural Perspective.* Albany, NY: State University of New York Press.

Rotter, J. B. (1954). *Social Learning and Clinical Psychology.* Englewood Cliffs, NJ: Prentice Hall.

Rotter, J. B. (1966). Generalized Expectancies for Internal versus External Control of Reinforcement. *Psychological Monographs, 80*(1, Whole No. 609).

Rousseau, D. M. (1978). Characteristics of Departments, Positions, and Individuals: Contexts for Attitudes and Behavior. *Administrative Science Quarterly, 23,* 521–40.

Rowan, B. (1981). The Effects of Institutionalized Rules on Administrators. In S. B. Bacharach (Ed.), *Organizational Behavior in Schools and School Districts* (pp. 47–75). New York: Praeger.

Rowan, B. (1982). Organizational Structure and the Institutional Environment: The Case of Public Schools. *Administrative Science Quarterly, 27,* 259–79.

Rowan, B. (1990). Commitment and Control: Alternative Strategies for the Organizational ‚Design of School. *Review of Research in Education, 16,* 353–89.

Rowan, B. (1993). Institutional Studies of Organization: Lines of Analysis and Data Requirements. Annual Meeting of the American Educational Research Association, Atlanta, GA.

Rowan, B. (1998). The Task Characteristics of Teaching: Implications for the Organizational Design of Schools. In R. Bernhardt, C. Hedley, G. Cattari, and V. Svolopoulos (Eds.), *Curriculum Leadership: Rethinking Schools for the 21st Century* (pp. 37–54). Creskill, NJ: Hampton Press.

Rowan, B. (2002). Rationality and Reality in Organizational Management: Using the Coupling Metaphor to Understand Educational (and Other) Organizations—a Concluding Comment. *Journal of Educational Administration,* 40, 604–11.

Rowan, B., Bossert, S. T., and Dwyer, D. C. (1983). Research on Effective Schools: A Cautionary Note. *Educational Researcher,* 12, 24–31.

Rowan, B., Correnti, R., and Miller, R. J. (2002). What Large-Scale, Survey Research Tells Us About Teacher Effects on Student Achievement: Insights from the *Prospects* Study of Elementary Schools. *Teachers College Record,* 104(8), 1525–67.

Rowan, B., and Miskel, C. (1999). Institutional Theory and the Study of Educational Organizations. In J. Murphy and K. S. Louis (Eds.), *Handbook of Research on Educational Administration* (2nd ed., pp. 359–83). San Francisco: Jossey-Bass.

Rowan, B., Raudenbush, S. W., and Cheong, Y. F. (1993). Teaching as a Nonroutine Task: Implications for the Management of Schools. *Educational Administration Quarterly,* 29, 479–99.

Rumelhart, D., and Ortony, A. (1977). *The Representation of Knowledge in Memory.* In R. Anderson, R. Spiro, and W. Montague (Eds.), Schooling and The Acquisition of Knowledge. Hillsdale, NJ: Erlbaum.

Russ, G. S., Daft, R. L., and Lengel, R. H. (1990). Media Selection and Managerial Characteristics in Organizational Communication. *Management Communication Quarterly,* 4, 151–75.

Russell, R. D., and Russell, C. J. (1992). An Examination of the Effects of Organizational Norms, Organizational Structure, and Environmental Uncertainty on Entrepreneurial Strategy. *Journal of Management,* 18(4), 639–56.

Rutter, M., Maugham, B., Mortimore, P., Ousten, J., and Smith, A. (1979). *Fifteen Thousand Hours: Secondary Schools and Their Effects on Children.* London: Open Books.

Ryan, R. M., and Deci, E. L. (2000). Intrinsic and Extrinsic Motivation: Classroom Definitions and New Directions. *Contemporary Educational Psychology,* 25, 54–67.

Ryan, R. M., and Grolnick, W. S. (1986). Origins and Pawns in the Classroom: Self-Report and Projective Assessments of Individual Differences in the Children's Perceptions. *Journal of Personality and Social Psychology,* 50, 550–58.

Sackney, L. E. (1976). The Relationship between Organizational Structure and Behavior in Secondary Schools. Doctoral diss., University of Alberta, Edmonton.

Salancik, G. R., and Pfeffer, J. (1977). Constraints on Administrative Discretion: The Limited Influence of Mayors on City Budgets. *Urban Affairs Quarterly,* 12, 475–98.

Salas, E., and Klein, G. (2001). *Linking Expertise and Naturalistic Decision Making.* Mahwah, NJ: Erlbaum.

Sanchez, P. (1999). How to Craft Successful Employee Communication in the Information Age. *Communication World,* 16(7), 9–15.

Sanders, W. L. (1998). Value-Added Assessment. *The School Administrator,* 55(11), 24–32.

Sashkin, M., and Burke, W. W. (1990). Understanding and Assessing Organizational Leadership. In K. E. Clark and M. B. Clark (Eds.), *Measures of Leadership* (pp. 297–325). West Orange, NJ: Leadership Library of America.

Sayles, L. R., and Strauss, G. (1966). *Human Behavior in Organizations.* Englewood Cliffs, NJ: Prentice Hall.

Scheerens, J., and Bosker, R. (1997). *The Foundations of Educational Effectiveness.* Oxford: Permagon.

Schein, E. H. (1985). *Organizational Culture and Leadership.* San Francisco: Jossey-Bass.

Schein, E. H. (1990). Organizational Culture. *American Psychologist,* 45(2), 109–19.

Schein, E. H. (1992). *Organizational Culture and Leadership* (2nd ed.). San Francisco: Jossey-Bass.

Schein, E. H. (1999). *The Corporate Culture.* San Francisco: Jossey-Bass.

Scherkenbach, W. (1991). *Deming's Road to Continual Improvement.* Knoxville, TN: SPC Press.

Scherkenbach, W. (1992). *The Deming Route to Quality and Production*. Washington, DC: CEEPress.

Schermerhorn, J. R., Hunt, J. G., and Osborn, R. N. (1994). *Managing Organizational Behavior*. New York: Wiley.

Schmidt, F. L., and Hunter, J. E. (1992). Development of a Causal Model of Processes Determining Job Performance. *Current Directions in Psychological Science, 1*(3), 89–92.

Schmitz, J., and Fulk, J. (1991). Organizational Colleagues, Media Richness, and Electronic Mail. *Communication Research, 18*(4), 487–523.

Schmuck, R. A., and Runkel, P. J. (1985). *The Handbook of Organization Development in Schools* (3rd ed.). Prospect Heights, IL: Waveland Press.

Schraw, G., and Moshman, D. (1995). Metacognitive Theories. *Educational Psychology Review, 7*, 351–71.

Schunk, D. (1991). Self-Efficacy and Academic Motivation. *Educational Psychologist, 26*, 207–31.

Schunk, D. H. (2000). *Learning Theories: An Educational Perspective* (3rd ed.). Columbus, OH: Merrill/Prentice. Hall.

Schunk, D. H. (1996). Goal and Self-Evaluative Influences During Children's Cognitive Skill Learning. *American Educational Research Journal, 33*, 359–82.

Schwartz, B., and Reisberg, D. (1991). *Learning and Memory*. New York: Norton.

Scott, W. R. (1977). Effectiveness of Organizational Effectiveness Studies. In P. S. Goodman and J. M. Pennings (Eds.), *New Perspectives on Organizational Effectiveness* (pp. 63–95). San Francisco: Jossey-Bass.

Scott, W. R. (1981). *Organizations: Rational, Natural, and Open System*. Englewood Cliffs, NJ: Prentice Hall.

Scott, W. R. (1983). Introduction: From Technology to Environment. In J. W. Meyer and W. R. Scott (Eds.), *Organizational Environments: Ritual and Rationality* (pp. 13–17). Beverly Hills, CA: Sage.

Scott, W. R. (1987a). The Adolescence of Institutional Theory. *Administrative Science Quarterly, 32*, 493–511.

Scott, W. R. (1987b). *Organizations: Rational, Natural, and Open System* (2nd ed.). Englewood Cliffs, NJ: Prentice Hall.

Scott, W. R. (1991). Unpacking Institutional Arguments. In W. W. Powell and P. J. DiMaggio (Eds.), *The New Institutionalism in Organizational Analysis* (pp. 164–82). Chicago: University of Chicago Press.

Scott, W. R. (1992). *Organizations: Rational, Natural, and Open Systems* (3rd. ed.). Englewood Cliffs, NJ: Prentice Hall.

Scott, W. R. (1995). *Institutions and Organizations*. Thousand Oaks, CA: Sage.

Scott, W. R. (1998). *Organizations: Rational, Natural, and Open Systems* (4th. ed.). Englewood Cliffs, NJ: Prentice Hall.

Scott, W. R. (2001). *Institutions and Organizations* (2nd ed.). Upper Saddle River, NJ: Prentice Hall.

Scott, W. R. (2003). *Organizations: Rational, Natural, and Open Systems* (5th ed.). Upper Saddle River, NJ: Prentice Hall.

Scott, W. R., and Meyer, J. W. (1991). The Organization of Societal Sectors: Propositions and Early Evidence. In W. W. Powell and P. J. DiMaggio (Eds.), *The New Institutionalism in Organizational Analysis* (pp. 108–40). Chicago: University of Chicago Press.

Selznick, P. (1949). *TVA and the Grass Roots*. Berkeley: University of California Press.

Selznick, P. (1957). *Leadership in Administration*. New York: Harper & Row.

Selznick, P. (1992). *The Moral Commonwealth*. Berkeley: University of California Press.

Semb, G. B., and Ellis, J. A. (1994). Knowledge Taught in School: What Is Remembered? *Review of Educational Research, 64*, 253–86.

Senatra, P. T. (1980). Role Conflict, Role Ambiguity, and Organizational Climate in a Public Accounting Firm. *Accounting Review, 55*, 594–603.

Senge, P. M. (1990). *The Fifth Discipline: The Art and Practice of the Learning Organization*. New York: Doubleday.

Sergiovanni, T. J. (1992). *Moral Leadership: Getting to the Heart of School Improvement*. San Francisco: Jossey-Bass.

Sergiovanni, T. J. (1994). *Building Community in Schools*. San Francisco: Jossey-Bass.

Shakeshaft, C. (1986). *Women in Educational Administration*. Newbury Park, CA: Sage.

Shamir, B., and Howell, J. M. (1999). Organizational and Contextual Influences on the Emergence and Effectiveness of Charismatic Leadership. *Leadership Quarterly, 10*(2), 257–83.

Shamir, B., House, R. J., and Arthur, M. B. (1993). The Motivational Effects of Charismatic Leadership: A Self-Concept Based Theory. *Organization Science, 4*(4), 577–94.

Shamir, B., Zokay, E., Breinin, E., and Popper, M. (1998). Correlates of Charismatic Leader Behavior in Military Units. *Academy of Management Journal, 41*(4), 387–409.

Shanker, A. (1989, May 14). Does Money Make a Difference? A Difference over Answers. *New York Times.*

Sharma, C. L. (1955). Who Should Make What Decisions? *Administrator's Notebook, 3,* 1–4.

Shelby, A. N. (1986). The Theoretical Bases of Persuasion: A Critical Introduction. *Journal of Business Communication, 23,* 5–29.

Shuell, T. (1996). Teaching and Learning in a Classroom Context. In D. Berliner and R. Calfee (eds.), *Handbook of Educational Psychology* (pp. 726–64). New York: Macmillan.

Shuell, T. J. (1986). Cognitive Conceptions of Learning. *Review of Educational Research, 56,* 411–36.

Sickler, J. L. (1988). Teachers in Charge: Empowering the Professionals. *Phi Delta Kappan, 69,* 354–56.

Silins, H. C. (1992). Effective Leadership for School Reform. *Alberta Journal of Educational Research, 38,* 317–34.

Silver, P. (1983). *Educational Administration: Theoretical Perspectives in Practice and Research.* New York: Harper & Row.

Simon., H. A. (1955). A Behavioral Model of Rational Choice. *Quarterly Journal of Economics, 69,* 99–118.

Simon, H. A. (1956). Rational Choice and the Structure of the Environment. *Psychological Review, 63,* 129–38.

Simon, H. A. (1957a). *Administrative Behavior* (2nd ed.). New York: Macmillan.

Simon, H. A. (1957b). *Models of Man.* New York: Wiley.

Simon, H. A. (1968). Administrative Behavior. In D. Suls (Ed.), *International Encyclopedia of the Social Sciences* (pp. 74–79). New York: Macmillan.

Simon, H. A. (1987). Making Management Decisions: The Role of Intuition and Emotion. *Academy of Management Executive, 1,* 57–64.

Simon, H. A. (1991). Keynote Address. UCEA Conference, Baltimore, MD.

Simon, H. A. (1993). Decision-Making: Rational, Nonrational, and Irrational. *Educational Administration Quarterly, 29*(3), 392–411.

Sinden, J. E., Hoy, W. K., and Sweetland, S. R. (in press). Enabling School Structures: Principal Leadership and Organizational Commitment of Teachers. *Journal of School Leadership.*

Sinden, J. E., Hoy, W. K., and Sweetland, S. R. (2003). A Qualitative Analysis of Enabling School Structure: Theoretical, Empirical, and Research Considerations. Working Paper. The Ohio State University.

Sirotnik, K. A., and Clark, R. (1988). School-Centered Decision Making and Renewal. *Phi Delta Kappan, 69,* 660–64.

Skinner, B. F. (1950). Are Theories of Learning Necessary? *Psychological Review, 57,* 193–216.

Skinner, B. F. (1953). *Science and Human Behavior.* New York: Macmillan.

Skinner, B. F. (1989). The Origins of Cognitive Thought. *American Psychologist, 44,* 13–18.

Slater, R. O., and Boyd, W. B. (1999). *Schools as Polities.* In J. Murphy and K. S. Louis, (Eds.), *Handbook on Research of Educational Administration* (pp. 297–322). San Francisco: Jossey-Bass.

Slavin, R. E. (1995). *Cooperative Learning* (2nd ed.). Boston: Allyn and Bacon.

Slavin, R. E., Karweit, N. L., and Madden, N. A. (1989). *Effective Programs for Students at Risk.* Boston: Allyn & Bacon.

Smith, F. (1975). *Comprehension and Learning: A Conceptual Framework for Teachers.* New York: Holt, Rinehart & Winston.

Smith, J. F., and Kida, T. (1991). Heuristics and Biases: Expertise and Task Realism in Auditing. *Psychological Bulletin, 109,* 472–89.

Smith, L. (1993). *Necessary Knowledge: Piagetian Perspectives on Constructivism.* Hillsdale, NJ: Erlbaum.

Smith, M. S., and O'Day, J. A. (1991). Systemic School Reform. In S. H. Fuhrman and B. Malen (Eds.), *The Politics of Curriculum and Testing* (pp. 233–67). London: Falmer.

Smith, P. A., Hoy, W. K., and Sweetland, S. R. (2001). Organizational Health of High Schools and Dimensions of Faculty Trust, *Journal of School Leadership, 11,* 135–51.

Smylie, M. A. (1988). The Enhancement Function of Staff Development: Organization and Psychological Antecedents to Individual Teacher Change. *American Educational Research Journal, 25*, 1–30.

Smylie, M. A. (1994). Redesigning Teachers' Work: Connections to the Classroom. *Review of Research in Education, 20*, 129–77.

Smylie, M. A., and Brownlee-Conyers, J. (1992). Teacher Leaders and Their Principals: Exploring the Development of New Working Relationships. *Educational Administration Quarterly, 28*(2), 150–84.

Smylie, M. A., and Hart, A. W. (1999). School Leadership for Teacher Learning and Change: A Human and Social Capital Development Perspective. In J. Murphy and K. S. Louis (Eds.), *Handbook of Research on Educational Administration* (pp. 421–41). San Francisco, CA: Jossey-Bass.

Smylie, M. A., and Smart, J. C. (1990). Teacher Support for Career Enhancement Initiatives: Program Characteristics and Effects on Work. *Educational Evaluation and Policy Analysis, 12*(2), 139–55.

Snowman, J. (1984). Learning Tactics and Strategies. In G. Phye and T. Andre (Eds.), *Cognitive Instructional Psychology.* Orlando, FL: Academic Press.

Sousa, D. A., and Hoy, W. K. (1981). Bureaucratic Structure in Schools: A Refinement and Synthesis in Measurement. *Educational Administration Quarterly, 17*, 21–40.

Spector, P. E. (1997). *Job Satisfaction: Application, Assessment, Cause, and Consequence.* Thousand Oaks, CA: Sage.

Spencer, B. A. (1994). Models of Organization and Total Quality Management. *Academy of Management Review, 19*(3), 446–71.

Spenner, K. I. (1988). Social Stratification, Work, and Personality. *Annual Review of Sociology, 14*, 69–97.

Spillane, J. P., Hallett, T., and Diamond, J. B. (2003). Forms of Capital and the Construction of Leadership: Instructional Leadership in Urban Elementary Schools. *Sociology of Education, 76*(1), 1–17.

Spillane, J. P., Halverson, R., and Diamond, J. B. (2001). Investigating School Leadership Practice: A Distributed Perspective. *Educational Researcher, 30*(3), 23–28.

Spillane, J. P., Halverson, R., and Diamond, J. B. (2004). Distributed Leadership: Toward a Theory of School Leadership Practice. *Journal of Curriculum Studies, 36*(1), 3–35.

Spillane, J. P., and Jennings, N. E. (1997). Aligned Instructional Policies and Ambitious Pedagogy: Exploring Instructional Reform from the Classroom Perspective. *Teachers College Record, 98*, 449–81.

Spiro, R. J., Feltovich, P. J., Jacobson, M. L., and Coulson, R. L. (1991). Cognitive Flexibility, Constructivism, and Hypertext: Random Access Instruction for Advanced Knowledge Acquisition in Ill-structured Domains. *Educational Technology, 31*(5), 24–33.

Sproull, L. (1981). Managing Educational Programs: A Microbehavioral Analysis. *Human Organization, 40*, 113–122.

Sproull, L., Weiner, S., and Wolf, D. (1978). *Organizing an Anarchy: Beliefs, Bureaucracy, and Politics in the National Institute of Education.* Chicago: University of Illinois.

Starkie, D. (1984). Policy Changes, Configurations, and Catastrophes. *Policy and Politics, 12*, 71–84.

Staw, B. M. (1984). Organizational Behavior: A Review and Reformulation of the Field's Outcome Variables. *Annual Review of Psychology, 35*, 627–66.

Stearns, T. M., Hoffman, A. N., and Heide, J. B. (1987). Performance of Commercial Television Stations as an Outcome of Interorganizational Linkages and Environmental Conditions. *Academy of Management Journal, 30*, 71–90.

Stedman, L. C. (1987). It's Time We Changed the Effective Schools Formula. *Phi Delta Kappan, 69*, 214–24.

Steers, R. M. (1975). Problems in the Measurement of Organizational Effectiveness. *Administrative Science Quarterly, 20*, 546–58.

Steers, R. M. (1977). *Organizational Effectiveness: A Behavioral View.* Santa Monica, CA: Goodyear.

Steers, R. M., and Porter, L. W. (Eds.). (1983). *Motivation and Work Behavior* (3rd ed.). New York: McGraw-Hill.

Steers, R. M., and Porter, L. W. (Eds.) (1991). *Motivation and Work Behavior* (5th ed.). New York: McGraw-Hill.

Steinfield, C. W., and Fulk, J. (1986). Task Demands and Managers' Use of Communication Media: An Information Processing View. Meeting of the Academy of Management, Chicago.

Stevenson, H., and Stigler, J. W. (1992). *The Learning Gap*. New York: Summit Books.

Stinchcombe, A. L. (1959). Bureaucratic and Craft Administration of Production. *Administrative Science Quarterly, 4*, 168–87.

Stipek, D. J. (1993). *Motivation to Learn* (2nd ed.). Boston: Allyn and Bacon.

Stogdill, R. M. (1948). Personal Factors Associated with Leadership: A Survey of the Literature. *Journal of Psychology, 25*, 35–71.

Stogdill, R. M. (1981). Traits of Leadership: A Follow-Up to 1970. In B. M. Bass (Ed.), *Stogdill's Handbook of Leadership* (pp. 73–97). New York: Free Press.

Stohl, C. (1995). *Organizational Communication*. Thousand Oaks, CA: Sage.

Strang, D. (1987). The Administrative Transformation of American Education: School District Consolidation. *Administrative Science Quarterly, 32*, 352–66.

Strauss, G. (1964). Workflow Frictions, Interfunctional Rivalry, and Professionalism. *Human Organization, 23*, 137–49.

Strube, M. J., and Garcia, J. E. (1981). A Meta-Analytic Investigation of Fiedler's Contingency Model of Leadership Effectiveness. *Psychological Bulletin, 90*, 307–21.

Suchman, M. C. (1995). Managing Legitimacy: Strategic and Institutional Approaches. *Academy of Management Review, 20*, 571–610.

Sutcliffe, K. M. (1994). What Executives Notice: Accurate Perceptions in Top Management Teams. *Academy of Management Journal, 37*(5), 1360–78.

Sutton, R. I., and Staw, B. M. (1995). What Theory Is Not. *Administrative Science Quarterly, 40*, 371–84.

Swanson, H. L. (1990). The Influence of Metacognitive Knowledge and Aptitude on Problem Solving. *Journal of Educational Psychology, 82*, 306–14.

Sweetland, S. R., and Hoy, W. K. (2000a). School Characteristics: Toward an Organizational Model of Student Achievement. *Educational Administration Quarterly, 5*, 703–29.

Sweetland, S. R., and Hoy, W. K. (2000b). Varnishing the truth in schools: Principals and teachers spinning reality. Unpublished research paper, The Ohio State University, College of Education.

Tagiuri, R. (1968). The Concept of Organizational Climate. In R. Tagiuri and G. H. Litwin (Eds.), *Organizational Climate* (pp. 11–32). Boston: Harvard Graduate School of Business Administration.

Tannen, D. (1990). *You Just Don't Understand: Women and Men in Conversation*. New York: Ballantine.

Tarter, C. J., and Hoy, W. K. (1988). The Context of Trust: Teachers and the Principal. *High School Journal, 72*, 17–24.

Tarter, C. J., and Hoy, W. K. (1998). Toward a Contingency Theory of Decision Making. *Journal of Educational Administration, 36*, 212–28.

Tarter, C. J., Hoy, W. K., and Bliss, J. R. (1989). Principal Leadership and Organizational Commitment: The Principal Must Deliver. *Planning and Changing, 20*, 139–40.

Tarter, C. J., Hoy, W. K., and Kottkamp, R. (1990). School Health and Organizational Commitment. *Journal of Research and Development in Education, 23*, 236–43.

Taylor, F. W. (1947). *Scientific Management*. New York: Harper.

Teddlie, C., and Reynolds, D. (Eds.). (2000). *The International Handbook on School Effectiveness Research*. New York: Falmer.

Terreberry, S. (1968). The Evolution of Organizational Environments. *Administrative Science Quarterly, 12*, 590–613.

Thomas, A. R., and Slater, R. C. (1972). The OCDQ: A Four Factor Solution for Australian Schools? *Journal of Educational Administration, 12*, 197–208.

Thomas, H. (1984). Mapping Strategic Management Research. *Journal of General Management, 9*, 55–72.

Thomas, K. (1976). Conflict and Conflict Management. In M. D. Dunnette (Ed.), *Handbook of Industrial and Organizational Psychology* (pp. 889–936). Chicago: Rand McNally.

Thomas, K. (1977). Toward Multi-Dimensional Values in Teaching: The Example of Conflict Behaviors. *Academy of Management Review, 20*, 486–90.

Thompson, D. P., McNamara, J. F., and Hoyle, J. R. (1997). Job Satisfaction in Educational Organizations: A Synthesis of Research Findings. *Educational Administration Quarterly, 33*(1), 7–37.

Thompson, J. D. (1967). *Organizations in Action.* New York: McGraw-Hill.

Tichy, N. M., and Devanna, M. A. (1986). *The Transformational Leader.* New York: Wiley.

Tiegs, R. B., Tetrick, L. E., and Fried, Y. (1992). Growth Need Strength and Context Satisfactions as Moderators of the Relations of the Job Characteristics Model. *Journal of Management, 18*(3), 575–93.

Tjosvold, D. (1997). Conflict within Interdependence: Its Value for Productivity and Individuality. In C. DeDreu and E. Van De Vliert (Eds.), *Using Conflict in Organizations* (pp. 23–37). London: Sage.

Tobias, S., and Duchastel, P. (1974). Behavioral Objectives, Sequence, and Anxiety in CAI. *Instructional Science, 3,* 232–42.

Toth, E., Klahr, D., and Chen, Z. (2000). Bridging Research and Practice: A Cognitively Based Classroom Intervention for Teaching Experimentation to Elementary School Children. *Cognition and Instruction, 18,* 423–59.

Trentham, L., Silvern, S., and Brogdon, R. (1985). Teacher Efficacy and Teacher Competency Ratings. *Psychology in Schools, 22,* 343–52.

Trevino, L. K., Lengel, R. H., and Daft, R. L. (1987). Media Symbolism, Media Richness, and Media Choice in Organizations: A Symbolic Interactionist Perspective. *Communication Research, 14,* 553–74.

Trice, H. M., and Beyer, J. M. (1993). *The Culture of Work Organizations.* Englewood Cliffs, NJ: Prentice Hall.

Trusty, F. M., and Sergiovanni, T. J. (1966). Perceived Need Deficiencies of Teachers and Administrators: A Proposal for Restructuring Teacher Roles. *Educational Administration Quarterly, 2,* 168–80.

Tschannen-Moran, M. (2001). Collaboration and the Need for Trust. *Journal of Educational Administration, 36,* 334–52.

Tschannen-Moran, M., and Hoy, W. K. (2000). A Multidisciplinary Analysis of the Nature, Meaning, and Measurement of Trust. *Review of Educational Research, 70,* 547–93.

Tschannen-Moran, M., Uline, C., Woolfolk Hoy, A. and Mackely, T. (2000). Creating Smarter Schools through Collaboration. *Journal of Educational Administration, 38,* 247–71.

Tschannen-Moran, M., Woolfolk Hoy, A., and Hoy, W. K. (1998). Teacher Efficacy: Its Meaning and Measure. *Review of Educational Research, 68,* 202–48.

Tsui, A. S. (1990). A Multiple-Constituency Model of Effectiveness: An Empirical Examination at the Human Resource Subunit Level. *Administrative Science Quarterly, 35,* 458–83.

Tubbs, M. E., Boehne, D., and Dahl, J. G. (1993). Expectancy, Balance, and Motivational Force Functions in Goal-Setting Research: An Empirical Test. *Journal of Applied Psychology, 78,* 361–73.

Turban, D. B., and Keon, T. L. (1993). Organizational Attractiveness. An Interactionist Perspective. *Journal of Applied Psychology, 78*(2), 184–93.

Tversky, A. (1969). Intransitivity of Preferences. *Psychological Review, 76,* 31–84.

Tversky, A., and Kahneman, D. (1973). Availability: Heuristic for Judging Frequency and Probability. *Cognitive Psychology, 5,* 207–32.

Tversky, A., and Kahneman, D. (1974). Judgment under Uncertainty: Heuristics and Biases. *Science, 185,* 1124–31.

Tversky, A., and Kahneman, D. (1981). The Framing of Decisions and the Psychology of Choice. *Science, 21,* 453–58.

Tyler, T. R. (1994). Psychological Models of the Justice Motive: Antecedents of Distributive and Procedural Justice. *Journal of Personality and Social Psychology, 67,* 850–63.

Udy, S. H. (1959). "Bureaucracy" and "Rationality" in Weber's Organization Theory. *American Sociological Review, 24,* 791–95.

Uline, C. L., Miller, D. M., and Tschannen-Moran, M. (1998). School Effectiveness: The Underlying Dimensions. *Educational Administration Quarterly, 34*(4), 462–83.

Uline, C., Tschannen-Moran, M., and Perez, L. (2003). Constructive Conflict: How Controversy Can Contribute to School Improvement. *Teachers College Record, 105,* 782–816.

U. S. Department of Health, Education and Welfare (1973). *Work in America, Report of a Special Task Force.* Cambridge: MIT Press.

Urwick, L. F. (1937). Organization as a Technical Problem. In L. Gulick and L. F. Urwick (Eds.), *Papers on the Science of Administration* (pp. 47–88). New York: Institute of Public Administration, Columbia University.

Vance, V. S., and Schlechty, P. C. (1981). Do Academically Able Teachers Leave Education: The North Carolina Case. *Phi Delta Kappan, 63,* 106–12.

Vance, V. S., and Schlechty, P. C. (1982). The Distribution of Academic Ability in the Teaching Force: Policy Implications. *Phi Delta Kappan, 64,* 22–27.

Van de Ven, A. H., and Ferry, D. L. (1980). *Measuring and Assessing Organization.* New York: Wiley.

Van Eerde, W. and Thierry, H. (1996). Vroom's Expectancy Models and Work Related Criteria: A Meta-Analysis. *Journal of Applied Psychology, 81,* 575–86.

Van Meter, P. (2001). Drawing Construction as a Strategy for Learning from Text. *Journal of Educational Psychology, 93,* 129–40.

Van Meter, P., Yokoi, L., and Pressley, M. (1994). College Students' Theory of Note-Taking Derived from Their Perceptions of Note-Taking. *Journal of Educational Psychology, 86,* 323–38.

Vecchio, R. P. (1977). An Empirical Examination of the Validity of Fiedler's Model of Leadership Effectiveness. *Organizational Behavior and Human Performance, 19,* 180–206.

Vecchio, R. P. (1988). *Organizational Behavior.* Chicago: Dryden Press.

Vecchio, R. P. (1993). The Impact of Differences in Subordinate and Supervisor Age on Attitudes and Performance. *Psychology and Aging, 8*(1), 112–19.

Vera, A. H., and Simon, H. A. (1993). Situated Action: A Symbolic Interpretation. *Cognitive Science, 17,* 7–48.

Verdugo, R. R., Greenberg, N. M., Henderson, R. D., Uribe, O. Jr., and Schneider, J. M. (1997). School Governance Regimes and Teachers' Job Satisfaction: Bureaucracy, Legitimacy, and Community. *Educational Administration Quarterly, 33*(1), 38–66.

Vinovskis, M. A. (1999). *History and Educational Policymaking.* New Haven: Yale University Press.

Vroom, V. H. (1960). *Some Personality Determinants of the Effects of Participation.* Englewood Cliffs, NJ: Prentice Hall.

Vroom, V. H. (1964). *Work and Motivation.* New York: Wiley.

Vroom, V. H. (1976). Leadership. In M. D. Dunnette (Ed.), *Handbook of Industrial and Organizational Psychology* (pp. 1527–51). Chicago: Rand McNally.

Vroom, V. H., and Jago, A. G. (1988). On the Validity of the Vroom-Yetton Model. *Journal of Applied Psychology, 63,* 151–62.

Vroom, V. H., and Yetton, P. W. (1973). *Leadership and Decision Making.* Pittsburgh: University of Pittsburgh Press.

Waller, W. (1932). *The Sociology of Teaching.* New York: Wiley.

Wang, M. C., and Walberg, H. J. (Eds.). (2001). *School Choice or Best Systems: What Improves Education.* Mahwah, NJ: Erlbaum.

Watkins, K. E., and Marsick, V. J. (1993). *Sculpting the Learning Organization.* San Francisco, Jossey-Bass.

Webb, N., and Palincsar, A. (1996). Group Processes in the Classroom. In D. C. Berliner and R. C. Calfee (Eds.), *Handbook of Educational Psychology* (pp. 841–76). New York: Macmillan.

Weber, M. (1947). *The Theory of Social and Economic Organizations.* In T. Parsons (Ed.), A. M. Henderson and T. Parsons (Trans.). New York: Free Press.

Weick, K. E. (1976). Educational Organizations as Loosely Coupled Systems. *Administrative Science Quarterly, 21,* 1–19.

Weick, K. (1995). What Theory Is Not, Theorizing Is. *Administrative Science Quarterly, 40,* 385–90.

Weick, K. (1999). Theory Construction as Disciplined Reflexivity: Tradeoffs in the 90s. *The Academy of Management Review, 24,* 797–808.

Weick, K., and Westley, F. (1996). Organizational Learning: Affirming the Oxymoron. In S. Clegg, C. Hardy, and W. Nord (Eds.), *Handbook of Organization Studies* (pp. 440–58). Thousand Oaks, CA: Sage.

Weiner, B. (1972). *Theories of Motivation: From Mechanism to Cognition.* Chicago: Academic Press.

Weiner, B. (1985). An Attributional Theory of Achievement Motivation and Emotion. *Psychological Review, 92,* 548–73.

Weiner, B. (1986). *An Attributional Theory of Motivation and Emotion.* New York: Springer-Verlag.

Weiner, B. (1990). History of Motivational Research in Education. *Journal of Educational Psychology, 82,* 616–22.

Weiner, B. (1992). *Human Motivation: Metaphors, Theories, and Research.* Newbury Park, CA: Sage.

Weiner, B. (1994a). Ability versus Effort Revisited: The Moral Determinants of Achievement Evaluation an Achievement as a Moral System. *Educational Psychologist, 29,* 163–72.

Weiner, B. (1994b). Integrating Social and Persons Theories of Achievement Striving. *Review of Educational Research, 64,* 557–75.

Weiner, B. (2000). Interpersonal and Intrapersonal Theories of Motivation from an Attributional Perspective. *Educational Psychological Review, 12,* 1–14.

Weinert, F. E., and Helmke, A. (1995). Learning from Wise Mother Nature or Big Brother Instructor: The Wrong Choice as Seen from an Educational Perspective. *Educational Psychologist, 30,* 135–43.

Wendel, F. C., Kelley, E. A., Kluender, M., and Palmere, M. (1983). *Use of Assessment Center Processes: A Literature Review.* Lincoln, NB: Teachers College, University of Nebraska.

Westphal, J. D., Gulati, R., and Shortell, S. M. (1997). Customization or Conformity? An Institutional Network Perspective on the Content and Consequence of TQM Adoption. *Administrative Science Quarterly, 42*(2), 366–94.

Whitehead, A. N. (1925). *Science and the Modern World.* New York: Macmillan.

Wietz, S. (1974). *Non-Verbal Communication.* New York: Oxford.

Wilensky, H. (1964). Professionalization of Everyone? *American Journal of Sociology, 70,* 137–58.

Wilkins, A., and Patterson, K. (1985). You Can't Get There From Here: What Will Make Culture-Change Projects Fail. In R. H. Kilmann, M. J. Saxton, and R. Serpa (Eds.), *Gaining Control of the Corporate Culture* (pp. 262–91). San Francisco: Jossey-Bass.

Wilkins, B. M., and Andersen, P. A. (1991). Gender Differences and Similarities in Management Communication: A Meta-Analysis. *Management Communication Quarterly, 5*(1), 6–35.

Williams, L. B., and Hoy, W. K. (1973). Principal-Staff Relations: Situational Mediator of Effectiveness. *Journal of Educational Administration, 9,* 66–73.

Willis, Q. (1980). The Work Activity of School Principals: An Observational Study. *Journal of Educational Administration, 18,* 27–54.

Willoughby, T. Porter, L., Belsito, L, and Yearsley, T. (1999). Use of Elaboration Strategies by Grades Two, Four, and Six. *Elementary School Journal, 99,* 221–31.

Willower, D. J. (1963). The Form of Knowledge and the Theory-Practice Relationship. *Educational Theory, 13,* 47–52.

Willower, D. J. (1975). Theory in Educational Administration. *Journal of Educational Administration, 13,* 77–91.

Willower, D. J. (1979). Some Issues in Research on School Organization. In G. L. Immegart and W. Boyd (Eds.), *Currents in Administrative Research: Problem Finding in Education* (pp. 63–86). Lexington, MA: Heath.

Willower, D. J. (1987). Inquiry into Educational Administration: The Last Twenty-Five Years and the Next. *Journal of Educational Administration, 24,* 12–29.

Willower, D. J. (1991). Values, Valuation and Explanation in School Organizations. *Journal of School Leadership, 4,* 446–83.

Willower, D. J. (1993). Explaining and Improving Educational Administration. *Educational Management and Administration, 21,* 153–60.

Willower, D. J. (1994). Values, Valuation, and Explanation in School Organizations. *Journal of School Leadership, 4*(5), 466–83.

Willower, D. J. (1996). Inquiry in Educational Administration and the Spirit of the Times. *Educational Administration Quarterly, 32,* 341–65.

Willower, D. J. (1998). Fighting the Fog: A Criticism of Postmodernism. *Journal of School Leadership, 8,* 448–63.

Willower, D. J. (1999). Values and Valuation: A Naturalistic Inquiry. In P. J. Begley (Ed.). *Values in Educational Leadership.* Albany, NT: State University of New York Press.

Willower, D. J., Eidell, T. L., and Hoy, W. K. (1967). *The School and Pupil Control Ideology.* Monograph No. 24. University Park: Pennsylvania State University.

Willower, D. J., and Forsyth, P. B. (1999). A Brief History of Scholarship on Educational Administration. In J. Murphy and K. S. Louis (Eds.), *Handbook of Research on Educational Administration* (2nd ed.). San Francisco: Jossey-Bass.

Willower, D. J., and Jones, R. G. (1967). Control in an Educational Organization. In J. D. Raths, J. R. Pancella, and J. S. V. Ness (Eds.), *Studying Teaching* (pp. 424–28). Englewood Cliffs, NJ: Prentice Hall.

Willower, D. J. and Licata, J. W. (1997). *Values and Valuation in the Practice of Educational Administration*. Thousand Oaks, CA: Corwin Press.

Wilson, T. D., Houston, C. E., Etling, K. M., and Brekke, N. (1996). A New Look at Anchoring Effects: Basic Anchoring and Its Antecedents. *Journal of Experimental Psychology: General, 125* (4), 382–407.

Wimpelberg, R. K., Teddlie, C., and Stringfield, S. (1989). Sensitivity to Context: The Past and Future of Effective Schools Research. *Educational Administration Quarterly, 25*, 82–107.

Wise, A. (1988). The Two Conflicting Trends in School Reform: Legislated Learning Revisited. *Phi Delta Kappan, 69*, 328–32.

Wiseman, C. (1979a). Selection of Major Planning Issues. *Policy Sciences, 12*, 71–86.

Wiseman, C. (1979b). Strategic Planning in the Scottish Health Service—A Mixed Scanning Approach. *Long Range Planning, 12*, 103–13.

Wittrock, M. C. (1992). An Empowering Conception of Educational Psychology. *Educational Psychologist, 27*, 129–42.

Wolin, S. S. (1960). *Politics and Vision: Continuity and Innovation in Western Political Thought.* Boston: Little, Brown.

Wood, D. J., and Gray, B. (1991). Toward a Comprehensive Theory of Collaboration. *Journal of Applied Behavioral Science, 27*(2), 139–62.

Wood, R., and Bandura, A. (1989). Social Cognitive Theory of Organizational Management. *Academy of Management Review, 14*, 361–84.

Wood, S. E., and Wood, E. G. (1999). *The World of Psychology.* Boston: Allyn and Bacon.

Woolfolk, A. (2004). *Educational Psychology* (9th ed.). Boston: Allyn & Bacon.

Woolfolk, A. E. (2000). *Educational Psychology* (8th ed.). Boston: Allyn and Bacon.

Woolfolk, A. E., and Hoy, W. K. (1990). Prospective Teachers' Sense of Efficacy and Beliefs about Control. *Journal of Educational Psychology, 82*, 81–91.

Woolfolk, A. E., Rosoff, B., and Hoy, W. K. (1990). Teachers' Sense of Efficacy and Their Beliefs about Managing Students. *Teaching and Teacher Education, 6*(2), 137–48.

Woolfolk Hoy, A., and Murphy, P. K. (2001). Teaching Educational Psychology to the Implicit Mind. In R. Sternberg and B. Torff (Eds.), *Understanding and Teaching the Implicit Mind* (pp. 145–85). Mahwah, NJ: Erlbaum.

Worthy, J. C. (1950). Factors Influencing Employee Morale. *Harvard Business Review, 28*, 61–73.

Wright, P. M., O'Leary-Kelly, A. M., Cortinak, J. M., Klein, H. J., and Hollenbeck, J. R. (1994). On the Meaning and Measurement of Goal Commitment. *Journal of Applied Psychology, 79*, 795–803.

Wright, R. (1985). Motivating Teacher Involvement in Professional Growth Activities. *Canadian Administrator, 24*, 1–6.

Yamagishi, T., Gillmore, M. R., and Cook, K. S. (1988). Network Connections and the Distribution of Power in Exchange Networks. *American Journal of Sociology, 93*, 833–51.

Yekovich, F. R. (1993). A Theoretical View of the Development of Expertise in Credit Administration. In P. Hallinger, K. Leithwood, and J. Murphy (Eds.), *Cognitive Perspectives on Educational Leadership* (pp. 146–66). New York: Teachers College.

Yuchtman, E., and Seashore, S. E. (1967). A System Resource Approach to Organizational Effectiveness. *American Sociological Review, 32*, 891–903.

Yukl, G. A. (1971). Toward a Behavioral Theory of Leadership. *Organizational Behavior and Human Performance, 6*, 414–40.

Yukl, G. A. (1989). *Leadership in Organizations* (2nd ed.). Englewood Cliffs, NJ: Prentice Hall.

Yukl, G. A. (1994). *Leadership in Organizations* (3rd ed.). Englewood Cliffs, NJ: Prentice Hall.

Yukl, G. A. (2002). *Leadership in Organizations* (5th ed.). Upper Saddle River, NJ: Prentice Hall.

Yukl, G. A. (1999). An Evaluation of Conceptual Weaknesses in Transformational and

Charismatic Leadership Theories. *Leadership Quarterly, 10*(2), 285–305.

Yukl, G. (2002). *Leadership in Organization* (5th ed.). Upper Saddle River, NJ: Prentice Hall.

Zahn, C. L. (1991). Face-to-Face Communication in an Office Setting. *Communication Research, 18*(6), 737–54.

Zald, M. M., and Berger, M. A. (1978). Social Movements in Organizations: Coup d'Etat, Insurgency, and Mass Movements. *American Journal of Sociology, 42*, 823–61.

Zammuto, R. F. (1982). *Assessing Organizational Effectiveness.* Albany: State University of New York Press.

Zand, D. (1997). The Leadership Triad: Knowledge, Trust, and Power. New York: Oxford University Press.

Zbaracki, M. J. (1998). The Rhetoric and Reality of Total Quality Management. *Administrative Science Quarterly, 43*(3), 602–36.

Zenger, T. R., and Lawrence, B. S. (1989). Organizational Demography: The Differential Effects of Age and Tenure Distributions on Technical Communication. *Academy of Management Journal, 32*, 353–76.

Zey, M. (1992). *Decision Making: Alternatives to Rational Choice.* Newbury Park, CA: Sage.

Zielinski, A. E., and Hoy, W. K. (1983). Isolation and Alienation in Elementary Schools. *Educational Administration Quarterly, 19*, 27–45.

Zucker, L. (1987). Institutional Theories of Organization. *Annual Review of Sociology, 13*, 443–64.

NAME INDEX

SUBJECT INDEX